CorelDRAW™ 8
Secrets®

CorelDRAW™ 8 Secrets®

William Harrel and Winston Steward

IDG Books Worldwide, Inc.
An International Data Group Company

Foster City, CA ♦ Chicago, IL ♦ Indianapolis, IN ♦ Dallas, TX

CorelDRAW™ 8 Secrets®

Published by
IDG Books Worldwide, Inc.
An International Data Group Company
919 E. Hillsdale Blvd., Suite 400
Foster City, CA 94404
www.idgbooks.com (IDG Books Worldwide Web site)

Copyright © 1998 IDG Books Worldwide, Inc. All rights reserved. No part of this book, including interior design, cover design, and icons, may be reproduced or transmitted in any form, by any means (electronic, photocopying, recording, or otherwise) without the prior written permission of the publisher.

Library of Congress Catalog Card No.: 97-078212

ISBN: 0-7645-3182-4

Printed in the United States of America

10 9 8 7 6 5 4 3 2 1

1E/RZ/QT/ZY/FC

Distributed in the United States by IDG Books Worldwide, Inc.

Distributed by Macmillan Canada for Canada; by Transworld Publishers Limited in the United Kingdom; by IDG Norge Books for Norway; by IDG Sweden Books for Sweden; by Woodslane Pty. Ltd. for Australia; by Woodslane New Zealand Ltd. for New Zealand; by Addison-Wesley/Pte Longman Singapore Ltd. for Singapore, Malaysia, Thailand, and Indonesia; by Distribuidora Norma S.A.-Colombia for Colombia; by Intersoft for South Africa; by International Thompson Publishing for Germany, Austria, and Switzerland; by Toppan Company Ltd. for Japan; by Distribuidora Cuspide for Argentina; by Livraria Cultura for Brazil; by Ediciencia S.A. for Ecuador; by Addison-Wesley Publishing Company for Korea; by Ediciones ZETA S.C.R. Ltda. for Peru; by WS Computer Publishing Corporation, Inc., for the Philippines; by Unalis Corporation for Taiwan; by Contemporanea de Ediciones for Venezuela; by Computer Book & Magazine Store for Puerto Rico; by Express Computer Distributors for the Caribbean and West Indies. Authorized Sales Agent: Anthony Rudkin Associates for the Middle East and North Africa.

For general information on IDG Books Worldwide's books in the U.S., please call our Consumer Customer Service department at 800-762-2974. For reseller information, including discounts and premium sales, please call our Reseller Customer Service department at 800-434-3422.

For information on where to purchase IDG Books Worldwide's books outside the U.S., please contact our International Sales department at 650-655-3200 or fax 650-655-3297.

For information on foreign language translations, please contact our Foreign & Subsidiary Rights department at 650-655-3021 or fax 650-655-3281.

For sales inquiries and special prices for bulk quantities, please contact our Sales department at 650-655-3200 or write to the address above.

For information on using IDG Books Worldwide's books in the classroom or for ordering examination copies, please contact our Educational Sales department at 800-434-2086 or fax 817-421-5012.

For press review copies, author interviews, or other publicity information, please contact our Public Relations department at 650-655-3000 or fax 650-655-3299.

For authorization to photocopy items for corporate, personal, or educational use, please contact Copyright Clearance Center, 222 Rosewood Drive, Danvers, MA 01923, or fax 978-750-4470.

is a trademark under exclusive license to IDG Books Worldwide, Inc., from International Data Group, Inc.

ABOUT IDG BOOKS WORLDWIDE

Welcome to the world of IDG Books Worldwide.

IDG Books Worldwide, Inc., is a subsidiary of International Data Group, the world's largest publisher of computer-related information and the leading global provider of information services on information technology. IDG was founded more than 25 years ago and now employs more than 8,500 people worldwide. IDG publishes more than 275 computer publications in over 75 countries (see listing below). More than 60 million people read one or more IDG publications each month.

Launched in 1990, IDG Books Worldwide is today the #1 publisher of best-selling computer books in the United States. We are proud to have received eight awards from the Computer Press Association in recognition of editorial excellence and three from *Computer Currents'* First Annual Readers' Choice Awards. Our best-selling *...For Dummies*® series has more than 30 million copies in print with translations in 30 languages. IDG Books Worldwide, through a joint venture with IDG's Hi-Tech Beijing, became the first U.S. publisher to publish a computer book in the People's Republic of China. In record time, IDG Books Worldwide has become the first choice for millions of readers around the world who want to learn how to better manage their businesses.

Our mission is simple: Every one of our books is designed to bring extra value and skill-building instructions to the reader. Our books are written by experts who understand and care about our readers. The knowledge base of our editorial staff comes from years of experience in publishing, education, and journalism — experience we use to produce books for the '90s. In short, we care about books, so we attract the best people. We devote special attention to details such as audience, interior design, use of icons, and illustrations. And because we use an efficient process of authoring, editing, and desktop publishing our books electronically, we can spend more time ensuring superior content and spend less time on the technicalities of making books.

You can count on our commitment to deliver high-quality books at competitive prices on topics you want to read about. At IDG Books Worldwide, we continue in the IDG tradition of delivering quality for more than 25 years. You'll find no better book on a subject than one from IDG Books Worldwide.

John Kilcullen
John Kilcullen
CEO
IDG Books Worldwide, Inc.

Steven Berkowitz
Steven Berkowitz
President and Publisher
IDG Books Worldwide, Inc.

Eighth Annual
Computer Press
Awards ≥1992

Ninth Annual
Computer Press
Awards ≥1993

Tenth Annual
Computer Press
Awards ≥1994

Eleventh Annual
Computer Press
Awards ≥1995

IDG Books Worldwide, Inc., is a subsidiary of International Data Group, the world's largest publisher of computer-related information and the leading global provider of information services on information technology. International Data Group publishes over 275 computer publications in over 75 countries. Sixty million people read one or more International Data Group publications each month. International Data Group's publications include: **ARGENTINA:** Buyer's Guide, Computerworld Argentina, PC World Argentina; **AUSTRALIA:** Australian Macworld, Australian PC World, Australian Reseller News, Computerworld, IT Casebook, Network World, Publish, Webmaster; **AUSTRIA:** Computerwelt Osterreich, Networks Austria, PC Tip Austria; **BANGLADESH:** PC World Bangladesh; **BELARUS:** PC World Belarus; **BELGIUM:** Data News; **BRAZIL:** Annuário de Informática, Computerworld, Connections, Macworld, PC Player, PC World, Publish, Reseller News, Supergamepower; **BULGARIA:** Computerworld Bulgaria, Network World Bulgaria, PC & MacWorld Bulgaria; **CANADA:** CIO Canada, Client/Server World, ComputerWorld Canada, InfoWorld Canada, NetworkWorld Canada, WebWorld; **CHILE:** Computerworld Chile, PC World Chile; **COLOMBIA:** Computerworld Colombia, PC World Colombia; **COSTA RICA:** PC World Centro America; **THE CZECH AND SLOVAK REPUBLICS:** Computerworld Czechoslovakia, Macworld Czech Republic, PC World Czechoslovakia; **DENMARK:** Communications World Danmark, Computerworld Danmark, Macworld Danmark, PC World Danmark, Techworld Denmark; **DOMINICAN REPUBLIC:** PC World Republica Dominicana; **ECUADOR:** PC World Ecuador; **EGYPT:** Computerworld Middle East, PC World Middle East; **EL SALVADOR:** PC World Centro America; **FINLAND:** MikroPC, Tietoverkko, Tietoviikko; **FRANCE:** Distributique, Hebdo, Info PC, Le Monde Informatique, Macworld, Reseaux & Telecoms, WebMaster France; **GERMANY:** Computer Partner, Computerwoche, Computerwoche Extra, Computerwoche FOCUS, Global Online, Macwelt, PC Welt; **GREECE:** Amiga Computing, GamePro Greece, Multimedia World; **GUATEMALA:** PC World Centro America; **HONDURAS:** PC World Centro America; **HONG KONG:** Computerworld Hong Kong, PC World Hong Kong, Publish in Asia; **HUNGARY:** ABCD CD-ROM, Computerworld Szamitastechnika, Internetto online Magazine, PC World Hungary, PC-X Magazin Hungary; **ICELAND:** Tolvuheimur PC World Island; **INDIA:** Information Communications World, Information Systems Computerworld, PC World India, Publish in Asia; **INDONESIA:** InfoKomputer PC World, Komputek Computerworld, Publish in Asia; **IRELAND:** ComputerScope, PC Live!; **ISRAEL:** Macworld Israel, People & Computers/Computerworld; **ITALY:** Computerworld Italia, Macworld Italia, Networking Italia, PC World Italia; **JAPAN:** DTP World, Macworld Japan, Nikkei Personal Computing, OS/2 World Japan, SunWorld Japan, Windows NT World, Windows World Japan; **KENYA:** PC World East African; **KOREA:** Hi-Tech Information, Macworld Korea, PC World Korea; **MACEDONIA:** PC World Macedonia; **MALAYSIA:** Computerworld Malaysia, Publish in Asia; **MALTA:** PC World Malta; **MEXICO:** Computerworld Mexico, PC World Mexico; **MYANMAR:** PC World Myanmar; **NETHERLANDS:** Computer! Totaal, LAN Internetworking Magazine, LAN World Buyers Guide, Macworld Netherlands, Net, WebWereld; **NEW ZEALAND:** Absolute Beginners Guide and Plain & Simple Series, Computer Buyer, Computer Industry Directory, Computerworld New Zealand, MTB, Network World, PC World New Zealand; **NICARAGUA:** PC World Centro America; **NORWAY:** Computerworld Norge, CW Rapport, Datamagasinet, Financial Rapport, Kursguide Norge, Macworld Norge, Multimediaworld Norge, PC World Ekspress Norge, PC World Nettverk, PC World Norge, PC World ProduktGuide Norge; **PAKISTAN:** Computerworld Pakistan; **PANAMA:** PC World Panama; **PEOPLE'S REPUBLIC OF CHINA:** China Computer Users, China Computerworld, China InfoWorld, China Telecom World Weekly, Computer & Communication, Electronic Design China, Electronics Today, Electronics Weekly, Game Software, PC World China, Popular Computer Week, Software Weekly, Software World, Telecom World; **PERU:** Computerworld Peru, PC World Profesional Peru, PC World SoHo Peru; **PHILIPPINES:** Click!, Computerworld Philippines, PC World Philippines, Publish in Asia; **POLAND:** Computerworld Poland, Computerworld Special Report Poland, Cyber, Macworld Poland, Networld Poland, PC World Komputer; **PORTUGAL:** Cerebro/PC World, Computerworld/Correio Informático, Dealer World Portugal, Mac*In/PC*In Portugal, Multimedia World; **PUERTO RICO:** PC World Puerto Rico; **ROMANIA:** Computerworld Romania, PC World Romania, Telecom Romania; **RUSSIA:** Computerworld Russia, Mir PK, Publish, Seti; **SINGAPORE:** Computerworld Singapore, PC World Singapore, Publish in Asia; **SLOVENIA:** Monitor; **SOUTH AFRICA:** Computing SA, Network World SA, Software World SA; **SPAIN:** Communicaciones World España, Computerworld España, Dealer World España, Macworld España, PC World España; **SRI LANKA:** Infolink PC World; **SWEDEN:** CAP&Design, Computer Sweden, Corporate Computing Sweden, Internetworld Sweden, it branschen, Macworld Sweden, MaxiData Sweden, MikroDatorn, Nätverk & Kommunikation, PC World Sweden, PCaktiv, Windows World Sweden; **SWITZERLAND:** Computerworld Schweiz, Macworld Schweiz, PCtip; **TAIWAN:** Computerworld Taiwan, Macworld Taiwan, NEW ViSiON/Publish, PC World Taiwan, Windows World Taiwan; **THAILAND:** Publish in Asia, Thai Computerworld; **TURKEY:** Computerworld Turkiye, Macworld Turkiye, Network World Turkiye, PC World Turkiye; **UKRAINE:** Computerworld Kiev, Multimedia World Ukraine, PC World Ukraine; **UNITED KINGDOM:** Acorn User UK, Amiga Action UK, Amiga Computing UK, Apple Talk UK, Computing, Macworld, Parents and Computers UK, PC Advisor, PC Home, PSX Pro, The WEB; **UNITED STATES:** Cable in the Classroom, CIO Magazine, Computerworld, DOS World, Federal Computer Week, GamePro Magazine, InfoWorld, I-Way, Macworld, Network World, PC Games, PC World, Publish, Video Event, THE WEB Magazine, and WebMaster; online webzines: JavaWorld, NetscapeWorld, and SunWorld Online; **URUGUAY:** InfoWorld Uruguay; **VENEZUELA:** Computerworld Venezuela, PC World Venezuela; and **VIETNAM:** PC World Vietnam. 3/24/97

Credits

Acquisitions Editor
Andy Cummings

Development Editors
Ron Hull
Susannah Pfalzer

Technical Editor
Susan Glinert

Copy Editors
Nate Holdread
Timothy J. Borek
Suki Gear

Production Coordinator
Ritchie Durdin

Graphics and Production Specialists
Jude Levinson
Linda Marousek
Hector Mendoza
Christopher Pimentel

Quality Control Specialists
Mick Arellano
Mark Schumann

Proofreader
C² Editorial Services

Indexer
Liz Cunningham

Book Design
Draper and Liew, Inc.

Cover Photography
Eugen Gebhardt/
FPG International

About the Authors

William Harrel is a freelance writer and graphics designer based in Southern California. He has written 17 books on computer graphics-related topics, including coauthoring IDG Books Worldwide's *Macworld PageMaker 6.5 Bible, Freelance Graphics 96 for Windows 95 For Dummies,* and *Acrobat 3.0 For Dummies.* He has also written hundreds of articles for computer magazines, including *PC World* and *Publish.*

Winston Steward is the author or coauthor of several computer books on such subjects as computers for the family, WordPerfect Suite 7, Macromedia Backstage Designer, and Word for Windows 97.

This book is dedicated to my wife, Heidi. She didn't really understand what it would be like being married to a computer journalist. Her adjustment has been the result of admirable and endearing patience.

William Harrel

For Barbara, Larisa, Trevor, and Irma.

Winston Steward

Preface

Once again Winston and I find ourselves engrossed in another book about CorelDRAW, this time CorelDRAW 8. And once again we find ourselves amazed at what the brilliant folks at Corel have done in this latest upgrade. Both of us have been using CorelDRAW since version 1. And I know I speak for Winston when I say that Corel has again found ways to make this fantastic graphics application do things we once never thought possible.

More so than ever, CorelDRAW is an extremely versatile graphics product that grows more and more powerful with each new release. In addition to being a full-featured graphics application suite, CorelDRAW has continued to provide new features to help the nonartist, middle-management, and small business owner to create professional-looking graphics — without having a lot of artistic know-how. In fact, when I started my desktop publishing firm several years ago, having CorelDRAW in the firm's software arsenal provided an edge. It had the automatic drawing, type manipulation, and special effects features we needed to create graphics that often looked as though they were created by a professional design studio. CorelDRAW still provides those automatic tools today, but on a much larger scale.

And this says nothing of the tools provided for the professional designer. This product in the hands of a graphics artist is nothing short of awesome. A perfect match of talent and tools.

In the Macintosh-dominated computer graphics field, CorelDRAW has made graphics in a Windows environment a viable, less-expensive solution. Many Windows draw programs have come and gone, and some others hold on by the skin of their teeth. Meanwhile, CorelDRAW maintains at least a 75 percent market share of the Windows graphics applications.

Part of the reason for this success is Corel's unrelenting commitment to value. With each new version of CorelDRAW, its power and versatility have increased dramatically. In addition to providing some very fine draw, paint, and special effects tools, CorelDRAW 8 comes with everything you need to create spectacular graphics with minimal fuss (including thousands of clip art, stock photography, and 3D model images), hundreds of fonts, and several useful utilities. And now you can use CorelDRAW to create colorful Web pages, resplendent with animation and myriad other special effects.

New Features

In reality, we could write an entire book this size dedicated solely to pointing out and explaining the scads of new features in version 8. But some in particular are worth pointing out here. First is the new dockers windows CorelDraw and Photo-Paint now sport. You can now display often-used commands and images in scrapbook-like windows, allowing you to select and apply them with a mouse click or two, almost eliminating the need to wade through cumbersome menus, dialog boxes, and roll-ups. In addition, all of the programs' setup and configuration options are now contained within one Options dialog box, and you can create and save workspaces for working on different types of projects.

In the flagship application, CorelDraw, you'll also find additional new interactive tools for creating blends, fills, drop shadows, perspectives, envelopes, and extrudes. Once you get the hang of them, you'll find these interactive tools much more convenient than dialog boxes and roll-ups. CorelDraw also has a new Distortion tool that will no doubt enthrall you for countless hours as you experiment to grasp the countless possibilities.

Corel Photo-Paint also has many enhancements, including the capability of creating even more sophisticated animated GIF files for use on your Web pages. And you'll really like the cool new enhancements to the Property Bar — more options than ever are a mere mouse click away. CorelDream 3D is also greatly enhanced, making it an even more full-featured and relatively easy-to-use 3D modeling program.

This brief mention of the new features and enhancements in CorelDRAW 8 barely scratches the surface. The entire package seems to run and load faster, and it has fewer quirks than version 7. If you've recently invested in one of the new MMX systems, you'll surely appreciate the speed with which complicated images redraw on your monitor. Once again, Corel has outdone itself. Version 8 is even more of a magnificent feat of software engineering than version 7.

Who Should Read This Book?

CorelDRAW 8 Secrets is designed for advanced and intermediate users — people who are already familiar with the basic ins and outs of CorelDRAW. In this book we emphasize the seldom-used but highly beneficial features and techniques of the program. Winston and I use CorelDRAW in our daily work and we know how to get results. With the secrets we provide, you can quickly get the results you need too.

In addition, as CorelDRAW users, we know that most other users of this highly versatile graphics program usually confine their work to one, sometimes two, applications in the suite; only CorelDraw, for example, or maybe CorelDraw and Photo-Paint. With this in mind, we've tried to produce a book that helps you use all of the programs and utilities in the suite — even if you usually focus on only two or three. Unlike most other CorelDRAW books, in this one you'll find extensive coverage of Photo-Paint, Dream 3D, and chapters on how to use CorelScan, the templates, clip art, and more. We think this is the most well-rounded and useful book on CorelDRAW available — even if we are just a little biased.

So, even if you are already familiar with CorelDraw (the suite's drawing application), you need this book so you can get the most from the *entire* suite.

How This Book Is Organized

CorelDRAW is so powerful and versatile that it's almost impossible to learn everything about the entire application suite. We use it almost daily and we're still learning. In addition, Corel's yearly update schedule means that you always have new features to contend with.

You can read this book in two ways: from cover to cover, or as needed as a reference. Frankly, we don't know anybody who reads after-market software books from cover to cover, especially one this size. With that in mind, we've arranged the book according to task and application so you can dive in wherever you want and find exactly the information you need. We've divided this book into four parts, as follows:

- **Part I** consists of several chapters covering just CorelDraw, the vector-drawing part of the application. Here you'll find numerous tips and secrets for working with type, fills, and special effects, as well as invaluable information on preparing your images for various destinations, including the computer screen and prepress. Much of this information is also pertinent to working with Photo-Paint and Dream 3D, so try not to skip it, especially Chapter 7.

- **Part II** concentrates on the other full-featured applications in the suite, namely Photo-Paint and Dream 3D. If you have never used or installed these two quite useful and powerful programs, here's your chance to fire them up. Photo-Paint, of course, enables you to edit and enhance photographs and create Web graphics. Dream 3D lets you create both still and animated 3D models.

- **Part III** deals with the utilities, clip art, clip media, and templates included on the CDs. You'll learn how to scan and trace bitmaps, as well as use OCR-Trace to turn scanned text into editable text. And you'll learn how to use the suite's useful scripting language to automate several aspects of your work.

- **Part IV** brings into focus a relatively new but ultimately important forum for computer graphics—the World Wide Web. You'll learn about using Web browser color palettes, creating multimedia events for the Internet, and much more.

Conventions

As I've said, *CorelDRAW 8 Secrets* is designed to provide in-depth and insightful coverage of the CorelDRAW graphics suite. To help you find information quickly, the text is annotated with the following icons. Use them as navigational aids.

Secret

The **Secret** icon highlights information about CorelDRAW that is not documented well or not widely known.

The **Design** icon highlights information relating to or affecting decisions you make regarding image and document design issues and principles.

The **Note** icon marks additional information about a feature or task, providing more insight on the standard procedure topics. Notes sometimes direct you to other parts of the book or other sources for finding additional information.

The **Tip** icon points out hints that can help you work easier and faster.

The **Version 8** icon points out features or procedures new and unique to version 8 of the software. If you are a seasoned user of the program, thumb through the book and look for these icons to pump up on the new stuff.

The **Expert Advice** icon marks information, techniques, or preferences from design experts and CorelDRAW experts.

The **Warning** icon warns you about procedures to which you should pay particular attention. Do yourself a favor — don't skip these.

The **Remember** icon reminds you about points that are easily over-looked or forgotten.

Finally, to assist you in reading and learning the material in this book, we use the following formatting conventions throughout the text:

■ Alternative command paths are formatted in stylized brackets. For example, the command you use to open a dialog box would appear like this: Choose File ➪ Open [Ctrl+O].

■ Text that you are asked to type appears in **bold.**

By now we're sure you're more than ready to learn all you can about CorelDRAW 8. That's what this book is for, so let's get started.

Acknowledgments

Heartfelt thanks go out to the editors at IDG Books Worldwide, Andy Cummings and Ron Hull. If it were not for their efforts in keeping me focused during this enormous task, there might never have been a *CorelDRAW 8 Secrets*. And that would have been a shame.

I'd also like to thank Winston Steward for his exhaustive efforts.

Most important of all, however, I'd like to thank my wife Heidi for putting up with the late nights and ill-temper these projects invariably produce. This time she did so all-the-while giving birth to and taking care of our new baby, Samantha. Also, Heidi's help putting together the CD-ROM material for this book was invaluable.

William Harrel

I would like to thank Ron Hull, Ellen Camm, Andy Cummings, and Nate Holdread for superb editorial support and accepting setbacks with good humor and grace. Thanks also to Margo Maley, agent extraordinaire. A special thanks to MegaImage, of Pomona, California, for building a laptop computer that would rise to this significant challenge.

Winston Steward

Contents at a Glance

Table of Contents

Part I

Drawing with CorelDraw

Chapter 1

The CorelDraw Interface

In This Chapter

You learn about the interface of the CorelDraw module of the CorelDraw 8 suite. The topics covered include the following:

▶ Creating and using multiple workspaces

▶ Customizing your keyboard, menus, toolbars, roll-ups, and color palette

▶ Touring the Property Bar

▶ Working more efficiently in CorelDraw

When the folks at Corel created CorelDraw, they designed the program to be as useful as possible for the largest number of users. The problem is that no two users work the same way. Consequently, Corel has made CorelDraw completely customizable. You can create your own menus, add buttons to the toolbar, create your own shortcut keys, and perform all sorts of customization wizardry to make the program's interface fit your needs. And, in version 8 you can now save sets of customization settings for different types of projects — a feature Corel calls *workspaces*. Workspaces allow you to completely customize the interface, save the settings, and load them whenever you need them. Wow! In this chapter you learn how to make CorelDraw work more like you do.

If you're like most computer program users, you learn one way to perform a task and then use the same method over and over to achieve the same results. If it works, don't fix it, right? Well, no — not necessarily. CorelDraw provides several ways to achieve the same results, and usually one method is faster and more efficient than others. In the last part of this chapter we'll look at some of the program's shortcut features, such as using pop-up menus, dragging and dropping between documents, and so forth. One feature that can really speed up your work is the CorelDraw Property Bar and the new dockers palettes, which we'll also look at in this chapter.

Customizing the Interface

The CorelDraw interface is based on a drawing-table metaphor. Picture yourself sitting at a drawing easel. You arrange your tools — pencils, pens, rulers, and so on — in a manner that best suits the way you work. Working in

CorelDraw is the same. You can customize the user interface to adapt the program to the type of work you do. For example, you can add, delete, and modify the following:

- Workspaces
- Keyboard shortcuts
- Menus and menu commands
- Toolbar options
- Dockers
- Colors on the color palette

You can also customize the way roll-up palettes work. You perform each type of customization option in the Options dialog box, shown in Figure 1-1, which you access by choosing Tools ⇨ Options.

Note

As you read this chapter, keep in mind that many of these customization options are also available in the other CorelDraw applications, such as Photo-Paint and Dream 3D. Furthermore, notice that the Options dialog box lets you configure virtually every aspect of not only CorelDraw, but also several aspects of the specific document you're working on, HTML options, and a slew of others. This chapter deals primarily with customizing the interface. Other chapters discuss other customization options. Chapter 20, for example, covers customizing HTML features, while Chapter 3 covers customizing grids, guidelines, layers, and so on.

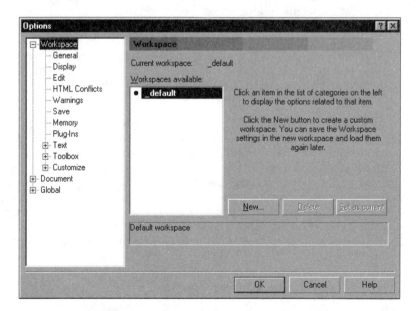

Figure 1-1: Use the Options dialog box to rearrange interface options.

As you can see in Figure 1-1, the Options dialog box contains several different categories, which you access by selecting options in the list on the left. To customize Keyboard, Menu, Toolbars, Roll-Ups, and Color Palette, you open the Customize option. Then click on each one of the suboptions to display the associated sheet as we go over the options available on these sheets one at a time. First, however, we want to show you version 8's new Workspace option.

Using multiple workspaces

Think of workspaces as separate workstations. For example, you would use (or change) one workstation for page layout, another for graphics design, and yet another for Web page construction. In CorelDraw 8 you can create and save entire work environments based on the task at hand. Combine this ability with templates (discussed in Chapter 16), and you can get CorelDraw to complete virtually all of your preliminary setup and preparation automatically.

Creating a new workspace is easy. Simply select the Workspace option in the list on the left in the Options dialog box, and then click on the New button in the Workspace window. This displays the New Workspace dialog box, which contains the following four options:

- **Name of New Workspace.** This one speaks for itself. Simply give the new workspace a descriptive name.

- **Base New Workspace On.** Here's a handy option. Use this dialog box to create workspaces based on other, or like, workspaces, which saves time. For example, say you have a workspace for creating a certain newsletter. Then you want to create another newsletter workspace with similar but not exact requirements. Rather than starting from scratch with the default work space, you can base the new workspace on an existing one, making only the changes you need to create the new workspace.

- **Description of Workspace.** You know what this means, right?

- **Set as Current Workspace.** This dialog box simply makes the new workspace active in the current document.

This concept of workspaces is an easy one. However, the changes you can make to a workspace are numerous and intricate. We're sure some possibilities have already occurred to you.

Changing Default Attributes

In addition to enabling you to customize menu, keyboard, toolbar, and roll-up options, CorelDraw also lets you modify virtually all aspects of the interface, including the default line weight, fill, text size, and typeface. To change these default attributes, you simply make a change without selecting an object. For example, to change the default typeface to Garamond 14-point, with nothing selected simply choose Text ➪ Format Text. CorelDraw displays a dialog box informing you that you are about to make a change to the default text attributes. The dialog box also gives you the option to assign the new default to artistic text, paragraph text, or both. (If you were working with a line or fill attribute, CorelDraw would provide a different message, of course.)

When you click on OK, the Format Text dialog box appears, enabling you to set text attributes. The changes you make at this point are changes to the default settings. As you can imagine, this is a powerful way to customize CorelDraw to work the way you do. We'll look closer at this feature in the next chapter.

When you get the settings exactly to your liking, you make the changes permanent with the Settings for New Documents command on the Tools menu. This option reconfigures the default new document settings, including the changes you make to the interface.

Saving time with keyboard shortcuts

Keyboard shortcuts (sometimes called *hot keys*) are keystrokes that execute commands, often saving you the trouble of opening menus and wading through nested dialog boxes. CorelDraw comes with several keyboard shortcuts already assigned. You can see many of these shortcuts simply by viewing the menus. On the Text menu, for example, the shortcut that opens the Format Text dialog box (Ctrl+T) appears to the right of the Format Text command.

Secret

You can get and print a list of all the keyboard shortcut keys in the current workspace.

STEPS:

Printing Your Keyboard Shortcuts

Step 1.   Select Tools ➪ Options.

Step 2.   In the list of categories on the left, double-click on Customize, and then click on Shortcut Keys.

Step 3.   Click on the View All button. This brings up the Shortcut Keys, shown in Figure 1-2. From here you can scroll to view your shortcuts.

Step 4.   Click on the Print button to print the list.

Figure 1-2: To view a list of keyboard shortcuts, display the Shortcut Keys dialog box, which is nested in the Options dialog box.

Although you'll find many of CorelDraw's preassigned keyboard shortcuts to be useful, you can speed up your work by modifying the preassigned shortcuts and adding your own. You can add, remove, and change the keyboard shortcuts using the Shortcut Keys sheet in the Options dialog box. Choose Tools ⇨ Options, and then double-click on Customize and select Shortcut Keys.

In the list on the left, labeled Command, you'll find an index of CorelDraw menus, styles, and scripts. To view the list of commands, styles, or scripts, click on the small plus sign (+) to the left of the menu name (or double-click on the name). To add a keyboard shortcut—or to modify or remove an existing shortcut—click on the appropriate item in the Command list. If the command already has a keystroke shortcut assigned, the key-combination shows up in the Current shortcut keys field near the center of the dialog box, as shown in Figure 1-3.

To delete a currently assigned shortcut, simply select the keystroke combination in the Current shortcut keys field and click on Delete. To add a keystroke shortcut, make sure the appropriate item is selected in the Commands list, move the cursor to the Press new shortcut key field, and then press the keystroke combination you want to assign. Keystroke shortcuts can consist of the following kinds of combinations:

- Ctrl+key or function key
- Ctrl+Shift+key or function key
- Ctrl+Alt+key or function key
- Ctrl+Alt+Shift+key or function key
- Alt+key or function key
- Alt+Shift+key or function key

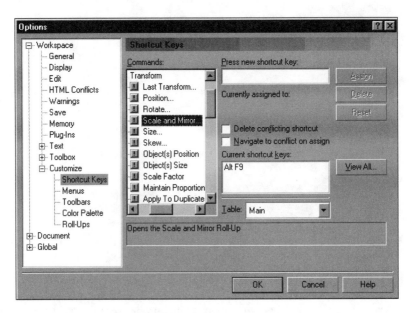

Figure 1-3: To see the keyboard shortcut(s) assigned to a command, highlight the command in the Commands list.

If you choose a keystroke combination already assigned to another command or option, the existing assignment appears in the portion of the dialog box labeled Currently assigned to. Because the same keyboard shortcut cannot be assigned to two different commands or options, you need to either choose a new keystroke combination or change the existing keyboard shortcut that conflicts with the new assignment. (If you check the Navigate to conflict on assign check box, CorelDraw automatically takes you to the command with a conflicting keyboard shortcut so you can change that assignment. In version 8 you can also check the Delete conflicting shortcut check box to tell CorelDraw to automatically remove the conflicting shortcut.) To complete the procedure, click on the Assign button. You can make as many assignments and changes as you want before leaving this dialog box, but remember to click on OK. If you click on the Cancel button, you lose your new keyboard shortcut assignments.

If you assign keyboard shortcuts to many commands, styles, and scripts, you can conceivably run out of keystroke combinations — or you might forget which keyboard shortcuts have already been assigned. CorelDraw provides a way to expand the number of combinations and at the same time logically organize your shortcuts. Unlike many other Windows applications, CorelDraw supports multilayered shortcuts. In other words, your keystroke combinations can consist of many consecutive keys, up to four levels deep, such as Ctrl+Alt+1, 2, 3, 4. In this example, you would press Ctrl+Alt and then press 1, 2, 3, and 4 in succession.

Assigning Keyboard Shortcuts to Styles and Scripts

If you've been using CorelDraw awhile, then you probably already know about the program's powerful style and scripting capabilities. (If not, Chapter 4 discusses text styles, Chapter 5 discusses color styles, and Chapter 19 covers scripting.) Styles, of course, enable you to define several attributes (such as typefaces, type styles, point sizes, outlines, and fills), assign them to a style name, and then apply them to an object with a mouse click or two. Scripts are macros you can record to execute several commands or functions at once, much like the macro function in word processors.

In addition to assigning commands, you can also assign styles and scripts to shortcut keys. Doing so enables you to apply a style or run a script simply by pressing a key-combination. You can assign styles and scripts in the Customize dialog box, as shown in the figure. To assign a style to a keyboard shortcut, scroll in the Commands list until the Apply Styles folder appears. Open the folder to display a list of styles defined for the current template. Now use the same method described earlier in this section for assigning shortcuts to commands. You assign scripts in the same manner, except you need to use the commands listed in the Apply Styles folder in the Commands list.

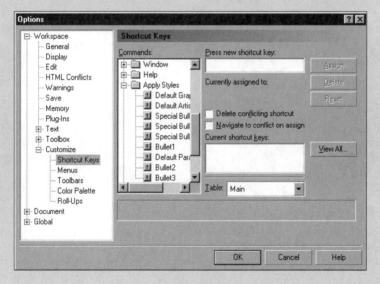

To assign shortcuts to styles and scripts, open the Apply Styles folder to view a list of available styles and scripts.

Multiple layers are especially useful for organizing script and style shortcuts. For example, if you have several styles for headings, subheads, and so on, you may decide to number your heading styles in layers. You can give level-one headings the shortcut Ctrl+Alt+1; level-two headings Ctrl+Alt+1,1; level-three headings Ctrl+Alt+1,1,1; and so forth. With a little ingenuity, you can create multilayered shortcuts that are organized in a way that enables you to work most efficiently.

Using menus and menu commands

Okay, so CorelDraw has numerous features that can turn even unartistic people into illustrators. But let's face it, all those features translate into far too many menus and choices. This is especially true of CorelDraw 8, which has even more menus and choices than previous versions. With version 8, however, you can get rid of the menu options that you never use.

You may also decide to create custom menu structures for certain kinds of documents that involve similar tasks. For example, if you perform repetitive tasks in a document, such as creating a monthly catalog or brochure, you can create a menu structure for that kind of document with only the commands and scripts you need.

In addition to letting you add and modify menus, CorelDraw 8 enables you to change the pop-up menus that you access with the right mouse button. These menus pop up when you right-click during certain functions or operations. Figure 1-4 shows an example. In versions 7 and 8 you can determine which options appear in the different pop-up menus. Neat, huh?

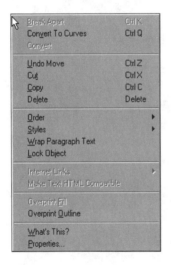

Figure 1-4: CorelDraw 8 makes pop-up menus fully customizable.

You can modify CorelDraw's menus from the Menus option in the Customize sheet of the Options dialog box, as shown in Figure 1-5. Choose Tools ⇨ Customize ⇨ Menus.

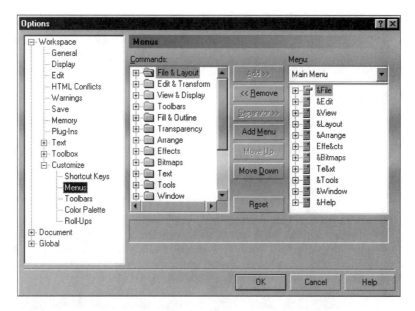

Figure 1-5: Use the Menus portion of the Customize sheet of the Options dialog box to modify CorelDraw's menu structure.

From here you can perform the following tasks:

- Add and delete menus on the menu bar
- Change the order of menus on the menu bar
- Add and delete submenus
- Rearrange submenus on a menu
- Add and delete commands on a menu
- Rearrange the commands on a menu
- Move commands or submenus from one menu to another
- Add styles and scripts to menus

In the next few sections we'll look at each of these tasks related to customizing the menus.

Adding, deleting, and moving menus

When you open the Customize sheet in the Options dialog box and open the Customize and Menus folders, CorelDraw displays your current menu structure (refer to Figure 1-5). The Commands list on the left displays all the available functions, including options on many of the roll-ups and any styles or scripts you may have created. In this list you choose objects for inclusion in your new menu structure. In the Menu list on the right you build new menus and modify existing ones.

When you're customizing the menu bar itself — the row of menus across the top of the screen — make sure that Main Menu is selected in the Menu drop-down list. (The other items in the drop-down list are your pop-up menus, grouped by context.)

To add a menu, click on the Add Menu button. This creates a new menu on the list. The space for the menu's name is automatically selected so you can name the menu, as Figure 1-6 shows. Because the menu is brand-new, it does not contain any commands or options. You'll see how to add those a little later.

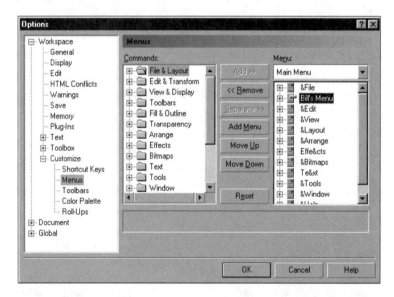

Figure 1-6: When you add a new menu, its name is automatically highlighted so you can customize it.

To delete a menu, simply select it in the Menu list and then click on Remove. Keep in mind that deleting a menu removes not only the menu name but also all the commands on it. Those commands will not be available while you work (unless they are available in roll-ups or through shortcut key assignments). You can assign the deleted commands and options to other menus.

To change the position of a menu on the menu bar, select it and then click on the Move Up and Move Down buttons to position the menu where you want it, as shown in Figures 1-7 and 1-8.

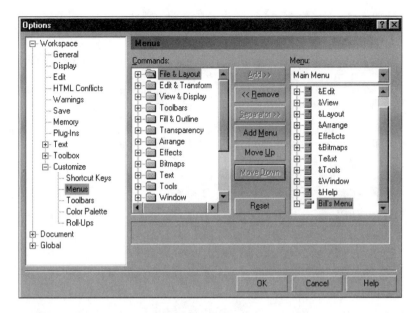

Figure 1-7: Use the Move Up and Move Down buttons to position a menu on the menu bar.

Figure 1-8: When you click on the Move Down button enough times, the selected menu moves to the end of the menu bar.

Adding, deleting, and moving submenus

Submenus, also called *flyouts*, are menus within menus. Submenus can add a wide variety of options to a menu. For example, a typical submenu is the Order submenu on the Arrange menu, with which you can choose from a list of layering options, such as Send to Back, Send to Front, and so on. Submenus can hold commands, scripts, and styles. They can also contain other submenus. The procedure for adding, deleting, and moving submenus is similar to adding, deleting, and moving menus, except that the drop-down list on the Menu portion of the Customize sheet in the Options dialog box must display the name of the menu you want to customize.

To add a submenu, double-click on the menu where you want to add the submenu. Click on Add Menu and then give the menu a name, just as you do when you add a new menu to the menu bar. (You can add as many submenus as you like, but at some point it becomes counterproductive.)

Delete submenus by selecting them and then clicking Remove. As with menus, when you delete a submenu, all the commands and options on the menu are also deleted. You can change a submenu's position on a menu by clicking on the Move Up and Move Down buttons.

Adding, deleting, and moving commands, styles, and scripts

When talking about menu entries, Corel calls everything that can be placed on a menu a command; these items include styles, scripts, roll-up options, and regular commands. Menu commands can include the styles and scripts you create within a document template as well as predefined options.

You can add menu commands (styles, scripts, commands, and so forth) to either submenus or menus. The following procedure shows you how.

STEPS:

Adding and Removing Commands on a Menu

Step 1.   In the Menu list, double-click on the menu or submenu in which you want to add or remove a command.

Step 2.   In the Commands list on the left, scroll to the command you want to add or remove, and then highlight it.

Step 3.   Click on the Add button or the Remove button.

Step 4.   To move an item up or down on a menu, use the Move Up or Move Down buttons.

Working with Templates and Styles

Most experienced CorelDraw users are familiar with templates. Templates are predefined shells, or layouts, you can use to create drawings and documents. CorelDraw ships with several predesigned templates for various projects, such as newsletters, brochures, and other documents. Each template contains its own set of predefined text, graphics, and color styles. You can also create and save your own templates for use in repetitive or similar projects.

When you start a new CorelDraw document, unless you choose another template you'll work in a style set based on the default template. While working in the default template, if you change existing styles or create additional ones, these styles are added to the style list for that template. This is also true when you work in templates other than the default. Each template has its own set of styles. When assigning styles to menus, you can work only with those contained in the current template.

Corel DRAW 8   With the addition of workspaces, discussed earlier in this chapter, you can greatly expand on the templates concept by saving separate workspace layouts to use with your various templates. While this can be extremely helpful, at some point it could become counterproductive — you'll spend all your time customizing workspaces and layouts, neglecting your work. Keep in mind that these options are designed to enable you to make CorelDraw's interface more adaptable to your work habits and projects. More often than not, however, the default interface works just fine. And many jobs do not require a template.

The procedure for adding styles to menus is similar. The only variation to this procedure is that you add the items in the Apply Styles folder in the Command list to your menus in the menu list.

You can further customize your menu by adding *separators*. Separators are those narrow lines on a menu that break the menu into sections, as shown in Figure 1-9. To add a separator, highlight the command or submenu directly above the point where you want the separator to appear, and then click on the Separator button.

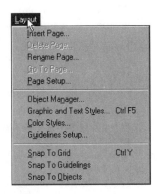

Figure 1-9: When designing menus, you can use separators to mark off groups of commands and make them easier to read.

Customizing pop-up menus

Seasoned Windows 95 users are no doubt familiar with pop-up menus accessed by clicking the right mouse button. These menus give you quick and easy access to commands and options according to context. In CorelDraw, for example, when you right-click the text I-beam on selected text, you get the menu shown in Figure 1-10. This menu enables you to perform text formatting and editing tasks quickly, without shunting to the menu bar.

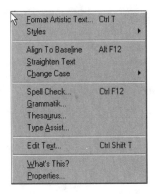

Figure 1-10: Clicking the right mouse button displays a pop-up menu.

Of course, the menu that appears depends on the tool selected and what you click on. CorelDraw ships with several predefined pop-up menus. To see a list of these menus, in the Menus portion of the Customize sheet of the Options dialog box, click on the Menu drop-down list. To edit a right-mouse button menu, scroll through the list and select the option you want to edit. CorelDraw displays the menu layout for that selection. To add, delete, and rearrange the pop-up commands, simply follow the procedure you learned earlier in this section.

Secret

At first glance, the capability to customize pop-up menus may seem ho-hum. But give it some more thought. One use for this option is to assign scripts to the pop-ups. Then, when you right-click on an object, all the scripts appear. All you have to do is choose the one you want to run on the selected object.

Toolbars

Toolbars are palettes of buttons and fields that give you quick and easy access to commands and other features. CorelDraw ships with several predefined toolbars that you can modify to suit your needs, or you can create your own. Over the years, we have found that many CorelDraw users don't even know that CorelDraw has toolbars in addition to the ones that appear automatically. If you're one of those people, you're not alone.

Controlling how toolbars are displayed

To see the available toolbars, choose View ➪ Toolbars. An Options dialog box pops up, shown in Figure 1-11. From here you can choose which toolbars to display, control how the toolbars appear, and create new toolbars.

By default, CorelDraw displays several toolbars, including the Property Bar, toolbox, and the standard toolbar. To display additional toolbars, select them in the Toolbars dialog box. You can also change the appearance of the toolbars by dragging on the sliders or choosing one of the options below the sliders. You can change the button size and the width of the borders around the buttons. This option is handy if you need to adjust the size of buttons to fit better on your monitor.

When you click on OK, the toolbars and the options you select appear on the application desktop. Depending on the toolbars you choose, they will display either at the top of the window (docked) or as a separate entity (floating) in the application window. You have several options for changing the appearance and location of toolbars. Figure 1-12 shows the Text toolbar displayed two different ways: floating and docked.

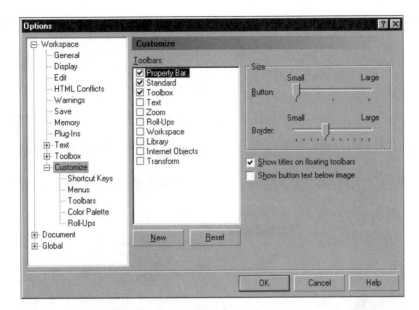

Figure 1-11: Use the Options dialog box to choose the toolbars you want to display.

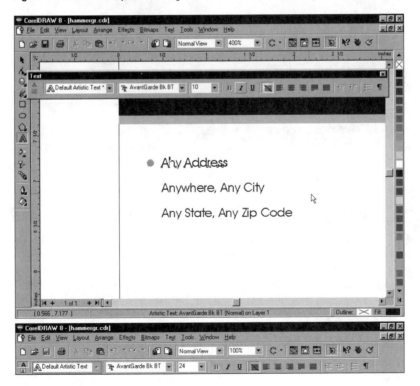

Figure 1-12: You can float or dock any toolbar.

To float a docked toolbar, move it from its docked position by dragging on a portion of the bar that is unoccupied by a field or button. To dock a floating toolbar, drag it to the position at the top or bottom of the window where you want it to remain docked. To resize a toolbar, drag its sides or corners, as shown in Figure 1-13.

Pull here to lenghten   Pull here to widen

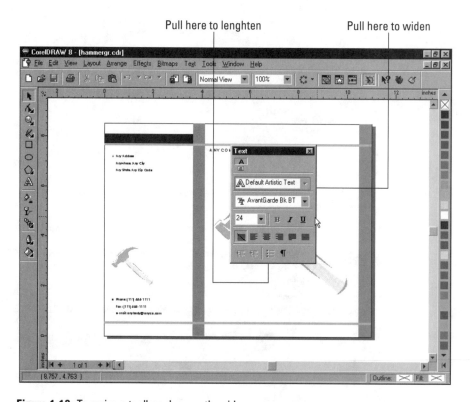

Figure 1-13: To resize a toolbar, drag on the sides or corners.

Adding and removing toolbar buttons

You can add, remove, and rearrange toolbar buttons using the Customize portion of the Options dialog box. You can get there by choosing View ⇨ Toolbars or by double-clicking on the Customize folder in the Options dialog box. Both methods bring up the dialog box shown in Figure 1-14. With either option, you must first display the toolbar you want to modify by selecting it in the Toolbars list. When the toolbar is displayed, double-click on the Toolbars folder in Customize to display the dialog box sheet shown in Figure 1-15. From here you customize your toolbars.

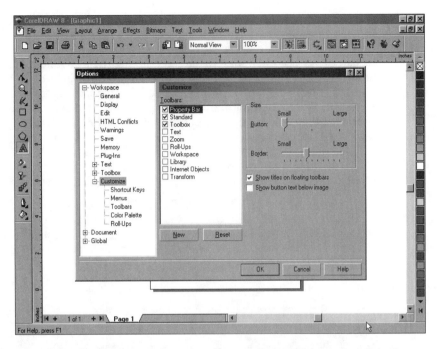

Figure 1-14: Use the Toolbars sheet of the Customize sheet of the Options dialog box to add buttons and fields to toolbars.

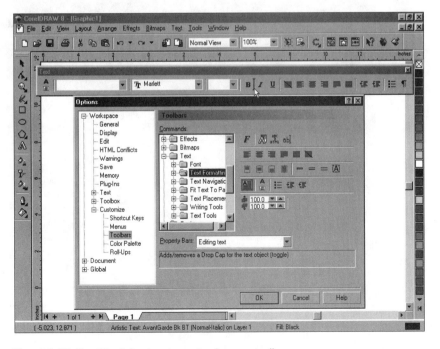

Figure 1-15: Use this dialog box to customize your toolbars.

The Commands field of the dialog box contains all the available commands and options you can assign to toolbars (not all options in the list can be assigned to toolbars—next, we'll show you how to see which ones are available). As you open folders and subfolders, the available toolbar options show up on the right side of the toolbox. The Buttons palette on the right shows the available buttons for the selected category. For example, when you select Text ➪ Text Formatting in the Commands field, you see the buttons and fields designed for changing text attributes. To add a button or field to the Text toolbar, simply drag the button or field from the dialog box onto the toolbar, as shown in Figure 1-16. To remove buttons or fields, simply drag them off the toolbar. You can change the positions of buttons on a toolbar simply by dragging them while the dialog box is open.

Easy enough to drag and drop, right? One thing: No matter how long you've been using CorelDraw, you probably don't know what all the available buttons mean. To find out, simply click on the icon. A message appears at the bottom of the dialog box, telling you what the button does.

Add a button by dragging it to the toolbar

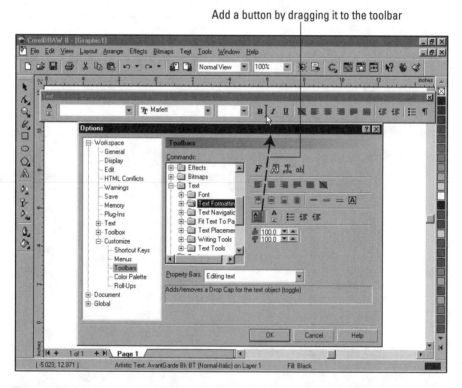

Figure 1-16: To add buttons and fields to a toolbar, simply drag them from the dialog box onto the toolbar. Here, the Add/Remove Dropcap option is being added to the Text toolbar at the top.

Instead of using obscure little icons on your toolbar buttons, you can put text on them. In the Customize portion of the Option dialog box, select the Show button text below image check box. The problem with this option is that the text takes up much more room. When you use text buttons, you cannot fit as many buttons on a docked toolbar.

Creating new toolbars

In addition to modifying existing toolbars, you can create your own new toolbars. From the Customize ⇨ Toolbars portion of the Options dialog box, simply drag an icon to the desktop. A new toolbar is automatically created — Toolbar 1. You can further customize the toolbar by dragging additional icons onto it. To rename the toolbar, close the Options dialog box, reopen it, and return to Customize ⇨ Toolbars. Right-click on the new toolbar in the list and choose Rename, as shown in Figure 1-17.

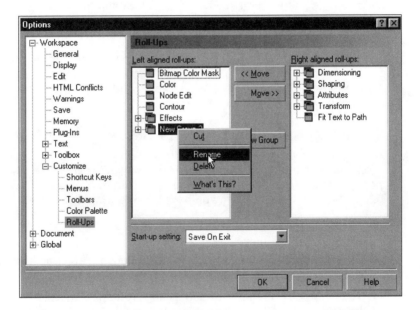

Figure 1-17: To rename a new toolbar, simply right-click and choose Rename.

Roll-up groups

One of the most useful features of CorelDraw is *roll-ups*. Roll-ups are palettes of commands that make it easy to modify the objects in your drawings. The Blend roll-up, for example, enables you to create blends between two or more objects.

Unlike menus and toolbars, you can't really add and remove options from roll-ups. You can, however, create groups of roll-ups specific to your own personal work habits. You can also specify the default location for each roll-up in the application window.

Roll-up groups are combinations of several roll-ups with related functions. The Effects roll-up group, for example, contains all the roll-ups you would use to create special effects, such as adding perspective, blending, creating 3D extrudes, and so on. The Attributes roll-up group contains the Special Fill and Pen roll-ups for modifying an object's lines and fills. You'll find roll-up groups useful because they reduce the clutter caused by the large number of roll-ups CorelDraw has accumulated over the years.

CorelDraw ships with several roll-up groups you can modify, or you can create your own groups. You can modify or create roll-up groups in the application window using the mouse to drag and drop, or you can create new groups in the Roll-Ups sheet of the Customize dialog box.

Creating roll-up groups using drag-and-drop

While CorelDraw's current roll-up configuration is probably fine for most uses, you may find it convenient to create your own task-specific sets. To modify a roll-up group, open the group you want to change by clicking on Tools ⇨ Roll-up Groups. Then you have the following three choices:

- **To separate** a roll-up from its current group, simply drag it from the roll-up list in the group, as shown in Figure 1-18.

- **To move** a roll-up from one group to another, simply drag it from one roll-up group list to another, as shown in Figure 1-19.

- **To combine** two roll-ups or add a single roll-up to an existing group, hold down the Alt key as you drag to the title bar of the roll-up or group you want to combine with, as shown in Figure 1-20. The cursor changes to an arrow with a roll-up icon as you drag the roll-up.

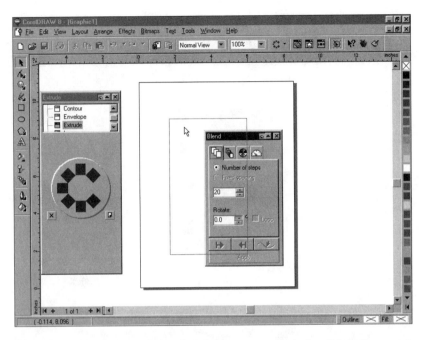

Figure 1-18: To separate a single roll-up from a group, simply drag it from the group to the desktop.

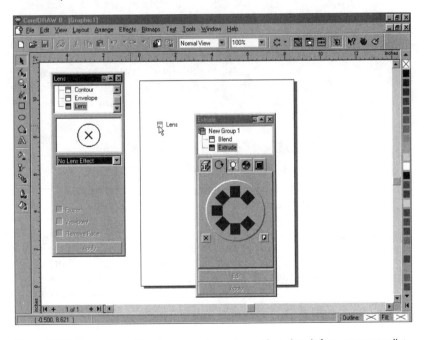

Figure 1-19: To move a roll-up from one group to another, drag it from one group list to another.

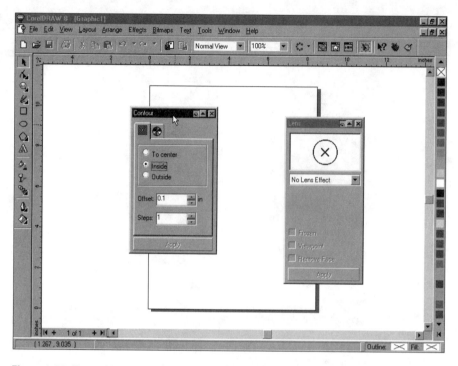

Figure 1-20: To combine two single roll-ups, hold down the Alt key and drag one roll-up to the other's title bar.

When you combine two single roll-ups, CorelDraw lets you name the new group whatever you like. Simply open the Options dialog box (Tools ➪ Options), open the Customize and Roll-Ups folders, and then click on New Group 1 to select it. Then click the right mouse button on the label, choose Rename, and retype the name.

Creating roll-up groups using the Customize dialog box

In addition to creating and modifying roll-up groups in the application window, you can also make changes to group configurations in the Options dialog box. The Roll-Ups subfolder of the Customize folder in the dialog box (Customize ➪ Roll-Ups), shown in Figure 1-21, displays roll-ups and groups according to how they appear in the "arranged" position on the left and right sides of the application window. In other words, the roll-ups and groups are listed based on the position they line up in when you choose Arrange All from any roll-up flyout menu. Figure 1-22 shows all the roll-ups in the Arrange All position. If you compare Figures 1-20 and 1-21, you can see what we mean.

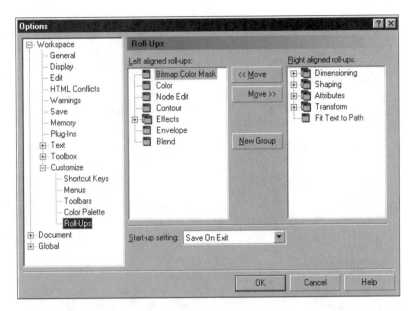

Figure 1-21: Use the Roll-Ups portion of the Options dialog box to customize roll-up groups.

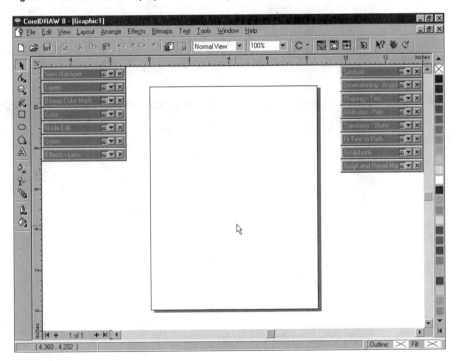

Figure 1-22: All of CorelDraw's roll-ups are organized here according to their Arrange All position.

Modifying roll-up groups from this dialog box is a lot like creating new menus and arranging menu options. To add a roll-up to an existing group, open the group by double-clicking on it, and then use the Move buttons or drag and drop a roll-up into the group. You can also use this dialog box to change on which side a roll-up lines up when you invoke Arrange All. To change the stacking order, simply drag the roll-up icon up or down the list. To create a new group, click on the New Group button, name the group, and then move the desired roll-ups into the new group.

You can also direct CorelDraw to display all roll-ups and groups upon opening the program. Choose the All Roll-Ups Arranged option in the Start-up setting drop-down list in the lower-left corner of the Roll-Ups portion of the Customize dialog box. Choosing No Roll-Ups instructs the program to open with no roll-ups displayed. Save On Exit saves the roll-up layout when you close CorelDraw. The next time you open CorelDraw, you get the same arrangement.

Dockers

One of the common complaints about dialog boxes is that you must open them, make your changes, and close them; if you don't like the changes the settings made to an object, then you must open the dialog box and start over again. Eh! Corel has addressed this problem by providing a number of interactive dialog boxes, called *dockers*. Dockers are dialog boxes that act similarly to toolbars and roll-ups in that they let you view your changes without opening and closing dialog boxes. Figure 1-23 shows an example of a docker. You can get a list of available dockers by choosing View ⇨ Dockers.

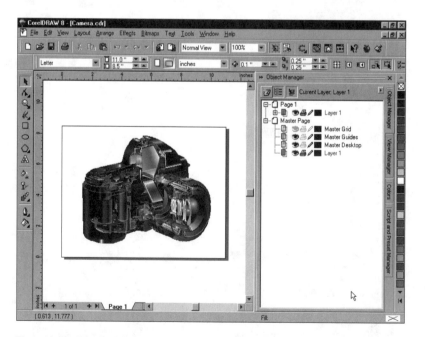

Figure 1-23: Use dockers to avoid the tedium of opening and closing dialog boxes.

You can open one docker or several, as shown in the figure. When several dockers are open, all but the active one display as tabs along the side of the dockers. By default, dockers open and dock on the left side of the applications window. However, like toolbars, you can move them to the right, top, or bottom, or you can float them. Similar to roll-ups, you can also create groups of dockers, displaying more than one docker session, by dragging on the dockers tab.

Unfortunately, dockers are not customizable — allowing you to remove and add options or create totally new dockers — in the same fashion as toolbars, roll-ups, and menus. But dockers are a new feature. Watch for customizable dockers (and a slew of new ones, if we know Corel as we think we do) in the next version.

The color palette

You have many ways to work with color more efficiently in CorelDraw. In this section you learn how to modify the display of the color palette. Chapter 5 provides a more in-depth discussion of applying and using colors.

You probably already know that you can add and remove colors from the color palette that spans the left side of the CorelDraw window. (If you don't know how to do this, we show you in Chapter 5.) But did you know that you can also change the appearance and position of the color palette? This can make it easier to get to, and you can access all the colors at once rather than having to scroll back and forth. You can adjust the appearance of the color palette by clicking the Color Palette folder in the Customize sheet of the Options dialog box (Tools ⇨ Options ⇨ Customize ⇨ Color Palettes), shown in Figure 1-24.

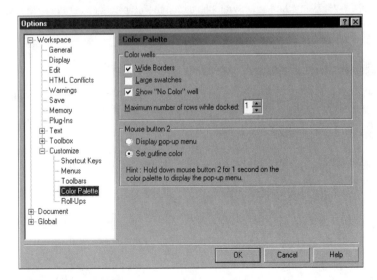

Figure 1-24: Use the Color Palette folder of the Options dialog box to modify the appearance and behavior of the color palette.

Changing the size of the color swatches

If you're working on a relatively small, high-resolution monitor, color swatches in the palette may be difficult to see. You can remedy this problem with the Large Swatches option in the Color Palette sheet of the Customize dialog box. Figure 1-25 shows what large color swatches look like on the color palette.

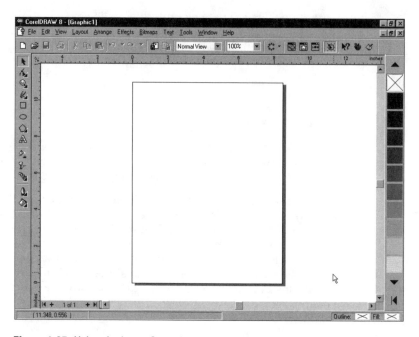

Figure 1-25: Using the Large Swatches option makes colors easier to see in the color palette along the bottom or side of the window.

Displaying more colors at once

Secret

Having to scroll back and forth in the color palette can be tedious. In fact, when we're feeling lazy, we sometimes choose one of the visible colors rather than scrolling through the palette to find the exact hue we need. CorelDraw provides a remedy to temporary bouts of sloth by enabling you to display *all* the colors on the color palette. You do so by using the Color Palette sheet of the Customize dialog box to adjust the number of rows displayed. You control this setting using the Display *x* rows while docked option. Figure 1-26 shows the color palette with four columns displayed.

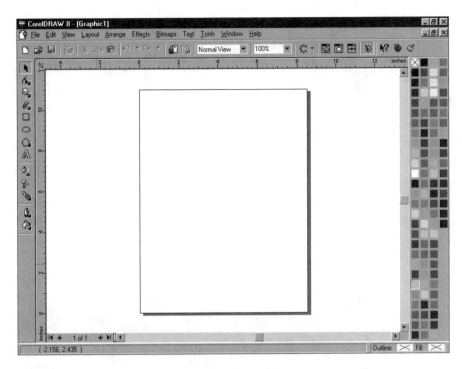

Figure 1-26: See more colors at once by adjusting the number of columns displayed in the color palette while it's docked. You can even display all the colors this way.

If you use a small, low-resolution monitor, you may be more interested in saving screen real estate than displaying more colors. An alternative is to place colors you use most at the front of the color palette. You can use the right-mouse button pop-up menu to move a color by selecting the Move to Front command. In addition, you can temporarily display all the colors on the palette by clicking on the upward-pointing scroll arrow in the lower-right portion of the application window, as shown in Figure 1-27. The full palette remains visible until you release the mouse button.

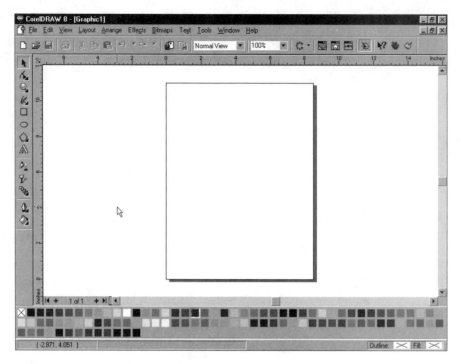

Figure 1-27: Clicking on this scroll button temporarily displays all of the colors on the palette.

Note

To display a right-mouse button pop-up menu on the color palette, you must first turn on Display Pop-Up Menu in the Mouse Button 2 section of the Color Palette sheet of the Options dialog box. Otherwise, clicking the right mouse button sets the outline color for a selected object; or, when nothing is selected, it sets the default outline color.

Changing the location of the color palette

On large, high-resolution monitors, you sometimes have to drag the mouse a long way from the drawing area to the color palette. CorelDraw provides relief by letting you float the color palette or dock it at the top, bottom, or left side of the screen. After you've floated the palette, you can resize it just like a toolbar. To float the palette, simply drag on the gray area around the swatches. To resize a floated palette, drag on a side or corner of the palette, just as you would a toolbar.

To dock the palette at the top or left side of the application window, drag the palette into the position you want, as shown in Figure 1-28. You can tell when the palette is in place when the outline of the palette pops into the new docked position. When you release the mouse button, the palette docks.

As you can see, the customization options for the color palette are extensive. You should experiment to find the right settings for the way you work.

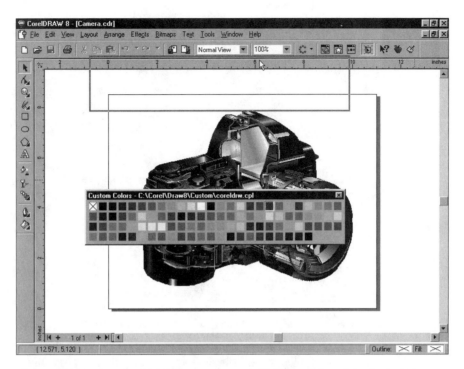

Figure 1-28: To move the color palette to a new position, drag it into place. To dock the color palette, drag it into position and release the mouse button.

Filters

Many CorelDraw users save their graphics files in several different formats. For example, you may need .TIFF or .EPS for printed material, .GIF or .JPEG for the Internet, and .BMP for presentations and multimedia. In addition, you often need to import various formats into CorelDraw and supporting applications, such as Photo-Paint or Dream 3D. Hence, CorelDraw comes with a trove of import and export filters.

Filters are little pieces of software that translate file formats non-native to an application into a format the application can use. For example, when you import an MS Word file into CorelDraw, a filter tells CorelDraw how to read and format the text.

CorelDraw comes with so many filters that sorting through them in the Import and Export dialog boxes can be annoying and time-consuming. You can use the Filters sheet in the Options dialog box (Tools ⇨ Options ⇨ Global ⇨ Filters), shown in Figure 1-29, in the Customize dialog box to remove and add filters as needed.

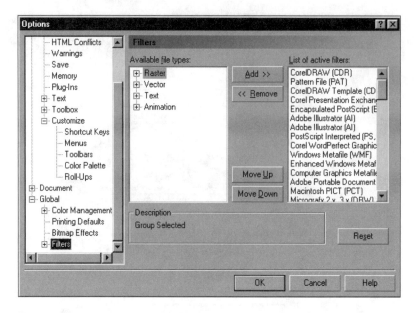

Figure 1-29: Use this sheet to add and remove import and export filters.

The list on the left shows the available file, or filter, types. They are separated by group, or type of file—raster, vector, text, and animation. The list on the right shows active filters, or the filters currently available when you invoke either the Import or Export commands on the File menu.

To add a filter to the active list, simply open a group in the left list, find the desired filter, select it, and then click on the Add button. (When you select a filter, CorelDraw displays a description of the filter in the Description portion of the dialog box.) To remove filters, simply select them in the right list and then click on Remove. You can also change the order in which the filters appear in the Import and Export dialog boxes with the Move Up and Move Down dialog buttons. Simply select the filter you want to move up or down, and then click on the appropriate button.

Associations

A nifty benefit of CorelDraw is that because of the vast array of applications and utilities included with the package, you can import, use, or edit almost every kind of computer file—without having to purchase another application. You do not, for example, need a copy of Adobe Illustrator to edit .AI and .EPS files. All you need is CorelDraw. To edit raster, or bitmap graphics, you can use Photo-Paint.

As with most of the other Customize functions we've looked at in this chapter, Associate works not only with CorelDraw itself, but also with all the other applications included in the CorelDRAW package. What this option allows you to do is tell a specific CorelDraw application which files it controls, or is associated with.

When you associate a file with an application, you tell not only CorelDraw! but also Windows 95 which file types are associated with which applications. If, for example, you associate .EPS files with CorelDraw, then whenever .EPS files are displayed in Explorer on in a dialog box, they will display as CorelDraw files. In Explorer you can double-click on an .EPS file to launch CorelDraw and open the file.

Associations are made from the Associate portion of the Options dialog box (Tools ⇨ Options ⇨ Global ⇨ Filters ⇨ Associate). This window is shown in Figure 1-30. To associate any file type in the list with CorelDraw, simply click in the check box beside the file type in the Associate list.

Note

To associate files with other CorelDraw applications, such as Photo-Paint, open that application and perform the same procedure.

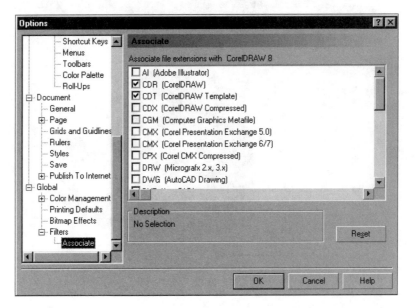

Figure 1-30: Open this folder in the Options dialog box to associate specific file formats with the current (open) CorelDraw application.

Using the Property Bar

Many professional desktop publishers and designers use graphics programs such as CorelDraw to create graphics for their layouts and then use a desktop publishing program, such as Adobe PageMaker or QuarkXPress, to lay out their pages. People who use desktop publishing programs are familiar with global control palettes that enable you to modify objects according to context. In PageMaker, for example, the Control Palette provides users with readily available controls for modifying selected objects according to which object is selected with what tool.

CorelDraw's Property Bar, introduced in version 7, is a similar device; however, it goes far beyond the palettes found in popular layout packages. It includes not only the traditional size, placement, rotation, and attributes options, but all sorts of other features as well. For example, when you select multiple objects, the Property Bar changes automatically. You get controls for grouping, combining, and aligning objects, and more. Figure 1-31 shows what the Property Bar looks like when multiple objects have been selected.

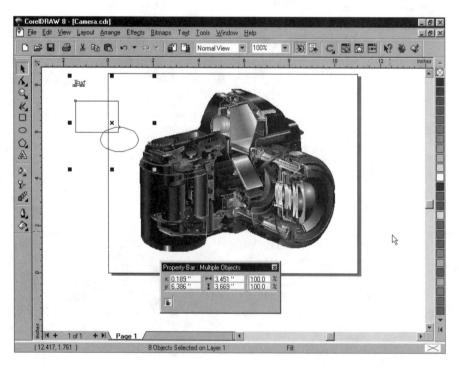

Figure 1-31: When you select multiple objects, the Property Bar provides options for working in that context.

When you apply special effects, such as blends or extrudes, the Property Bar changes to provide special options for modifying the effect, as shown in Figure 1-32.

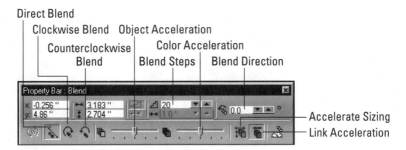

Direct Blend
Clockwise Blend   Object Acceleration
Counterclockwise   Color Acceleration
Blend   Blend Steps   Blend Direction

Accelerate Sizing
Link Acceleration

Figure 1-32: When you select an object containing a special effect, such as a blend, the Property Bar adapts to work with the effect.

Note

In all, over 20 Property Bar contexts exist—more than this chapter has room to discuss. Instead, we'll mention the different Property Bar configurations where they are relevant to the discussion at hand.

After you specify the context, you can make your changes to the Property Bar for working with text. Just follow the same methods described earlier in this section for working with the other toolbars.

Using the Property Bar is pretty straightforward. You modify objects much the same way you would modify objects with palettes and roll-ups. To change an object's size, for example, you can either type new values or use the arrows to change values incrementally. To maintain proportional sizing, be sure to turn on the Maintain Proportional Sizing/Aspect Ratio option. (As with all CorelDraw buttons and fields, you can get a description of the options on the Property Bar by hovering the mouse over the button or field.)

Note

If this brief discussion of the Property Bar has piqued your interest, you can learn more about this new feature of CorelDraw (and discover many techniques for using it) throughout the remainder of this book.

Customizing the Property Bar

Technically speaking, the Property Bar is a toolbar, and you modify it pretty much in the same way you do the others. (Toolbar customization is discussed earlier in this chapter.) You customize the Property Bar by opening the Customize folder in the Options dialog box and then opening the Toolbars folder.

The primary difference between the Property Bar and other toolbars is that the Property Bar is context sensitive. In other words, it adapts itself according to the context in which you're working. If you're formatting text, for example, the Property Bar displays options pertaining to text attributes, such as point size, type style, and so on.

(continued)

(continued)

When adding, deleting, and rearranging options on the Property Bar, you make changes according to specific contexts. To add buttons for working with text, for example, you first select the Text context from the Property Bars drop-down list. Doing so configures the Property Bar for the desired context, as shown in the figure. As discussed earlier in this chapter, you can also create your own property bars.

Property Bar context list

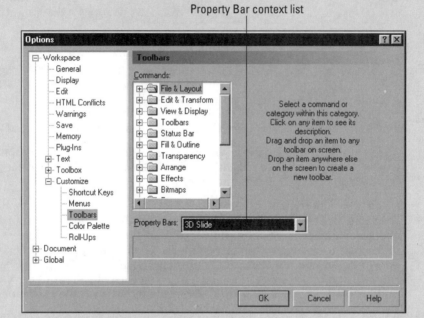

Before modifying the Property Bar, first select the desired context from the context list.

Working More Efficiently

This section explains a few ways to work efficiently. Here you learn about a few of the interface tools that can make your life easier:

- Protecting your work with automatic and last-saved backups
- Telling CorelDraw to print only the current page automatically
- Saving time with drag-and-drop

Backing up your work

CorelDraw supports two options for protecting your work—automatic backups and last-saved backups. Both backup methods can help you use CorelDraw more efficiently by protecting your work from being lost by mistake.

Automatic backups

The first backup method — automatic backups — happens in the background while you work. By default, CorelDraw automatically backs up every ten minutes to the directory where the original drawing files reside. The program saves the files with an .ABK extension. If you've ever lost work because of a system crash or power failure, you'll appreciate this feature. In the event of a minor disaster, all you need to do is go to the directory where the .ABK file is saved, change the extension to .CDR, and open the file in CorelDraw. All of your work (up to the last automatic save) is restored.

 You can change the location where CorelDraw saves its files and adjust how often the program backs up your work by selecting Tools ⇨ Options ⇨ Workspace ⇨ Save. The Save folder of the Options dialog box appears as shown in Figure 1-33. To change the time between backups, simply enter a new value in the Auto-Backup field. To change the directory the backup is saved to, select Always back-up to, and then choose a new directory using the Browse button.

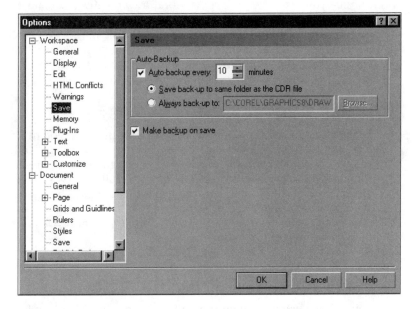

Figure 1-33: In the Save section of the Options dialog box, you can specify backup frequency and set other defaults.

Keep in mind when changing the time between backups that this setting constitutes reconciling a trade-off. If you set too long a time, you may lose a lot of work should disaster strike. If you set too short a time, when working with complicated drawings you could spend too much time having to wait for the program to create backup files.

Last-saved backups

Picture this: You spend hours creating a drawing. Then after showing it to your client, you return to the office and spend a few more hours making corrections based on the client's requests. Later, the client says, "I liked it better the other way." How on earth will you get the other copy back?

The obvious remedy to this problem is to save separate versions of the drawing with different names. Unfortunately, CorelDraw does not have a feature for automatically making incremental copies of your work.

Here's another scenario that we have experienced first hand: You work hard on a drawing and get it to look pretty good. Then you start tweaking it — trying this and that. Before you know it, you've completely messed up the drawing you once thought was good. You can easily resolve this problem by retrieving a copy of the last saved version of your work. If you want to be able to do this, you must first adjust a setting in the Options dialog box (Tools ➪ Options ➪ Workspace ➪ Save). After clicking on the Advanced tab of the Options dialog box, mark the Make backup on save check box. Now, each time you use Save or Save As, CorelDraw creates a second copy of the file with a .BAK extension. To open the backup copy, all you need to do is change the extension to .CDR. Keep in mind, though, that you can't have two files in the same folder with the same name. This procedure will not work, of course, if you have saved the document after making changes.

Printing only the current page

In many situations you often want to print only the page you're working on. We do it myself, often. We tweak this or that aspect of a page, and then print it to see how it looks. Often, however, we forget to set the Current Page option in the Print dialog box, and, before we realize it, two, three, or more pages roll out of the printer. You can avoid this scenario by checking the Print Only the Current Page by Default option in the Advanced sheet in the Options dialog box (Tools ➪ Options ➪ Global ➪ Printing Defaults). This option is the last option in the dialog box.

Saving time with drag-and-drop

If you've been using Windows for awhile, you are probably familiar with drag-and-drop, the capability of moving or copying an object from one place to another. But did you know that you can drag objects between multiple documents, or even from one application in the CorelDRAW graphics suite to another? This is a quick and easy way to place copies in multiple documents.

STEPS:

Dragging Objects Between Drawings

Step 1. Use Tile Vertically or Tile Horizontally (Window menu) to view two or more documents at once.

Step 2. Select the object(s) you want to drag to another drawing.

Step 3. To drag the object(s) to another drawing, simply drag from one document to another (see Figure 1-34). To drag a copy to more than one drawing, hold Ctrl as you drag, and drop a copy in each document.

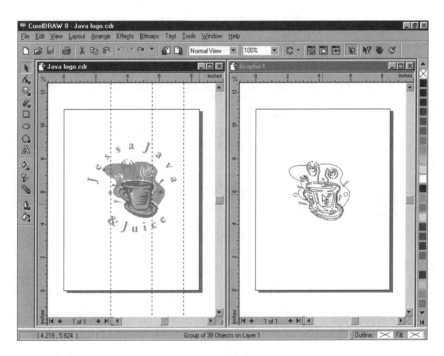

Figure 1-34: Dragging and dropping objects between drawings is easy.

STEPS:

Dragging Objects Between Applications

Step 1. To drag object(s) from one application to another, first resize the application windows so both are accessible on your screen. (You can do this quickly by choosing Windows ⇨ Tile Vertically.)

(continued)

STEPS *(continued)*
Dragging Objects Between Applications

Step 2.   Select the object(s) you want to move from one document
to another.

Step 3.   Drag to move the object(s) from the current document to
another, and hold Ctrl as you drag.

Note

Drag-and-drop is actually part of the Windows feature known as Object
Linking and Embedding (OLE) — a big time-saver. Check the Windows 95
Help menu (located under the Start menu) for more information about OLE.

Whatever you use CorelDraw for, the more you use it, the more you'll find
yourself needing specific features. With the Customize options, it's easy to
tailor CorelDraw to fit the way you work.

Summary

▶ You can customize CorelDraw to work the way you do by modifying shortcut
keys from the Keyboard sheet of the Options dialog box.

▶ CorelDraw's menu structure can be modified from the Menu sheet of the
Options dialog box.

▶ To modify or create new toolbars, use the Toolbars sheet of the Options
dialog box.

▶ Roll-up groups can be created or modified in the application window or from
the Roll-Ups sheet of the Options dialog box.

▶ Version 8's new dockers feature enables you to keep dialog boxes open as
you experiment with changes.

▶ You can change the appearance of the color palette from the Color Palette
sheet of the Options dialog box, and you can float or dock the color palette
by dragging it.

▶ Using the Filters sheet in the Options dialog box, you can tell CorelDraw
which filters to make accessible in the Import and Export dialog boxes.

▶ Setting file associations enables you to tell CorelDRAW! applications and
Windows which applications to open when you double-click on a filename in
Explorer, or when you open a dialog box from an application.

▶ CorelDraw's Property Bar provides ever-present, context-sensitive controls
for quick and easy access.

▶ Using CorelDraw's automatic backup option can save you much aggravation.

Chapter 2

Toolbox Secrets

In This Chapter

You learn handy secrets for:

▶ Selecting and manipulating objects with the Pick tool

▶ Reshaping objects with the Shape tools

▶ Creating shapes with CorelDraw's drawing tools

▶ Getting better views with the Zoom tool

emember when CorelDraw had only about nine or ten tools? Just one or two of the icons in the toolbox had flyout menus for additional tools and features. Today the program has about 30 tools (see Figure 2-1, where many are shown). And they do things you probably never could have imagined back when the program was new.

Figure 2-1: The CorelDraw 8 toolbox.

In fact, there's so much power behind these toolbox icons that it would be difficult to explain everything you can do with them. This chapter, however, gives you a lot of useful information on how to harness the mostly undocumented power of the toolbox. Each tool in the toolbox has hidden functions and includes features unavailable in other Windows-based graphics applications.

This chapter focuses on how you can configure the tools to behave in different ways. We'll also show you some tricks for using tools. For example, you can use the Pick tool to manipulate objects in a number of different ways. And the Shape tool has many features that seem almost magical. Another feature, the new Digger option, makes selecting stacked objects easier than ever.

Because so many tools exist, they can't all be discussed in one chapter. Many tools — such as the Text, Line, and Fill tools — are related to topics that are the subjects of entire chapters. Chapter 4, for example, is about working with text, so we've saved the discussion of the Text tool for that chapter. Some tools, such as the Interactive tools, are actually extensions of specific features in CorelDraw. In these instances, we discuss the tools in the chapters that cover those features.

The Pick Tool

The Pick tool — now there's a funny name. Sounds like you should use it to pitch hay or clean your teeth, not manipulate graphics. Other programs call their version of the same tool the Selection tool or Arrow tool. Whatever you call it, you can't really work in CorelDraw without it. And you probably already know how to use it — right?

More specifically, you probably know that clicking on objects with the Pick tool selects them. You move and resize objects with it, and if you click twice on an object with the Pick tool, the object goes into rotation & skew mode. And most people know that you can select multiple objects by Shift-clicking on them consecutively or by dragging a marquee around the objects you want to select. That's about the extent of what most CorelDraw users know about the Pick tool.

But you can use the Pick tool in all kinds of other ways, such as using the Tab key to select objects, performing tasks with the Property Bar, and a host of other useful functions. In addition, you can modify the way the Pick tool behaves. For example, you can change the arrow to crosshairs, enabling more precise moving and resizing. You can also make the Pick tool behave more like tools in other Windows applications.

In addition, the new Digger feature makes it easy to select hidden objects, or objects obscured by overlaying objects. And, as you'll soon see, Corel has added a nifty new feature — a new way to resize objects. When you create an object with one of the program's many graphics or text tools, you can resize it without going to the toolbox for the Pick tool, which will save some time.

You can adjust the Pick tool by opening the Toolbox folder in the Options dialog box (Tools ⇨ Options ⇨ Toolbox ⇨ Pick Tool), as shown in Figure 2-2. As you can see, you have several options for changing the way this tool behaves.

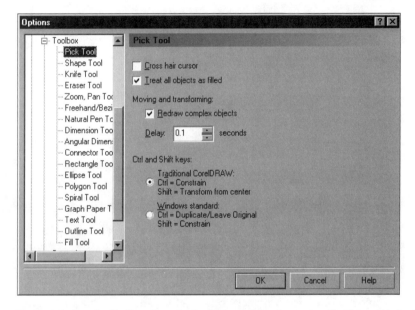

Figure 2-2: Use the Toolbox sheet in the Options dialog box to modify Pick tool behavior.

Using a crosshair cursor

Secret

Turn on this option by placing a check mark next to the Cross hair cursor option. Figure 2-3 shows what a crosshair cursor looks like. The crosshair cursor works like a T-square on a conventional drafting table. It's like having crossing straightedges that glide effortlessly across your work area. You can use the crosshairs to align objects in relation to other objects or to align them using the rulers.

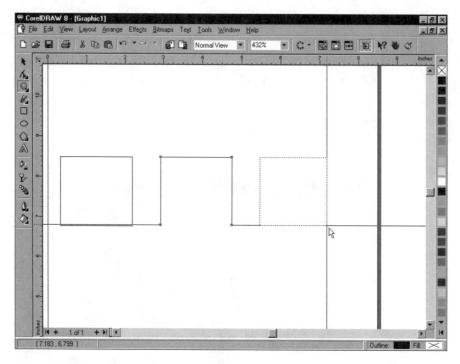

Figure 2-3: The crosshair cursor makes it easier to align and resize objects properly.

If you're accustomed to the conventional Pick tool, the crosshair cursor may seem a little confusing at first. It's actually very simple to use. The intersection of the crosshairs is used for selection and manipulation. To select an object, simply click the intersection point of the crosshairs on the object. To resize an object, drag the intersection point on the object's handles, the same as you would use the tip of the Pick tool arrow.

Crosshairs are ideal when using CorelDraw for schematics, floor plans, flowcharts, and other drawings where symmetry and precision are crucial. For example, in Figure 2-4 the crosshairs make it easy to align the drawing objects precisely. Even if you don't use the crosshair cursor all the time, many situations make it far more effective than the traditional Pick tool arrow.

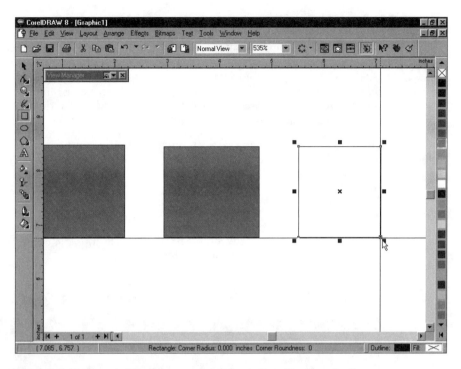

Figure 2-4: The crosshair enables you to draw and align objects on the fly.

Treating no fill as a solid

Even after many years of using CorelDraw, we still occasionally click in the center of objects with no fill to move or select them. And what happens then? Nothing, of course. Objects with no fill have nothing in them, so there's nothing to select. To select or move the object you must click on the object's outline.

The people at Corel are aware that CorelDraw users are sometimes forgetful, and they have included an option that accommodates users' absent-mindedness. You can tell the program to let you select and move no-fill objects like filled objects by placing a check mark next to the Treat all objects as filled option in the Toolbox sheet of the Options dialog box. Then, when you click or drag in the center of an object with no fill, you'll get the result you want.

In version 8, this feature is turned on by default. In addition, Corel has added another feature to make moving unfilled objects easier — a small X in the middle of selected objects that you can use to drag objects around. This X is actually part of the new Diggers feature, which you'll look at a little later in this section.

Using Windows mouse actions

If you use other Windows applications, you're probably used to certain things happening when you use your mouse. For example, in many programs, when you hold Ctrl and drag on a selected object, you get a duplicate of the original. In CorelDraw, the Ctrl key has a different function. When you resize or draw with the Rectangle tool while holding Ctrl, CorelDraw enables you to draw a perfect square.

In version 8 you can also resize an object from the center, meaning that instead of stretching or reducing proportionally on two sides, the object resizes on all four sides, from the center outwards. You perform this action by holding Ctrl+Shift as you resize.

If you'd rather use the traditional Windows keyboard functions, you can tell CorelDraw to use the standard Windows mouse actions by selecting Windows standard in the Toolbox sheet of the Options dialog box (Tools ➪ Options ➪ Toolbox ➪ Pick Tool), as shown in Figure 2-5.

Select this radio button to make your mouse conform to Windows conventions

Figure 2-5: Use this option to make your Ctrl and Shift keys conform to standard Windows conventions when using the Pick tool.

Right-clicking

A feature in CorelDraw you should be sure to take advantage of is the added functionality of the right mouse button. CorelDraw has greatly exploited the power of right-clicking in version 8. Now when you right-click, a bunch of useful options pop up, literally at your fingertips.

Remember

You can add commands to the different right-mouse button pop-up menus for different contexts. If you're already a seasoned right-mouser, you can greatly improve the convenience of this feature by adding the commands you use most.

Depending on which object(s) you've selected with the Pick tool, a number of useful options show up by default when you right-click. When a single block of text is selected, for example, right-clicking produces the menu shown in Figure 2-6, enabling you to instantly convert the text to curves (transform it from editable text to a graphic), apply a style, change the stacking order (Send to Back, Bring to Front, and so on), and perform several other readily available options.

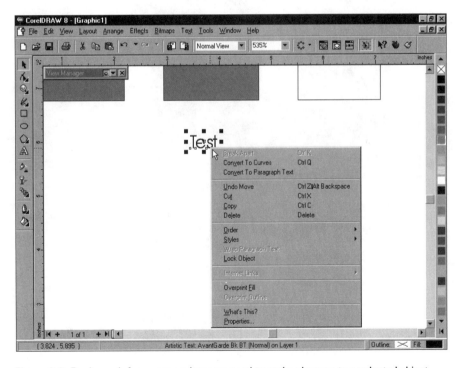

Figure 2-6: Don't reach for a menu when you need to make changes to a selected object. First try right-clicking on the object for a list of pop-up options.

Note

If, while looking over the commands on the right-click pop-up in Figure 2-6, you find yourself wondering about some of the commands you see, we discuss most of them in the next chapters. Overprint Fill and Overprint Outline, for example, are prepress options pertaining to successful reproduction on a printing press. They are discussed in Chapter 5, which deals primarily with color.

The Properties option at the bottom of the pop-up menu is particularly handy. Selecting it displays the Object Properties dialog box shown in Figure 2-7. From there you can modify almost every aspect of the object, including typeface, size, style, alignment, fill, outline weight, color, and style—you name it. In addition, you can use the Object Properties dialog box much like a roll-up. By clicking the Apply button as you make changes, you can perform numerous functions without closing the dialog box. Talk about control.

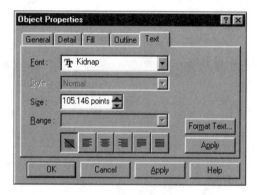

Figure 2-7: When you select Properties from a pop-up menu, you get this extremely useful Object Properties dialog box.

Right-clicking on a graphic or paragraph text object, of course, brings up slightly different menus. As we progress through CorelDraw's enormous wealth of features and shortcuts in the remainder of this book, we'll point out when you can use a right-click pop-up command instead of going to a menu. For example, when you right-click on two or more selected objects, you get options for grouping and combining multiple objects. On the other hand, when you right-click on grouped or combined objects, you get commands for ungrouping and uncombining. Group, Combine, and other arrangement and alignment features are discussed in Chapter 3.

Selecting hidden objects with Digger

While Digger is a simple concept, it sure can make life easier. If you've ever tried to select and move one object obscured by another (or several), you'll appreciate Digger. To select obscured objects with Digger, all you do is hold the Alt key while you click on the stack of objects. Because CorelDraw selects objects in the order they are stacked, you will get to the hidden object, as shown in Figure 2-8. Now all you do is drag on the X in the center of the object to move it into view for editing.

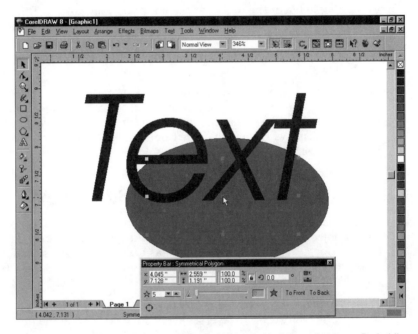

Figure 2-8: In this example, the polygon is hidden behind several objects. By holding the Alt key and clicking on the stack of objects, the polygon is selected, displaying the object's nodes and the center X. Now it can be moved into view for editing.

Selecting objects with Node Tracking

For years (no matter which program we use) we've been drawing objects with one tool, and then going back to the toolbox for another to edit it. Some programs, including CorelDraw, have tried to provide some relief by allowing users to choose an option to automatically select the selection (Pick) tool after you create an object with another tool (line, rectangle, text, and so on). But this is a nuisance if you want to draw more than one object—you have to go back and select the object's tool.

Corel has come to the rescue with Node Tracking, another simple but useful feature. When you create an object, all of its nodes (those used with the Pick tool and the Shape tool, discussed next) are displayed. All you do to edit the object is hover your cursor over the node. If it's a Pick tool node (resizing), the cursor changes to allow you to resize the new object. If you hover over a Shape tool node, the cursor changes to the Shape tool.

In addition to allowing you to edit nodes with an object-creation tool, you can also use Node Tracking with the Pick and Shape tools selected. In other words, you can edit Shape tool nodes when the Pick tool is selected and vice versa. Simply hover the tool over the node you want to edit. This does not, however, provide as much functionality as working with the actual tool selected. You do not, for example, get Shape tool options on the Property Bar when Pick tool is selected, and so on. But you do get right-mouse button functionality.

Think of all the time you'll save! However, if all these options being available at once is too much for you, you can turn off Node Tracking from the Standard toolbar (the one at the top of the window, below the menus, that CorelDraw displays by default). The Node Tracking button looks like the Shape tool (eighth from the right).

Selecting objects with the keyboard

Secret

In addition to the Digger selection option, you can still use Tab to toggle among objects, which, now that CorelDraw displays nodes and the center X (as described earlier in this chapter), has become a Digger selection in itself. To toggle among objects, simply select one object and then press Tab repeatedly until the object you want to select is highlighted.

Note

The most efficient way to keep objects separate in complicated drawings is to place them on separate layers. Layers are discussed in the next chapter.

Context-Specific Options on the Property Bar

Because you have so many different options for selecting and modifying objects with the Pick tool, you may have some trouble keeping all the shortcuts straight. We believe the best way to get fast results is by using the new Property Bar.

When working with the Pick tool, the Property Bar changes context according to the type of object you select, as shown in the following eight figures. In the order they are shown, the following objects are selected: text, rectangle,

ellipse (circle), graph paper, polygon, outlines, multiple objects, and dimensions.

In several of these Property Bars, the first six options — Position, Size, Scale Factor, Maintain Proportional Sizing/Aspect Ratio, Angle of Rotation, and Mirror — remain constant, no matter what you've selected. Numerous other options on the Property Bar change according to the context to help you manipulate the object. See Figures A through H.

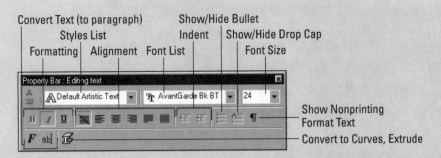

Figure A: When you work with text, the Property Bar shows the Font List, Font Size, Format Text, and Edit Text options. Click on any of these and other options to change text attributes.

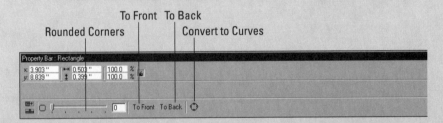

Figure B: When you're working with rectangles and squares, you get options to round the corners of the selected object and to convert the object to curves. (The Convert to Curves button changes the shape from a rigid, four-sided box to a more pliant graphic object that you can manipulate with the Shape tool. The Shape tool is discussed later in this chapter.)

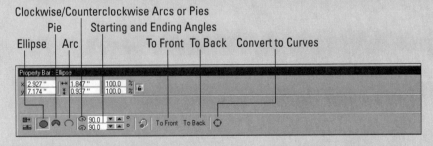

Figure C: When you work with ellipses, you get a wealth of options on the Property Bar. For instance, you can convert a circle to a pie shape or an arc. You can also control the starting and ending angles of a pie or arc, and you can determine whether the pie or arc displays clockwise or counterclockwise.

(continued)

(continued)

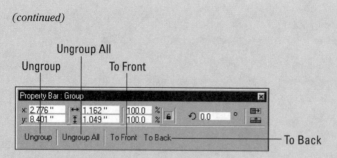

Figure D: When working with graph-paper objects, the Property Bar lets you set group and ungroup options and control the stacking order. To control the number of columns and rows, you would make changes on the Property Bar *before* you draw the graph. Other options become available when a spiral is selected. (Stacking order is discussed in the next chapter.)

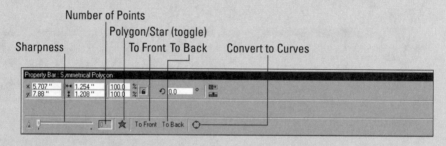

Figure E: For polygons, the Property Bar enables you to set the number of points on the polygon, and toggle between a star shape and polygon shape. When in star-shape mode, you can manipulate the sharpness of the points.

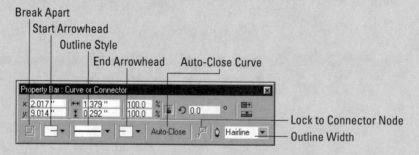

Figure F: When you're working with lines and spirals, the Property Bar gives you several options. You can choose line and arrowhead styles, and you can break a line into segments.

Combine   Ungroup   Weld   Intersect
   Group   Ungroup All   Trim   Align

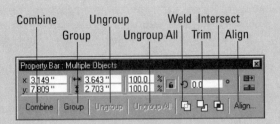

Figure G: When you select multiple objects, the Property Bar provides options for combining, grouping, ungrouping, welding, trimming, intersecting, and aligning objects. (The next chapter discusses these features.)

Units   Show Units   Style   Precision
Dimension Tool Modes| Prefix   Suffix | Dynamic Dimensioning

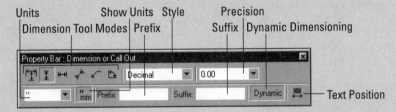

Text Position

Figure H: For dimension lines, the Property Bar enables you to toggle among the various Dimension tool types, determine the style of text displayed with the dimension line, adjust the level of precision, control the units after the decimal, change the unit of measurement, display unit symbols, use dynamic dimensioning, set suffixes and prefixes, and alter the position of the text on the dimension line. (All of these options are explained later in this chapter.)

You can set up CorelDraw so that the Property Bar displays when you open the program. (By default, if you close the program with the Property Bar displayed, the next time you open CorelDraw the Property Bar will be in the same place you left it.) Try to get in the habit of using this handy feature.

The Shape Tools

When we first started using CorelDraw, only one tool lurked in the Shape tool position in the toolbox. In those days it was called the node-editing tool. Today, four tools exist on the Shape tool flyout: the Shape tool, which is basically a node-editing tool; the Knife tool, which enables you to cut objects into sections; the Eraser tool, which enables you to remove parts of objects; and the Free Transform tool, which allows you to make several transformations to selected objects, including rotation, angle reflection, and scaling and skewing specific nodes.

Node-editing has always been an intricate part of vector drawing programs such as CorelDraw. The capability of cutting and erasing portions of vector objects, though, is relatively new. These features first appeared in version 6 of CorelDraw. They are truly remarkable feats of programming, and they're extremely useful, too. You'll also appreciate version 8's Free Transform tool. It offers quick and easy alternatives to other more cumbersome methods in previous versions.

In the next sections we look at the three tools in the order they appear on the Shape tool flyout.

The Shape tool

Perhaps one of the most overlooked features in vector-drawing programs is the node-editing tool, such as CorelDraw's Shape tool. The beauty of the Shape tool is that it enables you to manipulate lines in just about every way imaginable. In fact, so much can be said about node editing that we can only scratch the surface in this chapter.

Remember

Keep in mind that many of the options discussed in this section are now also available with Node Tracking. For example, when you create an object, you can edit nodes by hovering your mouse over the node you want to edit. Or you can perform many node-editing functions when the Pick tool or Text tool is selected.

Nodes are control points on the outline of an object that mark a change in a line's direction or the intersection of two lines. On a square, for example, nodes exist at all four corners. Depending on the type (or mode) of the node, you can manipulate the lines on either side of a node in different ways. You can move the intersection of two lines (as shown in Figure 2-9), or you can curve a line (as shown in Figure 2-10), smooth it, or make it straight and rigid. You do all this by manipulating the nodes.

You can create nodes on outlines in two ways. Any time you draw a line with the Freehand tool or another line-drawing tool (discussed in the "Line-Drawing Tools" section later in this chapter), nodes are added automatically where the line changes direction. Nodes are also automatically added when you convert text, shapes (boxes, ellipses, polygons, and so on), or symbols into curves (by selecting Arrange ➪ Convert to Curves). Converting an object to curves automatically places nodes at points where lines change direction or intersect. Once you have the nodes, you can begin shaping the object by manipulating its outline. The nodes are also available with several other tools selected when you have Node Tracking turned on.

While you can manipulate nodes in perhaps hundreds of ways, the methods fall under categories, or modes. In this section we'll look at some of the more useful modes, including To Curve, To Line, Smooth, Join, and Elastic.

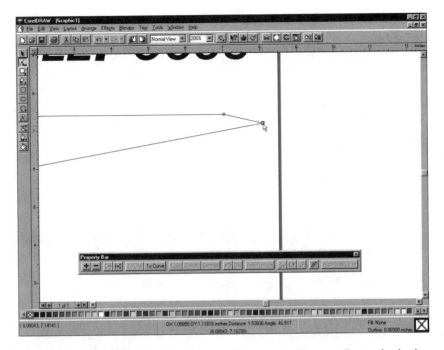

Figure 2-9: Node editing enables you to move the control points on a line, reshaping it by extending the node to a new position.

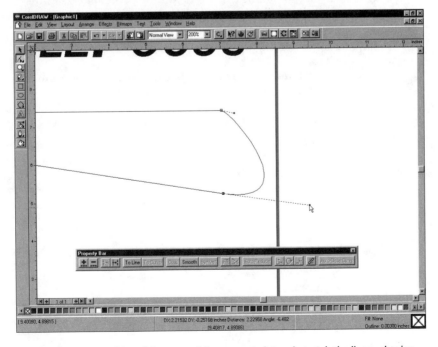

Figure 2-10: When node editing curved lines, you twist and stretch the lines, shaping them exactly as you like.

Node Edit roll-up versus the Property Bar

When working with the Shape tool, should you use the Node Edit roll-up (press Ctrl-F10), shown in Figure 2-11, or the Property Bar, shown in Figure 2-12.

Figure 2-11: Use the Node Edit roll-up to change the mode of nodes. To display it, simply double-click any node.

Figure 2-12: The Property Bar in node-editing mode.

This is one of those instances when CorelDraw offers too many choices. In this situation the Property Bar is simply a duplication of the Node Edit roll-up. The roll-up takes up less screen real estate and is easily accessible — all you do is press Ctrl-F10. On the other hand, the Property Bar is always available, and, because many of the buttons contain text rather than those enigmatic little icons, it's somewhat easier to use.

You already know our position — fly the Property Bar and leave it visible for all to see! But then, you might be used to the roll-up.

You may be wondering why only a few of the options in Figures 2-11 and 2-12 are available. When you select a node, it is in a certain mode — curve, line, cusp, and so on. When in one mode, only certain other options are available. If you change a node's mode, other options become available.

Okay, are you ready for yet another choice? If you're like us, you don't like a lot of clutter on the screen covering up your work. In many cases, you can avoid using the Node Edit roll-up and the Property Bar by simply clicking the right-mouse button on the node you want to edit. The ensuing pop-up menu contains most of the options available in both interactive palettes.

Using To Line mode and To Curve mode

We discuss these two modes together because they are mutually exclusive. A node cannot be in curve and line modes at the same time. To Line mode makes the line to the left of the selected node rigid. To Curve mode makes the line to the left of the node pliant, enabling you to bend and curve it.

An example should help make these modes clear. In Figure 2-13 we've converted some text to curves. The letters TELEF consist of straight, rigid lines, while the letters OCUS contain several curves. The straight lines behave differently from the curved lines when you edit them with the Shape tool.

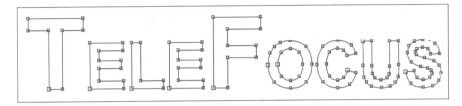

Figure 2-13: An example of nodes in To Line and To Curve modes.

To move or reshape a line attached to a To Line node, you must drag on the node itself, as shown in Figure 2-14. The line can only be shortened or lengthened. No matter how hard you try, CorelDraw will not let you put a curve in the line.

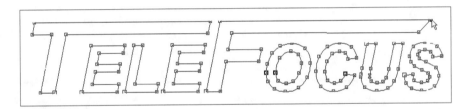

Figure 2-14: Nodes in To Line mode enable you to reshape lines only in straight, rigid movements.

Lines connected to a To Curve node, however, are flexible. You can arch and bend them as though they were made of rubber or wire, as shown in Figure 2-15.

Let's look a little closer at how to manipulate these nodes, in particular the To Curve nodes. No matter how much we tell you about these nodes, you still have to practice to learn how to finesse them. But let's see if we can't at least shorten the learning curve. (Or is that learning curves?)

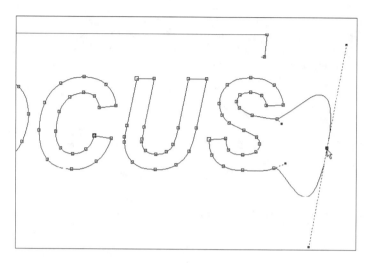

Figure 2-15: Nodes in To Curve mode are flexible and pliant.

Secret

When a node is in To Curve mode, you can manipulate it by moving not only the node itself but also the control points that extend from the node, as shown in Figure 2-16. You can also reshape the line by dragging on the line itself. At first, shaping a line in this manner may seem strange, but once you get used to it you'll find this method to be quite handy.

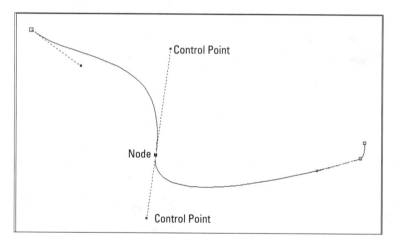

Figure 2-16: Practice shaping a line using a To Curve node and control points.

You have several ways to manipulate a To Curve line:

- Moving the node itself
- Manipulating the control points
- Dragging on the line

When you move the node itself, you can drag perpendicular to the line, parallel to the line, or use a combination of both movements. A perpendicular motion extends the curve, as shown in Figure 2-17. Dragging along the line enables you to move a node's position on the line and straightens the curve, as shown in Figure 2-18.

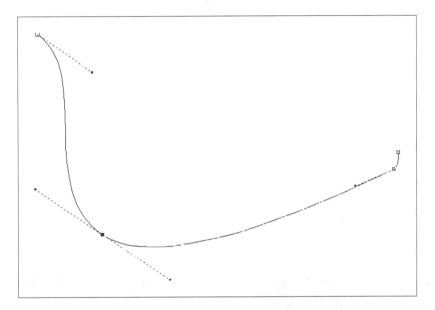

Figure 2-17: To increase the curve, drag the node perpendicular to the line.

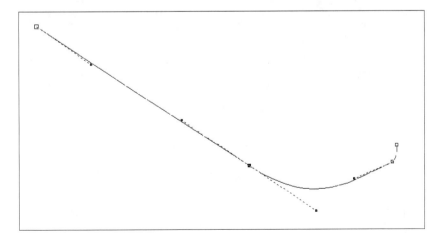

Figure 2-18: To straighten a curve and move the point of control, drag the node with the line.

Manipulating the control points enables you to increase or decrease the severity of the curve in two directions, in an S pattern, as shown in Figure 2-19. However, there's a bit more to it than that. You can also lengthen and shorten the control points as you drag. Lengthening the control points stretches the curve and reduces the severity of the curving action, as shown in Figure 2-20. Shortening the distance of the control point to the node makes the curving action more radical.

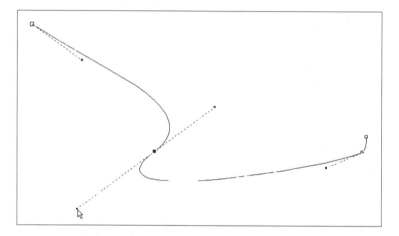

Figure 2-19: Dragging the control points in a swinging motion causes the line to bend in two directions, in an S curve.

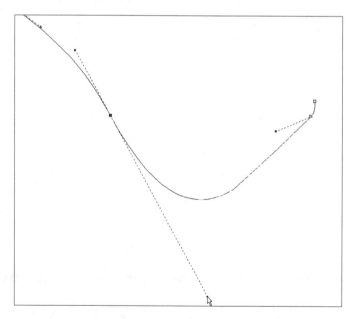

Figure 2-20: Increasing the distance from the control point to the node increases the length of the curve and reduces the curving action.

When you drag on the line itself, as shown in Figure 2-21, you get a similar action to dragging on the control points. The line moves in two directions, teetering on the node.

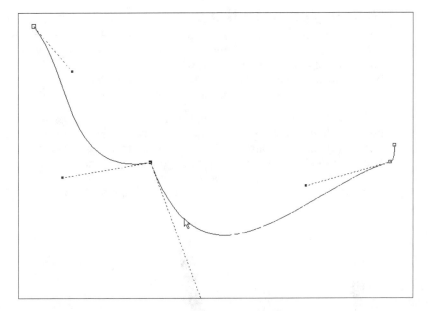

Figure 2-21: Dragging on the line itself works similarly to dragging on the control points. The farther from the node you drag, the longer the curve and the less radical the curving action.

After learning so many ways to curve lines, you may be wondering how to straighten one. It's simple. Select the node to the right of the line you want straightened and click To Line on the Property Bar. In Figure 2-22, we straightened both of the line segments that do all that curving in the previous figures simply by selecting the nodes and changing them to To Line mode.

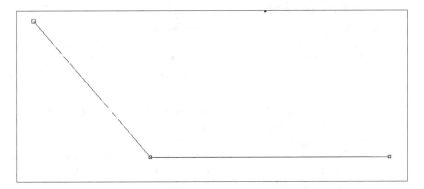

Figure 2-22: You can quickly straighten lines with the To Line mode.

And if you want to manipulate only one side of a curve, or a segment on the right side of the node, use the Cusp option on the Property Bar (or Node Edit roll-up).

Drawing smooth lines

If you're like us, you have a hard time drawing with a mouse (we have a hard time drawing with a pencil, too). Your lines wind up bumpy, with too many line segments, or nodes. CorelDraw provides several ways to smooth out bumpy lines. One of these is the Smooth option, also on the Node roll-up. Smooth irons the wrinkles out of your lines.

In Figure 2-23, we stretch the rigidity of the line by first converting all the nodes with To Curve and then choosing Smooth. You, too, can get the kinks out with this simple option. (You don't need to convert one node at a time. You can select multiple nodes just as you would select objects, by Shift+ clicking or by dragging a *marquee* around them. A marquee is the box you draw around objects with the Selection or Shape tools to select the objects.)

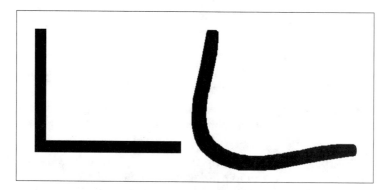

Figure 2-23: Use Smooth to take the kinks out of your lines.

Joining nodes

You can draw two kinds of outlines: open and closed paths. A path is the outline itself. An open path, though it can take many twists and turns, is a single line. It has a beginning and an end. A closed path, on the other hand, is continuous. Perhaps the simplest example of this is a circle, which really has no beginning or end.

The primary difference between open and closed paths is that you can't fill an open path. In other words, you can't make the area surrounded by the outline a color or assign it a gradient fill, and so on. A closed path, then, is a kind of container. Figure 2-24 shows the difference between an open and closed path. While both are circles, the second one is not closed and thus cannot contain a fill.

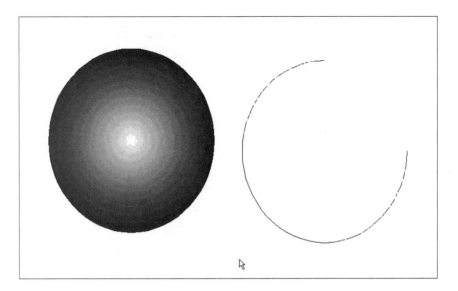

Figure 2-24: An open path cannot hold fills; a closed path can.

The Join option (the third option from the left on the Property Bar) connects two nodes and closes the path. The fourth option on the Property Bar is Break Curve, which you can use to disconnect, or separate, a set of joined nodes. Actually, Break Curve will split any node into two nodes, regardless of whether the path is closed or not. But it's still the option you use to open a closed path.

Another option you can use to close paths is Auto Close, which is the last option on the Property Bar. This option works without your having to select the two end nodes. However, what Auto Close does is draw a line between the two end nodes to close the path, which can severely misshape your path. To avoid this predicament, you should place the two end nodes close together or on top of each other before clicking on Auto Close.

Using Elastic mode

Elastic mode (second to last option on the Property Bar) affects the behavior of lines when you move a node connected to two or more selected nodes. If Elastic mode is turned off, all nodes move by the same amount. If Elastic mode is on, nodes move in proportion to their distance from the base node (the node you drag). The end result is that the curve appears to behave like elastic, expanding and contracting in response to mouse movement.

If you're inexperienced at using Elastic mode, it can be difficult to predict how an outline in elastic mode will behave when you manipulate it. However, once you get the hang of it, this is a great way to proportionately stretch and reduce segments of an outline.

The Knife tool

The Knife tool, located on the Shape tool flyout, is pretty straightforward. It enables you to cut a closed path into two closed paths. To do so, you simply click the Knife tool once on the path where you want to start the cut, and then again where you want the cut to end. Voilà! You get two closed path objects. The Knife tool also enables you to cut a closed path in half without closing the two paths. In version 6, this option was turned on from the Tool Properties dialog box. In version 8 you can toggle this option on and off from the first button on the Property Bar (when the Knife tool is selected, naturally), as well as from the Toolbox section of the Options dialog box. Having these controls on the Property Bar is a great time-saver.

Another option in the Toolbox section of the Options dialog box is Auto Reduce on Cut, which automatically reduces the number of nodes when you cut a curved line. This function is similar to applying Auto Reduce to a path from the Property Bar when the Shape tool is selected. Auto Reduce removes nodes and smoothes the path, which is faster and more efficient than removing nodes manually.

The Eraser tool

The capability of erasing parts of paths, much the way Eraser tools work in paint-type applications, is relatively new to drawing programs. It's quite useful, too. The Eraser tool lets you swipe through a closed path and create two closed paths, or swipe through an open path and create two separate open paths. This feature is straightforward and easy to use. However, you should know that you can adjust the width of the eraser tip and turn on Auto Reduce nodes on Erase from the Property Bar, rather than having to go into the Tool Properties dialog box.

The Free Transform tool

Here's a cool addition to CorelDraw — the Free Transform tool. This tool is actually four tools in one: Free Rotate, Free Reflection, Free Scale, and Free Skew. You choose which mode the tool works in with the first four buttons on the Property Bar when the Free Transform tool is selected. In the next sections, we'll look at each Free Transform mode and how to use it.

Free Rotate

We know what you're thinking—*CorelDraw already has a good rotation tool*. And you're right, it does. The difference between Free Rotate and the Pick tool's rotation mode is that Free Rotate makes it easier to pick a center of rotation, and it works more closely to the rotation tools in other graphics and page-layout programs. In fact, if you use PageMaker, you'll know exactly how to use this tool.

To use Free Rotate, simply select an object or group of objects that you want to rotate with the Pick tool, select the Free Transform tool, and click the Free Rotate (first) button on the Property bar. Then simply click and hold (drag) on the spot you want as your center of rotation, and rotate the object, as shown in Figure 2-25.

Figure 2-25: To rotate an object, simply click and drag.

Secret

Notice the line extruding out from the center of rotation. You can control the severity of your rotation movements by moving your mouse in and out on this line. The closer your cursor to the center of rotation, the more radical the movement. The farther away, the more subtle.

Free Reflection

Free Reflection (second button) allows you to reflect (mirror) and rotate simultaneously from a center of rotation you choose, similarly to the Free Rotate tool — by clicking and dragging where you want the center of rotation to land. This tool also allows you to control the size of the rotation movements by dragging your cursor along the dotted rotation line. Figure 2-26 shows the Free Reflection tool in action.

Free Scale

Free Scale (third button) allows you resize objects from any given center. In other words, where you click and drag on the object(s) becomes the center of scaling. The object will resize in all four directions from the point. In Figure 2-27, for example, we're dragging from near the left end of the object. Notice that the object resizes more radically on the far right end and less dramatically on the left end, or smaller end from the center of scaling.

Free Skew

Free Skew (fourth button) works similarly to Free Scale in that you can choose your center of skewing simply by dragging the point you want the object to skew from. Free Skew also allows you to rotate as you skew, as shown in Figure 2-28.

Figure 2-26: To mirror and rotate, simply click and drag from the desired center of rotation.

Figure 2-27: To use Free Scale, drag from the point where you want the scaling to center.

Figure 2-28: To use Free Skew, choose a center of rotation and drag in the direction you want to rotate and skew.

Okay, all of this interactivity is great. If you're like us, you'll use it all the time. But sometimes you need precision. And when you do, you'll find the controls on the Property Bar in Free Transform mode very handy. Almost any of the effects you can achieve by dragging on objects can be obtained by entering values in the many fields along the Property Bar. Pay particular attention to the Angle of Rotation (fifth option from the right) and the Center of Rotation Position (fourth option from right) fields. Entering values in these fields provide precise editing controls. Entering positive values rotates clockwise, and negative values rotate counterclockwise.

Line-Drawing Tools

If you've been using CorelDraw for awhile, you are probably familiar with most of the tools on the line-drawing tools flyout. However, version 7 (and carried into version 8) includes some significant changes to these tools. First, you may have already noticed that the Dimension tools are now on the same flyout as the Freehand and Bézier tools. Actually, an icon called Dimension Tool is on the flyout — the buttons that used to be on the Dimension flyout now display on the Property Bar when in the Dimension context. Once you get used to this, it makes working with the Dimension tool much easier.

But first, let's look at the Natural Pen tool, an addition to version 7 that many designers have found highly useful.

The Natural Pen tool

The Natural Pen tool lets you draw closed paths that look like curves. This tool is supposed to emulate a felt-tip or fountain ink pen, and it does a reasonable job. The four types of Natural Pen modes, which you choose from the Property Bar, are as follows:

- **Fixed Width mode** draws curves that are the same thickness along their entire length, similar to a thick line or outline. The difference is that the stroke created with the Natural Pen tool is actually a closed path that you can fill with any of CorelDraw's several fill options. The procedure for drawing fixed-width paths with this tool is as follows: Open the Curve flyout and click on the Natural Pen tool. Click on the Fixed Width Natural Pen Type button on the Property Bar. Type a width in the Natural Pen Width box on the Property Bar. Position the cursor where you want the curve to start. Click and drag along the desired path, like a pencil on paper.

- **Pressure mode** draws curves that change thickness based on a pressure-sensitive pen or keyboard input. Basically, this enables you to mimic the effect you achieve when drawing with a felt-tip or fountain pen by hand. This mode works best when working with a pressure-sensitive tablet, but you can also use your up- and down-arrow keys on the keyboard to adjust the width of the stroke interactively. The following steps are for using the Natural Pen tool in Pressure mode: Open the Curve flyout and click on the Natural Pen tool. Click on the Pressure Natural Pen Type button on the Property Bar. Position the cursor where you want the curve to start. Click and drag along the desired path, like a pencil on paper. If you are using the mouse, press the up-arrow and down-arrow keys to vary the pen pressure. If you are using a pressure-sensitive tablet, simply vary the pressure on the tablet, as you would when drawing by hand.

- **Calligraphic mode** draws curves that change thickness based on the direction of the curve. This creates an effect similar to using a calligraphic pen. The procedure for creating lines with this mode is as follows: Open the Curve flyout and click on the Natural Pen tool. Click on the Calligraphic Natural Pen Type button on the Property Bar. Type a width in the Natural Pen Width box on the Property Bar. Type an angle in the Natural Pen Nib Angle box on the Property Bar. Enter 0 degrees if you want the pen nib to be horizontal, and enter 90 degrees if you want the nib to be vertical. If you want the pen nib to be slanted, enter a value between 0 and 360 degrees. The nib will slant in the direction you set. Then click and drag along the desired path, like a pencil on paper.

- **Preset mode** draws curves that change thickness based on preset line types that you choose from a drop-down list on the Property Bar. Here is the procedure for drawing lines in the Preset mode: Open the Curve flyout and click on the Natural Pen tool. Click on the Preset Natural Pen Type button on the Property Bar. Choose a preset curve shape from the Natural Pen Presets list box. Position the cursor where you want the curve to start. Then click and drag along the desired path, like a pencil on paper.

Figure 2-29 shows the Property Bar in Natural Pen mode and calls out the various options.

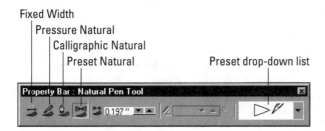

Figure 2-29: Here is what the Property Bar looks like in Natural Pen mode.

The Freehand tool and the Bézier tool

When you draw lines in CorelDraw, you usually use either the Freehand or Bézier tool — unless, of course, you need dimensions; then you would use the nifty Dimension tool. The Freehand tool, of course, enables you to draw fluid strokes, from one end to another, as though you were using a pen or pencil. With the Bézier tool you draw lines from point to point, or from Bézier to Bézier. Béziers, sometimes called Bézier curves, are the line segments between the nodes on lines drawn with the Freehand or Bézier tool (or text and shapes converted to curves).

Which tool you should use depends on what kind of outline you need. If you're like us, you have difficulty drawing lines, be they curved or straight, with a mouse. When we need a straight line, we use the Bézier tool. The beauty of this method is that all you do is click where you want the line to begin, and then click again where you want it to end. If you need a connecting line segment going in a new direction, simply click again where you want the line to end. CorelDraw automatically connects the new segment to the existing segment. And you can continue to add new segments, ad infinitum. Dot-to-dot drawing was never so easy! To close the path, simply click on the node where you first started.

Secret

Use the Freehand tool when you need curved or sloping lines. CorelDraw automatically places a node at each place where the line changes directions. If your line has too many ridges and bumps, simply use the Smooth option on the Property Bar to iron them out. You can also smooth lines by deleting nodes at the points where a line makes undesired bends. An easy way to delete nodes is to double-click on them.

You can modify the behavior of these tools from the Toolbox section of the Options dialog box (Tools ⇨ Options ⇨ Toolbox ⇨ Freehand/Bézier Tool), shown in Figure 2-30.

- **Freehand tracking** controls how closely a freehand curve matches the movement of the mouse. The lower the number you set, the more accurate the match. Setting this option too low will cause every little bump and ridge to show up, giving you lots of nodes. Setting it higher tends to smooth the line.

- **Autotrace tracking** determines the accuracy of the Bézier tool's bitmap autotrace feature. The lower the value, the more accurate the trace. Autotrace enables you to create outlines based on imported bitmap images. You can then edit the outline as a vector image, enabling you to fill, node-edit with the Shape tool, and generally treat the outlines as a CorelDraw drawing. As you know, bitmaps are virtually uneditable in CorelDraw. (This fact excludes, of course, the effects you can set with version 7's new Bitmap menu, discussed in Chapter 6. In addition, a more advanced autotracing of bitmaps is available in OCR-Trace, covered in Chapter 16.) Figure 2-31 shows an example of an autotraced bitmap. To use Autotrace, import a bitmap (File ⇨ Import), and then, with the bitmap selected, click on the object in the bitmap you want to autotrace.

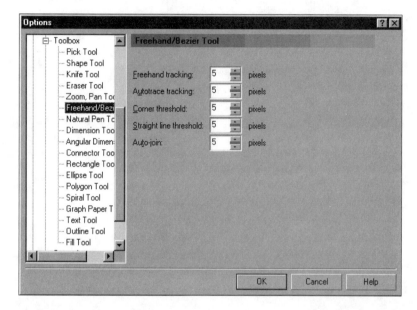

Figure 2-30: Use these options to control the behavior of the Freehand and Bézier tools.

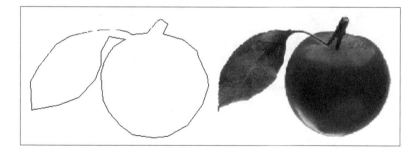

Figure 2-31: This bitmap was traced with Autotrace.

Manual Tracing

Because of the way they are constructed, many bitmaps cannot be autotraced with the Bézier or Freehand tool. You'll know whether you can autotrace all or a portion of a bitmap when you select the Freehand or Bézier tool. If the mouse cursor displays as crosshairs with a thin straight line on the right side of the horizontal crosshair, you can use autotrace on the image. If a small wavy line accompanies the crosshair cursor, you cannot use autotrace.

In these instances you can trace all or portions of the image manually. Here's how: Find a place where you want to begin. Click the mouse at that point. Now move along the edge of the object to a second point, and click again. Continue this procedure until the object is traced. The last click should close the path, as shown in the figure. To optimize your chances for success with this procedure, you should click at each spot where the object being traced curves or changes direction. After you've traced the object, you can

then use the Shape tool to manipulate the nodes and line segments to customize the trace. This is a great way to turn scanned images into vector objects editable in CorelDraw.

To trace bitmaps manually, click repeatedly to add nodes around the edge of the object.

- **Corner threshold** affects when corners, or bends in the outline, are cusped (as opposed to smoothed). Remember that cusped nodes enable you to manipulate Bézier curves on each side of the node independently. A node is more likely to be cusped if the value is lower.

- **Straight line threshold** determines the extent to which a line can vary from a straight path and still be drawn perfectly straight. The higher the value, the less accurate the line needs to be. This is a great option for those of us who can't draw straight lines.

- **Auto-join** sets the distance at which two end nodes join automatically. In other words, when you place an end node close to a node that begins a path, this option sets the distance (in pixels) where CorelDraw forces the two nodes to join and close the path.

The Dimension tool

This tool separates CorelDraw from most other drawing programs. The Dimension tool (which was actually a set of tools in version 6) makes CorelDraw much more adept at creating technical drawings and schematics, even simple blueprints. If you haven't used these tools before, you'll find them remarkably simple—especially with the advent of the Property Bar.

To draw a dimension line, simply select the direction you want from the Property Bar—horizontal, vertical, or diagonal—and then click where you want the line to begin. Click again where you want the line to end, and then click again where you want the text, or label, for the line displayed. Figure 2-32 shows the three types of lines.

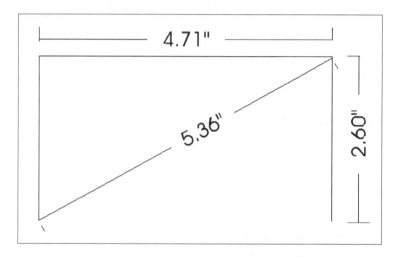

Figure 2-32: CorelDraw has three dimension lines: horizontal, vertical, and diagonal.

The other two line options on the left side of the Property Bar are Callout and Angular Dimension. Callout enables you to quickly direct attention to objects in a drawing, as shown in Figure 2-33. The Callout option works similarly to the other dimension modes. Click once to start the line, and then click again where you want the line to end. Click one more time. At that point, you can then type a label.

The Angular Dimension option lets you call out angles, as shown in Figure 2-34. To use this tool, click first at the point where your angle begins. In the figure, for example, we clicked at the point of the pie slice. Click again at the point where the angle will be measured from, and then click again where the angle is measured to. Now click to place the label. Voilà! You have angular dimension lines.

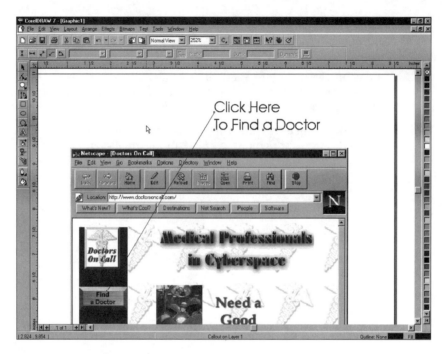

Figure 2-33: The Callout option enables you to quickly create callouts in your drawings.

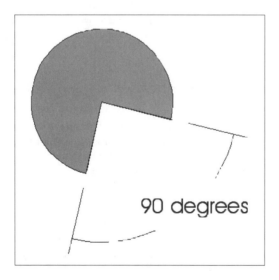

Figure 2-34: Use Angular Dimension lines to quickly call out angles.

Changing the Dimension tool options

You're probably already convinced that the Dimension tool is great. But it would be even better if you could make some changes to how it works. For example, wouldn't it be much handier if you could control where the text label lands in relation to the line itself? Also, by default, the text on the dimensions is much too large for most applications. Oh yeah, and how do you change the scale? Granted, the drawing on the screen is in inches, but floor plans and the like are measured in feet, meters, or yards.

In version 6, to change dimension tool (or any other tool) options you had to go into Tool Properties to change items such as label size, scale, units of measurement, and most other options. This really was a pain, because it entailed opening a dialog box for each change you needed to make. Things are much improved in versions 7 and 8.

Once again, the Property Bar comes to the rescue. Now you can change all aspects of how the tool (and the ensuing dimension line) displays and measures. Figure 2-35 shows the Property Bar when in Dimension mode. Let's look at each option in detail.

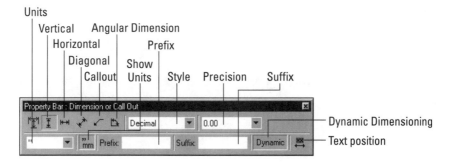

Figure 2-35: The Property Bar contains a number of useful options in Dimension tool mode.

- The **Vertical, Horizontal, Diagonal, Callout,** and **Angular** buttons determine which type of dimension line you draw.

- The **Style** field enables you to select how the dimension label is displayed. The choices are Decimal, which displays partial units behind decimal points; Fraction, which displays partial units as fractions; U.S. Engineering; and U.S. Architectural.

- The **Precision** field enables you to determine how finite a measurement is displayed in the dimension line label; in other words, how many numbers after the decimal point—tenths, hundredths, thousandths, and so on.

- The **Units** field lets you set the type of measurement, such as inches, millimeters, yards, miles, and so on. Go ahead, click on the drop-down arrow. You have a bunch of options here—one for every type of drawing you can imagine.

- The **Show Units** button determines whether the measurement symbol or abbreviation displays on the dimension line label. When the button is depressed, the unit shows; when not depressed, it does not show.

- The **Prefix** and **Suffix** fields enable you to include additional information with the dimension line label — a brief description, your own symbol, you name it. Prefix, of course, places the text you type into the field before the default label, and Suffix places it after.

- The **Dynamic Dimensioning** button lets you edit the text label on the dimension line. You can change the label to display virtually anything you want. To edit the label, select the dimension line, click on Dynamic to enable it (enabled is the up position), and then select the text label with the Text tool and type the new text.

- The **Text Position** drop-down list enables you to change the position of the text in relation to the line. You have three position options — above, on, and below the dimension line — and two angle options for diagonal lines: slanted with the line or horizontal. The horizontal option makes the text on a diagonal line slightly easier to read. Figure 2-36 shows the different options available from the Text Position drop-down list.

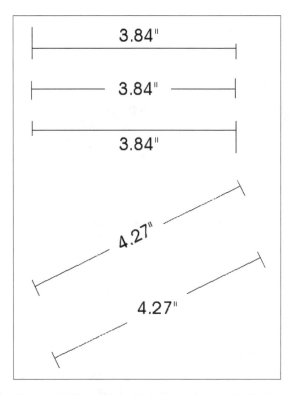

Figure 2-36: The label positions available from the Text Position drop-down list when the Property Bar is in Dimension mode.

Changing the dimension line scale

Secret

Dimension lines are great, but they measure in inches relative to the size of the page you are drawing on. This is of little value if, for example, you are laying out the floor plan for a 600-square-foot office. In this and other design situations, you need to change CorelDraw's units of measurement and scale. Unfortunately, you can't do this from the Property Bar. Instead, you have to change the program's defaults from the General section of the Options dialog box (Tools ➪ Options ➪ Document ➪ Rulers).

STEPS:

Changing CorelDraw's Units of Measurement and Scale

Step 1.   Open the Options dialog box and make sure the Document section is active, and then click on Rulers. This displays the Rulers sheet in the Options dialog box, shown in Figure 2-37.

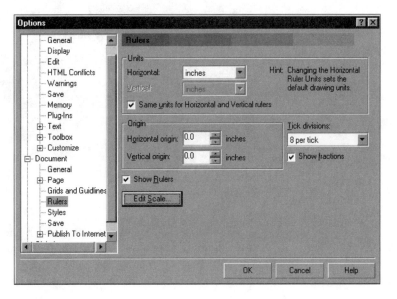

Figure 2-37: Use the Rulers sheet to set the units of measurement used in drawings.

Step 2.   Use the Horizontal and Vertical drop-down lists in the Units section to change the unit of measurement. The Horizontal option changes the horizontal ruler, and the Vertical option changes the vertical ruler. However, when you change the drawing scale in CorelDraw, both rulers will always depict the same unit of measurement. The only time you can use different units of measurements on two rulers is when the scale is 1:1. If you plan to change the scale, all you need to set for this step is horizontal units.

Step 3. Click on the Edit Scale button. This button brings up the Drawing Scale dialog box, shown in Figure 2-38. From here you can choose a scale from the Typical scales drop-down list. You have lots of options. Depending on the relative scale of your drawing, you may have to do some math to figure the right scale for your drawing. But most of the more common scales are built in. To show inches as feet, for example, choose 1"=1'. To show inches as yards, choose 1"=3'. You get the idea. If the scale you need is not on the Typical scales list, you can set it by entering the ratio in the Page distance and World distance fields. Page distance is the measurement for the drawing, and World distance represents the real-world scale.

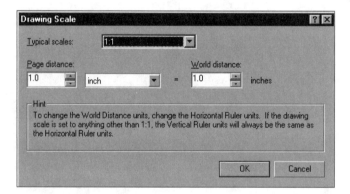

Figure 2-38: Use the Drawing Scale dialog box to set the scale for your drawings.

Step 4. Close all dialog boxes to return to the drawing screen. Your drawing and dimension lines will now reflect the new scale.

Note

Changes to the drawing scale do not affect only dimension lines, but also the rulers, grid, and all aspects of measurement within the drawing. This is the method you should use to change scaling for any type of drawing in CorelDraw, including floor plans, schematics, product designs, packaging, you name it. Note, too, that changing this option while a drawing is open changes the setting for that drawing; setting this option while designing a template enables you to automatically use the new scale settings each time you use the template.

In version 8, the procedure for changing settings for new drawings has changed. Now, instead of the Settings for New Drawings command, you use the Document sheet in the Options dialog box. This lets you create a basic work environment that is the same every time you create a new drawing or document. CorelDraw saves settings based on the selections you make on the Document page and uses them for each new document you create. For example, if you need inches displayed on the rulers, the Snap To Grid command enabled, and a drawing scale of 1"=1', you can enable the Grid And Rulers check box so that these settings are used each time you start a new document.

STEPS:

Setting New Default Settings for All New Documents

Step 1. Select Tools ⇨ Options.

Step 2. In the list of categories, click on Document.

Step 3. Make changes to the settings you want to use with your new documents.

Step 4. Close the dialog boxes.

Each new drawing will open with the new settings

Secret

The problem with this method is that you are making changes to CorelDraw's default workspace. At some point you may make so many changes that CorelDraw no longer works the way you want. To avoid this possibility, rather than making changes to CorelDraw's default workspace, try creating separate workspaces for each type of document you create, as discussed in the previous chapter.

Shape-Drawing Tools

On the surface, the shape-drawing tools — Rectangle, Ellipse, Polygon, Spiral, and Grid — seem pretty straightforward. You select one of them and draw your shape, right? However, there's a big difference in how you control each tool's performance in versions 7 and 8. All the options you once had to go to Tool Properties to change — such as rounded corners for rectangles, or changing the Ellipse tool to draw pies or arcs — are now available from the Property Bar.

Let's look at each tool and see how you can modify its behavior from the Property Bar. Before doing so, however, we want to remind you that you can constrain any of these tools to draw proportionally by holding Ctrl. When constraining the Rectangle tool, for example, it draws perfect squares; the Ellipse tool draws perfect circles, and so on.

The Rectangle tool

The Rectangle tool draws rectangles and squares. The Property Bar options when the Rectangle tool is selected are the same as when a rectangle is selected with the Pick tool, as discussed earlier in this chapter. One nifty feature is that you can round the corners of objects drawn with this tool by using the Corner Roundness slider or field.

The Ellipse tool

The Ellipse tool draws circles, ovals, pies, and arcs. As with the Rectangle tool, the options on the Property Bar when this tool is selected are the same as when you select an ellipse object with the Pick tool. What's hot about the Property Bar is that you can now switch between ellipse, pie, and arc modes without having to open a dialog box.

The Polygon tool

This tool has a lot of power. It lets you draw polygons (multisided shapes) or multipointed stars with a single mouse stroke. You can control what kind of shape, the number of sides or points, and the sharpness of a star's points, all from the Property Bar. The Property Bar options when you select the Polygon tool are the same as when you select a polygon or star with the Pick tool. Again, for those options, see the section "The Pick Tool" earlier in this chapter.

The Spiral tool

If you've tried to draw a spiral with a mouse or a pressure-sensitive tablet, you'll appreciate this tool. It draws spirals. From the Property Bar you can control several aspects of how the tool does its magic, such as the number of revolutions or tightness of the spiral. You can also control the same properties from the Toolbox section of the Options dialog box (Tools ➪ Options ➪ Toolbox ➪ Spiral Tool), which, in the case of the Spiral tool, may sometimes be more efficient, as you'll see in a moment.

First, let's look at controlling how the Spiral tool draws using the Property Bar, shown in spiral context in Figure 2-39.

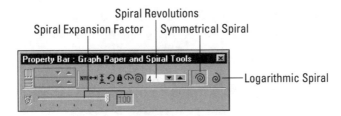

Figure 2-39: Here's what the Property Bar looks like in Spiral tool mode.

- **Spiral Revolutions** controls the number of lines, or loops, from the center of the spiral to the end.

- **Symmetrical Spiral** and **Logarithmic Spiral** are opposites. Symmetrical Spiral makes revolutions that are an equal distance from each other. Logarithmic Spiral creates a spiral where the distance between the loops widens from the center out. Figure 2-40 shows the difference between the two types of spirals.

- **Spiral Expansion Factor** becomes available when you select the Logarithmic Spiral. It controls how radically the revolutions expand as they draw outward. A factor of 1 is the same as Symmetrical Spiral, and a factor of 100 is a full expansion.

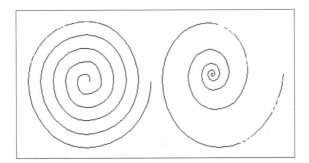

Figure 2-40: Note the difference between a symmetrical spiral (left) and a logarithmic spiral (right).

Secret

When adjusting the number of revolutions and expansion factor, you may find it more useful to do so from the Toolbox section of the Options dialog box (Tools ⇨ Options ⇨ Toolbox ⇨ Spiral Tool), because you can adjust the factor with the aid of a preview, as shown in Figure 2-41.

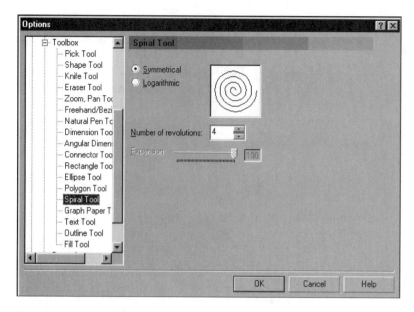

Figure 2-41: When adjusting Spiral tool options from the Options dialog box, you get a preview of how your changes will affect the behavior of the tool.

CorelDraw 8 makes it easy to turn a spiral into a closed path. Simply select the spiral with either the Pick tool or Shape tool, and then click on the Auto Close Path button. You can now fill the path with a solid fill, a fountain, or however you like. Figure 2-42 shows two closed-path spirals, one with and one without an outline.

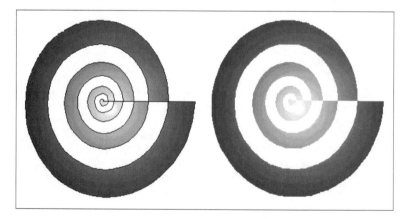

Figure 2-42: Examples of filled closed-path spirals, with an outline (left) and without an outline (right).

Using the Esc Key with the Property Bar

Secret

Many people find it convenient to use the Esc key along with the Property Bar. When you press Esc, the currently selected object is deselected, but the Property Bar and the current tool stay selected. This enables you to change tool properties more rapidly and continue drawing (rather than selecting the Pick tool, selecting the object, and then reselecting the drawing tool). For example, you can draw several dimension lines, press Esc to deselect the last one, change a tool property, and then continue drawing with a new setting.

The Zoom-and-Pan Tool

The Zoom-and-Pan tool (which we'll simply call the Zoom tool) controls your view of the current page. It's heartening to see that Corel has performed some maintenance on the Zoom tool. The View Manager and Zoom tool flyout in version 6 had so many choices that they had become mind-boggling. Another tremendous improvement in versions 7 and 8 is the Zoom tool context on the Property Bar. This addition is so nifty that you may never find a need to fly the Zoom Manager again. And this says nothing of the new and improved right-mouse pop-up menu, which also provides a rich group of zoom options.

Note

If you liked all those options on the Zoom tool flyout, have no fear. You can get them back again. Here's how: Go to the Toolbox section of the Options dialog box (Tools ⇨ Options ⇨ Toolbox ⇨ Zoom/Pan Tool), and then select Use Traditional Zoom Flyout. Close the dialog box and check out the flyout —there are all your beloved icons. And one of the things we've missed from CorelDraw versions past is the capability of right-clicking to zoom out, rather than using the right-click pop-up menu. You can get that shortcut back, too, by selecting Zoom Out in the Mouse Button 2 For The Zoom Tool option in the Options dialog box.

We're not going to go over all the Zoom tool options. To see what they are, hover the mouse cursor over each option on the Property Bar when it's in Zoom tool context to see the pop-up descriptions. (If you don't know what the descriptions mean, click them—you can't hurt your document with these tools.) Instead of covering all the Zoom tool options, it's more productive to cover just panning, marquee zoom, and saving views with the View Manager.

Using the Pan tool and marquee zoom

No matter what type of document you're working on, you often need to zoom in on and center certain objects on your monitor, making them easier to work on. Granted, you can click the Zoom tool directly on an object to enlarge your view of it, but this is hardly precise and is less useful when you want to center several objects at once on your screen.

Two of CorelDraw's features, Pan and marquee zoom, make getting a precise view easy. The first, Pan (the little hand on the Zoom tool flyout and the Property Bar in Zoom context), enables you to drag your document left, right, up, and down, simply by dragging on the screen. All you do is select the Pan tool and drag in the direction of the portion of the page you want to center, as shown in Figure 2-43.

Perhaps even more useful is the capability of marquee zooming on a specific area on the page. If you're familiar with marquee selecting with the Pick tool, using this feature should be a snap. All you do is select the Zoom tool and then drag a marquee around the area of the page you want to zoom in on, as shown in Figure 2-44. Easy enough, right?

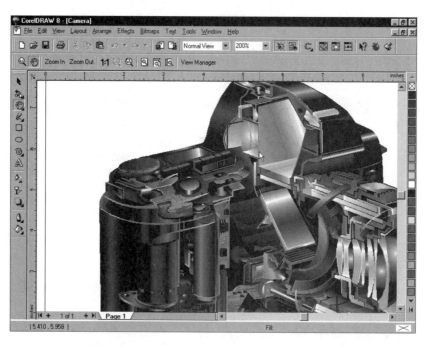

Figure 2-43: Use the Pan tool to drag your document page into the desired position on your monitor.

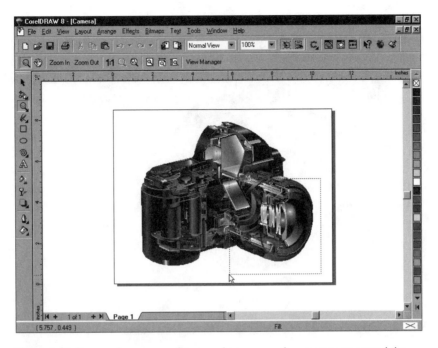

Figure 2-44: To zoom in on a specific area of your page, drag a marquee around the area with the Zoom tool, and then release the mouse button.

Saving views with View Manager

When working on intricate drawings, it's sometimes necessary to intermittently zoom in and out on several specific areas, going to one place, and then another, and then back again. This is especially critical when working on large pages, such as posters and banners, or when working with multipage documents. When you perform these operations manually, you often find yourself zooming in, out, panning, and repeating a lot of time-consuming, tedious steps. You can avoid a lot of this hassle by saving views in CorelDraw's View Manager docker (previously a roll-up), as shown in Figure 2-45.

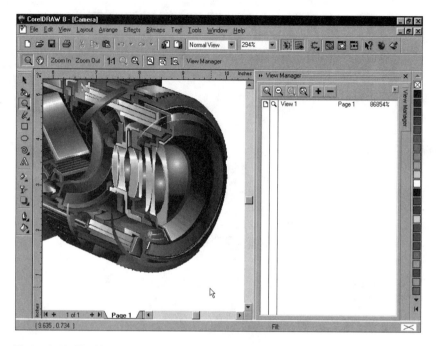

Figure 2-45: The View Manager docker lets you save specific views and reuse them to navigate around your document.

To display the View Manager docker, click on the View Manager button on the Property Bar when it's in Zoom tool context, or double-click on the Zoom tool in the toolbox.

STEPS:

Saving Views

Step 1.   Use the standard zoom and pan options to get the view you want.

Step 2.   Click on the pop-up menu arrow (shown in Figure 2-46) on the View Manager docker to display a list of Options.

Step 3.   Choose New from the pop-up menu. CorelDraw places a new view on the list, naming it View 1, View 2, or whichever is next, according to the views you've already set for this document.

Step 4.   Click on the name of the view and type a meaningful name for the view. (This step is especially critical in documents where you save a lot of views. After a while, View 1, View 2, and so on are easily forgotten.)

That's it. You can now return to a specific view — just as you saved it — at any time simply by double-clicking on it in View Manager. You can also add a view by clicking on the plus (+) button in the View Manager.

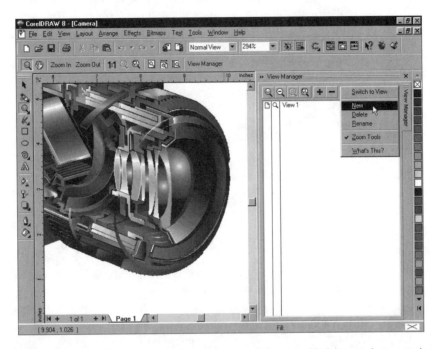

Figure 2-46: Use this menu on the View Manager docker to add, delete, and rename views.

Secret

One more thing about View Manager. Have you ever wondered what those little icons on the left side of the list of views do? You know, the page and magnifying glass? For a long time we thought they didn't really do anything — although we did wonder why we could turn them on and off.

Actually, they're quite useful. They enable you to modify how your saved views work. When you turn off the page icon (click on it and it dims), for example, you can use the corresponding view to go to the same view on the current page, rather than jumping to the page defined in the view. When you turn off the magnifying glass, double-clicking on the associated view takes you to the page defined in the view, but at the current zoom level, or the zoom level you were in when you double-clicked the item in View Manager.

In other words, if you want to go to the same zoom level on a different page, turn off the zoom icon. To go to a saved zoom level on the current page, turn off the page icon. It just doesn't get any more customizable.

Summary

- ▶ You can modify how the Pick tool behaves, such as changing the cursor to crosshairs or treating unfilled objects and filled objects, from the Toolbox section of the Options dialog box. Two new features, Node Tracking and Diggers, make it easier to edit and select objects

- ▶ The Shape tool enables you to poke and nudge outlines, getting them into exactly the right shape, by manipulating and changing the modes of nodes. You'll also find a lot of help for modifying the behavior of the Shape tool and Béziers themselves on the new Property Bar.

- ▶ The Knife tool lets you cut open and closed paths into sections, and you can greatly control how the Knife tool works from the Property Bar.

- ▶ CorelDraw's Natural Pen tool enables you to create closed-path pen strokes that emulate an artist's pens. The Natural Pen tool is pressure-sensitive, meaning that you can control the thickness of the stroke from a pressure-sensitive tablet or from your keyboard with a mouse.

- ▶ The New Free Transform tool allows you to free rotate, mirror, scale, and skew selected objects from any center point you choose.

- ▶ The behavior of the Freehand and Bézier tools is easily controlled from the Property Bar or the right-click pop-up menu, making it easier to draw and manipulate the desired type of outline.

- ▶ Dimension lines provide a wealth of options for drawing floor plans and other types of technical documents, such as schematics and architectural renderings. You can change the scale of a drawing from the Rulers section of the Options dialog box.

- ▶ CorelDraw lets you control various aspects of the shape-drawing tools from the Property Bar, including rounding the corners of rectangles and turning ellipses into pies and arcs.

- ▶ The View Manager docker lets you save various zoom levels on different pages to quickly navigate through complicated documents.

Chapter 3

Aligning and Arranging Objects

In This Chapter

You learn great secrets that can help you work more effectively with the following tools, commands, and features:

- ▶ Grids
- ▶ Rulers
- ▶ Child objects
- ▶ Break Apart, Combine, and Separate commands
- ▶ Guidelines
- ▶ Align and Distribute command
- ▶ The Trim and Weld tools
- ▶ The Separate command
- ▶ Object Manager
- ▶ The Intersection tool
- ▶ Grouping and ungrouping
- ▶ The Nudge and Duplicate commands

CorelDraw comes with a host of grids, guides, rulers, layering tools, and ordering options to help you manage objects and maintain total control over your drawings. In this chapter we'll explain these features, as well as describe some artistic tools such as Weld, Trim, Intersect, Combine, and Break Apart. We'll show you how to use these tools to create some interesting effects. For example, you'll see how to use Layer Manager to quickly create a watermark graphic that appears beneath the text of a document.

Lining Up Objects

CorelDraw includes a number of tools to help you line up objects in your drawing. The main tools are grids, rulers, guidelines, and Align and Distribute.

Setting up grids

To access the Grid Setup, right-click on the ruler, click on Grid Setup, and choose Grid Setup. You'll see the Grids and Guidelines dialog box. Here you can set up grid spacing, visibility, and whether to display the grids as dots or as lines. You can also right-click on the Master Grid in the Objects Manager (found under Master Page). (To see the Master Grid, you may have to expand Master Page by clicking on the plus sign next to it.) Then click on Properties ⇨ Setup. You'll see a two-tab dialog box called Grid and Ruler Setup. You'll have access to the same set of controls as contained in the Grids and Guidelines dialog box. Grids provide a visual reference for the size of objects on your page. When you require exactness, such as with blueprints or scaled street maps, grids are a must. Grids are very flexible and can be resized with a few mouse clicks. You can also turn on Snap to Grid (press Ctrl+Y) to make objects you draw conform to the grids you set up on your screen.

Grids are not always visible on your screen. To see them, select View ⇨ Grid from the menu bar, right-click on Master Grid in Object Manager and select Visible, or click on the Eye icon next to Master Grid in the Object Manager. See Figure 3-1.

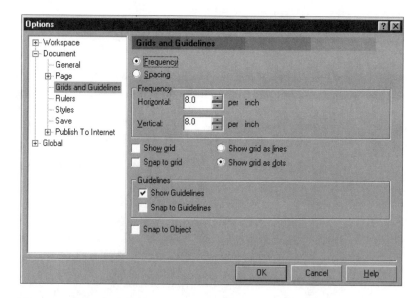

Figure 3-1: Use Grid Setup to control grid options for your drawing.

Secret

When objects have been selected on the page, you can make your objects snap to a grid by clicking on the Property Bar's Snap to Grid. When you save a document, the current Snap to Grid setting is saved along with that document.

Tip

Right-clicking on Master Grid in the Object Manager also provides options to print your grid. Printing your grid essentially turns the background of your document into grid paper. If you want to make your grid appear as solid lines rather than dots, after right-clicking on Master Grid you can either select Printable, select Properties and click on Printable, or choose Tools ➪ Options ➪ Document ➪ Grids and Guidelines.

Figure 3-2 shows three stars drawn with Snap to Grid enabled. By maintaining the same number of grid dots on either side of the stars, one can be sure of their alignment. Snap to Grid is also extremely helpful when drawing rectangles within other rectangles.

Figure 3-2: These three stars are evenly spaced because they were drawn with Snap to Grid enabled.

Changing grid frequency and color

You can change the space between grid dots by right-clicking on the ruler, selecting Grid Setup, and changing the Frequency number. The Spacing and Frequency numbers have the same effect on grid dot placement. If you have the Show grid as lines option selected, then your grid line frequency will be changed according to your new settings.

To change the color of your grid dots or lines, right-click on the Master Grid icon in Object Manager, and then change the Layer color. This can be helpful when working in Wireframe mode, because in Wireframe mode each object becomes a single color. If you've changed the grid color to something distinctive, it's easier to tell your grid dots or lines from your drawing.

Secret

The Snap to Grid, Snap to Guidelines, and Snap to Object commands are available on the Property Bar. Click on any white space to deselect any object, and then turn your attention to the icons at the far right of the Property Bar. Also, you may have noticed that, as your drawing grows in complexity, objects take longer to redraw after they are moved. Make sure the Draw Complex Objects icon (to the far right of the Property Bar) is not selected, and when you move or transform objects, you'll see only their outlines, which speeds the moving process. Click on the icon to the right of that icon, and you're able to click anywhere in an unfilled object and move it to a new location. If the icon is not depressed, you have to click on the unfilled object's outline.

Using rulers

CorelDraw's rulers are very flexible. Both the horizontal and vertical rulers can be moved to any part of your page. You can change the measurement units, drag unlimited numbers of guides from your ruler onto the page, or turn off the rulers altogether. You can access the Rulers dialog box by right-clicking on the ruler and choosing Ruler Setup. See Figure 3-3.

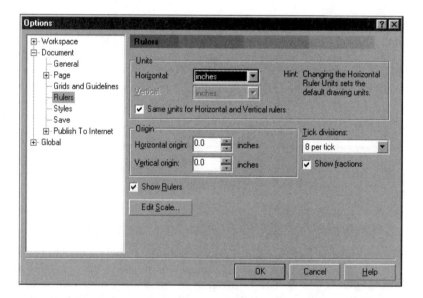

Figure 3-3: Use the Rulers dialog box to control ruler options for your drawing.

From the Rulers dialog box, you can also change the measurement units on your rulers. For example, if a client wants a drawing measured in millimeters rather than inches, CorelDraw's rulers can oblige. In fact, the Ruler menu offers 13 measurement systems, including pixels. Measuring in pixels can be helpful if your final product will be viewed on a computer screen rather than printed onto a page. Oversized work can be measured in meters or yards as well. When working with paragraph text, the rulers mark the height and width of the paragraph. The upper ruler contains sliding bars that enable control over paragraph indents, margins, and tabs. (See Figure 3-4.) Chapter 4 explains more about formatting paragraph text.

This is a frame containing paragraph text with the default Avant Garde font.|

Figure 3-4: This is what rulers look like when you select paragraph text.

Note the changing numbers in the bottom-left corner of the status bar, shown in Figure 3-5. These numbers are the mouse coordinates. These numbers always display the location of your mouse cursor relative to the bottom-left corner of your page. For example, if your mouse cursor is approximately five inches up and three inches to the right of the bottom-left corner of the page (known as "0, 0"), the mouse coordinates will read something like "3.239, 5.053" (the comma separates the horizontal x-axis value from the vertical y-axis value). If you've changed your measurement unit to millimeters, for example, these two reference numbers will also display millimeters. In fact, right above these reference numbers is a label telling you what measurement system you are currently using. By right-clicking on the status bar, you can remove the mouse coordinates or have the status bar display other helpful information. Editing toolbar properties is covered thoroughly in Chapter 9 of this book.

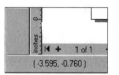

Figure 3-5: Mouse coordinates appear on the status bar.

The Drawing Scale dialog box

Figure 3-6 shows the Drawing Scale dialog box. You open this dialog box by right-clicking on the Ruler, selecting Ruler Setup, and then clicking on Edit Scale. You can alter the drawing scale to make maps, architectural designs, and other documents that need precise scale measurements. In this example, one inch of Page Distance equals 63,360 inches of World Distance; in other words, the scale is one inch to the mile.

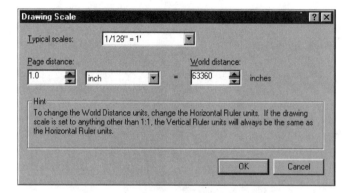

Figure 3-6: Use the Drawing Scale dialog box to create scaled maps with CorelDraw.

Moving the rulers

You can change the position of the rulers by pressing Shift while dragging the rulers in toward your drawing. This makes drawing precision shapes much easier. Figure 3-7a shows a rectangle drawn to exact specifications using moved rulers. CorelDraw comes with a complete set of tools to label measurements on your page. They are Dimension tools, and they are covered in Chapter 2 of this book. Figure 3-7b shows the rectangle we just created labeled with Dimension tools.

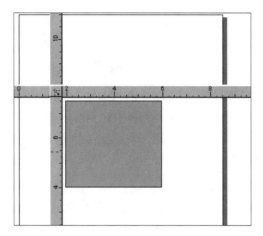

Figure 3-7a: A rectangle can be more easily drawn to exact specifications with rulers moved close to it.

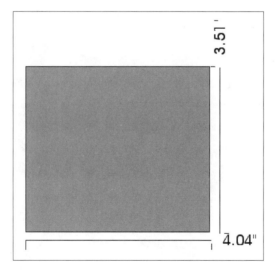

Figure 3-7b: The Dimension tools make it easy to label object dimensions.

No matter where they are on the screen, rulers can be moved back to their default locations by pressing Shift and double-clicking on the ruler.

Changing the ruler origins

The Ruler sets its origins at the bottom left of the page. If you want the ruler measurements to originate from a particular object on your page instead, you can

- Click and drag from the point where the rulers intersect at the upper-left of the screen (see Figure 3-8), moving towards the point of the object where you want the new ruler origins to be, and release the mouse button. (For example, the new 0, 0 could be at the bottom-left corner of a rectangle you've just created, rather than the bottom-left corner of the page itself.) After doing this, you'll notice the ruler numbers now originate from the point where you released to mouse.

- Right-click on the ruler and select Ruler Setup. Type new numbers in the Origin panel. Your ruler's 0, 0 points will now begin at those values. This is helpful, for example, if you know you want a one-inch border around you entire page. You can set the rulers to *zero out* exactly at one inch into the page.

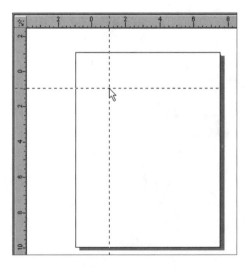

Figure 3-8. Clicking and dragging from the ruler's intersection point creates new ruler points of origin.

Guidelines

Guidelines are visual markers that you set up to help position objects on your page. They are vertical and horizontal lines that can be positioned and repositioned anywhere you like. They can be freely moved, rotated, and slanted. If you've taken the time to set up some precise guides, you'll be happy to know that guidelines can also be copied and pasted to other documents.

In CorelDraw 8, guidelines now have some of the features of objects. Guidelines can have text-wrap qualities; a guideline that cuts through paragraph text will push the intersecting text out of the way (see Figure 3-9). Like other objects in CorelDraw, guidelines can be locked into place (right-click on the guideline and select Lock Object).

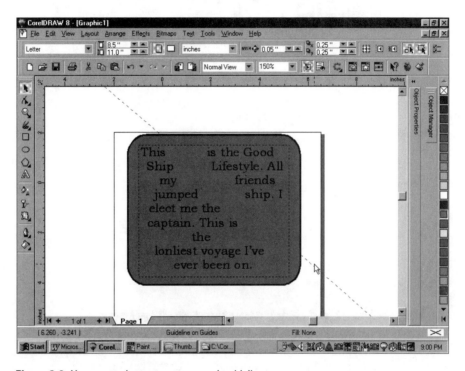

Figure 3-9: You can make text wrap around guidelines.

To create guidelines, simply begin dragging from any place along your ruler's edge into your drawing. When you stop dragging, a dotted red line appears. A guideline normally appears blue, but it will appear red when selected or newly created.

Using guidelines

After you have created guidelines, you can use them as visual guides, or you can make objects "snap" to them. For example, you may wish to have a newly created object adhere to the upper border of a rectangle already on your page. You can enable this by placing a guideline along that upper border and selecting Layout ⇨ Snap to Guidelines from the menu bar, or deselecting any object and clicking on the Snap to Guidelines button on the Property Bar.

Guidelines are also useful for arranging text on a page. Figure 3-10 shows horizontal guidelines used to line up and size artistic text to an exact height.

Figure 3-10: Use horizontal guidelines to make sure text conforms to an exact height.

Rotating and slanting guidelines

Clicking twice on your guideline places a rotation icon at either end of the guideline and a movable *center point* marker at the center of the guideline. Clicking and dragging at either end of the guideline will rotate it around the center point. You may move the center point anywhere, causing the guideline to rotate around that new position (see Figure 3-11). You can even move the center point away from the guideline itself. To slant a guideline (move one end of the guideline while the other remains stationary, rather than rotate it), click on the Node tool and then move the tiny square that appears at either end of the guideline. That end will now move independently of the other.

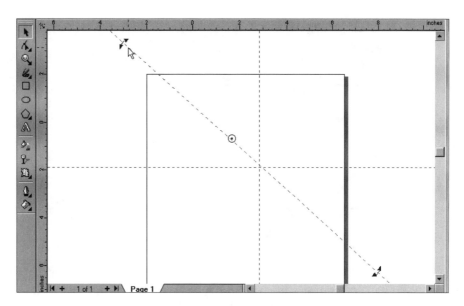

Figure 3-11: Guidelines on a page can be horizontal, vertical, or diagonal.

Modifying your guidelines

To access CorelDraw's Guidelines Setup dialog box, you have three methods available:

- Select Layout ⇨ Guidelines Setup from the menu bar.
- Right-click on Master Guides in Object Manager, and then select Properties ⇨ Setup.
- Select the guideline and then double-click on it.

The first method is usually more convenient. However, the second method gives you the option to print your guidelines or change their color.

You can maintain more precise control over your guidelines by using the Guidelines Setup dialog box pictured in Figure 3-12. You have three tabs to choose from. Use the dialog box to enter exact numerical values for guideline locations, rather than using your mouse and eyeballing it. Each type of guideline (horizontal, vertical, or slanted) is given its own tab for entering guideline numbers. You may use one of the 13 provided measuring systems for your guides, and set your diagonal guidelines by exact x, y coordinates or by degree of angle. The Guidelines Setup box enables you to create new guidelines or move and edit already existing ones.

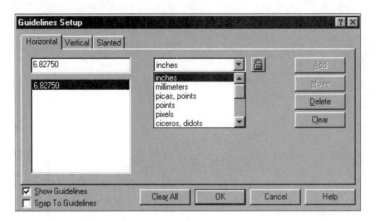

Figure 3-12: The Guidelines Setup dialog box enables you to position guidelines precisely.

You can quickly erase all guidelines from your screen by double-clicking on any guideline and selecting Clear All.

You can also use Object Manager (explained later in this chapter) to edit guidelines. If you use Object Manager, make sure a new layer is selected when you are finished editing your guidelines. Otherwise, any objects you create will apply only to the Guideline layer. Your screen will be covered with guideline objects! If you accidentally did this, cut the object and move it to Layer 1, for example, and it will then be a true object and not a guideline.

Using objects as guides

You can also create objects in the Guideline layer and use them as you would other guides. For example, you can create a circle as a guide and make sure everything else you create stays clear of that circle. Or you can create text as a guide, turn on Snap To Guidelines, and make sure other layers of text you create snap to that guideline. Figure 3-13 shows text as a guideline.

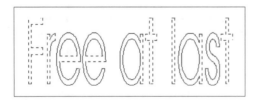

Figure 3-13: You can even use text as a guideline.

Using text as a guideline can be helpful if you want certain objects to align exactly to text — such as making sure drawn objects fall directly beneath a text heading. Similarly with using objects as guidelines, you can make sure one object is aligned with another. Later, you can group them and align them both to the page.

Tip

When you want objects to line up exactly, select Layout ⇨ Snap to Objects, or deselect any objects and click on Snap to Objects on the Property Bar.

Using the Object Manager

The Object Manager, shown in Figure 3-14, provides thumbnail views of all the objects and layers in your document. By default it is a docker (a window that attaches itself to the right of your screen), and thus when you minimize it (by clicking on the right-facing arrow at the upper right), it becomes a tab, expandable by a single click. The Object Manager groups all objects according to page, which may not be evident when you first begin to create a document. Every time you create an object in your document, a new thumbnail appears in the Object Manager. Holding your mouse over the thumbnail reveals a description of that object; for example "Control Ellipse-Fill: Texture, Outline: Black hairline." Changes you make in the object's properties (converting to curves, changing the outline size, applying special effects, and locking the object) will appear in this short description. Adding a URL does not appear in the description.

Tip

If you'd rather not view the icon descriptions, click on the middle icon at the upper left of Object Manager.

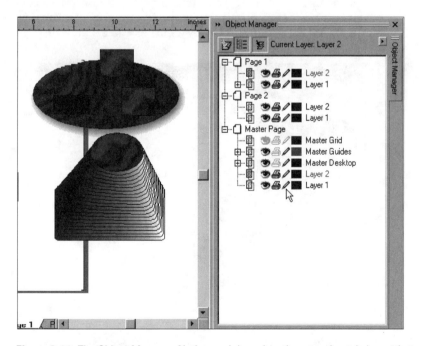

Figure 3-14: The Object Manager. Notice each layer has three toggle-style icons that enable you to print, view, or lock each layer.

How Object Manager is organized

Object Manager is organized under level headings or branching trees: the Master Page, individual pages, and layers. The Master Page contains items that will appear on all pages, such as guides and grids. As you add pages to your document, new page icons appear. When you create a page, layers for that page are also created. Therefore, Object Manager shows at least one layer icon beneath each page. When you create draw objects, such as rectangles or text, you are creating them on a layer. Object Manager reflects this by creating thumbnails of each created object under its appropriate layer heading.

Tip

To reveal any objects beneath a heading, click on the heading's plus sign. For example, clicking on the plus sign next to Page 1 reveals the layers beneath it. A minus sign indicates that nothing is hidden beneath that current branch or heading.

Special effects that create new objects such as blends will create a new "group object" icon in the Object Manager (see Figure 3-15). This can be helpful when you've created a blend and want to quickly reopen the Blend dialog box and edit the blend further. Just right-click on the Blend Group icon in Object Manager and select Current Effect Rollup. The Blend roll-up appears, open to the Blend settings you used on those objects. When you apply Shape effects such as Weld or Intersect to objects, the object qualities will change. When welding, the affected object will become a curve, for example. This change is reflected in the Object Manager. You'll notice the effect shape is now represented by a curve rather than a shape.

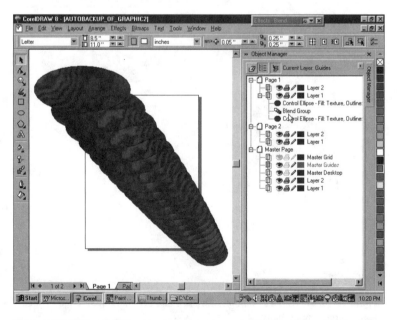

Figure 3-15. Using the Blend tool creates a group of intermediate objects. Here they are represented by a thumbnail in Object Manager.

Grouping with Object Manager

Use the Object Manager to group objects by dragging one object on top of the other. While dragging, you'll notice a group object icon appear. Release your mouse, and the object is then grouped. To group multiple objects, press Ctrl while clicking on the relevant objects in the Object Manager. (You'll notice bounding boxes surrounding the objects in your drawing area, but no change will appear yet in the Object Manager.) Right-click and select Group from the pop-up menu.

Changing order with Object Manager

To change object order using Object Manager, just reposition the object icon, either above or below the other objects. Look at your drawing area workspace. If the objects are overlapping, you'll immediately notice the change in object order. This will have the same effect as if you had used the menu commands under Arrange ⇨ Order. However, the Order menu has some new sophisticated commands that are not available from Object Manager, such as reversing the order of all objects or relocating a corresponding object to any other object on your screen.

Editing fills and outlines with Object Manager

You can edit object properties such as fills and outlines by keeping the Object Properties dialog box open as you move through your objects in the Object Manager. You do not need to edit one object, close the dialog box, select a new object, and then reopen the dialog box. Using Object Manager, click on one object, alter its fill and outline properties, and then simply select another one, without closing the dialog box in between.

To apply a fill or outline style to several objects, first create an object with the fill or outline style you want to copy. Then, using Object Manager, select all the objects to which you want to apply the new fill and outline. Next select Edit ⇨ Copy Properties From. From the resulting dialog box, select fill, text, or outline properties, or some combination thereof. Finally, click on the source object, the object that contains the property information you want to copy. All the objects you selected in Object Manager will now have the same chosen properties as the source object.

Secret

To quickly copy the properties from one object onto another, right-click on and drag the target object onto the source object. You'll see a dialog box asking which properties you want to take with you. After selecting, click on OK, and the object you clicked and dragged will now have the properties of the source object.

Creating styles with Object Manager

You can also use the Object Manager to speed up creating and applying styles. For example, after creating a fill and outline style that you want to save and apply later, right-click on the object in Object Manager and select Styles ⇨ Save Style Properties. You're prompted to name your style. Again, specify which properties to save as a style for later use. Next, click on the objects in Object Manager to which you want to apply this style. Right-click and select Styles ⇨ Apply. You'll see the style you just created in the list of applicable styles.

To apply a style you created some time ago, or one of CorelDraw's included styles, select Layout ⇨ Graphic and Text Styles. A Docker opens, showing as icons all available Styles. (The Object Manager's docker is momentarily obscured. To bring it back, click its tab, at the far right of the screen.) Now select the object (or objects) to which you want to apply a style. Finally, click on a style icon in the Graphic and Text Styles docker. Your chosen style is applied to all the objects you selected. You can also right-click on an object, select Styles ⇨ Apply, and select the style you want to apply to the current object (see Figure 3-16). You can also use this right-click method to save an object's attributes as a style.

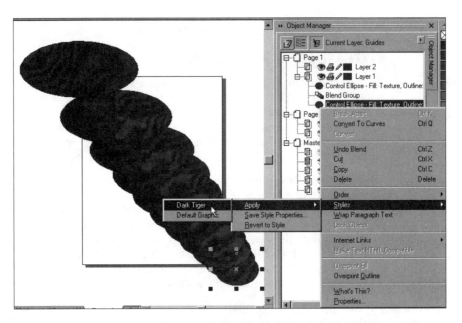

Figure 3-16: When applying a style, first click on the style, and then click on the object to which you want to apply the style.

Selecting and Moving Objects

In past versions of CorelDraw, after creating an object, you could not move it until you selected the Pick tool from the toolbox. In CorelDraw 8, a small X appears in the center of every object you create. You can move an object with any tool by clicking and dragging on this X. You need not select the Pick tool simply to relocate objects.

Secret

If you find that it takes too long to redraw objects after moving or transforming them, click on the Draw Complex Objects button on the Property bar. (First make sure nothing is selected.)

To select buried objects — objects obscured because something else is closer to the surface — press the Alt key while clicking on the surface object. While doing so, the object beneath is then selected. If you are seeking a third object, one buried even farther below the surface, press the Alt key again.

Using Align and Distribute

The Align and Distribute dialog box (Arrange ⇨ Align and Distribute) enables you to make sure all your document's objects — including captions — are properly aligned. You can use this dialog box, shown in Figure 3-17, to align objects to each other, to the edge or center of the page, or to grids.

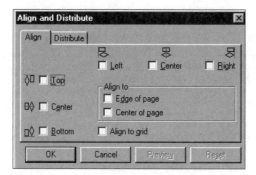

Figure 3-17: The Align and Distribute dialog box lets you align objects in various ways.

You have three ways to access the Align and Distribute dialog box:

- Select Align and Distribute from the Arrange menu.
- Press Ctrl+A.
- Select the word Align on the far right of the Property Bar. (It becomes visible only if two or more objects are selected.)

If you align objects to each other, all objects will be aligned to the last object selected.

The Align sheet of the Align and Distribute dialog box enables you to set a horizontal parameter (Top, Center, or Bottom) and a vertical parameter (Left, Center, or Right), and to choose the Align to page (Edge or Center) or Align to grid options. Preview your results on the page itself by clicking on Preview, and then click on Reset to try another option. Actually, you need not click on the Reset button to try another type of alignment. Just place checks by your new parameters and click on Preview. Use Reset to return your page to the way it was before you began editing. Click on OK to apply your effect.

Aligning objects

When you are selecting objects to be aligned, think about where you want the objects to end up, and place the last object to be selected on that part of the page. The last object you select will be what the others are aligned to. If you select only one object, you'll need to select one of the Align to page options, or no action will be taken.

You can combine check boxes to come up with a great number of alignment options, and the following figures provide a couple of examples of how the Align command works. If you work through these examples yourself, make sure to use the Order command to bring the "Pac-Man" circle to the front, put the triangle in the middle, and set the rectangle to the back. Figure 3-18 shows three unaligned objects with Center selected for both the horizontal and vertical parameters. Clicking on OK makes the objects look like Figure 3-19.

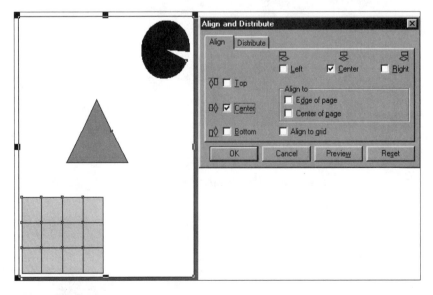

Figure 3-18: These three unaligned objects are about to be centered.

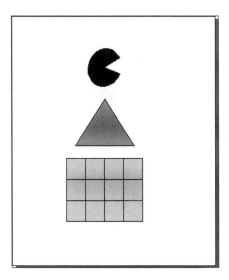

Figure 3-19: The same objects are now center-aligned.

Figure 3-20 shows what happens if you select Top, Left, and Edge of page. Objects will be aligned to the top left of the last object selected (the triangle), and also aligned to the top left of the page. Notice that the rectangle is not aligned in Figure 3-20 because it is not selected.

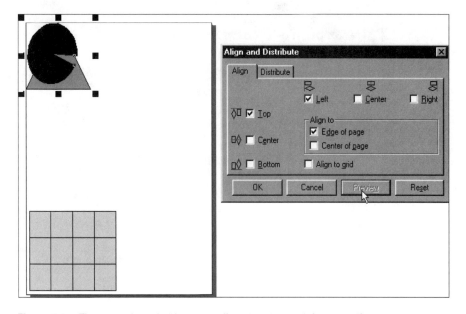

Figure 3-20: The two selected objects are aligned to the top-left corner of the page.

Figure 3-21 shows two objects centered to each other as well as to the page.

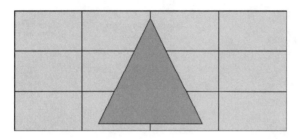

Figure 3-21: These two objects are centered to each other (horizontally and vertically) and to the page.

Figure 3-22 shows how to use Align to center a caption exactly under a rectangle object.

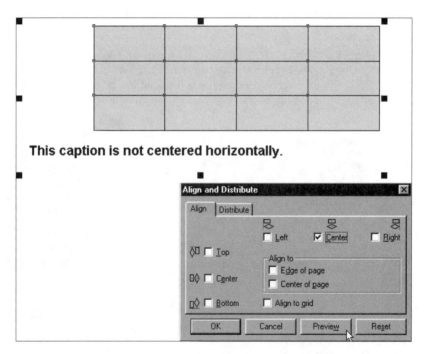

Figure 3-22: To center the caption under the rectangle, select the horizontal Center check box.

Distributing objects

Click on the Distribute tab of the Align and Distribute dialog box to adjust the distribution of selected objects, as shown in Figure 3-23. If you select several objects, you can use Distribute to space them evenly across your page or across a selected area. As with Align, you can set horizontal parameters, vertical parameters, or both to distribute your objects. For example, if you've just duplicated a CorelDraw object several times, the Distribute command can spread these copies across the top of a page at even intervals.

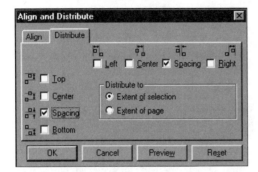

Figure 3-23: The Distribute sheet of the Align and Distribute dialog box lets you evenly distribute selected objects in various ways.

As with Align, you can click on the Preview button to test-run your choices before selecting OK. The Distribute option is only available when you have more than one object selected on your page.

Here are some examples of how to use Distribute. Figure 3-24 shows a five-dollar bill that has been duplicated six times using the Duplicate command. Unless you've edited your tool options, this is exactly how duplicated objects look: Each new copy is placed slightly above and to the right of the previous duplicate. The Distribute dialog box is shown with three options checked: horizontal and vertical Spacing, and Extent of page. Selecting OK spreads the dollar bills diagonally across the entire page, as shown in Figure 3-25.

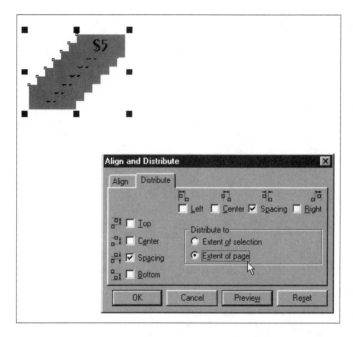

Figure 3-24: Duplicated CorelDraw objects are ready for even distribution.

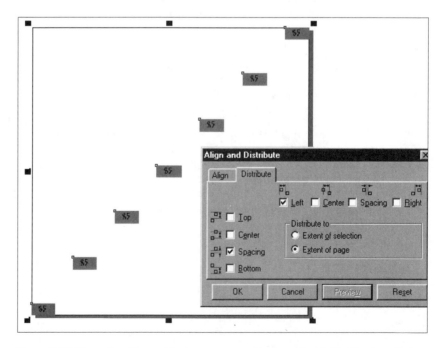

Figure 3-25: These CorelDraw objects are now evenly spaced with Distribute applied.

The Extent of selection option has an effect only if objects are selected that have room to move within the selected area. If you've just duplicated some objects, as in Figure 3-24, and then choose Extent of selection, nothing happens.

Figure 3-26 shows the result of choosing the same objects, selecting the horizontal Spacing option, and choosing Extent of page. The bills are distributed evenly across the top of the page.

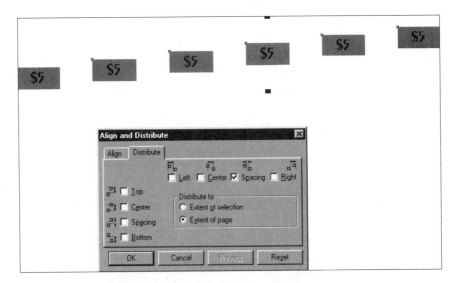

Figure 3-26: This art is now distributed across the top of the page.

Figure 3-27 shows one way you can use the Extent of selection option. First deselect the five-dollar bills and then reselect one. Now drag the bill farther up the screen. Doing so marks the path that the remaining bills will travel after you use the Distribute command.

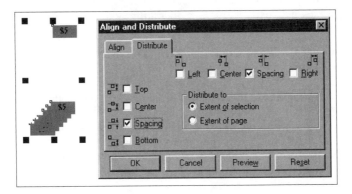

Figure 3-27: Before Extent of selection is performed, most of this art is bunched together.

Now select all the bills and choose the vertical Spacing option and Extent of selection. The results appear in Figure 3-28.

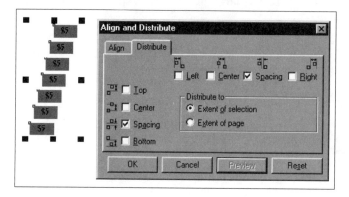

Figure 3-28: The art is evenly distributed after Extent of selection is performed.

The remaining CorelDraw object pieces are now evenly spaced across a path led by the first CorelDraw object, bounded within the selected area.

CorelDraw provides many tools for controlling the positioning and order of objects on your page. Still, it's not always easy to keep track of what is supposed to go where. For that task, CorelDraw has provided Layering controls.

Working with Layers

Layers are like the transparencies that many people use with overhead projectors. You can place one on top of another to gradually create a completed image. You can draw objects or type text on each layer, and then create a new layer for other objects in the same drawing. Each new layer you create is automatically placed on top of previous layers. While you're working with the new layer, you can choose whether you want to view underlying layers. Also, to prevent accidentally changing the work you did on an earlier layer, you can "lock" it in place.

CorelDraw's layers enable you to create one portion of your drawing at a time. For example, for a landscape drawing you may decide to work only on the sky at first and call that portion Layer 1. You could then create a new layer of mountains and call that Layer 2, and then put foliage on the mountains as Layer 3. Why keep them separate? By using layers (found in Object Manager), you could make the Mountain Layer invisible while working on the foliage, and make the Sky Layer uneditable, so that you don't have to worry about accidentally moving a chunk of your sky while repositioning a mountain. Layering is great for protecting selected portions of your drawing that you don't want to change.

Layering can also be useful for creating watermark graphics. A watermark graphic is a faint background picture that usually appears behind text or another image on a page. (Such graphics are meant to look like real watermarks that are pressed into paper during the paper-making process.) By using layers in Object Manager, you can create a watermark graphic without having to specifically duplicate the same picture manually. Also, Layer Manager enables you to specify portions of your work as nonprinting. For example, if you wanted to quickly print out the text portion of a lengthy newsletter but not the graphics, you could copy all the graphics to their own layer and temporarily render that layer "nonprinting."

In Object Manger, look at Master Page (see Figure 3-29). You'll see three default layers that are part of every CorelDraw page. These layers are the Master Grid, Master Guides, and Master Desktop. As you saw earlier, you can use these icons to edit Grid and Guideline features for your entire project or for one individual page. You use these three icons to change the color of guidelines and grids, make them printable, and change their spacing and properties.

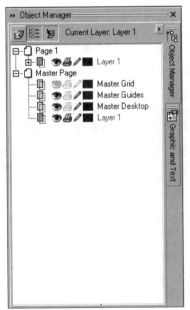

Figure 3-29. Click on Properties on a Master to change its color and spacing, and to specify if your changes should apply to all layers or only the selected one.

You'll also notice Layer 1, which is where all your drawing takes place until you create additional layers. All objects you create and edit will appear here. The Eye icon controls the visibility of the layer, so clicking on it temporarily makes it unseen. Click on the Printer icon to make this layer unprintable, and click on the Pencil icon to make it uneditable, which locks the layer in place, preventing accidental editing. All these icons are toggle switches, meaning that clicking on them again reverses the setting. Figure 3-30 shows a disabled layer.

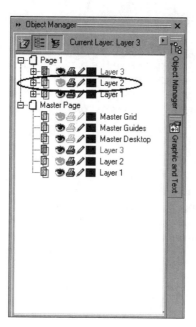

Figure 3-30: In Object Manager, the visibility of Layer 2 has been disabled. Editing is done on the selected layer.

Secret

You can make any layer into a Master layer by right-clicking on it and selecting Master. If a layer is a Master, then every object on that layer will appear on each page of your document. This is a fast way to create a document watermark, or a document heading that appears on all pages.

Tip

Master layers, such as the Guides layer, repeat on each page. If you want to make a change (right-click on one of the Masters and select Properties) but not apply the change to all pages in your project, place a check mark by Apply Change to Current Page Only.

Tip

As you're working, if suddenly you cannot select or edit anything on your picture, check Layer Manager. You may be attempting to edit an inactive layer or a layer that has been protected.

Changing the layer color

To choose a new layer color, right-click on a layer, click on Properties, and select the Layer Color drop-down menu. When working in Wireframe mode, objects on this layer will appear in this chosen color. With the Wireframe option, you can move objects around quickly by viewing only their outlines — it's like looking at the object's skeleton. To view only the outlines, select View ➪ Wireframe. This view is helpful because seeing all of the shapes in your drawing in the default blue wireframe can be confusing. Specifying a separate color for each layer helps make each more distinct.

Using the Object Manager flyout menu

The Object Manager flyout menu, shown in Figure 3-31, enables you to move or copy drawings from one layer to another, as well as rename, delete, and add new layers. On this menu are options to show all the pages and layers as one long list, or show only the current page (Show Pages). You can also specify whether editing you perform will affect all layers or only the current layer (Edit Across Layers).

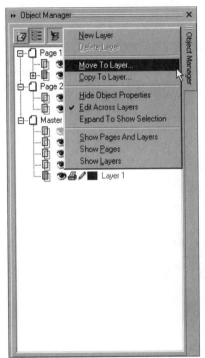

Figure 3-31: The Object Manager flyout menu gives you control over your drawing's layers.

Editing across layers

When you are working with layers, normally you cannot select an object that is not in the current layer. In fact, if you find yourself clicking repeatedly on an object and cannot select it, check to see whether the object is on a different layer. If so, you won't be able to select it unless you either move to the other layer or select Edit Across Layers. Edit Across Layers enables you to select any object on any layer that is not locked. A locked layer cannot be edited until it is unlocked.

Selecting and adding layers

By default, CorelDraw creates one layer for each new picture (in addition to the Grids, Guides, and Desktop layers). If you want to add more layers, click on the Add Layer icon at the upper-left of Object Manager, or open the Object Manager flyout menu by clicking on the arrow facing right at the upper right. Select New Layer and notice that Layer 2 will now be created. To select any layer, click on the Paper icon to the left of the Eye icon. To view layers, pages, and masters that may be hidden from view, click on the plus sign to the left of any icon in Object Manager.

Using the Properties menu

Click on any layer icon in the Object Manager to access its Properties dialog box, as shown in Figure 3-32. Here you make a layer printable, visible, and available for editing. It also includes two invaluable tools: Override full color view and Apply layer changes to the current page only.

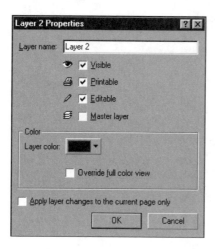

Figure 3-32: The Layer 2 Properties dialog box lets you control the behavior of an individual layer.

Overriding full color view

If you ever want to view only the wireframe of part of a drawing but see another part in full color, move the portion to be viewed as a wireframe to its own layer, and select Override full color view. From now on, that portion of the drawing will be viewed as if you had selected Wireframe from the View menu, while the remainder of the drawing will be viewed in full color. If a particular portion of your drawing takes very long to refresh, you may want to consider this option.

Applying layer changes to the current page only

This command enables you to make exceptions to your layer rules. For example, if you have a drawing that repeats on each page, and you'd like to skip the drawing on page 8, then move to page 8 of your document, make that layer invisible, open the Settings dialog box, and then apply this command. For another example, if you would like to print your guidelines only on page 1 of your document, then turn on the Guideline Layer Print icon while on page 1. Open the Settings dialog box and select this command.

As you can see, the various layering options are extremely useful for creating and editing complex drawings. Another important tool that affects the arrangement of objects is the Group command.

Grouping and Ungrouping Objects

The Group and Ungroup commands appear under the Arrange menu. These commands can also be accessed by right-clicking on the selected objects and bringing up the Object Properties menu. (For a keyboard shortcut, press Ctrl+G.) As mentioned earlier, objects can be grouped in the Object Manager. As drawings grow in complexity, this thumbnail "birds-eye view" of grouped objects can be helpful.

Figure 3-33 shows a CorelDraw picture of a sailboat. This picture is really a group of nine objects. The sail was drawn separately and then grouped with the mast. These objects were later grouped with the hull, and so on.

Figure 3-33: A single CorelDraw object is often really a group of objects.

Group of 9 Objects on Layer 1

The boat, when combined with other objects, might later become a harbor scene, which might be a collection of objects grouped together as a *master group*. A master group is a complete drawing. It can be resized, exported as a different file type, or copied and pasted to another file, all as a group. You do not have to ungroup objects in order to edit them individually. You can select any object within a group and recolor or reshape that one object, without affecting the others in the group. To select one object from a group, press Ctrl and then click on the group repeatedly until the object you want is selected. Pressing Ctrl enables you to click and drill down through all the objects in a group, selecting each individually. The boat could then be edited individually, recolored and reshaped all on its own, and then grouped again with the rest of the master group. Figure 3-34 shows the layout of the grouping of a typical CorelDraw project.

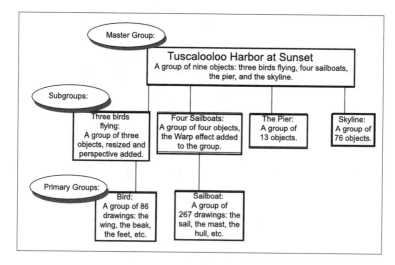

Figure 3-34: A layout of the grouping of a typical CorelDraw project.

Grouping enables you to "section off" portions of your drawing and treat each section as a single object. For example, if you created a sky scene with a complicated artistic text pattern on top of it, you could select only the text, group it, move it to a new page of your drawing, and edit the text without the sky getting in the way.

Even after you've grouped objects, you can still select an object within that group to perform simple editing, such as recoloring. If you wish to perform special-effects editing, however, such as Extrude, Rotate, and Contour, you first need to make the object into a child object. When you create a child object, you can edit a grouped object without accidentally editing the entire group. For example, while working with a complex drawing of a person, you might decide to rotate only one arm of the person. One approach would be to ungroup the entire drawing, but you might end up editing more of the drawing than you intended. Then you might have trouble properly grouping the drawing again. To quickly edit a small portion of a group, a better approach is to select only the part of the group you want to edit and press the Ctrl key to create a child object. Here's how it's done.

STEPS:

Creating a Child Object

Step 1. Hold down the Ctrl key and select the portion of the object to be edited.

Step 2. Check the status line. It should report that the selection is now a child object.

Step 3. Release the Ctrl key. You can now perform special-effects and transform editing on the selected portion without worrying about it affecting the entire group.

Step 4. You have no need to unchild the selected portion when you are finished. Simply move on to the next step in your project.

An example of creating a child object is shown in Figure 3-35, in which the enveloping effect has been applied to only a portion of the pencil object on the right. (Enveloping, by the way, is one of CorelDraw's special effects. See Chapter 6 for more information about enveloping.)

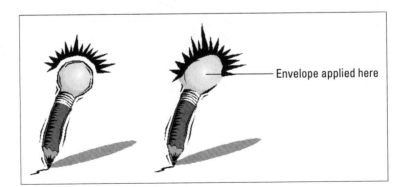

Figure 3-35: Here a portion of the pencil object is selected and made into a child object, and the Envelope effect is applied.

Combining and Breaking Apart Objects

Combining objects is different from grouping objects. The Combine command creates a single object out of two or more selected objects. With grouping, the objects maintain the shape qualities they possessed before they were grouped. The Group command is used to conveniently select objects for moving around the page as a unit. Grouping does not alter the characteristics of the individual objects involved in the group. When you use the Combine command, each object is converted to curves to form one object.

The Combine command

When you apply the Combine command, the areas where the objects overlap become transparent, enabling anything underneath to show through. Figure 3-36 shows how this works. The rectangles and text overlapping each other leave holes where they overlap, enabling a fountain-filled pattern behind the objects to show through.

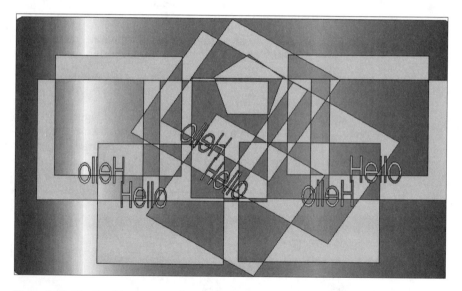

Figure 3-36: The Combine command at work: A series of overlapping rectangles and text shows how the Combine command enables the fill behind to show through.

Here's another use of the Combine command: Suppose you group a number of objects, and one of those objects is a shade of green that you've worked hard at getting just right. It turns out that you would like all the objects, when grouped, also to take on that exact shade. Simply select all the objects, and then select the green object last. Choose Arrange ⇨ Combine. All the objects will be the same color.

The Combine command can also be used to quickly make text transparent. In Figure 3-36, the word "Hello" is transparent, just like the rectangles. To try this yourself, create a text object and then make a transparent rectangle. Then select the text first, followed by the rectangle. The text will now be transparent. This procedure is the first step in creating a text mask. A text mask works like a cookie cutter that leaves a hole in an object in the shape of the text — as in the word "Hello" in Figure 3-36. A text mask is handy for enabling a bitmap buried beneath the first object to show through where the text mask is. Figure 3-37 shows another example of a text mask.

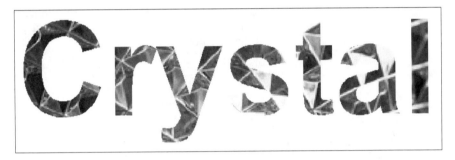

Figure 3-37: A bitmap showing through a text mask using the Combine command produces this interesting result.

Here's how you can use the Combine command to create a text mask like the one shown in Figure 3-37.

STEPS:

Creating a Creative Text Mask

Step 1. Import a bitmap image into CorelDraw. Make it an interesting, repeating pattern such as honeycomb or brick.

Step 2. Create a rectangle large enough to cover the image you imported. Do not fill the rectangle with any color.

Step 3. Type a word with a bold, clear font. In the example shown in Figure 3-37, we imported an image of crystal as the bitmap and typed **Crystal** to form the mask.

Step 4. Drag the word you've typed to the center of the rectangle. The word should be large enough to nearly fill it.

Step 5. Select both the typed word and the rectangle, and click on Arrange ⇨ Combine. You now have a transparent rectangle and transparent text.

(continued)

STEPS *(continued)*

Creating a Creative Text Mask

Step 6.   Fill the rectangle around the text with white. (If your background color is something besides white, use it instead.) You now have a mask of text that you can place over any image, and the underlying image will show through the text.

Step 7.   Drag the word over the bitmapped image you imported. In the example shown here, the word Crystal was placed over a bitmapped picture of crystal. The white surrounding the letters creates the illusion that the rectangle no longer exists, because it is filled with background color.

Note

To again work individually with these pieces, you must choose Arrange ⇨ Break Apart, not Ungroup.

Text masks are only one example of how you can use the Combine command. Here's another: If you want to apply a single fill across several objects, first select them, choose the Combine command, and then apply your fill.

Secret

Have you ever tried to apply a blend to three objects? You can't. However, if you select two of the objects you want to blend, apply the Combine command to those two objects, and then select the third object, you can now apply Blend to the three objects. One more use: If you have created an extremely complex drawing, choose Combine to reduce its complexity. The drawing will not take as long to render onto the page each time you make a change.

The Break Apart command

The Break Apart command, found under the Arrange menu, undoes the work of the Combine command. Say you have combined two sails on a drawing of a ship. Then you decide to change the color of one of the sails. Because the two sails are combined, if you were to recolor one, the other would change as well. To recolor only one sail, select both sails and choose the Break Apart command. (You can't use the Ungroup command in this procedure, because the objects are combined, not grouped.) Now apply the color to the one sail, and then combine them again, if you wish.

Note

If you use clip art and are trying to edit only a part of the clip art, you'll find yourself using the Break Apart command quite a bit. That's because clip art is often made up of individual drawn pieces that are combined.

Secret

If you break apart combined objects, it may appear as though the smaller objects suddenly disappear. For example, look again at the Hello image in Figure 3-36. If we applied Break Apart to that object, each Hello text would then be an independent object apart from the rectangles. You would see only the rectangles because the text would be underneath. To see the text again, you must select the rectangles and choose Arrange ➪ Order ➪ Send to Back. This, in effect, brings the text to the front, where you can see it.

You can also use Break Apart with the Trim command to fully separate objects that have been trimmed. We explain the Trim procedure next.

Using the Trim Tool

The Trim tool, found under the Arrange menu, is only available if two or more objects overlap. The Trim tool cuts overlapping areas out of selected objects. Here's how it works: If you select an object that overlaps another and then choose the Trim command, the area where the first object cuts into the second object will be removed from the second object. Put more simply, the first object you select trims the second object. The Trim tool is often referred to as the "cookie-cutter tool."

The roll-up for the Trim tool is shown in Figure 3-38.

Figure 3-38: You access the Trim roll-up from the Arrange menu.

STEPS:

Trimming an Object

Step 1.   Select a CorelDraw object and place it on top of another.

Step 2.   Choose Arrange ➪ Trim to display the Trim roll-up. Make sure both of the options in the Leave Original area are unchecked.

Step 3.   Click on the Trim command, and an arrow appears.

Step 4.   Click on the Target Object arrow, the object that is to receive the cookie-cutter cut. The first object disappears, leaving only its shape as a hole in the first object. If you've used a rectangle and a star, the results should look something like Figure 3-39.

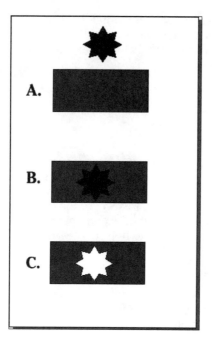

Figure 3-39: Here's the Trim tool in action. A: The star and rectangle are created. B: The star is placed on top of the rectangle. C: The Trim command is applied, leaving a hole where the star used to be.

Figure 3-40 shows an hourglass created by trimming the sides away from an oval. This example shows the use of two shapes to create a third shape. The oval object used as a cookie cutter is no longer visible.

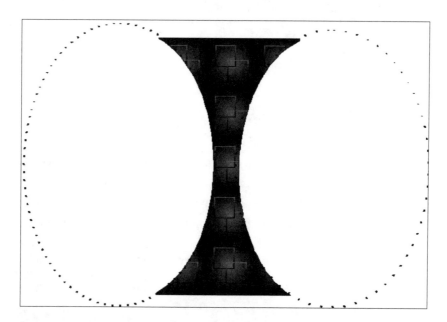

Figure 3-40: An hourglass shape created by using two ovals as trimming tools.

The Trim dialog box provides options to leave both the Target Object and Other Object (the cookie-cutter object) untouched. You can use shapes for editing, and still have the originals just as they were before you began. Remember, though, that you may have to move the originals out of the way to see your cookie-cutter results.

Secret

You can also use the Trim command to divide a single object into two. Use the Freehand Pencil tool to draw across an object and then select the line. Click on the Trim command, point the big black arrow at the object under the line you drew, and click the mouse. Select Arrange ⇨ Break Apart, and you can now drag the two pieces away from each other for a broken effect, as shown in Figure 3-41.

Figure 3-41: A CorelDraw object with Trim and Break Apart applied. Don't try this on Valentine's Day.

Note

The Trim command cannot be used with bitmaps; you can only use it with objects created in CorelDraw.

Welding Objects

The Weld tool, which you access from the Arrange menu, erases all internal lines and leaves only the outline when you weld one object to another. Figure 3-42 shows the Weld dialog box.

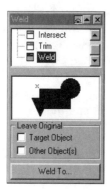

Figure 3-42: The Weld dialog box lets you attach objects together.

One good application of the Weld tool is for drawing street maps. Figure 3-43 shows a series of intersecting lines. It's not hard to create a street map from this gridlike arrangement. After combining the lines (select them all and then click on Arrange ⇨ Combine), select the Node tool (the second tool from the top on the toolbar). Click on the grouped objects. When you select an object with the Node tool, you'll find that, instead of seeing bounding boxes, you'll see nodes placed throughout the objects. You can reshape the objects by moving the nodes to a new location, or change the node curve angle with the handles. After arranging the nodes to resemble the streets you want to simulate, apply the Weld tool. (Click on Apply in the Weld roll-up, and then click the black arrow on the combined objects.) The Weld tool eliminates all common boundaries, simulating the appearance of contiguous streets rather than a bunch of grids on a page. (See Figure 3-44.)

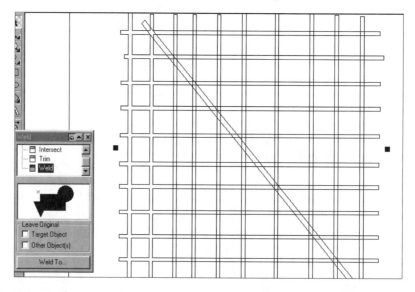

Figure 3-43: A series of intersecting lines such as these are prime candidates for the Weld operation.

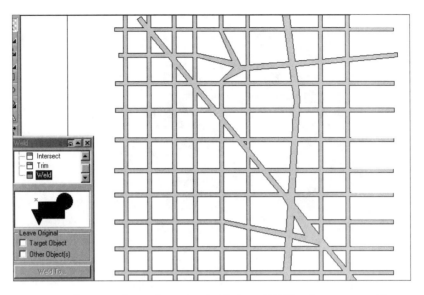

Figure 3-44: The same lines, after using the Node and Weld tools, now resemble a street map.

To use the Weld tool, select the objects you want to weld and then click on the Weld command (under the Arrange menu). The selected objects must overlap at some point, or the Weld command will not be available. The cursor becomes a black arrow. With this arrow, click on the object group, and every boundary that the objects share will disappear.

When you use the Weld tool on a group of touching shapes, the shapes are reduced to the outline of their combined shape. No lines will exist inside the new shape.

The Weld dialog box has a section labeled Leave Original. By selecting an object in this section, you are in essence duplicating the group you wish to weld, and carrying out the Weld command on this exact copy. For example, if you selected Leave Original when creating the map shown in Figure 3-44, the result would be a "before and after." One object group would be transformed, while the original object group would be left unedited by the Weld command.

Here's an example of what you can do with the Weld tool. Figure 3-45 shows a picture of a flower created by using one ellipse and the Weld command (along with the Rotation, Combine, and Extrude commands).

Figure 3-45: This flower was created using the Weld command.

STEPS:

Creating an Object with the Weld Command

Step 1.   Create a simple, vertically-oriented ellipse. Double-click on it and drag the rotation center to the bottom center of the ellipse.

Step 2.   Select Arrange ⇨ Transform ⇨ Rotate. The Rotate dialog box appears.

Step 3.   Set the Angle value in the Rotate dialog box to –25 degrees, as shown in Figure 3-46. Click on the Apply to Duplicate button once and your ellipse will be duplicated, but at the angle specified.

Step 4.   Click on the Apply to Duplicate button repeatedly until you've gone in a full circle duplicating the ellipse.

Step 5.   Place a circle in the center of the ellipse group. Now press the Shift key and select each of the ellipses, making sure none are left out of the selection process. Watch the status bar to make sure the Number of Selected Objects increases each time you try to select one. You should end up with 14 selected ellipses.

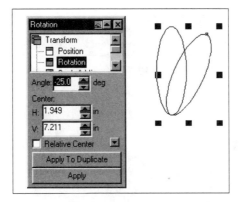

Figure 3-46: A simple ellipse has had the Rotation
dialog box's Apply to Duplicate command applied once.

Step 6.   Select Arrange ⇨ Weld. Make sure none of the Leave Original
buttons are checked, and click on Weld. You'll see an arrow as
shown in Figure 3-47.

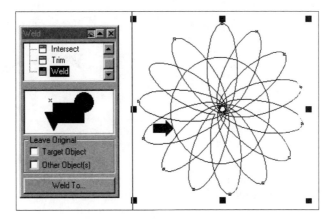

Figure 3-47: Apply the Weld command to the ellipses group and
the circle by clicking with the large arrow.

Step 7.   Click the arrow on the circle. Your ellipses and circle should now
be one solid object. If some portions remain unwelded, just click
on Weld again and select the unwelded portions with the arrow
until everything is solid.

(continued)

STEPS *(continued)*

Creating an Object with the Weld Command

Step 8. Color the welded object gray. Place another circle in the center of the object. Select the circle and the object and click on Arrange ⇨ Combine, as shown in Figure 3-48.

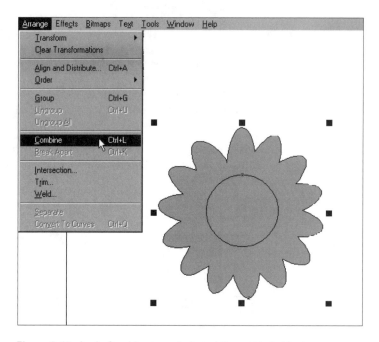

Figure 3-48: Apply Combine to a circle and the welded object.

Step 9. Select Effects ⇨ Extrude and set the Depth parameter to 35, as shown in Figure 3-49. Set the options to Big Back and VP Locked to Object, as shown. Click on Apply.

Recolor portions of the petals with lighter shades of gray to create a more dramatic effect.

Remember

The next time you create objects and want to join them, leaving only their common outline, the Weld tool can do the trick.

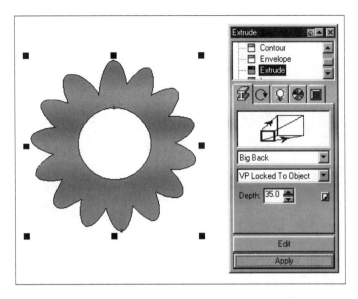

Figure 3-49: Use the Extrude dialog box to apply the Extrude command and create the flower.

Using the Separate Tool

Sometimes when using the Blend, Contour, or Extrude tool, you may wish to separate the effect portion from the original object. For example, after using the Extrude effect on a star, suppose you want to move the face of the star to a new location. Before you can ungroup the star, use the Separate command (Arrange ⇨ Separate) to make the star face a separate object from the extruded portion. Then use the Ungroup command, which gives you the freedom to move the star face to a new location. Similarly, after using Contour, you can use the Separate command to pull the new contoured lines out from the original object. Then use Ungroup to make them movable on their own. Next, move the Contour lines to a new location, if you wish. Figure 3-50 shows an extruded star with its face moved away from the extruded portion. The same figure shows Contour lines pulled away from a star, duplicated and moved around the star at various angles. These effects are made possible by the Separate command.

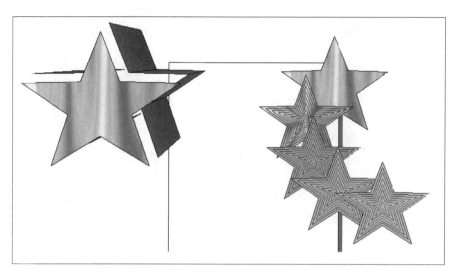

Figure 3-50: Two objects treated with effects. Applying the Separate command enables you to move the original object away from the effect portion.

You can use Separate with the Blend command. Figure 3-51 shows the two original objects being pulled out of a blend. Now those two objects, and the blend itself, can be treated as objects unto themselves.

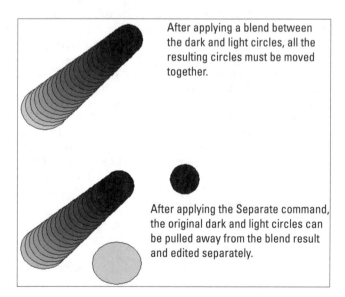

After applying a blend between the dark and light circles, all the resulting circles must be moved together.

After applying the Separate command, the original dark and light circles can be pulled away from the blend result and edited separately.

Figure 3-51: Use Separate to extract the original objects used in a blend effect.

Using the Intersect Tool

The Intersect command, found under the Arrange menu, creates a new object out of the area where two or more objects overlap. If part of a rectangle overlaps with a triangle, click on the Intersect command, and only the portion where the two overlap will be left.

Selecting the Intersect command from the Arrange menu calls up the Intersect dialog box, shown in Figures 3-52, 3-53, and 3-54. You must click on an object, click on the Intersect command, and then click on the second object with the arrow. And as with the Trim and Weld commands, you are given the option of leaving the target or other (original) object untouched by the process. In essence, this means you perform the command on a duplicate object. As with the other two commands in this group, Intersect only works with CorelDraw objects. Bitmaps cannot be used.

Figures 3-52, 3-53, and 3-54 show how to use the Intersect tool to create a shape from the area where two circles intersect.

Figure 3-52: One circle overlaps another before the Intersect command is applied.

Figure 3-53: Applying the Intersect command with Other Object checked results in this image.

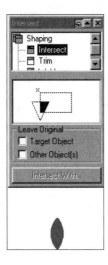

Figure 3-54: Applying the Intersect command with no option checked results in this image.

Figure 3-55 shows several rectangles and diamonds intersecting with text. When Intersect was applied, the text overlapping the rectangles became a new object. In this example, the objects that were created as a result of Intersect were recolored. This example demonstrates how new objects are created only where the letters actually overlap the rectangles.

Let's create a 3D text object horizontally split in half. Because you're actually going to extrude two split text objects, this technique gives the 3D effect even more substance.

Figure 3-55: The Intersect command creates new objects out of text that overlaps other objects.

STEPS:

Creating a 3D Text Object Split in Half

Step 1. Type a word with a big, bold font. The size should be about 86 points.

Step 2. Draw a rectangle over the top half of the text, and select the rectangle.

Step 3. Select Arrange ⇨ Intersection and put a check mark by both Target Object and Other Object.

Step 4. Click on the Intersect With button and click the arrow on the text.

Step 5. Although you've invoked the Intersect command, nothing looks different because you've elected to leave both original objects alone. Change the color of the text in the rectangle to a dark gray. Only the upper half will be recolored, because you are actually recoloring the copy that was "cut off" by the rectangle.

Step 6. Drag the rectangle down over the lower half of the text, and remove both Leave Original option check marks in the dialog box.

(continued)

STEPS *(continued)*

Creating a 3D Text Object Split in Half

Step 7. Select the text, and again apply the Intersect command, this time by pointing the big black arrow at the rectangle. If you select the rectangle first, apply the command, and point the big black arrow at the text, you'll get an error message saying that the command cannot be carried out. That's because it's very hard to select the text behind the rectangle after the rectangle is selected.

Step 8. You now have two text halves. The method you used to carry out the previous command eliminated the originals. Color the bottom half a light gray. Now you have two text objects. Apply a light-gray "hairline" outline to both halves of text.

Step 9. Select Effects ⇨ Extrude and select the lower half of the text. From the Extrude dialog box, the parameters should read Small Back and VP Locked to Object.

Step 10. Apply the Extrude effect.

Step 11. Drag the vanishing point X upward and to the right for a more dramatic effect (you'll learn more about perspective and vanishing points in Chapter 6). Click on Apply again.

Step 12. Repeat the entire Extrude procedure for the upper half of the text.

Step 13. This procedure causes the top half to be sent to the back. Before you deselect the top half, select Arrange ⇨ Order ⇨ Send to Front. Your top text will now be positioned where it should be.

Step 14. You may now group your text together as you would any finished piece. The results should resemble the text shown in Figure 3-56.

The Intersect tool is similar to the Trim tool, except it takes the process one step further. Rather than simply removing the area where two objects overlap, it creates a third object out of the space where the objects overlap. This is a great tool for creating objects that look like they're being sliced, such as the effect of a piece of cheese falling forward after being sliced by a knife. This final example is merely a drop in the bucket of what's possible. The applications are endless.

Figure 3-56: You can create a two-tone text object like this using Intersect and Extrude.

Duplicating Objects

The Duplicate command is available from the Edit menu (or by pressing Ctrl+D while an object is selected). If you've used CorelDraw for any length of time, you've probably discovered that Duplicate is faster than using Copy and Paste. However, if you are not happy with the way CorelDraw automatically positions an object after duplicating it, you can select Tools ⇨ Options ⇨ Workspace ⇨ Edit and adjust Duplicate Placement and Nudge (see Figure 3-57). You can change these numbers to make CorelDraw deposit the duplicate item a bit closer to or farther from the original.

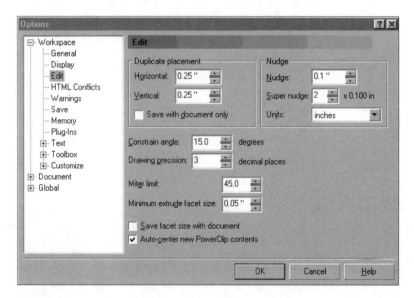

Figure 3-57: Click on Workspace ⇨ Edit in the Options dialog box to access the Duplicate and Nudge controls.

Using the Property Bar with Duplicate

You can also adjust Duplicate Distance from the Property Bar. When no objects are selected, the Property Bar becomes a menu of options for adjusting paper size, "snap to" settings, as well as Duplicate Distance amounts. Hold your mouse momentarily over the set of numbers slightly to the right of the page on the Property Bar. One set of numbers will read Duplicate Distance. Here you can adjust both the vertical and horizontal settings for where duplicates are placed on your page.

Using Duplicate with other effects

The Duplicate command is also built into several of CorelDraw's effects and transform commands. For example, the Position, Rotate, and Mirror commands all contain options that perform their edits on duplicate objects rather than affect the original. The Weld, Intersection, and Trim commands all contain Leave Original options that are, in effect, forms of the Duplicate command.

Use Leave Original and Apply to Duplicate to perform these tasks:

■ Perform your effects on a duplicate object so that you can view "before" and "after" objects on your screen simultaneously.

■ Apply effects to the duplicate after duplicating, to speed up complicated editing chores.

It's standard Windows practice to automatically look for Copy and Paste when you want to reproduce an object on your screen. Not only is using the Duplicate command faster, but using the Copy and Paste commands needlessly places the object on the Windows Clipboard. You can avoid this drag on your system's memory by duplicating onscreen objects using the Duplicate command.

Nudging Objects

If you've ever wanted to move a CorelDraw object just a little bit in a particular direction, you'll love the Nudge tool. You can nudge selected objects by using the arrow keys on your keyboard. As you may have noticed, however, the problem with the Nudge tool is that the preset nudge amount is usually never quite right.

Secret

You can adjust how far objects are nudged by changing the Nudge Offset amount, which can be set from the Property Bar. Make sure no objects are selected, and the Property bar will display the Nudge Offset amount. Adjust this number to your liking. Both Nudge Offset and Duplicate Distance amounts will be displayed in units matching the measuring system currently being used by the rulers.

Summary

▶ Using grids and guidelines is key to making sure all your CorelDraw objects line up on your page. Grids and guidelines can be turned on or off and are fully adjustable.

▶ Rulers also can be repositioned to suit your needs. The ruler measuring system can be changed. Rulers can be altered to reflect a map scale (for mapmaking).

▶ The Align and Distribute command helps you keep control of complicated documents by providing tools to keep everything straight.

▶ Object Manager enables you to view and edit all the objects and layers in your document as thumbnails, arranging them just as they appear in the document itself.

▶ Grouping and ungrouping drawn objects makes it easy to copy, cut, paste, and move complicated composite objects.

▶ Break Apart, Combine, and Separate make it easy to set apart a portion of an complicated object for special-effects editing, without having to ungroup the object.

▶ Trim, Intersection, and Weld provide tools for cutting pieces out of CorelDraw objects, slicing them down the middle, and joining them entirely, removing all the boundaries between them.

▶ The Duplicate command is far superior to cutting and pasting duplicate objects. By understanding the Duplicate command, you can create special effects on multiple objects quite quickly.

▶ The Nudge command makes it easy to move CorelDraw objects even a fraction of an inch with your arrow keys.

Chapter 4

Typesetting Secrets

In This Chapter

We cover secrets about:

▶ Typesetting terminology

▶ Typefaces

▶ Manipulating artistic text

▶ Manipulating paragraph text

▶ Using different font features

Computers have put the power of typesetting at nearly everybody's fingertips. Unfortunately, having an arsenal of fonts—CorelDraw 8 comes with over 900—does not qualify you as a designer or typographer. For the novice, having too many fonts can be a hindrance. Using too many fonts (or using the wrong ones) can make your work look ridiculous, even disastrous.

Numerous books dedicate themselves to the subject of typesetting and design. This chapter covers only the basics of font usage and typesetting. In most cases, font usage in business communications is relatively conservative, so deciding which fonts to use is fairly simple. In graphics and fine art settings, however, almost anything goes—as long as it works.

Many CorelDraw users are unsure about some basic typesetting questions. What exactly is a font? What's a typeface? When should you use TrueType or Type 1 PostScript fonts? The answers may surprise you. After exploring some of these basic questions, we'll explain some of CorelDraw's special text features, such as fitting text to a path, converting text to curves, and so forth. CorelDraw's text effect features are very powerful, so hang on tight.

Typefaces and Fonts

Before we start talking about type, let's make sure we're speaking the same language. A *typeface* is a style of type, such as Times or Helvetica. Most typefaces can have at least four different attributes: normal (often called "Roman" or "Book," depending on the typeface), **bold**, *italic*, and ***bold-italic***. Some, however, only have one or two styles. Others, such as ITC Goudy Sans, have as many as eight styles or more. Figure 4-1 shows some different typefaces with their various attributes. Each typeface is a family. The fonts that make up a typeface family look similar, but they each have different attributes.

Baskerville
Baskerville Bold
Baskerville Italic
Baskerville Bold-Italic

Arial
Arial Bold
Arial Italic
Arial Bold-Italic
Arial Narrow
Arial Narrow Bold
Arial Narrow Italic
Arial Narrow Bold-Italic
Arial Black

Brush Script

Giddy Up

K i d N a p

Figure 4-1: Typefaces generally come in families made up of text with different attributes.

The term *font* refers to the members of a typeface family that have specific sets of attributes, such as Helvetica Italic.

Another term you should be familiar with is *point size*. The height of text is often measured in units called points. Approximately 72 points equal one inch.

Serif and sans serif typefaces

Most typefaces are either serif or sans serif. Serifs are the "feet" (or "foundations") at the ends of letter strokes. The most common serif typeface is Times. Others include New Century Schoolbook, Palatino, Garamond, and Goudy Old Style. Most serif typefaces work well for body text because they are easy on the eyes. The serifs help move the reader's eyes from character to character. When used in larger type, serif typefaces appear more decorative.

Sans serif is French for "without serifs." The most common sans serif typeface is Helvetica. Others are Avant Garde, Futura, and Helvetica Black. Traditionally, sans serif typefaces are used for headlines and subheads. Some also work well for contemporary-looking body copy—as long as they are not used for large blocks of text spread across several pages (sans serif text is harder to read at such lengths). Figure 4-2 shows the difference between serif and sans serif typefaces.

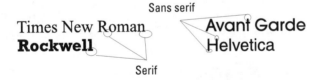

Figure 4-2: Serifs are tiny feet at the ends of letter strokes. Sans serif type has no serifs.

Decorative typefaces

Decorative typefaces can be elegant or fun, or they can fall somewhere in between. On the whole, decorative typefaces are hard to read. They work well for short headlines, but rarely for body text. Use them in ads, flyers, and newsletter nameplates. Figure 4-3 provides some examples of decorative typefaces.

The decorative typefaces come in a wide range of varieties. For example, there's elegant, and then there's really elegant. Compare Bernard Tango to Brush Script, as shown in Figure 4-3. Bernard Tango is ornate and elegant, whereas Brush Script gets its grace from its simple, hand-lettered look. Both are fun and serve distinct purposes, but they would be difficult to read in large blocks of text.

Bernard Tango

Brush Script

Dom Casual

Binner Gothic

Figure 4-3: Decorative fonts such as these are usually more difficult to read than nondecorative fonts.

Again, decorative typefaces work best in short, attention-grabbing headlines, such as those in ads and flyers. Some also work well in invitations and announcements, including the more elegant, hand-tooled typefaces such as Park Avenue and Letraset Hollow.

Typeface tone

Some desktop designers don't realize that typefaces have distinct tones. As you have seen, typefaces can be serious, ornate, or elegant; others can be simple, fun, or cartoonish. Note the differences in the typefaces in Figure 4-4. The words are the same, but the tones vary tremendously. Note that in a couple of the examples, the words Serial Killer seem inappropriate.

Serial Killer

Serial Killer

Serial Killer

SERIAL KILLER

Serial Killer

Serial Killer

SERIAL KILLER

Figure 4-4: The tone of a typeface adds greatly to the impact of the words.

Keeping it simple

Using elegant or funny typefaces for headlines and subheads is fine if they fit the tone of your work. If your work is not meant to be particularly elegant, ornate, or funny, play it safe by using a simple, sans serif typeface for headlines, and serif typefaces for body text. My personal favorite is the combination of Arial Black (Helvetica Black equivalent) for headlines, and New Century Schoolbook for body text. Swiss Black is stronger than Helvetica, and Schoolbook is a little less formal than Times.

Remember

Remember that you do not want to use your entire typeface library on each page, or even in each document. A good rule is to use no more than four typefaces per document. Also, you should not use many different point sizes. Avoid confusion by making all headlines the same font. All subheads and body copy should be the same also. Using a variety of typefaces and sizes frequently produces an incoherent hodgepodge that looks more like a ransom note than an effective business document.

Type 1 versus TrueType

Since the advent of Windows 3.1's built-in TrueType font rendering system, many users have become confused about which type of font file is best. Having too many choices can sometimes make computing more difficult.

Actually, whether you use one or the other is not that critical. The speed and quality differences between the two formats are negligible. Many people use both. Depending on the application, we often switch back and forth between them. The type you should use depends on what you're doing with your computer.

Both TrueType and Type 1 fonts are *outline* fonts. Font outlines use a font manager, such as Adobe Type Manager (ATM) and Windows's built-in system for TrueType, to *rasterize*, or *render*, fonts. Both terms simply mean reading information from a font file and then displaying type on a monitor or sending font information to a printer.

Type 1 fonts

Originally, Type 1 fonts were created for use with Adobe's PostScript page description language. To use them in Windows, you must have a third-party type manager, such as ATM, installed. Having to use a third-party utility is a bit of an inconvenience, but once installed it's almost invisible to the user, except when it's time to install or uninstall fonts.

The primary advantage of Type 1 fonts is that they have been around a while longer than TrueType and are therefore the font of choice for desktop publishers and designers. Most desktop publishing service bureaus (establishments where users take their high-resolution printing, slides, and color-proofing jobs for printing) use Type 1 fonts. This means that if you use Type 1 fonts in your documents, the service bureau is more likely to have your fonts.

Wait a minute! The last statement is not entirely true. Not all service bureaus have all fonts by all vendors. Some, including our service bureau here in Ventura, California, support only Adobe Type 1 fonts. The fonts on the CorelDraw CD-ROMs are Bitstream fonts (which are fine fonts, by the way). Even though our service bureau and many others have CorelDraw, they don't install the fonts on their system. Getting around this situation entails providing the fonts you use in your document with the document file, which is discussed in Chapter 7.

However, an increasing number of service bureaus have TrueType font collections. If yours doesn't, Windows and TrueType provide several solutions. (TrueType font embedding, discussed in the next subsection, is one solution. Embedding TrueType fonts in print files, discussed in Chapter 7, is another.)

TrueType fonts

TrueType, a component of Microsoft's TrueImage, is a PostScript clone. The one area where TrueType prevails over Type 1 is in compatibility, not only among different Windows systems but also across platforms. Apple has incorporated TrueType at the system level in Macintosh System 7, and some software fixes even make it backward compatible to System 7.

For a while we hoped TrueType technology would catch on, making PageMaker, Word for Windows, and other Windows documents (and CorelDraw Mac documents) more readily transportable across platforms. Keep in mind that in Windows and on the Mac, we're talking about a built-in type manager, not a third-party overlay. Think of TrueType as system fonts. Another example of system fonts is those that appear when you enter commands at the DOS prompt — you take them for granted. TrueType is not quite that simple, but it's a step or two closer.

TrueType font embedding

Transporting documents from one computer running Windows to another has always been a headache. The only way it works well is if both systems have the same fonts and font manager installed, which, considering all the font products available, is not always the case. TrueType addresses this problem with a feature called *font embedding*. With font embedding, when you create a document that will be read or printed on another computer, you can include the fonts in the file. To do so, when you save a document with Save As, simply select Embed TrueType Fonts using TrueDoc, as shown in Figure 4-5.

Click here to embed True Type fonts

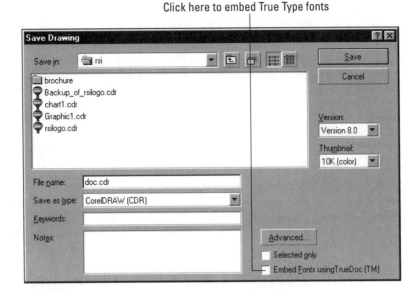

Figure 4-5: Embedding TrueType fonts with your documents.

Working with Text

CorelDraw provides a number of ways to use text in your drawings. Although the options for manipulating type are extensive, you really have only three major categories: artistic, paragraph, and symbols. We cover the following topics:

- Artistic text
- Paragraph text
- Using text styles
- Converting type to curves
- Using the Property Bar for text formatting

Artistic text is entered directly onto the page or drawing area, while paragraph text is entered into a text frame. Paragraph text usually consists of larger blocks of text, and the controls you have over it are similar to those in a word processor or desktop publishing package. Use paragraph text to add blocks of text to brochures, flyers, and illustrations.

Artistic text

Artistic text can be manipulated in many ways; for example, it can be colored, filled with patterns or fountain fills, stretched, extruded, or blended. Artistic text is usually decorative and fancy. To enter artistic text, simply click on the Text tool in CorelDraw. The cursor changes to a cross. Click where you want to enter the text and begin typing. You can then edit and manipulate the text in more ways than you can imagine. This section concentrates primarily on manipulating text with the Node Editing (Shape) tool. As you'll see, you can do lots of magical things with this simple tool, which most CorelDraw users don't know. We'll also look briefly at fitting text to paths and converting to curves.

When you select text with the Node Editing tool, each character is given its own node, and the text block is given spacing control handles. Characters can be moved individually with the nodes — up, down, left, and right — to create special effects. Text can be spaced interactively with the spacing control handles.

Changing character and word spacing

To increase the space between characters, drag the right spacing control handle to the right. To decrease the space between characters, drag the right spacing control handle to the left. Simple enough, right? Figure 4-6 shows the procedure in action.

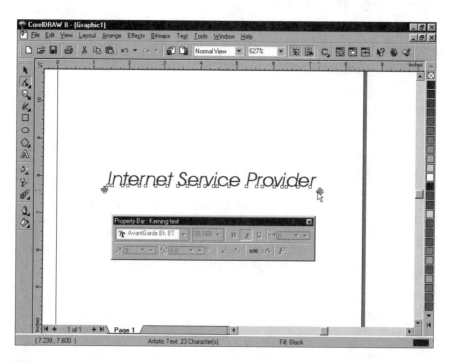

Figure 4-6: Dragging on the right spacing control handle increases the spacing between characters.

To increase the space between words, hold the Ctrl key down and drag the right spacing control handle to the right. To decrease the space between words, hold the Ctrl key down and drag the right spacing control handle to the left. Figure 4-7 shows you how to space words with the Node Editing tool.

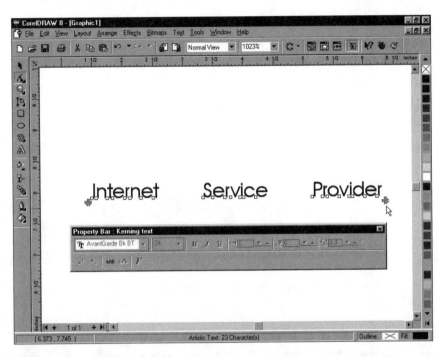

Figure 4-7: To increase or decrease the space between words interactively, hold down the Ctrl key as you drag on the right spacing handle.

Changing line spacing

To increase or decrease the space between lines of text, drag the left spacing control handle up or down. Figure 4-8 shows you how to increase the space between lines with the Node Editing tool.

Secret

Horizontal text spacing (*tracking*) and vertical text spacing (*leading*) can also be adjusted with the Spacing option in the Edit Text dialog box. We discuss tracking and leading later in this chapter. Use the Shape tool to edit interactively by appearance; use Spacing when you need precise settings.

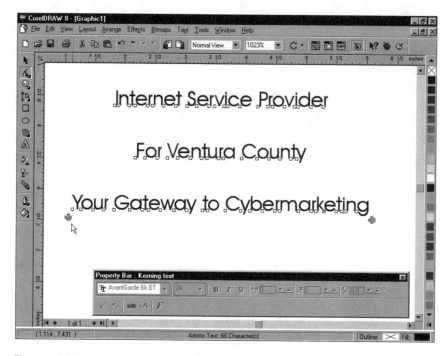

Figure 4-8: You can increase the space between lines by dragging the left handle down.

Dragging characters off the baseline

You can use the Node Editing tool to move individual characters, or groups of individual characters, off the baseline to create special effects (the baseline is the imaginary line on which a line of text sits). To move one character, select the node to its left. To move a group of characters, marquee select the nodes to the left of each character, or hold the Shift key and click on each node. Figure 4-9 shows an example of dragging text from the baseline with the Node Editing tool.

As you become more familiar with CorelDraw, you'll find hundreds of uses for manipulating text this way. Some may have already occurred to you.

Manipulating text by dragging individual nodes is a trial-and-error process. Whenever you go too far and want to start over, simply choose Align to Baseline from the Text menu. The text jumps back into its original position. To move a single letter back to the baseline, simply select it before you select the Align to Baseline command. To realign all the text, make sure the text is selected but no individual letters are selected.

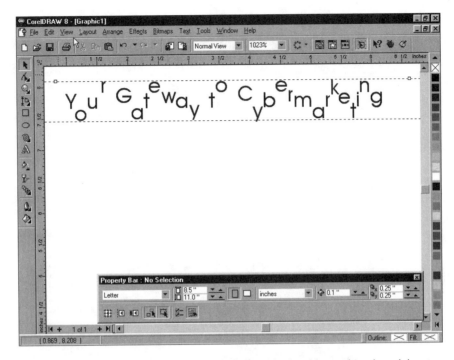

Figure 4-9: To drag a character from the baseline, select the character's node and drag to the desired position.

Fitting text to a path

The Fit Text to Path option is used mostly for creating artistic text in logos and other drawings. This tool is very powerful. Achieving the same effects manually can take a long time, especially if you're not artistically inclined.

To fit text to a path, type your text and add the desired attributes, such as font, size, bold, and so on. Then use a drawing tool to draw the path. You can also use a path from any other graphic, such as a symbol, clip art, or a text letter that has been converted to curves. (If you are not familiar with converting text to curves, refer to the section that covers it later in this chapter.) When you finish creating text and the path, select them both and choose Fit Text to Path from the Text menu.

In previous versions of CorelDraw, the previous action would have displayed the Fit Text to Path roll-up. Version 8 automatically fits the text to the path using the default settings — placing the text on top of the path and spacing it accordingly — shown in Figure 4-10. It also displays the Property Bar in Text on Curve/Object mode. With the Property Bar you can then make several adjustments to the manner in which text conforms to the path, including where on the path the text string starts and whether the text sits in the middle of the outline or below it.

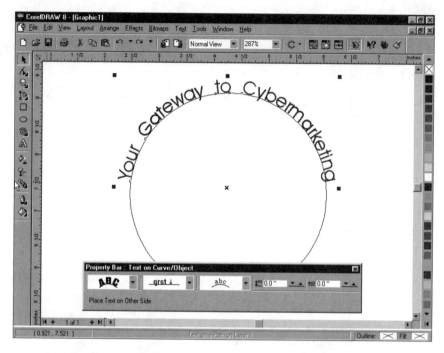

Figure 4-10: The Text on Curve/Object Property Bar gives you several options for controlling how text contours to the path. The options are visual to help you decide.

Most of the options in the Text on Curve/Object Property Bar are displayed on the various drop-down lists graphically. To choose where a text string begins on a path, for example, use one of the four options on the Text Placement drop-down list (third option from left). The graphical depictions show you where the text will land on the path.

Also new in version 8 is the ability to adjust incrementally where the text sits in relationship to the path. You can change how far the text is offset from the path (the distance from the text baseline to the path) and the horizontal offset. These are the last two options, respectively, on the Property Bar. The first option actually moves the text away from the baseline by the increment you put in the field. The second option allows you to determine where the text begins on the path, providing much more precision than Text Placement, described in the previous paragraph. In Figure 4-11, for example, we have set the Horizontal Offset to 1.0".

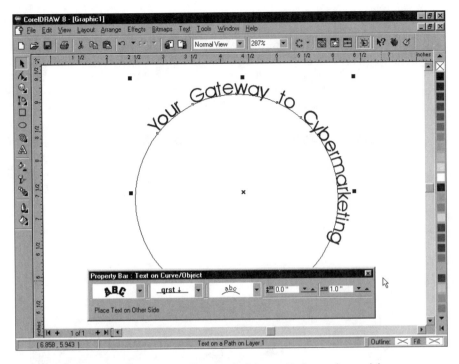

Figure 4-11: Use Horizontal Offset (last option in Property Bar) to make precision adjustments to where text sits on the path.

After text has been fit to a path, you can edit it with the Text tool. If you change the shape of the path, the text automatically adjusts to the new shape. You can use the Node Editing tool to fine-tune character placement along the path.

STEPS:

Fitting Text to a Path

Step 1. Type the text you want to fit to path.

Step 2. Using the Ellipse or another drawing tool, draw the path to which you want the text to conform. (Remember to hold the Ctrl key down to draw a perfect circle or square.)

Step 3. Marquee-select the text and the path with the Pick tool.

Step 4. Select Text ⇨ Fit Text to Path.

Step 5. Using the Text Placement option (the third option on the Property Bar), click in the quadrant where you want the text to appear.

The text conforms to the path. To change where the text string begins, simply click on a different quadrant in text placement, as shown in Figure 4-12. If you change the shape of the path, the text will follow, as shown in Figure 4-13. You can place text on the other side of the path, or turn it over with the Place Text on Other Side option, as shown in Figure 4-14. Use this option for making text that would otherwise be upside-down, right-side up. You can fit text to virtually any path. But remember, text should always remain legible.

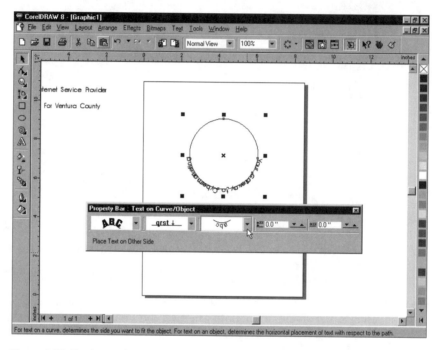

Figure 4-12: To change the position of text, simply click a different quadrant in the Fit Text to Path roll-up, and then click Apply.

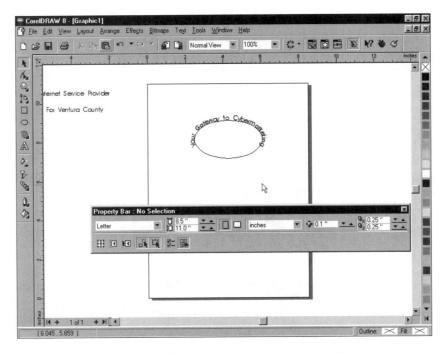

Figure 4-13: When you change the shape of the path, the text reconforms.

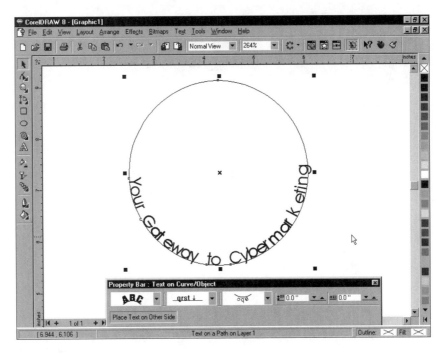

Figure 4-14: When you want to flip the text right-side up, use Place Text on Other Side in the Fit Text to Path roll-up.

Secret

You can also type text directly on a path.

STEPS:

Typing Text Directly on a Path

Step 1. Click on the Text tool.

Step 2. Using the mouse, move the Text cursor near the object.

Step 3. When the cursor changes to the insertion point cursor, click in your drawing.

Step 4. Type the text along the object's path, as shown in Figure 4-15.

Figure 4-15: To type text directly on a path, simply click the Text tool on the object's path and begin typing.

If you need to specify values such as the distance between text and object, or change the placement of text along the object's path, use the Text on Curve/Object Property Bar as described earlier in this section. You can fit artistic text to the path of objects with open and closed paths.

Converting text to curves

Converting text to curves turns the text into a graphic, complete with nodes and other graphics qualities. This enables you to shape the text with the Node Editing tool in ways you cannot shape regular text. You'll want to be careful, though. This is a one-way street. Text that has been converted to curves cannot be converted back to text.

To convert text to curves, simply select the text string and choose Arrange ⇨ Convert to Curves.

Warning

When you convert text to curves, you can no longer edit it as a text string. Make sure words are spelled properly and that you have assigned all the desired attributes before converting the type to curves.

STEPS:

Converting Text to Curves

Step 1. Type the text you want to convert to curves.

Step 2. Make all attribute changes, such as font, size, and so on. Remember that you cannot change attributes after you convert.

Step 3. Choose Arrange ⇨ Convert to Curves. The text is now a graphic. Notice that the status line no longer calls it text. You can use Convert to Curves to manipulate type in almost any way you can think of.

Step 4. Select the Node Editing tool.

Step 5. Select Arrange ⇨ Break Apart. This separates the text into separate editable entities. If you don't understand Break Apart, turn to Chapter 3. You now have several objects with many nodes. You can treat these objects as graphics.

Step 6. Manipulate the nodes as desired.

Step 7. Fill and color the graphic as desired.

Figure 4-16 shows a text graphic we manipulated using the preceding method. In this case, we extended the top horizontal bars of the *T* and *F* letters and added a gradient fill.

Figure 4-16: An example of text that has been converted to curves and reshaped.

Paragraph text

Paragraph text usually consists of larger blocks of text than artistic text. To enter paragraph text, click and drag a box with the Text tool. When you release the mouse, a text box appears with the text cursor blinking at the top-left corner of the box. You can type text directly into the frame, or you can import text from a word processor file or paste from the Windows Clipboard. Paragraph text can be moved anywhere on the page, and the frame can be resized and manipulated with the Selection (sometimes called Pick), Node Editing, or Enveloping option, and with many other options.

If you use Microsoft Word, Corel WordPerfect, QuarkXPress, Adobe PageMaker, Microsoft Publisher, or any other text editor or page-layout program, you should have no trouble using paragraph text in CorelDraw. In many ways, it's identical. You can justify it right and left, center it, break it into columns, adjust the tracking (the space between characters and words), adjust the leading (the space between lines), and so on. You can even assign styles and *jump* text from one paragraph frame to another. Jumping is when you continue blocks of text on new pages, as you've seen in magazines and newspapers.

Because paragraph text in CorelDraw behaves similarly to text blocks in other programs, such as Microsoft Word or QuarkXPress, we assume that you already understand how to create, import, and perform basic formatting on paragraph text. So, rather than boring you with old information, this section concentrates on using the Property Bar to format paragraph text, and applying some of CorelDraw's special effects features on paragraph text.

Formatting Text with Styles

Picture this scenario: You've laid out a 50-page document in CorelDraw. You take it to your client (or boss) for approval. She says, "Looks great, but I need all the heads switched from Arial to Arial Black, and the body copy needs to be Garamond 12-point, not Times 10-point. And I need it in 30 minutes, please."

So what will you do, rush back to your workstation, select each paragraph one at a time, and change them? Wrong! If you formatted your paragraphs with styles, all you need to do is change the style definitions, and CorelDraw does the rest, changing each paragraph tagged with the style to the new format.

CorelDraw supports two text style types: artistic text and paragraph text. Similar to styles in a word processor or desktop publishing package, CorelDraw's styles enable you to use predefined formatting information to instantly format strings of artistic text or blocks of paragraph text. Text styles are managed from the Styles Manager docker (View ⇨ Dockers ⇨ Graphic and Text Styles). You create them by choosing New from the docker's pop-up menu. You have three ways to create a new style. First, select the text containing the attributes that you want to incorporate into a new style, and then choose New from the docker's pop-up menu. Second, select Copy Properties From from the docker's menu, and then click on the paragraph containing the attributes you want in your new style. And third (this is perhaps the easiest method), use the right mouse button pop-up menu, which is discussed later in the process description.

With either method, CorelDraw creates a new style and adds it to the list in the docker. You can then rename the style to anything you like. Once you've created your styles, you can apply them from the Styles Manager docker (shown in Figure A), the Property Bar, or from the right-mouse button pop-up menu.

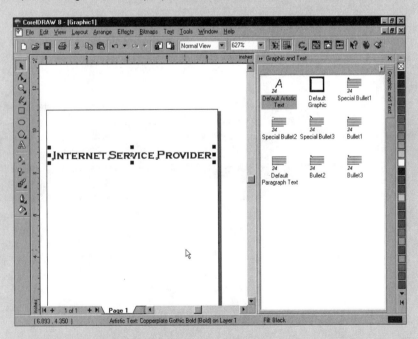

Figure A: You can apply styles you've created by using the Styles Manager docker.

You can create styles for the default template—the one that appears when you open a new document—or you can save them in groups as a new template. This capability of creating multiple style sheets, or templates, enables you to prepare predefined shells for creating similar multiple documents, such as a flyer that changes only slightly from month to month. Creating and using templates is covered in Chapter 16.

(continued)

(continued)

In addition, in version 8 you can create styles and add them to workspaces, as discussed in Chapter 1.

The following is an overview of creating and using text styles:

- Create the text from which you will create your style.

- Format the text as desired.

- Click and hold the right mouse button on the text from which you want to create a style until the menu flies out. Then choose Style ➪ Save Style Properties as shown in Figure B.

- In the Save Style As dialog box, shown in Figure C, name the style. Notice that you can adjust the properties of the new style by expanding the folders and turning on and off attributes. In Figure C, for instance, you can expand Text and turn off aspects of the new style by unchecking boxes. You can also turn fill and outline formatting on and off.

- Click OK.

To rename the style, select it in the Styles Manager docker, click the right mouse button, and choose Rename. You can import styles from another template by choosing Template ➪ Load from the docker's pop-up menu and then choosing the desired template. To assign a keyboard shortcut to the new style, choose Edit Hotkey from the pop-up menu. This option displays the Options dialog box (described in Chapter 1). Click the cursor in the Press New Shortcut Key field, and then press the key combination you want as a shortcut.

If you define styles on CorelDraw's default style sheet, they become part of the default new document setup. If you create new styles, you should save them under a new name with the Template ➪ Save As option in the Styles Manager docker pop-up menu.

Figure B: To save a text style, right-click on text for which you want to save the style, and then choose Styles ➪ Save Style Properties.

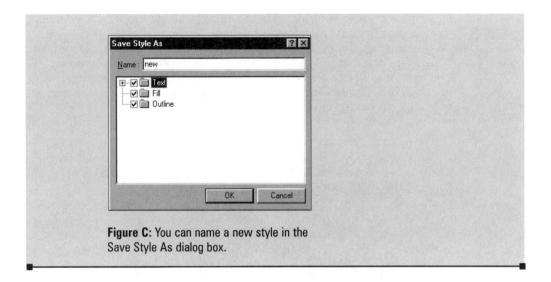

Figure C: You can name a new style in the Save Style As dialog box.

Using the Property Bar to format text

When does CorelDraw look like Microsoft Word? When you edit paragraph text from the Property Bar. Look at Figure 4-17. Notice the word processor-like configuration across the top of the screen. From here you can apply styles, change typefaces, change size and other attributes, set alignment, and alter a bunch of other options, including setting tabs and margins from the ruler.

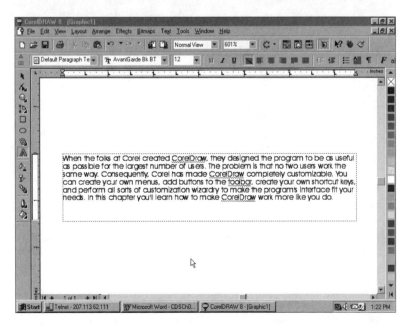

Figure 4-17: The new Property Bar enables you to format paragraph text with word processor-like ease.

Unfortunately, you cannot set columns from the default Property Bar. Instead, to set columns in paragraph text frames, choose Text ➪ Format Text ➪ Frames and Columns, which brings up the dialog box shown in Figure 4-18. From here you set your columns by typing a number in the Number of Columns field. You can choose to let CorelDraw maintain uniform column sizes by making sure that Equal Column Width is selected, or you can uncheck this option and set individual column and gutter (space between columns) sizes in the Width and Gutter fields.

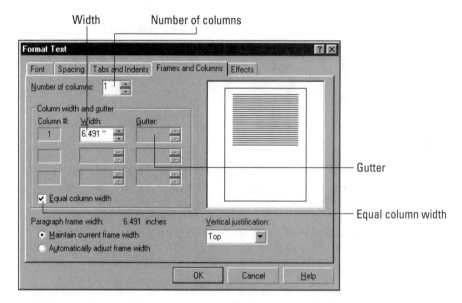

Figure 4-18: Use the Format Text dialog box to set columns in CorelDraw paragraph text frames.

Enveloping text

An exciting feature CorelDraw first offered in version 4 was the capability of placing paragraph text in a container and then reshaping the container with the Envelope roll-up. The purpose is to sculpture text in various shapes — stars, octagons, Christmas trees, whatever. This feature is different from PowerClip, which we cover in greater detail in Chapter 6. The PowerClip feature clips, or masks, the text that doesn't fit into the container. Enveloping paragraph text, on the other hand, actually reshapes the text block, adjusting the text flow, to the container. You can create and shape your own envelopes, or you can create an envelope from an existing shape or symbol.

To use an envelope, first create or import a block of paragraph text. Then add a container for the text with the Envelope roll-up. You can then shape the text container according to the type of envelope you choose. As you'll see in Chapter 6, there are four types of envelopes: straight line, single arc, two curves, and unconstrained. You can tell how each works by the icon on its respective button in the roll-up. The icons are labeled in Figure 4-19.

Straight line

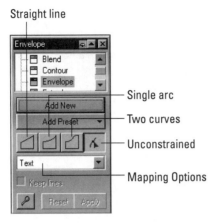

Single arc

Two curves

Unconstrained

Mapping Options

Figure 4-19: The Envelope roll-up provides four types of envelopes. You can further modify how an envelope behaves with one of the mapping options directly below the envelope types.

Note

This section looks briefly at using envelopes to reshape paragraph text. For a more complete description of envelopes, see Chapter 6.

The following is an overview of a procedure for reshaping a block of text with an envelope.

STEPS:

Reshaping Text with an Envelope

Step 1. Type or import the text you want to reshape.

Step 2. Use the Format Text (Text ⇨ Format Text) dialog box to make the necessary attribute changes to the text. This is important because making these changes after you assign the envelope can change the look of the text inside the envelope container. Keep in mind, too, that you'll get a better-looking text block if you set alignment to Full, so that your text will fill the shape on the right side.

In both drawings and documents, you should not try to justify text over 14 points. You'll get too many unsightly gaps, like broken teeth. In fact, in most cases, enveloping text larger than 14 points probably won't give you the effect you're after.

Step 3. Reshape the box around the text to its best fit, as shown in Figure 4-20. As a reminder, paragraph text boxes are reshaped similarly to graphics and artistic text objects — by resizing the control handles.

(continued)

STEPS *(continued)*

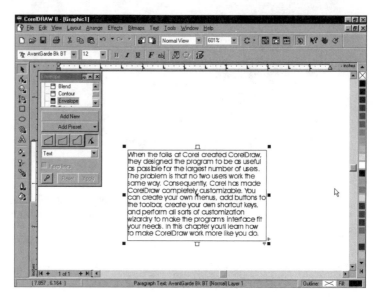

Figure 4-20: Once you have created your text and assigned the desired formatting attributes, reshape the box so it fits better around the text.

Step 4. Select Effects ➪ Envelope to display the Envelope roll-up.

Step 5. In the Envelope roll-up, click on Add New.

Step 6. Select the desired envelope type from one of the buttons, or use Add Preset to use one of the predefined envelopes. To assign an envelope from a specific shape (closed path), use Create From (eyedropper) in the lower-left portion of the roll-up. To do so, make sure the text you want to shape is selected, click on the eyedropper, and then click on the shape from which you want to create an envelope.

Step 7. If you chose one of the shaping objects, rather than a preset or custom shape, reshape the envelope as desired. Note that you can also add additional envelopes, as Chapter 6 explains in further detail. Notice that the nodes on envelopes are quite similar to outline nodes editable with the Node Editing tool.

Step 8. When you finish reshaping the envelope, click on Apply.

Add additional envelopes as desired, reshaping and clicking Apply as needed. Remember that you can use Clear Envelope to reverse undesirable effects. Clear Envelope removes envelopes in the order you apply them, from the most recent backwards.

You can make text containers conform to just about any shape imaginable. It's important to remember, however, that too much distortion can make the text difficult to read. Remember that good design is a balance between aesthetics and legibility.

Font Features

The practice of configuring type to print on paper is known as *typesetting*. Nowadays computers enable almost everybody to be "typesetters." However, the difference between professional typesetters and novice desktop publishers is that the pros use several conventions that nonprofessionals don't know about. The result is a better-looking page — more polished.

This section discusses some basic typesetting concepts that can help you polish your drawings and other documents. The following topics are discussed:

- Special characters
- Character spacing
- Leading
- White space
- Drop caps

Special characters

Many computer software publishers call uncommon characters *special characters*. There's nothing really special about them. They simply are not on your keyboard — which does give them a certain distinction. If you're not familiar with special characters and how to use them, getting at them may seem like magic.

Most Windows applications let you enter special characters by holding down the Alt key and typing the character's ANSI address on the number pad (DOS programs generally use ASCII, IBM's character set). The software manuals for Windows and many desktop-publishing programs have tables showing ANSI address codes. However, this can be cumbersome, requiring too much fumbling around.

Instead, you can use the Windows Character Map, shown in Figure 4-21, to look up character addresses. To find a character's address, simply select a font from the font list, and then select the desired character. If it can be accessed through the keyboard, the keystroke is displayed in the lower-right Keystroke portion of the Character Map window. If a decimal address is required, the address is displayed. You'll find Character Map on the Accessories submenu on the Windows Start menu.

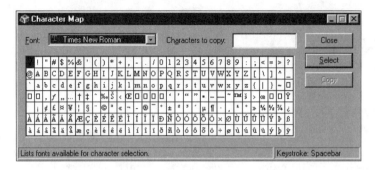

Figure 4-21: Use the Windows Character Map to look up special characters. Choose Start ⇨ Accessories ⇨ Character Map.

You can use Character Map to insert characters into a drawing or document by using the Copy button to copy them to the Clipboard. First highlight the character you want with the arrow keys or by clicking on it with the mouse. Then click on the Select button (the character appears in the Characters to Copy field). Next, click on the Copy button. Then return to your document, select the same font you selected in Character Map, and select Edit ⇨ Paste. Or you can simply remember the Alt+Number Pad address; however, when using this method, make sure Num Lock is turned on.

Unless your documents contain non-English words or math and science formulas, you will not use most special characters. The following subsections describe some of the more common special characters.

Em dash (—)

The em dash should be used for the dash. It replaces the double hyphen (—) that you probably use on a typewriter or in your word processor. In most font sets, the em dash's decimal address is Alt+0151. I recommend that you use Type Assist to enter this character. (See the sidebar "Using Type Assist.")

Quotation marks

You probably use straight quotation marks ('or "). These are actually foot and inch symbols (typewriters could have only so many keys, so some characters like these had to be used to represent others). Single and double quotation marks should be opened (' or ") and closed (' or "). By default, CorelDraw automatically opens and closes quotation marks. When you need foot and inch markers, you should find them in Character Map and enter them directly.

Built fractions

Most people make fractions like this: 3/4. This format is not only confusing (compare 22 3/4 and 22¾) but also does not look right. Your character set might have fraction characters for all quarter-inch and eighth-inch increments. You can make others with your software's superscript and subscript features (for example, $^{16}/_{32}$). You can also create keystroke combinations in Type Assist for fractions that you use often.

Using Type Assist

Okay, so Character Map is easier than fumbling through a manual. Still, it requires leaving CorelDraw and invoking another application, and then toggling back and forth. CorelDraw and many other Windows applications provide further relief with a handy feature called Type Assist.

If you use Word or WordPerfect, you might be familiar with features that are similar to Type Assist. What this feature does is automatically insert characters or character strings in response to keyboard input. While writing this book, for example, we used Word's AutoCorrect (similar to Type Assist) to embed special characters, such as an arrow for the following characters: =>. Each time we typed =>, Word substituted ⇨. Each time we entered cd, Word entered *CorelDraw*.

To access Type Assist, choose Text ⇨ Type Assist (here's a case where Type Assist helped automate this writing). This command brings up the dialog box shown in this sidebar. From here you can configure Type Assist. Notice that Corel has configured several special characters for you, including several commonly misspelled words. When you enter the characters on the left side of the list, Type Assist replaces them with the character or text string on the right.

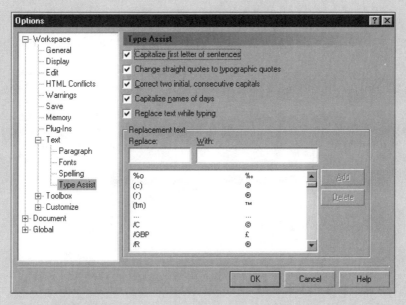

You have two ways to get Type Assist entries into this dialog box. You can type them directly, filling the Replace and With fields, or you can type the character or string in your document that you want in the With field, select it, and then open the Type Assist dialog box and complete the Replace portion of the pair. To add special characters, use the Alt+Number Pad method described earlier in this section.

Legal characters

The registered name and registered trademark symbols should be set superscript next to the product or company name (for example, Microsoft® Windows™). The copyright symbol usually appears after the word Copyright (Copyright © 1998 by IDG Books). Corel has built-in Type Assist replacements for most of these symbols. For the most common, ®, ©, and ™, simply enter the characters (r, c, or tm) surrounded by parentheses.

Bullets

Why use hyphens (-) or asterisks (*) as bullets? These characters are dull, and you have so many other wonderful characters available. You can even use the hollow box as a check box.

☐ Shoes

☐ Shirts

☐ Socks

CorelDraw comes with several sets of special characters you can use as bullets. But keep your head about you. Too many cute little bullets can look ridiculous. You can create bullets in CorelDraw automatically from the Effects portion of the Format Text dialog box (Text ⇨ Format Text ⇨ Effects), as shown in Figure 4-22. Simply select Bullet Effect Type list, choose the symbol font character, and then select the desired bullet from the scrolling palette. This works on the paragraph where the cursor is blinking or on several selected paragraphs, or you can assign the bullet to a paragraph text style. You can also embed the bullet in the paragraph, or you can create a hanging indent bullet by choosing one of the placement options.

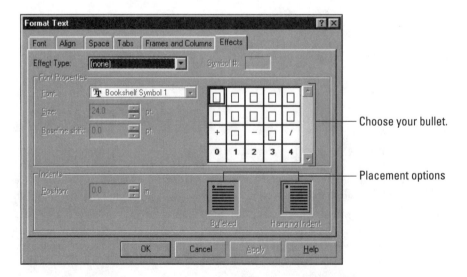

Choose your bullet.

Placement options

Figure 4-22: Use the Effects portion of Format Text to create bullets automatically.

In version 8 you can use the Symbols docker to create a new symbol font. To do so, simply select your object (Tools ⇨ Create ⇨ Symbol), and then name the new symbol font. It is now installed in the Symbols docker, and you can use it at will. This is much easier than the procedure used in previous versions, which entailed exporting the font to a font file. With this method, CorelDraw will create the font and install it for you.

Dingbats

Dingbats are a font set of stars, boxes, arrows, and other characters useful for sprucing up a layout. A common dingbat is the pointing hand (☞) used to bring the reader's attention to something, usually a callout, note, tip, or some other special point. Another is the little phone (☎) that advertisers use to indicate a phone number. A standard favorite in a bulleted list is the check mark:

We offer the following services:

✔ Embalming

✔ Grave site beautification

✔ Lifetime guarantee

Nowadays several dingbat fonts, including Wingdings, come with Windows, and several come with CorelDraw. Resist the temptation to use them just because you have them. Although dingbats look nice, they should serve a purpose. A layout sprinkled with cute little dingbats for no apparent reason looks juvenile.

Drop caps/raised caps

Drop caps are enlarged first characters at the beginning of an article, as demonstrated here. Their purpose is to indicate the beginning of a story or the start of a new or important section within a story. But they are also attractive design elements that can break the monotony of large blocks of text. Drop caps can be raised (set high on the line), dropped into the text block, or adjacent (set beside a text block).

Another technique is to use a graphic as a drop cap. Simply create the letter and embellish it in CorelDraw. Then bring it into your layout on the Clipboard.

The possibilities for drop caps are nearly limitless. In a two-color newsletter, you can add color to drop caps. This professional touch adds a little polish to the publication. Another professional technique is to use the color on the logo or nameplate for drop caps.

CorelDraw 8 lets you create drop caps automatically, from the Effects section of the Format Text dialog box (Text ⇨ Format Text ⇨ Effects), as shown in Figure 4-23. You can set either Dropped style or Hanging Indent from the Indents portion of the dialog box, as well as set how many lines the drop cap extends into the text in the Dropped lines box.

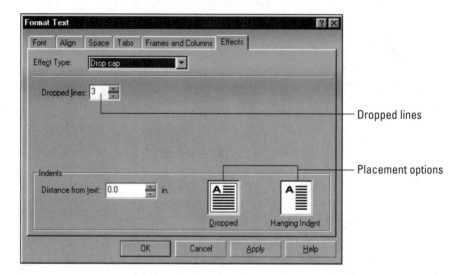

Figure 4-23: Use the Effects portion of the Format Text dialog box to create drop caps automatically.

Character and word spacing

Tracking is the spacing between letters and words. *Kerning*, on the other hand, refers to the space between specific characters — which is something else altogether. Let's look at them both.

Most software measures spaces between letters and words in *ems*, the space occupied by the lowercase *m*, which is considered to be square. Desktop publishing programs and vector draw programs such as CorelDraw provide extensive control over tracking. The main reason for adjusting tracking is to improve the appearance of type. But you can, at times, adjust it slightly to squeeze more type into an area, or to widen spacing to fill in a blank space. When using it for the latter, though, be careful not to compromise the legibility or overall appearance of your text.

Font sets have default tracking. When you bring text into layout software, it is given the default, except when text is fully justified (each line is then adjusted separately), or if your text style specifies otherwise. Most of the time the default is fine. But at times you'll want to adjust tracking, usually to improve the appearance of headlines and body text.

Adjusting tracking

You adjust the tracking in CorelDraw in the Space section of the Format Text dialog box (Text ➪ Format Text ➪ Space), as shown in Figure 4-24. You can also adjust tracking with the Node Editing tool, as discussed earlier in this section. CorelDraw provides options for adjusting the tracking between letters and words separately. And you can also adjust tracking for each type of alignment. To do so, simply select the type of alignment for which you want to adjust the tracking, and then make your setting changes.

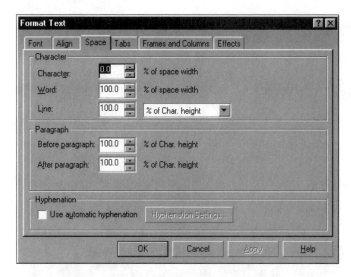

Figure 4-24: Use the Space options in the Format Text dialog box to adjust tracking.

In most cases, the default tracking is fine for headlines. There may, however, be times when you want to adjust it. Use tracking to make headlines more attractive and easier to read. Tracking comes in handy for improving the appearance of body copy, especially for tightening loose type (too widely spaced), and vice versa.

Adjusting kerning

Many people confuse tracking and kerning. Kerning refers to specific pairs of characters, called *kerning pairs*. Kerning pairs are character pairs with combined shapes that can cause unsightly gaps, such as *To, AV, Ta, ff,* and many, many others. Most fonts come with compensation for kerning pairs built in, automatically compensating for the shape inconsistencies. However, sometimes you may find it necessary to make your own kerning changes.

Unlike some desktop publishing software, CorelDraw does not let you make permanent kerning changes to your fonts. Instead, each time you need to change a pair relationship, you must do it by hand. You can make the change manually, by selecting the character you want to kern with the Node Editing tool, and simply moving it left or right, remembering to hold the Ctrl key so that you don't shift the character from the baseline. The second method is to select both characters with the Node Editing tool, and then make adjustments in Spacing (Text ⇨ Format Text ⇨ Spacing).

Leading

Leading refers to the white space between lines of type measured baseline to baseline. Most publishing programs have a default leading of 120 percent of the point size. Ten-point type, then, has a 12-point leading. For smaller point sizes (6–12), 120 percent is just right. Larger sizes tend to look peculiar and take up too much space with 120 percent leading. You will usually want to adjust the leading (set it in your styles) for headlines to about 100 percent.

Another reason to adjust leading is to achieve special effects. This is a matter of taste, and you will want to be careful to avoid making text hard to read.

You adjust the leading in CorelDraw with the Spacing option from the Format Text command on the Text menu, as shown in Figure 4-25. You can also use the Node Editing tool, as discussed earlier in this chapter.

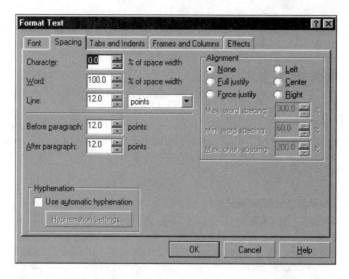

Figure 4-25: Use the Line option in Spacing to set leading for selected text or for text styles. Setting this option with no text selected changes the program's default.

White Space

Pick up any book or magazine article on document design and layout, and you will soon find a discussion of white space. The blank spaces — or what you do not put on a page — are just as important as the ones containing elements. The mentality that we had to overcome was that blank spaces are wasted ones. Blank spaces are, instead, breaths of fresh air. Each element — headlines, pull quotes, columns, and so forth — should have its own space. Do not crowd elements together so the reader cannot tell where one begins and the other ends.

True, some design elements break up the page, such as graphics and photographs. But a page covered with ink is too full. It is difficult to say exactly how much white space you need. But it is easy to tell when you don't have enough. If it comes down to crowding things together or omitting something, leave something out.

No hard-and-fast formula exists for discerning the right amount of white space. What we do is evaluate our emotional response to the page. If our initial reaction is, "Gee, that sure does look like a lot to read," we find ways to break up the text with visuals and by spreading elements out to give them breathing room.

Summary

- A typeface is a style of type, such as Times or Helvetica. Most typefaces have four different attributes or styles: normal (often called Book or Roman, depending on the typeface), **bold**, *italic*, and ***bold-italic***. Some, however, have only one or two styles. Others, such as ITC Goudy Sans, have as many as eight or more styles.

- Fonts come in all shapes and sizes but can be broken into four broad categories: serif, sans serif, display (or decorative), and symbol. Each sort of font has different uses. Serif fonts have little feet at the ends of the character strokes, called serifs. Sans serif fonts have no feet, or serifs. Display fonts can be fancy, frilly, fun, and even formidable; symbol fonts are special figures and icons that usually aren't available in regular fonts.

- Some typefaces are serious, some are ornate, and some are elegant; others are simple, fun, or cartoonish. The tone of a typeface can greatly affect the weight of the message.

- You have several ways to manipulate type in CorelDraw, including artistic text and paragraph styles. You can also use artistic text with the Node Editing tool. And you can manipulate the paragraph text frames themselves for a wide range of special effects.

- When using type in your document, you should be mindful of several industry standard conventions, including the following: Using special characters, adjusting tracking, adjusting leading, using white space effectively, and making effective use of drop caps and dingbats.

Chapter 5

Working with Colors and Fills

In This Chapter

You learn useful secrets about:

- ▶ Color models and color-matching systems
- ▶ Corel Color Manager
- ▶ CorelDraw's color palettes
- ▶ Using CorelDraw's color styles
- ▶ CorelDraw's fountain fills
- ▶ CorelDraw's prefabricated textures and patterns

Although it's not as hard as it used to be, getting colors to reproduce properly in electronic-publishing environments requires some special knowledge and a lot of patience. The reason for this is, of course, the differences in the ways various devices — desktop printers, monitors, scanners, printing presses, and so on — create color. Some devices, such as computer monitors, use combinations of red, green, and blue (RGB) to create different hues, while others use cyan, magenta, yellow, and black (CMYK). These and other differences between devices make for a wide range of variables that affect reproduction of color.

The documentation for many graphics programs lacks clear explanations of how to achieve good color results. Consequently, we've dedicated part of this chapter to explaining the mechanics of getting good results when you use CorelDraw's colors and fills. (In addition, Chapter 7 explains how to use CorelDraw to reproduce colors for a printing press — a process known in the graphic art business as *prepress*.)

The remainder of this chapter covers CorelDraw's immensely useful color and fill tools. One of the great things about CorelDraw is that it provides so many tools for automating tasks. In this chapter you'll learn how to automate many of the tasks related to colors and fills.

Note

Throughout this chapter we'll throw in some tips on how to use color effectively in your documents and presentations. Although our examples focus on CorelDraw, much of this discussion also pertains to the other applications in the CorelDraw 8 graphics suite.

Color Models

A color model is a method for representing color as data. In the world of electronic publishing and graphics design, color models provide a way to consistently describe color with number values. CorelDraw applications support several different color models. In this section we look at the ones used most often: the color models RGB, CMYK, and the up-and-coming HiFi (LAB).

RGB

RGB stands for red, green, and blue. By mixing these three colors, you can create just about any color possible — well, any color possible on a computer monitor, anyway. RGB is the model used by your monitor. The screen mixes colors by illuminating red, green, and blue phosphorous lights with an electron gun at the back of the monitor screen. Varying the intensity of each light on the phosphors produces different colors.

RGB, then, is the color model you should use when creating graphics for reproduction or display on a computer monitor. (Or it's the model you should at least start with. Some other variables also apply, such as the type of application in which you plan to use the image. Images designed for the World Wide Web, for example, often require color reduction through indexing. But we're getting ahead of ourselves. You should turn to Chapter 21 for a discussion of using images on the Web, and Chapter 22 discusses using images in multimedia titles and presentations.)

CMYK

CMYK stands for cyan, magenta, yellow, and black (yes, the K stands for black). CMYK is the process used by most print shops for full-color, or four-color print documents. CorelDraw and other applications separate the four colors into plates, one for each color. The printing press then prints percentages of the colors (actually, percentages of each color), one over the other, to mix the desired colors.

Traditionally, CMYK is the model of choice for creating documents bound for a printing press, a color-proofing printer, dye-sublimation, full-color poster printer, or print-on-demand applications. In fact, by default the colors you apply in CorelDraw from the color palette are defined with CMYK values.

Note

Printing CMYK separations is discussed in Chapter 7. When printing separations from CorelDraw, the program automatically converts RGB information to CMYK, so you don't need to worry about making sure to use CMYK colors when assigning colors in your drawings. This is also true when you export your drawings to EPS format for placement in a layout. However, if you export to a bitmap format, such as PCX or TIFF, RGB values are maintained. Whenever you export from any CorelDraw application to a DTP layout, you should use either EPS or CMYK TIFF. These points are made much clearer in Chapter 7.

Warning

Wait a minute! Did we say that you don't have to worry about RGB colors getting converted to CMYK? This process works reasonably well for documents printed on desktop inkjet and color printers. But the leap from monitor to printing press is a huge one, with plenty of obstacles along the way — not the least of which is the inherent difference between how colors display on computer screens compared to how they print on printing presses. When working in an environment where the integrity of your color selections is critical, do not rely blindly on CorelDraw to make these conversions for you. Instead, read the section in this chapter on the Corel Color Manager, and then turn to Chapter 7 and read up on printing and prepress.

HiFi (Hexachrome)

The HiFi, or LAB, color model is not new. HiFi color printing uses additional process inks to reproduce more colors. PANTONE's Hexachrome system is the most common — it uses green and orange inks in addition to CMYK. This allows for colors not attainable in the standard CMYK models, most notably, when using Hexachrome, bright oranges and greens.

While HiFi color can give printed documents a wider range of colors, it requires two additional prepress separations, requiring additional film and additional press plates — making for a considerably more expensive print run. If you don't understand *prepress* and *color separations*, these terms are discussed later in this chapter.

Color-Matching Systems

Color-matching systems are different from color models. Color-matching systems provide a consistent way for choosing and talking about colors. Color models provide a way to translate colors into numeric values. (A color model is a way of representing colors as data.) As you'll see, color-matching systems are very useful tools for designers and artists.

PANTONE Matching System (PMS)

Often, you use a color-matching system to choose a color before you create it with a color model. As you know, color models define colors through values or by mixing percentages of color — usually RGB or CMYK. But this can be confusing. Color-matching systems are composed of predefined colors that you typically select from swatch (or sample) books. When you go into a print shop and choose a color from a chart or swatch book, such as the PANTONE Matching System swatch book shown in Plate 5-1 in the color insert, you are using a color-matching system.

Two types of color-matching systems are available: *spot* and *process*. Spot colors usually consist of premixed inks. On the printing press, ink is applied to the paper in the premixed color. Process color-matching system swatches, on the other hand, show colors as they appear when they have been mixed during the print run. A process color swatch book, then, shows the results of mixing the four CMYK values.

Color-matching swatch books take the guesswork out of selecting colors by enabling you to see how they look on both coated and uncoated paper — a much more precise method than trying to choose colors from a monitor.

PMS is the spot color-matching system used in most print shops. You should use spot colors when your documents contain one or two colors, because it's cheaper and more precise than process color. When you choose a color from a swatch book at your local printer, it is usually PMS.

CorelDraw has a complete PANTONE color system built in. To use it you should switch to PANTONE Matching System in the Uniform Fill dialog box (click on the Fill tool, and then choose the first option on the flyout), shown in Figure 5-1. To select colors interactively, without having to go in and out of a dialog box, you can use the Color roll-up (the second to last option on the flyout). To get to the PANTONE palette in the roll-up, choose Palette in the top list, shown in Figure 5-2, and choose PANTONE MATCHING SYSTEM from the third list, the one directly above the color swatches.

In version 7 you had to wade through several menus to bring up the PMS colors. In version 8 the route is much swifter. After you open the Uniform Fill dialog box, simply click on the third button in the upper-left corner, the Fixed Palettes button — the one that actually looks like a PMS swatch book. PANTONE Matching System is the first option in the list, as shown in Figure 5-2.

Click here to switch to
PANTONE Matching System

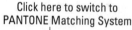

Figure 5-1: The Uniform Fill dialog box can be set up to use the PANTONE Matching System.

Figure 5-2: To use PANTONE colors in the Color roll-up, choose the Palette option, and then select PANTONE MATCHING SYSTEM in the third list in the roll-up.

Usually, you match PANTONE colors by names and numbers. To see a list of PANTONE numbers, click on the More button in the Uniform Fill dialog box. (This is also new to version 8. In version 7 you chose Show Color Names from a menu.). Figure 5-3 shows the PANTONE swatches with corresponding names. In the Color roll-up, the names are displayed above the swatches, as shown in Figure 5-4. Notice that the names and numbers match those on the PANTONE swatch book shown in Plate 5-1.

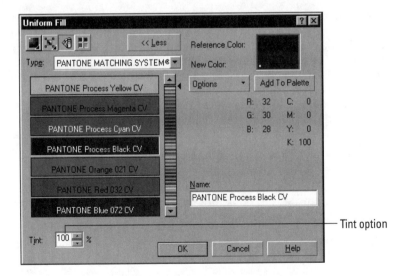

Figure 5-3: You can choose More to display each PANTONE color with its matching system name and number.

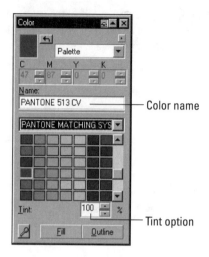

Color name

Tint option

Figure 5-4: In the Color roll-up, the PANTONE names are displayed above the swatches.

Secret

This list of colors is quite extensive. PANTONE specifies virtually hundreds of colors. If you know the name (or number) of the color you want, you can find the color by typing the name in the Name field. CorelDraw displays the appropriate swatch in the list of colors. Unfortunately, in version 8 Corel has done away with the Search option, which we found quite helpful.

Often, it's tempting to select a PANTONE color from the list in the Uniform Fill dialog box. Before you do, however, try this experiment. Grab your PMS swatch book (you really should have one if you're working with PMS colors) and open the Uniform Fill dialog box in CorelDraw, go to the PANTONE Matching System section, and then click on the More button. In the Name field, type **PANTONE Reflex Blue**. Open your swatch book to the first strip of colors and find the one labeled PANTONE Reflex Blue. Hold the swatch book up to your monitor and compare the two colors.

Warning

Depending on the quality of your computer's display system and the color calibration and color-management options you've set up, the difference between the swatch in the swatch book and the color in the CorelDraw list will be more or less dramatic. In any case, you'll see our point: Choose your colors from the swatch book, not your monitor! The swatch book will always be correct; your monitor may not.

Note

You can choose PMS colors from the Property Bar when using the Interactive Fill tool, as discussed in the "Interactive Fill Tool Magic" sidebar toward the end of this chapter.

Using Spot Colors Effectively

Designers often use spot colors to effectively enhance the message contained in their documents, rather than merely as an aesthetics tool. Using spot colors improperly can detract from the message. Following are a few do's and don'ts for using spot color.

Use bright spot colors to attract reader attention or make a point. Colors can signify priorities. People tend to look first at the brightest colors on a page or in a graphic. You can control where their eyes go first by putting the most important material in the brightest colors. This is especially true of charts or other graphics designed to make comparisons, as shown in the color insert, Plate 5-2.

Use spot colors to map information. Use spot color to explain or to enhance the message, not to decorate. Do not use color merely because it's at your disposal. Instead, lead the reader's eye to the significant portions of a page. In a newsletter, for example, use color to draw the reader's attention to the banner or table of contents. In a flyer, highlight important parts of the message with color. Plate 5-3 in the color insert shows an example of effective use of spot color in a newsletter, letterhead, and brochure. When readers look at the page, the colored elements draw them into each piece.

Use spot colors to emphasize. Colors can make new points or different points of view stand out. On a brochure page, for example, use color to introduce a change in topics. On a newsletter page, use color for sidebars or sections containing contrasting arguments. Again, see Plate 5-3 in the color insert.

Use spot colors to symbolize: Certain colors can symbolize the nature of data. The most obvious associations are green for go, red for danger, and amber for caution.

Use spot colors to emphasize distinguishing characteristics. Almost all documents have elements that refer to the document rather than the subject matter. The most obvious are page numbers, headers and footers, frames, boxed backgrounds, and other recurring objects. You can use spot color to set these objects off from the rest of the document, making it easier for the reader to find them.

Use spot colors as navigation tools. In multisectioned documents, many designers use locators to tell the reader where he or she is in a publication. Using color to mark the beginning of each section and subsection helps the reader find material, which makes using the document more pleasurable. Advertising data in particular is much more effective if information is easily located. You can also use colors to highlight section numbers and locator tabs. You can use different colors to identify separate sections, making each section distinguishable from the others. Plate 5-4 in the color insert shows several examples of using different colors for navigation tools.

Use percentages (tints) of spot colors to make a document appear more colorful. Sometimes called poor-man's color, percentages of spot colors (called *tints* in CorelDraw) make an image or document seem as though you have used many colors. Tints are simply the same colors at lower saturation, which produces lighter shades of the spot color. In CorelDraw, you apply tints from either the Uniform Fill dialog box or Color roll-up (or from the Property Bar when using the Interactive Fill tool), as shown in Figures 5-3 and 5-4 earlier in this chapter. You can set tints at any percentage from 1 to 100. However, you should use at least a 5 to 10 percent variance between tints; otherwise you don't really get the appearance of multiple colors. Plate 5-5 in the color insert shows examples of using tints to create the illusion of multiple colors.

When to Use Spot or Process Color

You should consider several factors before deciding whether to use spot or process colors to print a publication. The three key factors are time, money, and design. Process colors usually require more resources, such as time and cost, than spot colors. Sometimes you can't avoid using process color. Color photographs and full-color drawings, of course, require four-color printing (process colors).

You should use spot colors if you have a limited budget and can accomplish your design using three or fewer colors. If you need to print four or more spot colors, you should use process colors instead, as this color choice then becomes the more cost-saving. The most effective way to get a process spot color is to use PANTONE Process or one of the other color-matching systems. You should also use spot colors when you need to make a precise color match in a corporate logo or some other graphic, or when you want to use a special spot-color ink, such as fluorescent or pearlescent.

Other color-matching systems

You may be wondering about all those other names in the list of matching systems. Granted, there's a bunch, including FOCOLTONE, TRUMATCH, PANTONE Process, and others. Mostly these are process color-matching systems for which you can find corresponding swatch or match books at art supply stores. Some print shops and service bureaus also sell them.

Basically, these systems are similar to PMS in that you choose colors based on swatches on a printed page. The difference is that many of these are not premixed inks that you call out at a print shop as spot colors. Instead, they are created on process printing presses, usually with mixtures of cyan, magenta, yellow, and black. These color-matching systems are primarily designed to enable you to choose colors based on how they will print, instead of how they look on a monitor.

Corel Color Manager

Because you can't depend on colors coming out on a printing press exactly as they appear on your monitor, you need a way to match colors reliably. An excellent way to get all your output devices in sync is to use a color-management system (or CMS). CorelDraw comes with its own CMS, called Corel Color Manager. Before going into how to use Corel Color Manager, let's first take a look at what it does.

CIE color spaces

Secret

Output devices such as printers, monitors, and scanners all define colors differently. The color model used for color definitions is known as the device's *color space*. Most offset presses and many color desktop printers, plotters, and large poster printing devices, for example, specify colors as percentages of cyan, magenta, yellow, and black (CMYK). The color blue in the CMYK model uses the following values: C:97, M:96, Y:18, K:5. The same color on your monitor, which specifies colors with red, green, and blue (RGB) percentages, displays using these values: R:48, G:28, B:102, as shown in Figure 5-5.

Colors defined using CMYK and RGB models are *device dependent*. In other words, they appear a certain way on a particular device. The color defined in Figure 5-5 would look different on monitors made by different manufacturers — you would see different shades of blue. A color printer would give you yet another color. Depending on paper and some other conditions, the same blue might reproduce in a different shade even when printed on a process-color press.

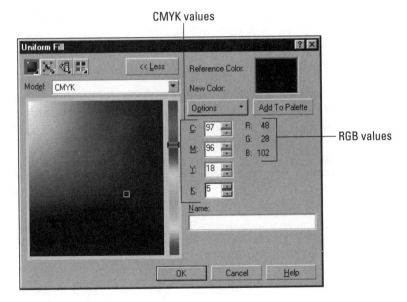

Figure 5-5: Color models define colors in different ways.

People in the printing and motion picture industries dealt with this problem long before computer graphics came along. In 1930, the Commission Internationale de l'Eclairage (International Commission on Color), or CIE, came up with a system of color standards. Making color models specify color in the same way was an impossible task, so the commission created CIE color spaces that specify color by using the human eye as the rendering method. The CIE specifies colors as people see them. CIE color spaces use mathematical values that aren't dependent on inconsistent variables, such as the design of a particular printer or the composition of a particular ink. It is on these CIE values that color-management systems such as Corel Color Manager (and others) base their definitions of colors.

How Corel Color Manager works

To understand how color-management systems work, you need to be familiar with two important concepts: *gamut* and *profiles*.

Gamut

A device's color gamut describes the range of colors that the device can create or, in the case of scanners, sense. Each color device — printing press, monitor, scanner, or printer — has its own color gamut. The CIE color space, based on the human eye, describes the most colors. It has the largest gamut. Color devices cannot reproduce this wide range of colors. In other words, their gamut is smaller than the CIE gamut. In the case of a 300-dpi inkjet printer, for example, the gamut is significantly smaller. Plate 5-6 in the color insert shows the color range for each type of color model and specific devices for reproducing color.

Profiles

Corel Color Manager and other color-management systems use device profiles to record the color gamut of specific devices. A profile describes the characteristics of each device, as well as other information about its capabilities and limitations. These profiles may be created either by the manufacturer of the color management system or by the manufacturer of the device.

Corel Color Manager uses device profiles to adjust colors between printers, monitors, and scanners. It converts the color data to and from CIE color-space formats. If the proper device profiles are installed on your system, the Corel Color Manager can turn the colors on your monitor into CIE colors and then convert them to similar colors for your printer, imagesetter, or another output device.

CorelDraw ships with many profiles, including profiles for several different printers and monitors. If your printer or monitor is not included, you can select a similar device, or contact the device maker to try to obtain one, or get information on which included profiles match (or are close to) an included profile. Unlike many color-management systems, Corel Color Manager also lets you create your own profiles through a system known as *calibration*, which is explained later in this chapter.

Limitations of color-management systems

Corel Color Manager, like other color-management systems, does not eliminate the need for traditional color proofing. (If you're not sure what we mean by *color proofing*, you should refer to Chapter 7.) Corel Color Manager works best when defining gamuts downward — in other words, when decreasing the number of colors. Computers are much better at reducing information from existing data rather than increasing it. That makes sense, when you think about it, because increasing data would entail some guesswork. Color-management systems reduce one device's gamut to match another — from, say, a monitor to a printer. This is convenient because color monitors have greater gamuts than desktop color printers. The most useful conversion is from what you see on your monitor (RGB) to what rolls out of the color-proofing printer and then, finally, the printing press (CMYK). Corel Color Manager transforms RGB color to its internal CIE format and then creates a CMYK equivalent, a process that works reasonably well but is hardly perfect — as you'll see when we look at actually using color management in your CorelDraw documents.

Preparing to use Corel Color Manager

Getting color right in a graphics environment depends on several factors, including not only the use of a color-management system and installing the proper device profiles, but also the proper calibration of your monitor. These steps increase the reliability of colors created and applied in CorelDraw. This section looks at setting up a work area conducive to color management, choosing and setting up a Corel Color Manager, and calibrating your monitor, scanner, and printer.

Tip

Your work environment plays an important role in how you see color on your monitor. The lighting in the room where you work and your monitor's contrast and brightness settings should remain constant for a consistent display of colors. If your work area lighting changes throughout the day, when working with color on your computer you should draw the blinds and work in artificial lighting. If you use fluorescent lights, which can cast a yellow tint, you might consider investing in 5,000-degree Kelvin lighting. But all this depends on how critical color consistency is to your application.

When you've got, the lighting in the room right, adjust the contrast and brightness on your monitor. Contrast adjusts intensity and brightness adjusts the level of black. To make the adjustments, display an image containing a lot of black, and then adjust the brightness until you get the best black available, making sure that the black is not surrounded by a gray shadow. Then adjust the contrast until you're pleased with the intensity.

After going to all that trouble of adjusting monitor settings in the correct lighting, it wouldn't be good if somebody came in and readjusted your monitor. (Or if you bumped the controls with a book or software package.)

You'd have to go back and do it all over again. To avoid this, tape down the contrast and brightness controls on your monitor.

When your monitor is adjusted, it's time to fire up the Corel Color Profile Wizard, as shown in Figure 5-6. Depending on the devices and drivers you have installed on your system, the first time you launch Corel Color Manager, the wizard configures itself the best it can by checking out your equipment.

 However, depending on how you installed CorelDraw, the Corel Color Manager's profiles may not be installed on your system. If not, you can follow the procedure in this section for installing them.

In Figure 5-6, for example, Color Manager was not able to find any installed profiles. Rather than install all the profiles during installation, we have chosen to install only those we need from the CorelDraw CD-ROM. To do so, you first choose the device for which you want to install a profile — monitor, scanner, composite (proof) printer, or separations printer — in the Device list. Then choose Get Profile from Disk in the Profile drop-down list. The box below the Profile list shows current settings for that device.

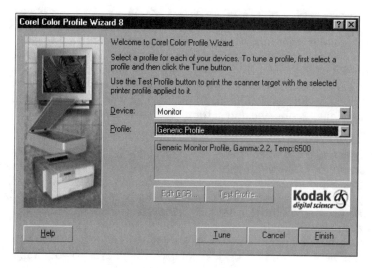

Figure 5-6: The Corel Color Profile Wizard helps you set up Corel Color Manager.

Corel Color Manager enables you to use device profiles written specifically for your devices, or you can create your own or modify the predefined profiles. For most applications, the predefined profiles work fine. However, if you use devices for which Corel has not bundled profiles, or if your application requires highly accurate color correction, you should read the information in the "Calibrating your output devices" section that follows.

Before going into creating your own profiles, let's look at the options in Corel Color Profile Wizard and what they mean. In the Device list there are four options. While these options may seem self-explanatory, they can use some defining in terms of color management.

- **Monitor.** When you choose Monitor from the device list, the Profile drop-down provides a list of installed profiles, or a list of profiles chosen during installation of CorelDraw. If your profile isn't in the list, you can choose Get Profiles from Disk and choose a similar monitor, get one from the monitor vendor, or generate one, as described in the next section. What many people don't know about monitors is that although there are plenty of manufacturers, many of them use the same picture tubes. The monitor vendor should be able to help you find a monitor profile among those shipped with CorelDraw.

- **Scanner.** This option, of course, enables you to tell Corel Color Manager which scanner you use. CorelDraw ships with profiles for most popular scanners. If yours isn't in the list, you can choose Generic Profile, contact the maker of your scanner to obtain a profile, or choose the Tune option to create your own profile or edit an existing one. We'll look at creating and editing a scanner profile in the next section.

- **Composite Printer.** Use this option to choose a profile for your color proofing printer, either your own desktop model or the profile for the device your service bureau uses for composites. (If one is not included with CorelDraw, perhaps you can get one from the service bureau.) If you use your desktop printer for final output, you would still use this setting to choose a profile for your printer. Like the other profiles in this list, you can get one from the printer vendor or generate one.

- **Separations Printer.** Use this option to choose the separation device on which you proof separated film — usually your service bureau's separation proofing device for creating color keys or match prints. If you don't know what color keys and match prints are, be sure to read Chapter 7. (If a separation device profile is not included with CorelDraw, perhaps you can get one from the service bureau.) Again, these profiles may be available from the device vendor, or you can create your own. However, creating or editing profiles at this level is a somewhat intricate process.

When you've chosen all your profiles, choose Finish. CorelDraw will use these settings to correct the color among your various devices and to simulate the final output on your monitor. Keep in mind that if you are creating graphics for display on a monitor, you should not use Corel Color Manager to correct color.

When you have your profiles set, CorelDraw and the other applications in the suite know what colors your output devices are capable of producing. When working in these applications, Corel Color Manager can now warn you when you define a color beyond the gamut of your printing devices.

After you choose your profiles and exit the Corel Color Profile Wizard, color management goes to work in the CorelDraw suite. For example, when you define colors in the Uniform Fill dialog box, the Color roll-up, or one of the many other CorelDraw suite application dialog boxes, you can turn on the gamut alarm (usually on the dialog box flyout menu), and the program shows you which colors are not available on your printer, as shown in Figure 5-7.

Figure 5-7: Corel Color Manager profiles enable you to set a gamut alarm to warn you as to which colors are available on your printer. The blotted area (which shows as a bright color on your monitor) shows the colors in current range that your printer cannot produce.

You should not choose colors outside your printer's gamut. The resulting color shift will most likely be one you won't like.

Calibrating your output devices

As we mentioned earlier, for most applications Corel Color Manager's built-in profiles work fine. However, if you don't have a profile for your device — or if you work in an environment where color precision is critical — you can use Corel Color Manager to manually calibrate each of your devices. This section covers the process for each type of device.

Monitor calibration

The profiles in Corel Color Manager assume that the devices adhere to a set of standards. (Printers and scanners are calibrated during manufacturing.) Monitors, however, are subject to so many variables, such as work-area lighting, graphics adapters, and so on, that often a predefined profile is simply not accurate enough. Often it's advantageous to calibrate monitors manually. This section shows you how to use Corel Color Manager's monitor calibration utility to get the colors right on your monitor.

Begin by making sure your work area is set up as you normally use it, as explained previously. Before going any further, make sure your monitor has been on about an hour, so that all the phosphors are warm. Now fire up Corel Color Profile Wizard and make sure that Monitor is displayed in the Device drop-down list.

Now scroll in the Profiles drop-down list and choose either Generic Profile or one that you've installed that you believe is close to a profile for your monitor. (Choosing a similar profile can shorten the calibration process.) Now click on Tune. The subsequent dialog box, shown in Figure 5-8, enables you to choose the manufacturer and make of your monitor. Keep in mind here that if you select the exact name and model number from the lists, you'll actually be editing the predefined profile for your monitor. If you're not happy with the results, you'll have to reinstall it. What we suggest you do is choose the manufacturer and then, under Monitor Model, type something descriptive, such as **My Profile**. Remember, too, that you can create several monitor profiles for the same monitor for different types of graphics work. Use the text box below Monitor Model to make notes about the current profile. If you are creating a profile for an unsupported monitor, of course, you'll have to give it a name.

After naming the new profile, clicking on the Next button brings up another dialog box asking if you want to calibrate your monitor with a calibration device, such as a Colortron. (If you are using a calibration device, you've gone beyond the scope of the discussion in this book and should consult the device's documentation.) When you click on Next again, the dialog box shown in Figure 5-9 displays. It is from here that you actually calibrate your monitor. So rummage through your CorelDraw box and find the scanner target, which you'll need to complete the calibration process. (The scanner target is easy to recognize — it has the same picture of the woman shown in Figure 5-9.)

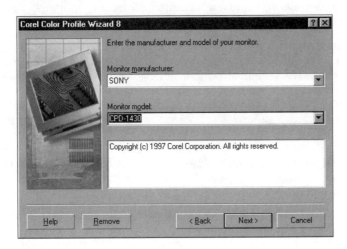

Figure 5-8: Use this section of Corel Color Profile Wizard to name your new monitor profile.

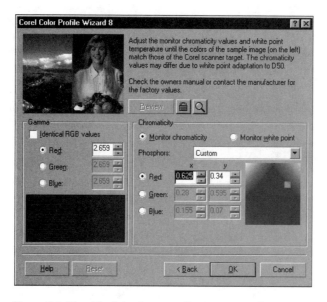

Figure 5-9: Use this dialog box to calibrate your monitor.

Basically, the goal is to get the two pictures — the landscape and the woman holding fruit — in the upper-left corner of the dialog box to match the target. You do this by making adjustments to the various settings in this dialog box. The three settings you adjust are Gamma, Monitor chromaticity, and Monitor white point. Following is a list of the settings and what each does:

- **Gamma** controls the monitor's brightness. Adjusting gamma values for your image affects midrange values most. Dark and light values change more slowly. You adjust gamma values using the Gamma box as a reference. The square on the left represents the natural gamma of your monitor, and the square on the right shows current gamma settings. Your monitor's gamma is set correctly when these two boxes match each other. You can adjust gamma one color channel at a time by clicking on one of the three radio buttons. When adjusting gamma, you should move back from the monitor until the horizontal lines in the left side of the gamma box appear as a solid color. Now adjust the sliders or enter numerical values until the two sides match. You can adjust all three channels at once by selecting the Identical RGB values check box.

- **Monitor chromaticity** defines hue and saturation, or chroma levels, for your monitor. Chromaticity is a quality of color corresponding to the monitor's color gamut, or the number of saturated colors that the monitor is capable of reproducing. Because chromaticity values are relatively stable and do not vary greatly between monitors, they usually do not need to be adjusted. In most cases, it's simpler just to select a phosphor, or tube type, from the Phosphors drop-down list, which usually automatically makes the right chromaticity settings for your monitor.

■ **Monitor white point** measures the light produced by the monitor when all electron guns are firing at full intensity. It enables you to define the quality of *pure* white for your monitor. Pure white is expressed as a temperature in degrees Kelvin (K) corresponding to the reflective qualities of different types of light sources, such as the lighting in your office or at your workstation. Different types of lighting affect the cast reflected on your monitor. *Cold* light (Cool White Fluorescent or Fluorescent Three-band), for example, casts a violet tint, so it reflects from white with a bluish tinge. *Warm* light reflects with more of a red tinge. You can use the slider (that appears when you select the Monitor white point radio button) to compensate for the type of lighting at your workstation, or you can simply choose a lighting type from the Illuminate drop-down list.

While making your adjustments, click on the Preview button now and then to see how they affect the targets in the upper-left corner of the dialog box, using your hard copy target as a guide. You can get a larger preview (shown in Figure 5-10) by clicking on the button with the magnifying glass icon, making it easier to see how your changes affect the match between the target and your monitor. When you finish making adjustments, click on OK to save your changes and return to the Corel Color Manager main dialog box.

Figure 5-10: Click on the magnifying glass icon to get a blow-up of the target image.

Scanner calibration

The procedure for calibrating your scanner is much like the one for calibrating a monitor. The primary difference is that for scanners, instead of making adjustments for a preloaded target, you first scan the target and then make adjustments based on the scanned image.

If you haven't already done so, find the scanner target in the CorelDraw box. Place it on the scanner bed and fire up Corel Color Profile Wizard. In the Device list, scroll Scanner. Choose a scanner profile from the Profile list and click on Tune. This brings up the dialog box that lets you choose your scanner make and model, or you can type in your own identifying information. Then click on Next.

As we've pointed out several times, different levels of users have different requirements. In version 8 you can click on How To Order a High Quality Target button in this dialog box. If your work requires precision color scanning, you should consider this option.

The ensuing dialog box, shown in Figure 5-11, lets you choose whether to retrieve a prescanned target or scan the target now.

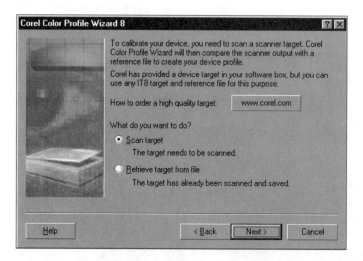

Figure 5-11: To scan the target for the first time, choose Scan Target.

If you've never calibrated the scanne before, you'll need to scan the target before you can proceed. Select Scan target and click on Next. The following dialog box, shown in Figure 5-12, lets you choose the driver for your scanner and, if you want, the TWAIN-compliant scanner interface. You can choose one of the drivers Corel has supplied, but they are all 32-bit drivers. If you don't have a 32-bit scanner, you should use the interface software that came with your scanner. In our case, for example, we use HP's DeskScan.

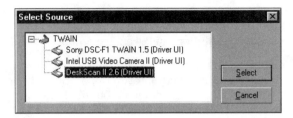

Figure 5-12: Use the Select Source dialog box to select the driver for your scanner.

After you click on Select, Corel Color Manager launches the TWAIN-compliant interface you chose and, depending on which interface software you're using, either prescans the target or waits for you to initiate a prescan.

Here's what we mean. In our case, with DeskScan, the target is automatically prescanned. If you use another driver, it may not prescan the target. In this case, simply click on Prescan (or whatever command initiates the prescan to tell the scanner to make a pass over the target). The purpose of this pass is to enable you to define the area to be scanned. After the target has been prescanned, you use the mouse cursor to position the selection box around the target, as we're doing in Figure 5-13.

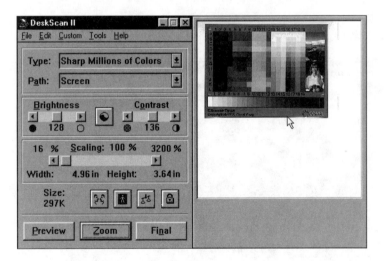

Figure 5-13: Use the scanner interface to define the area to be scanned.

In most cases, the scanner interface automatically adjusts itself to the proper color depth for the image being scanned. However, you may need to adjust the resolution. When calibrating a scanner, you should scan the image at the resolution you'll most often use for final output. This depends primarily on how you'll use the image. Images destined for hard copy, high-quality brochures, for instance, are typically scanned at much higher resolutions than images destined for the Internet. (If you don't know which resolution best suits your application, check out the discussion in Chapter 7 about image resolution.) For most full-color images destined for the printing press, you usually scan at resolutions between 200 and 300 dpi.

To set the image resolution in Corel TWAIN, simply choose Custom from the Resolution drop-down list and type in the resolution in the field below the drop-down list. (If you are using your scanner's bundled interface, you should refer to the documentation for setting resolution prior to scanning.) Now click on Scan (or whatever initiates your scanner software).

Corel Color Manager now asks you about the target — is it the Corel-supplied target or one supplied by somebody else? Some scanner manufacturers and image-editing programs provide their own target. Choose the target you are using and click on Next.

Now you must define the target area so that Corel Color Manager knows which portion of the scanned image to calibrate to. If you placed the target in the scanner straight and defined the scanning area properly, this is an easy task. However, if the target image is crooked, you should first use the rotation buttons (the two buttons with arrows on them) to straighten the target.

To define the target area, click the mouse cursor on the white crop marks in the lower-right, upper-left, and upper-right corners, as shown in Figure 5-14 (and in case you're wondering why just three of the corners, it's because Corel Color Manager finds the fourth one on its own).

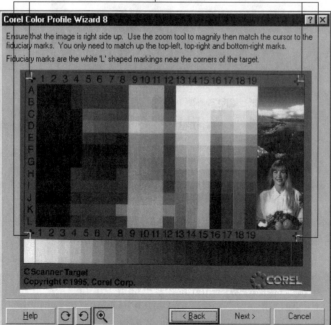

Figure 5-14: Use this dialog box to define the target area.

On the first click, the corner you click in magnifies, as shown in Figure 5-15. Then the mouse cursor turns into an L-shape. Line up the L on the white crop marks and click again. You need to repeat this process for all three corners, and then click on Next.

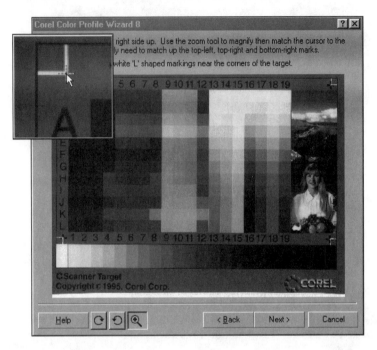

Figure 5-15: When you click on the first corner, you'll see a magnified view of the crop mark.

Corel Color Manager provides two options for calibration, as shown in Figure 5-16. You can either let the software perform the calibration for you (Use Defaults), or you can make some minor adjustments yourself (Use Preset Tonal Settings). The method you choose depends on how happy you are with the results of default calibration.

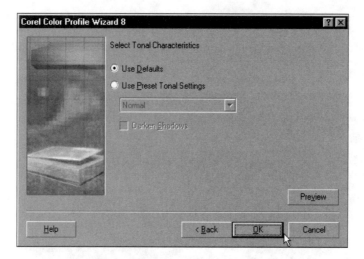

Figure 5-16: The first option accepts the default calibration, and the second option lets you make adjustments based on preset values.

Take the target out of the scanner, and then click on the Preview button in Corel Color Profile Wizard. Now hold the target up to the screen. If you're happy with the match between the target and the Calibrated Image (right), you're finished calibrating your scanner. If not, click on Close and then select Use Preset Tonal Settings. In the drop-down list, choose Lighten, Darken, or Reduce Contrast, or (if the calibrated image looked like it needed it) click on Darken Shadows. Now click on Preview again.

You don't have many choices for adjusting the calibration, so experiment with them, using the drop-down list options in conjunction with turning Darken Shadows on and off, until you get the best match with the target. When you click on OK in the Corel Color Profile Wizard, you are returned to the main Corel Color Profile screen and the profile for your scanner has been saved. You're done.

Printer calibration

Depending on where you get your proofs and color keys, calibrating a proof and separation printer is a little more involved than calibrating a scanner and monitor. If you get color proofs and separation proofs at a service bureau, for example, you'll have to work in conjunction with them to print calibration targets. With that in mind, we'll go over the process for calibrating a proof printer and creating (or editing) a profile. Remember that if your color proof printer and separation proof printer are separate devices, you'll have to go through the process twice, once for each device.

In the Corel Color Profile Wizard main dialog box, scroll through the Device list and choose Composite Printer (or Separation Printer, if you're calibrating it). Then, in the next dialog box, choose your printer make and model, or Generic Profile. Now click on Tune. (Remember, from the discussion about calibrating monitors, that if you choose a Corel Color Manager-supported device, you will alter the default profile for that printer.) Click on Next.

In previous versions, Corel Color Manager provided two methods for obtaining a target: the Scanner Method, which allowed you to use your scanner to measure a printer's output, or using a calibration device such as a Colortron II. The scanner method never was too accurate, so Corel has dropped it. Now you must use a color-calibration device, which you can either purchase or perhaps rent from your service bureau. You can print a target (test pattern file) or use a preprinted one. This procedure can be time-consuming and requires special equipment. You print a target sheet, measure each color square using a spectrophotometer, type the results into a measurements file, and then make some final adjustments. From this point forward, the steps involved depend largely on the type of device you use to calibrate.

Note

When creating your target, you can select the number of patches to be printed, which can be any number from 40 to 200. The larger the number of patches, the wider the range of samples you give Color Manager to calculate your printer's color characteristics. Corel has set the default number at 200 for maximum accuracy, but 60 or more samples provide adequate results.

In addition, when calibrating for final printing press output, the process becomes even more involved. To obtain the best accuracy, you really should print separations from the target imagesetter, and then have your service bureau create a color key (discussed later in this chapter), and use it to take your color measurements.

Secret

When you print the target, Corel Color Manager launches the Print Setup dialog box for your printer. From here you should make the settings with which you print graphics. For example, on an HP DeskJet 855C, we would click on Properties and set the graphics quality to Best. The settings you make depend, of course, on your printer.

Using Color Manager

After you have set up all your profiles, you can use Corel Color Manager in any of the graphics-editing programs in the CorelDraw 8 suite. The procedure is essentially the same in all the programs — you turn on color correction from the Options dialog box (Tools ➪ Options ➪ Color Management) and uncheck Calibrate for Display.

Remember that the purpose of Corel Color Manager is to try to get your monitor to simulate as closely as possible what will finally roll out of your printer, your service bureau's printer, or from a printing press. When you turn on Color Correction, Corel Color Manager tries to show you onscreen how the document will print. The Fast setting performs an approximation to give you a rough idea of how colors will look, and Accurate tries to give you an accurate portrayal. To avoid heart failure, when working on documents you know will be printed on paper, we suggest you work in Fast mode while creating your drawing, and then switch to accurate before printing. The color shift will not be nearly as dramatic. And you can easily go back and tweak colors that don't look right.

Corel Color Manager isn't foolproof. In no way does it relieve you from having to take the standard precautions to avoid unpleasant surprises at the print shop. This includes using CorelDraw's gamut alarm (discussed earlier in this chapter under "Gamut") to make sure you do not select colors beyond the range of the printing press, and printing color proofs before dropping the job off at the print shop.

Color Palettes

Secret

The use of color palettes involves more than just selecting an object and then clicking on a swatch. For example, as you may already know, to change the color of an outline, you simply select the outline and then open the Outline Color or Pen roll-up from the Pen tool flyout. But you can avoid the extra steps of opening the Outline Color dialog box or Pen roll-up by changing the right-mouse button configuration of the color palette options in the Customize dialog box (Tools ⇨ Options ⇨ Customize ⇨ Color Palette). In version 8, this option is turned on by default. However, with the other option — Display Pop-up Menu — Set Outline Color is the first option in the list as shown in Figure 5-17. You can alter this so that CorelDraw changes the color of a selected outline when you right-click on a color swatch. Simply select the Set Outline Color option in the Mouse Button 2 portion of the Color Palette section in the Options dialog box.

Figure 5-17: By default, you get this menu when you right-click on the color palette. You can change this so that CorelDraw colors the outline of selected objects when you right-click on a specific swatch.

Using Color Effectively in Charts, Graphs, and Presentations

CorelDraw is perhaps the most versatile of available drawing programs. Not only is the drawing program itself capable of laying out multiple-page documents such as newsletters and reports, but it also comes with a wide selection of chart and graph clip art you can recolor and use in your presentations. The purpose of charts, graphs, and diagrams is to make concepts easier to understand. The purpose of presentations is to explain or persuade. Color contributes to the clarity, impact, and memorableness of a presentation. Again, when using color in business documents, the primary goal is to convey your message, not make the piece pretty. Color should be used as a tool. Its aesthetic value is secondary.

It's tempting when using color to use every hue in your arsenal. Remember that you want to make your point. This section lists several rules for using color in charts and presentations. The color insert contains several examples of these points.

Use Color to Make a Point. Use color to emphasize a single point—one pie segment, one trend line, one row of figures, one bullet, one bar or column. Unless you are comparing data, avoid showing two sets of data on the same slide. See Plate 5-7 in the color insert.

Use Color to Make Points Stand Out. Use color to make emphasized elements stand out. Use dark colors—black, blue, purple—for backgrounds. Use bright colors—white, yellow, orange—for the most important words and items. And use neutral colors, such as light blue or green, for unimportant elements.

Use Colors to Bring in New Points. Use color to emphasize new points. Assign the brightest

(continued)

(continued)

colors to new data and use duller colors to play down information you've already covered. One of the more common uses for this technique is to "build" slides in which new bullet points are bright and old points are grayed out, or "dimmed." You can also use dull colors to play down negative or unimportant points. Plate 5-8 in the color insert shows an example of using color to bring in new points.

Use Color to Establish Relationships. Use color to identify recurring or related themes. You can, for example, assign green to all positive aspects of your presentation and orange to all negative data. It doesn't take long for an audience to recognize these trends, especially if you point them out early in the presentation.

Use Color to Build Excitement. You can use color to build your presentation to a climax. Start with a dull neutral color and then gradually build to a bright one. Or start with a dark shade of a color and gradually lighten it until it's a bright hue.

Use Color Coding. Much like using color to establish relationships, you can also color code information. In a series of charts you should use the same colors for related data. If, for example, you want to show trends for a certain department throughout your presentation, use the same color each time you display data for that department. See Plate 5-9 in the color section.

You can also add and remove colors from existing color palettes, or create all-new color palettes. We especially like to use this last option to create palettes for drawings that contain colors not on CorelDraw's built-in palettes, or for creating palettes of spot-color tints. Once you've created the palettes, it's much easier to apply tints and custom color to objects, rather than re-creating the colors each time you need them.

Adding and removing colors

Different types of drawings and documents require different colors. In fact, we seldom use the colors on CorelDraw's built-in color palettes. Instead, when working on artwork destined for a printed document, we find it safer (now that we're used to it) to choose colors from color swatch books. The problem with this method is that usually the colors we want are not on the color palette. So first we must create them and then, to use them again in the same drawing (or another one), add them to the color palette.

Whether you are creating colors for print media or for an electronic document, the procedure is the same (except that the swatch book is irrelevant when publishing for multimedia or the Internet).

In previous versions of CorelDraw, you added colors to the color palette from either the Uniform Fill dialog box or the Color roll-up. Version 8 provides a bunch of new ways for adding colors to existing palettes or creating all new palettes. The most notable are the Palette Editor, New Palette from Selection, and New Palette from Document, all on the Tools menu. We'll take a look at the Palette Editor in this section and the other two in the next section. Also, because you can create new palettes with the Palette Editor, we'll look at that procedure in the next section.

To add or remove colors from the default palette (coreldrw.cpl) or any other, the procedure is primarily the same. It all starts in the Palette Editor (Tool ⇨ Palette Editor), which is the dialog box shown in Figure 5-18.

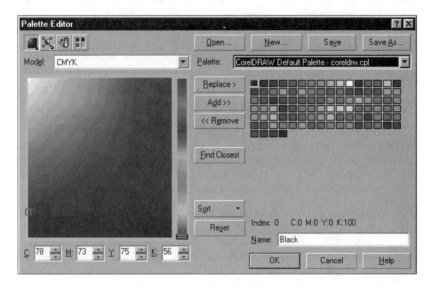

Figure 5-18: Use the Palette Editor to add and remove colors from your color palettes.

The current palette is shown in the Palette drop-down list. To edit this palette, don't change the setting. To edit another palette, choose the palette from the list. This list is drawn from the Custom folder inside the Graphics8 folder. If you have created and saved palettes in another folder, use the Open button to find and open it.

From this point, using this dialog box should be self-evident to most CorelDraw users — most Windows users, for that matter. You choose a color model from the Model list, and then define your color in the window or enter color values below the window. When you finish, click on Add to add the color to the palette. To replace an existing color, select the swatch for the color you want to replace and then click on Replace. To remove a color, select the swatch and click on Remove.

Easy, right? Here are few other things you should know about the Palette Editor:

- Use the Sort drop-down list to change the order in which you sort colors. You can sort by name, hue, brightness, and a bunch of other options.

- Use the Find Closest option to find and replace colors on the palette that are nearest to the one you are defining.

- Use the Name option to name your new colors.

We find naming colors especially helpful when creating palettes of spot-color tints—you know, descriptive names such as PMS 363 90%, PMS 363 80%. This convention makes it much easier to choose the right tints in a color scheme. Names are also helpful when designing a series of drawings based on the same color scheme, especially when the drawing contains many similar colors, such as several shades of green for plants and flowers. Using color names is also helpful if you view and edit documents on computers with different display systems and monitors.

Creating new color palettes

The main reason we like to create new palettes in CorelDraw is that the existing one has far too many colors on it already. We don't like scrolling through them. Many of my documents and drawings don't contain a lot of colors, so we like to create palettes containing only the colors I need. Plus, frankly, Corel's default colors are colors we use often anyway.

In addition to some of the methods in previous versions for creating new color palettes, such as right-clicking on the Color Palette and choosing New, version 8 has several new, slick ways to create new color palettes: Palette Editor, New Palette from Selection, and New Palette from Document. Let's take a look at all three.

New palettes from the Palette Editor

To create a new palette from the Palette Editor, you can either start from scratch or modify an existing palette and save it with a new name. To use the first method, open the Palette Editor (Tools ⇨ Palette Editor) and click on the New button. Then name and save the palette. This will give you a new, blank palette, as shown in Figure 5-19. Now simply define and add colors as discussed in the previous section, "Adding and removing colors." When you finish, click on Save to save your new palette.

To use the second method, from the Palette Editor choose Open. Open the palette you want to modify, and then choose Save As and rename the palette under its new name. Now make the changes to the palette as described earlier in this chapter, and click on Save to save your changes.

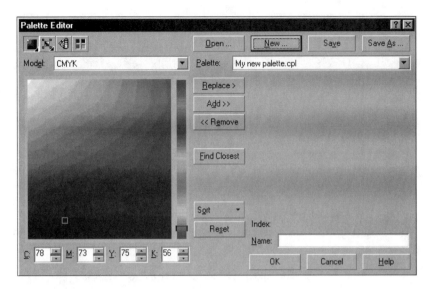

Figure 5-19: Starting a new palette from scratch.

New palettes from selections

This option does exactly what it says — creates a new palette from objects you select within a drawing. It doesn't get much easier than this. Simply make your selection and then choose Tools ⇨ New Palette from Selection. Type a name in the New Palette dialog box and click on Save. CorelDraw creates a new palette containing all the colors in the selection.

To use the new palette, right-click on the existing palette and choose Open. Find the new palette in the Open Palette dialog box and click on Open.

New palettes from documents

This option, too, does exactly what it says. The difference between this one and New Palette from Selection is that it creates a palette from all the colors in the document rather than just from what you select. Aside from that, it works the same.

You can use either of these methods to create a color palette from existing images, such as, say, clip art. Using the colors contained in tried and proven clip art images (such as those bundled with CorelDraw) is one way to make sure that your colors print properly. It's also a way to make sure that objects you create in CorelDraw, such as text and boxes, match the colors in the clip art images you use.

A practice run

As mentioned earlier, a favorite of ours is to create palettes containing PMS tints. This helps us remember which tints we've used and keeps us from having to redefine them each time we need a tint.

STEPS:

Adding PMS Tints to a Palette

Step 1.   In the Palette Editor, click on Fixed Palettes (third button).

Step 2.   Create and save a new palette.

Step 3.   Find the PMS colors for which you want to create a series of tints.

Step 4.   Set the first tint percentage in the Tint field.

Step 5.   Click on the Add button.

Step 6.   Type a descriptive name in the Name field.

Step 7.   Repeat the process, adding colors and tints until you have all the desired colors defined in your new palette.

Step 8.   Save the palette.

That's it! Figure 5-20 shows the Color roll-up containing several new colors we defined for PANTONE Reflex Blue.

Figure 5-20: An example of a new color palette with custom-defined colors.

Color Styles

One of the more exciting new features in CorelDraw 7 was color styles. If you are already familiar with text styles and graphics styles, then using this feature will be a snap. However, in version 8 the Styles roll-up, Color Style, is now a docker.

Basically, this feature lets you assign style sheets to the colors you create in the Color roll-up, the Uniform Color dialog box, or Palette Editor. You can then reuse each color simply by assigning the style to selected objects. You can also create parent-child styles with other similar colors. If you create a style for the color blue, for example, you can create child colors for other hues of blue, such as light blue, sky blue, and so on. The beauty of the parent-child relationship is that should you decide to change the color scheme, for example, from blue to red, all you do is change the parent style; the child styles will follow suit. You can also tell CorelDraw to automatically create styles and parent-child relationships as you work, which we'll show you in a moment.

As with text and graphics styles (both are sometimes called *object styles*), you can create specific color styles for individual templates and copy them between templates. This is a great way to ensure consistent color schemes among documents and to create templates, drawings, and documents with colors you use often.

Creating a color style

It's actually very simple to create a color style. Color styles are created from the Styles docker, shown in Figure 5-21. To open the Styles docker, choose Layout ➪ Dockers ➪ Color Styles.

To create a color style, simply click on the New Color Style button (first button on the left in the Colors style docker). This brings up the New Color Style dialog box shown in Figure 5-22. From here you create a color as you normally would, type a name in the Style field, and then click on OK. (If you forget to name the style, CorelDraw names it Color Style. You can then rename it by right-clicking on the name and then choosing Rename.)

You can edit a color style by selecting it in the list and then clicking on the Edit Style button (third from the left), which brings up the Edit Color Style dialog box. In addition, you can create color styles from existing objects by clicking on the Automatic Create button (last one), which brings up the Automatically Create Color Styles dialog box shown in Figure 5-23. To use this option, you must first select a colored object in your drawing. The style will be based on the color of the object, either fill or outline, depending on which you choose in the Automatically Create Color Styles dialog box.

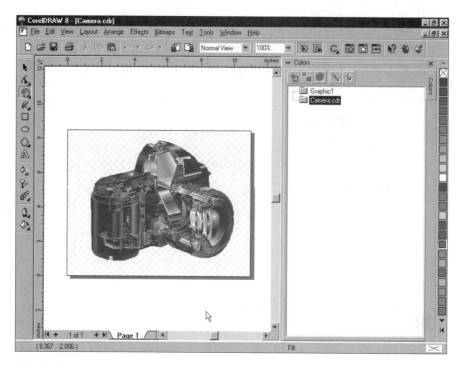

Figure 5-21: Use the Colors docker to create and manage color styles.

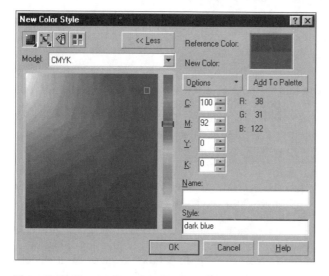

Figure 5-22: Use the New Color Style dialog box to create color styles.

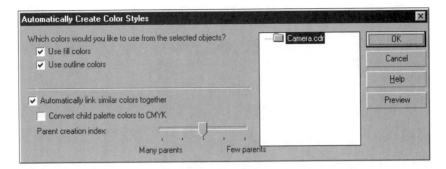

Figure 5-23: Use this dialog box to create a color style from an existing color in your drawing.

From here you can choose to create a color style based on either a fill or outline color, or both. You can also create child styles automatically (explained next).

Creating parent-child relationships

Many drawings call for different shades of the same color. In CorelDraw, related color styles can be linked through a parent-child relationship. You can manually create your own child color styles, or you can have CorelDraw create them for you automatically (from existing colors in your documents).

The manual method

This method enables you to create only one child color style at a time, but gives you far more control over the resulting color associated with the color style than the automatic method. Let's face it, CorelDraw's built-in decisions are not always right for the task at hand—they can't always anticipate your precise needs. To create a child color style, select the color for which you want to create a new child and then click the Create a New Child button (second from the left). This brings up the Create a New Child Color dialog box shown in Figure 5-24. From here you can use the color window to select a hue or the Saturation and Brightness controls to edit the new color. You can also use the Color Name field to assign a color style name other than CorelDraw's default. When you click on OK, the child is added to the Styles docker.

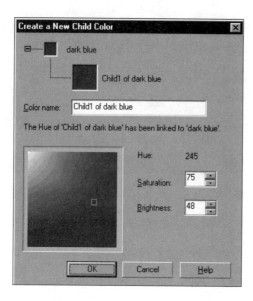

Figure 5-24: Use this dialog box to create the color and name for a child style.

The automatic method

You can instruct CorelDraw to create child styles automatically from an existing style by clicking on the Create Shades button (second from the right) in the Colors docker. This brings up the Create Shades dialog box shown in Figure 5-25. From here you tell CorelDraw how many child colors to create, whether they should be darker or lighter than the current color, and how widely they should vary from the current color.

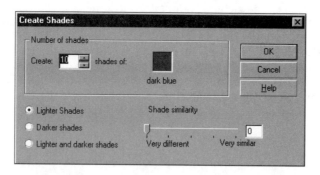

Figure 5-25: This dialog box lets you create child color styles automatically, enabling you to control the number of child colors and the variant colors.

The different options are clearly labeled. About the only aspect of this dialog box that is not readily self-explanatory is Shade similarity. You can adjust the slide to varying degrees of difference and similarity. We've played extensively with this option, and what we've learned is that if you need precision, you should choose your child colors manually. Create Shades is seemingly a bit random, but this option works great if your coloring does not need to be exact. It also works well for creating shades (or tints) of spot colors, saving you from having to do it manually, although you may find yourself engaged in a bit of trial and error before you get the colors you need. But then a big part of graphics design and layout is trial and error anyway, right?

Fountain Fills

One of the most impressive things about computer draw programs is their capability of automatically creating gradient fills, or what CorelDraw calls fountain fills. A gradient is two or more colors blending, or graduating, in steps into one another. One exotic type of gradient is a rainbow fountain fill, which consists of several colors graduating into one another.

If you don't already know how to create different types of fills, you should check the online documentation that comes with CorelDraw. Look under "fountain fills." This section focuses on adjusting fills for just the right effect. It also explains the Interactive Fill tool and the Interactive Transparency tool—two great time-savers.

Before these two tools debuted in version 7, you controlled fountain fills from either the Fountain Fill dialog box or from the Special Fills roll-up. And, when you need the largest set of controls, you still use the Fountain Fill dialog box or Special Fills roll-up. The benefit of using the dialog box is that it provides more controls than the roll-up, such as the capability of adjusting a fill's edge pad and fountain steps (edge pads and fountain steps are explained later). On the other hand, the roll-up provides a level of interactivity not available in the dialog box. In the dialog box, you must make your adjustments, click on OK to apply them, and then reopen the dialog box to make further changes.

However, the Property Bar (in Interactive Fill tool mode) provides most of the controls available in the Fountain Fill dialog box. You can, for example, control edge pad and fountain steps interactively, almost making the need to open the Fountain Fill dialog box obsolete. About the only thing you need to open the dialog box for is to create two-color custom fills or to select one of CorelDraw's preset PostScript fills. Let's talk about those two options first.

Two-color rainbow fills

Rainbow fills enable you to create multicolored gradients. Rainbow fills are configured from the color wheel in the Color blend area in the Fountain Fill dialog box, which you access by choosing the second option on the Fill tool flyout. The Fountain Fill dialog box is shown in Figure 5-26. The three arrow buttons next to the color wheel indicate three options. These options enable you to create a straight blend directly from one color to another, a blend that selects colors clockwise around the color wheel, or counterclockwise around the color wheel.

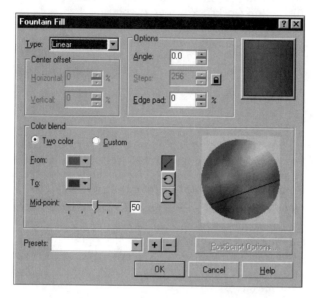

Figure 5-26: You use the options in the Color blend section of the Fountain Fill dialog box to configure rainbow blends.

The following procedure creates a blend:

STEPS:
Creating a Blend

Step 1. Select the type of blend — Linear, Radial, Conical, or Square — from the Type drop-down list.

Step 2. Use the From and To color palette drop-down lists to select the begin and end colors.

Step 3. Select one of the color wheel options: straight blend, clockwise, or counterclockwise. Color Plate 5-10 shows the difference in how the three options create a blend.

Step 4. Adjust the midpoint and angle (if you don't know what these are, read the "Midpoint, edge pad, and fill angle" section that follows).

Step 5. Click on OK.

Preset fills

Presets are preconfigured fills you can apply to objects, eliminating a lot of experimentation. The reason we like to use presets is that Corel has already optimized them for printing, so we don't get any surprises at the print shop. You apply presets from the Fountain Fill dialog box. There's a bunch of them, and we'll bet you can find one for your needs. Plate 5-11 shows some examples using presets on extruded text.

Fountain steps

Fountain steps refers to the number of increments in the fill, or the number of gradation steps from one color to another. Changing the number of steps affects the fill in two ways: It can increase the overall quality of the fill, and it can actually change the overall look of the blend. Using many steps creates a smooth flow in the blend from one color to another. Using fewer steps creates a banding effect, making the gradation increments more apparent.

You have two ways to change fountain steps: either from the Fountain Fill dialog box, or from the Property Bar when using the Interactive Blend tool. Because the major focus of this book is to show you how to create artwork in CorelDraw more efficiently, let's look at changing fountain steps from the Property Bar.

Depending on whether you select an object that already has a fountain fill or one that has a solid fill, when you select the Interactive Fill tool from the toolbox, the Property Bar may or may not show the Fountain Step option (last option on the right end). Fountain Step becomes available when you select Fountain Fill from the Property Bar with the Interactive Fill tool selected. To change the number of fountain steps, click on the Fountain Step Lock/Unlock button, and then use the controls to set the number of steps. Your changes show onscreen automatically.

Secret

As with all of your work in CorelDraw, when working with fountain fills you must be mindful of the difference between what's displayed on your monitor and what will finally roll off the printing press. By default, CorelDraw displays only 50 fountain steps. If you set your fountain steps higher than 50, you won't see the difference. The reason for the default of 50 is twofold. One, the higher the number of fountain steps, the slower your display system redraws them. Two, depending on the resolution of your display system, most computers cannot really display more than 50 steps. How many steps a device can produce depends on its resolution capabilities. Hence, desktop printers, proof printers, and printing presses are capable of reproducing more steps than you can see on your monitor.

Also keep in mind that at some point too many steps is overkill and can even cause some older output devices to crash. By default, when you print from CorelDraw or export to a PostScript format, the maximum number of fountain steps is 128, which is plenty for most drawings. Anything higher than that can really bog down a printing device. You also need to consider some other things when printing fountain steps, which we'll look at in Chapter 7.

Midpoint, edge pad, and fill angle

In some of your drawings you may want your fills to flow from certain points in the selected object rather than from end to end. And in radial, conical, and square fills, you may want to change the center of the fill. When you make these kinds of adjustments, you are changing the fill's midpoint. CorelDraw also lets you change where a blend begins and ends, or adjust the edgepad. And sometimes the effect you're after calls for changing the angle of the blend. In version 7 of CorelDraw you changed the midpoint and edgepad in the Fountain Fill dialog box. Fill angle could be changed in either Fountain Fill or from the Special Fill dialog box. Those options are still available in version 8, but the easiest way to adjust them is with the Interactive Fill tool.

Adjusting the midpoint

The midpoint is where the two colors are at their highest point of blending. In a fountain fill between yellow and red, for example, the midpoint would be where the two colors mix at 50 percent each, or orange. In a rainbow blend, the midpoint is the place on the color wheel halfway between the From and To colors. One of the more common uses for changing the midpoint is to adjust color shading.

Still not sure of what the midpoint is? Perhaps an example will help. Figure 5-27 shows the same rectangle with a fountain fill set at different midpoints. To change a fill's midpoint with the Interactive Fill tool, make sure that you have the tool (and the object) selected, and that Fountain Fill is active on the Property Bar. And make sure that the type of fill you want—Linear, Radial, Conical, or Square—is also selected on the Property Bar. Now simply drag the Fountain Fill Midpoint slider left or right to increase or decrease the midpoint. For a precise setting, simply type the desired midpoint setting in the field next to the slider.

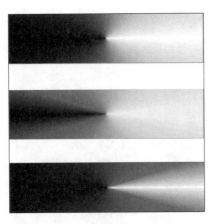

Figure 5-27: Examples of various midpoint settings: 50 percent (top), 10 percent (middle), and 90 percent (bottom).

Changing the edge pad

The term *edge pad* refers to the distance from the edge of the filled object to the point where the fountain fill begins. In other words, you can have a solid color at the edge of the object and a fountain fill nearer the middle, or you can have a solid color on one side of the object and fountain fill at the other.

The Interactive Fill tool enables you to adjust the edge pad in two ways: from the Property Bar or with your mouse. Both methods adjust the edge pad in two directions or, in the case of radial, conical, and square fills (which blend from the center outward), in four directions.

To change the edge pad with the Property Bar, change the value in the Edge Pad field, which is the field next to the Midpoint field. When you hover your mouse over it, the label says Fountain Fill Angle and Edge Pad, which actually refers to both fields. Edge Pad is the one on the bottom. To adjust the edge pad interactively with your mouse, drag on the arrow side of the interactive adjuster (the arrow with a square box on one end and an arrow at the other), as shown in Figure 5-28. As you move the arrow inward, the edge pad increases. As you move it outward, the edge pad decreases.

To adjust only one side of an edge pad, you move the square end of the interactive adjuster, as shown in Figure 5-29. As you can see, you can use this method to create blends in virtually any portion of your selected object. And you can move the edge pad to any portion of the object by moving the square end of the interactive adjuster. You can also create a two-sided edge pad by first moving the square end of the adjuster, and then dragging on the arrow end to shorten the adjuster.

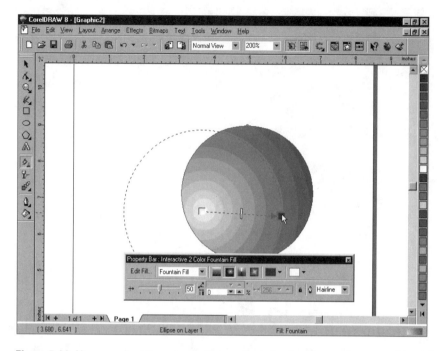

Figure 5-28: You can adjust the edge pad interactively by dragging on the arrow side of the interactive adjuster.

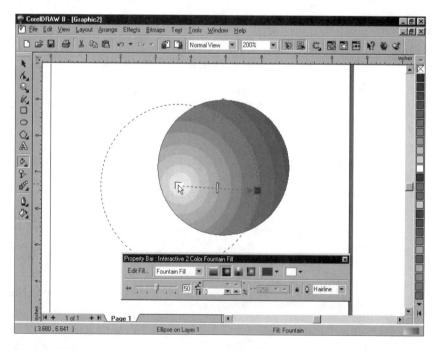

Figure 5-29: To create one-sided edge pads, move the square end of the adjuster, as shown here.

Interactive Fill Tool Magic

Few things in life are slicker than making changes directly on the page with the Interactive Fill tool. Depending on the type of fill you're working with, the Interactive Fill tool gives you a whole mess of options for manipulating your fills. We'll take a brief look at the various options by type of fill.

When you work with a uniform (or solid) fill, you can adjust your colors by percentages, as shown in Figure A.

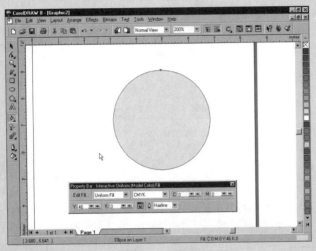

Figure A

When you work with PANTONE colors, the Property Bar lets you change colors and tints interactively, as shown in Figure B.

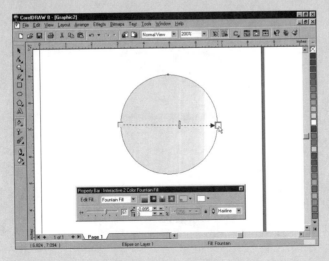

Figure B

When you work with a fountain fill, you can change the edge pad and angle interactively with the adjuster, and make numerous other changes, such as type of fill, with the Property Bar, as shown in Figure C.

(continued)

(continued)

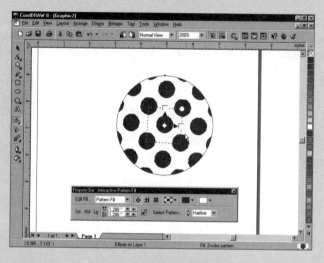

Figure C

When you work with pattern fills, you can interactively switch between two-color and full-color patterns and adjust the size of the pattern, as shown in Figure D.

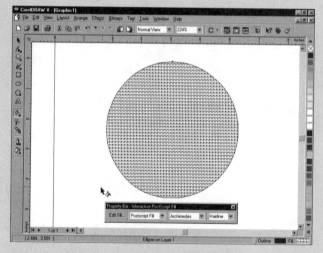

Figure D

Also, in version 8 you can adjust the angle and size of the pattern interactively. Notice in Figure D the small icons to the left of the circle — the three squares and the arc. To increase the size pattern, drag on either the upper-left or lower-right square. Hold the Ctrl key to adjust proportionally. To change the angle, drag one of the in the direction you want the pattern to change.

When working with PostScript fills, you can quickly switch between the various fill types, as shown in Figure E.

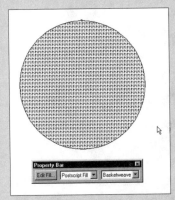

Figure E

Note

If you don't know what some of these fill types are, you can find an explanation of them later in this chapter.

Adjusting fountain fill angles

Depending on the type of fountain fill you are working with, adjusting the angle of the fill can dramatically change the effect of your graphic. In Color Plate 5-12, we adjusted the angle in five different directions to make this point.

You can adjust a fountain fill's angle from the Fountain Fill dialog box or from the Special Fill roll-up. But by far the easiest method is with the Interactive Fill tool. When you select a fountain-filled object with the Interactive Fill tool, you get the interactive adjuster. To change the direction of the blend, simply drag the arrow in the direction to which you want the fountain fill to flow, as shown in Figure 5-30.

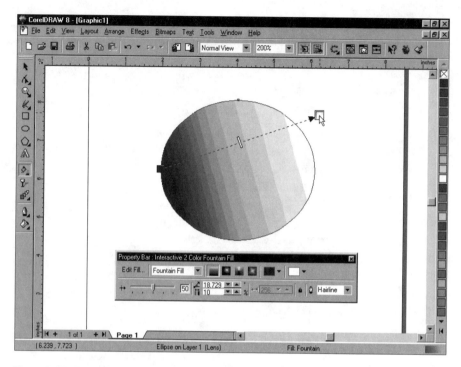

Figure 5-30: To change the angle of a fill interactively, drag the arrow in the direction you want the fill to flow.

You've seen throughout this section how to modify fountain fills in different ways. In many cases you can improve the overall quality of your fountain fills by using a combination of these techniques. Although the fountain fill options are quite helpful and enable you to create effects that might otherwise take a long a time to achieve manually, this feature requires trial and error to achieve that just-right effect, and it takes practice to master.

Creating multicolor fountain fills

Earlier in this chapter we showed you how to create rainbow fills from two-color fountain fills. If you need more control over which colors are contained within a fill and where they appear, you can use the Interactive Fill tool to create multicolored (or custom) fills. Note that you can also do this from the Fountain Fill dialog box with the Custom option, which is well documented in Help. But you get far more control with the Interactive Fill tool.

You won't believe how easy this is. Say you have a two-color blend, perhaps red and orange, and you want to add another color. All you do is select the color in the color palette (or from one of CorelDraw's many other color creation options) and then drag it to the filled object. To add the color in the fountain fill, simply place the tip of the mouse cursor on the interactive adjuster dotted line (precisely where you want the color to appear) and release the mouse button. Voilà! You've got a third color in your fill. You can add as many colors as you like with this method.

Figure 5-31 shows a filled object with several colors added. Each square along the adjuster dotted line designates a different color and acts as control point for moving the color in the fill and adjusting its width and midpoint. With the capabilities of stretching the adjuster with the arrow, moving the square at the opposite end of the adjuster, and dragging on the individual color-control points, you have extensive control over the placement, width, and midpoints of your fills.

To delete a color, simply right-click on the corresponding square.

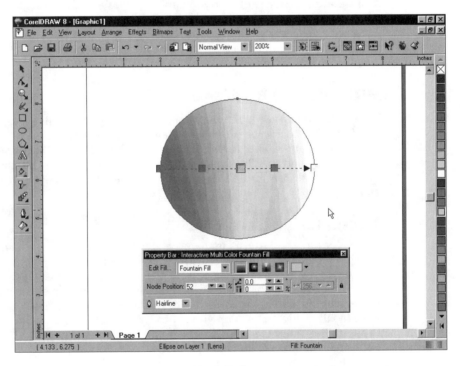

Figure 5-31: An example of a custom blend. Each square control point represents a new color. You can control the midpoint of each color by dragging on the squares.

Predefined Patterns and Textures

As mentioned earlier, one of CorelDraw's strengths is that it provides not only the power the professional artist needs but also many features the nonartist can use. CorelDraw's prefabricated textures and patterns are a case in point. With just a few mouse clicks you can wind up with some rather spectacular effects. But this is not to say that the professional artist cannot also use these impressive fills in his or her artwork, too. They are robust, completely customizable, and can save hours of tedium in trying to create the same or similar effects by hand.

In this section we take a brief look at CorelDraw's Pattern, Texture, and PostScript fills. Plate 5-13 in the color insert shows several examples of the effects available through using these fills, and these examples don't even scratch the surface of what's available. We're assuming that you already know that they exist and that you apply them as you would any other fill — by selecting an object and then selecting the fill you want. Consequently, what we'll concentrate on here is modifying the fills to suit your needs and using them in conjunction with the Interactive Fill tool.

Using pattern fills

CorelDraw ships with two types of prefabricated pattern fills — two-color and full-color. Each type provides rather extensive controls over the size and tiling of the pattern and, in the case of two-color fills, the colors used to compose the pattern. The full-color fills come in two flavors, bitmap and full-color, providing for a wide range of options. We'll look at each type separately.

Two-color pattern fills

Two-color fills are patterns made up of different-colored foregrounds and backgrounds. CorelDraw ships with several two-color fills, and you can create your own or import them from other graphics files, such as other CorelDraw drawings or Photo-Paint .PCX files. You can adjust the size and placement of a two-color pattern with the size and tiling options in the Pattern Fill dialog box, which you get to by clicking on Edit Fill in the Property Bar when the Interactive Fill tool is selected. Figure 5-32 shows the Pattern Fill dialog box in two-color mode.

To use this option, select a pattern from the pattern flyout. Choose whether you want the pattern to be small, medium, or large, and then select the desired colors. If you're not happy with the results of the small, medium, or large options, you can adjust the pattern more precisely with the Width and Height options to set precise measurements for the pattern. Or, as discussed earlier in the "Interactive Fill Tool Magic" sidebar, you can adjust size and angle interactively.

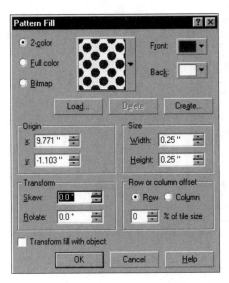

Figure 5-32: The Pattern Fill dialog box in two-color mode enables you to adjust the size of the pattern and the foreground and background colors.

You can further adjust the look of the pattern by adjusting the pattern's Size, Row or column offset, and Origin settings. To make the pattern larger or smaller, change the values in the Width and Height fields. Smaller values make tighter patterns, and larger values make larger patterns. Row or column offset actually lets you shift the pattern tiles in relationship to one another, distorting the pattern, as shown in Figure 5-33. Similar to edge pads for fountain fills, Origin enables you to set where the pattern begins in relation to the object being filled. You adjust the values in the x and y fields to shift the pattern right or left.

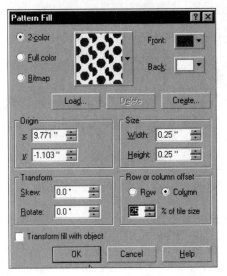

Figure 5-33: Offsetting a pattern's tile by column or row enables you to distort the pattern for some interesting effects.

Finally, you can conform the pattern to the size and shape of your object with the Transform fill with object option. This option tries to make the pattern fit the object. Depending on the shape of your object, sometimes this works and sometimes it just makes a mess.

Secret

You have two ways to add new two-color fills to your collection: Create and Load. Create enables you to design fills by filling in a grid, and Load lets you use another graphics file to create a pattern. (Our favorite way to create new fills is to scan them. We created a wood-grain pattern, for example, by scanning a section of a picture of a bookcase.) Let's look at both procedures.

STEPS:

Creating a Two-Color Pattern Fill

Step 1. Make sure the object for which you want to create a fill is selected. (Note that you can create a pattern without selecting an object by selecting the Pattern Fill button on the Fill tool flyout.)

Step 2. In the Pattern Fill dialog box, select the 2-color fill option.

Step 3. Click on Create. This brings up the Two-Color Pattern Editor shown in Figure 5-34. In this dialog box you create patterns by filling in squares. As you can see, you have three grid size options and several pen sizes available. Pen sizes refer to how many squares are filled when you click in the grid. To erase a filled square, click the right mouse button. Figure 5-35 shows a simple pattern we created.

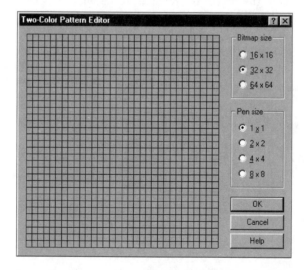

Figure 5-34: Use the Two-Color Pattern Editor to create patterns.

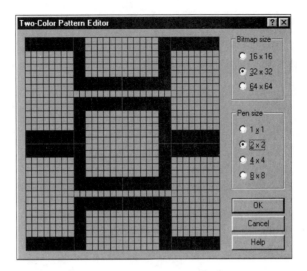

Figure 5-35: Here is a simple pattern created in the Two-Color Pattern Editor.

Step 4.   When you finish creating your pattern, click on OK.

If your pattern is not displayed on the pattern button, scroll through the pattern palette and select it. It will be the last pattern in the palette. To delete the pattern, choose Delete in the Pattern dialog box.

Here's how to import a pattern:

STEPS:

Loading a Two-Color Pattern

Step 1.   In the 2-color section of the Pattern Fill dialog box, click on the Load button.

Step 2.   In the Import dialog box, find the bitmap image from which you want to make a pattern and double-click on it. CorelDraw automatically converts it to black and white. (If you want to use part of a graphic, you should cut the section you want to use out of the graphic and save it in a separate file—before you begin this procedure.)

When you've imported the image, you can adjust the size with the Size or Row or column offset options.

Full-color pattern fills

Full-color fills are similar to two-color fills, except they consist of many colors instead of just two. You can use them to fill objects, or as backgrounds, and you can import your own. You access them by choosing either the Full color or Bitmap option in the Pattern Fill dialog box. Full-color fills are created from vector, draw-type images; bitmap fills are created by importing paint-type images (or pieces of images that you snip out).

As with two-color patterns, you can adjust the size and placement of the pattern with the small, medium, and large options; you can also adjust the pattern more precisely with tiling. And you can create your own patterns by importing virtually any graphics file.

Using textures

CorelDraw's texture fills, sometimes called fractal textures, are bitmaps that work well as backgrounds and as fancy fills for special effects. CorelDraw ships with several textures that you can use in both CorelDraw and Photo-Paint. You can also modify existing textures or create your own.

Each texture has a different set of options and colors, as in the Texture Fill dialog box shown in Figure 5-36. To change a texture, simply change the values in the text boxes, or click on the desired color button. If an option is locked, as designated by the lock icon to the right of the option, you must click on the lock to unlock it. To save a texture after modifying it, click on the plus button; to delete a texture, click on the minus button (at the top of the dialog box).

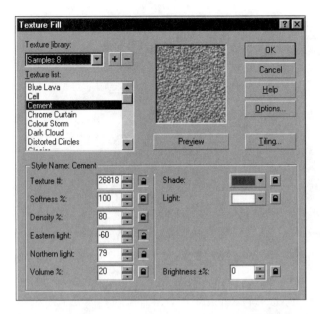

Figure 5-36: Use the Texture Fill dialog box to modify texture fills. The options for each type of fill are extensive and different for each texture. Experimenting is the best way to get the right fill.

PostScript textures

CorelDraw ships with several PostScript textures, such as Bars, Basket Weave, and Bubbles. Some of them are quite useful. Note, however, that CorelDraw does not export PostScript textures to .EPS files well, which makes placing drawings and containing them in other applications difficult, and at times impossible. About all they're really good for is printing from CorelDraw. PostScript textures are accessed by selecting the PostScript Fills option on the Property Bar with the Interactive Fill tool active (or by choosing PS from the Fill Tool flyout).

You can adjust the size and patterns of the fills by adjusting values in the PostScript Texture dialog box (as shown in Figure 5-37). To see them on your display, you have to use Enhanced Mode.

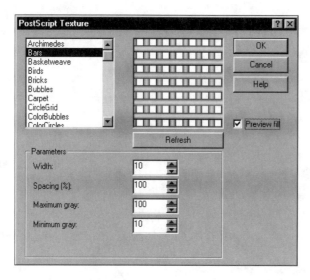

Figure 5-37: Use the PostScript Texture dialog box to edit and apply CorelDraw's PostScript texture fills.

Summary

▶ CorelDraw and other graphics and layout programs support various color models for defining color to accomodate the different ways output devices create color. Printing presses and desktop printers, for example, use percentages of cyan, magenta, yellow, and black (CMYK) to produce color. Computer monitors, on the other hand, use an RGB color model.

▶ The human eye, computer monitors, desktop printers, and printing presses all have different limitations (or gamuts) when it comes to defining color. Hence, programs such as CorelDraw provide color-management systems to help compensate. CorelDraw uses Corel Color Manager, which relies on profiles of your hardware to help ensure that what you see on your monitor matches what comes out of the printer.

▶ CorelDraw's new Palette Editor enables you to create and save your own sets of colors as custom color palettes. You can then use the palettes in any of your CorelDraw drawings or documents.

▶ The Color Styles feature enables you to create and apply styles to objects, similarly to the same CorelDraw feature for graphics and text styles. As with object styles, color styles can easily be copied between templates, and you can create parent-child relationships between styles for easy updating.

▶ CorelDraw's new Interactive Fill tool makes applying and editing fountain fills — which consist of two or more colors flowing, or graduating, into one another — much more easily than wading into multiple dialog boxes.

▶ CorelDraw's prefabricated fills, patterns, and textures provide quick and easy ways to create dramatic special effects. You can edit the patterns to suit your needs, and you can even add and create your own patterns to the fill palettes.

Chapter 6

Automatic Special Effects Features

Have you ever looked at a document — flyer, poster, magazine ad — and wondered: How did they do that? Often when we see the work of other designers, we are awestruck. Nowadays, however, many of the stunning artistic effects are not necessarily the result of great talent. Instead, a lot of amazing effects can be achieved if you can simply recognize what looks good. Computer graphics programs — once you understand some of their hidden power — have literally given almost everybody the power to create spectacular-looking graphics. And CorelDraw certainly excels in providing tools to help designers whip out some dramatic effects — without needing a lot of art background.

The term *special effects* is a convenient catchall. This chapter is titled "Automatic Special Effects Features" because it covers CorelDraw's automatic drawing capabilities. (Besides, Corel also calls them special effects.) Not only do these features enable you to create special effects, but they also let you perform standard drawing functions — effects that graphic artists take for granted — easily and automatically. Figure 6-1 provides several examples of effects that CorelDraw enables you to perform automatically, without any particular training. You'll find even more examples of various special effects in Plates 6-1a through 6-1e in the first color insert.

Envelope (A),

PowerClips (B),

and Lens (C).

Figure 6-1: Here are examples of three different special effects

The possibilities provided by the special effects options are nearly limitless. This chapter discusses many of them, but mostly it shows you how to use these powerful features. When you've learned how the special effects work, you can experiment further with the automatic draw options to create your own effects.

You'll find all seven special effects options on the Effects menu, as follows:

- **Perspective** enables you to create perspective views, such as objects appearing as though they recede away from you. Simply drag the nodes on a *bounding box*, or the dotted box surrounding the object, to change its view.

- **Envelope** enables you to distort and warp objects in almost any direction by dragging on bounding-box nodes.

- **Blend** enables you to blend two objects into one. You can also use this feature to create airbrush effects and shading.

- **Extrude** creates 3D effects by extruding multiple planes and surfaces from a selected object.

- **Contour** allows you to create contoured duplicates of an object — to either the inside or outside. This is another way to create blends for shading, gradients, artistic frames, and a wealth of other neat effects.

- **PowerClips** is an incredibly useful masking feature that lets you clip objects inside other objects.

- **Lens** enables you to apply special effects to designated areas. A prime example is to use the magnify option to blow up part of a map or technical drawing.

When you master these features, you'll have a new toolbox of effects for sprucing up your documents and presentations. CorelDraw also supplies several interactive special effects tools, which we'll also look at in this chapter. These tools include the following:

- **Interactive Blend tool.** This tool works similarly to the Blend option, except it allows you to create and manipulate your blends interactively, onscreen, with your mouse and the Property Bar.

- **Interactive Distortion tool.** Use this tool to distort any object's shape in just about any way imaginable. This tool actually turns a selected object's outline into a rubber band that you can stretch and bend to your heart's content.

- **Interactive Envelope tool.** This tool expands on the same concept as the Envelope roll-up, except that it provides much more interactivity onscreen.

- **Interactive Extrude tool.** This tool is an extension of CorelDraw's 3D extrude capabilities. Like the Interactive Envelope tool, the Interactive Extrude tool lets you manipulate the effect onscreen.

- **Interactive Drop Shadow tool.** This tool lets you create and manipulate drop shadows onscreen. A drop shadow, of course, makes objects seem 2D by casting a shadow behind an object.

- **Interactive Transparency tool.** This tool lets you adjust the opacity of your fills, making them semitransparent. This is a great way to create overlaying objects that appear to be see-through.

A few of these interactive options are, again, extensions of existing options or options you can control from roll-ups or commands on the Effects menu. Others are standalone effects. As we move through this discussion of effects, those tools, such as Interactive Extrude and Interactive Envelope, that are also roll-up options are discussed together. Standalone interactive effects are contained in their own sections.

In addition to covering these features, this chapter also looks at a few items on the Arrange menu, such as Rotate, Skew, Mirror, and Stretch, as well as the bitmap effects options on the Bitmap menu.

Perspective

This feature is called Perspective because it changes the view of an object. Basically, Perspective enables you to make objects appear to recede away or loom toward the viewer, giving drawings a 3D aspect. You can get a similar effect by rotating and skewing, but not nearly as easily — without trial and error, that is. This feature makes the 3D creation process almost foolproof.

When you add perspective to an object, an eight-node bounding box surrounds it. You then adjust the nodes to change the object's *vanishing point*. The vanishing point is the place in the background or foreground where the object disappears at the horizon.

Perspective drawings can have several vanishing points, as shown in Figure 6-2. You can also adjust perspective by dragging on the vanishing points themselves.

Vanishing points

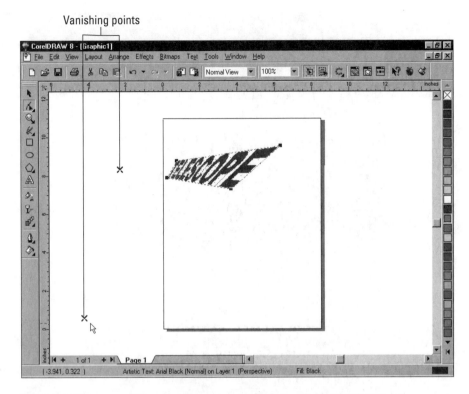

Figure 6-2: When you add perspective, you can adjust an object's vanishing point.

To add perspective to a selected object, follow these steps:

STEPS:

Adding Perspective to an Object

Step 1. Using the Pick tool, select the object to which you want to add perspective.

Step 2. Select Add Perspective from the Effects menu. The object now has a bounding box.

Step 3. You can manipulate perspective by dragging on one of the nodes, as shown in Figure 6-3. As you drag on a node, a vanishing point "X" appears. Move the X to adjust the vanishing point up or down. Depending on where you drag the bounding box's handles or the vanishing point X, your vanishing horizon will move.

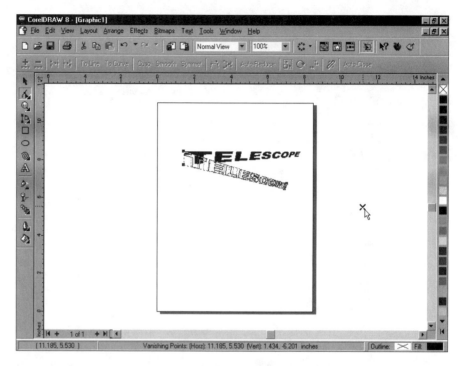

Figure 6-3: To move an object's vanishing point, drag the vanishing point X or the bounding box's handles.

Secret

To create a two-point vanishing horizon, drag directly on one of the square handles on the perspective bounding box or the second vanishing point X, as shown in Figure 6-4. (Each object with a perspective assigned to it has two vanishing points, left and right. If you cannot see one or the other, you can bring either into view in your drawing area by dragging on a corner bounding box handle.) Depending on the size and shape of the object you are applying perspective to, you may have to drag one of the bounding box handles (on the side for which you want) to bring both vanishing point Xs into view.

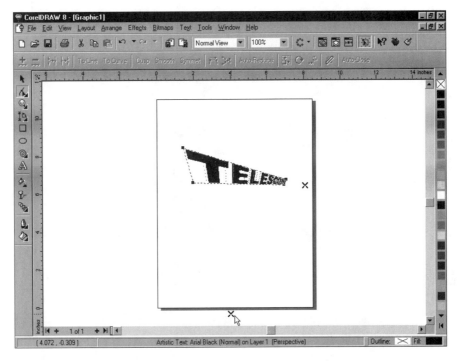

Figure 6-4: Use the second vanishing point arrow to create a two-point perspective.

Figure 6-5 shows the result of creating a two-point perspective on each of two objects (both objects exhibit two-point perspective).

Figure 6-5: For an interesting effect, you can create a two-point perspective.

Envelopes

Envelopes are bounding boxes you manipulate to reshape objects. Envelopes enable you to bend and warp objects in various ways, as shown in Figure 6-6. The possibilities are limited only by your imagination.

Figure 6-6: You can manipulate objects with the Envelope option in many creative ways.

The Envelope roll-up, shown in Figure 6-7, shows four options as icons: Straight Line, Single Arc, Two Curve, and Unconstrained Editing.

Figure 6-7: Use the Envelope roll-up to apply envelopes for manipulation with your mouse.

The first three options primarily affect the sides of objects. The fourth option lets you mold the bounding box similar to the way you manipulate points with the Node Edit tool (discussed in Chapter 2). You'll find the fourth option handy for shaping objects to conform to the shape of other objects, such as sculpturing text to conform and fill an outline, as shown in Figure 6-8.

Figure 6-8: You can use the Unconstrained Editing option in the Envelope roll-up to conform objects to selected objects. In this case, the word *Cheese* has been conformed to the shape of the cheese's side.

You can also use one of several preset shapes by selecting the Add Preset option in the Envelope roll-up. Envelopes can be created from individual shapes with Create From, similar to the way you use Copy Style From. An object can have more than one envelope, meaning you can bend an object one way, assign a new envelope, and bend the object another way, while still maintaining modifications from previous envelopes.

Creating envelopes

Here is a brief overview of using the Envelope feature.

STEPS:
Creating and Applying an Envelope

Step 1.   Select the object you want to warp.

Step 2.   Select Effects ⇨ Envelope.

Step 3.   Click on Add New.

Step 4.   Drag a node in the direction you want to distort the object, as shown in Figure 6-9.

Step 5.   After manipulating the envelope bounding box square, click on Apply in the Envelope roll-up. The object warps according to the shape of the selected envelope size.

(continued)

Creating and Applying an Envelope

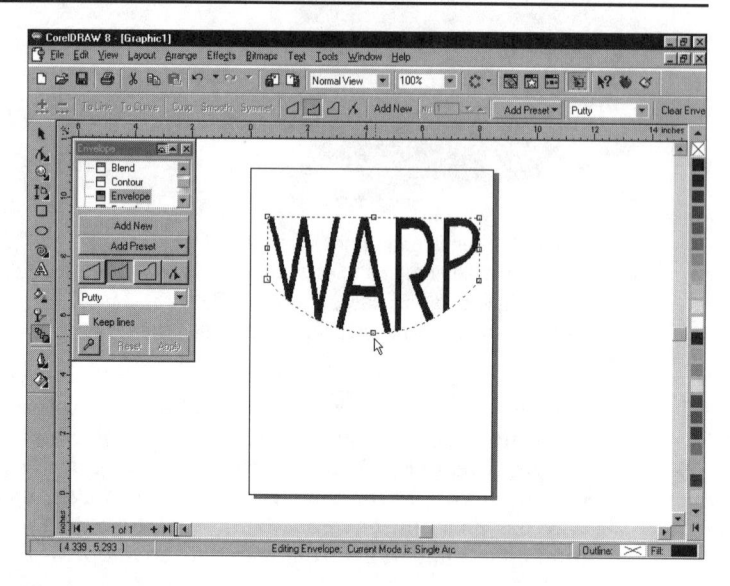

Figure 6-9: To warp an object with Envelope, drag on a node as shown here.

Depending on the mode you are in when you click on Add New, the envelope will behave in a certain way. Figure 6-10 shows how each mode affects the warping of the object. To select a specific mode, simply click on the button representing it in the roll-up. Single Line mode enables you to warp the object with straight edges. Single Arc mode warps an object with curved edges on one side of a control node. Curve mode warps on both sides of a node. And Unconstrained Editing mode enables you to reshape an envelope in virtually any direction, as with the Shape tool, discussed in Chapter 2.

After you apply an envelope, you can apply more envelopes to shape the object further, or you can continue to adjust the existing envelope. When you apply additional envelopes, the previous envelope disappears but the warp remains.

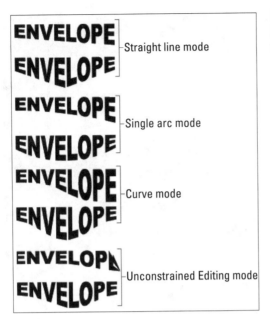

Figure 6-10: Choosing different Envelope modes results in a variety of interesting effects.

Secret

Editing envelope nodes is much like editing nodes on an outline with the Shape tool, as discussed in Chapter 2. The nodes on the envelope bounding box work similarly to Shape tool nodes. In fact, when you double-click on these nodes, the Node Edit roll-up appears, enabling you to set node properties to curve, to line, and so on.

Click on Create From and you can use the shapes in CorelDraw's symbols library to contour text and objects to almost any shape you can imagine. To do so, get the desired shape from the symbols palette, and then follow the preceding techniques.

Interactive envelopes

Primarily, the Interactive Envelopes tool works similarly to the roll-up, with two dramatic distinctions: The changes you make happen dynamically, and you can add and edit nodes as you would with the Shape tool, as discussed in Chapter 2. At first glimpse this may not seem like much, but it adds dramatically to the shape of envelopes you achieve — without going through all the hassle of using multiple envelopes (although you still use multiple envelopes if you need to).

The Interactive Envelope tool works in conjunction with the Property Bar, as shown in Figure 6-11. Notice that you have all the options in the Envelope roll-up and several others, such as Add Node, Delete Node, To Line, Cusp, and other node-editing options. We don't cover these options here because they are discussed in Chapter 2 in the discussion of the Shape tool. We should point out, however, that you add nodes by first clicking on the envelope line and then clicking on the Add Node button. You subtract nodes and make other changes to them on the Property Bar by first clicking on the node (or nodes, by Shift+clicking) to select it.

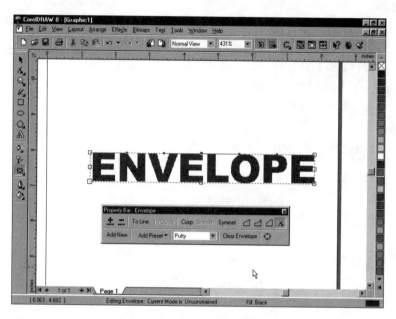

Figure 6-11: The Interactive Envelope tool relies heavily on the Property Bar.

Figure 6-12 shows an envelope we created with the Interactive Envelope tool; it would have taken at least two envelopes using the traditional method. All we did was add nodes.

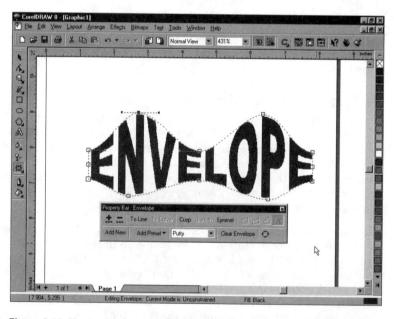

Figure 6-12: You can warp and stretch in all directions with the new Interactive Envelope tool.

Clearing envelopes

If at any point you don't like the effect of your envelope manipulations, you can retrace your steps with Clear Envelope (Effects ⇨ Clear Envelope, or Clear Envelope on the Property Bar in Interactive Envelope mode). This command clears one envelope at a time, starting with the most recent and working backward. You can use this command to undo modifications without losing all of them. Clear Envelope is available only when an object containing one or more envelopes is selected. Another option is Clear Transformations, but it removes all modifications, including any other effects, such as perspectives and extrudes. It also removes font attributes, such as typeface and size. So experiment with Clear Envelope to see how it can help you in ways Clear Transformations can't.

Extrude

Extruding an object gives it the illusion of depth. To create this 3D effect, CorelDraw projects points along the edges of an object and joins them to form surfaces. The results are dramatic, as you can see in Figure 6-13.

Figure 6-13: Use extrudes to give flat objects the illusion of depth.

Extrude works best with text and simple shapes. You control extrudes with the Extrude roll-up and your mouse — or, in versions 7 and 8, with the Interactive Extrude tool. The success of your extrude depends on several factors, including how you set options such as extrude depth, light source, shading, coloring, and rotation.

Granted, creating extrudes with the Extrude roll-up is easier than creating them manually, but it's not always easy to get the effect you're after. CorelDraw ships with several predefined extrudes. To see them, simply click on the Extrude Presets button (first in roll-up), and then scroll through the list.

If you have used previous versions of Extrude, you'll get a kick out of the Interactive Extrude tool. When used in conjunction with the Property Bar, the Interactive Extrude tool contains almost all of the options in the Extrude roll-up, shown in Figure 6-14. The benefit of the Interactive Extrude tool is that most of your changes happen automatically, without your having to click on the Apply button in the roll-up. Also, the Property Bar contains some controls for setting such options as vanishing-point angle, page location, and size of the extruded object with precise values and coordinates unavailable in the roll-up.

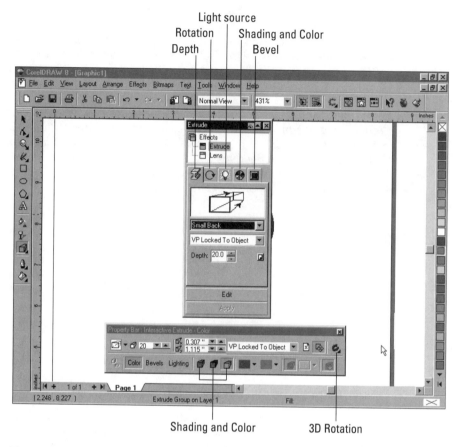

Figure 6-14: The Property Bar (when in Interactive Extrude mode) includes almost all of the options on the Extrude roll-up.

Controlling extrude depth

Extrude depth refers to the length of the extrude planes behind the extruded object. You can control the depth from either the Extrude roll-up or the Property Bar when in Interactive Extrude mode. When you control extrude depth in conjunction with the extrusion type drop-down list, which contains such predefined options as Small Back, Big Back, Back Parallel, and several others, you can dramatically change the size and shape of your extruded planes. You can also adjust the depth interactively when using the roll-up with your mouse by dragging the vanishing-point X away from and toward the extruded object. When using the Interactive Extrude tool, the X controls the length of the extrude, and the slider on the extrusion control line controls the depth.

The options for depth range between 1 and 99, with 1 being the shortest depth and 99 being the longest. Figure 6-15 shows the differences you can achieve by changing the depth. These examples are of the Small Back type. They would look quite different if we used a different type.

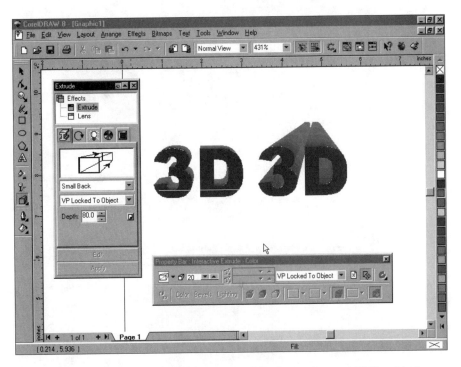

Figure 6-15: The object on the left contains a Small Back extrude set at 10. The object on the right is small-backed with a depth value of 80.

When adjusting your planes with Extrusion Type and Depth, you can also determine the vanishing point angle of your extrude. In other words, you change the direction of the 3D angle, making your extrude appear to go to the right, left, above, or below the extruded object. You can adjust these options from the Vanishing Point Coordinate fields on the Property Bar (third control from left), or you can change them interactively with your mouse by adjusting the vanishing point X, similarly to working with Perspective, as shown in Figure 6-16. In Interactive Blend mode, you would also drag on the X to change the vanishing point perspective.

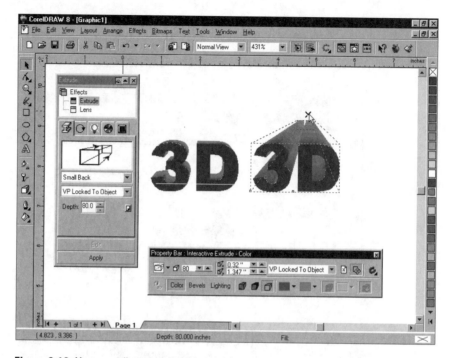

Figure 6-16: You can adjust the vanishing point angle of an extruded object interactively with your mouse.

Rotating extruded objects

Here's a feature that rescues us artistically challenged CorelDraw users — the capability of rotating extruded objects in 3D space. You can pick up an object and move it around — as though you held it in your hands. To do so, click on the Rotation option in either the Extrude roll-up or on the Property Bar. Figure 6-17 shows the Extrude roll-up in rotation mode.

Figure 6-17: To rotate extruded objects, you can use the Rotation mode of the Extrude roll-up.

You have two options for rotating the object: either by entering rotation values or interactively. To use the first method, click on the icon that looks like a sheet of paper on the right side of the roll-up, and then enter rotation values. We prefer the interactive method, which entails moving the large C-shaped object in the center of the roll-up, as shown in Figure 6-18. It's that simple. As you click and drag on the C, each time you release the mouse button, a dotted replica of the object appears over the original to show you how your adjustments will affect the object. In version 8 there is also a second interactive method, manipulating a rotation circle with your mouse onscreen, as shown in Figure 6-19. To enter rotation mode with the Interactive Extrude tool, click on the center X of the object's controls and then manipulate the object using the dotted circle and rotation arrows.

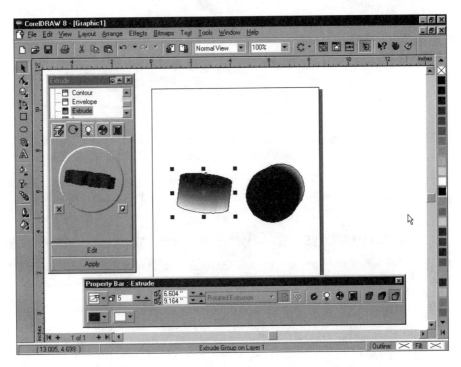

Figure 6-18: The left object in this example is a rotated version of the object on the right.

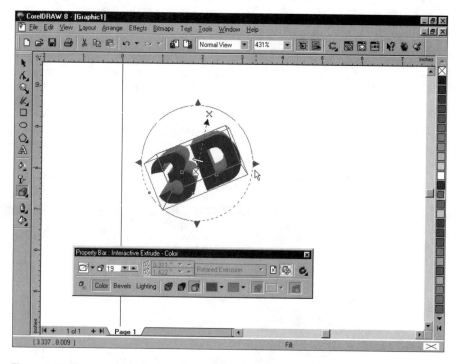

Figure 6-19: To rotate an extruded object interactively with the Interactive Extrude tool, click the center arrow and then use the dotted circle and arrows to rotate the object.

Adjusting shading on extruded objects

When you first start using Extrude, you may not immediately get the effect you expect or want. For example, look at the two extruded objects in Figure 6-20. The left one is an extrude without the shading adjusted, and the one on the right is the result of some minor shading adjustments. Shading can be adjusted either from the options on the Property Bar — Use Object Fill, Use Solid Color, and Use Color Shading — or from the same settings in the Fountain Fill dialog box, which you access from the Fill tool flyout. The first two Property Bar options do very little — they simply apply either the fill of the object being extruded to the extrude planes, or some other solid color. These options are more effective when used in conjunction with Lighting, which the next section discusses.

The third option is more versatile. Click on Use Color Shading in the Property Bar to color shading controls, which are the two-color drop-down palettes next to the Use Color Shading button. From here you can assign From and To colors to the extrude fills, further enhancing the 3D effect, similarly to fountain fills discussed in the previous chapter. These same controls are also available on the Extrude roll-up by clicking on the color wheel button (fourth button from left).

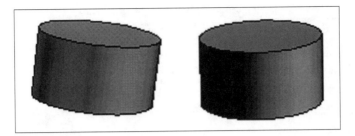

Figure 6-20: Examples of extruded objects with nonshaded (right) shaded planes (left)

Secret

You can set virtually any color you want in the From and To palettes, but you may end up with some rather bizarre shading. A favorite effect of ours is to use the same color in From as the fill in the original object, or the object you've extruded, and then to use white or a light percentage of black in the To palette. This gives the extrude the appearance of 3D shadows.

Note

These two options have different names in the roll-up and on the Property Bar. They are called From and To in the roll-up, and Solid/Shade From Extrude Color and Shade to Extrude Color on the Property Bar. We like From and To better.

DESIGNER

Extrudes almost always look better if you add a hairline to them with the Pen tool. The lines delineate the planes. The hairline is the fifth tool on the Pen tool flyout.

Lighting

The Lighting option allows you to simulate a light source on your extruded object. In fact, you can create up to three light sources. By *light source* we mean making the object appear as though light is shining on it from a specific direction or directions.

Lighting is controlled from the Light Source sheet in the Extrude roll-up. You can access the Light Source sheet in two ways. You can click on the light-bulb icon, shown in Figure 6-21, and the Light Source sheet appears. You can also access the sheet from the Extrude Light pop-up on the Property Bar when in Lighting mode, which you get to by clicking on the Lighting button when in Interactive Extrude mode, shown Figure 6-22. In either case, the lighting options work nearly identically. To create a light source, simply click on one of the 1, 2, or 3 light-bulb icons, and then use your mouse to move the corresponding icon in the preview area to where you want the light source to originate. The preview will provide a simulation of how the lighting will look. To add another light source, click on another light bulb and adjust the source. In Figure 6-23, for example, the object on the right has one light source originating in the upper-right corner. The object on the left has two light sources — upper-right and lower-left.

Figure 6-21: Use the lighting section of the Extrude roll-up to adjust to simulate light source effects.

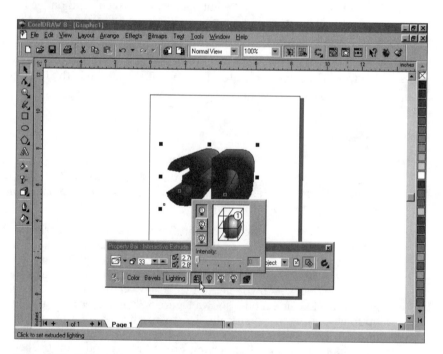

Figure 6-22: When performing extrudes interactively, you can use this pop-up to configure your light sources.

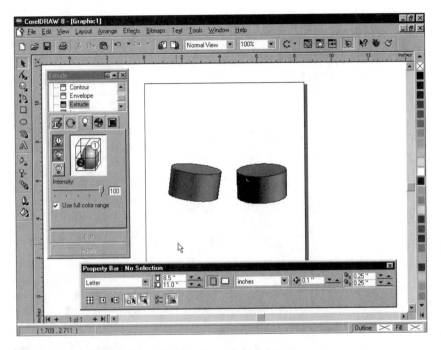

Figure 6-23: Examples of one (right) and two (left) light sources.

Blends

The controls in the Blend roll-up and in the Property Bar (when the Interactive Blend tool is selected) blend one object into another through a series of intermediate shapes. Remember that a blend is a graduation, or gradation, of one object into another. If the blended objects are different colors, the blend steps will also contain intermediate colors. You can specify the number of intermediate steps created and the range of colors blended. You can also fit objects you've blended to a path.

Using blends to create shading

Blending has many applications, but the most common is to create shading, as shown in Figure 6-24 and in the color insert (see Plates 6-2a and 6-2b).

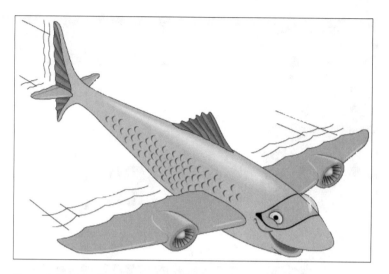

Figure 6-24: One of the most useful applications of blending is to create shading. In the flying fish, for example, the shading effect is achieved by blending an object containing the lighter fill into another shape containing the darker fill.

You may be thinking that blends are a lot like fountain fills (discussed in Chapter 5). In one regard, they are: They enable you to create a fountain fill-like effect with one or more colors graduating into another. However, the difference that makes this feature more appropriate for shading is twofold. With blends you control the shape of the gradation, and by adjusting the blend steps you have much greater control over how shades are placed.

You create a blend for shading as you would any other, except that the shape and placement of your control objects, or the two objects being blended, is critical to the effect you'll achieve. Notice the cool shading on the fish in Figure 6-24.

What you can't see in this picture is that blend steps exist between the outer and center control objects. The blends on the fish are many and complicated. We can get a better view of this concept if we look at a simpler blend. In Figure 6-25, for example, the lemon appears with outlines that show the steps between the outer outline and the final center outline.

To achieve a shading blend, you simply draw your outer and inner shapes, and then assign the outer and inner colors. Remember that the two objects do not need to have the same shape. In fact, you'll get a more interesting and lifelike effect if you alter the shapes. You can also control the light source simulation by placing the center, or lighter-colored shape, off center, or from where you want your light source to emanate. In the picture of the lemon, for example, the light source is set at the top-center of the lemon.

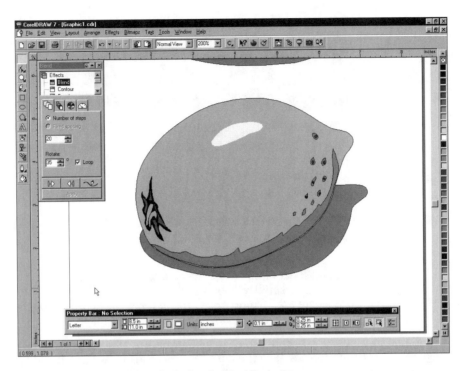

Figure 6-25: A lemon with outlines showing the blend steps.

In a blend, the intermediate shapes are dynamically linked, which means you can edit either of the blended (control) objects and the blend conforms automatically. (Note that you cannot blend objects on different layers. Layers are discussed in Chapter 3.) Say, for example, that in the lemon blend you want to change the size or reposition the lighter portion of the blend. All you do is select the control object and manipulate it — CorelDraw conforms the blend to your changes.

Finally, keep in mind that CorelDraw blends objects in the order they were drawn or selected.

Remember

Using the Interactive Blend tool

The Blend roll-up is pretty handy, but not nearly as slick as the Property Bar in Interactive Blend tool mode. You get all the controls of the roll-up plus a wide range of interactivity, including the capability of creating blends automatically from one object to another, and adjusting the properties of your blends onscreen. The Interactive Blend Property Bar is shown in Figure 6-26.

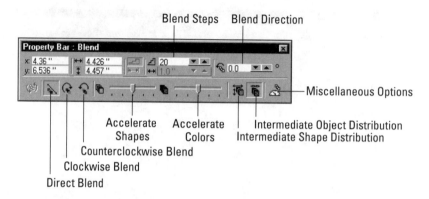

Figure 6-26: The Property Bar in Interactive Blend tool mode gives you great control over your blends.

The slickest aspect of this tool is its capability of creating a blend between two closed paths interactively — by simply dragging from one object to another, as shown in Figure 6-27. Simply select the first path with the Interactive Blend tool and then drag to the other path. It just doesn't get much easier.

In version 8 you can also change intermediate shapes and colors interactively with your mouse. (See the description in the following bulleted list for Intermediate Shape Distribution and Intermediate Color Distribution.) Notice the two triangular control objects in the middle of the blended objects in Figure 6-28. You can move the lower one to redistribute colors and the upper one to redistribute (or reshape) objects.

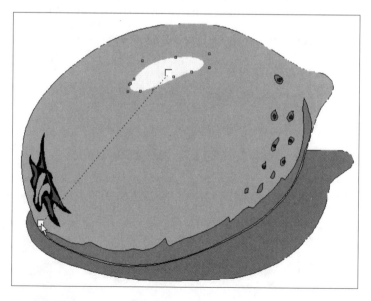

Figure 6-27: To create a blend with the Interactive Blend tool, drag from one object to another.

Intermediate Color   Intermediate Object
Distribution   Distribution

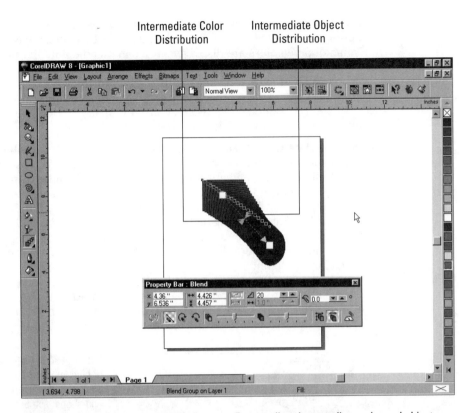

Figure 6-28: In addition to using the Property Bar to adjust intermediate color and object distribution, you can also use these controls on the Interactive Blend tool.

Now we'll look at the other options available on or through the Interactive Blend tool Property Bar and how they affect your blends:

- **Blend Steps/Blend Spacing**. Use these options to select the number of intermediate shapes you want in the blend. When blending on a path (discussed later), you can specify the spacing between the intermediate shapes. Changing the steps and spacing affects the gradation and the angle of your blends, providing control over light source and other properties.

- **Blend Direction**. Use this option to form an arc or spiral between the start and end objects. Specifying negative values changes the direction of the arc or spiral. Basically, this option rotates the intermediate steps between the two control points, modifying the blend in a circular motion. The problem with using this option when shading is that it actually turns the intermediate objects, which can distort the shape of your image. In most cases you'll want to make very small changes with this setting. You'll have better luck rotating blends used in shading with the Loop option (first button to the right from Blend Direction), which rotates at the halfway point between the two control objects. This can help you change light source without a lot of trial-and-error manipulations.

- **Direct Blend/Clockwise Blend/Counterclockwise Blend.** Use these options to specify how colors are blended. If either object has a fill of None, outline colors are displayed. You can blend colors normally with the shortest distance from the start to end colors on the color wheel, or choose a multicolored blend, which blends the colors either clockwise or counterclockwise on the wheel, similar to fountain fills, as discussed in Chapter 5. Rainbow blends can consist of many colors. Use the buttons to blend either clockwise or counterclockwise.

- **Intermediate Objects Distribution/Intermediate Color Distribution.** When you blend objects on a path, these options let you adjust the distribution of intermediate shapes and colors. To blend on a path, select the two objects you want to blend and then click on Miscellaneous Options pop-up, which is the last button on the Property Bar. Select Blend to Full Path. Clicking on this option displays a menu with commands for blending objects along a path. You can edit the path with the Shape tool, and CorelDraw redraws the blend. New Path displays a special mouse pointer for specifying a new path for a blend group. You can also specify a new path for a blend group already blended on a path. Detach from Path separates the blend group from its path. Now use the Intermediate Shapes and Intermediate Color Distribution sliders on the Property Bar. Figure 6-29 shows the results of adjusting these options.

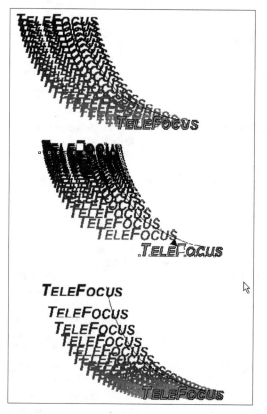

Figure 6-29: Three examples of blending on a path. The first shows default intermediate color and shape distribution. The second shows intermediate shape distribution manipulation, and the third shows intermediate color distribution manipulation.

Remember

- **Map Nodes.** An option you should know about on the Miscellaneous Options pop-up is Map Nodes. Use it to make your blends different shapes by mapping them to various Bézier nodes. Selecting this option displays a special mouse pointer for specifying which node on the start and end objects you want CorelDraw to use as the objects' starting node. You can use Map Nodes on an existing blend group or on a new one before blending.

Note

Depending on the fills, some blends may perform differently from what you expect. For a description of how CorelDraw treats various fills, refer to CorelDraw's Help under the Blends.

Contour

The Contour effect places evenly spaced concentric lines inside or outside the borders of a selected object, as shown in Figure 6-30. The concentric lines conform to the same shape as the outline of the original object. Depending on the options you choose, the lines are smaller or larger, depending on where they are created (inside or outside the object). Figure 6-30 shows an example of a square with a contour applied. Figure 6-31 shows the Property Bar in Contour mode and calls out the options. The Contour roll-up contains the same options in two sheets, one for controlling the contour lines and steps, another for controlling fill and outline colors.

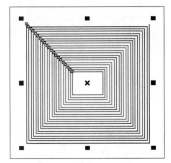

Figure 6-30: An example of an object with the Contour effect applied.

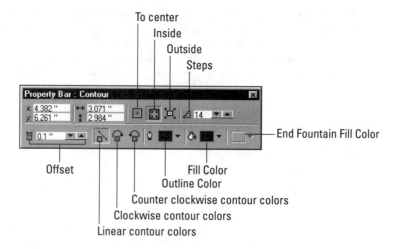

Figure 6-31: The Property Bar in Contour mode.

In many ways, a contour acts similarly to a blend or fountain fill. When you fill the object to be contoured, the spaces between contour lines are filled with colors that follow a progression from the original object to the last contour created. In other words, the shapes are filled along a color continuum — linear, clockwise, or counterclockwise — or color wheel, as we discussed in the preceding chapter on colors and fills. If there is a difference in color between the contour lines and the original object's outline, a second progression occurs for the outlines. You can modify both color progressions to get the look you want by manipulating the steps, offset, and color options.

Drop Shadows

Although automatic drop shadows are common in paint programs such as Photo-Paint and Adobe Photoshop, CorelDraw 8 is the first draw program to implement them, via the Interactive Drop Shadow tool. Drop shadows, of course, are copies of an original object placed and shaded in a manner that makes the object seem 3D, or as if it is suspended in space with a light source shining on it. Adjusting placement and shading changes the simulation of the light source. This is a slick new feature and will save you countless hours of creating drop shadows manually. Figure 6-32 shows a drop shadow and the Property Bar in Interactive Drop Shadow mode.

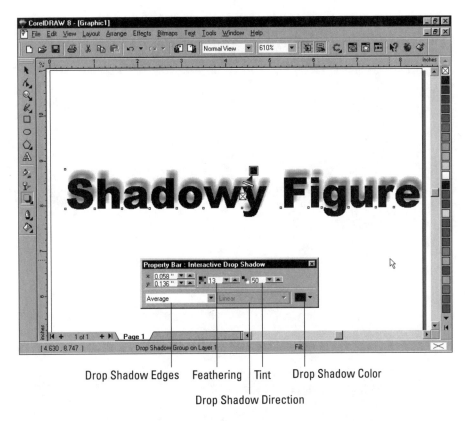

Drop Shadow Edges   Feathering   Tint   Drop Shadow Color

Drop Shadow Direction

Figure 6-32: An example of a drop shadow and the Property Bar in Drop Shadow mode.

There are two ways to use this feature — interactively with your mouse or by making adjustments in the Property Bar.

To use the first method, simply select the object, and then select the Interactive Drop Shadow tool and drag out a drop shadow, as shown in Figure 6-33. Use the black box on the interactive controls to adjust placement of the shadow. Use the slider on the interactive controls to adjust the tint, making the shadow lighter and softer.

Adjusting from the Property Bar achieves similar results and allows for more options, such as adjusting feathering and the shape of the shadows (drop shadow edges).

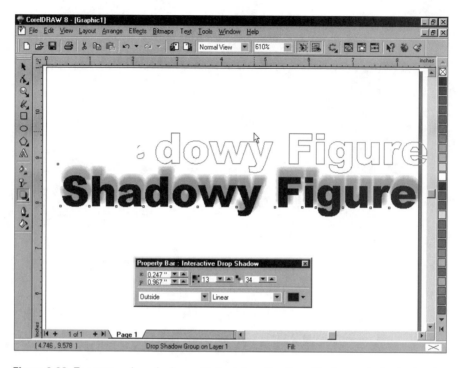

Figure 6-33: To create a drop shadow with the Interactive Drop Shadow tool, simply drag in the direction you want the shadow to appear.

The darkness and placement of your drop shadow is primarily a matter of taste. Adjusting the tint, for example, changes the harshness (or brightness) of the simulated light source. Darker tints simulate a brighter light source. We prefer lighter, or softer tints, for more subtle drop shadows. Another way to adjust the simulated brightness of the light source is by changing the *feathering*. Paint program users are probably more familiar with feathering than are users who work primarily in draw programs. Feathering blurs the edges of the drop shadow, further softening the simulated light source.

You can also affect the direction, or origination point, of the light source by changing the feathering direction with Drop Shadow Direction options on the Property Bar. While we can't determine your taste in drop shadows, we can give you this little bit of advice: When using several drop shadows in the same drawing, you'll get better results, making the drop shadows seem more realistic, if you create the shadows in a manner that makes the shadows appear as though the light source is emanating from the same direction with the same level of brightness.

Distortion

Another new interactive tool you'll have lots of fun with is the Interactive Distortion tool. This tool allows you to manipulate objects in more ways than you can think of. In fact, before going into this discussion of the Interactive Distortion tool, we should point out that the effects you can achieve with this tool are vast. This tool certainly deserves some time for experimentation.

Figure 6-34 shows the Property Bar in Interactive Distort mode. The figure is followed by descriptions of the different options.

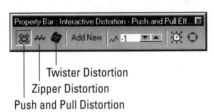

Figure 6-34: The Property Bar in Interactive Distort mode.

Twister Distortion
Zipper Distortion
Push and Pull Distortion

- **Push and Pull Distortion.** This option allows you to push or pull on any node on the object to distort the outline, as shown in Figure 6-35. The outline will distort between all nodes, and the effect is determined by two factors: whether the line between nodes is a rigid, straight line (To Line mode) or a curve, and how drastically you push or pull the node. When you distort the line in this mode, several other options become available on the Property Bar: Add New for stacking distortions, similar to the Add New option for Envelopes, discussed earlier in this chapter; Distortion Amplitude, which lets you control your distortion numerically; and Clear Distortion, in case you change your mind.

- **Zipper Distortion.** This effect is aptly named. It creates a bunch of zipperlike ridges on the outline, as shown in Figure 6-36. When you select this option, the Property Bar changes and provides several options, including Distortion Amplitude, Distortion Frequency, Random Distortion, Smooth Distortion, and Local Distortion. The first two, Distortion Amplitude and Distortion Frequency, enable you to create the zipper distortion numerically. Random Distortion applies the zipper based on preset algorithms built into CorelDraw, which you can then alter interactively or numerically. Smooth Distortion smoothes out hard ridges and points. Local Distortion enables you to use the interactive tools (or numeric controls) to centralize the zipper distortion, or confine it to certain portion of the object.

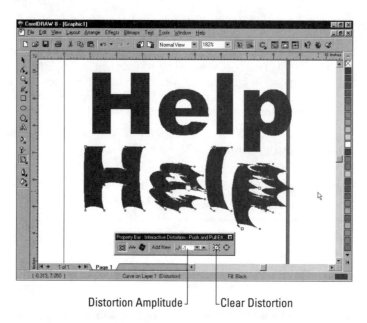

Distortion Amplitude ┘   └Clear Distortion

Figure 6-35: An example of Push and Pull Distortion.

Random ┘   └Local
Smooth

Figure 6-36: An example of the zipper distortion effect.

■ **Twister Distortion.** Use this distortion option to bend and twist an object on any node. The distortion can be clockwise or counter-clockwise and as radical as you want, as shown in Figure 6-37.

Keep in mind that to distort text objects, you must first convert them to curves.

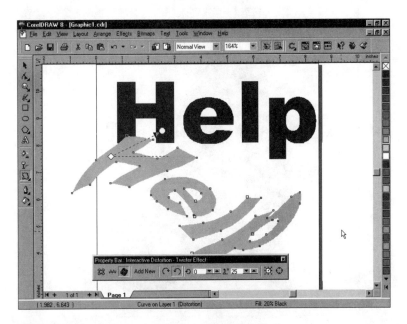

Figure 6-37: An example of the Twister Distortion effect.

PowerClips

Introduced in CorelDraw 5, the PowerClips feature is a great special effects feature that places enormous power at your fingertips. Use PowerClips to paste selected objects into containers, masking out areas of the original object that don't fit into the container, as shown in Figure 6-38.

Figure 6-38: The PowerClips feature enables you to paste objects inside other objects, creating an automatic mask.

In Figure 6-38 we PowerClipped the image of a computer into the letters PC. The image shows through only in the areas contained within the letters; the rest of the computer is masked out. The possibilities of PowerClips are limited only by your imagination. Another effect we like is to use PowerClips for clipping text into an object, shown in Figure 6-39.

Figure 6-39: You can use PowerClip to create all types of effects, such as PowerClipping text into shapes, as shown here.

Lenses

The Lens roll-up contains several lenses that you can apply to objects in your drawings. Applying a lens to an object causes the object to display through the lens. You can only apply a lens to objects with closed paths. Plates 6-3a and 6-3b in the color insert show examples of the Magnify and Tinted Grayscale lenses.

Using the Lens roll-up

Using the Lens roll-up is easy. Simply select one or more objects you want to use as a lens. Scroll through the list of lens effects in the roll-up, and then select the one you want. Depending on the effect you choose, the roll-up provides controls for the effect. Magnify, for instance, supplies a field for setting the magnification level. Tinted Grayscale lets you set the tint color. Transparency lets you set the level of transparency and the lens color, and so on.

In addition to applying basic settings for each lens, you can make several other adjustments from the roll-up, or you can copy a lens or remove a lens altogether. The roll-up's Frozen, Viewpoint, and Remove Face options help you get the exact effect you want for any type of lens. The first option, Frozen, captures the lens's current contents so that you can move the lens and a copy of the contents beneath it. This is a great feature for creating blowups of portions of maps and technical drawings. The second option, Viewpoint, enables you to use the mouse to change the area covered by the lens. You can move the viewpoint to display a specific part of a drawing through a lens without having to move the lens. The third option, Remove Face, enables you to show a lens only where it covers other objects. In other words, blank areas are not affected by the lens; for example, you don't get a tinted lens where you don't need it. Copying a lens, of course, enables you to make quick duplicates of lens effects for use elsewhere in your drawings.

When working with the Lens feature, remember the following pointers:

- The object (outline or closed path) you use as the lens cannot be a grouped object. You can apply a lens to a group of objects, however.

- When a lens is applied to a group of objects, it is applied to each object individually. You could get some rather bizarre effects.

Here's some good news. In previous versions of CorelDraw, you could not apply a lens on one layer to an object on another layer. Version 8 changes that. In complicated drawings you may find it handier to place your lenses on a separate layer. If you don't know about layers, you should check out Chapter 3.

Choosing a lens

Lenses are powerful features providing for a wide range of special effects. In this section we've provided brief explanations of what each lens does. But to get a good grasp of how each lens actually works, you should create a lens, place it over an object, and then go through the list in the roll-up, selecting each type of lens and fiddling with the settings. Let's take a closer look at the following ten lens options:

- **Color Add lens.** With this lens you can mix the colors of overlapping objects. The color you choose in the Color box overrides the color of any object under the lens that is filled with a nonuniform fill. If you place a

Color Add lens over an object filled with white, the lens retains its settings; however, the lens color will not display. Basically, this lens lets you tint the objects beneath it with any color (or percentage of a color) you choose.

- **Color Limit lens.** Color Limit works similarly to a color filter on a camera. It filters out all colors under the lens except the one you specify in the Color box. For example, if you place a green lens over an object, all colors except green appear filtered out within the lens area. You control the strength of the filter by the value you specify in the Rate box. A rate of 100 percent lets only green show through. A lower setting lets other colors show through.

- **Brighten lens.** Colors under the Brighten lens are brightened by the factor you specify in the Rate box. You can specify a Brighten rate between –100 percent and 100 percent. At 100 percent, the colors approach white. At 0 percent, the lens has no effect, and at –100 percent, the colors approach black. You can use this effect for highlighting portions of an image, as shown in Figure 6-40. You can also use this option to correct output brightness. Consider using this lens if one object or area prints too dark or too light.

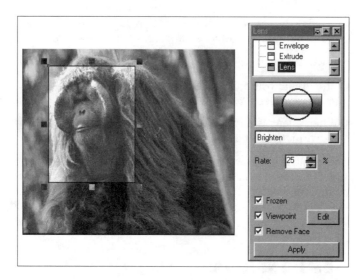

Figure 6-40: Use the Brighten lens to highlight portions of an image.

- **Custom Color Map lens.** This lens sets all underlying colors to a color range between any two colors you select in the To and From palettes. You can also choose the progression between the colors. By default, the lens uses a direct route between the two colors. However, you can create interesting effects by selecting the Forward Rainbow or Reverse Rainbow options. These options map colors using a progression that follows a forward or backward route through the spectrum between the two colors you've selected. Areas of the lens that do not cover other objects are filled with the color at the end of the color map.

- **Fish Eye lens.** Fish Eye distorts and either magnifies or shrinks the objects behind it, depending on the percentage value you specify in the Rate box. Lenses with positive rates distort and magnify objects by increasing amounts as their rate settings progress from 1 to 1,000. Lenses with negative rates shrink and distort objects by increasing amounts as their rate settings progress from –1 to –1,000. A rate of 0 results in no change to the appearance of objects behind the lens.

- **Heatmap lens.** This lens changes colors to those in a predefined Heatmap palette, creating a heatmap or infrared look. Bright, or hot, colors are mapped to hot colors (yellow, orange), and dark colors are mapped to cooler colors (blue, cyan, red, and purple). The palette rotation value determines where the color mapping begins. For example, a value of 0 or 100 percent causes mapping to begin at the start of the palette (white) and move to the right (through cyan, blue, and so on). A value of 50 percent causes mapping to begin halfway through the palette (red) and move to the right and then back to the start of the palette. You'll get some interesting effects from this lens.

- **Invert lens.** This lens inverts the colors under the lens to their complementary colors based on the CMYK color wheel. For example, red becomes cyan, green becomes magenta, and yellow becomes blue.

- **Magnify lens.** This lens causes the objects under the lens to be magnified by the factor you specify in the Amount box, creating the illusion that you've placed a magnifying glass over the drawing. The maximum magnify factor is 10. Use this option to blow up portions of drawings and images. See Plate 6-3a in the color insert.

- **Tinted Grayscale lens.** Objects under this lens appear as if they've had a tonal scale setting applied to them. Colors under the lens are mapped from the lens color to an equivalent tonal color of that lens. For example, a blue lens over a light-colored object creates light blue, while the same lens over a dark-colored object creates dark blue. You can use this option to create duotones. See Plate 6-3b in the color insert.

- **Transparency lens.** Colors of objects under this lens are mixed with the lens object's color, creating the illusion that you've placed a piece of transparent film over the object. You enter a transparency rate from 1 to 100 percent for the lens object in the Transparency Rate box. The greater the value, the more transparent the lens object. At 100 percent, the lens fill disappears. The color you choose in the Color box overrides the color of any object under the lens that is filled with a nonuniform fill. With the addition of the Interactive Transparency tool, this lens becomes a bit obsolete. The new tool, as you'll see in the next section, is much more adept at creating transparent objects.

- **Wireframe lens.** This lens displays only the frame or outline of the object beneath the lens, removing the fill's outline line weights. If you don't understand CorelDraw's wireframes, you can see what we mean by choosing View ⇨ Wireframe. In effect, wireframes are the bounds within which your drawing objects reside. Placing a wireframe lens over an object gives you the same effect — except only in the area beneath the lens.

Secret

Here's a trick you can use to blow up and call out portions of maps, tables, and diagrams, as the color insert shows in Plate 6-3c. To achieve this effect, you use two lenses, Magnify and Transparency. First we placed the circle path over the portion of the map we wanted to blow up, and then used the Magnify lens set at x2. We then clicked on the Frozen option in the Lens roll-up, which duplicates the area covered by the lens and pastes it into the mask object, enabling us to move the magnified area anywhere in our drawing. (Note that the Frozen feature works with all the lens effects.)

To create the shaded backdrop, we drew a triangle with the Bézier tool, filled it with a light gray, and then applied a Transparency lens set at 75 intensity. Voilà! A professional-looking blow-up.

The Interactive Transparency Tool

CorelDraw's new Interactive Transparency tool lets you apply uniform, fountain, pattern, or texture transparencies to objects with your mouse for some dramatic effects. You control the direction and position of the transparency using transparency arrows, which you drag across the surface of the selected object. You control the opacity of the beginning and end of the transparency using the Property Bar.

To use this tool, start by selecting the closed path for which you want to change transparency. The Property Bar takes on the look and feel of the Interactive Fill tool mode (discussed in Chapter 5), except that you are provided with Opacity sliders (Starting Transparency and Ending Transparency) that control the transparency levels of the fill. Starting Transparency controls the more opaque areas in the fill, and Ending Transparency controls levels in less-opaque areas.

Figure 6-41 (see Plate 6-4 in the color insert) shows one application for the Interactive Transparency tool. In this example, we simply selected the filled object, assigned it a solid fill, and adjusted the level of transparency with the slider.

Figure 6-41: Use the Interactive Transparency tool to place transparent fills in objects.

When working with fountain fills, discussed in the preceding chapter, you can also drag the control arrow across the filled object to control the direction of the fill flow, much like the same feature of the Interactive Fill tool. In addition, you can use the Freeze button (similar to Frozen in the Lens roll-up) to capture the image (or portion thereof) beneath the object containing the transparent fill. This enables you to move the filled object and the captured portion of the underlying object to a new position in your drawing.

Rotating and Skewing Objects

This section discusses CorelDraw's traditional Rotate and Skew tools. You should also check out the new Free Transform tool discussed in Chapter 2.

Although it's easiest to rotate and skew objects with the Pick tool (click twice on a selected object to put it in Rotate and Skew mode), using the Transform roll-up gives you precise control over the amount an object is rotated or skewed by enabling you to enter angles and percentages in text fields. You'll also find performing the same tasks with the Property Bar quite handy.

You can also rotate or skew a copy of an object with the Apply to Duplicate option on the Rotate section of the Transform roll-up or, when working with the Property Bar, by pressing Ctrl+R (Edit ⇨ Repeat) repeatedly. This procedure works well for creating special effects, such as rotating several copies of an object to create a pinwheel effect, as shown in Figure 6-42. Simply set the amount of angle rotation for the first object, and then click on Apply To Duplicate until you have the desired number of copies.

Figure 6-42: Use the Apply To Duplicate option in the Transform roll-up to create a pinwheel effect like this one.

Scaling and Mirroring

This section discusses CorelDraw's traditional Scale and Mirror tool. You should also check out the new Free Transform tool discussed in Chapter 2.

Note

The stretching and mirroring options in the Transform roll-up stretch, scale, or mirror (flip horizontally or vertically) selected objects. Use this command instead of using the mouse when you want precise control over the amount of stretching or scaling. Objects are stretched from both sides of their highlighting box. Values greater than 100 shrink them, and values less than 100 enlarge them.

DESIGNER

To scale an object, enter equal values in the Scale Horizontally and Scale Vertically boxes. With the Leave Original option, you can stretch or mirror a copy of selected objects, which is helpful for creating shadows and other special effects. Creating a shadow may seem like a simple task, but many CorelDraw users don't know how easy it can be with Scale and Mirror.

STEPS:

Creating a Shadow with Scale and Mirror

Step 1.   Create the word or object for which you want to create a shadow, and then enlarge, reduce, or shape it as desired.

Step 2.   If it's not already open, open the Transform roll-up.

Step 3.   Select Scale and Mirror in the Transform roll-up list.

Step 4.   Click on the Vertical Mirror button (bottoms of the two buttons on the list).

Step 5.   Click on Apply to Duplicate. A copy of the original is flipped and placed over the original.

Step 6.   Drag the top object down until the bottoms of the letters are matched up, as shown in Figure 6-43. To constrain the object so that it moves in a straight line, hold down the Ctrl key while you drag the object down. This ensures that you align objects precisely.

Step 7.   Click on the currently selected object to put it in Rotate and Skew mode.

Step 8.   Using the bottom-center arrows, drag to the right or left, depending on the direction you want your shadow to lean, as shown in Figure 6-44.

Figure 6-43: Drag the duplicated mirrored object to the bottom of the original, as shown here.

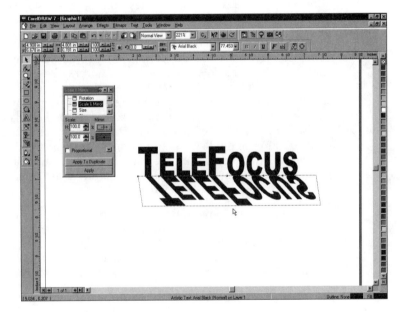

Figure 6-44: Skew the object by dragging to the left or right.

Step 9. Now you can make whatever changes you want to affect the height and length of your shadow. You can also make it a lighter shade of the same color to give it a more realistic shadow appearance.

Bitmap Effects

Someday, graphics programs may treat vector draw-type and bitmapped paint-type images the same way, eliminating the need for two types of graphics programs. In the meantime, CorelDraw has a slew of bitmap editing features, enabling you to perform all sorts of bitmap-editing wizardry right in CorelDraw documents.

Granted, for the most part these effects are merely duplications of the same features in Photo-Paint. The benefit of having these features is that you don't have to do your bitmap work in Photo-Paint and then import the images into your CorelDraw drawings and layouts. This really is a time-saver and enables you to make adjustments to your bitmaps based on how they look in the final document.

Again, most of the bitmap effects are the same special effects plug-ins you'll find on the Effects menu in Photo-Paint. Plug-ins are covered in Chapter 11. This section here concentrates on the application of bitmap effects in CorelDraw. For a more detailed description of how to use the plug-ins themselves, refer to Chapter 11.

If you understand the difference between vector and bitmapped images (see Chapter 8), you may be wondering why you would want to convert vector images to bitmaps. Yes, vectors are more versatile in terms of scalability, file size, and print times. However, here are some other things to consider. First, if you want to use your images on the Internet or in multimedia presentations, the images must be in a bitmapped format, such as GIF, JPEG, or BMP. Granted, CorelDraw's Publish to Internet feature (discussed in Chapter 22) will publish an entire CorelDraw page to HTML format, converting the graphics on the page as needed. But if all you need is a graphic, not the entire page, you'll get more utility from Convert to Bitmap (Bitmap ⇨ Convert to Bitmap).

After an image is converted to bitmap format, you can then change its color model (Grayscale, Paletted, RGB, CMYK, and so forth). For World Wide Web graphics, you would use the Paletted option (Bitmap ⇨ Convert To Paletted) to map the colors before saving the image as a GIF file. You would then use Export (File ⇨ Export) to save the image to the desired format.

However, electronic publishing is not the only reason you would convert a vector graphic to a bitmap. If you know anything about prepress procedures (discussed in Chapter 7), the following may seem obvious. Sometimes you can get better results on a printing press if you assign different resolutions to certain portions of your documents. In a newsletter layout, for example, photographs can be optimized if you set their resolution separately from the rest of the document. You can do this by converting portions of your document to bitmaps.

When you choose Convert to Bitmap, CorelDraw lets you control resolution (and color depth) during the conversion from the Convert to Bitmap dialog box, shown in Figure 6-45. You can also use this feature to resample resolution and color depth of existing bitmaps, or images that you import into your CorelDraw documents.

Figure 6-45: Use the Convert to Bitmap dialog box to convert vector objects to bitmaps, or to resample existing bitmaps.

When you convert text and other objects that contain well-delineated edges, such as text, you should also check either the Normal or Super-sampling Anti-aliasing option. The difference between the two is that Super-sampling provides optimal edge smoothing.

Summary

▶ Use Perspective to create objects that appear 3D by moving toward a vanishing point. Perspective provides two possible vanishing points, enabling you to create objects that seem to move in two directions.

▶ Use Envelope to warp objects in any way you can imagine. CorelDraw has several types of envelopes that let you create straight-edged warps, curved-edge warps, and even freehand or warps with Bézier control points. You can also apply multiple envelopes, enabling you to apply additional warps to previously warped objects.

▶ Use Extrudes to apply 3D planes to objects, making them appear as though in 3D space. Extrude works well on simple objects, such as one line of text or simple shapes. You can control an extrude's depth, shading, and light source to further enhance the appearance of a three-dimensional object.

▶ Use Blend to blend one object into another. The most common use for this feature is to create shading in drawings and fine art. Controlling various aspects of the blend, such as object shape, blend steps, and acceleration, provides extensive controls over your shading and other blend applications.

▶ Use the Contour tool to create concentric lines and fills outside of or inside selected shapes, similarly to using blends and fountain fills.

▶ Use the Interactive Drop Shadow to create 2D drop shadows interactively. You can then use the Property Bar to create that just-right shadow effect.

▶ Use the Interactive Distortion tool to apply Push and Pull, Zipper, and Twister distortion to selected objects. This new tool allows you to distort and reshape in more ways than you can imagine, and then some.

▶ Use PowerClips to mask objects inside containers, such as text outlines or simple CorelDraw shapes (for example, boxes, polygons, or stars). This is a great way to create special effects.

▶ Use Lens to place closed paths over objects and then create one of several effects through the container, such as magnify, grayscale, heat lamp, and many others.

▶ Use the Interactive Transparency tool to apply uniform, fountain, pattern, or texture transparencies to objects with your mouse for some dramatic effects.

Chapter 7

Printing Secrets

In This Chapter

You learn the ins and outs of:

- ▶ Resolution and screen frequency
- ▶ Printing on slide recorders
- ▶ Printing on laser printers
- ▶ Printing on color inkjet printers
- ▶ Getting camera-ready
- ▶ Printing color separations
- ▶ Using CorelDraw graphics in your layouts

Each output device — laser printer, monitor, slide recorder, imagesetter — works differently and requires you to prepare graphics in a particular way. Each reproduction device also has its own requirements, as do the media — paper, slides, transparencies, and so on — on which it prints. For example, a grayscale photograph printed on newsprint requires line screen and resolution settings different from those used to print the same photograph on glossy paper.

With this in mind, note that basically graphics reproduction devices can be separated into two types: hard copy and electronic. *Hard copy* is anything you print out — in one way or another. *Electronic publishing* refers to software reproduction, in the form of Web pages, electronic presentations, and multimedia titles. This chapter tells you how to get the best results in reproducing your graphics on hard copy devices, such as laser printers and printing presses. Electronic output is covered in detail in Part IV.

Note

Most of the discussion of graphics output in this chapter pertains not only to CorelDraw but also to all CorelDraw graphics applications, all graphics applications in general, and all DTP applications, such as Adobe PageMaker, Corel Ventura, and QuarkXPress.

The issues involved in going from computer monitor to paper or another hard copy output medium are many, and your knowledge of them determines the success you'll achieve. As you saw in Chapter 5, transferring color from a computer to some other type of medium brings up many issues, such as color shifts, color models, and color management. Being aware of these potential pitfalls is only half the battle. You must also understand several printing and prepress concepts, such as resolution and screen frequency, and several other issues. In this chapter we'll attempt to clear the fog on the road from computer file to printed document, equipping you for a safer trip.

Screen Frequency and Resolution

More than any other variable, screen frequency and resolution play essential roles in how well your graphics reproduce. The purpose of this section is to familiarize you with these terms and to present an overview of their importance. A combination of screen frequency and resolution affects image quality. Resolution is important because it determines the printer's capability of printing higher screen frequencies.

Screen frequency

Screens and *halftones* (these terms are used interchangeably) are percentages of solids. When you tell a program to shade a box at 20 percent, you are creating a screen. Grayscale photographs, where shades of gray are made up of percentages of black, are also screens. So are the percentages of colors that make up a four-color drawing or photograph. Four-color images are created on a printing press by mixing percentages of cyan, magenta, yellow, and black.

Conventionally, halftones are created with a camera. Fine-mesh screens (measured in *lines per inch*, or *lpi*) are laid over the object to be screened. The mesh separates the image into lines of tiny dots. The size and frequency of the dots determine where the printing press puts ink on paper, thus creating halftones.

Computers and scanners have all but eliminated the need for the fine-mesh screens, but printing presses still work much as they always have. It is important to consider screen frequency when preparing documents for the printing press, for a variety of reasons.

The most important consideration is how ink spreads on different paper types (this is called *dot gain*). For example, taking into account the difference in how soft newsprint and coated glossy paper accept ink is crucial. On soft paper, ink soaks in and spreads, running together. Glossy paper is much more forgiving. Ink tends to sit on top of the coating, eliminating much of the spreading.

To compensate, halftones printed on newsprint require a loose screen, about 75 to 90 lpi, so that ink dots do not spread together, muddying the image. Coated paper, where ink spread is minimal, works best at 133 lpi or higher so that the coarseness of the screen is not noticeable. The trick is to match the lpi to the paper's absorbency so that as little as possible of the screen's coarseness shows, without degrading the halftone through ink spread.

Another aspect of halftone printing affected by lpi (and resolution) is *grayscale*, which most people call *black and white*. Manipulating screen frequency and grayscale can make a tremendous difference in the quality and clarity of each black and white photograph. As we move through this discussion of graphics output, the importance of this relationship between dpi and lpi will become increasingly clear.

Secret

When preparing a document for slide recorders and the print shop, work closely with your service bureau and print shop. Before creating the graphics and laying out the document, decide on which medium (or media) the work will be reproduced (such as paper type, slides, or copier). Then consult your service bureau and print shop regarding the best resolution and lpi settings for that medium. Oh yeah, and don't worry about seeming like a beginner. All professional designers work closely with their vendors to ensure the best results.

Resolution

Most computer users are familiar with printer resolutions. Hard copy output devices — printers, imagesetters, slide recorders, and plotters — print at various rates of *dots per inch* (dpi). Most laser printers, for example, print at 300 or 600 dpi. Imagesetters (photo-quality typesetters) print from 900 dpi up to 3,000 dpi and beyond. The benefit of higher resolution is smaller dots. Smaller dots mean more detail and subtleties — sharper lines and curves — and, more important, cleaner halftone screens and photographs.

Calibrating Your Output Devices with Color Management

It certainly makes sense that in desktop publishing, what you see on your monitor should match (as closely as possible) what rolls out of the printer, imagesetter, or printing press. The closer your computer screen matches the completed work, the less guessing you'll need to do. If what you see on your monitor is precise, you save time by avoiding numerous proofs and revisions.

In other words, the computer display should be WYSIWYG, or what-you-see-is-what-you-get. Unfortunately, as any desktop publisher will attest, there really is no such thing as WYSIWYG computing — not entirely.

However, if all you publish is black-and-white text and monotone graphics, your computer's display does a decent job of representing what pops out of your printer. The problem arises when you work with color. Seldom do the colors on your monitor look the same when printed on a color printer or when you run the print job on a printing press.

(continued)

(continued)

The difference arises from the way each device inherently handles colors, making it nearly impossible for them to match. In fact, the same colors look different on each device, and when you move to a printing press, the type of paper the document is printed on also affects how colors appear. These discrepancies have made getting colors right from a desktop system a grueling (and sometimes expensive) proposition, requiring painstaking trial and error and lots of experience. You'll have much better luck if you calibrate your input and output devices, as discussed in Chapter 5.

If you save your CorelDraw drawings in *vector* file formats, which include CorelDraw's native formats and EPS, you don't need to worry much about resolution while creating your documents. These formats are *device independent*; in other words, they reproduce at the resolution at which they are printed. (An exception, of course, is EPS files in which you embed a photograph or bitmap image. This portion of your EPS file will maintain the resolution of the embedded image.)

However, sometimes it's better to save graphics in bitmap format (TIFF, PCX, or BMP) using CorelDraw's export filters. When exporting from CorelDraw, you are given an opportunity during the setup process to select a resolution. After you choose a bitmap format in the Export dialog box (select File ⇨ Export) and click OK, the Bitmap Export dialog box in Figure 7-1 is displayed. From here you can change the dpi in the Resolution drop-down list. You can also set color depth from the Color drop-down list, enabling you to adjust colors for electronic publishing, including such forms as Web pages and multimedia titles (as discussed in Chapter 21). You can also export in a CMYK format, which contains the information necessary for creating four-color separations.

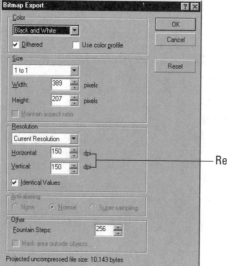

Resolution Controls

Figure 7-1: When exporting bitmaps from CorelDraw, you set the resolution during the export process.

The Convert to Bitmap option (Bitmap ⇨ Convert to Bitmap) also lets you adjust resolution and color depth without exporting the entire document to a bitmap format, as shown in Figure 7-2. You'll find a number of reasons to convert specific objects inside a CorelDraw document to bitmap format, as discussed in Chapter 6. However, exporting drawings as bitmaps provides much more extensive control over the attributes of the bitmap than does converting objects using Convert to Bitmaps. When exporting bitmaps, for example, you can control not only resolution and color depth but also image size and separate settings for horizontal and vertical resolutions. The importance of setting pixel size for an image is discussed in Chapters 21 and 22.

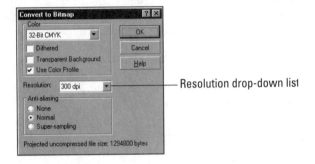

Resolution drop-down list

Figure 7-2: When using Convert to Bitmaps, you can set resolution and color depth.

Printing on Slide Recorders

Slide recorders print documents as 35mm slides. Believe it or not, preparing graphics for slides is easier than preparing them for monitors. For example, you don't have to worry about color depth. Since the primary mechanism in slide recorders are 35mm cameras, these devices can print a wide range of colors.

When using vector, device-independent graphics, don't worry about resolution. The image will print at the highest possible setting. The only type of image you should treat specially is bitmap. The image you see on your monitor is shrunk several times to fit on a slide. Remember that making a bitmap image smaller usually increases quality.

When scanning or resampling an image for slides, be it a line drawing or a 24-bit photograph, set the resolution to 75 dpi and then resize the image on the slide to fit. Higher settings accomplish nothing, except to slow down the slide recorder. If you choose too high a setting, you may overload the slide recorder, causing it to crash. To get the slides to print, you'll have to go back and lower the resolution of the bitmaps.

There is, however, an exception (isn't there always). Nowadays, most people print slides directly from applications designed to do so, such as Microsoft PowerPoint. These programs perform the reduction and resolution increase for you. Sometimes, though, some users do design slides in other applications, such as CorelDraw, creating the slide to scale. As you know, 35mm slides are small. If you design a slide to scale — which means you'll be using small graphics — you will then want to scan or create high-resolution graphics, as high as 1,200 to 2,400 dpi, depending on the resolution of your slides, which we'll look at in a moment.

Line screen and dpi settings for slides are controlled from the Windows printer driver for the slide recorder, which is usually controlled by the service bureau at the time of printing. Actually, when printing slides, resolution or lpi is measured in thousands, or Ks. A 2K slide, then, is 2,000 lines per inch. Slides can be printed at 2K, 4K, 8K, and so on. The higher the K setting, the higher the resolution of the slides. The higher the resolution of the slides, the larger you can magnify the image with a slide projector without degradation. If, for example, you display 2K slides in a large auditorium with an audience of thousands, your slides will appear rough and jagged. You should set the resolution of your slides according to the size of the auditorium and your audience.

Table 7-1 shows usable slide resolutions for various representative audience sizes.

Table 7-1   Audience Size Versus Slide Resolution

Audience Size	Slide Resolution
100 to 500 people	2K to 4K slides
500 to 1,500 people	4K to 8K slides
1,500 people or more	8K to 12K slides

Although Table 7-1 provides some guidelines for printing slides, you should also keep in mind the size of the screen and the room where your slides will be presented. If you have no control over placement of the projector and projection size, you'll have to adjust your slide resolution accordingly. Keep in mind, too, that service bureaus charge more as the resolution size increases. An 8K slide can cost more than twice as much as a 2K slide. If you're printing your slides in-house on a desktop slide recorder, chances are it will print at only 2K, or at best 4K (this resolution is set with the printer driver supplied with the device).

Laser Printers

A laser printer is, of course, a common desktop printer that works much like a copy machine. The laser heats spots on the paper, to which toner sticks. A few years ago, they were the desktop printers of choice, until inkjets got so darned good at providing quality output.

Laser printers versus imagesetters

In the early and mid-1980s, it was common to use 300-dpi laser sheets for camera-ready art. In 1984, when we first started publishing, we used my laser printer to print text and line art and let the print shop shoot the tricky stuff—screens and halftones. At first, we didn't know we had an alternative. Then we noticed service bureaus springing up all over the place. (A *service bureau* is a vendor where desktop publishers and designers go for output not available at the home office, such as imagesetter film, slides, oversized prints. Today, many service bureaus also create CD-ROMs.) One of them offered to print out a sample document for us, and we were hooked. Service bureaus have machines called *imagesetters*, which are high-resolution output devices for prepress.

A tremendous difference separates 300-dpi laser output from 1,200-dpi (or higher) imagesetter output. Today we use my laser printer primarily for printing proofs. We use a laser sheet for the final output only on occasional small jobs that consist of text and a few rules. As you will see, 300- and 600-dpi printers cannot print screens and halftones well, especially if you plan to reproduce them. However, the latest generation of PostScript Level 2 600-dpi printers are getting much better at it. Recently, 1,200-dpi laser printers have become more commonplace, and they're coming down in price.

Here is a list of guidelines for determining whether 300- or 600-dpi output is right for your documents:

- Use a 300- or 600-dpi laser printer for black elements only—text, rules, boxes, line art, and so on—not for screens or halftones.
- Use 300- or 600-dpi output for small jobs (less than 1,000 one-page copies). If you are printing 20,000 one-page copies, the added cost (under $10 per plate) of imagesetter output is negligible.
- If the print shop must screen and place many elements (more than one per page), imagesetter output may turn out to be less expensive than laser output.
- Use 300- or 600-dpi output only if you cannot afford imagesetter output. This is especially true if your newsletter targets the marketing departments of other businesses. Chances are good that they know and can tell the difference.

High-resolution laser printers

Some laser printers boast 600, 800, 1,000, or even 1,200 dpi. However, these figures can be misleading. Often, the processors in these machines are simply fooled into squeezing more toner into smaller areas. And that's the problem with laser printers in general — they use toner. They spread powder on paper. This process has inherent limitations. The dots are big at any resolution, which restricts their capability of creating halftones.

However, the output from some of them is much crisper and cleaner than that from 300-dpi machines. Edges are smoother, sharper. Screens are tighter. Often this output is quite acceptable. Whether you should use a laser printer for final camera-ready output depends on whether you are pleased with the results. We do not use them for photographs. However, if you have one in-house, and the output is acceptable, that is an entirely different situation.

You should never attempt to use laser printer output for four-color documents. Dot placement is not precise enough.

Setting screen frequency

Whether you use a laser printer or an imagesetter, you'll occasionally need to adjust screen frequency. (Note: The terms *screen frequency* and *line screens* can be used interchangeably.) In CorelDraw, as in many other Windows applications, you usually set screen frequency through the Windows PostScript printer driver in the Graphics portion of the Print Setup dialog box, shown in Figure 7-3. You can also set Screen frequency inside CorelDraw's Print dialog box, discussed later in this chapter.

Figure 7-3: You can set your line screens from your PostScript Printer driver's Properties dialog box. Most laser printers automatically install the optimal settings.

You can get to this dialog box by selecting File ⇨ Print Setup ⇨ Properties ⇨ Graphics. To change line screens, choose Use Settings Below and type in the lines per inch you want. Note, however, that this dialog box is slightly different for each type of laser printer.

What screen frequency is right for your printer? If your printer came with its own Windows driver, the installation program usually installs the driver with optimal screen settings. Notice in Figure 7-3 that my TI Pro 600 is set at 75 lpi. That's because it is a 600-dpi PostScript Level 2 device. Most 300- and 600-dpi Level 1 printers work best when set between 50 and 60 lpi. Imagesetter documents bound for the print shop should be set according to the type of paper planned for the job.

When using spot colors, you can adjust screen frequency for each individual spot-color object. The reason for this is that spot colors are often printed in percentages, or screens (as you learned in Chapter 5). Sometimes it's beneficial to adjust screens separately from the rest of the document. Sometimes, for example, you'll need to adjust screen frequency for paper types.

Printing on different paper types is discussed later in this chapter, under the "Offset Presses" section. Be sure to read this section before printing camera-ready art for the printing press.

In most cases, you shouldn't need to change these settings. If you do, however, get to this dialog box by selecting File ⇨ Print Setup ⇨ Properties ⇨ Graphics. Again, different laser printers have different dialog boxes.

Color laser printers

Another type of device that is becoming increasingly popular and less expensive is the color laser printer. Frankly, while these devices are faster than inkjets (discussed next), my experience is that their quality is dubious (though getting better all the time), especially when considering the excellent quality achieved by the newer inkjets. All conditions must be right to get good quality from laser printers, and the output is still much too expensive. Some people swear by them, but if we need quick and dirty copies from a desktop printer, we'll go for an HP DeskJet or Epson Stylus any day — and we'll save a bunch of money to boot.

Laser-printed reproductions

Because of laser printers' resolution and line screen limitations, their effectiveness for reproduction is dubious. Two additional concerns present themselves when you use laser printers for reproduction: expense and cracking.

Expense

Most people think it is less expensive to make copies on a laser printer than at the print shop. Unless your document run is small — say, 100 or 200 copies — this is not so. Toner and laser developer cartridges are expensive, as is wear and tear on your printer. For large runs, the print shop cost (per copy) is small, and it decreases with larger print runs.

Cracking

What would you think if the ink cracked and chipped off your finished documents? Depending on the paper you use, this problem is a distinct possibility. One desktop publisher we know learned the hard way. After paying over $500 for beautiful stone-colored stationery, he discovered that the paper did not hold laser toner. At every fold, the toner fell off, sometimes leaving two or three lines of illegible text. Graphics chipped off as much as a quarter of an inch on either side of the folds. The chipping and cracking were especially embarrassing because the person used the stationery to advertise his desktop publishing business.

One way to avoid this problem is to use paper designed for laser printers. If your local stationer's store does not carry it (most have only white), the store may be able to order some for you. However, because of the enormous amount of toner color lasers put on paper, cracking sometimes cannot be avoided no matter what paper you use.

You should also first test the paper you plan to use for reproduction. Simply print out a page of words and graphics and then fold it several times (or better yet, wad it up). If the toner cracks, use a different paper. Use laser paper even if you do not plan to fold the document. The reader may fold it, and toner may work itself off in other ways. After all that work, your drawings should be durable. They should stand up to time, being passed around, and being thrown into briefcases.

Grayscale images

Just because your scanner, monitor, and graphics package are capable of up to 256 shades of gray does not mean that an equal number of shades will come out of your printer. For example, 300-dpi printers can achieve only about 25 shades of gray, because of their resolution and screen frequency restraints. Their highest screen frequency, before quality degradation, is about 60 lpi. The dots are too big to set screen frequency any higher.

You can calculate what grayscale level an image will print at with this formula:

$$\text{Screen Frequency} = \frac{\text{Printer Resolution}}{\sqrt{\text{Gray Levels}}}$$

In other words, 60 lpi on a 300 dpi printer gives you 25 levels of gray. A number of reasons exist for adjusting shades of gray, the most important being continuous tone quality, or how well graduating shades of gray run together. Other reasons include file size and printing time. The higher the resolution and lpi, the bigger the computer file and the longer it takes to print.

If you set line screens higher than 60 lpi on a 300-dpi printer, the image can become muddied, or blotchy. You can set screen frequency somewhat higher on higher-resolution devices and get improved quality, but for top-quality grayscale images you really should use an imagesetter for final output.

Color Inkjet Printers

Not long ago, you wouldn't see much written about graphics printing on inkjet printers — the output was so poor. However, inkjets have come of age. When you use coated paper designed specifically for inkjet printers, the quality is surprisingly good. So good, in fact, that we have used them for promotions for my own graphics design firm.

With that said, these devices still have some serious limitations. You cannot, for example, use the output for reproduction at a print shop — unless, of course, you use a color copier, which can be quite expensive. You can use the printer itself to make multiple copies of your artwork and documents; however, the cost of ink cartridges and the special paper required to get good output makes this solution cost-prohibitive for all but short runs — less than 100 copies.

If you use color management (discussed in Chapter 5), however, your colors will print relatively true to what you see on your monitor. And the output is respectable.

Setting resolution for inkjet printers

Most of the newer inkjet printers have two resolution settings, 300 dpi for color output and 600 dpi for black and white. Some claim resolutions of 700 or 800 dpi and beyond. When printed from CorelDraw, text and vector graphics print at the highest possible resolution, and bitmaps print at the resolution to which you set them. That does not mean, however, that you gain quality by setting your bitmap graphics to 300 or 600 dpi. These devices have the same screen frequency limitations as the laser printers discussed earlier in this chapter. You'll get the best results by scanning and saving your bitmap images at between 150 and 200 dpi for color graphics and at about 300 dpi for black-and-white images. Anything higher simply takes up too much disk space and memory and takes too long to print for little or no gain.

Most of these devices enable you to set print quality with somewhat generic terms, such as "Draft," "Normal," and "Best." You then match the output quality to the type of paper, such as regular copy or printer paper, premium inkjet paper, transparencies, or glossy paper. My Hewlett-Packard 855C, for example, provides some simple but useful controls for controlling output, as shown in Figure 7-4. You'll get the best results by tweaking these settings and matching them to the paper you use. What we usually do is use a normal setting and copy paper for printing drafts and then bump up the quality settings and paper type for printing the final outwork. You can get to these settings by clicking the Properties button in the Print dialog box.

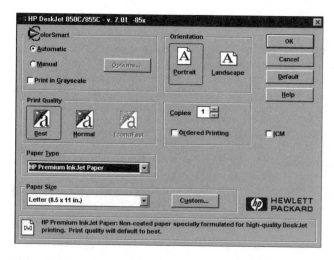

Figure 7-4: You can dramatically affect print quality on most inkjets by adjusting settings in the device's Properties dialog box.

The convenience of these types of printers is that they enable you to easily revise and print materials on demand, as needed, a few pieces at a time. We find this a useful and cost-effective way to print occasional proposals, stationery, and other quick and dirty documents as needed, rather than getting multiple copies at the print shop and then throwing a bunch of them away when they're outdated.

Adjusting screen frequency for inkjet printers

Unless your inkjet printer is a PostScript device, you can't really make adjustments to line screen settings, apart from adjusting the print quality as described in the previous section. If your inkjet is a PostScript device, however, you change line screen settings as you do for PostScript laser printers, as discussed earlier in this chapter.

Oversized-Poster Printers

Occasionally, you may benefit from a relatively new class of print devices, the oversized-poster printers, such as LaserMaster's DisplayMaker. Basically, these devices print on continuous sheets 36 inches wide or more, enabling you to create huge posters and murals directly from your CorelDraw files. In effect, these are really big inkjet printers, at least in terms of the resolution and line screens settings you make in your documents.

When you need just a few posters or other oversized artwork, these devices are much more cost-effective than offset printing, and the output is superb. When designing for these devices, you should use the same settings that you would for your desktop inkjet. You should also get color profiles for Corel Color Manager from the printer manufacturer or your service bureau to ensure good color correction.

Print-On-Demand Devices

Yet another new breed of devices that can make you and your company's life easier is the high-speed print-on-demand color printers designed to turn out small four-color runs. One of the more popular is the Spontane. Basically, these devices replace four-color printing presses when you need quick copies and small quantities. This is not to say, however, that they give you the same quality as offset presses. My experience is that the quality is about half as good — acceptable sometimes.

The thing to remember about these devices is that they all have different requirements that depend largely on the program you use. The Spontane, for example, cannot reliably handle TIFF files. If you plan to use one of these devices, you'll need to work closely with your service bureau.

Getting Camera-Ready

After you complete a drawing, a newsletter, or some other document, you need to make it "camera-ready." Making a layout camera-ready requires attention to detail — fine tuning. This section explains how to successfully transfer documents from your computer to the print shop.

Offset presses

In conventional printing, *camera-ready* means exactly what it implies — creating a layout ready for the printer to take pictures of. The printer then uses the negatives to create metal plates for the printing press. For most print shops, "camera-ready" means no other preparation work is necessary before photographing. If the printer must paste up, shoot halftones, mask, or white-out areas — in short, do anything — you'll incur an additional charge. And you lose control of that part of your layout.

Camera-ready also means having a separate board, or plate, for each color. For example, say your four-page newsletter is black and blue. Your camera-ready art will have eight pages — one for each color on each page. Color separations are discussed in detail later in this chapter. For now, just be aware that they are part of the process of making work camera-ready.

Today, most camera-ready art is created from computer files on imagesetters. Nevertheless, you can still use the conventional paste-up method, and you can adequately reproduce some documents and graphics from laser printer output, especially output from high-resolution laser printers.

Imagesetters Versus Printers

Imagesetters are never used as mass reproduction devices. Instead, they are used for printing camera-ready art for an offset printer or for silk-screening processes. Throughout this book the terms printer and imagesetter are used more or less interchangeably. However, a big difference distinguishes them. Imagesetters are the output devices of choice for desktop publishers and graphics designers. Unlike laser printers, they do not use toner. Instead they use a process similar to photography. The page, a plastic-coated paper (or film), is actually developed in chemicals. The result is higher resolution (because the dots are much smaller). This means cleaner output — crisp and clear lines and type, as well as fine screens and halftones. Also, most laser printers are not capable of hairlines and crisp small (under 10 point) text. Imagesetter output contains finer lines and more detail. Although high-resolution lasers improve subtleties somewhat, they still print dark and are not really capable of hairlines.

Today, several manufacturers make imagesetters, but their output quality levels are comparable. They print at several resolutions from about 900 dpi to over 3,000 dpi. The higher resolution is more expensive and takes longer to print.

Windows 95 supports most imagesetters, except for the latest. The few that are not supported usually supply their own printer driver. Be sure to check with your service bureau to see which imagesetter they use. If a third-party printer driver is required, the service bureau can provide it for you.

When you're making a document camera-ready for an offset printer, you need to adjust the screen frequency appropriately. You should take two factors into consideration: the paper to be used and the camera that the print shop will use to create the negatives.

Compensating for the paper

The most critical issue here is the paper's absorbency. The most significant absorbency factor is whether the paper, or stock, is coated — one or both sides treated with a sealant. Many kinds of coatings are in use. For our purpose, the most common are gloss and dull gloss.

Coated stock is less absorbent than uncoated because ink does not seep into the paper's fibers. Instead, it sits on top of the coating. On uncoated stock, the paper absorbs the ink, spreading out the dots. To allow for the spreading, a coarser screen is needed. Use higher screen frequencies for coated stock and lower frequencies for uncoated stock.

Another factor in paper absorbency is softness. Thousands of paper types continue to flood the market. A good rule of thumb is to use lines per inch frequencies from 70 to 90 for newsprint; 90 to 100 for bond, such as stationery; and about 133 or higher for coated or glossy stock. If you need more precision, your print shop should be able to tell you what screen frequency works best for the paper you choose.

Taking the camera into account

If you will be having negatives and metal plates made from your camera-ready output (a necessity for documents containing photographs and screens), consider the limitations of the print shop's camera. If your screens are tight (say, over 120 lpi), some cameras cannot discern the dots, making the image blotchy and ugly. Other cameras, however, can handle such frequencies adequately. Consult the print shop for the best lpi setting for the shop's equipment.

If your final layout will be from a 300-dpi laser printer, have the print shop prepare all images except monotone line art (and, perhaps, some black-and-white drawings, if you are pleased with how they print). The coarse screens and halftones that 300-dpi devices produce may have been acceptable a few years ago, but not today, not with so many high-resolution imagesetters available at service bureaus.

Printing to film

One powerful alternative to conventional offset printing is *printing to film*. This is exactly what it sounds like—the document comes out of the imagesetter as a negative. The procedure (which is explained in more detail later in this chapter) is not much different from printing positive paper sheets on a high-resolution imagesetter, and the benefits are many. In this section we examine the advantages of printing your documents on negatives.

No matter how good your print shop's camera (and the person operating it) may be, some clarity and detail are lost during shooting. Printing to film ensures the best possible reproduction of your layout (except for, perhaps, full-color photographs, which are still a bit tricky to reproduce on a computer unless you have some experience). When high quality and a professional appearance are important, print your layout to film.

Screens and halftones are screened exactly as you set them. When you print to film, you eliminate the possibility of underexposure, overexposure, camera alignment problems, and a number of factors that can be influenced by human error. Once you learn the intricacies of printing to film, you'll find no substitute for transferring print data directly from your computer to a negative.

Printing to film is most advantageous when you need tight, high-resolution screens and halftones for reproduction on coated paper. Imagesetters are capable of much higher line screen frequencies than the cameras used in conventional prepress printing.

Printing camera-ready art

To print in CorelDraw (and other CorelDraw applications), select File ⇨ Print, which opens the Print dialog box shown in Figure 7-5.

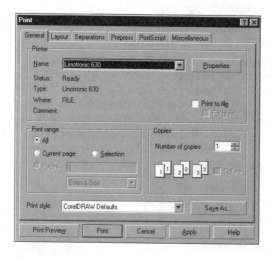

Figure 7-5: The Print dialog box is the gateway to a wealth of print options.

Monotone, spot color, and process color printing

Camera-ready art can be prepared as any of three types: monotone, spot color, and process color. Each type requires slightly different treatment.

To print a black-and-white composite on a laser printer, simply click OK. You can also choose to print a range of pages or to print to a file. Notice also the For Mac option. When you select Print To File, For Mac becomes available. This option prepares the print file for processing on a Mac-based system.

To print color separations, click the Separations Tab. As you can see in Figure 7-6, this is a useful sheet in the dialog box. In fact, it is so powerful that all of its uses are not immediately apparent. Although often you need only to click OK to print a drawing, the process can be a little more complex when you're printing camera-ready art.

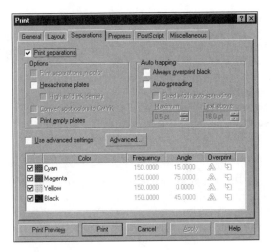

Figure 7-6: The power behind CorelDraw's printing options becomes apparent when you look at the Separations sheet in the Print dialog box.

Preparing camera-ready art for the print shop can entail a number of steps, depending primarily on the drawing and the type of reproduction.

If you are proofing on a PostScript laser printer and printing final output on an imagesetter, the first step is to select the correct printer, the paper size, the resolution, and the line screen, for example. If you are printing to a file or making separations, you have several other options to set.

Secret

When proofing a drawing larger than your laser printer supports, you can use the Fit to Page option in the Print dialog box to force the page to fit the current page size, or you can use the Scaling option in the Windows PostScript printer driver Options dialog box.

Printing options

To set prepress options in earlier versions of CorelDraw, you use the Prepress toolbar in Print Preview. While you can still set these options in Print Preview in Version 8, you may find it much handier and quicker to set them from various sheets within the Print dialog box, using Print Preview only when you aren't sure what the changes you make in the dialog will do to your print run. Let's take a look at the various sheets in the Print dialog box and how to use them.

General

This is a rather standard Print dialog box sheet. From here you perform basic print functions, such as choosing a printer and determining which pages to print. You also set Print to File and the number of copies options from this sheet. If you've used Windows at all, these options are self-evident. (Printing to a file is discussed later in this chapter.)

Some graphics designers print on a variety of printers and imagesetters using different settings for each one, as well as a variety of settings for each type of document. Rather than wading through CorelDraw's voluminous print options each time you print, you can instead create *print styles* for each type of print job. Notice the Print Style option at the bottom of the General sheet in the Print dialog box. After you've set up a specific type of print job, use the Save As button next to Print Style to save the settings. The next time you need to print using the same settings, simply choose the print style you saved. You can save as many print styles as you want.

Layout

The Layout sheet in the Print dialog box, shown in Figure 7-7, allows you to control how your graphic or page prints on the paper, slide, or imagesetter film. The options include repositioning the image on a page, resizing the image, and setting up *signatures*. Let's look at this option and how to use it.

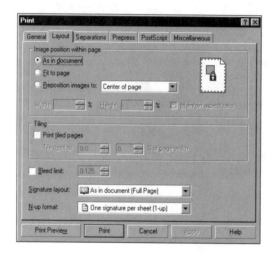

Figure 7-7: Use this section of the Print dialog box to control how a document prints in relation to the output media.

- **Image position within page** allows you to resize and reposition an image on the paper, slide, and film to which you are printing. A handy use for this option would be to force an image to resize to fill a slide or transparency, for instance. The As in document option speaks for itself. Fit to page forces the image to resize to the size of the media on which you are printing. Reposition images to allows you to reposition the document to a specific place on the page, such as upper-left corner, lower-right, and so on. When you click this option, the Position drop-down box becomes available, as do the Width and Height fields, which allow you to resize the image on the page by percentages. When using Fit to page or the Height and Width fields, make sure that Maintain aspect ratio is checked. Otherwise your graphic will be resized disproportionately, distorting your image.

- **Tiling** is used to print documents too large to fit on the printer on which you are printing. The document is printed in pieces, or *tiles,* that you can then glue or tape together. Once you've clicked on Tiling, the Tile overlap and % of page width options become available, allowing you to set the amount of overlap for each tile and the percentage of a page each tile should use. (As an aside, we've tried this in several documents. Matching up the tiles is not easy, making this an impractical means for producing camera-ready art. It's best used for creating mock-ups for proofing.)

- **Bleed limit** lets you tell CorelDraw how far to extend bleeds beyond the edge of the paper. A *bleed* is any object on the page that prints to the edge of the paper. (See the sidebar "Preparing Oversize Pages and Bleeds.") To achieve bleeds on offset presses, the portion of the image being bled is actually printed a bit beyond the edge of the paper, usually a wee bit, between $^{1}/_{16}$" and $^{1}/_{8}$". The print shop then trims the page to it's proper size, slicing off the extended portion of the bleed.

- **Signature layout** lets you use one of CorelDraw's specially designed print layouts to position the image for special treatment, such as folding for a brochure or inclusion in a booklet. *Signature* is the term printers use to define the nature of a layout. A tent-card signature, for example, is used to create those tent flyers you see on restaurant tables advertising wines and deserts. Typically these are created with the information on one side of the fold upside-down, so that the image is upright after folding. CorelDraw's Tent-Fold signature can help you perform this feat without figuring out the logistics prior to printing. (Call me a control freak, but we still prefer to do these types of layouts by hand across a single page. CorelDraw's signature layouts are designed for people with little or no layout experience and don't often provide the precision required by high-end designers.)

- **N-up format** controls the number of pages that print on a sheet of paper or film. There are many applications for this, such as several business cards on the same sheet or placing several pages for a booklet on the same piece of film. The primary advantage of using an N-up format is that it can save production costs in terms of imagesetter output and setup costs at the print shop. You should always consult the print shop for instructions before using this feature.

Separations

The Separations sheet allows you to control many aspects of how your color separations print. Rather than go into a lengthy description here, you'll find information vital to printing color separations later in this chapter in the section "Color separations." You should notice, however, the Auto Trapping section of the Separations sheet. This can save you a lot of time and fuss. It, too, is discussed later in this chapter.

Prepress

The Prepress sheet of the Print dialog box, shown in Figure 7-8, allows you to control the marks used by the print shop to set up your document for printing. These items include crop marks, registration marks, and several others. Let's look at each one separately.

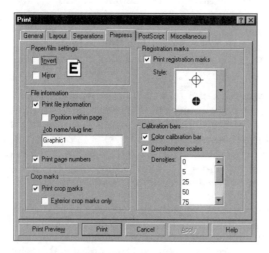

Figure 7-8: Use this sheet in the Print dialog box to setup prepress marks to be used at the print shop.

- **Paper/film settings.** In most cases you print positive images on paper and negative images on film. Remember that negative film is the best way to print in full color. (However, my service bureau likes to control the negative switch on the imagesetter, so we don't make my separations negative.) Note also that if you are creating art for silk screening (T-shirts, sweatshirts, and so on), your separations should be positive. The Invert option causes the image to be printed negative. The Mirror option toggles between emulsion up and emulsion down. (In most cases you will always use emulsion down, which is the default.)

- **File information.** This simply tells CorelDraw to print the name and location of the file, page numbers, and other information on the page, as shown in Figure 7-9. This is simply a housekeeping feature allowing you to match file info to printouts.

- **Crop marks.** To ensure that pages are the right size and that they are straight, the print shop will need some guidance: crop marks. Crop marks are required for almost all offset press runs, including black and white. On letter-sized pages, however, some print shops can use the edges of the laser printout as crop marks. Crop marks are lines in the corners of pages that tell the print shop where to crop (or cut) the pages, as shown in Figure 7-10.

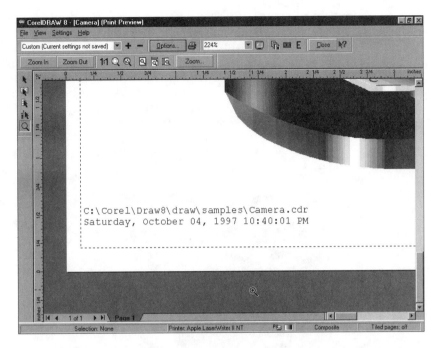

Figure 7-9: Use File information to print file, date, and other information on your plates.

Crop marks   Registration marks

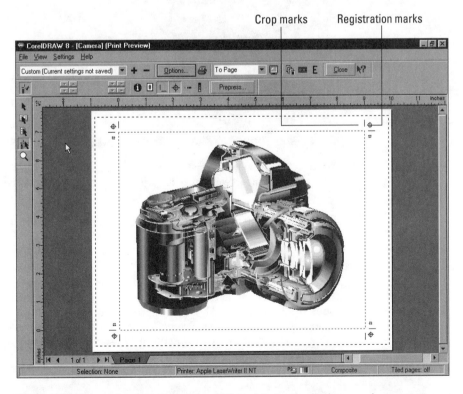

Figure 7-10: Crop and registration marks aid the print shop in aligning your document and color separations properly.

- **Registration marks.** These marks are required for color separations. They are small target-like figures that print on each separation, also shown in Figure 7-10. To ensure proper overlay, the print shop aligns the plates on the registration marks. As mentioned under Crop marks, when printing letter-sized documents on letter-size sheets, the print shop can use the edges of the paper as crop marks. If the document contains spot color, however, the printer may still require registration marks on separations. If so, you can place them directly on the page. You can draw registration marks and place them in white space at the top, bottom, and sides of the page, as shown in Figure 7-11. The printer can mask them out after creating plates.

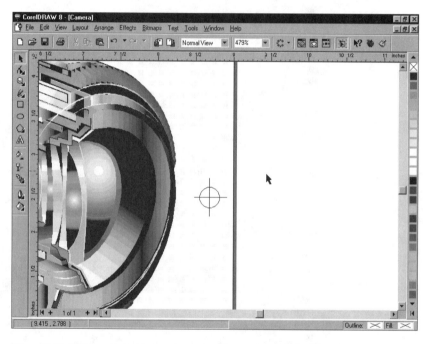

Figure 7-11: When printing spot color pages that are the maximum size your printer allows, you can draw registration marks in blank spaces on your document.

Remember

Remember to place your marks inside a quarter-inch margin. Most lasers cannot print to the edge of the paper.

- **Calibration bars.** See Figure 7-12. These bars help the print shop ensure that inks mix properly. For color documents, click Color Calibration. To get a screen densitometer for measuring screen densities, click Densitometer Scales. These bars are also helpful when printing to a proofing device, such as a dye-sublimation printer, discussed later in this chapter, or when printing color keys, also discussed later.

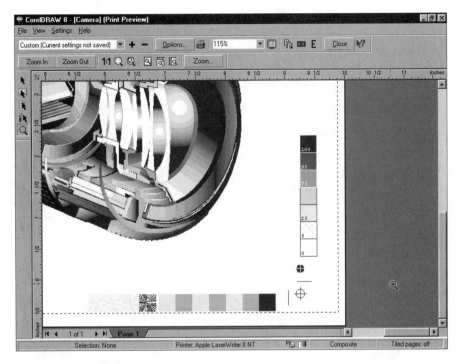

Figure 7-12: Use calibration bars to aid your print shop and service bureau to gauge color and grayscale accuracy.

When your pages are smaller than the printer's paper size, you can use CorelDraw's Crop mark and Registration mark settings, as long as your drawing is at least one-half inch or so smaller than the actual paper size.

Printing Oversize Pages and Bleeds

To get crop marks when printing pages, especially color separations, to the edge of the paper supported by your desktop printer, you really should take your job to a service bureau for output on oversized paper. For example, if your page is 8½ by 11 inches and you need crop and registration marks, your service bureau can print your plates on oversized, or "extra-sized," sheets. Your letter-sized document would actually be printed on 9½" by 12" paper, making space for crop and registration marks. This is also true of legal (8½" by 14") and tabloid (11" by 17") pages, which should be printed on extra-sized paper to accommodate the crop marks.

Another design element that requires special treatment is bleeds, which is an unfortunate term for documents on which the artwork (ink) runs to the edge of the paper, such as the cover of this book. To achieve a bleed, you design your artwork so that it runs slightly over the edge of the page, as shown in the figure. The actual bleed is achieved during trimming. When the print

(continued)

(continued)

shop cuts the paper, it slices off the portion of the artwork that extends past the edge of the page. This method ensures that you don't get any white slivers on the edge of the paper, a possibility were you to design the page with artwork abutting the edge of the paper.

Your bleed doesn't need to extend far over the edge of the paper; about an eighth of an inch will do.

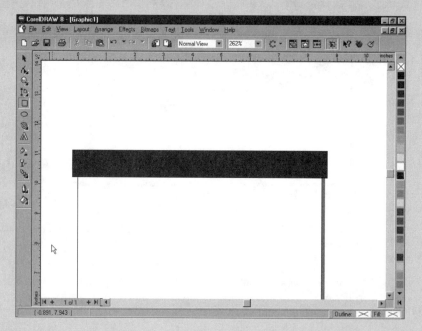

When designing pages on which the artwork extends to the edge of the paper, place the art so that it slightly overlaps the edge.

PostScript

When printing to a PostScript printer (the printer language of choice for high-end designers), CorelDraw provides several options in the PostScript sheet of the Print dialog box, shown in Figure 7-13, to ensure the best quality. Some of the options in this dialog box allow you to resolve issues related to somewhat antiquated technology, such as DCS file formats. We've taken the liberty to skip options we don't think apply to printing documents you are creating today. In addition, many of these options pertain primarily to printing on high-end devices usually found in service bureaus, which we've also left out.

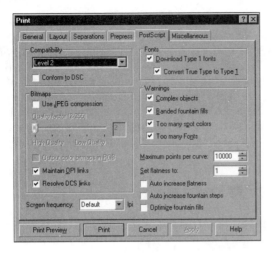

Figure 7-13: Use this sheet in the Print dialog box to control PostScript options.

- **Compatibility.** Nowadays, there are three versions of PostScript: 1, 2, and 3. This option simply enables you to choose the version used by the printer to which you are printing.

- **Screen frequency.** This option allows you to set the screen frequency for the current document. Screen frequency was discussed earlier in this chapter. Remember that screen frequency is usually set according to paper type. Keep in mind, though, that the lower a device's resolution, the lower the screen frequency it can print effectively.

- **Fonts.** Use this option to tell CorelDraw when to download fonts to either the printer or to PostScript print file. In most cases, you would leave this option on. The Convert True Type to Type 1 option is used primarily when printing to a file, as discussed later in this section. (If you don't know the difference between Type 1 and TrueType, check out Chapter 4.)

- **Warnings.** The options in the Warnings section provide two functions: To notify you when a document may not print properly or to notify you when you are in danger of overloading the printer (which can also cause documents to print improperly or not at all.) Complex objects and Too many fonts, for instance, can cause a printer to overload and crash without printing a document or only portions thereof. Banded Fountain fills warns you when your fountain fills will probably not print properly, that your fills will not flow evenly from one color to the next, a phenomena known as *banding* where you can actually see the steps in your fills. This option uses a formula based on the resolution of the output device and the screen frequency that you set in the Screen frequency field in this sheet in the dialog box. Too many spot colors simply warns you as to when it would be more cost effective to use process colors.

Miscellaneous

The options in the Miscellaneous sheet of the Print dialog box, shown in Figure 7-14, allow you to choose a color profile for your target output device (see Chapter 5 for a discussion of color profiles), as well as set proofing options and generate reports about the document itself. The Proofing options let you to turn off various aspects of a document, allowing it to print faster. Turning off bitmaps, for example, can speed up printing considerably. Also, printing all text in black allows you to proof text that might otherwise print in light gray on a grayscale composite printer, making it difficult to read.

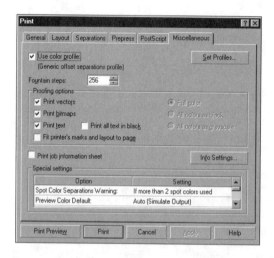

Figure 7-14: Use this dialog box to set up miscellaneous options, such as proofing settings and generating print reports.

One of the more useful options in the Miscellaneous sheet is the ability to generate information reports regarding a current document. You can get a variety of useful information, such as which printer driver is used, what fonts the document contains, what settings are turned on and off (and their variables) in all the Print dialog box screens, and so on. To generate the report, simply click Info Settings. Doing this brings up the dialog box shown in Figure 7-15. As you can see, you can turn off various aspects of the reports, and you can print it or save it to a file.

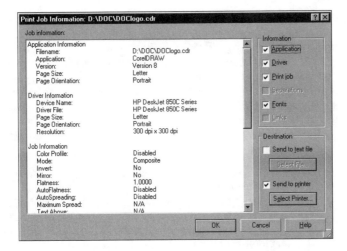

Figure 7-15: Use this report as a checklist to make sure all is well before printing your document.

Working with a service bureau

Not so long ago, desktop publishing service bureau operators hated to work with non-Macintosh users. "Oh," they would say dourly, "you use *Windows*," as if it were some kind of disease. For a while we were the only desktop publishers in our area that used IBM-compatible equipment. Everybody else used Macintoshes. Today, many people use IBM-compatible electronic publishing stations. But most service bureaus still lean toward Macintoshes.

This section explains how to prepare your documents to be printed on a high-resolution imagesetter. Different service bureaus have different requirements as to how documents should be prepared. Some service bureaus can print directly from CorelDraw or your layout program. Others require you to print to a PostScript file. Similarly, some service bureaus have a large inventory of fonts available, whereas others require you to include the fonts with your documents.

You will need to find out what your service bureau's particular requirements are. Often, all you need to do is call up the service bureau and say "I want to bring in a CorelDraw file for output." The service bureau personnel will tell you what format they prefer.

Before taking any of the following steps, call your service bureau. Ask them what type of imagesetter they use, and find out whether the fonts you use (all of them) are available. If Windows does not ship with a Windows printer driver for the imagesetter, ask the service bureau to supply you with the proper printer driver. If you are using fonts other than Adobe Type 1 PostScript fonts (those included with the CorelDraw package are supplied in both Adobe Type 1 and TrueType formats), you should also find out if the service bureau has the same brand (such as Bitstream, Z-Soft, and TrueType). If they do not, you'll have to include the fonts with each job so the service bureau can install them.).

Secret

If you have been working with a service bureau for a while, your system is probably already set up for configuring documents for that vendor. If not, or if you are new to this aspect of prepress, you might find version 8's Prepare For Service Bureau wizard useful. This nifty feature helps you find the right printer profile and gather everything you need to prepare the file for transport to the service bureau, including collecting fonts.

Configuring your printer setup

When working with a service bureau, keep in mind that you are actually creating your document on one computer and printing from another. In this situation, you may need to compensate for the configurations of the different devices.

Adding printers in Windows

In order to use a printer, you must first install it from Printer Setup or from the Printers dialog box. You can get to Printers from the Windows task bar (Start ➪ Settings ➪ Printers). To further modify or adjust a printer's settings, you can get to Printer Setup from the Print or Print Setup commands in almost any Windows application. Use the Printers dialog box's Add A Printer icon to create separate printer definitions for each printer. Use Printer Setup to switch printers from within an application or during a printing session.

Adding a printer is not as complicated as you may think. Figure 7-16 shows the Printers window, which you access from the Settings submenu on the Windows Start menu. You begin all printer installations from here by clicking the Add Printer icon, which invokes the Add Printer Wizard. Now simply follow the step-by-step directions. If the printer you are installing is physically connected to your computer, you'll set the printer port to LPT1; however, if the service bureau does not support CorelDraw (or your version of CorelDraw), you'll want to direct the printer's output to a file, as explained later. (You can also change the printer's port from Print Setup after it's installed.).

Figure 7-16: Use the Printers window to install a printer.

Printer drivers

A *printer driver* is software that mediates between an application and a printer. Basically, it translates the document into code the printer uses. Hundreds of printers divvy up the market, and Windows 95 and Windows NT ship with many different printer drivers.

Windows defines all of its PostScript drivers in one file, PSCRIPT.DRV. This makes it easy to switch between the different PostScript printers.

Printing to a file

After adding a printer, you'll need to tell Windows where to send the data. If the document will be printed on a printer located at the service bureau, you should send the data to a file. You can do this using the Add Printer Wizard by selecting File as the port. (See Figure 7-17.) Then you can give the service bureau a self-contained PostScript print file.

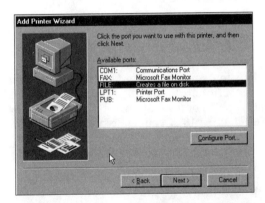

Figure 7-17: If your service bureau does not support CorelDraw (or your version of CorelDraw), you can set the printer's output to a file.

If you did not set the output to File during installation, you can do so during printing from the Print dialog box from within CorelDraw. Simply select Print to File in the Print dialog box, as shown in Figure 7-18. If you are taking the file to a service bureau that uses only Macs, be sure also to click the For Mac option. Now when you click Print, you will be prompted to name the print file.

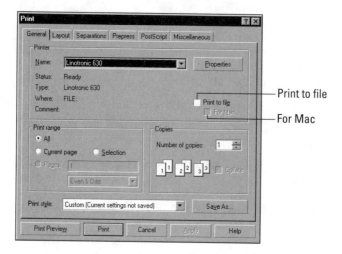

Figure 7-18: You can print to a PostScript print file by choosing the Print to File option in the Print dialog box.

If your document contains fonts not supported by the service bureau, you should also go to the PostScript portion of the Print dialog box and make sure that the Download Type 1 Fonts and Convert True Type to Type 1 check boxes are selected. (See Figure 7-19. If you don't know the difference between these two types of fonts, refer to Chapter 4.) This will ensure that the proper fonts are printed when the service bureau runs the file.

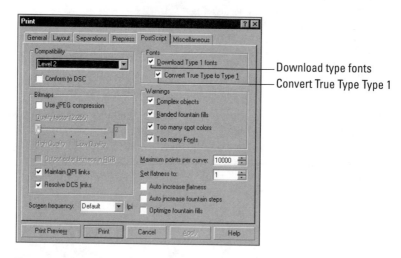

Figure 7-19: Use the PostScript Preferences dialog box to download fonts if the service bureau does not have them.

Before printing to a file, be sure to also check the proper separation and printer mark settings, as discussed in the section named "Color separations" later in this chapter.

Secret

If you have a desktop PostScript printer, you can ensure that the file prints properly by copying the file to your printer—which is essentially the same thing your service bureau does with your print files. To copy a PostScript print file to your printer, follow these steps:

STEPS:

Copying a PostScript Print File to Your Printer

Step 1. In Windows Explorer, find the print file you created from CorelDraw.

Step 2. Right-click on the file.

Step 3. From the pop-up menu, select Copy.

Step 4. Scroll in left window of Explorer until My Computer is visible, then double-click the icon to open My Computer.

Step 5. In the right window of Explorer, double-click Printers to open the folder.

Step 6. Right-click on the PostScript printer to which you want to copy the file.

Step 7. Choose Paste from the pop-up menu.

Windows copies the file to your printer and the document prints, enabling you to check your separations, and to make sure fonts and printer marks print properly. (Printer marks are discussed in the "Color separations" section that follows.)

Note

You have a number of different ways to setup a print file. This is the method I use because I find it to be the most convenient.

Secret

Here's another hint. Many designers use Adobe Acrobat Distiller as a PostScript proofing device. Distiller will catch and report many problems that may slip by on your local printer. In fact, many of the printers I deal with require we send the Distiller logs along with our PostScript files. If you are familiar with Acrobat, be sure and check out Bill Harrel's *Adobe Acrobat 3 for Dummies* (IDG Books Worldwide, Inc.).

Getting your files to the service bureau

If the service bureau has a PC with your program installed, and the fonts you use, it can print your documents directly to an imagesetter from the original document file. If the service bureau does not have your program or fonts, you should print your document to a PostScript print file, as explained earlier.

I prefer this latter method, because I maintain control — and my service bureau gives me a 20 percent discount. The one drawback is that if for some reason your file doesn't print, the service bureau can't do much to help. In most cases, either a PostScript print file prints or it does not. With document files, the service bureau can open a document and try to figure out why it does not print, but time is money, and having them do the troubleshooting can be expensive.

However, print files tend to be huge, often much larger than will fit on a conventional 1.44MB floppy disk. In these situations you will need some kind of removable medium, such as a SyQuest SyJet or Iomega Zip or Jaz drive, to transport your files to the service bureau. You should check with your service bureau to see which devices they support before investing in a removable drive. (Removable media are discussed in Chapter 23.)

As an alternative to removable media, most service bureaus have electronic bulletin board services or Web sites to which you can transmit your files via modem. If that is the case, you'll probably want to compress the file using some kind of compression utility. The most common are PKZIP and WinZip.

Quick press reproduction

Many cities have small "quick" or instant press print shops. What usually makes them quick is they don't use the negative and metal plate method on their printing presses. Instead, they use *paper* plates, eliminating a few steps. In some cases, this can be a little less expensive. The paper plates reproduce halftones and screens much better than a photocopier, but not as well as metal plates.

This process is good for short press runs that do not require the highest quality. For longer runs, the cost of the negatives and plates used in the more conventional method becomes negligible, because the per-copy price drops substantially as the quantity rises. A major cost factor in printing is the number of *passes* (times paper runs over the press) required. Quick presses tend to run small sheets, increasing the number of passes. Large presses use large sheets that hold several pages, decreasing the number of passes. Many of them can also print more than one color at a time, further eliminating additional passes.

If you want the final document to reproduce your camera-ready art as closely as possible, use the metal plate process, which requires film, from either your computer or your print shop's camera. As you know, in the conventional process, the print shop shoots negatives and uses them to "burn" plates for the press. These extra steps cost a little more (from $10 to $20 per plate), but you gain substantially in quality. Screens and halftones reproduce clearly. Small type and fine lines print crisper and cleaner. You will be more pleased with the results.

If your document requires a large press run (say, more than 1,000 copies), look for a volume print shop with a large press. You will save money on the number of passes. Once, on a 9,000-copy press run, I found a $3,000 price difference between a quick press shop and a volume printer.

Color separations

As you saw in Chapter 5, you have two basic ways to print color on a commercial printing press: using spot-color inks or process-color inks. When you use color in your documents, print shops often require a separation for each color used. This process is not always as straightforward as it seems. This section looks a little closer at preparing your documents for the printing press.

Both processes — spot and four-color — have slightly different requirements. We will look at spot color first.

If your final layout will be printed on an imagesetter, print the separations on a laser printer first. Make sure that each of the colored elements is on the right plate.

Preparing spot color documents

Spot color differs from process color in that instead of mixing inks to get colors, the printing press uses premixed ink in the desired color. This approach poses some special problems, especially in printing one spot color over another, such as in logos, or, say, newsletters with sidebars and announcements in colored boxes.

Knockouts

Printing spot separations in graphics and layout software works fine, except when colors overlap. Depending on the colors involved, a solution can be tricky. When printing a light color, such as yellow, over a dark one, such as black, the black will show through — unless you create a *knockout*. Because the black shows through the yellow, discoloring it, you do not want black ink directly under the yellow ink. A knockout is white space, or paper (rather than ink), in the area where the top color will print. Color Plate 7-1 illustrates a knockout. Notice that no black ink prints where the yellow overlaps.

This problem occurs only when you have a lighter color over a darker one. You can, for example, print black over almost any color without the color showing through. And overprinting, or printing one spot color over another, works just fine for several other color combinations. No hard-and-fast rule exists here. The best approach is to check with your printer before trying to overprint colors.

Knockouts are important when you are working with screens and halftones. You cannot put any color behind a grayscale halftone without a knockout.

By default, CorelDraw automatically knocks out overlapping spot colors, which is good, but this feature poses another problem — the possibility of press misregistration, which you eliminate by trapping, as discussed a little later in this chapter.

Overprinting in CorelDraw

Although CorelDraw automatically knocks out overlapping colors, sometimes you'll get better results from overprinting.

You can tell CorelDraw to overprint using the right mouse button Overprint Fill menu option, shown in Figure 7-20. Simply select the object you want to overprint, click and hold the right mouse button, and then select Overprint Fill. If the object has an outline, you should also select Overprint Outline.

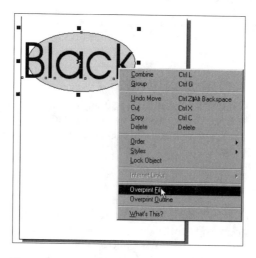

Figure 7-20: Overprinting is controlled from the right mouse menu pop-up.

You can tell CorelDraw applications to overprint all black objects by choosing Always Overprint Black in the Separations area of the Print Preview dialog box. This saves time by eliminating the need to set all black items in a drawing to overprint.

STEPS:

Setting the Always Overprint Black Option

Step 1.   Click File ⇨ Print Preview.

Step 2.   Click Options.

Step 3.   Click the Separations tab.

Step 4.   Enable the Print Separations check box.

Step 5.   Enable the Always Overprint Black check box.

Trapping

The problem with knockouts in graphics software is that they are too precise. They knock out exactly the overlapping areas. Printing presses, on the other hand, do not register precisely; that is, they do not print in exactly the same place on each piece of paper. As paper passes through the press, it stretches and moves slightly. Most presses register to within .005 of an inch. This may not seem like much, but it is enough to leave undesirable white gaps between two colors. So if, for example, you are printing yellow text inside a black box, some of the copies may have noticeable white lines between the colors.

To ensure that knockouts print without registration gaps, you should trap them. A *trap* is a small outline around the darker element that prints over the lighter one. It compensates for the press's lack of accuracy. Color Plate 7-2 in the color insert shows an example of a trap. In CorelDraw you can create traps in several ways. Creating a trap is easy: simply use the Outline Pen tool to create .005-inch outline around the object being trapped, and then change the color of the outline to the color of the object being trapped. Next, from the right mouse button pop-up, choose Overprint Outline.

Secret

Until you've done it a few times, you may find trapping to be a little tricky. But you don't have to do it yourself. You have four options: you can take your drawing file to a service bureau that supports CorelDraw and let the technician there do the trapping. Or if your service bureau uses Macs, export the drawing to Adobe Illustrator 3.0 format (select File ⇨ Export) and provide it to the service bureau for a technician to trap. (If your service bureau uses CorelDraw Macintosh, save the file as a CorelDraw 6.0 file.) Your third option is to print the drawing to a file and let the service bureau use its automatic trapping software to do the trapping. Figure 7-21 shows the Auto trapping options in the Print dialog box.

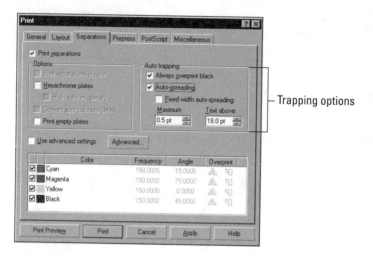

Figure 7-21: Use these options to setup CorelDraw's automatic trapping.

Warning

One word of caution, though — if you export to Adobe Illustrator format, be sure to convert your text to curves (as described in Chapter 7). The service bureau's Macintosh system probably will not have your CorelDraw fonts installed.

Additionally, you can tell CorelDraw to automatically trap objects. Here's how:

STEPS:

Automatically Trapping Objects

Step 1.   Click File ⇨ Print Preview.

Step 2.   Click Options.

Step 3.   Click the Separations tab.

Step 4.   Select the Print Separations check box.

Step 5.   Select the Always overprint black check box.

Step 6.   Select the Auto-Spreading check box.

Choose either to type a maximum trap value or always to use a fixed trap amount. When you use the Maximum Trap Value option, the size of the trap assigned to an object depends on the maximum trap value and the object's color. The lighter the color, the larger the trap. The darker the color, the smaller the trap. If you want the spread width to be fixed, then enable the Fixed width check box. The Maximum Value box changes to the Width box when you select the Fixed Width check box. Use this box to set the width of your traps.

I prefer using fixed traps rather than letting the software determine the size of the trap. If you choose fixed traps, call your print shop to see what size traps they recommend. Keep in mind, though, if you set this value too low, small text may be illegible when auto-spreading is applied. And some small objects may be distorted. The fact that CorelDraw tries to trap everything in the document is a good reason to exercise extreme caution when using fixed traps.

You can also set Always overprint black and auto-spreading when exporting to EPS format. Simply select them in the Auto-trapping section of the EPS Export dialog box.

Process (four-color) color separations

CorelDraw has the power to do terrific process color separations, especially when you use the color management system, Corel Color Management, discussed in Chapter 5. In process-color printing, the printer uses four translucent inks — cyan (C), magenta (M), yellow (Y), and black (K) — to reproduce colors. By printing different sizes and combinations of CMYK ink dots close together on a page, the printing press simulates hundreds of different colors.

If the dots are positioned properly, the result is a rosette pattern that helps to create the color illusion. If the dots are off even slightly, an unsightly moiré pattern prints instead, breaking the color illusion. Halftone dots also vary in size — small dots are used to print lighter areas, and larger dots, to print darker areas. In the final printed piece, your eye uses the dots to perceive dozens of different colors.

Don't take my word for it. You can see what we're describing by picking up any magazine and flipping to a color photograph. If you look closely at the color photograph (you may even want to grab a magnifying glass to help), you will notice small dots of color that make up the image. Up close, those dots look like cyan, magenta, yellow, and black dots. From a distance, though, your eye merges those colored dots to perceive a simulation of the range of colors from the original photograph.

Prepress tools

Corel Color Management, discussed in Chapter 5, is not so efficient that it eliminates the need for conventional prepress tools, such as color proofs, color keys, and press checks. These traditional devices are often still required to make the transition from screen to paper. They can help you, your service bureau, and print shop professionals to get the desired results. You should know, however, that CorelDraw provides most of the tools you'll need to correct these and other problems.

Color proofs

Color proofs assure you that the colors you see on your monitor match the data sent to the printer or imagesetter. The best color proofing device is a dye-sublimation printer. Your service bureau probably has one. If the colors in your dye-sublimation printout look right, you're well on your way to good reproduction.

Color keys

Color keys are created from the final separated film you give to the print shop. For an additional fee (usually about $60 per full-color page), your service bureau or print shop can create a key consisting of acetone sheets, one sheet for each separation plate. When the four clear plates are overlaid, you get a good representation of how the final page will look.

Press checks

A press check is the only foolproof method for getting the results you desire. This is exactly what it sounds like. The print shop sets up the press, runs off a couple of copies, and invites you to check the colors. Some print shops charge for press checks. Some shops do the checks themselves, comparing the copies to the color key.

Whether you use one or all of these methods, once you get the output in hand, your service bureau or print shop professional should be able to tell you what adjustments you need to make. As any graphics designer will tell you, the only way to get good four-color processing is through communication with all the parties involved.

Printing CorelDraw Graphics Using Other Applications

The concepts covered in this chapter are also important when you import CorelDraw graphics into other applications, such as PageMaker or WordPerfect. Resolution and screen frequency settings are just as important in a PageMaker layout as they are when printing from CorelDraw. The overprinting and trapping concerns also remain. To get spot and process color separations, you must print from an application that supports these features. The application must also be capable of separating imported graphics, which few layout applications can do. (As of this writing, no word processors support color separations.)

Note

Many of the settings you choose in CorelDraw are maintained when you import them into other applications. Screen frequency settings, traps, and overprints that you set in CorelDraw, for example, are maintained when you export to an .EPS file and then import the graphic into a Ventura Publisher layout. You should note, however, that it is necessary to use EPS format — no other. You can also use the Adobe Illustrator export filter, which is, in fact, also Encapsulated PostScript (EPS).

Size, color, and resolution settings made in CorelDraw, CorelDream 3D, and Photo-Paint are maintained when exporting to bitmap formats, such as .PCX, .TIFF, and .BMP. However, layout programs do not separate all bitmap formats. In most cases you'll need to export as a CMYK TIFF, although some layout programs do have the capability of converting other formats. PageMaker, for example, can convert RGB TIFFs to CMYK, and it can also separate Photoshop files.

Check out compatibility issues before you attempt to print with a layout or word processing program.

Summary

▶ In offset press printing you should note two important settings: resolution and screen frequency. Resolution refers to the dots per inch of an image, and screen frequency refers to the lines of dots per inch. Note that these two types of dots are different. Resolution is defined in machine dots, that is, the dots made by an imagesetter. Halftone dots are made up of machine dots. Lpi refer to halftone dots; dpi refer to machine dots. Getting the optimal reproduction results requires a balance between these two settings.

▶ When printing to slide recorders, remember to keep the resolution of your graphics low, about 75 dpi. Slide resolution and line screens call for settings such as 2K, 4K, and so on.

▶ When printing on laser printers, keep in mind that they have limitations in respect to screen frequency, thereby limiting the number of shades of gray they can print. Remember too that laser printer output does not always reproduce well on a printing press and you can never use it for four-color separations.

▶ When printing on color inkjets, match graphics quality to paper quality through the Properties dialog box, and keep in mind that printing multiple copies on an inkjet can be expensive.

▶ Camera-ready art is artwork ready for the print shop or service bureau to create negatives from with their camera. Nowadays, many designers go beyond camera-ready by printing to film.

▶ When printing color separations, you will often find it necessary to knock out and trap your colored objects to avoid discoloration and press misregistration snafus. When printing process separations, be sure to use Corel Color Manager, and take advantage of the other proofing tools at your disposal, such as dye-sublimation proofs, color keys, and press checks.

▶ When you are using CorelDraw graphics in your layouts in other software programs, many of the trapping, knockout, and other separation issues remain relevant.

Part II

Supporting Applications

Chapter 8

Corel Photo-Paint

In This Chapter

We go over some of the basics about Corel Photo-Paint and introduce you to some little-known facts and features of the program, including:

▶ What you can do with Photo-Paint

▶ Managing raster format versus vector images

▶ Navigating the Photo-Paint interface

▶ Basic image-editing techniques

What Is Corel Photo-Paint?

Corel Photo-Paint is a powerful image-editing tool that functions along the same lines as Adobe Photoshop. It helps you complete several different graphics editing tasks, including:

■ Working with nontechnical illustrations

■ Enhancing images and photographs

■ Using a scanning interface

■ Using special plug-in filters to edit, enhance, and apply special effects to images

■ Resampling raster graphics for various types of output, including offset press, multimedia titles, slides, and World Wide Web graphics

■ Converting images between several color models, including CMYK, RGB, grayscale, and the Internet-ready GIF format

Before reading this chapter, you should have a basic understanding of CorelDraw, the vector image editor included in the CorelDraw package.

You can create many different types of graphics with Photo-Paint. Plate 8-1 in the color insert shows a few examples of the many different types of images you can create in Photo-Paint.

Nontechnical illustration

Photo-Paint and programs like it are the applications of choice for creating aesthetically pleasing images, such as those you see all over the World Wide Web and on magazine covers. The program gives you access to a host of tools that help you paint much as an artist paints on canvas. In addition to its simulations of artists' tools such as pens, pencils, and brushes, Photo-Paint provides you with several tools and techniques that were certainly not available to the old masters — tools such as air brushes and special effects plug-ins (discussed in Chapter 11). Color Plate 8-2 shows an example of an aesthetically satisfying image created with a computer.

Photographic image editing

If you've ever wondered how ad designers and Hollywood types place one person's head on someone else's body, or how they recolor the sky, sea, or eyes in photographs, now you know — they do it with programs such as Photo-Paint. This program gives you the power to control the inferences your audience draws from photographs.

The capability of enhancing and editing photographs and other raster images includes correcting the exposure in underlit or overexposed images and removing imperfections such as dust, scratches, and stains. You can also patch tears, delete or add objects — you name it. In the course of this chapter and the three that follow it, we'll show you how.

Scanning

Photo-Paint is fully TWAIN (Technology Without An Interesting Name) compliant, meaning that it works with most desktop scanners. Photo-Paint interfaces readily with the software that comes with many scanners, with any TWAIN-compliant third-party software, and with CorelScan (another application that comes with CorelDRAW 8), permitting you to scan images directly into Photo-Paint from any of these sources.

During the scanning process, you can resize, adjust brightness and contrast, adjust shadows, and make any number of enhancement settings to improve the quality of the image so that it prints or displays on a Web page optimally.

Plug-in filters

Here's an aspect of Photo-Paint that conventional artists and painters could surely have used. Plug-ins are small applets that you can install in Photo-Paint. They enable you to provide a wealth of enhancements to your images, such as embossing, beveling, textures, and more — much more. Photo-Paint comes with a number of plug-ins and you can purchase several others, including Alien Skin's Eye Candy and MetaTools's KPT Power Tools.

Plug-in filters are so handy that we've included an entire chapter (Chapter 11) about them. In the meantime, Figure 8-1 shows an example of a Web banner created with Alien Skin's Bevel plug-in, just to get you interested.

Figure 8-1: In this Web banner, an Alien Skin plug-in was used to bevel the edges of the banner and the text.

Resampling raster graphics

As you've seen repeatedly throughout this book, different types of media require different graphics resolutions and line screens. Images headed for the printing press should be set to much higher resolutions than images designed to display on a computer screen. You can use Photo-Paint to prepare images for the various media types you'll be using. To do so, choose Image ⇨ Resample. This brings up the Resample dialog box shown in Figure 8-2. From here you can adjust image size and resolution.

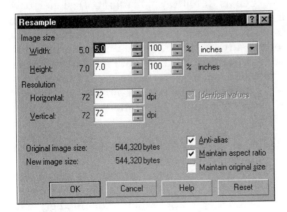

Figure 8-2: Use the Resample dialog box to change the resolution and size of your raster images.

Color model conversion

Various media types require specific color models just as they require specific resolutions. Printing presses, for example, might require CMYK separated. Multimedia titles and the Internet require RGB or indexed-color images. In addition to editing, enhancing, and resampling images, you can use Photo-Paint to convert your raster graphics between various color models. Part IV of this book covers preparing images for electronic media. In the meantime, you should know that you change color models in Photo-Paint using the Convert To command on the Image menu. The various models Photo-Paint supports are on the Convert To submenu.

Raster Graphics Versus Vector Graphics

The tasks introduced in the previous sections have one major aspect in common: They directly relate to raster images. Before using the Photo-Paint interface, you should understand what raster images are and how they differ from the vector images you create in CorelDraw.

The major difference between vector images and raster images is that vector graphics represent shapes mathematically, whereas raster graphics represent shapes as patterns of dots or pixels. This difference explains why both formats are necessary — each type has its own particular uses.

Vector graphics

Drawing programs — such as CorelDraw, Micrografx Designer, or Adobe Illustrator — are used to create vector graphics. Vector graphics are drawn mathematically, using lines and curves rather than the fixed dots used in bitmaps. The immediate advantage is that the drawing prints at the resolution of the printer, because these files are resolution independent and can create objects with precise outlines. Another advantage of this format is that the files are generally much smaller than bitmaps and usually don't take as long to print. (However, a complex illustrations can take much longer to print than a simple bitmap.)

More important than file sizes and print times is the fact that vector graphics are scalable and support many aesthetic qualities better than bitmaps. (When an image is scalable, you can resize it without degrading quality. This concept is discussed in further detail later in this section.) Vector graphics are much better adapted than bitmapped graphics for handling drawings consisting of lines and arcs, or images in which elements are well defined, such as the one shown in Figure 8-3.

Figure 8-3: The vector graphics format used by CorelDraw is more efficient at creating graphics with intricate details, such as text and smooth lines.

Notice the detail of the drawings in Figure 8-3. Fine lines are truly fine, text is sharp, and flat surfaces are well defined. The vector format's capability of resolution independence (also called *device independence)* enables more control over detail, also making it ideal for technical drawings and diagrams.

Vector graphics also provide more control over the final output resolution. Because they are *device independent*, they do not have a fixed resolution. In other words, you can print a graphic at whatever resolution, measured in dots per inch (dpi), your final output device supports. Bitmapped graphics, on the other hand, retain the resolution at which they were created.

Often, the quality of a graphic depends largely on the resolution. This happens for many reasons. The most significant is that as resolution increases, dots get smaller, allowing for more flexible dot placement within an image. This translates into smoother lines and more evenly spread fills.

Vector graphics are also better at high-resolution fountain fills, such as CorelDraw's linear and radial fills and blends, shown in Figure 8-4, and at all sorts of other special effects you can't achieve with the same level of success in bitmapped graphics.

Figure 8-4: Vector graphics are capable of smooth fountain fills, blends, and other special effects that require high resolution.

Another advantage of vector graphics is that many of the variations on this format, such as CorelDraw's CDR files, Encapsulated PostScript (EPS), Designer's DRW files, and some others, provide direct support for Type 1 and TrueType fonts. What this means is that, as with a word processor or desktop publishing file, you can open and close a file as often as you like, even import it into other programs, and the text remains editable.

When you use type in a bitmap editor, it becomes part of the graphic, a bitmap itself, and is no longer editable as a text string.

Because vector graphics are drawn mathematically and retain their resolution, they, unlike bitmapped graphics, can be resized without losing quality. (To a certain extent, bitmapped images can be reduced without loss of quality. However, reducing them too much can cause loss of clarity. You will have little or no luck, on the other hand, enlarging them in your layouts.)

When you enlarge a bitmapped graphic, you'll notice that jagged edges appear. This effect increases as the image gets larger. The vector graphic, by contrast, retains its quality no matter how big you make it.

Encapsulated PostScript graphics

Although Encapsulated PostScript graphics don't directly pertain to Photo-Paint, we can't really talk about vector graphics without mentioning them. Adobe's Encapsulated PostScript (EPS) graphics format is the most widely used and most versatile form of vector graphics. It is the graphics format of choice for desktop publishers and designers for a number of reasons. EPS graphics are mentioned in this discussion of the vector format (as well as several times throughout this book) because it is important to keep in mind that they are the standard CorelDraw-type graphics format.

PostScript is the format used by most of today's high-resolution typesetting equipment and slide recorders. As you saw in the discussion of graphics output in Chapter 7, PostScript is a must for reproducing quality four-color documents on an offset printing press.

A drawback to EPS graphics is that you need a PostScript printer or other PostScript interpreter, such as a PostScript cartridge used with older Hewlett-Packard LaserJets or PostScript conversion software (Graphx RasterPlus 95, for instance), to print them.

Other vector formats

Other vector formats include CGM, DRW, and the default formats of several other programs, including CorelDraw's CDR. Many of these formats do not require PostScript printers; however, they are not as versatile as PostScript in handling type and providing numerous resolutions and fills. You cannot take full advantage of many of CorelDraw's fills and special effects without a PostScript printer. An exception is CorelDraw's native CDR format (which is actually a superset of PostScript). Not many applications support the CDR format. For example, such leading desktop publishing packages as QuarkXPress and PageMaker are just beginning to support it.

Note

The times they may be a changin'. Version 6.5 of Aldus PageMaker and version 5.5 of FrameMaker now support CorelDraw files directly, eliminating the need to convert them to EPS before placing them in layouts.

If you have a non-PostScript laser or inkjet printer, such as an HP-compatible (a printer that uses Hewlett Packard's Printer Command Language, or PCL), you can still print almost anything you create in CorelDraw, with a few limitations.

Raster (bitmapped) graphics

Raster graphics (also called bitmapped graphics) are created in bitmap editors, or paint programs, such as Photo-Paint. Nowadays, however, most paint programs are referred to as image-editing, photograph touch-up, or digital darkroom software. Granted, most of them have become much more adept at photograph enhancement, but no matter what you call them, they're still bitmap editors.

Vector graphics have several advantages over bitmapped graphics. Bitmapped graphics consist of grids of dots in fixed patterns and print in blobs, much like a rubber stamp. Each dot is programmed into a computer file. If a graphic contains a lot of grayscale or color information, the file can be gigantic and take a long time to print. Depending on the image, bitmapped graphics can also lack some of the aesthetically valuable features offered by vector formats. They do not, for example, reproduce curved and fine lines or text nearly as well. Nor are they as flexible in creating intricate shadings and certain special effects.

Bitmapped graphics are *device dependent*, which means they retain the same resolution, no matter the capabilities of the device you print them on. This is not to say that bitmapped formats are all bad. In fact, they are essential to desktop design and publication of electronic documents, such as multimedia titles, presentations, and documents to be posted to the Internet. The same characteristics that make them unsuitable for some images make them perfect for others. The way bitmapped formats use dots makes them ideal for lifelike images, such as photographs and some sketches and paintinglike graphics.

Grayscale and color photograph scanning require bitmapped formats. In fact, print shops have used a similar procedure to prepare photographs for printing for years. Using special cameras (today, many shops use scanners), they turn a photograph into a halftone (or into color separations for color pictures). A halftone is a translation of the picture in dots, which makes it possible for the printing press to reproduce it. A closer look is taken at halftoning in Chapter 7, where we discuss preparing images for printing and layout.

Raster graphics differ radically from vector graphics. A bitmap editor can modify each individual pixel on the screen, changing the hue, saturation, and color for each pixel that needs to be modified. (This process is also called *mapping*; hence the name bitmap graphics.)

Full-color bitmaps at high resolutions create huge files. Here's why: As the number of colors (and the resolution) goes up, the information in the file increases dramatically. The address of a simple black or white pixel contains the location of the pixel and whether the pixel is black or white. The address for an 8-bit image must contain the location of the pixel and which of 256 possible colors or shades of gray the pixel is; and the address for a 24-bit image must contain the information about which of 16.7 million possible colors the pixel should be. As color depth increases, so do the address information and the file size.

Bitmapped Graphics and CorelDraw

As mentioned, Photo-Paint is the program you should use to create and edit bitmaps. However, you can also import and export some bitmap file formats to and from CorelDraw. CorelDraw 8 is now capable of applying special effects to bitmaps as well, and you can do some moderate touch-up (sharpening and so on).

Although you can't edit bitmaps in CorelDraw, you can import them into your drawings. An example is including a photograph on a flyer. Another reason to import them is for tracing, either with CorelDraw's Autotrace feature or manually with your mouse or a pen stylus. Once a bitmap is traced, you can delete it and edit the outline in CorelDraw as you would any other vector element.

You can export anything you create in CorelDraw to any of several bitmap file formats, including PCX, TIFF, and BMP. You can also convert any object in a drawing to a bitmap without saving the file to another format. For example, you may want to edit bitmap images in Photo-Paint or another bitmap editor, or use them in computer presentations on a monitor. Bitmaps work better on computer monitors than do some vector formats.

Another important aspect of raster images is resolution, or the number and size of the pixels used to construct the image. Bitmaps often define resolution in numbers such as the following: 640×480, 800×600, and 1024×768, which are basic monitor resolutions in pixels. However, when you create high-resolution (200 to 300 dpi) image bitmaps for printing, the number of pixels increases dramatically. The larger the numbers, the smaller the pixels, and smaller pixels mean higher resolution and finer detail — as well as larger files. If you combine high resolution and high color, you can easily wind up with files that exceed 100MB.

This concept is dramatically demonstrated by a simple exercise:

STEPS:

Seeing the Effect of Resolution on File Size

Step 1. Open a high-resolution file in Photo-Paint, and then choose Image ⇨ Resample. You see a dialog box similar to the one shown in Figure 8-5.

Figure 8-5: Image information for a high-resolution graphic appears in the Image Info dialog box.

Step 2. Notice that this graphic consumes just about 5MB of memory. (File sizes vary greatly. Your graphic's size will differ.)

(continued)

STEPS *(continued)*

Seeing the Effect of Resolution on File Size

Step 3. Now convert the image to an 8-bit (256 color) image by choosing one of the 8-bit options from Image ⇨ Convert To. Reopen the Image ⇨ Resample dialog box, shown in Figure 8-6. Notice that the file size has been cut to almost one third of the original.

Figure 8-6: Image information is revised after the image has been converted to 256 colors.

Step 4. Now change the resolution to 72 dpi by choosing Resample from the Image menu. (Be sure the Maintain aspect ratio check box is checked.) Reopen the Image Info dialog box. As shown in Figure 8-7, notice that our original nearly 5MB file is now only 885K.

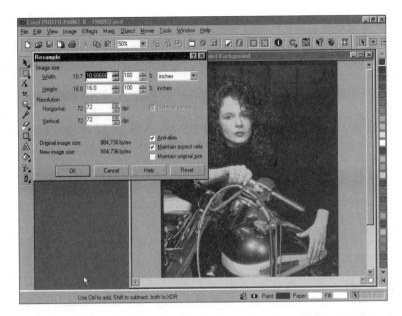

Figure 8-7: Image information is further revised after the resolution has been decreased to 72 dpi.

Unfortunately, there is no such thing as a free lunch, and each step in the preceding exercise diminishes the quality of the image as well as its size, especially if you're printing the image on a printing press. Notice that the image's physical size remains the same, but the pixel resolution has changed. The image's resolution has changed, but not its dimensions.

Because raster graphics are constructed of pixels, they do not magnify with great success. Zooming in, increasing the size of the photo, or decreasing resolution also increase the size of each pixel. This can result in an unacceptable condition called *pixelization*.

Secret

Images almost always scale down without any significant loss of quality. Unfortunately, they seldom scale up without suffering quite a bit. Here, then, is one valuable rule of thumb to keep in mind when working with raster graphics: Always attempt to scan or acquire your images in a size that is as big as, or bigger than, what you will be using.

Saving raster images as vector images

Saving a raster graphic as a vector graphic isn't as easy as the opposite process, and usually the conversion is not successful. What typically happens is that you wind up with a raster image inside a vector format, leaving the image virtually uneditable in a vector application.

The typical raster-to-vector conversion occurs when you save a raster image as Encapsulated PostScript (EPS). While this doesn't actually convert the image to vectors, it does have its uses. Some programs, such as QuarkXPress, are not particularly raster-friendly, especially when it comes to CMYK TIFFs. Converting CMYK raster images to EPS can provide better color separations in some layout programs. If you need spot-color separations, saving as EPS is crucial — raster formats do not support PMS and other spot-color separations.

Some tracing programs, such as OCR-Trace (discussed in Chapter 15), can actually convert raster graphics to vector graphics — the program traces the edges of the vector image to produce objects that can be edited directly in CorelDraw — but the results are often less than perfect, especially with full-color photographs. You can give it a try with OCR-Trace, but don't say we didn't warn you.

In Chapter 5 you learned about manipulating color in CorelDraw. Most of the information in that chapter applies to Photo-Paint as well, but note one significant addition: When you are drawing in a four-color mode, CMYK for example, or using process or spot colors, always remember that the monitor is displaying the images in the RGB model. What you see on the screen is seldom what you get when you take your work to a printing press. Corel Color Manager tries to simulate what will roll out of the printer or off the printing press, but as you saw in Chapter 5, Color Manager is hardly perfect.

Always have a sample book of colors near you, and frequently check your image against it; post-press surprises are seldom pleasant ones. More important — calibrate, calibrate, calibrate, and use the gamut warning function discussed in Chapter 6.

Introduction to the Photo-Paint Tools

At first blush, the CorelDraw and Photo-Paint interfaces look a lot alike. But if you look a bit closer, they suddenly start to appear distressingly dissimilar. The toolbars have different items on them, the Property Bar looks as if it has had one too many, and extra tools are even stuck here and there about the interface.

Once you realize that the two programs are designed to do two quite different things, you can start to appreciate the differences. We're assuming that you bought this book because you own and use CorelDraw, and that you don't know much about Photo-Paint. Poring over the manual is of doubtful value, so we will approach Photo-Paint on a slightly more introductory level. Realize, however, that Photo-Paint is a highly complex program, one that takes a lot of effort on your part to learn. We can't cover all the information you need to become proficient at image manipulation in just four chapters. Our purpose is to introduce you to some basic concepts and techniques.

Fortunately, you already know many of the elements of Photo-Paint, because quite a few elements in the interface are the same as in CorelDraw. Fortunately, too, Photo-Paint is a first-class gas, a whale of a lot of fun, and well worth any time that you can spend with it.

Familiar CorelDraw tools

If you have learned CorelDraw, you already know three sets of Photo-Paint tools pretty thoroughly: the zoom tools, the shape tools, and the fill tools. All these tools operate much like their CorelDraw counterparts. You also know quite a bit about the object, node, and text tools, even though Photo-Paint's work in some substantially different ways. We'll start by looking, quite briefly, at some of these differences.

The Object Picker tool

You already know about the selection, or Pick, tool, which is called the Object Picker tool in Photo-Paint, the first tool on the Toolbox shown in Figure 8-8. The second tool on this flyout, Transform Mask, allows you to work with Photo-Paint's powerful masks, a topic covered in depth in Chapter 10.

Figure 8-8: The second tool on the Object Picker tool flyout is the Transform Mask tool, much different from what you're used to in CorelDraw.

The Zoom tool

The Zoom tool is the fifth button down and performs the same duties for Photo-Paint as it does for CorelDraw. However, you'll notice one major difference that you're sure to love. When you activate the Zoom tool by clicking on the Zoom Tool button, you can then operate it entirely by left-clicking your mouse to zoom in and right-clicking to zoom out. The second tool on the Zoom tool flyout is the Hand tool. Use it to pan within an image. If you are familiar with PageMaker, this tool is similar to the Grabber Hand. It allows you to shift objects or layers around on the screen as though you have actually picked them up. (Note that if you have the Microsoft IntelliPoint mouse, you can zoom with the wheel.)

The Node tool

Here again, the first tool on the flyout (the Path Node Edit tool, similar to CorelDraw's Node Editing or Shape tool) is familiar to you. The difference here is that your objects in Photo-Paint do not have editable outlines. The Node tool is used instead to edit object boundaries, paths, and masks. Objects are discussed in Chapter 9, and paths and masks are discussed in Chapter 10.

The Text tool

The Text tool operates much as it does in CorelDraw. However, note one significant difference: The Photo-Paint Text tool creates rasterized images of the fonts. What this means is that once the text is created, it can no longer be edited as text with the text cursor.

Secret

Photo-Paint is not intended for typesetting. If you need to include text in a document, it is highly recommended that you perform all image editing in Photo-Paint and then move the finished image into CorelDraw, where you can add vector-based text. Your letters will be cleaner and sharper, and the file will not be bloated with a lot of excess information.

At times, however, it's easier to add text directly to an image, so that the text will become an integral part of the design. In these cases, go ahead and do it, but don't count on the same level of quality that you can get by using vector-based tools.

The Fill tool

The Photo-Paint Fill tool is similar to the Fill tool in CorelDraw. You can fill an irregular object with any color selected. You can also make a solid fill or a gradient fill across a mask or a masked area. These techniques are discussed in Chapters 9 and 10. You need to learn to use them both to make good use of the Fill tool.

The Property Bar

You may already be familiar with context-specific Property Bars in CorelDraw. The Property Bars in Photo-Paint work essentially the same way, but you will want to become familiar with all the new options, which change with each tool you select. The same information in the Property Bar is also available in the various roll-ups for each particular tool. (See Figure 8-9.) This is how the folks at Corel built even more flexibility into your paint area — mix and match your use of the Property Bar or the roll-ups — it's your choice! Chapter 9 explains the Photo-Paint Property Bar in detail.

Figure 8-9: The Photo-Paint Property Bar is shown for the Mask tool. As with CorelDraw, the Property Bar in Photo-Paint changes with each tool selected.

Secret

Many times when you are working with tools in Photo-Paint, you will want to use a combination of settings from the Property Bar and a tool's settings dialog box. Double-click on the tool you want to use, and the appropriate Settings roll-up menu opens. You can then display or hide the Property Bar with the Show/Hide Property Bar command on the View menu.

Unique Photo-Paint tools

Although artistic masterpieces are not traditionally crafted from scratch in paint programs, Photo-Paint does give you some powerful tools that enable you to create works from scratch. To get a feel for these new gadgets, go to File and select New to open a new image. You'll see the dialog box shown in Figure 8-10. Notice that the Create a New Image dialog box enables you to set the color depth, resolution, and size of the image you want to work with. The last two lines in the dialog box let you know how much memory the image will consume, and how much you have available.

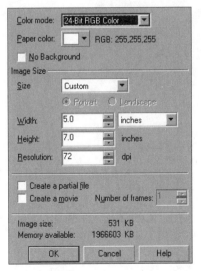

Figure 8-10: The Create a New Image dialog box controls basic image properties.

Quite a few tools you haven't seen before appear in the toolbar — masking tools, the Crop tool, the Eyedropper tool, Eraser tools, the Image Sprayer tool, the Paint tool, the Effect tool, and the Clone tool. Many of these tools are quite simple to use, and many aren't. In this section you learn about some of the really cool capabilities of this program.

The Paint tool

Have you ever asked yourself why artists always seem to have a zillion brushes sticking up from old coffee cups? As any artist knows, each brush does a special thing because it has a special shape or texture. Every artist knows that each brush has a function, and you just can't do anything without the proper tools.

You can now go those artists one better. Double-click on the Paint tool — it's the last one on the bottom of the Toolbox, and it looks like a paintbrush. The Tool Settings roll-up opens, shown in Figure 8-11, revealing the paint tools available to you. Now click on the Type drop-down list to see the many brushes.

Figure 8-11: You can choose from among several possible expressions for different paint tools.

You can set the characteristics of the brush shape, including the texture of the paint laid down by the brush, and you can control other properties of brushes; for example, you can turn a brush stroke into a series of dabs. Also, using the Property Bar you can select brush type, paint mode, nib shape and size, transparency, softness of the brush edge, and anti-aliasing. Click on the last icon on the right to pull down the Tool Settings roll-up, which provides a wealth of options for modifying how brushes behave.

It is tough to describe the flexibility and types of paint tools available in Photo-Paint. Open the brush Tool Settings dialog box by double-clicking on the Brush tool. With a blank new file open, select any medium type you want and experiment — moving from spray can to watercolor to air brush. Many predefined types are already available. If you are an experienced artist and do not find a tool to your liking, customize one as your own and save it to use again by clicking on the Save Brush button and giving your new tool a name. You can now use this tool anytime in the future.

You'll need to experiment with all of the various tool settings. Bear in mind as you go along how different this is from CorelDraw. For example, you have settings for brush transparency and soft edge. When you are painting, one color bleeds into another, and paint seldom completely covers what is underneath. If you are artistically inclined, you will be tempted to lock yourself up with your computer, appearing only now and then to feed yourself. This can be great fun.

If you haven't discovered the fact already, note that Photo-Paint is much more demanding of your computer than is CorelDraw. Creating works of art on a memory-challenged 80486 can become an exercise in frustration, and even the fastest CPU can and will bog down when it attempts to perform some of the more intense Photo-Paint tasks, such as painting with complex brushes and performing masks. We talk about masks in a bit, and in full in Chapter 10.

As a rule, you need a pretty quick CPU (80586 or Pentium), as much uncompressed hard-drive space as you can afford, and as much memory as your borrowed bucks can buy. If you have 32MB of RAM, you should do all right when you start getting into intensive Photo-Paint operations.

The Crop tool

Everybody knows what cropping is. It's simply cutting away unwanted portions of an image, leaving a desired portion. Using the Crop tool (fourth from the top) is a piece of cake.

STEPS:

Using the Crop Tool

Step 1.   Select the Crop tool.

Step 2.   Drag a marquee box around the part of the image you want to keep.

Step 3.   Adjust the size of the marquee box by dragging its sizing handles.

Step 4.   Double-click in the image area to accomplish the crop.

Figure 8-12 shows an example of what cropping can do for a picture.

Figure 8-12: Good cropping can turn a ho-hum photo (left) into a zinger (right)!

The Eyedropper tool

Many times you will want to load your brush with a particular color that appears in an image or in the mixing area, and you will have absolutely no idea what the name of that color may be. Using the Eyedropper tool, you can select the color you want.

STEPS:

Using the Eyedropper Tool

Step 1.   Select the Eyedropper tool.

Step 2.   Place the cursor on the color in the currently displayed image or the color in the mixing area that you want to use.

Step 3.   Left-click to set the paint color, or right-click to set the fill.

Note

When a large color sample is taken with the Eyedropper tool, the color result is an average of the colors included in the area sampled. So be aware—the end result may not actually exist within the sample. You can get a more precise color by narrowing the size of the Eyedropper brush tip from the Tool Settings roll-up (with the Eyedropper selected).

The Eraser tools

The Eraser tools flyout, shown in Figure 8-13, has three tools. The first tool (Local Undo) is used to undo the last action you did with one of the paint tools. The second tool (Eraser) works like a traditional eraser, except that it paints with any color you choose for the paper color. The third tool (Color Replacer) replaces only the current paint color in the image with the paper color. Slick!

Use the Eyedropper tool to select a new current color to replace with the Color Replacer tool. You can adjust the size and shape of the eraser brush from the Tool Settings roll-up or from the Property Bar (with the Eraser selected).

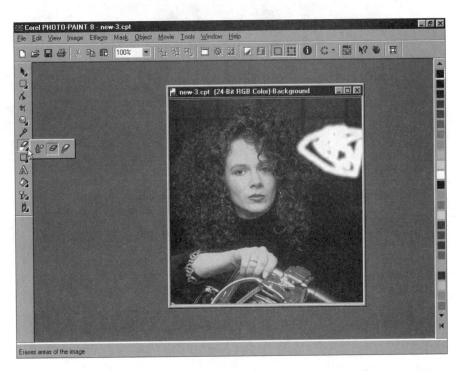

Figure 8-13: A suite of three tools in Photo-Paint averts many disasters. Try the Local Undo and the Eraser. The Color Replacer tool works in conjunction with the Eyedropper, which lets you select the color you want to replace.

The Image Sprayer tool

Most of the time when you paint, you lay down a path of color using one of the paint tools. However, it is possible to paint with images. Instead of laying down a swath of yellow, for example, you can lay down a swath of images of your favorite cat's face. Click on the Open File folder on the left side of the Property Bar to load any paint graphic. Then spray with the Image Sprayer tool (fourth tool on the Paint tool flyout). You can also edit the size, frequency, and transparency of the image you want to spray from the Tool Settings roll-up or the Property Bar (with the Image Sprayer tool selected). Figure 8-14 shows an example of the Image Sprayer's handiwork. Watch out, taggers, Corel's on your turf!

Using the tool effectively takes a little practice, though. See Chapter 9 for more information.

Figure 8-14: The butterflies were sprayed (superimposed) on the brick wall. The more quickly you move the cursor, the more transparent the sprayed images become.

The Effect tool

The Effect tool (second on the Paint tool flyout) is used to smear, smudge, alter brightness and contrast, and change the hue, as well as to sponge, tint, blend, sharpen, and undither images. Use the Effect tool much as you would use a brush or the Image Sprayer. (See Figures 8-15 and 8-16.)

Figure 8-15: The original image of a butterfly is blurred against the background.

Figure 8-16: The new image has been sharpened and brightened to bring out the butterfly against the background.

Chapter 11 describes effects further. For now, it is enough to know that you can build and use a zillion different way-out special effects to spice up your images.

The Clone tool

The Clone tool (third tool on the Paint tool flyout) is one of the most awesome and powerful tools in your Photo-Paint repertoire. You will use this tool to perform all manner of touch-up tasks on images, correcting flaws in negatives, removing scratches from film, or even removing unwanted elements from the background of an otherwise great photo.

The Clone tool copies things from one location in an image to another, so it has two cursors — one to show the origin and one to locate where the cloned information will be placed. Probably the best way to understand what the Clone tool does is to view an example of the tool in action. See Figure 8-17.

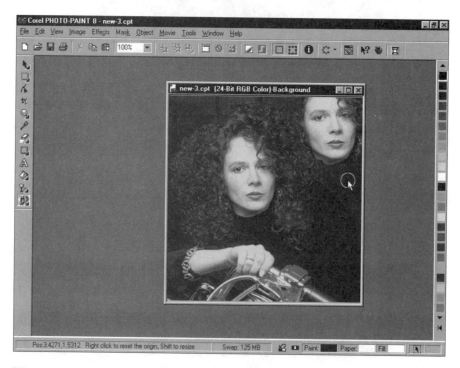

Figure 8-17: Here is an example of cloning with the Clone tool.

Secret

Perhaps the greatest secret to using the Clone tool is to work with the image displayed as large as possible. If, as in this example, you are taking pieces of the background from the close neighborhood of the element you want to paint over, get as close to the element as you can.

Three lesser secrets to using the Clone tool include selecting the proper origin, establishing a checkpoint, and patience. Selecting the proper origin comes with practice. Establishing a checkpoint is something that needs to be in your everyday bag of tricks.

Setting a checkpoint is a valuable practice — try it. When you start to get into some intense image manipulation, establish a place you can return to if everything suddenly goes wrong. You do this by choosing Checkpoint from the Edit/Undo Special menu. Now if something you do turns out wrong or you don't like its looks, you can always get back to where the image was right by choosing Restore to Checkpoint from the Edit menu. Cool.

STEPS:

Using the Clone Tool

Step 1. Zoom in on the area you want to change.

Step 2. Select the Clone tool from the drawing toolbar.

Step 3. Right-click on a location from which to copy an element.

Step 4. Paint with the new cursor.

It sounds easy, but it takes some practice.

Watch that tool size. The Clone tool, like all the other tools in Photo-Paint, has a settings dialog box, as well as special settings available on the Property Bar. Keep the nib size reasonably small. It is much easier to keep resetting the origin (right-click) than to try to go back and clean up. Figure 8-18 shows the Tool Settings dialog box for the Clone tool.

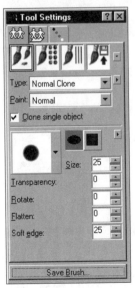

Figure 8-18: Use the Tool Settings dialog box for the Clone tool to adjust significant settings.

Masking tools

The purpose behind Photo-Paint is to let you mess around with raster images. Up until now, everything we have shown you could be directly applied to, or done on, the entire image that was displayed on the monitor. However, you will seldom want to work in such broad strokes.

Rather, you will want to modify one part of an image, say by making a brown eye blue. To do this, you need some method or tool that enables you to choose one small part of an image, while at the same time protecting the rest of the image from unwanted change.

This process is called masking, and you can use a whole series of tools in Photo-Paint to create small areas in an image for change. This beats the masking tape you use to protect your cabinets when you paint your kitchen!

The Masking mechanisms available to you are the Rectangular, Circle, Magic Wand, Brush, Lasso, Scissors, and Freehand masking tools (see Figure 8-19). You can also select similar colors over an area with the Magic Wand. Scissors creates an irregular mask by following edges, whereas the Mask Brush tool creates a mask from Brush Strokes. Last but not least, you can also Transform a Mask. For a detailed description of masking, turn to Chapter 10.

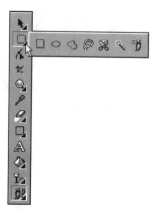

Figure 8-19: The Masking tools flyout offers a variety of means for masking.

Drawing tools

Unlike CorelDraw, Photo-Paint is pixel oriented and has only a limited selection of actual object-drawing tools. You can create a rectangle, an ellipse (or circle), a polygon (any irregular shape), and straight lines. When creating objects in Photo-Paint, you can choose to fill the object with a color or leave it hollow. You can also control the line weight (thickness) of the object border, just as you would in CorelDraw. (See Figure 8-20.)

Figure 8-20: The Photo-Paint Tools flyout offers access to the program's somewhat limited selection of drawing tools.

Summary

▶ Corel Photo-Paint is a bitmap editor rivaling Adobe Photoshop in power to create paint-type images. You can also use it to edit and scan photographs, apply special effects plug-in filters, and carry out a wealth of other bitmap image-editing procedures.

▶ Photo-Paint's raster format differs from CorelDraw's vector-image format in that images are created as grids of dots rather than as mathematically drawn arcs and lines. Raster is the ideal format for photographs and paintinglike images.

▶ The Photo-Paint interface differs from CorelDraw's in having many different tools for creating paint-type effects, such as smudging tools, painting brushes, and even an image sprayer, sometimes called an image hose.

Chapter 9

Advanced Photo-Paint Techniques

In This Chapter

You learn some advanced tips and techniques for working with:

▶ The Property Bar in Photo-Paint

▶ Photo-Paint's toolbars

▶ Photo-Paint's new Brush tools and paint modes

▶ The Docking window

▶ Colors

▶ Objects and Object Manager in Photo-Paint

▶ Other Photo-Paint features

▶ Photo-Paint's new special effects

Using the Property Bar in Photo-Paint

The Property Bar is an extremely powerful toolbar. It changes according to the context with any tool you select. By default, it is attached to the top of the screen, right beneath the standard toolbar.

The Property Bar changes with each of the tools found on the Photo-Paint toolbar (on the left side of the screen).The Property Bar enables you to quickly and easily make major adjustments or do some fine-tuning with any tool you use. If you select the Object Picker tool, for example, the Property Bar reveals options to adjust the alignment and opacity of the object, repositioning, and duplication. In this context, the Property Bar also provides a drop-down menu that changes the mode of the Object Picker, enabling you to distort and resize any object on your screen without digging through a menu to find the right tool. We've mentioned only a few options here. In all, the Property bar provides from 8 to 15 options for each of the Object Picker's seven modes.

You can float your mouse pointer over the Property Bar to reveal two different kinds of tool-tips:

- Tool-tips near the tools themselves
- Detailed descriptions that appear on the status bar

These tips are extremely helpful because the Property Bar can contain as many as 24 options per tool. (No floating tool-tips are available as you use the Tool Settings roll-up.)

The Photo-Paint Property Bar in different contexts

Let's take a look at how the Property Bar's features change depending on the tools that you're using in Photo-Paint.

The Object Picker tool

In Photo-Paint, the Property Bar has a drop-down menu for the Object Picker tool (sometimes called the "Object tool" for short), as shown in Figure 9-1.

Figure 9-1: Here is what the Property Bar looks like while the Object tool is selected. The corresponding drop-down menu is open.

You'll find a few more options on this drop-down menu than on the toolbox flyout for the Object tool. The additional icons on this drop-down menu rotate, scale, resize, skew, distort, and add perspective to the selected object. Keep your eye on the status bar to be sure which tool you have selected.

Secret

You need not go through the trouble of selecting a tool from the drop-down menu whenever you want to choose a different tool. Each time you click on an object with the Object tool, you can activate a different tool depending on the number of times you click. Click once to move the object, twice to rotate or skew the object, three times to distort the object, and four times to drag the object with the perspective tool. Notice that the type of bounding marker changes each time you click.

Selecting a tool within the Object Picker submenu causes the other options on the Property Bar to change. Look at the Property Bar each time you select a new Object Picker option. The Property Bar's adjustable parameters change according to your selection. Figure 9-2 shows the Property Bar with the Rotate mode selected. Some of the Rotate options are things you could do just as easily by double-clicking on the object itself and rotating by hand. But using the numerical values on the Property Bar gives you more accuracy. For example, using the Property Bar, you can move the "center point" around which an object rotates, and alter the transparency of an object.

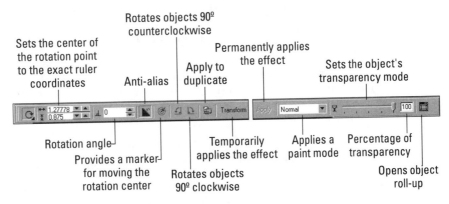

Figure 9-2: The Property Bar (split to show detail) shows these options with the Rotate mode selected for the Object Picker. Make sure you have an object selected, or you won't see these options.

The Mask tool

When you select a tool from the Mask tool drop-down menu, the Property Bar changes depending on the tool you have selected. With the Property Bar you can make your mask subtract from the selected area rather than add to it. You can also change your mask to an XOR mask tool, which enables you to make several unique masked areas on one picture. Feathering, Anti-Aliasing, and Float controls are available on the Property Bar. Masking options are explained in more detail in Chapter 10. You can also open the Channel and Objects roll-up from the Masking Property bar, and convert your mask to a path. Figure 9-3 shows the Property Bar with the Scissors mask selected.

Figure 9-3: The Property Bar appears this way with the Scissors mask selected.

The Path Node Edit tool

Paths are a series of curves and straight lines that can be stretched and twisted by nodes. You create paths by placing nodes down on your page. Lines connecting your nodes are automatically drawn. The space between two nodes is referred to as a *segment*, and by repositioning nodes you lengthen, shorten, or twist the line connecting the two nodes. Paths can always be edited, even after a document is saved.

Paths can be turned into masks and can be automatically stroked with the current paintbrush and color. Paths can be saved as EPS files and opened in Adobe Illustrator, or exported as vector images and opened in CorelDraw. The beauty of paths is their precision. A path created to outline the shape of an object or bitmap can be as exact as you like.

Paths can be saved and opened again later, and they can be opened in other Photo-Paint documents. In Photo-Paint, paths can be instantly converted to masks, and vice versa. If you are unhappy with the lack of precision of the masking tools, just create a path with the Path Node Edit tool and convert it to a mask.

Figure 9-4 shows how the Property Bar looks when the Path Node Edit Tool (or "Node" tool, for short) is selected.

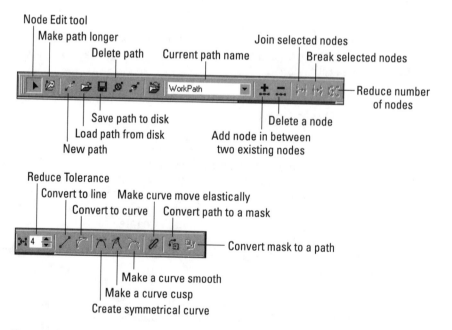

Figure 9-4: The Property Bar takes this form when the Node tool is selected. The icons will be grayed out unless you actually have a path selected.

The first button on the left of the Property Bar is the Node Edit tool. Use the Node Edit tool to create a path, reposition nodes you've already created, and turn line nodes into curved nodes. When the path is selected, you cannot add new nodes (new steps along the path) in your drawing, except by using the + button on the Property Bar.

The next button, New Node, activates your tool for placing new nodes on your picture. The next four buttons create new paths, save paths, open paths, and delete existing paths. You may have several paths open on one document simultaneously. You can save any path with the extension PTH and name it anything you like.

Note

The New Node tool is not the same as the Add Node button (the plus sign). The Add Node button inserts a new node between two selected nodes. The New Node tool lets you lay down new nodes on your picture by hand to extend your path.

The next menu item opens a drop-down menu, the Current Path Name menu. This menu shows the name of the path you are currently working on. Because you can have more than one path open in a document at once, that drop-down menu can contain several entries. "Work Path" is the default name for the first path created in any document.

The Add tool (the + button) places a new node between the selected node and the one right before it. The Delete tool (the – button) removes any node you have just clicked on. You can also use the plus and minus keys on your numeric key pad to add or delete nodes. The next three tools can be used to join, break apart, or reduce the number of nodes on a path. The Reduce button eliminates any nodes on a path that are not adjusting that path's direction in some way. Reduce Tolerance is the numeral next to the Reduce command. Set from 1 to 10, it affects how aggressively the Reduce command works to find nodes it can get rid of and still maintain your path's shape. Setting this number higher than 6 causes some real alteration in the way your path looks.

The next six buttons change the selected node into various kinds of curves or lines, such as sharp curves (cusps), symmetrical curves, or smooth curves. The "rubber band" button turns on Elastic mode, which makes the line near the selected node behave like a rubber band when manipulated.

The next two tools turn the selected path into a mask, or a mask into a path, and the final two tools stroke the selected path or mask. Stroking causes the currently selected paint tool to trace the path once. Your path or mask will then have a brush stroke around its perimeter. Repeating this command thickens and accents the brush stroke.

Secret

If you want to create a precise mask, because a path's segments are adjustable, try creating a path first and then converting it to a mask.

The Crop tool

Figure 9-5 shows the appearance of the Property Bar when the Crop tool is selected. When eyeballing an image with the Crop tool is not precise enough, the Property Bar provides a numeric entries dialog box for more precise cropping. The Tool Settings roll-up gives you an option to change the measuring system you use to crop your picture. That way, if you are using the Crop tool, you can switch to the metric system on the fly.

Figure 9-5: The Property Bar looks like this when the Crop tool is selected.

The Crop tool Property Bar also contains Crop to Mask and Crop to Border commands. Crop to Mask reduces the size of your picture to the area just surrounding the currently selected mask. The Crop to Mask command can also be found in the Image ⇨ Crop ⇨ To Mask menu. Crop to Border opens a dialog box that enables you to crop your image according to paper color, the current paint color, or a color picked from your picture with the Eyedropper. See Figure 9-6.

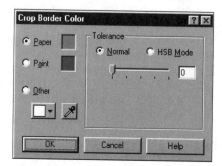

Figure 9-6: The Crop Border Color dialog box offers choices for cropping according to color.

The Zoom tool

Figure 9-7 shows the Property Bar while the Zoom tool is selected. It contains a numeric zoom option drop-down menu and magnifying buttons that enlarge or shrink your view of an object when you point and click. Also included are the Normal, Actual Size, to Width, to Height, and Zoom to Fit tools. If you want to see the entire width of a picture and don't really care if you see its entire height, click on the Zoom to Width tool. Conversely, if you care to see only the entire height of an image, click on Zoom to Height.

Figure 9-7: The Property Bar has this form while the Zoom tool is selected.

The Eyedropper tool

Figure 9-8 shows the Property Bar while the Eyedropper tool is selected. Normally, the Eyedropper tool samples one pixel of paint from the image. The active paintbrush color changes to the exact color that the Eyedropper tool lands on. The Property Bar enables you to select a range of pixels from your image. The average value of those pixels becomes your paintbrush's active color. Click on the Eyedropper tool while 3X3 is selected, and Photo-Paint averages the surrounding nine pixels. Select 5X5 and the surrounding 25 pixels are averaged. The average becomes your paintbrush tool's color. Select Custom, and you can click and drag an area as large as you like as your sample. Select Point, and Eyedropper returns to selecting single pixels.

Figure 9-8: The Property Bar takes this form while the Eyedropper tool is selected.

Secret

To change the fill color rather than the paintbrush color, right-click on your chosen color with the Eyedropper tool. Pressing Shift while clicking also changes the fill rather than the paint color. Pressing Ctrl while clicking changes the paper color.

The Eraser tool

Figure 9-9 shows the Property Bar while the Eraser tool is selected.

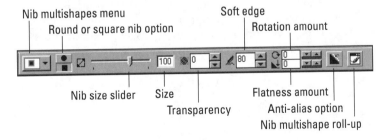

Figure 9-9: The Property Bar appears like this while the Eraser tool is selected.

Many of the erase features of the Property Bar have to do with nibs. A *nib* is a tool attribute that hasn't been discussed yet. For now, think of nibs as strands of hair on the tip of your paintbrush. The tip of your brush can be square and thick, skinny and round, or oddly shaped. Your brush tip can render "brushy" strokes that show off individual brush hairs, or it can apply paint in thick gobs. Or your brush tip can have a soft edge that gets rid of any jagged, pixelated edges to your brush strokes. By choosing the right nib, you can lay down hard lines like a No. 3 pencil. Figure 9-10 shows the different Eraser effects that can be achieved by changing the nib attribute.

Figure 9-10: A portion of this image on the left has been erased with a soft-edge eraser. The image on the right has no soft edge.

As you view the Eraser tool Property Bar from left to right, the first tool allows selection of the nib shape. Scroll all the way down to see all of the different shapes. (See Figure 9-11.) The number next to each shape is the nib size. Besides selecting interesting angles and orientations for your Eraser tool, you can insert pictures and symbols. The size and edge quality of these pictures takes on the properties you select with the other Eraser tool parameters.

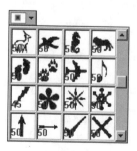

Figure 9-11: You can use either the Eraser tool Property Bar or the Nibs roll-up to select some interesting shapes for your nib. The number near each shape is the nib size.

The next two buttons assign a round or square shape to your eraser, and the slider bar determines eraser size. The Transparency number, set to zero by default, determines how much underlying image remains after you use the Eraser tool. If Transparency is set to zero, none of the underlying image shows through.

The next number, the Soft Edge setting, determines if the image next to the erased area fades out or stops abruptly. The next two buttons determine the angle and flatness of your eraser tool. You don't need to adjust any of these settings unless you aren't satisfied with the built-in eraser shapes.

The next button turns on the anti-aliasing feature. (Anti-aliasing smoothes out the edges of edited bitmaps. It is explained in more detail a little later.)

Secret

First double-click on the Paint tool, and then click on the Eraser (both in the toolbox). You'll see the Nibs roll-up menu. At first glance, this menu looks just like the first item, Nib Shapes. But look closely at the arrow pointing right on the right side of the Nibs roll-up. (See Figure 9-12.) Click on the arrow, and you'll see that you can save your edited brush tips (nibs) for later use. You do this by clicking on Add Current Nib.

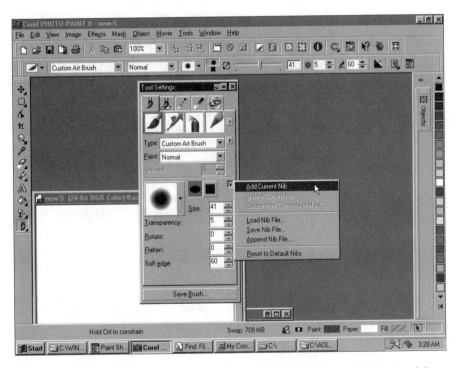

Figure 9-12: The Nibs roll-up menu is available by double-clicking on the Paint tool and then clicking on the Eraser tool. Here you can save eraser shapes for later use.

Tip

In Photo-Paint, an eraser is simply a style of brush that applies the paper color. When you save a shape you create (for example, a unique shape formed from a mask) as a brush, it can be used as an eraser as well. Conversely, any mask saved as an eraser can be used as a brush.

Drawing tools

The Property Bar changes depending on which shape is selected. It provides a unique selection of options for each shape, as well as a few options that are common to all shapes (such as opacity controls and scaling).

Figure 9-13 shows how the Property Bar looks when the Rectangle tool is selected. You can set the Fill and Outline types, do away with the Fill altogether, or change the transparency of the drawing itself. The Line Width value defaults to 20, which can be a little wide for most uses. The word "Normal" is part of the Paint Merge dialog box. Photo-Paint provides extensive control over special-effect color-merging modes that can create some rather striking effects. The Anti-Alias tool also appears on the Drawing tools Property Bar.

Figure 9-13: The Property Bar takes this form when the Rectangle tool is selected.

If you want to create a shape that is not immediately embedded into the background, click on Render to Object, near the far-right Drawing tool Property Bar. With Render to Object checked, your shape will be immediately converted to an object on its own layer, where it can be manipulated independently.

Secret

The way to make rounded rectangles in Photo-Paint is to increase the Roundness value. It's the third number from the left on the Property Bar. You cannot come back to a previously created rectangle and change its roundness amount.

The Fill tool

Photo-Paint's Fill tool enables you to fill a mask, an object, or an entire page with color, a fountain fill, bitmaps, or textures. The tools for editing and selecting Photo-Paint fills have greatly improved over the years. The Fill tool Property Bar provides Transparency and Paint modes, as well as Anti-aliasing options. You'll also find Color Tolerance controls, for determining how sensitively your fill will interact with colors surrounding the area to be filled. But to really edit your fill, you need to click on the Fill button on the far-right of the toolbar (or double-click on the Fill tool in the toolbox). This opens the Tool Settings dialog box, shown in Figure 9-14. We'll look at the Uniform Fill and then the Fountain Fill dialog boxes.

Figure 9-14: The Tool Settings dialog box offers access to various fill types.

The Uniform Fill dialog box

Choose Uniform Fill (the rainbow-colored, first button on the left) and click on Edit, and you'll see the Edit Uniform Fill dialog box. (See Figure 9-15.) The Uniform Fill dialog box has four ways to select colors for your fill. Pictured is the Color Viewer, which enables you to combine four colors into a custom blend.

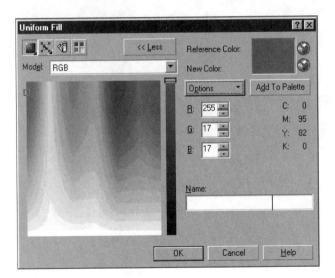

Figure 9-15: The Edit Uniform Fill dialog box controls colors and other attributes of uniform fills.

The four icons at the upper left of the Uniform Fill dialog box represent four ways to select a color, or to build a palette of colors based on various rules of color combining. The first icon opens a rectangle of color that gradually blends from one hue to the next. Drag your cursor in this rectangle, and watch the New Color rectangle to the right. Drag in the rectangle to choose a color. The color you see in the New Color rectangle will be your new fill color. Or click on Add To Palette to add this new color to your currently selected palette. The drop-down menu of this first icon lets you choose which type of Color Model to select a color from; for example, RGB, CYMK, or LAB.

The next icon provides a mixing area, where you can use an Eyedropper tool and brush to select and then blend colors in a palette-like environment (see Figure 9-16). Adjust the Blend Amount slider to specify how readily you want colors to combine when you paint with the brush. Use the provided Eyedropper tool to select a color. The drop-down menu of this second icon reveals two other ways to choose colors for blending—the Color Harmonies Wheel, which arranges colors according to their complements as you spin a wheel, and the Color Blend area. Here you can select four colors, and each of your four colors fades into a rectangle, creating unique blends. Click anywhere in the rectangle to select and save a new color for your palette or fill. As before, the color you see in the New Color rectangle is your new Fill Color. Click on Add To Palette to add your new color to the currently selected palette.

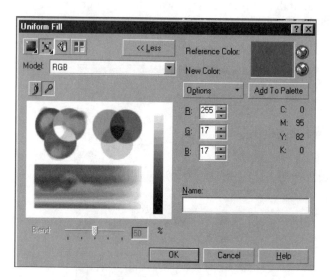

Figure 9-16: You can blend colors to create new ones in this palette-mixing area.

The third icon lets you choose colors by established color-matching systems, such as PANTONE, FOCOTONE, and Netscape Navigator palettes. Creating a palette from these colors is helpful if you are sending work to an outside printing bureau or building a Web page using specific, Web-aware colors.

The fourth icon allows you to load specific palettes (such as Corel's default CORELPNT.CPL) and see each color by name. You can change a color's name and build a separate palette based on any color scheme you design here.

While choosing a color, you may see a "crossed out" printer icon next to it. This icon indicates that your currently chosen printer cannot print the exact shade you have chosen.

The Fountain Fill dialog box

Fountain Fill enables you to adjust the fill's source colors, fill shape, spectrum direction, and number of steps. Pictured in Figure 9-17 is the Edit Fountain Fill dialog box with the Cylinder 19 preset being edited. Moving any of the seven fill points (pictured where the mouse cursor is) adds new color variations to the selected fill.

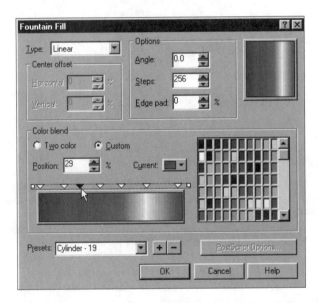

Figure 9-17: The Edit Fountain Fill dialog box affords access to further fill options.

Clicking on the "checkerboard square" icon on the Tool Settings roll-up enables you to choose a bitmap fill. You can import an image in any common picture file format to be used as a Photo-Paint fill. Options are included to stretch the bitmap so that it fits the selected area, or to tile it according to your specifications.

Click on the Texture icon (farthest from the left) on the Tool Settings roll-up and choose Edit. You'll see the Edit Texture Fill dialog box shown in Figure 9-18. Photo-Paint comes with hundreds of preset textures available from the four libraries included on the CD. As you can see from the number of options pictured in Figure 9-18, each texture can be edited within an inch of its life. This dialog box is one of Photo-Paint's most distinctive creativity tools.

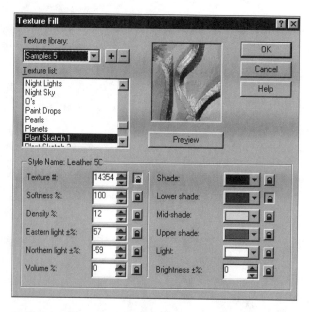

Figure 9-18: The Edit Texture Fill dialog box affords access to bitmapped textures.

The Interactive Fill tool

Working with the toolbox, press and hold the Fill tool. The tool to the right is the Interactive Fill tool. This tool has its own Property Bar. It contains an option to use two colors as starting and ending points on the spectrum for your fill. Thus, rather than simply fade from blue to red, your fill can consist of the entire color wheel from blue to red, either clockwise or counterclockwise. You can also fade from the paper color (usually white) to any other color. On your canvas, you'll notice markers that can be repositioned for editing the starting, ending, and color center of your fill. Manipulating the markers produces instantaneous changes on your paper. This can be done as often as you like. When you are happy with your results, click on the Apply button on the Property Bar.

Figure 9-19 shows how to apply an interactive fill that fades to transparent. Notice the Style settings on the Tool Settings roll-up next to the image. To mimic the angle of the candle, and to ensure that the text remains visible on the page, you need to use all the interactive controls. Notice that the fill starts from the bottom left and moves towards the upper right, as dictated by the arrow origin and direction. The tiny rectangle near the word *Birthday* controls where the colors begin to fade from one to the other. By manipulating the rectangle, we could see to it that the transparency started soon enough to make the text visible, while filling the bottom left with a good deal of color. Stretching the arrow all the way to the top of the page ensures that the fill blend is very gradual. Shortening the arrow completes the blend closer to the blend's origin. Again looking at the Tool Settings roll-up, you can change the Transparency amount by entering a digit or using the slider below. This affects how much of the underlying image shows through the fill.

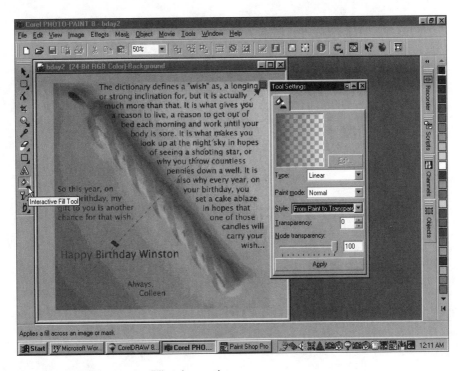

Figure 9-19: The Interactive Fill tool at work.

The Paint tool

When the Paint tool is selected, the Property Bar reveals options for brush type, nib size and shape, transparency and Soft Edge amount, and links to the Nibs roll-up, Brush reset options, and Tool Settings roll-up. Of particular interest are the Brush reset options. Having this tool handy enables you to edit existing brushes with total abandon, knowing that you can restore them at a moment's notice if you want.

Figure 9-20 shows the Property Bar for the Paint tool with the paint mode drop-down list open.

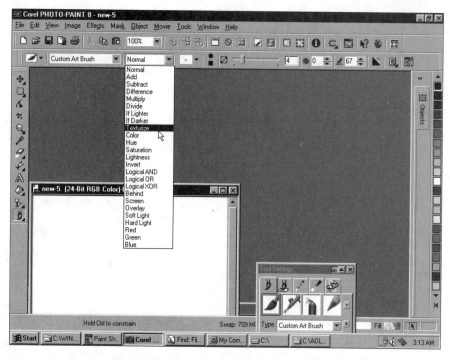

Figure 9-20: The paint mode drop-down list contains many different options.

Placement of the Property Bar

Because the Property Bar is rather long, often containing more than a dozen options, you may find it too cumbersome to work with as an attached bar. You can make it into a floating toolbar simply by pressing and holding down your mouse on any portion of it and dragging it into your image. Next, dragging inward from either side of the Property Bar causes the tools to double up in rows and become a wider, taller rectangle rather than a short, skinny one. To again anchor the Property Bar to the top of the workspace, drag it towards the top of the screen and quickly release it with a fast snap in that direction.

Working with Photo-Paint's toolbars

Photo-Paint has more than a dozen toolbars. Right-clicking on any open toolbar reveals a toolbar list. A check appears next to each of the toolbars currently open. Whereas the Property Bar contains options to edit and refine the selected tool, each toolbar contains single-click access to the tools themselves. For example, the Paint Tools toolbar contains 15 brush types. Often, each toolbar contains the same tools found on the toolbox at the far-left of the screen, but expanded to provide easier access. Photo-Paint's toolbars include the following:

- Property Bar
- Version 6
- Standard
- Mask/Object
- Movie
- Roll-ups/Dockers
- Toolbox
- Paint Tools
- Effects Tools

- Clone Tools
- Mask Tools
- Objects Tools
- Node Tools
- Zoom Tools
- Undo Tools
- Object Transparency Tools
- More Tools

Click on View ⇨ Toolbars to see all the toolbar types. You'll see a dialog box called Toolbars. Click on the Options button to view sliders that allow you to adjust the button size of a toolbar, as well as how much blank space should be left surrounding the toolbar buttons.

Note

The More Tools toolbar contains a menu for any personalized toolbars you create, as well as the Shape and Fill Tools toolbars.

When a toolbar appears on the screen, it appears as a floating toolbar. Pushing a floating toolbar rapidly up toward any side of the screen causes it to anchor there. Anchoring can sometimes cause toolbars to "double up" two-to-a-row. This causes some of the tools to be hidden below the screen-viewing area. Be careful not to anchor more than three or four toolbars at a time.

Arranging your toolbars

You can arrange your toolbars any way you like. If you want, you can reduce your work area to about an eighth of your screen space by filling it up with toolbars. (See Figure 9-21.) Photo-Paint forces you to spend a little time choosing the tools you really want to have handy. Access any toolbar by clicking on View ⇨ Toolbars. Place a check by any toolbar you want present on the screen. Remove the check from any toolbar you no longer want to see. You can also right-click on any blank toolbar space and select a toolbar from the pop-up menu.

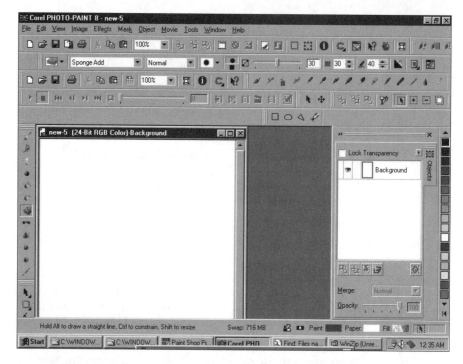

Figure 9-21: All Photo-Paint's toolbars have been placed on the screen.

Tip

Here are a few helpful tips for placing toolbars on your screen:

- Some toolbars, such as the Roll-Ups/Dockers toolbar, take up less than half a horizontal screen. Others, such as the Node and Repeat Stroke toolbars, take up only two spaces. If you drag these minitoolbars next to each other, they stay put and create one long toolbar. This is better than taking up lots of vertical space with tiny toolbars.

- Toolbars will snap to the position you drag them toward. They can be anchored up, down, right, or left. Any toolbar can be a floating toolbar.

- Whatever you do, don't put away the Property Bar.

- Get to know the Command Recorder (View ➪ Dockers ➪ Recorder). With it, you can automate routine tasks, making some toolbars unnecessary.

- Instead of having many toolbars up, learn some keyboard shortcuts for oft-repeated tasks. Use the Customize Toolbars dialog box (View ➪ Toolbars ➪ Customize ➪ Keyboard) to create new shortcut key commands.

Customizing your toolbars

Figure 9-22 shows the Customize dialog box with the Toolbars tab selected. Open it by Selecting View ➪ Toolbars ➪ Customize. In this example, the Tools folder is open, and the mouse pointer is hovering over the Pen Settings tool button. By dragging that tool button to any toolbar on the screen, you can cause it to remain there and be operative whenever the toolbar is opened.

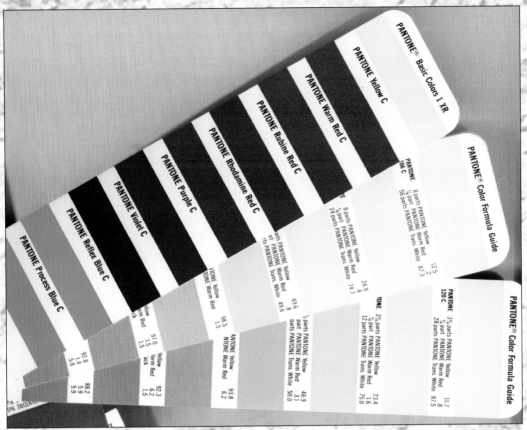

Plate 5-1: When choosing spot colors at the print shop, you'll more than likely use the PANTONE Matching System swatch book. This is a precise way of choosing premixed spot colors. You should use this method rather than relying on your monitor.

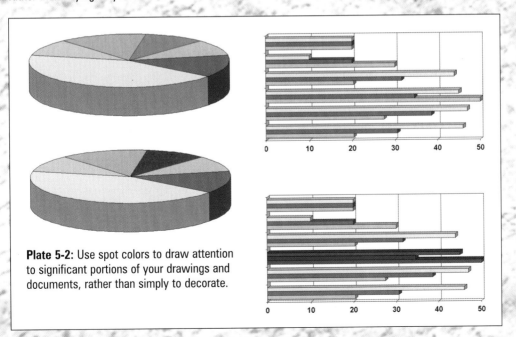

Plate 5-2: Use spot colors to draw attention to significant portions of your drawings and documents, rather than simply to decorate.

WestNet News

Resource Management News for Our Clients and Friends

Human Resource Management Consultants

1155 Port Avenue, Culver City, CA 92800   July, 1997- Vol. III   Tel: 805-240-1188, Fax: 805-240-1189, AOL: sjenson

Team Conflict: Taming the Savage Beast

What to do when your crews become unruly.

When your work team gets out of hand, it seems like an impossible beast to tame.

The federal education loans and grants Sue received while in college should have been enough to help her live and study in reasonable comfort--but she spent far too much on alcohol.

Sue started drinking when she was 16. She drank moderately at first, only on weekends, usually. This pattern followed her into college, where she continued to drink only on those nights when she didn't have school the next day. Sometime in her senior year, she started drinking during the week.

One year after she got out of college, Sue got married. Marriage, her two children and a career as a medical technician in a major California hospital was nothing like what she had expected--by the second year she was drinking every night and having a couple of drinks during her lunch breaks.

By age 25, Sue was spending hundreds of dollars a month on alcohol. But she didn't even suspect she had a problem. She began coming in late to work, making a lot of mistakes, and sometimes not showing up at all. Her dulled senses and negative

If They Would Just Grow Up

How to handle immature employees

Few things are less frustrating than an immature team member.

Ask Mike Lusk, Regional Sales Development Manager for Allstate Insurance, what he attributes his company's success to, and his answer is simple--traditional values. Allstate, both locally and worldwide, practices the concepts of service, value and community involvement, and it has paid off. From the writing of their first policy in 1931, the company has done nothing but prosper. According to Lusk, customer satisfaction are responsible for Allstate's tremendous growth.

Part of the reason for Allstate's enormous success can be found in its roots. Allstate Insurance is the brain child of General Robert E. Wood, who was the president of Sears & Robuck Co. in 1931. Allstate is a member of the Sears Financial Network. However, big companies do not always do well just because they are big. Allstate's growth is due primarily to the company's attitude toward its customers and a sense of civic duty.

The Allstate mission statement is:

a

WestNet

Human Resource Management Consultants

b

Australia
Decision Dynamics
61-2-442-232 (Telephone)
61-2-442-235 (Fax)
randsag@ibm.net

Canada
PMB. Consultants
416-425-6624 (Telephone)
416-425-2832 (Fax)

Mexico and Latin America
Quest
1-714-581-9478 (Telephone)
1-714-581-9456 (Fax)

US
West Net
Tel: 805-240-1188
Fax: 805-240-1189
AOL: sjenson

Helping People With People

WestNet
1155 Port Avenue
Culver City, CA 92800

Bulk Rate
U.S. Postage
Permit #DA0
Culver City, CA

Helping

People

With

People

WestNet

Human Resource Management Consultants

c

Plate 5-3: Rather than cluttering up your documents with random color, instead use color to direct the reader's eyes to specific portions of the page. In newsletters (a) and letterhead (b) you can use color to call out the newsletter name and company logo. In brochures (c), use color to label information, making topics easier to find.

Plate 5-4: Use color in longer documents to mark the beginning of each section to help readers find material and stay oriented. Use color to highlight section numbers, to distinguish individual sections, and so on.

Plate 5-5: Sometimes called "poor-man's color," different percentages or *tints* of spot colors create the illusion of multiple colors. In the pie chart, for example (a), the various tints make it seem as though several different colors are in use, rather than just one. When using black and a spot color, as in this annual report cover (b), you can use percentages of both colors, widening your range of color options.

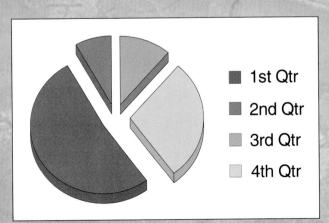

a

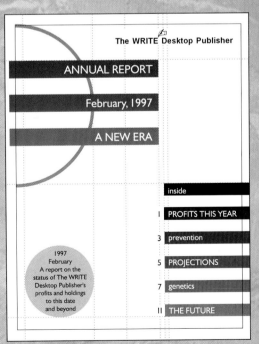

b

Plate 5-6: This graph shows the vast differences between what colors the human eye can see and what color devices are capable of reproducing. Notice that process printing presses have the most severe limitations.

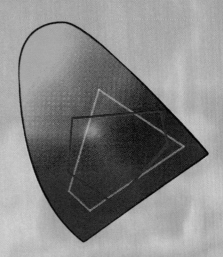

Plate 5-7: Use color in your charts to draw the viewer's eyes to the most important element on the chart.

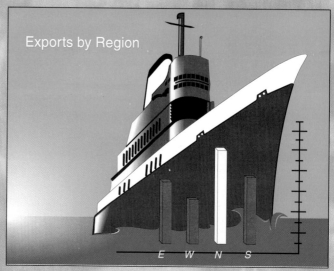

Exports by Region

E   W   N   S

Plate 5-8: Use bright colors to bring in new points and dull (dim) colors to play down points you've already introduced (a). You can also use the build effect with charts, enabling you to talk about one group of data at a time (b).

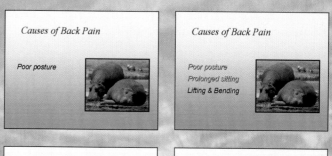

Causes of Back Pain

Poor posture

Causes of Back Pain

Poor posture
Prolonged sitting
Lifting & Bending

a

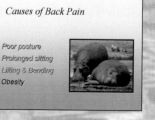

Causes of Back Pain

Poor posture
Prolonged sitting

Causes of Back Pain

Poor posture
Prolonged sitting
Lifting & Bending
Obesity

b

Sales By Region

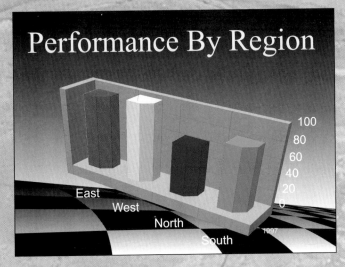

Performance By Region

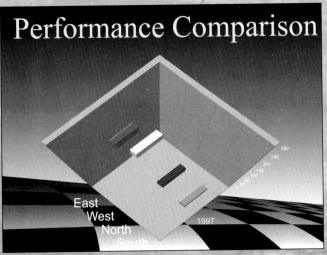

Performance Comparison

Plate 5-9: Use the same colors for related data. If, for example, you want to show trends for a certain department throughout your presentation, use the same color each time you display data for that department (compare a, b, and c).

Plate 5-10: Examples of how the straight (top), clockwise (middle), and counterclockwise (bottom) options affect fountain fills.

Plate 5-11: Here are a few example of effects you can achieve with fountain fills and extrude.

Stranger than Fiction
Stranger than Fiction
Stranger than Fiction
Stranger than Fiction
Stranger than Fiction

Plate 5-12: These examples show how changing a fill angle can affect the look of your drawing. The angles shown here are 90º, 180º, 270º, 360º, and a radial fill at 90º.

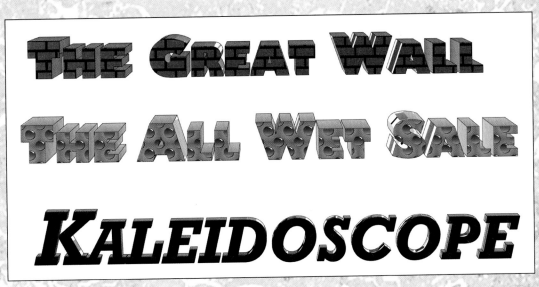

Plate 5-13: With CorelDraw's textures and patterns, you can create custom art with just a few mouse clicks. From two-color to full-color patterns to fractal textures, literally thousands of options are available from which to choose.

Plate 6-1: Here are some examples of what you can achieve with special effects: Envelope (a), PowerClips (b), Lens (c), Perspective (d), and Blend (e).

a

b

c

d

e

Plate 6-2: Examples of shading achieved with the Blend feature. Notice the highlights in the chicken's wings, the baseball, and so on. These effects were achieved by blending two colors together.

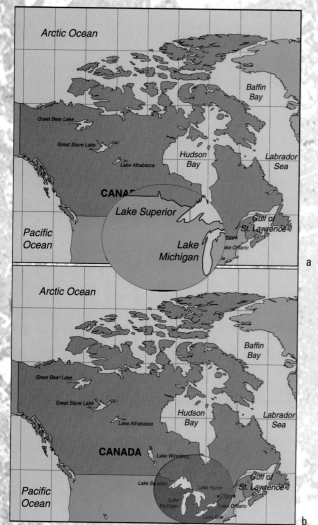

Arctic Ocean

Baffin
Bay

Great Bear Lake

Great Slave Lake

Lake Athabasca

Hudson
Bay

Labrador
Sea

CANADA

Lake Superior

Gulf of
St. Lawrence

Pacific
Ocean

Lake
Michigan

a

Arctic Ocean

Baffin
Bay

Great Bear Lake

Great Slave Lake

Lake Athabasca

Hudson
Bay

Labrador
Sea

CANADA

Lake Winnipeg

Lake Superior

Lake Huron

Gulf of
St. Lawrence

Pacific
Ocean

Lake
Michigan

Ottawa

Lake Ontario

Lake Erie

b

Plate 6-3: You can use lenses to highlight and call out portions of your drawings. In this example, the Magnify lens (a) zooms in on a portion of the map. The Tinted Grayscale lens (b) highlights a specific area on the map. In addition, you can use two lenses, Magnify and Transparency, to call out portions of a map (c). This third example shows the power of Lens. The circle path over the portion of the map uses a Magnify lens set at x2. The Frozen option in the Lens roll-up is selected, which duplicates the area covered by the lens and pastes it into the masking object. You can move the magnified area anywhere in the drawing.

Arctic Ocean

Baffin
Bay

Great Bear Lake

Great Slave Lake

Lake Athabasca

Hudson
Bay

Labrador
Sea

CANADA

Lake Winnipeg

Pacific
Ocean

Lake Superior

Lake Huron

Gulf of
St. Lawrence

Lake
Michigan

Ottawa

Lake Ontario

Lake Erie

Lake Superior

Lake
Michigan

c

Plate 6-4: Use the Interactive Transparency tool to place transparent fills in objects. Transparencies created with the Interactive Transparency tool give the appearance of placing tinted film over an object, making the transparent object seem opaque.

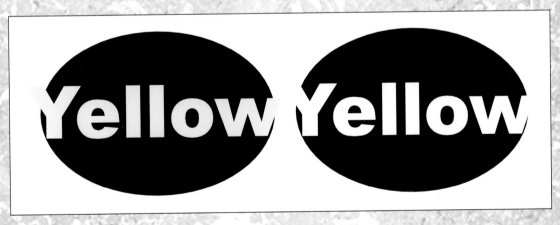

Plate 7-1: Unless you knock out the dark color under the light color, the dark color will show through.

Plate 7-2: When printing light colors over dark colors or two overlapping light colors, you can avoid unsightly gaps from press misregistration by trapping. In this example, we changed the trap to red so that you can see it.

Plate 8-1: You can create a variety of images with Photo-Paint. Here, a plug-in helped create the planing effect on the Statue of Liberty (a). Elements from two different pictures were combined to create the image of the hands and globe (b). The screen capture depicting Advanced Teamware's Web page contains several different effects you can achieve with Photo-Paint (c).

a

b

c

a

b

c

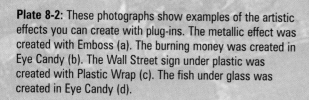

Plate 8-2: These photographs show examples of the artistic effects you can create with plug-ins. The metallic effect was created with Emboss (a). The burning money was created in Eye Candy (b). The Wall Street sign under plastic was created with Plastic Wrap (c). The fish under glass was created in Eye Candy (d).

d

Plate 11-1: Examples of special effects created with KPT Power Tools.

Plate 13-1: These examples of lumbar laser procedures are examples of the 3D drawing achievable in Dream 3D.

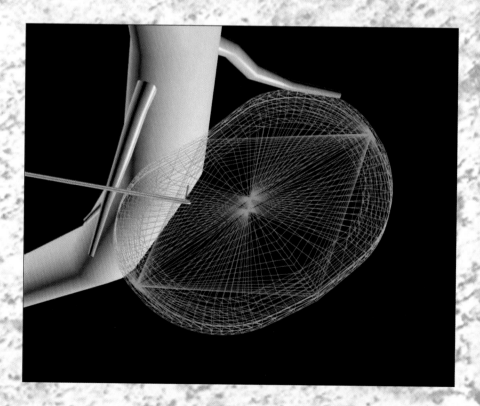

Patrick Lichty is an artist and writer, and a partner of Lichty Studios. His digital art and metal sculpture have been shown internationally, and he is an exhibitor at the 1996 New York Digital Salon. His commercial work has included multimedia titles, publication design, 3D animation, music videos, and Web design. Companies using his work include the Colin Riley group, IBM, Diebold, and MTV.

As a writer, Lichty has been published in computer art and academic circles. He has contributed most frequently to *Corel* and *3D Artist* magazines, and journals dealing with postmodern social theory. Lichty speaks frequently at academic conferences on cyberculture and the society of the Information Age. In his spare time, Lichty studies Asian flute music, martial arts, and popular culture.

Plate A-1: PowerLines were used to attain a variation in line necessary for facial expressions. Blends were also used to add realism to features such as eye glints.

Plate A-2: The source file contained over 2,500 discrete objects. To keep the machine from bogging down with excessive redraw times, we saved off the artwork in sections and merged them to build the final piece.

Plate A-3: Blends were used heavily to produce soft, flowing fabric folds that were unattainable through the use of fountain fills. However, use of blends resulted in a high object count.

Plate A-4: In many areas where precision blends were not necessary, radial and custom fountain fills (such as those in the hair) added a pleasing effect.

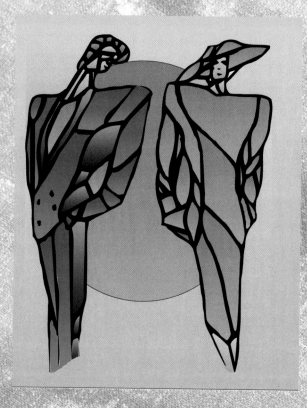

Sue Rodgers, an artist for 20 years, lives in Pittsburgh, Pennsylvania, with her husband, Randy, and their two children, Zachary and Tyler. She and her husband own two small businesses. They also do professional desktop publishing on the side.

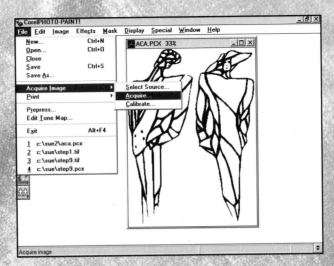

Plate B-1:
The picture was originally scanned in using Corel Photo-Paint, and then saved.

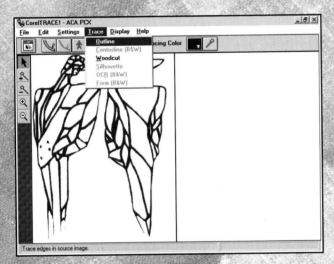

Plate B-2:
The file was then imported into CorelTrace in order to separate each piece so most of the work could be done in CorelDraw.

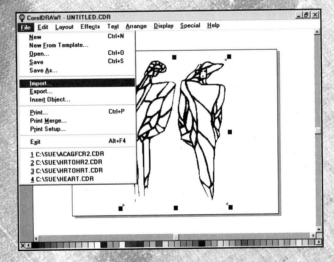

Plate B-3:
The graphic was imported into CorelDraw and reduced in size.

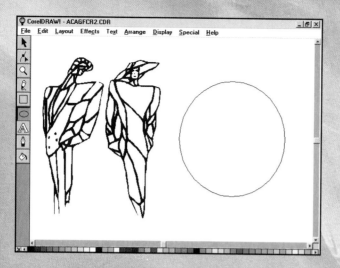

Plate B-4:
Using the Ellipse tool, a circle was drawn beside the graphic so it could be used behind the two people. The circle was then highlighted and moved to the back using Arrange ⇨ Order ⇨ To Back.

Plate B-5:
A rectangle was drawn with the Rectangle tool, and the graphic was sized and placed within the rectangle.

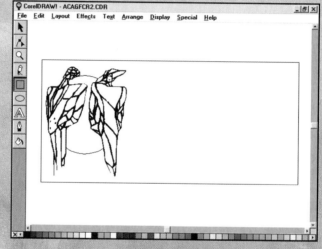

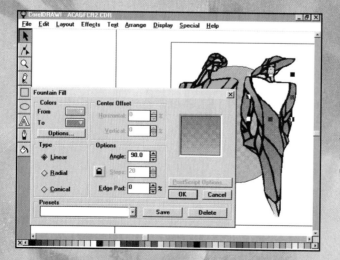

Plate B-6:
The people's clothes were highlighted using the Pick tool and then filled in using the Fill tool. A similar effect was applied with the circle behind them.

Timothy J. Moran is a graphic artist who lives and works in Elyria, Ohio. He uses CorelDraw for marketing and advertising projects, including logos, brochures, catalogs, and presentations.

Plate C-1: The eagle in the checker was a clip art image. All fills were changed to none and the eagle was made into a wireframe outline. Three copies of the image were staggered, each with a different color outline, to produce the embossed effect.

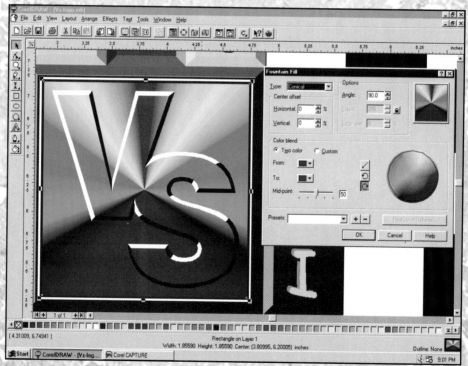

Plate C-2: The rainbow swirl is a conical fountain fill using a two-color, red-to-red blend with a clockwise path around the color wheel at a 90-degree angle.

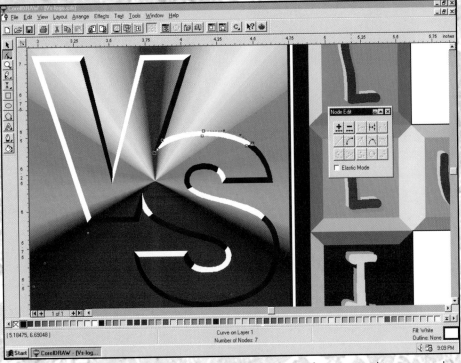

Plate C-3: The embossed "VS" was the Swiss 721 Black Outline font converted to curves and edited into several pieces using the Node Edit tool. Black and white fills were then applied.

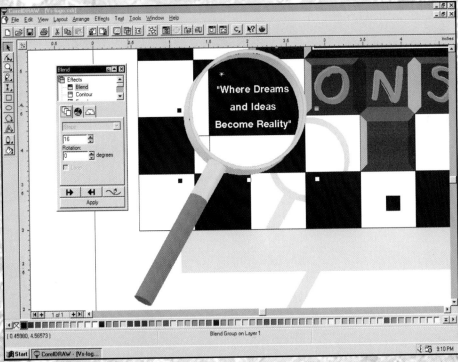

Plate C-4: The magnifying glass handle is a combination of objects with custom linear fountain fills. The rim is two circles of different yellow shades and line widths blended together.

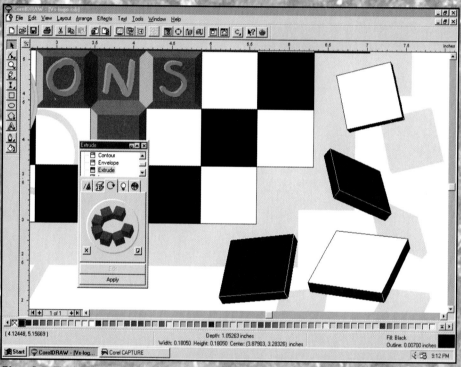

Plate C-5: The loose tiles were resized squares that were extruded slightly using solid fills. From within the extrusion options window, the squares were rotated in 3D.

Edward Fitzgerald is a freelance graphic designer and photographer who lives in the Kansas City, Missouri area. He retired several years ago from a 30-year career with Hallmark Cards, where he was a retail designer.

He has adapted the design in his logo to business cards, stationery, and note paper.

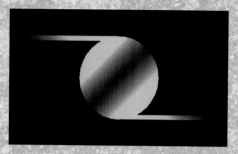

Plate D-1:
The logo is made up of circles and rectangles with fountain fill blends applied to achieve a reflected look. All of the blends are linear. The first circle was drawn and centered on the page. The circle is composed of a linear blend and two colors. The lower rectangle was created by mirroring the existing rectangle horizontally and vertically and applying it as a duplicate.

Plate D-2:
A second circle is centered on the page and reduced in size, allowing the first circle to appear as a band. The lower rectangle was duplicated as in the first step.

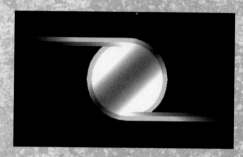

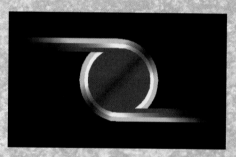

Plate D-3:
Another circle is centered on the page and reduced in size, allowing the first and second circles to appear as bands.

Plate D-4:
The final circle is a radial fill centered on the page. Three stripes were added at the top and bottom.

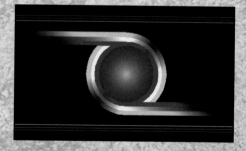

Anne Baker is a graphic designer who specializes in technical illustration. She lives in central Illinois. She uses CorelDraw on a daily basis, both at work and for fun projects, such as this illustration.

On a gray October day several years ago, she noticed a pair of antlers wired to a fence post, evidently forgotten by some hunter in a prior season. On the tip of one antler, a Monarch butterfly provided a splash of brilliant color. This illustration is an attempt to depict the subtle beauty of the scene.

Plate F-1:
The background is composed of two rectangular objects and one free-form object, all filled with gradient blends. These three objects were blended together to form one compound object.

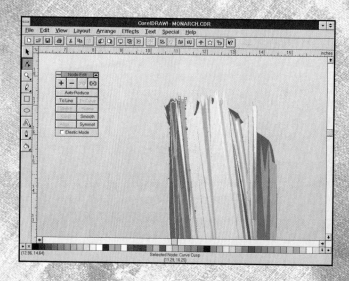

Plate F-2:
The fence post is a series of objects drawn freehand

Plate F-3:
Barbed wire was created entirely from power lines. After one section was completed, it was copied several times to form a continuous strand, and the colors were altered slightly. (Hint: Power lines can create large files. If you are limited on space, use the Separate and Ungroup features to convert power lines into smaller objects, and then reduce the number of nodes with the Autoreduce feature in the Shape menu.)

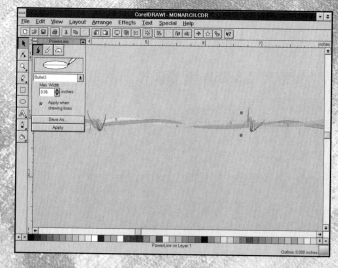

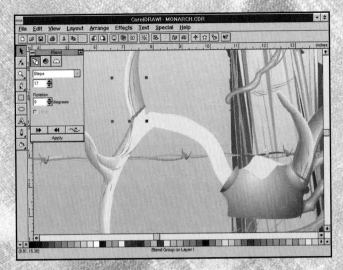

Plate F-4:
To create the antlers, the illustrator first drew some simple freehand shapes to serve as guides. The subtle shading and suggestion of different textures were accomplished by drawing lines of various widths and colors, which were then blended together.

Plate F-5:
The wireframe view demonstrates the pattern and technique used.

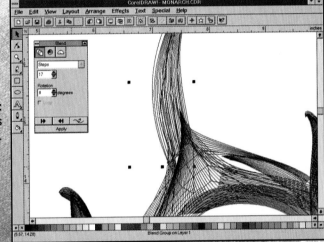

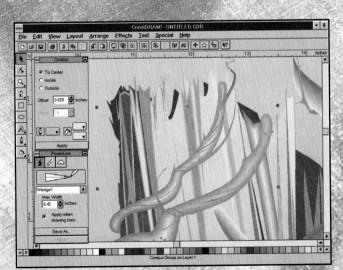

Plate F-6:
Vines were created by drawing freehand shapes. The Contour feature was used to create the gradient fills. Smaller vines were drawn using the power line feature.

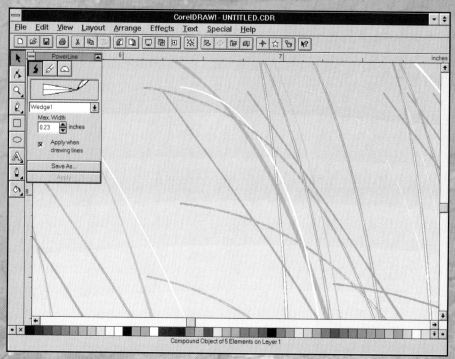

Plate F-7: Grass was drawn entirely with power lines.

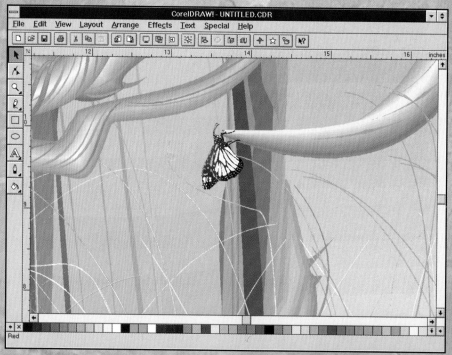

Plate F-8: As a finishing touch, a butterfly was imported from CorelDraw's clip art.

(By the way, if you own a stylus, this feature enables you to customize Photo-Paint to support your stylus's pressure settings and special features.) That's how easy it is to customize a toolbar.

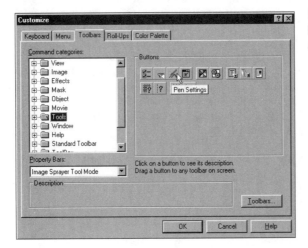

Figure 9-22: The Customize dialog box Toolbars tab can be attached to any toolbar.

The Toolbars tab is on top. From here you can take any menu function and place it on a toolbar. The folder icons to the left represent the menus. Click on any folder icon, and you'll see a ready-made icon for each command under that menu. If you want instant access to a command, just drag it to any toolbar on your screen. It's as easy as that.

Clicking on the Menu tab enables you to move commands from one menu to another. The Keyboard tab enables you to assign shortcut keys to almost any Photo-Paint function. The Roll-Ups and Color Palette tabs can be used to set new options for those features.

Customizing the status bar

Just as you can customize Photo-Paint's toolbars, you can modify the status bar to suit your own work habits. Right-click on the status bar and click on Customize. The Toolbar Customize dialog box appears. At this time, you may open any folder of commands, such as those found in the File or Edit menu. Notice that icons appear on the right, one icon for each command found in the opened menu folder. Drag any icon you like to the status bar, and it will stay there. You are not removing it from its "home" menu but merely making a copy of it and moving it. Figure 9-23 shows a modified status bar to which we added the "What's This?" icon, which is usually located in the Help menu. Any time we forget what a tool button or menu item does, we can simply drag this icon to that item and click.

Figure 9-23: A customized Photo-Paint status bar with the "What's This?" icon added.

The Docking Window

The Docking Window is a set of four panels positioned together on the right side of the Photo-Paint workspace (see Figure 9-24). They provide quick access to four features used frequently: Objects, Channels, the Command Recorder, and Scripts. Each panel is accessed by clicking on its tab. The Objects Panel provides a way to select each object, access its properties, link objects, lock transparency, and change object opacity. Clicking on the eye of any object thumbnail enables you to make the object visible or invisible. Click on the eye once to make it temporarily invisible. Click again to restore it. The Channels panel allows you to select a particular channel and create new ones. Select a mask in the Channel menu to see a semi-transparent mask in more detail than otherwise possible. The Command recorder panel lets you record Photo-Paint tasks as scripts, to be used later. And the Scripts Panel gives you access to any script.

Figure 9-24: The Docking Window, with all four panel tabs visible.

While accessing one of the panels of the Docking Window, the window changes to offer features relevant to that panel. However, you can minimize and close the Docking Window easily. Clicking on the right-facing two arrows on the upper-left portion of the Docking Window minimizes it, so that it only takes up a small portion of its normal size. Click on the X at the upper right to close the Docking Window. The tiny right-facing arrow on any panel offers relevant options. For example, to increase the size of the object thumbnails, click on this arrow while the Objects panel is open. To change a mask's indicator color from the default red (or to change how transparent this indicator color appears on your screen), click on this arrow while the mask is selected in the Channels panel, and then click on Channel Properties. You can also undock it and pull it into the page, where it takes up little space as a small modeless dialog box. This is done by quickly dragging it towards the center of your document.

Secret

If you close the Docking Window entirely, you'll have to open each panel separately from the menu (View ⇨ Dockers). If you minimize it, then each panel is still available at a single mouse-click.

Next we'll look at some of the unique features of the Docking Window.

Lock Transparency

While the Objects panel is visible you'll notice the Lock Transparency check box at the upper-left. With this box unchecked, you can use masking tools to change the shape of any object. As shown in Figure 9-25, a mask is selecting part of an object, which is a cartoon character (looks like an eyeball to us). The mask is allowed to select outside the cartoon character itself because Lock Transparency is not checked. If it were checked, then you would not be able to edit the mask beyond the object's boundaries, even if the mask's selection properties would normally allow it. With Lock Transparency checked, you will see selection marquees that extend beyond the object's boundaries. But you won't be able, for example, to fill the mask with a new color beyond the object's boundaries.

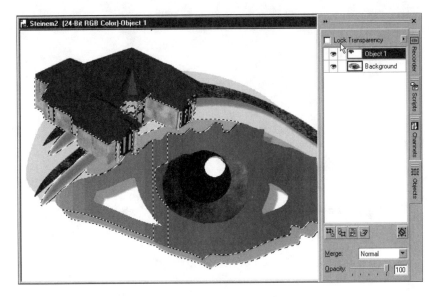

Figure 9-25: Without Lock Transparency checked, a mask can select outside the boundaries of the current object.

The Command Recorder

To record a task in Photo-Paint, such as resizing an image, painting brush strokes, or adding filters, make sure the Recorder panel is visible in the Docking Window (View ⇨ Dockers ⇨ Recorder). Click on the big red Record button and perform your task.

Scripts are thoroughly covered in Chapter 18 of this book, but for now we'll review some of the convenient features of the Command Recorder panel. As you perform your task, you'll see each step (for example, "Mask Rectangle" and "Fill Tool") listed in the panel. When you are finished recording, you can name and save your script for later use or use the two icons at the top of the panel (the ones that resemble pieces of paper; see Figure 9-26) either to delete or move steps. For example, if you decide you don't want to fill the rectangle with color in later uses of your script, you can simply delete that step before saving your script. If you reposition or delete steps, make sure your script still "makes sense" and doesn't try to perform tasks that are not possible because you've moved some essential part of the sequence.

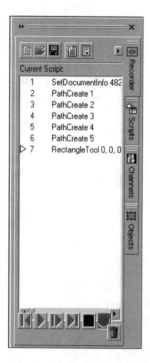

Figure 9-26: The Command Recorder dialog box.

Command Recorder records your actions, keyboard sequences, toolbar clicks, and paint strokes. It saves them as macros or scripts. Command Recorder displays your actions as single lines of text, and you can use the Command Recorder roll-up to relocate, edit, and delete any action. The record button (red) is pushed, and Insert New Commands is enabled. Then click on the right-facing arrow to access the Save ⇨ Load ⇨ New menu. After completing your command sequence, click on Stop (Command Recorder's buttons function like those of a tape recorder) and save your script. It will be saved as a CSC file, and it can be opened and executed by clicking on it.

The Command Recorder is similar to Corel Script Editor, which is examined later in this book. (See Chapter 18 for a more complete discussion of scripts.) Script Editor is a complete scripting tool that can be used to create large macros in Corel that include buttons, radio buttons, multiple-choice check boxes, and other Windows tools.

Secret

As with any graphic-based macro recorder, it is best to avoid mouse-oriented commands that involve clicking on a toolbar. A particular toolbar might not be in the same location the next time you use Photo-Paint. Use keyboard commands and menus rather than toolbars to design scripts.

The Photo-Paint Scrapbook

The Scrapbook is a collection of folders containing graphics, arranged as tabs, located on the right side of the Photo-Paint workspace. (See Figure 9-27.) Each tab is a link to folders containing one of the graphics collections included with Photo-Paint, such as Photos, Clipart, and such. Clicking on a particular tab opens a browse window for searching folders and locating just the image you want to import for your project. Images of all types will appear in the Browse window as thumbnails.

What makes this Scrapbook of particular importance to CorelDraw users is that many commercially available "image organizer" programs do not recognize the CorelDraw or Photo-Paint file type. This Scrapbook, then, is almost a must for quickly locating and opening native Corel graphics files. Although the Scrapbook's tabs are directly linked to clip art and photos from Photo-Paint's collection, you can use the Browse window to locate any file you want. Open the Scrapbook by selecting View ⇨ Scrapbook ⇨ Browse. To see all the images included with CorelDraw 8, you must have the proper CD in the caddie. You'll be prompted to place the right CD in the drive if it's not there already.

Notice that the Scrapbook contains a tab for single-click access to relevant FTP sites. For this feature to work, you must have an active Internet connection already in place when loading the Scrapbook.

Figure 9-27: The Photo-Paint Scrapbook.

After locating an image you want to import, just drag it to the Photo-Paint workspace. If you drag it to an existing document, it will open in the document as an object. If you drag it into Photo-Paint while no document is open, the image will open as a document itself.

At times, the size of the Scrapbook's thumbnails might not show enough detail. To increase the size of the thumbnails as they appear in the scrapbook viewing area, click on the right-facing arrow at the upper right of the Scrapbook and select View ⇨ Thumbnail Size. You'll see an image of a thumbnail surrounded by a resizable bounding box. Click any edge of the thumbnail and resize it to your liking. A numeric control is also available at the bottom of the thumbnail for more precise resizing. Keep in mind that larger thumbnails take longer to appear in the Scrapbook's viewing area, and because of size constraints, fewer thumbnails will appear at a time.

You can minimize the Scrapbook by clicking on the left-facing arrows at the top, which removes the Preview Area of the Scrapbook, but the tabs will remain on the screen. Clicking on any tab will restore the entire Scrapbook, so this arrangement is helpful because it saves screen space while giving you full access to the features. Click on the X on the right side of the Scrapbook to close it entirely. To restore it again, click on View ⇨ Scrapbook ⇨ Browse.

Advanced Opening and Saving Options

This section covers some advanced techniques for opening and saving images.

Opening only part of an image

Sometimes its desirable to open only a portion of an image. If the image you're planning to work on is particularly large, and if you know you are going to edit only a segment of it, you can use Photo-Paint's Partial Load feature. This feature presents the image divided into a grid, prompting you to select which part of the image you want to open.

To open only part of an image, click File ⇨ Open, and then turn your attention to the drop-down menu that reads Full Image. Click on it and select the Partial Load option. You'll then see the Partial Area dialog box (see Figure 9-28). Your image, divided into a grid, shows one section of your image blinking. If you proceed now, that portion of your image will be opened. Click on any other rectangular segment of your image to make it the active one. When the right segment of your image is selected, click on OK to proceed. If the available segment of your image is too small or large, then click on the Grid size drop-down menu. You can either select a new Grid size or click on Custom. The grid lines will then be movable, allowing you to resize the grid, as well as move the entire grid so that the portion of the picture you want to work with is more centralized and highlighted.

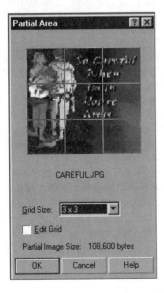

Figure 9-28: The Partial Area dialog box.

After using Partial Load, you can switch to another segment of the same image without having to use the Open dialog box again. Simply click on File ⇨ Select Partial Area, and you're prompted to choose a new segment from the gridlike preview you saw at first.

Note that Photo-Paint cannot load a partial mask, so if your file contains a mask, you have to load either the entire area containing it or a section sans mask.

Opening your image at a lower resolution

One way to examine your image without necessarily working on it at the moment is to open a lower-resolution version of your image. Click on File ⇨ Low Res, and you'll see a dialog box prompting you to select a new resolution for your image. Use the up- and down-arrows next to the percent symbols to change how large the Low Res version is.

Secret

When you open a Low Res version of an image, you are actually creating a new document. You can therefore save and edit this version without affecting the original.

Saving multiple versions of your document

Photo-Paint allows you to save an "archive" of your document, saved along various stages of completion. This archive can be compressed as a single group of documents, and you can specify that the first of the group will not be overwritten. This allows you to have a "safety" that is above any wanton experimental ideas that may occur to you.

To conveniently save several versions of the same document, click on File ⇨ Version Control ⇨ Archive Current, and you're prompted to save an initial version of your current work. After doing so, you'll see the New Archive Properties dialog box, shown in Figure 9-29. Here you can choose to compress your archive, which saves disk space but makes reloading a document take a bit longer, and choose a maximum number of archived documents before the program goes back and writes over the earlier versions. The more documents you allow, the larger the archive's file size. Later, when you want to open one of the archived versions, don't use the standard File ⇨ Open menu. This feature didn't work in our version. Instead, click on File ⇨ Version Control ⇨ Retrieve Document.

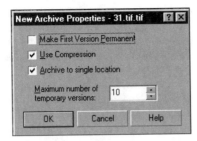

Figure 9-29: The New Archive Properties dialog box.

When you create a mask with a brush, the mask may have many levels of transparency. Any effect rendered through such a mask will be applied in degrees. Yet in normal viewing, when you look at a mask created with such a brush, you really cannot see this level of complexity. It just looks like a normal, "inside or outside" mask. You can view your mask's various levels of transparency by opening the Channels panel and clicking on the mask icon in the list of channels. Areas covered by the mask will appear clear. Areas not covered will appear red. You'll also see levels in between as well. Masks are covered thoroughly in the following chapter.

Working with Objects in Photo-Paint

Before getting into the secrets of working with objects in Photo-Paint, we'll review the difference between three of the most important elements you use in Photo-Paint: masks, paths, and objects.

A mask is a selection of pixels on the surface of an image. You make that selection by choosing color ranges (masking the reds or blues in your image, for example) or by area (carving out a shape with one of the masking tools). Masks are not necessarily sharply bordered, carved-out selections; they are simply temporary aids for setting aside a portion of an image for editing. A mask on your image allows you either to edit that area or protect that area from editing. However, masks can offer degrees of protection. You can set up a mask so that a little bit of your filtering or coloring can be allowed to seep through the mask, and affect the underlying image, to some degree. This is done by turning a grayscale image into a mask. Each level of "grayness" in the image, when applied as a mask, determines how much editing will be allowed to pass through the mask. Also, a mask can be feathered, meaning that it can taper off gradually around the edges. Masks can be empty until applied and can be moved around the surface of your image. Masks are covered thoroughly in Chapter 10.

A path is a shape or a line created by the Node tool. The Node tool is capable of great precision, and paths are usually highly detailed outlines of a portion of a bitmapped image. Paths can be lines. They need not be closed shapes. A path can be copied and reapplied to the same image, and it can be treated with special effects. A path can also be stroked with paint and then removed, leaving the paint behind on the canvas. Unlike a bitmap, a path never loses the integrity of its shape — no matter how much you enlarge it. Paths can be saved as EPS files and opened in other applications, even vector-based programs such as CorelDraw. (You can also import paths from any vector drawing, such as CDR and EPS files. You do this from the Property Bar when you are in the Path Node Edit mode.)

Objects are bitmapped images that occupy their own layer in front of a background image (or on top of it, if you like). They need never be merged or combined with the background image. They can be reshaped and edited, and they can be merged with other layers to create special effects. For example, in Photo-Paint you can create a drop shadow on an object with only a single mouse-click.

Note

Not all selecting tools have the same capabilities. The Object and Mask Transform tools are both used to select things, but if you click on a mask with the Object tool, nothing happens.

The Objects roll-up

Figure 9-30 shows the Objects docker, accessible by choosing View ⇨ Dockers ⇨ Objects. The Objects panel shows two objects and one background.

In Figure 9-31, the photo composition of a man in very warm clothing chasing balloons around the Easter Island statue was assembled using objects in Photo-Paint.

One object, the balloon group, is selected and available for editing. As an object, it is floating above the background image on its own layer. Consequently, it can be recolored and reshaped without affecting the underlying image. The man is also an object. To see a marquee around the objects on your page, select Object ⇨ Marquee Visible (or click on the Show Object Marquee button in the standard toolbar.) The Objects panel contains options to make chosen objects invisible, uneditable, and merged with the background image. You can also experiment with paint modes and transparency levels using the Objects panel. The object you are editing will have a red border around it in the roll-up.

Figure 9-30: The Objects docker is shown with a corresponding picture.

Figure 9-31: A photo composition created with objects in Photo-Paint.

Here's how you can recreate the image in Figure 9-31:

STEPS:
Creating a Composite Image Using Objects

Step 1. Open the image CLRCAST.CPT (found on the CD that comes with this book) and use the Magic Wand tool to select the man and his clothing. The Magic Wand tool is one of the Mask Selection tools, the second tool from the right on the toolbox. Press and hold your mouse button to see the drop-down menu of Mask selection tools. You'll have to play with the Tolerance settings to make sure you get only the pixels you want, with no white or blue. Remember that higher tolerance settings increase the likelihood of selecting unwanted pixels. Tolerance values can be adjusted from the Tool Settings dialog box for the Magic Wand tool (double-click on the Magic Wand tool to access Tool Settings). See Figure 9-32.

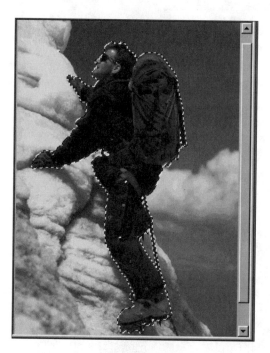

Figure 9-32: Extract the climber from the snow and turn him into an object.

Step 2. Select Object ➪ Create ➪ Object: Copy. This converts your mask into an object. Copy it to the Windows Clipboard.

Step 3. Open HEAVYRIP.CPT, also found on this book's CD. Open the Objects roll-up as well.

Step 4. Select Paste from the Edit menu and choose Paste as New Object. Position the man as he appears in Figure 9-31. You need to use the Object Rotate tools to obtain the angle shown. This is done by clicking twice on the man with the Object Picker tool and rotating him to your liking.

Step 5. Open the Balloon image. If you are not a fan of balloons, you may open a similarly sized object. We are going to be converting the balloon group to a mask and painting a shadow of the balloons on the Easter Island statue, so if you use a different image, keep that in mind.

Step 6. Using the Magic Wand tool again, select the balloons, convert them into an object, and copy them to the Windows Clipboard. Adjust the tolerance of the Magic Wand tool by double-clicking to bring up the Tool Settings dialog box, or use the arrows on the Property Bar.

Step 7. Paste the balloon group as an object into the Easter Island image. Position the balloons as shown in the picture. Notice your Objects roll-up shows two objects now. Instructions we now give for moving and copying the balloon group will not work unless the balloon group is selected in the Objects panel.

Step 8. While the balloons are selected, click on Mask ➪ Create from Object. Make sure there's a check mark by Marquee Visible in the Mask menu. You'll see "marching ants" around the balloons. Actually, the balloons haven't been touched. They're not selected at all. The mask you've just created from the balloon group object is actually selected.

Step 9. Using the Object Picker tool, select the balloons and choose Edit ➪ Cut.

Step 10. Switch to the Mask Transform tool. Make sure you're using the four-way arrow, which moves masks. Move the "marching ants" mask over to the lower middle of the Easter Island Statue, where you see the balloon shadow positioned in the final version of this picture (Figure 9-31).

Step 11. Use the Distort tool to stretch the balloon shadow downward slightly. Select Mask-Shape ➪ Feather, and choose 1 for Width and Middle for Direction.

(continued)

STEPS *(continued)*

Creating a Composite Image Using Objects

Step 12. Making sure the mask is still selected, choose the Fill tool and make the fill color black. Fill the mask with the shadow color. If the shadow edges appear too sharp and not natural enough, chose Mask-Shape ⇨ Feather again, use the same settings as in Step 11, and again fill the widened mask with black paint.

Step 13. Select Edit ⇨ Paste ⇨ Paste as New Object. The balloons will reappear. Reposition the balloon group with reference to the light source in the picture, making the shadow as realistic as possible. Position the man so that it looks as if he is truly after those balloons. By now I'm sure he wishes he'd brought something cooler to wear.

The Object menu

The Object menu contains three interesting commands that deserve special attention: Tag WWW URL, Clip Object to Mask, and Defringe.

Tag WWW URL

If you have an object selected with the Object tool, clicking on this command creates a clickable HTML map from it. (The command does not destroy or alter the object itself.) After clicking, you'll see a screen showing the object you clicked. You're asked to enter a Universal Resource Locator (URL) and make any comments that will help you remember where clicking on this image leads you. When you save your image, you're asked to save the image as an HTM file as well. The object's coordinates and image data are saved as a clickable region within the HTM file itself. Simply put, the Tag WWW URL command creates an HTML image map from your object. Creating Web pages from Corel documents is covered in Chapter 20.

Clip Object to Mask

Let's quickly review the difference between an object and a mask. An object is a bitmap that floats above the background image in its own layer. A mask is a way of setting aside a portion of the surface of an image for editing. So, yes, you can apply a mask to an object just as easily as you can to a background image. (The Clip to Mask feature is covered more thoroughly in Chapter 10.)

Here's how the Clip Object to Mask command works:

STEPS:

Using the Clip Object to Mask Command

Step 1.   Use a masking tool on an object to select an area for editing. When you are finished, use the Object Picker tool to make sure the object is selected.

Step 2.   Select Object ⇨ Clip Mask ⇨ Create ⇨ From Mask. Any part of the object that covers an area outside the mask will be clipped off.

Figure 9-33 shows an object on a background with a mask applied to it. The background is the crosshatch pattern. Above that is the archaeological site with the two tourists walking. The mask is the area surrounded by "marching ants." It was selected using the Magic Wand masking tool. The purpose was to select all of the archaeological site but leave out the blue sky.

Figure 9-33: The object is the archaeological site. The mask covers all of it except for the blue sky. "Marching ants" show the mask's boundaries.

Figure 9-34 shows the results of creating a clip mask. The sky is gone from the archaeological site. You see no more sky in the object because it has shrunk down to the size of the mask.

Figure 9-34: The object has shrunk down to the size of the mask.

Figure 9-35 shows the composite picture after the special effect, The Boss, was applied. Special effects are explained in detail in Chapter 11.

Figure 9-35: The composite picture is complete.

The Defringe command

The Defringe command (Object ⇨ Matting ⇨ Defringe) is used when a selection you imported as an object was not trimmed well. Sometimes a fringe of white pixels (not necessarily white, actually) gets imported along with your image. The Defringe command removes the fringe of pixels. You specify the width of the fringe to be removed. Figure 9-36 shows imported text as a bitmap sorely in need of defringing. Figure 9-37 shows the results of the operation.

Figure 9-36: The text bitmap was cut out of another picture and placed against the new backdrop. A white fringe got imported with the bitmap.

Figure 9-37: Here's how the same composition looks after the Defringe command was used.

Other Photo-Paint Features

Photo-Paint 8 includes so many new features that it's not surprising that a handful of tools defy easy categorization. For example, there's the Repeat Stroke tool and the Navigator pop-up.

The Repeat Stroke tool

The Repeat Stroke tool will not be available unless the Paintbrush tool is selected in the toolbox. To access Repeat Stroke, click on Edit ⇨ Stroke ⇨ Repeat Stroke (see Figure 9-38.)

Select Edit ⇨ Stroke ⇨ Repeat Stroke, and your mouse becomes a point-and-click paintbrush. Click on your canvas and a paint stroke appears. The Repeat Stroke dialog box, shown in Figure 9-39, enables you to edit your stokes. Increase the stroke number so that clicking once creates several strokes. You can also assign randomness to your brush stroke, which brings kind of a crosshatch, "driving rain" feel to your picture. You can assign a certain degree of random size and direction to your brush stroke, which can create an "impressionist" feel if applied with discretion. Use the available controls to alter the colors of the repeated strokes, and vary the angle. If you specify that one click of your mouse should create ten strokes, each varying its angle by 15 degrees, for example, the result will resemble a star. Figure 9-40 shows some interesting brush strokes generated with the Repeat Stroke tool.

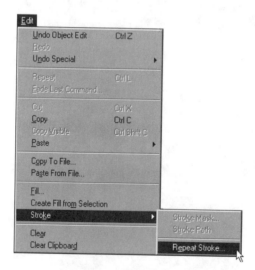

Figure 9-38:The Repeat Stroke command, found near the Stroke Mask and Stroke Path commands.

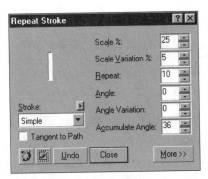

Figure 9-39: The Repeat Brush Stroke tool roll-up permits you to repeat brush strokes to achieve special effects.

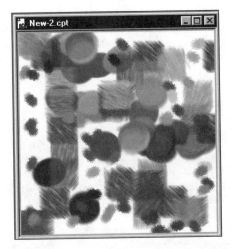

Figure 9-40: These strokes have been created using the Repeat Brush Stroke tool, with the Simple stroke selected.

Notice the Stroke drop-down menu in the Repeat Stroke dialog box. It says the word Simple. No other entries appear in the menu. That's because the only way to load an entirely new brush stroke is to load it from a path you have created with the Node tool. The following procedure explains how to make a new brush stroke that can be used as a Repeat brush stroke in your painting.

STEPS:

Making a New Brush Stroke Available as a Repeat Brush Stroke

Step 1.   Use the Node tool to create a path on your canvas.

Step 2.   Select Edit ⇨ Stroke ⇨ Stroke Path. Alternatively, you can load a saved path from an earlier session: Using the Node tool, make a path that looks like the brush stroke shape you'd like to make.

Step 3.   Save the path as a PTH file, as you would any path.

Step 4.   Select the Repeat Brush Stroke tool and click on the right-facing arrow above the Stroke drop-down menu. Select Load Path as Stroke. The path is loaded onto your canvas.

Step 5.   The next time you click on the canvas, the path will be stroked with the brush type and style you have selected.

If the brush stroke style you have selected is too "out there," you're likely to get undesirable results when you apply it to a path. Using a narrower, less diffuse brush can sometimes make a wild stroke look clearer.

The Navigator pop-up

If you open an image that is significantly larger than the screen, you'll notice a small white square at the bottom right of your picture. When you click and hold this square, a miniature version of your picture appears. Notice the gray bounding box inside the Navigator screen. You can maneuver this box in and around your picture to determine which portion you want to view. See Figure 9-41 for an example of the Navigator pop-up in action.

Figure 9-41: The Navigator pop-up is shown in action.

The Undo list

The Undo list, accessible by selecting Edit ⇨ Undo Special ⇨ Undo List, holds each edit you've performed on your picture, keeping them available for you to undo any procedure as far back as the most recent save. (See Figure 9-42.) Saving your work clears the Undo list. You may undo as many procedures at one time as you like. Selecting all procedures on the Undo list has the same effect as reverting back to your last saved version of the image.

If you have reapplied commands using Redo, then you also have generated a Redo list. To view and selectively again apply Redo commands, select Edit ⇨ Undo Special ⇨ Redo List. You can also undo each step, starting from the bottom of the list. If you select the last command on the list and click on Undo, Photo-Paint runs through the entire script, omitting the last step.

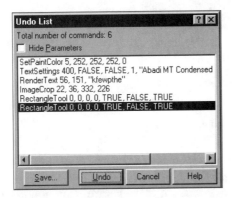

Figure 9-42: The Undo list lets you work back to your last save.

The Movie menu

The Movie toolbar contains buttons to stop, start, and record your movie. Photo-Paint's Movie tool creates a simple AVI file from a series of pictures you create. Figure 9-43 shows the Movie menu when you first open it.

Figure 9-43: The Movie menu appears like this when you begin your project.

Upon opening the menu, the only active control is Create From Document. Here's how it works:

STEPS:

Creating a New Movie

Step 1. After creating a picture, select Movie ⇨ Create From Document. Your picture now has plus and minus signs in its bottom-left corner. These are the Add Frame and Rewind to Beginning tools.

Step 2. Click on the plus sign at the bottom-left of your picture. The dialog box shown in Figure 9-44 appears.

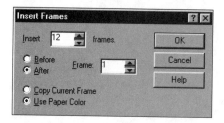

Figure 9-44: The Insert Frames dialog box lets you add frames to your movie.

Step 3. Add as many frames to your movie as you like. The new frames will be blank AVI frames, not CPT files. You can now go back and use any paint or editing tool to create a movie from your individual AVI frames.

Step 4. After creating a few frames, choose Movie ⇨ Control (see Figure 9-45). These are the controls for playing back, fast forwarding, and rewinding your movie. It's easier to open the Movie toolbar, which gives you all the controls without having to fool with the menus.

Step 5. Your AVI file's control menu (Minimize ⇨ Maximize ⇨ Move) now has a Close option in the upper-left corner. Select this option and you're prompted to save your AVI file on your hard drive.

Step 6. Your project can be played back on Windows Media Player or any device that plays AVI files.

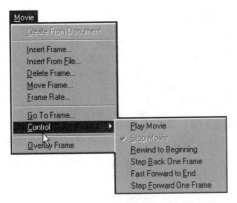

Figure 9-45: The Movie Control menu controls the movie's play.

Getting Your Colors Right

Just as important as editing your document with clever tools and special effects is the job of making sure your final color values are something to be proud of. Photo-Paint enables you to adjust color ranges in your document, select a palette from among many choices, change the overall hue of your document, and alter the color composition of your work in many ways.

Screen dithering

When you must work in 256-color mode, use screen dithering. Found under the View menu, screen dithering combines pixels to simulate colors available only in the 65,000 or 16-million color ranges. Two types of screen dithering are available: Ordered, which is fast, and Error Diffusion, which is more accurate but takes longer to render.

Color correction

Choose View ⇨ Color Correction to open the Color Correction menu. (This option will not appear if you have not set up Corel Color Manager. To do so, from the Windows Start ⇨ Programs menu, click on CorelDRAW 8 ⇨ Graphics Utilities ⇨ Corel Color Profile Wizard 8.) Color Correction helps keep your colors accurate in two ways:

- It ensures that the colors you select and use in a particular picture are allowable under the parameters you've set in Corel Color Manager.

- It enables your screen to display colors as they will appear in your printed work.

Within the Color Correction menu are four options:

- **Accurate.** This choice lets you trade speed for accuracy depending on the size of your image and your need for the most accurate color viewing.

- **Fast.** This choice lets you trade accuracy for speed depending on the size of your image and your need for the most accurate color viewing.

- **Gamut Alarm.** If you choose a color that is out of range according to your Color Manager system profile, your monitor will display that color as an ugly neon green. Gamut alarm permits you to choose a color besides neon green as your "alarm color." You can also reach the Gamut Alarm option by selecting View ⇨ Rollups ⇨ Color and clicking on the small right-facing arrow.

- **Simulate Printer.** When you choose a color to use in your picture, Photo-Paint replaces it with the nearest color that your printer can print.

Color hue control

Select Image ⇨ Adjust ⇨ Color Hue to open the Color Hue Control dialog box, shown in Figure 9-46. It always opens with the current picture on display.

Photo-Paint's Hue Control option enables you to increase the presence of a chosen hue in your picture. The effects are more subtle than simply tinting.

Each of the panels at the bottom half of the dialog box shows the results of accenting a particular hue in your picture; hence the panel names: More Green, More Red, and so on. Happily, you aren't simply adjusting the hue for the entire color range of the picture. Look at the check boxes in the Adjust section. You can increase magenta for the shadows of your picture and increase yellow for the midtones of your picture, for example. The flexibility of adding several subtle effects gives this tool a much wider application than tinting.

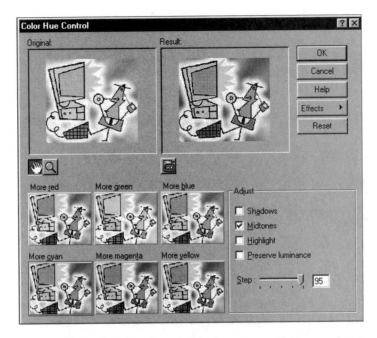

Figure 9-46: The Color Hue Control dialog box opens with the current picture.

Click on one of the six frames at the bottom, and the large frame at the upper right, Result, will show your picture with the adjusted hue value. The upper-left frame, Original, enables you to compare before and close up after. The upper-right frame will continue to show your updated hue choices if you've chosen more than one adjustment. You are not limited to adjusting only one parameter. The slider labeled Step controls how much More Green or More Yellow, for example, you apply by clicking.

The hand and magnifying glass icons enable you to pan across your picture, should it be larger than the screen can display, or zoom in on a particular portion. Click on the image itself if you want to view the Results twice as large. To zoom out, click the right mouse button.

The Color Balance option, accessed by selecting Image ⇨ Adjust ⇨ Color Balance, is just like Hue Control, except that it employs sliders rather than panels of pictures to click.

Color tone control

Select Image ⇨ Adjust ⇨ Color Tone to open the Color Tone Control dialog box, shown in Figure 9-47. It operates the same way as the Color Hue dialog box. Use this feature to make your image lighter or darker, to increase or decrease color saturation, or to raise or lower overall image contrast.

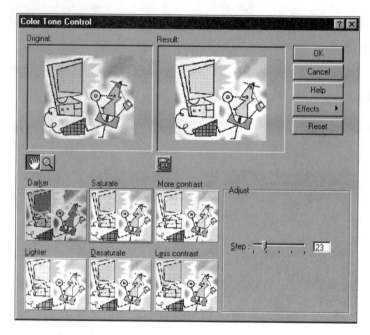

Figure 9-47: The Color Tone Control dialog box enables control of saturation and contrast.

Color transform commands

These commands, found under the Image menu, are useful for correcting lines in scanned images, inverting all the colors in your picture, and simplifying the shades of color in a complex picture.

Deinterlace

The Deinterlace command (Image ⇨ Transform ⇨ Deinterlace) removes lines created by scanning or capturing video images. To replace the discarded lines with color, choose one of the four methods provided. Experiment to see which brings the best results.

Invert

Invert reverses all the colors in your image, creating a photo-negative effect.

Posterize

Posterize reduces the number of colors in your image, creating a sixties pop-art effect, emphasizing bright tangerine, lime, and lavender-type shades.

Level equalization

Choose Image ⇨ Adjust ⇨ Level Equalization to bring up the dialog box displayed in Figure 9-48.

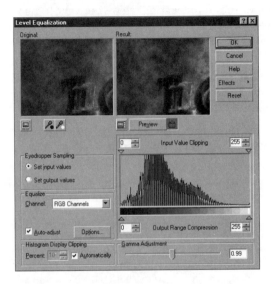

Figure 9-48: The Level Equalization dialog box offers choices to improve the color value of images.

Level Equalization improves the color value of images that appear too dark, too light, or too lacking in contrast. To let Photo-Paint make the adjustments for you, bypass this dialog box altogether and select Image ⇨ Adjust ⇨ Auto Levels instead. Level Equalization spreads the color pixels more evenly between the darkest and lightest portions of your picture. Three problems occur that Level Equalization can fix. Here are the techniques:

- If your picture is too light, your mission is to get Level Equalization to redistribute pixels along a darker scale.

- If your picture is too dark, you want to set up a lighter range, hopefully replacing some of the darkest pixels with lighter hues.

- If your picture is too muddy and lacks contrast, you'll want to increase the spread, making Level Equalization spread pixels across a larger range of color values.

Why not just use Brightness/Contrast or Darken/Lighten? Because you'll lose shadows and depth. If you overdo those controls, your picture will look flat. Level Equalization lets you redistribute the range of pixels rather than just add some at the top or the bottom.

You have an Eyedropper tool for selecting what you want to be the lightest and darkest colors in your picture. You will be using one eyedropper to select the lightest pixels in your picture and another eyedropper to select the darkest.

If you simply go ahead and select the lightest and darkest regions as they are right now, nothing will change. But your job is to use these eyedroppers to skew the scale in the right direction:

- If your picture is too dark, then you should use the **dark extreme** eyedropper to select a region of your picture that is not as dark as the darkest black.

- If your picture is too light, then you should use the **lightest color** eyedropper to pick out a color that is not quite as white as the whitest part.

- If your picture lacks contrast, then go ahead and select the true **darkest** and **lightest** regions with your eyedropper, but then set the Input Value Clipping values and the Output Range Compression values for wider ranges than you find them. Doing so spreads the colors in your pixels across a wider range.

You may have to experiment with eyedropper selection ranges to achieve optimal results.

Figure 9-49 shows a muddy picture before and after a trip to the Level Equalizer.

Warning

Don't select Color Correction unless you've already created a system profile with Corel Color Manager. When you create a system profile, Corel Color Manager creates a record of the colors your computer hardware and software are truly capable of producing. Until you've created a Color Manager system profile, Color Correction won't have anything to adjust to.

Figure 9-49: Level Equalization has improved a picture's contrast.

Color channels

A channel holds color information about your picture. If you're working with an RGB picture, your picture contains three channels: One describes how much red is in your picture; one, how much blue; and one, how much green. If you select Image ⇨ Split Channels To, your picture will display a new image for each of these three channels. These images were there all along, so to speak. That's because whenever you create a new image with Photo-Paint, channel information is automatically created for the image. In Figure 9-50, the Channels tab shows thumbnails of the original image and each separate channel. To view a particular channel, click on the thumbnail. Images can be split according to any of several color models: CMYK, HSB, HLS, YIQ, and LAB. Note that you don't need to split the image to see these channels. Physically splitting the image creates a separate image for each channel. This is different from using the Channel display in the Docker.

Looking again at Figure 9-50, you may remember the original, Figure 9-30. That picture had different fills applied to it through the three color channels. In this example, the texture fill Rings Hard 3C from the Styles Library is applied. We then clicked on the blue channel and applied Ripples Soft Embossed from the same library of textured fills. Then we made the moon into a separate object, selected it, clicked on the Green Channel in the Channels Docker, and applied Ripples Hard Embossed. This edit only affected the moon in the green channel. When you again click on the top icon, which allows you to see the combined channels, you'll notice that each blend applied is more like a special effect that occupies its own color space. Applying effects and fills to only one channel of a picture creates a type of "layered" appearance.

To make the effect more pronounced, the original image of the cliff, pathway, and moon was retrieved and pasted onto this image. It was actually pasted in twice — first with the Overlay paint mode, and then with the Multiply paint mode. Pasting twice caused the moon and path to seem to "leap up" from the background. This image is much more effective in color, and is included with the CD that comes with this book.

Secret

Notice that when you split your image into channels, each channel appears in grayscale. To have the channels appear in their respective colors, just use the Channels Docker.

Note

There's another type of channel called an alpha channel. Alpha channels are used for masks, which are the subject of the next chapter, Chapter 10.

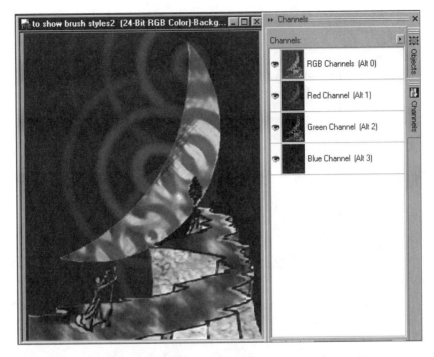

Figure 9-50: This image was created by applying fills to separate channels.

Advanced Photo-Paint Tools

In this section we'll look at some of the more adventurous and unique tools that Photo-Paint offers.

Paint modes

Paint modes, sometimes called merge modes or apply modes, are the rules you can choose when painting on a background, combining objects, or applying a mask to an image. Most often, "Normal" appears in the paint mode field because paint is usually applied (and objects are usually layered) according to the normal rules. For example, normally you want the color red to appear red. But when you apply an alternative paint mode, you can change the rules. Each mode in the drop-down list (Subtract, Texturize, XOR, and so on) represents a different algorithm that can be applied to the relationship between the selected object (or paint tool) and the background. Figure 9-51 shows a couple of examples of different paint modes. For example, click on Add, and the picture will be brightened according to the color value of the top object. Click on Multiply, and the values are multiplied together.

— Difference mode example

— Saturation mode example

Figure 9-51: Here are two examples of special effects created by special paint modes. Viewed in color, you could tell that the paint modes give the lettering almost a 3D appearance and an "internal glow" quality.

Paint modes come into play when you lay one object atop another. Paint modes set up rules for how colors from the object beneath affect the object above. Figure 9-52 shows several examples of applied paint modes; the mode at the upper left, Normal, has no paint mode applied at all. The leaf resting on the rose obscures the rose, pure and simple. The Difference mode, shown in the figure to the right of Normal, is a calculation of the difference between the two color values. This calculated difference is displayed where the two colors overlap. The Subtract mode subtracts one value from another and displays those color values where two colors overlap, even the background color of white.

The Hard Light / Green image represents what occurs when the leaf is set to Hard Light paint mode and the Drop Shadow beneath is set to Green paint mode. The image involving three objects shows what happens when you apply the Lightness mode and Hard Light.

Secret

Sometimes you want to apply one paint mode to an object, and another paint mode to its Drop Shadow. You can't do this unless you ungroup the Object / Drop Shadow group. To do this, select the object in Object Manager and click on Ungroup on the Property Bar. Or right-click on the group and click on Ungroup.

The picture in Figure 9-53, *Quarks and Ladders*, was created with three Photo-Paint fills, the Interactive Transparency tools, the Perspective and Whirlpool effects, and many applications of paint modes. The following procedure explains how it was created.

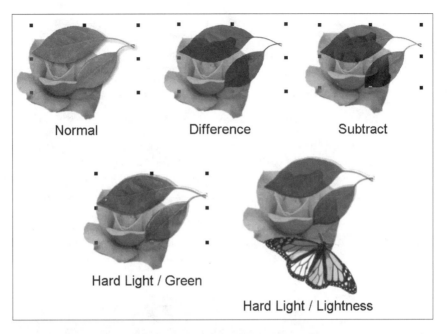

Figure 9-52: Examples of paint modes applied to two and three objects.

Figure 9-53: *Quarks and Ladders*, created with basic Photo-Paint tools such as paint modes and fills.

STEPS:

Creating *Quarks and Ladders*

Step 1. The background was filled with a conical blend: lighter colors on the bottom, browns and dark blue on the top.

Step 2. The first new object layer is a textured fill (Rock ⇨ Swirled ⇨ Cracked 2C from the Styles library). Before applying the fill, a new, blank object was created by selecting Object ⇨ Create ⇨ New. (This really amounts to creating an empty layer to work on.) You are creating a new object, and its default name should be Object 1.

Step 3. The Interactive Transparency tool was applied (second tool from the bottom on the toolbox, second tool on the flyout) using the Rectangular Type (see Figure 9-54). The Interactive Transparency tool has a drop-down menu that builds a transparency that reshapes your object into a rectangle, cone, or ellipse, for example.

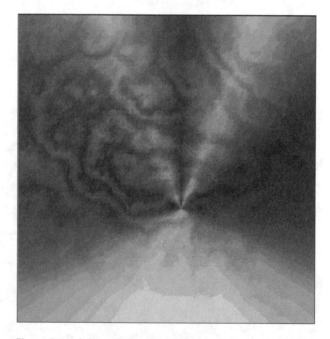

Figure 9-54: A fill applied and edited with the Interactive Transparency tool.

Step 4.   Next a new layer was applied, filling a new blank object with Textured Fill ⇨ Horizontal (also from the Styles library of the Textured Fills dialog box). Interactive Transparency was applied, so that the new texture is mostly constrained to the upper left of the canvas (see Figure 9-55). This should be Object 2.

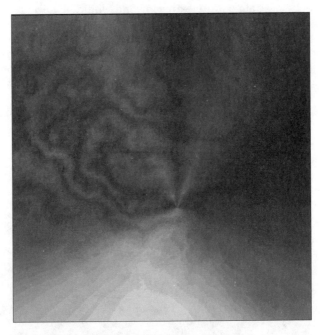

Figure 9-55: The second object, or layer, filled with a texture fill.

Step 5.   The curtainlike figure that extends from the upper-middle downward (see Figure 9-56) is a textured fill (Swirl 2, from the Styles library) which was treated with the Perspective effect (Effects ⇨ 3D ⇨ Perspective, with Best Fit selected). The transparency levels at the top and bottom of the "curtain" were painted on, using the Object Transparency Brush tool. The Transparency slider on the Property Bar was set to 38. We used a size 60 Nib circular brush with the Soft Edge setting turned up all the way. We could then control the amount of transparency along the edge of the curtain by brushing along the top with only the edge of the brush and not the center. This created a nice feathering, gradually blending the transparency. When we wanted

(continued)

STEPS *(continued)*

Creating *Quarks and Ladders*

to apply more transparency, we would dip down with the brush, applying a stroke from the brush's center. This center applied almost no feathering and would just about cleanly erase everything under it. Using this method, we could vary the amount of transparency we were applying without having to change brushes. We also painted highly feathered transparency near the middle, so that the center of the rainbow cone would show through clearly. In Figure 9-56, the recent textures are removed so you can see the curtain effect more clearly. This should be Object 3. If you are following along, copy this curtainlike figure to the Clipboard.

Figure 9-56: The curtainlike layer was created with the Perspective tool applied to a textured fill.

Step 6. The next object, which is the sideways rectangle receding in the distance towards the right, was created by pasting in a copy of the previous "curtain" object and rotating it 45 degrees to the right. It was applied with the Behind paint mode. It was treated with the Whirlpool effect (Effect ⇨ 2D ⇨ Whirlpool, with Style: Fountains, Spacing: 48, Smear Length: 15, Twist: 17, Streak Detail: 96). The rotation and whirlpool effect caused the previously feathered transparency to appear more like a tear in fabric. This should be Object 4. (See Figure 9-57.)

Figure 9-57: The Behind paint mode gives this rotated layer its ethereal appearance.

Step 7. In Object Manager, drag Object 4 so that it is positioned right after the background. It should appear in the list even before Object 1. The Object list for this whole project is shown in Figure 9-58. This is what Object Manager looks like when you are finished creating. Note that Object 4 is moved right above the background, preceding Object 1 in sequence.

(continued)

STEPS *(continued)*

Creating *Quarks and Ladders*

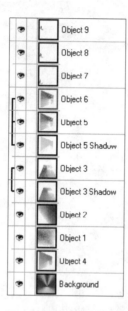

Figure 9-58: The Object list for this entire project. Note Object 4 is repositioned.

Step 8. The object that appears to be inside the sideways-receding rectangle is actually the same pasted-in and rotated, curtainlike object as before; but after rotating it, simply apply it with the Red paint mode. This should be Object 5. We applied a Drop Shadow to this object, and then we ungrouped this object from its shadow and applied the shadow with the Red paint mode as well. Set the Opacity to 59. This should be Object 5 Shadow. (See Figure 9-59.)

Step 9. Paste the same curtainlike object again into the same position, and apply it with Hard Light paint mode. Set the Opacity to 66. This should be Object 6. This simply has the effect of brightening up the receding rectangle and making the surface appear more reflective.

Figure 9-59: An object was pasted over the rotated "curtain," applied with the Red paint mode.

Step 10. Moving to the flames on the left side of the picture, We picked a flame from the CorelDraw CD-ROM. CorelDraw comes with a collection of objects, found on the same CD that has the extensive Photo collection. Open the Nature folder and choose one of the flames.

Step 11. The flame was pasted into the bottom-left corner of the rectangle, using the If Lighter paint mode. This should be Object 7. The same flame was pasted above it using the Overlay paint mode (Object 8). Above that, the same flame was pasted in, and painted with the Transparency Paint tool so that it appeared to blend in better with the rectangle. The Add paint mode was used (Object 9). See Figure 9-60.

(continued)

STEPS *(continued)*

Creating *Quarks and Ladders*

Figure 9-60: Adding flame to the edges of the sideways curtain.

Step 12. Right-click on Object 9 in Object Manager, and click on Duplicate Selected. You can't see it, but a new Object 9 has now appeared on top of the first. Click and drag on Object 9, the flame, and you'll see a new flame was indeed created. Drag it towards the top. The Transparency Paint tool was again used, to make the flame blend in with the rectangle. It was thinned out so it would not look like a copy of the flame below it.

If you've been following along with this project, try seeing how the final product looks with some of the layers turned off. Do this by clicking on the eye icon (in Object Manager) of any object you want to disable temporarily. Remember that, in Object Manager, if you click on the eye icon of the object you are currently selecting (the border around the thumbnail will be red), you will be making every object invisible except the selected one. To turn an object off, make sure it is not selected, and then click on the eye icon.

The Text tool

Figure 9-61 shows the Property Bar as it appears with the Text tool selected. Beyond the basic font and paragraph formatting options, notice that the Character and Line Spacing tools are immediately accessible, which is a real plus for creating aesthetically pleasing bitmapped text. When you start adding shadows and layering font masks, extra space between characters is needed.

Figure 9-61: The Property Bar assumes this appearance with the Text tool selected.

One feature worth pointing out is the Render to Mask option, which is available from the Property Bar as well as from the Tool Settings roll-up. Click on this button to turn your text into a mask, which allows you to stroke it with the currently selected paintbrush, fill it with any type of fill, and edit it with various 2D Effects such as Ripple or Puzzle. You can also save your text mask as a path and edit it as an EPS file in another program. The Text tool enables you to change fonts and font sizes even after the text appears on your picture, as long as you have not edited your text with resizing, rotating, or some other Transformation tool. The text remains fully editable in a bounding box until you select a different tool. To permanently apply your editing to your text, you must render it by clicking on the document outside the text itself.

Note

When Render to Mask is selected, text becomes a mask, repositionable on the current layer you've been working on. You can also select Edit ⇨ Copy to copy the mask to the Clipboard. When Render to Mask is not selected, text will become its own object on a new layer as soon as you click on the document outside the text.

A Specimen of Text Effects

This ominous tribute to premillennial anxiety (Figure A) is brought to you by Photo-Paint's totally revamped Text tool, which now converts text to objects or masks, performs lighting effects, and creates instant drop shadows.

Figure A: This is our basic image, 1999.

This image was created using the Fill texture called Mineral Speckled, Two Colors. Text was created and the Render Text to Mask command was used. The Spray Can paintbrush was applied to the text (see Figure B). The text was turned into an object, copied to the Clipboard, and pasted back into the image several times using various paint modes (see Figure C). Lighting effects and drop shadows were also applied. The image is included on the CD for you to edit and experiment with.

Figure B: Spray painting the text after it has been changed to a mask has this effect.

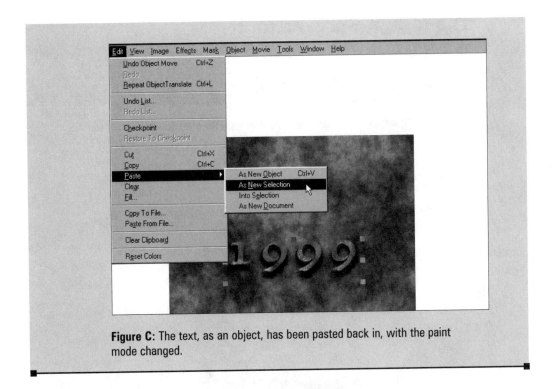

Figure C: The text, as an object, has been pasted back in, with the paint mode changed.

Secret

After entering text and clicking outside the text you created (which renders it as an object), you may find that the edges of your text are suddenly fuzzy. That's because, by default, the Anti-aliasing feature (the third icon from the right on the Text Property Bar) is turned on. This may not be desirable. Before rendering text, you may want to disable anti-aliasing.

Also, if you render text to a document and find that it's just not legible enough, sometimes the smallest amount of Drop Shadow can make artistic text in Photo-Paint appear a bit stronger and more distinct on a colorful background. (See Figure 9-62.) First render your text as an object by clicking outside it immediately after typing. Then select Object ⇨ Drop Shadow and try these settings: Offset: .06944, Opacity: 87%, Degrees: 225, Width: 4. These settings worked well with Arial text at 24-point font size.

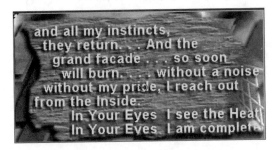

Figure 9-62: Text created with a slight, clarifying Drop Shadow.

The Image Sprayer tool

Figure 9-63 shows the Property Bar while the Image Sprayer tool is selected.

Figure 9-63: The Property Bar takes this form with the Image Sprayer tool selected.

Figures 9-64 and 9-65 give you some idea of what you can do with the different settings.

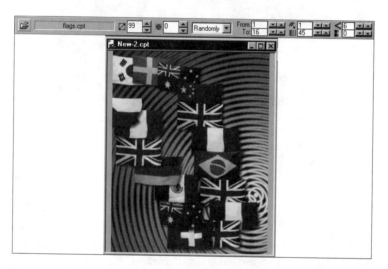

Figure 9-64: An image has been filled with the Moondrops texture, followed by three brush strokes. The brush was loaded with a Photo-Paint preset, Flags. Note the options selected on the Property Bar.

The Image Sprayer Property Bar enables you to adjust the size of each image as it appears on your picture. Because the Image Sprayer tool works with several pictures applied as one paintbrush stroke, the Property Bar provides controls for the sequencing of those images. For example, you can have Photo-Paint apply "blue butterfly, red butterfly, yellow butterfly" in a sequence, or you can have the images applied in a random order. The Property Bar offers you the choice of whether to spray on your images *thinly*, meaning with lots of space between each object, or *thickly*. Spraying on your images more densely, for example, creates an effect of thick foliage, or of rocks piled on top of each other. You can also specify how much *spray* your brush has, meaning how far from the brush the images land, as you paint a stroke. Adjust the Fade Out arrows to determine if your images should gradually fade into the canvas or end abruptly.

Figure 9-65: Before painting, these images of stamps were set to be sprayed smaller and spread farther apart than than the previous image. (These settings are adjustable with the arrows found on the Image Sprayer Property Bar.) Notice that without the background, the stamps appear more vivid.

The Image Sprayer Tool roll-up

The Image Sprayer tool roll-up has several settings that affect how the images appear on your page. The first tab allows you to change the paint mode, size of the sprayed images, and transparency amount. The second tab lets you choose how many images should be sprayed on the page each time you click your mouse (Number of Dabs). The Spread setting determines how big a "clump" or cluster of images should be sprayed as you drag your mouse on your canvas. Spacing determines how far apart each image should appear from its neighbor. A high Fade Out number causes your brush to gradually lose paint as you continue your stroke, just like a real brush would do near the end of a stroke.

Creating and Applying Your Own Image Sprayer

You can create an image similar to the one shown in Figure A. Here's how:

Figure A: *Feeding Frenzy*, created with a single image, converted to an Image Sprayer, and applied with various paint modes. The full-color image is included on the CD.

Create a single, small image and remove the white (or paper color) border around it, by selecting outside the image with the Magic Wand tool and then selecting Mask ⇨ Invert. Then convert the resulting mask into an object by selecting Object ⇨ Create ⇨ Object: Copy Selection.

Reproduce this image (right-click on it and choose Duplicate) using the Rotation tool to make each copy face various directions, resizing each new duplicate as well. Image Sprayers are very effective when they look like they are facing "every which way" when you paint with them, so arrows work quite nicely.

Each time you reproduce your image, make each one unique by painting it with a different color. Make each mini-image somewhat unique so that your page won't turn into a blurry mess when you spray the images on your page.

The document you are going to turn into an Image Sprayer will be composed of several of these images (in this case, arrows). Each image should be an object, with no white border. Take care to remove any paper color boundary around your objects. Select all the objects. This is easier by opening the Objects Docker and selecting them there, making sure you don't miss any.

With every object on your document selected, double-click on the Image Sprayer tool (one of the Paint Tool flyouts) to reveal the Image Sprayer tool Roll-up. Click on the tiny right-facing arrow and choose Save Objects as Image List (see Figure B). You're prompted to name and save your new Image Sprayer.

Your custom Image Sprayer will now be available in the same list as Photo-Paint's preset Image Sprayers. The one you just created will be loaded and ready to use. You can edit your new Image List by opening it, clicking on the right-facing arrow on the Image Sprayer Tools roll-up, and selecting Edit Current Image List. (Double-click on the Image Sprayer tool to open the roll-up.) You can paint them, but you cannot resize or move your component Image List images.

Figure B: Saving a custom Image Sprayer.

Here's what we did to create the picture in Figure B:

1. We filled a canvas with a faded rainbow gradient using the Paint Bucket tool, with a Transparency setting of 50. We then sprayed with our arrows using a Dab setting of 1, Spacing: 1. We used a circular, inward spiral motion (see Figure 9-C).

Figure C: Creating the first layer with the Image Sprayer against a faded rainbow gradient.

2. We cut the resulting image to the Clipboard, so it can later be pasted on top of the next canvas.

3. We created a new canvas with a contrasting texture and color scheme using a textured blend (Texture Fill ➪ Using the Styles Library ➪ Textured Blend Vertical) and applied the Swirl effect (Effect ➪ 2D Effects ➪ Swirl ➪ Using Whole Rotations: 1, Additional Degrees: 316).

(continued)

(continued)

4. We sprayed the arrow Image Sprayer using a Dab setting of 3 and a Spread setting of 7. This allows for some "clumping" of arrows along the path of our stroke. Again, we used a spiral pattern (see Figure 9-D).

Figure 9-D: The Image Sprayer applied and now set to spray with several dabs with one mouse click.

5. To get the feathery-soft look seen on this layer (see Figure 9-E), we used the Whirlpool effect, with the Fountains style applied and Warp turned off.

Figure 9-E: The Whirlpool effect applied to this layer gives it a feathery appearance.

6. We pasted the first canvas we had cut to the Clipboard onto this canvas, using the Multiply method. We sprayed a few additional arrows using the Hard Light paint mode, which made the arrows appear to blend into the lighting of the background canvas.

7. We pasted the same canvas again, layered on top of the two previous layers, and rotated this new layer 35 degrees clockwise. We then changed the paint mode to Soft Light, with an opacity of 86.

8. The line at the bottom of the canvas, moving up the right, was created by selecting the background in the Objects docker, choosing Mask ⇨ Select All, and then selecting Edit ⇨ Stroke Selection. We used Art Brush: Swirl, reducing the Nib Size to 8.

The Brush tool

With the Brush tool Property Bar, shown in Figure 9-66, you can adjust brush shape, size, softness amount, and anti-aliasing. The Property Bar provides a complete list of brushes. Although both the Brush tool Tool Settings roll-up and the Property Bar provide icons of the brush types, only the Property Bar enables you to pass your mouse over the brush icon to see a tool tip that tells you the name of the brush.

Figure 9-66: The Brush tool Property Bar.

Figure 9-67 shows some of the effects you can achieve with the various kinds of brushes.

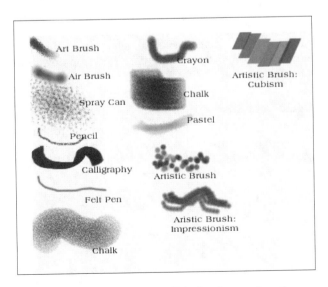

Figure 9-67: The standard Photo-Paint brushes produce these stroke examples.

With Photo-Paint 8, you modify each brush by selecting its brush type, perhaps more properly called a brush method. For example, within the Pencil category you must choose between 2B, HB, Sharp & Hard, and Sharp & Soft pencil types. Similarly, the Chalk brush can be further defined by choosing Soft Rub, Medium Rub, and Hard, Square Rub.

Some of these brushes might appear impractical coming right out of the box, but tweaking them with the provided tools pays great dividends (see the painting in Figure 9-68, created using Photo-Paint brushes from a scanned photograph). In Chapter 14 we explore the new brushes more thoroughly. From the Property Bar, you can adjust brush shape, size, softness amount, and anti-aliasing. Also, the Property Bar provides your only complete, labeled list of brushes.

Figure 9-68: *Sophia+Kitty* painted with the Superfine Cover brush and Dry Camel hair, and treated with the Impressionist effect.

Photo-Paint has more paintbrush types than ever. After selecting a brush from the far-left icon on the Property Bar, click the drop-down menu to the right of it to see what kind of variety is available for each brush.

Special brush nibs

As mentioned earlier in the Eraser tool section, the Nibs roll-up (which can be accessed from the Brush tools Property Bar) presents some unusual brush stroke possibilities. Figure 9-69 shows a handful of strokes applied using some of these nibs (brush tips).

Figure 9-69: Sample strokes use nibs from the Nibs roll-up.

Figure 9-70 shows a painting created using Photo-Paint's Water brushes and Artistic brushes. The moon was painted with the Medium Soft Bleed Water brush using a crosshatch nib from the Nib drop-down. The darkening around the edges was done with the Art Brush: Soft Wet Oil Blend. The pathway was created using the Art Brush: Raked Rough-in, with a Swirl nib. The drop-off sides of the cliff were created using the Sponge Brush Texture (textures are set on the second tab of the Brush Tool roll-up), loading the Sponge Texture. The texture setting was increased to 55. In each section, brush strokes were applied lightly, and large nib sizes were used (above 40, which shows lots of brush texture and nib shape) with very little going back over, slightly varying the colors each time.

Figure 9-70: An image painted with Photo-Paint's water and art brushes. Scroll deeply into the Nib Shapes menu to find lots of interesting brush tips to paint with.

Customizing a brush

From the Property Bar, click on the Tool Settings roll-up button and select the second or third tab. These tabs provide tools for painting with a bitmap or texture, adding watercolor properties to your brush, making color and hue variations to your brush stroke, and choosing options for saving your brush with the other preset brushes. Pictured in Figures 9-71 and 9-72 are the second and third tabs of the Brush tool Tool Settings roll-up.

Figure 9-71: The second tab of the Brush tool Tool Settings roll-up.

Figure 9-72: The third tab of the Brush Tool Settings roll-up.

From these menus you can add a texture to your brush or import a bitmap to use as a brush texture. Adding a brush texture does not add color to your brush but simulates raised areas and depressions on your painting according to the colors of your texture bitmap. Light colors are interpreted as raised areas; dark colors, as depressions. Figure 9-73 shows a painting employing the Coins texture, which is a preset texture included with Photo-Paint.

Figure 9-73: Some brush strokes are shown employing the Coins texture.

Secret

To make the texture show through more, increase the Soft Edge of your brush.

Watercolors

The second tab of the Brush tool settings roll-up shows options for adjusting Watercolor settings of your brushes. These controls only apply if you are currently using a Watercolor brush. The options control the Bleed and Sustain Color amounts. How wet do you want the painting to look? Should the colors bleed together aggressively or keep to their own? Figure 9-74 shows a few strokes using Photo-Paint's Watercolor brush. The canvas is sparse because we wanted to show the gradual fade that the Watercolor brush produces.

Figure 9-74: The Watercolor brush at work. Note the tapering of the brush stroke.

Dab, spacing, and color variation control

The third tab of the Brush tool Tool Settings roll-up controls how many dabs of paint should be applied when you apply a single stroke. When applied with color variation, this tool can be useful for creatively filling in an empty area. Spacing refers to the amount of space in between the brush hairs of your brush. This creates the appearance of one of your brush strokes creating two or three parallel strokes.

The color variation controls can provide many a "happy accident" on your canvas. Use these HSL sliders to control the introduction of random color into your brush strokes. For example, a high number means that your brush stroke is more likely to introduce a little blue or green if you are currently using red. Lower numbers keep to your chosen hue but still interject a bit of random color play into your painting.

Saving a custom brush

At the bottom of each tab of the Brush tool Tool Settings roll-up is a Save Brush option. You'll be prompted to provide a new brush name. Your brush will be saved as a new brush type under the brush category itself. Think of your new brush as a new style or iteration of the main brush group. For example, if you are working with the Pointillism brush and edit it and save it as your own, remember that the Pointillism brush is a brush type of the Artistic brush group. The next time you open Photo-Paint, look for your new brush: Click on the Artistic Brush icon and open the brush type menu. Your brush will be there. An easy-to-remember name will help you later locate your custom brush.

Using a Bitmap as Background for Gradient-Filled Text

The following image was created using multiple layers of text converted to objects and applied to a bitmap background. All these controls are available from the Text tool Property Bar. To make them accessible, click on the Text tool on the toolbox, and select View ⇨ Toolbox. Make sure Property Bar is checked. In this figure, character spacing has been increased to make room for the Drop Shadow effect. Wide letter-spacing also creates room for the letter contouring that occurs when you apply several layers of text with various paint modes, as was done here. This picture is also included on the CD, with all layers intact, for your experimentation.

Here is another fancy-text example.

The Stroke Attributes tab

The fourth tab of the Brush tool Tool Settings roll-up, shown in Figure 9-75, controls the appearance of your brush stroke. You can make your stroke anti-aliasing, which, together with the Smoothness setting, removes any jagged qualities from your stroke. If you want your stroke to taper off gradually, fading away near the end, then increase the numbers of the Fade out setting.

Figure 9-75: The Stroke Attributes tab of the Brush tool roll-up.

If you want your brush stroke to vary in color, move the Hue slider of the Stroke color variation panel to the right. Place a check next to Longer hue direction if you want your stroke to cycle through more colors, taking the long way through the spectrum as you apply a stroke. Move the Saturation and Lightness sliders to the right if you want to introduce variety in saturation and lightness amounts while you paint.

Photo-Paint's new brush tools

Let's take a look at two exceptionally interesting new Photo-Paint brush tools: Symmetry and Orbits. You may find these brush features useful as special effects rather than as workaday paintbrushes. Play with the settings. Experimentation is the key.

Painting with Symmetry

With Symmetry turned on, Photo-Paint will reproduce your brush strokes on another part of your canvas. Imagine creating an entire flower by drawing only one petal, while Photo-Paint draws the other petals, perfectly aligned and positioned. When painting with Symmetry, you can specify the number of exact reproductions of your brush strokes that are created; again, think of it as determining the number of petals that should be drawn as you draw. You can specify the starting point of the duplicated strokes — should they be centered and begin near your own brush stroke, or should they radiate out from a distant portion of your canvas? You can also make your brush strokes mirrored so that the brush stroke copies are created as exact opposites of your own stroke.

You can open the Symmetry dialog box by double-clicking on the Paintbrush tool in the toolbox, and then clicking on the right-facing arrow on the middle-right of the toolbox, next to the Brush Type drop-down menu. Then click on Symmetry. In the resulting dialog box shown Figure 9-76, you can set the number of Points, meaning the number of brush strokes created at the same time as your own. Click on the Mirror option, and determine numerically how far apart your other strokes should be from your original (using the Left, and Top units text boxes).

Figure 9-76: The Symmetry dialog box.

After you set the number of points, the best way to set the center of your symmetrical drawing is to click on the Set Center button. Your mouse cursor becomes a crosshair. Position the cursor over the canvas where you want your strokes to radiate from, and then click. Now choose a paintbrush and begin your design. As you can see in Figure 9-77, while your actual brush is represented by the brush's particular icon, the other strokes are created by an X that moves around as you move your brush. Clicking on the Mirror button enables you to create horizontal or vertical mirror images of your strokes.

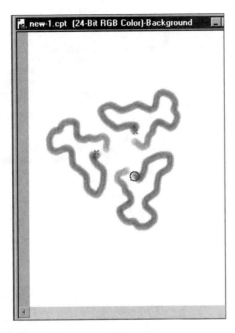

Figure 9-77: Each X represents an automatic stroke, created while you paint one stroke.

Painting with Orbits

Painting with Orbits automatically causes your stroke to rotate, drawing circular patterns while you move your mouse or stylus along. You can adjust the speed of the orbits, the radius, and the number of orbits emanating from one stroke. The effect is similar to those Spirograph drawings popular a few years ago. You can access the Orbits dialog box from Brush Options (double-click on the paintbrush icon in the toolbox). Orbits is the tab in the back. To paint with Orbits, you must first click on the Enable Orbits check box and then increase the Number of orbits setting to at least 2, or you won't see any effect. Click on the Include center point check box if you want a line to be drawn at the bottom of your Orbit chain, kind of connecting them together. Please note that Orbits will remain active as long as this check box is checked, even after you close the Orbits dialog box.

If the presets found in the drop-down menu seem too ornate for practical use, adjusting the Radius and Rotation speed settings downward can lead to something less frilly.

In Figure 9-78, the top line was created by beginning with the preset Muscle Fiber (click on the drop-down Presets menu at the bottom of the dialog box) with the following settings: Rotation speed: 5, Radius: 25, Grow speed: 9, and Number of orbits: 2. (The settings not mentioned are default values.)

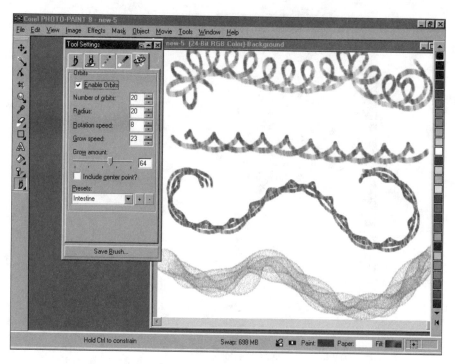

Figure 9-78: Several strokes created with the Orbit brushes.

In the next line in Figure 9-83, Grow speed was reduced to 2, Radius to 14, and Rotation speed was decreased to 4.

The stroke below that was made with the DNA preset with the Radius increased to 10, which allows for more space to be shown in between the strands. Notice how the stroke changes during a curve. This DNA preset uses the Include center point option, which accounts for the line going through the middle of the orbits.

And finally, the stroke at the bottom was created with the unedited preset Intestine. The stroke was repeated back on itself to show more detail. Because the effect is partially transparent, the stroke overlaps nicely.

To quickly create a page full of unique, symmetrical patterns, try using Orbits while drawing with the Symmetry feature on.

Summary

- The Property Bar changes with every tool you select. Knowing what's available on the Property Bar saves you from having to hunt for tool options from a list of menus.

- A myriad of paintbrushes come with Photo-Paint, and you can even create your own brushes, including Image Sprayer brushes. Layering objects with various paint modes gives you more creative options for your palette of ideas.

- Photo-Paint's color correction and color editing tools can make your image work successfully when you move it from the computer screen out into the world of printed material.

- The Object Manager, the Repeat Brush Stroke tool, the Navigator pop-up, and the Movie menu are among the tools that you'll find extremely useful.

Chapter 10

Photo-Paint Masks

In This Chapter

You look more closely at masks. You learn:

▶ What masks do

▶ How to create masks

▶ How to float masks

▶ How you can brush masks onto an image

▶ How to create a mask from text

▶ How to use color range masks

▶ How to feather masks

Masking Fundamentals

You use masks to select an area of your image you wish to modify in some way. After you apply a mask, your image is divided into two areas: the *selected area* and the *protected area*. The area where the mask is applied is the selected area. Any editing you do to the selected area affects only that area. The rest of the image is protected. No pixels outside the selected area will be altered. You can also select an area with a mask tool and then invert the mask. When you do that, the area that used to be protected becomes the selected area for editing, and vice versa.

Only one mask can appear on your image at a time, because masks are temporary selections. While your mask tool is selected, look at the upper-left corner of the Property Bar. If the arrow is depressed, then you are in Normal mask operations mode. Clicking outside the selection terminates the mask. Click on the plus sign, and any masking you do adds to the existing mask. Click on the minus sign to remove part of your mask with your next actions. And click on the XOR button to create a new mask segment where the overlapping areas are not masked, as shown in Figure 10-1.

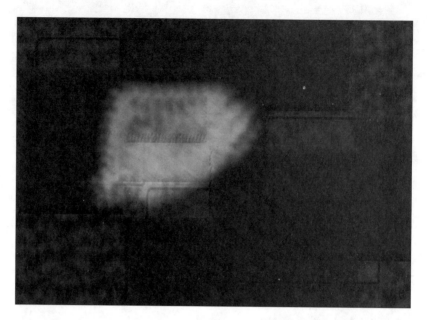

Figure 10-1: An image created using the XOR feature. Adding to a mask with XOR selected causes the overlapping areas to be unmasked, as shown where these two rectangles meet.

Figure 10-1 began as a simple rectangle mask. By clicking on the XOR button, another rectangle was drawn, overlapping the first. The area where they overlapped became a hole in the mask. The mask was stroked with a thin, dark line (Edit ➪ Stroke Mask), repeated with the Inside Mask setting selected, to create the double-line effect. Then the mask was turned into an object, duplicated, and painted with the Big Soft Cover brush with a high Transparency and Soft Edge setting. (These controls are found on the Property Bar.) The object copy was treated with the Paint Alchemy Effect Soft Pencil: Dark (Effects ➪ Fancy ➪ Alchemy ➪ Soft Pencil Dark). High Transparency settings were used on each object to make it possible to see all the way to the background under each object. The background is one of Photo-Paint's standard bitmap fills.

Creating masks

You have two methods for creating masks:

- Area selection
- Color range

For area selection, you use a tool to select a group of pixels conforming to the shape of your chosen tool (for example, a rectangle, an ellipse, or a polygon shape, and so on). You are selecting all the pixels within your tool's path, regardless of their color. You can add to your mask after you've created an initial shape. When you click on the plus sign and add to your existing mask, the new pixels you add to your mask do not have to be connected to the initial selection you created. In other words, a mask can be composed of noncontiguous segments. You can also use the Brush Mask tool to paint on a mask.

For color range masks, you select an area or areas based on the color of the pixels rather than selecting or painting a shape. For example, you might use the Color Mask tool or the Magic Wand tool to select areas of your picture that have a certain shade of red. A mask created by a color range tool does not have to be all the same color. You can use a tool to select a range of color — say, from orange to yellow — depending on the particular tool's capabilities. The Color Mask tool, for example, lets you use the Eyedropper to choose a large range of colors from your image for masking. Masks created by color range tools are not necessarily composed of contiguous pixels. You can select pixels for this type of mask that are not connected to each other at all.

Adjusting mask transparency

Every mask has a transparency value. As mentioned earlier, you use masking to select one area of your image and protect another. But you can set your mask so that a certain amount of the editing process will be blocked. For example, if you create a mask and fill the selection with red, you can adjust the mask so that the red fades out around the edges of the mask. This helps create much more realistic effects than sharp mask borders. A simple mask, one that allows the full result of an effect to show through, has a transparency value of 0.

Although you couldn't tell by looking at it, a mask is actually a grayscale cover applied on top of your image. (Think of it as being like a wire-mesh screen with loosely or tightly woven mesh.) A simple mask with no transparency would then be entirely black; its pixel value would be 0. Entirely transparent areas of the mask would be white, or have a pixel value of 255. Portions of your mask that allow half an effect to show through would have a pixel value of 127. For example, if you applied a cloud effect to an area where the mask began with no transparency and gradually became 50 percent transparent, you would see clouds begin to appear over the partially transparent portion of the mask. If you applied the same cloud effect to a masked area that moved dramatically from no transparency to full transparency, you would see a sharp border where clouds would suddenly appear. To apply these graduated effects, use the Interactive Transparency tool found on the toolbox. While your mask is selected, press and hold the mouse button over the Fill tool, and you'll see this tool fly out from the toolbox.

Moving masks

You can move a mask in any of three different ways:

- You can use the Mask Transform tool to move the boundary of the mask without affecting the underlying image.

- You can move both the mask and the portion of the image that is covered by the mask.

- You can move both the mask and a copy of the portion of the image covered by the mask. (This is called *floating* the mask.)

Using the Mask Transform tool

It's important to understand the difference between the mask itself and the image underneath. Figure 10-2 shows the Mask Transform tool. You use this tool to move the marching-ants boundary, which shows the outline of the mask itself. When you use the Mask Transform tool, you move the mask from one portion of the image and use the mask to protect pixels in another part of the image. The area of the image that was originally protected by the mask remains unchanged.

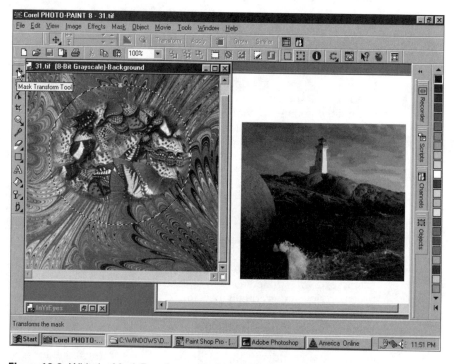

Figure 10-2: With the Mask Transform tool, this oval mask can be moved without affecting the underlying image. Any new editing performed will now affect the area where the mask is moved.

Remember

Remember that the Mask Transform tool has its own drop-down menu of shape-changing effects, such as Distort, Perspective, and Scale. (Figure 10-3 shows this drop-down menu, which is available from the Property Bar—not the toolbox.) When you repeatedly click on your image with the Mask Transform tool, you can scroll through these effects with each click. You will see the bounding boxes around your mask change depending on the particular effect selected. The status bar tells you which one is operative at a given moment. Move the bounding boxes to preview the effect. You'll find that the bounding boxes move differently depending on which effect you are applying. For example, the Perspective tool's bounding boxes move forward, then inward or outward, depending on whether you want a *narrowing* or *broadening* Perspective effect. The Distort tool allows you to move any bounding box irrespective of the others.

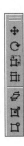

Figure 10-3: The Mask Transform tool's drop-down menu is reached from the Property Bar.

Tip

When manipulating a mask with one of the tools, click on Transform on the Property Bar to apply the change temporarily. If you are happy with the results, click on Apply. To discard the change, click outside the masked area. Remember, you can hold your mouse over any of the Mask Transform tool buttons for a tool tip describing what the button does. Also, the Status Bar prompts you through the process of permanently applying an effect

Moving the mask boundary and the underlying image

When you want to move the selection itself (the image under the mask), select any mask tool, such as the Magic Wand or Lasso tool, click inside the marquee, and drag. You'll cut out a portion of the image, leaving a hole where it used to be. (Before doing this, make sure the plus or minus signs are not selected on the Property Bar.) Unless you've changed the paper color, that hole will be white. This only works in Standard mode—if you don't have the + or - button selected.

Floating a mask

You can also float a mask. When you float a mask, you copy the selected portion of the image to the Windows Clipboard without leaving a hole in the image. To do this, click on Mask ➪ Float before moving the selection. You can use this feature to build an object from several identical smaller objects, such as creating a flower from petals, or achieve a checkerboard effect from a series of identical squares.

Saving masks

If you want to preserve your mask for later use, you can save the mask to disk or save it as a path or a channel.

To save a mask to disk, choose Save from the Mask menu. A mask can be saved as a PSD, CPT, 24-bit TGA, or TIF file. Adobe Photoshop 3 or 4 recognizes masks saved as PSD files. (The masks open as active selections.) A TIF or TGA file that contains an alpha channel opens in Fractal Design Painter 5 or Photoshop 3 or 4 with the mask as an active selection.

Secret

The advantage of saving a mask is that it can be applied to your document later. Remember, you can only have one mask open on your document at a time, but you can reload masks later. This is especially important if you have created a complex mask with an exact color tolerance, or perhaps with the Node tools, and then converted the path to a mask. After you save your mask (Mask ➪ Save ➪ Save to Disk), load it at any time when you want to continue working with it (Mask ➪ Load ➪ Load from Disk).

You can also save the mask as an *alpha channel,* referred to in Photo-Paint as a *mask channel.* Alpha channels are sections of your image set aside for storing mask information. These channels can be reopened later for editing the masked area. Saving complex masks as alpha channels means that you don't have to create the same mask later. You can save several alpha channels in a single painting. This practice is one way to work around the limitation of the software not being capable of having more than one mask open at once in your document. By saving and reloading masks as alpha channels, you at least don't have to create them again. Also, saving a mask as an alpha channel allows the mask to be edited in other programs that use them.

Secret

Sometimes you may want to quickly create a masked area on your canvas, apply a change using that mask, and then create another mask without entirely discarding the first mask. To keep a mask accessible, keep the Channel docker open, save your mask as a channel (middle icon at the bottom of the Channel docker), and then create a new mask. When you want to use that first mask again, click on its thumbnail in the Channel docker, and click on the Channel to Mask (lower-left-hand corner) icon. To keep your second mask available for later, save it as a channel, also. You can do this with as many masks as you like.

The Mask Overlay option

When you are creating a complicated mask on your image, it's often helpful to see only your mask selection. Select Mask ➪ Mask Overlay, and your entire image except the masked portion will be covered with a red tint. You can turn this overlay on or off without affecting the image itself. You can also change the color of the overlay in the Options ➪ General dialog box. This is useful if you are working with an image containing a lot of red.

The Invert Mask command

Secret

If the portion of your image that you want to mask is complicated, in terms of shape and color, and the other part of the image is simple, you can select the portion that's easily masked and then invert the mask (click on Mask ⇨ Invert). Now the difficult portion of your image will be masked. Performing this technique is much easier than spending hours trying to outline the exact shape of complex, irregular pictures. Figures 10-4a and 10-4b show the Invert Mask command at work.

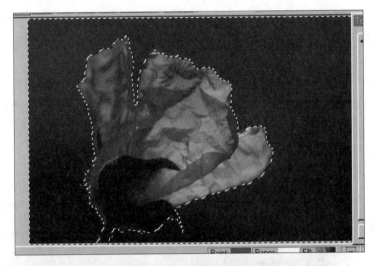

Figure 10-4: The background is masked on this image using the Magic Wand tool, which is explained later (a). After using the Invert Mask command, the flower itself is masked (b).

Area Selection Masks

Press and hold your mouse pointer over the main masking tool (near the top of the toolbox), and you'll see the seven area-selection masking tools on a flyout from the toolbox. These tools include the following:

- The Rectangular Mask tool
- The Elliptical Mask tool
- The Irregular Polygon Mask tool
- The Brush Mask tool
- The Scissors tool
- The Lasso tool
- The Magic Wand tool

Only the Rectangular, Elliptical, and Irregular Polygon tools select a simple bounded area without reference to the color of the pixels involved. The other three area-selection masking tools—Scissors, Lasso, and Magic Wand—have both area-selection and color-range capabilities. (Those tools are discussed later in this chapter.)

When you paint on an area with the Brush Mask tool, the feathery edges of the brush you use will create a mask with various degrees of transparency. Many brushes have feathery brush tips, allowing part of the underlying image to show through. Depending on how you paint, you can have transparent or opaque areas scattered throughout your mask. Adjusting the Transparency slider on the Property Bar also affects how much of the underlying image beneath the mask will show through.

Figure 10-5 shows an image created by painting on a mask over the intersection points of two objects. As you can see by where the mouse is highlighting the Soft Edge amount on the Mask Brush tool Property Bar, it's easy to make a mask using soft, feathery edges to prevent abrupt transitions between blended objects. The masked area where the two objects join was saved as a channel before being cut (Mask ⇨ Save ⇨ Save as Channel). The cutting allows some of the background to show through. To make the cut appear uniform across both objects, you must select one object, load the mask you saved as a channel by selecting Mask ⇨ Load, and then click on the name of the channel you saved your mask as. This mask now appears on the object you selected. You can then perform the same edit on the new object, but using the same mask you previously saved. This way, you don't have to recreate the same mask—just apply it on various objects.

As shown in Figure 10-6, the mask was loaded in and embossing was applied to the masked area (Effects ⇨ 3D Effects ⇨ Emboss). This shows that you can reload a mask later and perform special effects to the masked area only. The masked area is feathered and tapered because an unevenly shaped nib was used. The embossing look gradually fades into the more flat lettering.

Figure 10-5: You can apply a feathery mask anywhere you like on an image using the Mask Brush tool. Increase the Soft Edge, as shown, for a more blended appearance.

Figure 10-6: The mask was reloaded to apply embossing only to the area where the previous editing occurred. Notice the Channels docker is open, making it easy to save and load masks as channels by using the icons at the bottom of the docker.

If you are using a mask simply to create transparency, then use Photo-Paint's Object Transparency brush tool instead (second tool from the bottom on the toolbox). To use this tool, you have to convert the area you want to affect to an object first.

Secret

With the Brush Mask tool, you can paint levels of transparency anywhere in a mask, not just the edges. The next time you want to create a feathered mask using the Feather command in the Mask menu, consider painting on a mask with one of the more complex feather-tipped brushes instead. You have much more control over where the transparent areas occur in your mask. Using a Brush Mask tool, some mask areas can be more transparent than others.

Figure 10-7 shows the selection of tools when you click on and hold the masking tool button.

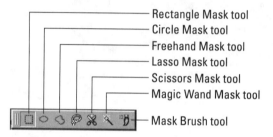

— Rectangle Mask tool
— Circle Mask tool
— Freehand Mask tool
— Lasso Mask tool
— Scissors Mask tool
— Magic Wand Mask tool
— Mask Brush tool

Figure 10-7: The flyout menu showing the area-selection masking tools.

Remember

The Property Bar and the Tool Settings roll-up change depending on the tool you select. Figure 10-8 shows the Property Bar's four tool options when you choose one of the area-selection tools.

Create a new mask
Add to an existing mask
Subtract from an existing mask
The XOR Mask button

Figure 10-8: These options are the first four on the Property Bar when an area-selection masking tool is activated.

If you are starting a new mask on your image, the arrow should be depressed. If you are adding to a mask, you should click on the plus (+) sign. Use the minus (-) sign to remove a portion of an existing mask. Use the double-squared tool for XOR masking, which is explained later in the section "Other area-selection masking tools."

The Area Mask Operations menu

The drop-down menu next to the first four tools (see Figure 10-8) is the Area Mask Operations menu. While using the Rectangle and Ellipse tools, you will find the following four settings available:

- **Normal.** The tool has no angular or scale constraints.

- **Fixed Size.** Clicking on your picture drops a mask of a specific height and width. Next to the drop-down menu are two numerical data boxes. You may input any number (measured in pixels) for the mask's width and height.

- **Row(s).** This option selects a small but wide strip of an area, similar in appearance to a row of spreadsheet data.

- **Column(s).** This option selects a tall but thin strip of an area, similar in appearance to a column of spreadsheet data.

When you are using the other area-selection mask tools, this drop-down menu enables you to switch between two types of Color Tolerance modes: Normal and HSB. The HSB mode is helpful for intelligently narrowing the scope of pixels you want to select with your tool. You can, for example, make your tool ignore an area that is particularly dark or highly saturated with color, while selecting pixels that are otherwise quite similar.

The Brush Mask tool

The Brush Mask tool paints a mask onto your picture. Using the paintbrush Property Bar and the Tool Settings roll-up, you can create any type of brush, brush size, number of bristles, transparency amount, or stroke quality; in fact, any brush parameter besides color can also be used to modify the Brush Mask tool. Using the Zoom tool with the Brush Mask tool, you can build a very precise mask.

Figure 10-9 shows some rather painterly strokes rendered with the Brush Mask tool.

Figure 10-9: The Brush Mask tool at work.

Other area-selection masking tools

Now we'll look at a handful of other tools that employ methods for selecting shapes and areas (rather than color ranges).

The XOR Mask tool

Figure 10-8 shows the XOR (pronounced X-O-R) Mask tool in action. When you create a mask using XOR and then add it to a prior mask, you unmask the area where your new selection overlaps with the preexisting mask. In Figure 10-10, the black area and the light-gray area are selected. The dark gray between them is no longer selected because it is the overlapping area. The XOR effect can be used for creating masks that overlap. The XOR effect allows an underlying image to show through where the masks converge.

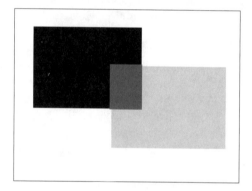

Figure 10-10: The XOR Mask tool is shown in action.

The Anti-Alias option

Anti-Alias is an option that can be used with almost all of Photo-Paint's mask tools. It is especially useful for area-selection masks. (The Anti-Alias button is found on almost every tool's Property Bar, usually toward the right end. By default, antialiasing is enabled.) With Anti-Alias enabled, the tiny jagged edges that are inevitably included with your mask selection are smoothed out. The need for antialiasing is simply part of the process of working with bitmaps rather than more precise vector images. Unless you have an affinity for jagged edges, leave the Anti-Alias option selected.

Expand/Reduce

Expand/Reduce expands or reduces the size of your mask according to the number of pixels you choose. This is a simple area command that takes no consideration of the colors of the surrounding pixels. Select Mask ➪ Shape from the Menu bar and then choose Expand or Reduce.

Text masks

Text is always created as an object. However, you can convert text to a mask to create a stencil effect with the text. Figure 10-11 shows four smaller pictures converted to objects and pasted onto a textured background. The text "Be Here Now" was created and then converted into a mask. (Type the text and then click outside the text, which makes the text into an object. Then select Mask ⇨ Create from Object.) The mask was cut, leaving only the hole for the underlying image behind the four pictures to show through. The phrase "Be Here Now" then became visible as a stencil cutout. You can create raised or embossed effects by pasting the previously cut text over the cutout area (which turns the selection into an object) and then applying Merge Modes. (The Object Property Bar has a drop-down menu that most often reads Normal. Experiment with other Merge Mode options, such as Multiply and Overlay, to see which modes bring the most interesting results.) The text in Figure 10-11 was created using this technique along with the Luminosity Merge Mode.

Figure 10-11: An image has been created by converting text to a mask.

STEPS:

Converting Text to a Mask

Step 1. Create a background with a fill or a bitmap.

Step 2. Paste in four square images as objects, and place them evenly over the background. You must select images that contrast highly against the background. (After you remove the text stencil, the background image shows through as text.) High contrast with the top images will make the results more legible.

(continued)

Converting Text to a Mask

Step 3.   Use the Text tool to create a brief text phrase. You may have to select a font size several times until you've covered just the right amount of image with your text.

Step 4.   For maximum effect, position your text evenly over all four square-image objects.

Step 5.   Because the text is an object, you must click on Mask ⇨ Create from Object and then cut the text (Edit ⇨ Cut), which leaves a hole, showing the underlying image, and copies the text to the Clipboard so you can apply it later.

Step 6.   Try pasting the text from the Clipboard, positioning it over the hole, and experimenting with Merge Modes.

You can also use objects as stencils, turning them into masks and removing the mask, leaving a hole in the image that matches the outline of your object.

Color Range Masks

Unlike area-selection masking tools, color range masking tools are based on the color of pixels rather than shape or contiguity. For example, if an image has lavender colors and you want to shift the lavender to more of a red, you can use a Color Range mask to select the lavender and change it to red. Also, if you were working with a picture of a man with gray hair and wanted to change the gray hair to black, it would be much easier to use a Color Range mask tool to select the hair than it would be to attempt following the hairline's uneven edges with an Area Mask tool.

Color tolerance

The color range masking tools in Photo-Paint include an option for you to assign a level of *color tolerance* to the tools. (The numeric data box that, by default, reads 10. Place your mouse over the data box, and it reads Color Similarity or Hue Level.) When using a color range masking tool, such as the Magic Wand, you can assign rules that tell the tool to select one shade of a color for masking and leave another shade untouched. For example, will your tool select only pixels similar to the red spot where you clicked the tool, or will it cast a wide net and pick up anything in your picture that is even remotely red? This is called setting the color tolerance level. The higher you set the color tolerance level, the more pixels will be selected by the mask. When you set a low color tolerance level, the tool selects only hues similar to the spot where you actually clicked the tool.

The Color Mask tool

Let's first take a look at the Color Mask tool. When you load a picture in Photo-Paint and select Mask ⇨ Color Mask, a dialog box appears that frames the picture you loaded. (See Figure 10-12.) You can create a color mask by clicking any area in the picture you want with the Eyedropper tool. The rectangular boxes on the right side of the dialog box fill up with your color selections. Click on the Eye icon to see a preview of your mask. You'll also notice that your mask grows larger with each color you choose from your picture. Figure 10-12 shows the Eyedropper tool (which automatically comes up with the dialog box) poised and ready to select an area of dark color. Notice that the top rectangle is filled with the same color that the Eyedropper is selecting. You may select as many (or as few) colors from your picture as you wish. Although the Color Mask screen shows only ten sample boxes, you can scroll down farther if you want to make more than ten selections

Figure 10-12: The Color Mask dialog box shows the Eyedropper at work.

You can use the Pan tool (the hand) to move other portions of your image into the viewing screen. The Smoothing slider bar changes how tolerant of color variances your Eyedropper tool should be. One helpful tool is the Overlay button (the eye). It places a red tint over all masked areas of your image. Any part of your image that is not tinted is not masked. This helps for spotting "holes" in masks that are supposed to cover a uniform area. If you'd rather have your mask appear as a Marquee, click on that drop-down menu and select Marquee.

Notice that the Create From field in Figure 10-12 shows a drop-down menu that says Sampled Colors. This indicates that you're creating your mask with colors sampled from your picture. The drop-down menu has other options, enabling you to create a mask from colors in any available color pallet. Click on the More button to select HSB values rather than normal Tolerance amounts.

Using the Color Mask Tool to Change a Background

Go into Photo-Paint and open the file named BRUSHES.CPT, an image that comes with Photo-Paint in the Samples folder. Use this file to practice changing the background by using the Color Mask tool.

STEPS:

Changing the Background Using the Color Mask Tool

Step 1.   Select the entire blue background using the Color Mask dialog box and Eyedropper, leaving the dog entirely untouched by the masking. Click on the Overlay button (the eye) to make sure all the blue is gone. See Figure A.

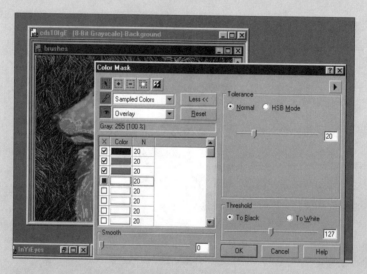

Figure A: The tinted overlay makes it easier to select unmasked areas.

Step 2.   After closing the Color Mask, you might see areas of blue that are not entirely masked. Use the Brush Mask tool to add to the mask, making sure that Additive mode is enabled. See Figure B.

Step 3.   Invert the mask so that the dog is selected by clicking on Mask ⇨ Invert, and then cut the mask to the Clipboard. This leaves an area of white where the dog was. See Figure C.

Figure B: Touch up the mask with the Brush Mask tool.

Figure C: Use the Invert Mask command.

Step 4.　Choose Effects ⇨ Fancy ⇨ Alchemy. This kind of effect makes changes to your whole image if an area is not selected. Using the default settings (Threads, Random), click on OK and close the Alchemy dialog box.

(continued)

STEPS *(continued)*

Changing the Background Using the Color Mask Tool

Step 5. Select Edit ➪ Paste ➪ As New Object, and reposition the dog so that all the white is covered. (See Figure D.)

Figure D: Paste the dog back in as a new object.

The finished image is shown in Figure E.

Figure E: Here is what the file named BRUSHES.CPT looks like after changing the background.

Other color range masking tools

Several other color range masking tools exist besides the Color Mask tool. Some of them work alone; others need to be used in combination with area-selection masking. Following is an overview of the other color range masking tools.

The Grow command

After using one of the area mask tools (such as the Rectangular Mask tool), select Mask ⇨ Shape ⇨ Grow. The mask expands to include all the pixels similar in color to the ones along the edge of the current marquee. The Grow command uses the color tolerance level of the current paintbrush or painting tool. Look at Figure 10-13. Clicking on the Grow command would expand the existing mask to include most of the lower rocks below the lighthouse, but not the lighthouse itself. In this case, to include the upper rocks near the lighthouse, the color tolerance level would have to be increased to about 25.

Figure 10-13: The Grow command expands this mask to include most of the lower rocks.

The Similar command

Select Mask ⇨ Shape ⇨ Similar, and your current mask grows to include pixels anywhere in your picture that are within the current color tolerance level. The difference between the Similar command and the Grow command is that Similar includes pixels anywhere in your picture, whereas Grow expands your mask only to contiguous pixels.

The best way to set a color tolerance level for working with commands such as Grow and Similar is to double-click on the Magic Wand tool in the toolbox. The Tool Settings roll-up appears. You can then easily set the color tolerance level in that dialog box for use with these commands.

The Smooth command

Select Mask ⇨ Shape ⇨ Smooth to find this command. If you've created a color range mask, the smooth command blends the colors in the pixels around the edges of the marquee. The result looks a lot like feathering, which is explained a little later. Rather than creating areas where the background shows through (which is what feathering does), you are blending the colors around the parameter of your mask. With the Smooth command, you need to enter a value in the Radius data box. The larger the number, the more the colors will blend together.

The Paint on Mask command

This command is easily confused with the Brush Mask tool. With Paint on Mask, you are not painting a new mask onto your image. You are painting degrees of protection onto a canvas. After you've selected Mask ⇨ Paint on Mask, your image turns black, except for the masked area, which is white. Your color choices are degrees of gray because the level of transparency of your mask is measured by the degree of gray present on the mask. Figure 10-14 shows a picture that was altered using the Paint on Mask command. The masked area, which is white, originally had no gray pixels because it was entirely masked. (In other words, there was no transparency to the mask at all.) The area surrounding the mask is black, because no mask is present there. The figure shows a stroke of a paintbrush on the mask area, in a shade of gray. After the Paint on Mask command is turned off, that mask will have a somewhat translucent area where it was painted with a brushstroke. If a lighter shade of gray had been used, it would be less transparent. Darker shades of gray would create almost total transparency.

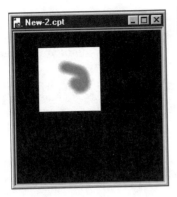

Figure 10-14: A masked area is shown with Paint on Mask turned on. One brushstroke is over the mask.

Figure 10-15 shows a powerful special effects tool associated with the Paint on Mask command. While Paint on Mask is turned on, if you paste any image onto the mask, the image will be interpreted according to its relative shades of gray and will thus modify the mask—just as if you had painted it on with brush strokes. You do not need to convert your image to grayscale to use this feature. For Figure 10-15, an oval mask was applied to the psychedelic background image and then filled with butterflies. While Paint on Mask was turned on, the apple object was pasted onto the mask. The apple had so many dark shades of gray that it behaved almost as a cutout, revealing almost all of the butterfly image provided by the mask. If there had been lighter shades of gray, you'd see more of the background image and less of the butterflies, which are found only on the mask.

Figure 10-15: An apple is pasted onto a mask, modifying only the mask's grayscale qualities. The mask shows through.

The Stroke Mask command

After creating a mask, select Edit ➪ Stroke ➪ Stroke Mask, and the Paint Tool dialog box appears. You can then select a brush style of your choice to stroke your mask's border. You can stroke with any color, and you can even instruct Stroke Mask to go around the mask more than once, to introduce an element of randomness to strokes after the first. Stroke Mask can place its stroke(s) inside, on top of, or outside the mask's border. Figure 10-16 shows some hearts that were masked and then stroked inside the mask border with the Stroke Mask tool.

Figure 10-16: The Stroke Mask Tool is shown at work.

Tools for Both Area and Color Range Selection

The Magic Wand, Lasso, and Scissors tools have color tolerance controls that allow them to select a broader or narrower range of pixels beyond what they would normally select as Area Mask tools. Figure 10-17 shows these three tools circled, as part of the Mask tools flyout menu.

Figure 10-17: These masking tools appear on the toolbox.

Figure 10-18 shows a mask created with the Freehand Mask tool (the third tool from the left). The mask was stroked with a single brush stroke. (Click on Edit ➪ Stroke ➪ Stroke Mask.) Remember that this tool requires you to double-click when you finish selecting.

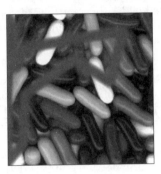

Figure 10-18: A mask is created with the Freehand Mask tool, with one brush stroke applied.

The Lasso Mask tool

The Lasso Mask tool deserves special attention because after you carve a mask around a particular area, the Lasso Mask tool shrinks down to select any obvious boundary or object inside the scissors marquee. How well it picks out the object inside the scissors marquee depends on your fine-tuning of the color tolerance settings.

Secret

You can apply constraints to several Shape masks using the Ctrl and Shift keys. Pressing Ctrl while using the Rectangular and Ellipse Mask tools constrains the shape to a square or a circle, respectively. The Shift key applied with the same tools expands your selection from the center rather than starting at the left or right. (Give it a try. This is a helpful option.) Using the Ctrl key with the Mask Brush tool constrains the brush to vertical or horizontal movement.

The Scissors Mask tool

The Scissors Mask tool finds the obvious edges in your picture (areas where the pixel colors change abruptly). If you "cut" with the scissors tool near the edge, the mask marquee will be placed right at the edge. The Scissors Mask tool is also helpful in adding freehand-selected areas to an already existing color-range-created mask.

The Magic Wand

Click on a pixel with the Magic Wand tool, and all nearby pixels will be included in the selection according to color tolerance levels that you define on the Tools Property Bar. With this tool, you simply click on the color you want as it appears in your picture. Click in an area that has direct, contiguous communication with the other pixels you want included in your mask.

Feathering

Feathering is probably the most important tool in working with masks.
Feathering gives fuzzy edges to your area selection. If you are working with a
Rectangular mask, for example, you may not want that rectangular shape to
remain as harsh and sharp when blended with other portions of your picture.
Feathering creates interesting collage effects where one image blends nicely
into the next. Feathering helps blend the pixels from one image into the next
with a nice tapered graduation.

Select Mask ⇨ Shape ⇨ Feather to open the Feather dialog box. (Note that both
Objects and Masks have their own feathering tool.) As shown in Figure 10-19,
the Feather dialog box enables you to select how wide the feathered area
should be. The feathering command creates feathered pixels on all sides of
your mask. This affects how deeply into the image you want the feathering
process to cut. Larger numbers cut deeper into the edges of your picture
to produce a highly feathered image. The drop-down menu (the default
is Average) controls how gradually you want the pixels to blend into the
background image, or how pronouncedly they should seem to rest on top of
the background. Choosing Average creates more blending into the background,
and Middle makes the mask appear to rest on top of the background.

Figure 10-19: The Feather dialog box controls blending options.

Figure 10-20 shows a portion of a complex image showing several blending
techniques. The trumpet, in the foreground, stands out, with several images
feathered behind it.

Figure 10-20: This composition features feathering.

Feathering one side of a mask

Here's a technique for combining two very different pictures into one image. Let's combine a picture of a lighthouse with a photo of downtown San Francisco to create a surrealistic landscape. Something similar to this can be done with the Stitch Command (Image ➪ Stitch; see Chapter 14), but with Stitch you have less direct control over the feathering amount.

Open the lighthouse image, cut it to the Windows Clipboard, and paste it as an object onto a New Image, leaving lots of blank paper around it. (We'll be squeezing two blended photos onto this canvas. Figure 10-21 shows a mask drawn widely around an image of a lighthouse. The mask cuts through the lighthouse image on the right side, because when you invoke the feather command, you'll want the feather to cut into only the right side of the image. Notice the huge feathering amount in the dialog box (144 pixels). If you put the mask any farther toward the center of the photo, you'd get some degree of feathering on all four sides.

Figure 10-21: A technique for feathering only one side of an image.

You can also perform this effect by applying the Object transparency tool to one image and then the other. The Object transparency tool is the second tool from the bottom in the toolbox. Of the three tools shown, click on the one with the tool tip Applies transparency to Objects. When you drag the Object Transparency tool across an object, the tool becomes an arrow facing the direction you drag. The transparency increases in the direction you drag the tool. Dragging a short distance results in abrupt, steep transparency curves. Dragging a long distance results in a more gradual tapering of transparency.

If you create the mask as it is in Figure 10-21, the deep feathering effect appears only on the right side of the image. After you click on OK, your image should show only the mask. Click on Object ➪ Clip Mask ➪ Create ➪ From Mask, as shown in Figure 10-22. The next figure, Figure 10-23, shows the results of this action. Only one side of the object is feathered. To permanently apply this clipping mask, click on Object ⇨ Clip Mask ⇨ Combine. Clipping masks are covered more thoroughly in Chapter 14.

Figure 10-22: After feathering a large mask, create a clipping mask.

Figure 10-23: The results of Clip Object to Mask: a feather on one side.

If you repeat this procedure on another photo, creating the feather on the left side, and then blend the two feathered images together, the final image should look something like Figure 10-24. This figure shows the mask boundary still visible, so you can see how the city photo was treated with the same effect, but on the opposite side. (Don't forget to experiment with the Interactive Transparency tool as well. For combining images in which large amounts of feathering is not important, use the Stitch Command.)

Figure 10-24: The finished composition combines two feathered images.

Blending images with feathering

Figure 10-25 shows a blend of two photographs for an ethereal composition. First the photo of the river was altered to accommodate the size of the door. Then the feathered door was added.

Figure 10-25: A composition shows a feathered object inserted into a river scene.

Here are the steps we took to create this image:

Adding a Feathered Image

Step 1. The original image (see Figure 10-26) was not tall enough to accommodate the sailing-into-the-door effect. To create a blank space on the canvas, we adjusted the paper size (select Image ⇨ Paper Size). Figure 10-27 shows the Paper Size dialog box. Making the Paper Size larger gives an image room to expand. In this case, we made it about twice as tall as the original and placed the existing image at Center Bottom

Figure 10-26: The original boat image is shown before it was altered to accommodate the door.

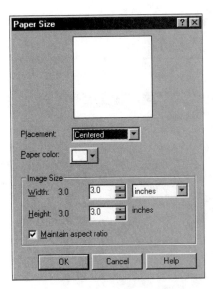

Figure 10-27: The Paper Size dialog box controls image size and placement.

Step 2. We then converted the river image into an object. We selected the entire image with the Rectangle Mask tool and then clicked on Object ⇨ Create Object: Create from Background.

Step 3. The Perspective tool was used on the river scene to create the illusion of the river's horizon being farther away. We selected the Object Picker tool and clicked on the river scene. We clicked on the object several times until the status bar showed Perspective on the Image. We then dragged the image's upper boundary toward the top of the paper. Making the image narrower while dragging created a deeper perspective effect. This procedure was followed once on the right side of the image and then again on the left.

Step 4. We then used the Distort tool to make the image into a true rectangle again.

Step 5. We opened a photo from Corel's Doors of San Francisco collection and pasted it at the top of the river photo. The door itself was selected and feathered at about 100 pixels. Figure 10-28 shows the feathered door before it was placed in the river image.

(continued)

Adding a Feathered Image

Figure 10-28: The feathered door is shown before being placed into the river image.

Step 6.   We then copied the feathered image to the Clipboard and pasted it as an object onto the river image.

Step 7.   Finally, we added a second boater behind the first one. Because the boater was a narrow figure, this contributed a long, deep journey feeling to the composition. To do this, we selected the boater with the Magic Wand tool, clicked on Object ⇨ Create ⇨ Object: Copy Selection, and pasted the copy a bit upriver and to the right of the original.

Whenever you want to blend images more naturally, diminishing any harsh lines between the images, think of the Feathering tool. Remember that higher feathering values cause images to fade together more gradually. Lower feathering values cause more abrupt combinations.

Using Masks to Create a Framed Picture

Here's a masking technique that enables you to create an interesting photo composition using a photograph of a piece of wood as a background.

STEPS:

Further Practice with Masking and Feathering

Step 1. Starting with a background photograph of a piece of wood with daylight shining across it, a mask was made by double-clicking on the Rectangle Mask tool. This selects the entire wood background.

Step 2. Select Mask ⇨ Shape and set the Reduce value to 80 pixels. If the wood background image you begin with is sized differently than this one, you may need to select a different pixel range to get the frame effect, as shown in Figure A.

Figure A: An image of wood has a mask around it to create a frame.

Step 3. Double-click on the Fill tool to bring up the Tool Settings roll-up, and then click on the Texture option (the first button on the right). Select Textured Blends Vertical from the list.

Step 4. Fill the outside border of the image with the Fill tool. It will be filled with the texture.

(continued)

STEPS *(continued)*

Further Practice with Masking and Feathering

Step 5. To create the thickening effect of the frame, Select Object ➪ Create ➪ Copy: From Selection. (Make sure the mask is still selected when you do this.) Select Edit ➪ Paste ➪ As New Object. Experiment with various Paint Mode tools as you blend the new frame you just pasted from the Clipboard with the existing one. We found that Texturize created a nice effect.

Step 6. Open an image of a flower with a dark background. The dark background makes it easy to use the Magic Wand tool to select the background. Click on Mask ➪ Invert so that the flower itself is selected. When selecting the background with the Magic Wand tool, make sure the Additive Mode (the plus sign) is active.

Step 7. While the flower is selected, again choose Object ➪ Create ➪ Object: Copy Selection and copy the flower to the Clipboard. Paste it as a new object into the framed wood image. Select Object ➪ Create Drop Shadow, if you like. Your results should look similar to Figure B.

Figure B: The finished product shows the flower on the wood.

Removing holes

Sometimes when you are selecting a large contiguous area of your image, small islands of nonselected portions remain. That's because the color tolerance settings of your tool have not been set broadly enough to pick up these stray pixels. Sometimes these holes in your mask are too small to be conveniently snapped up with the tool you are using. You can use the Mask Brush tool to paint over the holes or, while the mask is selected, choose Mask ⇨ Shape ⇨ Remove Holes, and all unselected areas enclosed in the mask will become part of it.

Setting the threshold

While a mask is selected, click on Mask ⇨ Shape ⇨ Threshold to remove feathering from a mask. You're prompted to select pixel values between 1 and 255, because feathering, as a component of your mask, is actually a shade of gray. By selecting a pixel value, you are actually choosing a cutoff value for your feathering effect. The result is sharper edges around your mask.

Summary

▶ Adjusting a mask's transparency can give you greater control over how images blend with special effects.

▶ The various mask tools such as Invert and the Mask Overlay option are useful for working with both area-selection and color range masks.

▶ With the Paint on Mask tool, you can paint degrees of transparency onto an existing mask.

▶ The Brush Mask tool is an area-selection masking tool you can use to paint masks onto an image.

▶ With feathering, you can get rid of harsh mask edges, and you can even blend two different images together.

Chapter 11

Plug-Ins for Photo-Paint and CorelDraw

In This Chapter

▶ Using plug-ins for enhancing and touching up images

▶ Using plug-ins for creating special effects

▶ Working with third-party plug-ins

Programs such as Photo-Paint are often referred to as having an *open architecture*. Open architecture means that other small applets (for example, plug-ins) can hook into the application, providing additional features and enhancements to the host application. In the case of Photo-Paint, the program supports standard Adobe Photoshop plug-ins. Many plug-ins ship with Photo-Paint, and you can purchase others from third-party vendors such as Alien Skin, Adobe, and MetaCreations.

Located on the Effects menu, plug-ins are arranged in groups (on submenus) by category. Some provide additional image enhancement, while others can apply complex special effects. Photo-Paint plug-ins include categories for blurring, sharpening, distorting, lighting, adding noise and texture, and applying stylistic effects, such as embossing, page curling, beveling, and many other effects.

Plug-ins can add tremendous new dimensions to your images and to your design process. Although a thorough discussion of every available plug-in lies beyond this book's scope, in this chapter you'll get enough information to get fired up and ready to use plug-ins with Photo-Paint and CorelDraw.

Using the CorelDraw 8 Plug-Ins

As you may already know, filters are important pieces of software that you use to import and export graphics and text files. In CorelDraw, for example, you can import several different file formats, such as EPS, TIFF, and Microsoft Word documents. CorelDraw also lets you export to several non-native formats. In paint programs, such as Photo-Paint, you can also open and save different formats through filters. In addition to using import and export filters, you can use special pieces of software called plug-in filters (also called plug-ins). Essentially, these plug-ins work the same as other filters; they hook into a host application and enhance its capabilities.

With CorelDraw 8 you have the capability of applying plug-in filters in both CorelDraw and Photo-Paint. Even though you cannot edit bitmaps directly in CorelDraw, you can apply plug-ins to bitmaps imported into your drawings. Consequently, this discussion of plug-ins pertains in large part to both Photo-Paint and CorelDraw. In CorelDraw, you'll find the plug-ins on the Bitmap menu.

In Photo-Paint, plug-ins are applied from the Effects menu, as shown in Figure 11-1. Although the arrangement of plug-ins on the menu seems to have no rhyme or reason, the plug-ins can be broken into two basic categories:

- Touch-up and enhancement plug-ins

- Effects plug-ins

Most of the plug-ins apply effects of one sort or another. The touch-up and enhancement plug-ins can be found primarily on the Adjust, Blur, Noise, and Sharpen submenus.

Many more plug-ins are available than this chapter can cover. In fact, plug-ins provide so many options that the only way to get a good handle on them is to experiment with them first-hand. Nevertheless, here is a brief overview of some of my favorites.

Secret

Note that Photo-Paint can use all plugs-ins designed for use with Photoshop. If you have Photoshop installed, you can set the plug-in path in Photo-Paint to Photoshop's plug-in directory, enabling you to use all these filters without having to install them twice on your system To set the plug-in path to Photoshop's plug-in directory, select Tools ⇨ Options ⇨ Workspace ⇨ Plug-ins, and then choose Add in the Plug-ins sheet and go to the path where your Photoshop plug-ins reside (usually C:\Photoshop\Plugins).

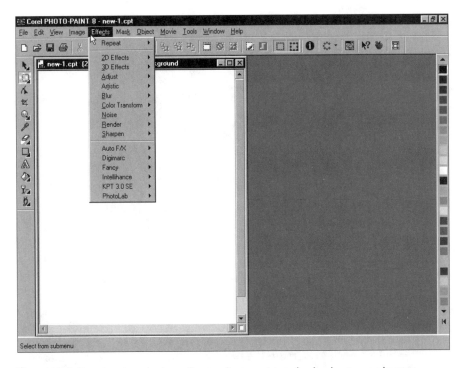

Figure 11-1: Use the commands on these submenus to apply plug-ins to your images.

Touch-up and enhancement plug-ins

A *touch-up and enhancement plug-in* is basically one that improves the quality of an image (rather than applying a special effect). These plug-ins enable you to adjust brightness, color, sharpness, and remove noise and flaws. You get the picture. And yes, believe it or not, blurring or softening an image can sometimes improve its overall appearance.

Whether you are applying a touch-up plug-in or an effects plug-in, the procedure is primarily the same. You simply select the plug-in you want from the Effects menu, which brings up a dialog box similar to the one shown in Figure 11-2. From here you can make adjustments to the plug-in's action and get previews, before you apply the filter, of how your changes will affect the image. The preview feature is a big help, as it can take a long time to apply some filters to large, full-color images.

When applying a plug-in, Photo-Paint provides a wide range of options. For example, you can move the image in the Original window with the hand tool to see how your settings affect a specific portion of the image.

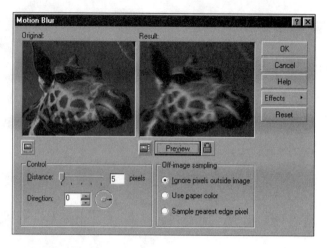

Figure 11-2: This typical plug-in dialog box for adjusting, applying, and previewing plug-ins introduces you to the available options.

When you move the mouse over the Original preview window, it automatically becomes a hand with which you can move the image around in the window. (In previous versions, you first clicked the Hand tool button.) To see the results on the portion of the image in the Original window, click Preview. Alternatively, you can click the little padlock and have the preview update automatically.

You can also zoom out on the image (right-click the mouse cursor in the Original window) to see how your changes affect more of the image, as shown in Figure 11-3. To zoom in, left-click without dragging. To zoom out, click the right mouse button.

Figure 11-3: Use the Zoom tool to zoom in on specific areas of the image and preview how plug-in settings will affect your image. (Here the image is zoomed out.)

You can also fill the viewing area with a preview image, giving you a larger, better view to judge the results, as shown in Figure 11-4. To use this option, click the button to the left of the Preview button. Aside from these basic instructions, each plug-in is different and performs varying tricks on the image; our best advice is to monkey around with the controls.

Figure 11-4: Click the button next to the Preview button to fill the viewing area with the preview window.

The Sharpen plug-ins

You'll find one of the most useful groups of plug-ins on the Effects menu on the Sharpen flyout. Although several good plug-ins lurk here, the two we find the most helpful are Find Edges and Sharpen. Find Edges does exactly what the name implies; it finds hard surfaces within an image and sharpens them. This plug-in is a great way to make objects within an image appear more clearly.

Sharpen attempts to eliminate blur, or to make an image more clear. Although it doesn't succeed on all images, it does a good job on many. Check out the images in Figure 11-5. We applied the Sharpen plug-in resulting in the after image. Pretty cool, huh? How much a picture needs sharpening depends totally on the image, of course. Too much sharpening can distort the image or cause pixelization. Our experience is that you should apply Sharpen incrementally, a little bit at a time. At the point you've gone a little too far, use Undo to go back a step.

458 Part II: Supporting Applications

Figure 11-5: Use the Sharpen plug-in to clear up blurry scans.

Dust and Scratches plug-in

Sometimes that just-right photograph for your project isn't in the best of shape. It might be scratched, or maybe you spilled coffee or ketchup on it. Who knows? Technology to the rescue. You can clean up many image flaws with the Dust and Scratches plug-in available on the Noise submenu. In Figure 11-6, for instance, the image was edited with this plug-in to remove scratches and stains.

Figure 11-6: Touch-ups made with the Dust and Scratches plug-in can help prepare this image for newspaper publication.

In most cases, you'll want to use this filter on the area that contains the flaw you want to remove, so select the area with one of the selection tools, as shown in Figure 11-7. Then open the Dust and Scratches plug-in and adjust the settings until you get the effect you want. You'll need to do this for each area of the image you want to touch up. This may seem tedious, but it's much better than using an image with glaring flaws or not being able to use the image at all.

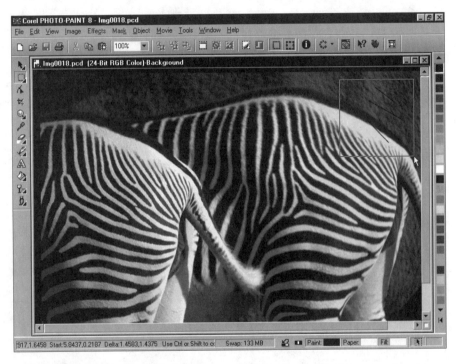

Figure 11-7: When using the Dust and Scratches plug-in, first select the area you want to touch up before invoking the plug-in.

You can get a similar effect by using the Sharpness plug-in on the Adjust submenu. In fact, this method provides several preview windows, allowing for a more interactive approach to cleaning up your images.

Secret

As the previous example demonstrates, you can apply plug-ins to selected portions of an image. Many of the plug-ins work within a selected area, on a mask, or on a separate object layer, enabling you to apply enhancements and effects with discrimination, making for some unique results. For more information about using masks, refer to Chapter 10.

Protecting Your Creations on the Internet

Secret

If you've spent much time cruising the Web, you've probably noticed that many of the same images are used by different designers. With stock photography, clip art, and shareware, this sometimes can't be avoided (which is why we usually always alter stock images in some way before we use them). However, you may want to protect the images you use from being copied, which you can do with the Digimarc Watermark plug-in. This plug-in enables you to mark images with secret codes that identify the images as your own. You can also use this plug-in to locate the creators of other images you find on the Internet and get contact information.

Photo-Paint comes with a demo copy of Digimarc, shown in the figure, which you can register for a trial period. Basically, here is how watermarks work: Images are digitally encoded with a registration number you obtain from Digimarc. You can add various attributes to the watermark, such as Do Not Copy or Adult Content. This code marks the image as belonging to you. If you (or Digimarc) finds this watermark on the Internet, the image is easily identifiable as yours.

The plug-in has two parts, Embed Watermark, which enables you to encode your images, and Read Watermark, which enables you to find contact information for images you download from the Web.

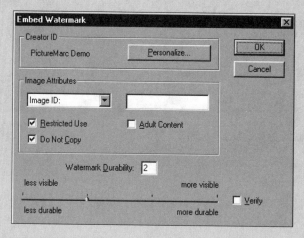

Special Effects Plug-Ins

If you're not familiar with Photo-Paint and plug-ins, you'll be pleasantly surprised by all the things you can do with Photo-Paint's special effects plug-ins. The CorelDraw package comes with hoards of them, and if they don't do everything you need, you can buy additional plug-ins from third-party vendors that produce just about every kind of effect imaginable, and then some. Again, each plug-in works differently. In this section, we list a few particularly cool plug-ins. But don't stop at just these favorites — try out some other plug-ins on your own.

Emboss

Using this plug-in, you can seem like a real artist without really trying. When you use Emboss on an image, you raise its hard edges, giving it a 3D effect. The Emboss dialog box, shown in Figure 11-8, enables you to adjust the depth and level of the 3D effect and the direction of the light source, and it provides four different color effects from which to choose.

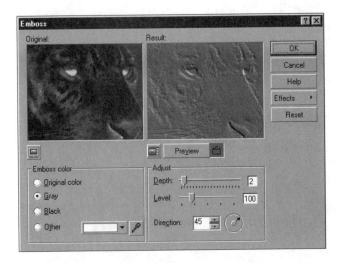

Figure 11-8: Set emboss depth, light source, and other options with the Emboss plug-in dialog box.

Figure 11-9 shows an image embossed with several different settings. You'll have fun using this effect.

Figure 11-9: The first image is the original. The second image was embossed with an Emboss color of Gray, a Depth of 3, a Level of 100, and a Direction of 90 degrees. The third image was embossed with an Emboss color of Paper, Depth 2, Level 100, Direction 0 degrees.

Page Curl

If you surf the Web, you've probably noticed this effect used frequently. It also shows up on many software packages and in magazine ads. You'll find Page Curl on the 3D Effects submenu on the Effects menu, which displays the dialog box shown in Figure 11-10. The effect re-creates the look of paper being curled, or peeled back, as shown in Figure 11-11.

To use the Page Curl dialog box, first specify which corner you want to curl, using one of the four Adjust buttons. Then specify whether you want the curl to be horizontal or vertical. Adjust the height and depth of the curl. If necessary, move the image in the Original window so you can see the corner you're curling. You can get a preview at any time by clicking on the Preview button, as shown in Figure 11-12.

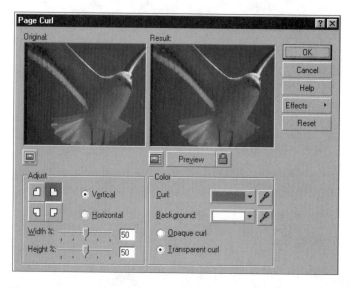

Figure 11-10: The Page Curl plug-in dialog box helps you create that curled page corner effect you see in magazines and on the Web.

Figure 11-11: Example of effect achieved with the Page Curl plug-in

Choose which corner you want to curl

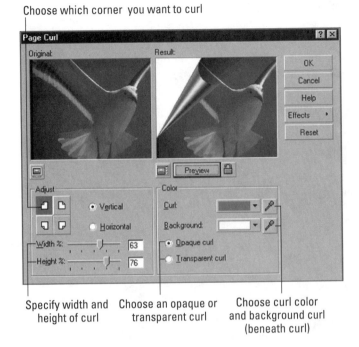

Specify width and   Choose an opaque or   Choose curl color
height of curl   transparent curl   and background curl
(beneath curl)

Figure 11-12: Use the Preview option to gauge your progress as you adjust the curl.

To change the color of the curl itself, or the background beneath the curl, simply choose new colors from the drop-down palettes. You can also set the curl to transparent, which is a cool effect, as shown in Figure 11-13.

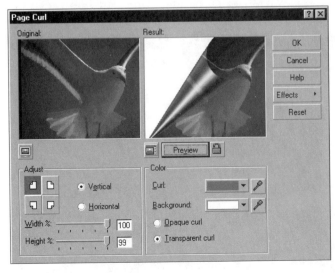

Figure 11-13: Use the Transparent option to create an interesting curling effect.

Perspective

Here's an attractive effect. This plug-in enables you to manipulate an entire image in 3D space. And it's remarkably easy to use, as you can see from the dialog box shown in Figure 11-14. All you do is adjust the corners on the little box in the lower-right corner of the dialog box.

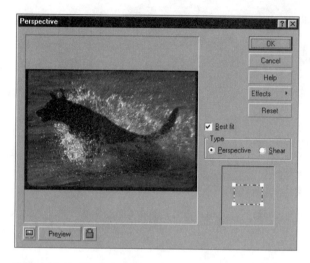

Figure 11-14: The Perspective plug-in dialog box makes it easy to adjust an image's perspective.

You have two ways to manipulate your image: Perspective and Shear. Perspective works similarly to the Perspective roll-up in CorelDraw (discussed in Chapter 6). Use it to narrow and widen the sides of the image, making it appear to be moving toward a vanishing point, as shown in Figure 11-15.

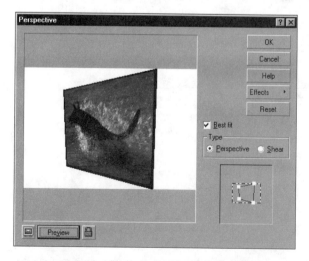

Figure 11-15: Use Perspective to tilt your images toward a vanishing point.

The Shear option enables you to manipulate the image as though you are rotating it in your hand, turning it to its side, on its back, and so on, as shown in Figure 11-16.

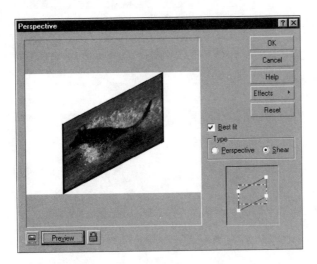

Figure 11-16: Use Shear to rotate the image in 3D space.

Using Third-Party Plug-Ins

In addition to the many plug-ins that come with Photo-Paint, several collections are also available from various third-party vendors, such as Alien Skin, MetaCreations, Adobe, and Pegasus. As a rule, Photo-Paint supports industry-standard, Adobe Photoshop, plug-ins. However, this technology changes all the time. Be sure to check for compatibility with Photo-Paint 8 before you buy.

Secret

As a rule, when you install a plug-in package, the installation program looks for Adobe Photoshop's plug-ins subdirectory. For your plug-ins to work with Photo-Paint (and CorelDraw), they must be installed in the plug-ins folder inside the Corel folder, or the folder where you've installed your CorelDraw files. If you use Photoshop or another image-editor, you can also access the plug-ins by creating shortcuts of your Photoshop plug-ins and placing them in the Corel plug-ins folder. You can also add any folder on your system to the list Photo-Paint uses to search for and access plug-ins in the Options dialog box (Tools ⇨ Options ⇨ Plug-In Filters ⇨ Add), as shown in Figure 11-17.

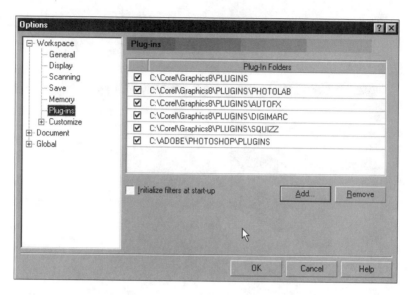

Figure 11-17: Use this dialog box to tell Photo-Paint where to find additional plug-ins.

While we can't begin to cover all the plug-ins available, this section lists and describes a few of our favorite collections. You can find several others by searching for "Photoshop plug-ins" on the World Wide Web.

Alien Skin's Eye Candy

This nifty set of 15 or so plug-ins is great for creating buttons and other graphics for the Web. This plug-in set enables you to create several cool effects, such as cutouts and carves. The three plug-ins we find most useful are Inner Bevel, Outer Bevel, and Drop Shadow. Figure 11-18 shows examples of all these effects.

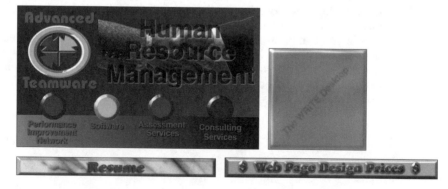

Figure 11-18: Example of bevels, drop shadows, and buttons created with Alien Skin's Eye Candy.

Another thing we like about Eye Candy is its easy-to-use, feature-rich interface, shown in Figure 11-19. The interface enables you to make all kinds of intricate changes to your special effects, and it shows you a helpful preview.

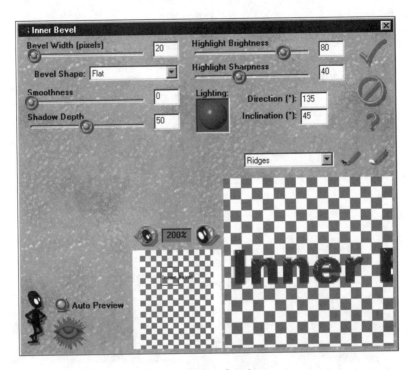

Figure 11-19: Eye Candy's feature-rich interface is easy to use.

You can obtain Alien Skin Eye Candy at http://www.alienskin.com.

Creating Web Buttons with Inner and Outer Bevel

Without a doubt, the Web has created a whole new venue for graphics designers. And every Web designer needs buttons — lots of buttons, right? Eye Candy provides two powerful tools — Inner Bevel and Outer Bevel — for making Web buttons of all shapes and sizes. Using these effects, you can create beveled buttons that simulate all kinds of materials, from plastic to metal, you name it. Here's a brief look at each effect:

Inner Bevel. This effect creates an embossed appearance by beveling the outer edges of a selected object and adding simulated lighting effects. You can create buttons with wide bevels, flat subtle bevels, or rounded bevels.

(continued)

(continued)

Outer Bevel. The difference between Inner Bevel and Outer Bevel is primarily this: Inner Bevel applies its effects only to the selected object, while Outer Bevel also applies its effects to the surrounding background, creating a kind of bubble or raised plastic effect. Notice in the figure that not only is the WDP beveled, so is the background around it, providing an interesting effect.

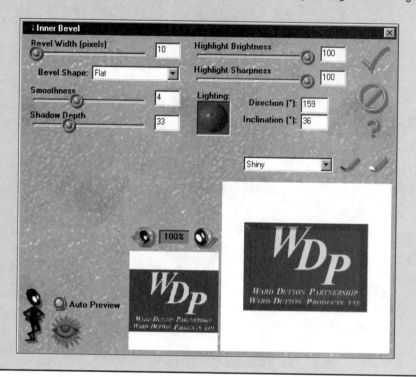

Kai's Power Tools

Perhaps the best known of all plug-ins, Kai's Power Tools from MetaCreations is a collection of texture and gradient designers with more options than you can imagine. You'll find KPT "lite" (a special version) in the CorelDraw box that installs when you install Photo-Paint. The full version provides a wider range of plug-ins and design options.

You can use the Texture Designer to create virtually any texture of any color. One of our favorite tools in the collection is KPT Planar Tiling, which actually creates an abstract tiling of the entire image, as shown in Figure 11-20 and in Plate 11-1 in the color insert.

Figure 11-20: An example of a KPT Planar Tiling effect from
Kai's Power Tools

You'll find a demo version of Kai's Power Tools on the CD-ROM included with
this book. You can contact MetaCreations at http://www.metacreations.com.

Extensis Intellihance

Extensis makes a bunch of plug-ins, and many of them are quite useful. The
one we find most useful and use most often is Intellihance. This is not a
special effects plug-in — Intellihance is designed to help you correct
problems on images, such as sharpness, brightness, remove cast, and a
bunch of others. What we like best about Intellihance is it enables you to
apply all these correctional functions at once, in the same preview window,
before committing to them. This saves you from a lot of trial and error and
back-and-forth trying to apply that just-right combination of enhancements.

You can reach Extensis at http://www.extensis.com.

Summary

▶ The terms *plug-in* and *filter* are often used interchangeably. They both do the
same thing — add functionality to an application, whether it's to enable a
program to import and export foreign file formats, enhance and touch up
images, or apply special effects.

▶ You can apply plug-ins to images in Photo-Paint from the Effects menu and in
CorelDraw from the Bitmap menu. The filters work similarly in each
program, except they work only on imported bitmaps or portions of your
drawing that you convert to bitmaps in CorelDraw.

▶ Plug-ins come in two basic flavors: enhancement/touch-up and special
effects. The former are for improving image quality, and the latter are for
special effects or stylizing images or portions of images.

▶ In addition to using the many plug-ins that come with CorelDraw, you can
purchase collections from various third-party vendors, including Alien Skin,
MetaCreations, Adobe, and Pegasus.

Chapter 12

Photo-Paint 8 Expert Advice

In This Chapter

▶ Working with clip masks and parent and child objects

▶ Exploring Photo-Paint 8 with a stylus

▶ Tracing in Photo-Paint 8

▶ Learning new Photo-Paint 8 features

Creating a Clip Mask

Many photo-editing programs do not let you place a mask on an object. You can't use a masking tool to carve a selection from an object itself. With Photo-Paint, you can use any shape or color-based masking tool to create a mask on an object. A clip mask is a way to trim the object down so that it only is visible inside the boundaries of the mask. Take a look at Figure 12-1. It shows an object in the background and a mask, which is in the shape of an angel, on top of it. Select Object ⇨ Clip Mask ⇨ Create ⇨ From Mask, and the object shrinks itself down to the borders of the mask, as shown in Figure 12-2.

Permanently applying the mask

The interesting thing about clip masks is that the arrangement doesn't have to be permanent. In Figure 12-3, notice that the Objects panel shows an object, followed by a plus sign, with a mask next to it. This represents a clipping group. You can remove the mask (Object ⇨ Clip Mask ⇨ Disable; or Object ⇨ Clip Mask ⇨ Remove), and the object returns to how it looked before the clip mask was applied. To permanently apply the clip mask to the object, select Object ⇨ Clip Mask ⇨ Combine. You can also disable the clip mask temporarily by right-clicking on the clip mask icon in the Object palette.

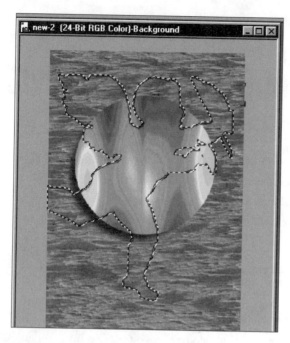

Figure 12-1: Starting to create a Clip Mask.

Figure 12-2: The object shrinks down to the borders of the mask.

Figure 12-3: How the Objects panel appears with clip masks.

Accessing object properties

While the clip mask is operative—while you can see both the mask and the object thumbnails connected by the plus sign in the object window—you can edit the object or the mask individually, to a degree. In the Object panel, click on the object thumbnail, for example, so that the red outline appears around it. Notice that Merge becomes available, as does the Opacity slider. Also, you can right-click on the object icon in the Object panel to access object properties such as URL features, Object naming, and Clip to Parent. Clip to Parent is only available if you have a clipping group.

Secret

Using object properties in the Objects panel is a thorough way to set URLs for every object in a Web page, because it's easier to use the thumbnails to check each object quickly and make sure each URL is the one you want.

Parent and Child Objects

In Photo-Paint, you can determine that one object take on the shape characteristics of an object positioned under it. In such a situation, one object becomes the *parent* and another becomes the *child*. This relationship between the two objects is created in the Object panel.

STEPS:

How to Create a Child Object

Step 1.   Open the Object panel from the Docking window and place the thumbnail for the object you want to be transformed *over* the other object's thumbnail. In Figure 12-4 you see two objects, a bird and a man. Notice in the Object panel that the bird's thumbnail is positioned above the man's.

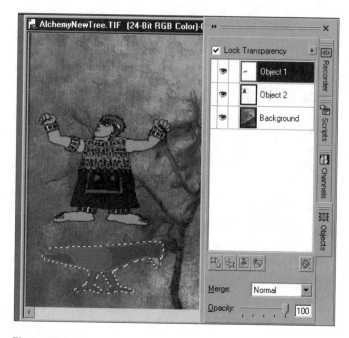

Figure 12-4: Beginning to create a parent/child object.

Step 2.   To create a child object, click once in the space directly to the left of the object's thumbnail, and you'll see a paper clip appear (see Figure 12-5). Notice in that same figure, looking at the canvas itself, that the bird has been positioned over the man. The bird is only visible where it overlaps the shape of the man.

Figure 12-5: The child object in place. Notice the paper clip icon near the object's thumbnail.

This is a dynamic relationship, meaning that the bird's visibility changes as you reposition it over the man. In Figure 12-5, the bird's object marquee is visible, which reveals that the bird as an entire object is still present. (Turning off the marquee would remove the bird outline from view.)

Step 3. To restore the child object so that it is entirely visible, click again on the paper clip in the object thumbnail area. You'll see the paper clip disappear, and the entire object will be visible.

The Effects tool

The Effects tool Property Bar looks a lot like the Brush tool Property Bar, but the drop-down menus provide completely different effects. Figure 12-6 shows the Property Bar with the Brush Type menu open.

Figure 12-6: The Effects tool Property Bar is shown with the Brush Type menu open. The Effects tool roll-up shows the tools to choose from. The Property Bar shows the Brush Type menu for the Swirl tool.

With Photo-Paint, brushes are not limited to painting color but can be used to apply effects such as Smudge, Hue, and Blend. Similarly, the Paintbrush tool doesn't have to be shaped like a traditional brush but can apply effects to your picture in the shape of a Swirl, a Motion Blur, or a Rake, for example. With the Photo-Paint Effects tool, you need to select two main parameters before painting on an effect:

- The Effects tool itself, such as Smudge, Tint, or Undither, as well as the usual Brightness and Contrast tools. These are accessed by clicking on the icon farthest to the left on the Effects tool Property Bar.

- The shape of the Effects tool, referred to as the brush type. The Brush Type menu is the first drop-down menu on the Effects tool Property Bar. Not only can you choose unusual shapes for your effect, but you can alter the effect mode by, for example, changing Sponge Add to Sponge Remove.

Figure 12-7 shows an image altered using Swirl, on the background, and Blend so that the color surrounding the horse itself appears to fade into the swirl background. This image is found on the accompanying CD-ROM, with all the layers intact, for your editing fun.

Figure 12-7: The horse is resting on a background that has been blended and swirled using the Effects tool.

The Clone tool

Click and hold the Brush Tool flyout, and select the tool with two brushes on it. This is the Clone tool. The Clone tool Property Bar provides options to change the clone type and method. Remember that any application of the Clone tool requires that you first right-click in your source image to select where your brush should begin "copying" from as you paint. The next strokes you paint will start picking up image data from that exact spot, literally painting with that source image.

Next we'll explore a few features of the Clone tool Property Bar. Clicking on the Clone Type drop-down menu enables you to select a brush type. Your stroke will apply colors and image information from the source image, but with the texture and shape of your chosen brush. Click on the drop-down menu farthest to the left on the Property Bar, and choose the icon that looks like a brush next to a floppy disk. This is the Clone from Saved tool, which enables you to open the previously saved version of your current file and clone a portion of that image back into your current image. The Clone tool Property Bar includes the usual Nib Shape and Size, Transparency, Anti-Aliasing, and Soft Edge tools, as well as links to the Brush Reset dialog box and the Clone Tool Settings roll-up.

Cloning brushes

When you double-click on the Clone Brush tool in the toolbox, you'll see the Clone Tool Settings roll-up that appears in Figure 12-8. The normal clone brush appears first — it's the icon at the upper left of the roll-up. To the right of that brush are the icons for the Impressionist Clone and the Pointillism Clone. When you paint a stroke with these clone brushes, the stroke picks up the paint color from the original image and continues with those colors as you complete your stroke. It does not update the new image as you move your brush, the same way a normal clone does. For example, if you begin a stroke with the Impressionist cloner, cloning from the green and blue sections of the car, it continues with those shades of green and blue until you finish your stroke. The stroke does not change colors while you are painting. When you again begin a new stroke, the brush picks up the corresponding clone colors from the original image. Therefore, when using these two clone brushes, use short strokes if you want to make your new painting look similar to the source. Figure 12-9 shows an image created by painting a stroke with the Hue Replacer Effect brush, with the effect turned up all the way. The musical note is a single stroke rendered with the Note Nib (click on the Nib Shape icon and scroll way down). The Tile effect (Effects ⇨ 2D Effects ⇨ Tile) was used to create the repeated effect.

Figure 12-8: The Clone Tool Settings roll-up.

Figure 12-9: An image created with a stroke with the Hue Replacer Effect brush, using the Note nib.

When one thinks of a cloning brush, what comes to mind most often is painting with a brush that transfers pixels from one painting to another. For example, with a Photo-Paint c482loning brush, right-click on your clone source and then begin painting on a new canvas. The image from the first painting will begin to appear as you paint with your brush.

Photo-Paint 8 includes many new brushes, and each creates unique strokes with unusual shapes and varying degrees of opacity. Photo-Paint enables you to use any of these brushes as a clone brush. Each brush brings its own characteristics to the cloned image. For example, if you paint a clone with a wispy, thin brush, the original image will not just be transferred with photographic clarity. Rather, the qualities of the brush will affect how the clone appears on your page. Figure 12-10 shows two trucks. The truck near the front is the original. The truck behind was painted with the Scalloped Dab brush. Notice that its edges are softer and the colors blend.

Figure 12-10: The lower truck was painted with a Clone brush.

Brushes That React to Stroke Style

Photo-Paint's Pen roll-up enables you specify what should happen when you vary the pressure on your pen. One stylus feature everyone enjoys is pressure sensitivity. Photo-Paint can respond to changes in pen pressure in a number of ways:

- Pressing lightly can create thin strokes, and as you bear down on your pen, a fatter line results.

- Alternatively, pressing hard can leave more paint on your canvas, while light pressure creates a faint coloration.

- You can specify that pressing hard makes your stroke change color as you paint, or the bristles of your brush to spread out farther apart.

Figure 12-11 shows the Pen Tools roll-up. On the left are the parameters than can be controlled by pressure, for example. On the right are the numerical values (1 to 100) that determine the degree of effect as you press harder. As you can see, pressing hard can result in a number of simultaneous changes to your brush stroke.

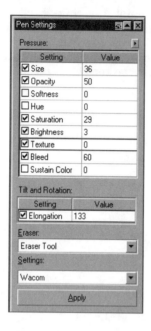

Figure 12-11: The Pen Tools roll-up.

Note

You can name and save Pressure settings and restore them later for particular projects. For example, one favorite brush might call for the hue and color to vary with your pen pressure, and another brush might require the stroke to widen.

Secret

Think in terms of combining pressure sensitivity settings with certain types of brushes. For example, try adding pressure-controlled stroke width to the Tempura Blend brush, since the brush already has a high degree of Bleed associated with it. Or try adding pressure-controlled Bleed to the Cubist brush.

Program your digital pen's eraser

Many digital pens have an eraser, especially Wacom tablets such as the ArtPad II. Photo-Paint lets you program the eraser's function. By default, using the stylus's eraser activates Photo-Paint's Eraser tool. But you can program the stylus eraser to create a mask, add a special effect, become the Eyedropper or Zoom tool, or perform just about any other tool-driven or menu-activated function. Looking again at the Pen Tools roll-up in Figure 12-6, use the drop-down menu below the word *Eraser* to affect changes in the eraser's action.

Examples of pressure-sensitive strokes

Figure 12-12 shows some strokes created with a pressure-sensitive stylus.

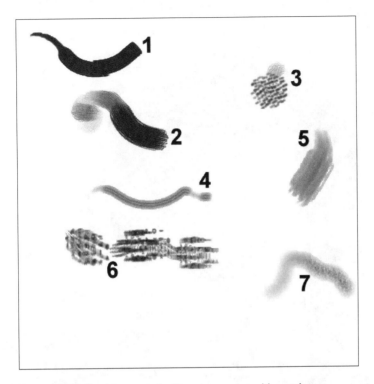

Figure 12-12: Strokes created with a pressure-sensitive stylus.

- **Stroke 1:** Pressure variability causes changes in the stroke width. In this case, high pressure causes a wider stroke, as you can see.

- **Stroke 2:** Transparency and size are influenced by pressure.

- **Stroke 3:** Pressing hard causes the brush bristles to spread out and increase in size.

- **Stroke 4:** You can see a narrowing and fading caused by decreasing the pressure on the stylus.

- **Stroke 5:** Brush bristles get wider when you press hard, just as what would occur with a real brush.

- **Stroke 6:** The colors change, although you can't see that in this grayscale picture here.

- **Stroke 7:** Pressing hard causes not only a thicker and deeper-colored line, but more Texture is apparent with higher pressure.

The female face study in Figure 12-13 was made easier by using a tracing paper technique, as explained in the sidebar. The shadows were much easier to draw using a pressure-sensitive stylus, deepening the color as more pressure was used.

Figure 12-13: A tracing painting done with a pressure-sensitive stylus. Brushes such as the Light Turin Cover, Scalloped Dab, and Dry Camel Hair are great at providing shadows and shading.

Building an Image Using Tracing Paper

Because the new Photo-Paint has many new painting tools, it's nice to have various ways to put them to use. Combining painting and drawing techniques with photographic filters can make an image stand out. Creating tracing paper, where a source photo with low opacity appears underneath the canvas you are actually working on, is a great way to facilitate mixing various methods while keeping a unified image.

After you set up tracing paper, you can draw or paint on a blank "canvas" (actually, a blank object that covers the whole page), while not losing touch with the original underneath.

STEPS:

Setting Up Tracing Paper

Step 1. Open the image you want to use as your source.

Step 2. Select Mask ⇨ Select All.

Step 3. Select Edit Í Cut, and paste the image back in as an object (Edit ⇨ Paste ⇨ As New Object). That means you can now reduce the image's opacity.

Step 4. Reduce this main object's opacity to 13. See Object 1 in Figure A. Remember that the background will now be blank, because you've removed the image.

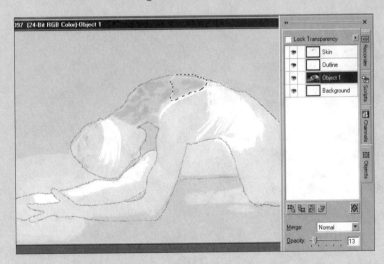

Figure A. Reduce the opacity of the original object to make it faint enough to draw over.

Step 5. Now you can create a new "working layer" for your painting and drawing over the faint original. This canvas is where your actual painting will be created. Select Object ⇨ Create ⇨ New Object (or click on the New Object icon in the Object Manager). In Figure 12-14, that Object was named Outline because it was used to trace the entire parameter of the ballerina in the image.

(continued)

STEPS *(continued)*

Setting Up Tracing Paper

Step 6. Adjust the opacity of either object, the outline, or the source object to make a more accurate tracing.

Later, you can paint in any portion of the source image you like, using Photo-Paint's new brushes, or you can copy portions of the original image and paste them in and combine them with the new Outline image, blending them with various Merge modes or effects. Use the tracing paper underneath to keep everything in its place. Notice in this same figure the object thumbnail near the top, labeled Skin. Painting in the skin of the ballerina was accomplished by masking off small areas based on lighting and color, and then selecting the right brush and color for that specific area.

When you are finished building your composite, discard the original tracing paper image and combine the outlines and painting layers into one object, if you like.

Completing the Image

Figure B shows the complete image using the composite ballerina we began creating above. Here are some particulars on how it was built:

Figure B. "Tesseract," created by combining painted layers with photographic filtered layers.

■ The shape containing the man in the middle was created using Auto FX's Photo/Graphic Edges, which is included with Photo-Paint. (Select Effects ⇨ Auto FX ⇨ Photo/Graphic Edges ⇨ Select Outset Effect ⇨ Apply. See Figure C.)

Figure C. The photograph of the singing man treated with Auto F/X Photo/Graphic Edges.

■ After the effect separates the man from the original, rectangular photograph of the man, the man was pasted into the ballerina image as an object. Returning to the remaining portion of the rectangle, it was selected with a masking tool, and then a linear blue-to-white fill was applied to that area.

■ The remaining rectangle portion was treated with Paint Alchemy's Sponge Print style (Effects ⇨ Fancy ⇨ Alchemy ⇨ Style ⇨ Sponge Print), copied, and pasted into the ballerina image.

■ The Wind effect (Effects ⇨ 2D Effects ⇨ Wind) was applied in two directions to this outer layer.

■ The legging pattern on the ballerina was painted with the Swirl brush using the Orbit brush setting, Dizzy.

New Photo-Paint Effects

In this section we'll take a closer look at some of Photo-Paint 8's new special effects.

Lighting effects

Photo-Paint enables you to position lights around your canvas, creating spotlight effects, or add subtle differences in color or brightness, which can be very effective when done with a light source. You can control any aspect of a light source, changing its angle, brightness, color, distance, lens aperture, and many other features as well. Figure 12-14 shows the Lighting Effects dialog box (Effects ➪ Render ➪ Lighting Effects). In the Preview area you can see an image being treated by five spotlights, shining from near the top of the canvas. You may reposition each of these five lights manually, clicking and dragging on each light icon with your mouse. Photo-Paint comes with many lighting presets, which are available by choosing from the Style drop-down menu at the bottom of the dialog box.

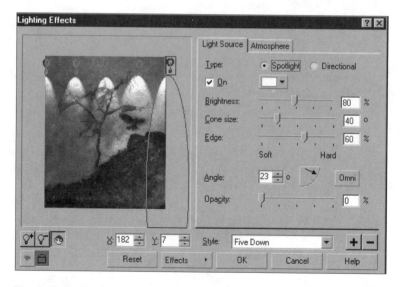

Figure 12-14: The Lighting Effects dialog box.

Altering lighting presets

It's easy to alter a preset, adding brightness, changing the width of the beam (Cone Size) and making the beam's focus more pronounced, or diffuse (Softness). Changing a light from Spotlight to Directional causes your whole canvas to be affected by the light, rather than a narrowly focused beam that you can reposition or control.

In the case of the document shown in Figure 12-14, we chose the lighting effect *Five Down*, as shown in the Style drop-down menu. The lights were brightened up a little by increasing the brightness slider, and the cone size of each light was widened a bit. It's easy to save a light you've edited. Just click on the plus sign at the bottom of the menu. You're prompted to name your new light, and then it will always be available from the Style list, along with the Photo-Paint preset lights.

The Atmosphere tab

The Lighting Effects dialog box also has an Atmosphere tab. Here you can add a Texture effect to your lighting. Select the RGB Channel and raise the Relief and Contrast sliders, and you'll see that the lighting effect will appear to accent raised and lowered areas on your canvas, simulating a textured quality (see Figure 12-15). The Ambient and Image Brightness sliders are helpful for adjusting a lighting effect that seems to "bleach out" the image too much.

Figure 12-15: Using the Relief and Contrast sliders created a raised lighting effect.

The Wet Paint effect

One of Photo-Paint 8's new special effects is the Wet Paint effect, which makes the surfaces of a painting look as if they are dripping (see Figures 12-16 and 12-17, before and after). To use the Wet Paint effect, click on Effects ⇨ 2D Effects ⇨ Wet Paint, and adjust the two sliders provided in the Wet Paint dialog box. The Percentage slider determines the amount of the picture affected by the wetness effect. The Wetness slider determines the extent of the effect itself, the amount of "drip."

Figure 12-16: A canvas before applying the Wet Paint effect.

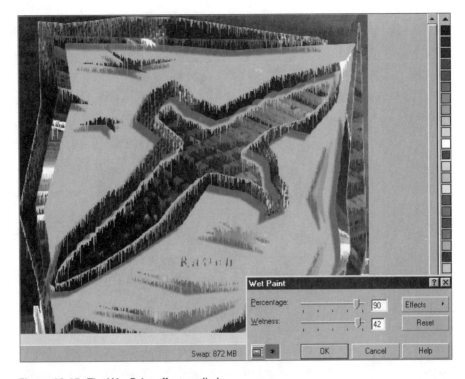

Figure 12-17: The Wet Paint effect applied.

The 3D Rotate effect

The 3D Effect, which was used to create the image shown in Figure 12-18, tilts a canvas to appear as if it is receding in a particular direction. Click on Effects ➪ 3D Effects ➪ 3D Rotate, and adjust the two sliders at the bottom right of the dialog box. One repositions the canvas so that it leans forward or backwards; the other, to the right or left. Please note that these changes affect the entire canvas, not an object or a masked area. Click on the Preview button to see how the edited canvas would appear. As shown in this figure, a single pane of the double wall was created using 3D Rotate, pulling the wall towards the right. Then the image was copied to the Clipboard, pasted again into the image, and flipped horizontally (Image ➪ Flip ➪ Horizontally). It was then joined with the original wall to create the dual receding effect shown in Figure 12-18.

Figure 12-18: Using the 3D Rotate effect.

Object Lenses

Object Lenses are movable shapes that "float" over the surface of the canvas and create special effects by altering the canvas underneath them. The fastest way to create an Object Lens is to create a mask with any masking tool, making it any shape you like, and then clicking on Object ⇨ Create ⇨ Lens From Mask. You'll see a menu prompting you to choose which special effect you'd like the lens to utilize. Look at Figure 12-19. The chosen effect, Solarize, is now applied to the rectangular object over the lower part of the rabbit. Clicking on any available effect opens a dialog box regulating it; for example, the amount of Brightness/Contrast or the Level of Psychedelic or Posterize filtering. When you move an Object Lens around on your canvas, the effect moves with it. Looking again at Figure 12-19, if the rectangular lens was moved up and to the left, the effect would be rendered over the rabbit's face and not where you see it now.

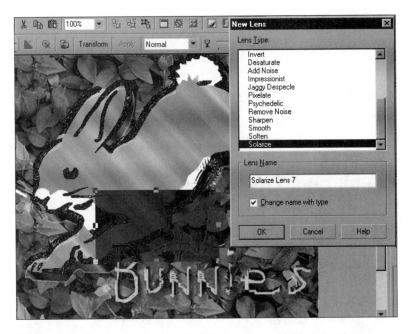

Figure 12-19: This effect is mobile, because it moves with the Object Lens.

You can create interesting effects with Object Lenses by importing a complex object, creating a mask from the object (Mask ⇨ Create from Object), and then creating an Object Lens from that mask (Object ⇨ Create ⇨ Lens From Mask ⇨ Psychedelic Lens). Next, import the same object again and position it over the mask you created from the previous, identical object. The effect will be similar to a Drop Shadow, but with more variety (See Figure 12-20).

Figure 12-20: Creating an Object Lens from a complex mask, after converting the mask to an object.

Like all objects, Object Lenses can be resized and distorted using any object tool or menu feature. Using Merge Modes with Object Lenses can also lead to some unique effects.

Photo-Paint 8's New Features

Here are a handful of the new Photo-Paint 8 tools that deserve special mention. Others have been covered in Chapters 8 through 11.

Combining two images

Photo-Paint includes a Stitch feature that enables you to line up two images horizontally or vertically and combine them along any edge. They can be blended with a precise border visible, or feathered. The Stitch feature is particularly helpful when you've scanned a picture that was too large for one pass, and you need to blend the two halves into one image. You can only blend two images at once (and they must be 24-bit color).

To use the Stitch feature, first open both images you want to combine, and then click on Image ➪ Stitch. You'll see the Select Images dialog box. You're prompted to select the two images for combining; specify if you want horizontal or vertical alignment. After clicking on OK, you'll see another dialog box that enables you to position the images anywhere along the edge you've chosen for combining. You can also choose a blending amount, determining the amount of feathering and overlapping between the two images. It's possible to get very precise with this, which is helpful when you have to line up two scans to appear as if they are one image, or when you want to create a natural-looking blend between one image and another.

After clicking on OK, you'll notice that you are actually creating a new image, leaving the two source images intact. You can now edit and save your new, combined image independently of the others.

Creating beveled buttons

Photo-Paint's new filter, The Boss, can create bevels on any masked object, as shown in Figure 12-21. These are great for unique Web page design, where clickable button objects play such a large role.

First create an object, perhaps using the rectangular Mask tool, and then fill the mask and turn it into an object (click on the Create Object from Mask icon on the Property bar, or click on the Object Manager). Why bother with this? Just use the Rectangle tool to automatically create an object. Then create a mask that rests entirely upon the object. In this case, the rectangular masking tool would be used. Next, click on Effects ⇨ 3D Effects ⇨ The Boss. You'll see a dialog box prompting you to select how pronounced you want your bevel effect to be. Adjusting the Smoothness slider has the most dramatic effect on the bevel's size and appearance. In the Lighting panel of The Boss dialog box, adjusting the Sharpness slider makes the bevels edges more obvious. Click on OK to close the dialog box. Your object will now be beveled.

Figure 12-21: Buttons created by the Photo-Paint filter The Boss.

Create Fill From Selection

The Create Fill From Selection command works exactly as the title indicates. Use any masking tool to create a selection, and then click on Edit ⇨ Create Fill from Selection. You're prompted to save your selection as a .CPT file. You can name it anything you like. Then, if you double-click on the Fill tool as it appears in the toolbox and click on the Bitmap Fill icon (the third from the left), you'll notice that your new fill will appear among the preset Bitmap fills provided with Photo-Paint, and it can be applied like any other. (See Figure 12-22.)

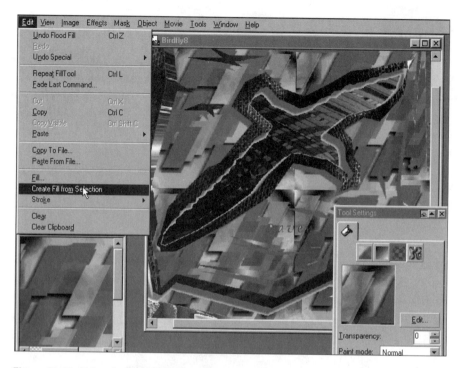

Figure 12-22: Using the Create Fill From Selection command.

Fade Last Command

Sometimes you can apply a filter or a special effect and realize that you've overdone it, but you don't necessarily want to remove the effect entirely. In such cases, the Fade Last Command feature can be useful. It works well with tasks that can be undone in degrees, such as the Smoked Glass effect, Posterize, or Lens Flare, but not with "all or nothing" mutations such as feathering and resizing. If Fade Last Command applies to a task you have just performed, then the command will be available (Edit ➪ Fade Last Command). If not, then the command appears grayed out. Figure 12-23 shows a painting with a feathered mask treated with the Find Edges effect. Figure 12-24 shows the same painting after applying Fade Last Command at 50 percent. The Fade Last Command dialog box provides a slider for choosing the percentage of Undo you want to apply. A higher percentage of Fade leaves less of the effect on the document. Also provided is a Merge Mode drop-down menu, with which you can apply the effect with alternative Merge techniques — the same techniques available for layering objects.

Figure 12-23: A figure with the Swirl effect.

Figure 12-24: The same effect reduced with Fade Last Command.

Designing text by altering background elements

In this exercise you'll learn how to create the image shown in Figure 12-25. It can be done with just one color element, a background filled with the Blur Rainbow Texture Fill. A blank object is created, filled, and manipulated in two different ways to create depth and texture. Text is created from this same background and converted to a mask so that special effects like The Boss and embossing can be used to make it stand apart from the background. We'll explore special effects found in the Effects menu, such as Mesh Warp, 3D Rotate, and Offset, and we'll add a canvas texture to an object with the Canvas command. We'll also explore some custom settings for Drop Shadow, The Boss, and Emboss.

Figure 12-25: "Night Music," created by manipulating a single rainbow-textured fill.

STEPS:

Creating "Night Music"

To start, our image was 8 × 5 inches, using a resolution of 72 dpi.

Step 1. Fill the background with the texture fill Blur Rainbow from the Style 5 Library.

Step 2. Apply Effect ⇨ 2D Effects ⇨ Offset, with a Horizontal setting of 25 percent and Vertical of 37 percent. (See Figure 12-26.)

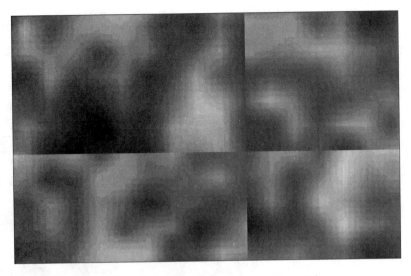

Figure 12-26: The Offset effect applied to a Rainbow background.

Step 3.   Create a new object, which will initially be blank. Fill this new object (which takes up the entire image area) with Blur Rainbow.

Step 4.   Apply the Offset Effect to the object, but change the Offset Horizontal and Vertical Settings significantly.

Step 5.   Apply the Saturation Merge Mode to this object. You'll notice the canvas now resembles a watercolor pattern divided into six random rectangles.

Step 6.   Duplicate this object, and select Effect ⇨ 3D Effects ⇨ 3D Rotate. Set the tilt for 39 degrees Vertical and –23 Degrees Horizontal. Change the Merge Mode to Normal to make the object easy to work with for now.

Step 7.   Shrink the object to 80 percent of its original size.

Step 8.   Making sure this rotated object is still selected, select Effect ⇨ Artistic ⇨ Canvas and choose the Marble2c canvas pattern from the list. Set the Transparency to 88 and the Emboss to 48. No other parameter need be changed. (See Figure 12-27.)

Step 9.   Create a Drop Shadow for this object.

Step 10.   Change this object's Merge Mode to Invert.

Step 11.   Click on the original object you've already duplicated, and duplicate it again. Change the Merge Mode of this new object to Normal.

Step 12.   With this new object selected, click on Effects ⇨ 3D Effects ⇨ Rotate, but this time, set the tilt for 39 Horizontal and 33 Vertical.

(continued)

STEPS *(continued)*

Creating "Night Music"

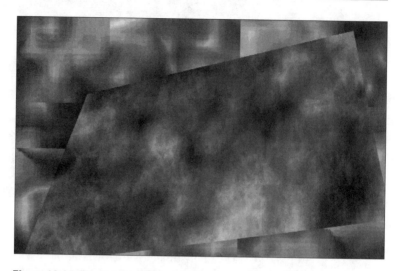

Figure 12-27: The Rainbow Blur rotated and treated with the Canvas Effect.

Step 13. To give this object that "flying carpet" look, select Effects ⇨ 3D Effects ⇨ Mesh Warp, and move the wire nodes to make the edges of the flat object look like they are being ruffled by the wind. Make sure the number of gridlines is set to 4. The effect will make the object look less flat.

Step 14. Apply a Drop Shadow to this object as well. (See Figure 12-28.)

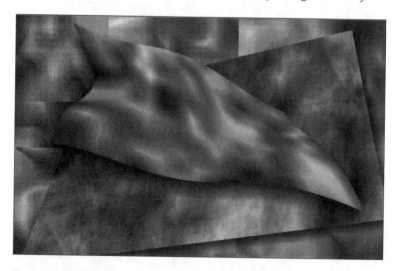

Figure 12-28: Two Layers and a background, so far.

Step 15. Make sure this object is still selected and type **Night Music**, using a font with some flair to it. The font should be wide and not too frilly, because you will be applying our own embossing and raised areas. We used the font Formal 436 BT, size 110, and we increased the horizontal spacing between the letters (see the Property Bar when the text tool is selected, the numeral next to the horizontal arrow) to 5.

Step 16. After typing your text, click on the Render Text to Mask Button on the Font Property Bar.

Step 17. Click outside the text box to render your text. It will appear as the blank "marching ants" mask marquee. If you have Mask ⇨ Make Marquee Visible unchecked, then you won't see anything at all.

Step 18. Click on the Create Object ⇨ Cut Selection icon on the Property Bar (or click on Object ⇨ Create ⇨ Object: Cut Selection from the menu).

Step 19. Reposition the letters to create contrast with what's behind them.

Step 20. Click on Effects ⇨ 3D Effects ⇨ Emboss, using these settings: Original Color, Depth 4, Level 23, Direction 243.

Step 21. Click on Mask ⇨ Create from Object on the menu. This gives you access to the Boss Effect.

Step 22. Click on Effects ⇨ 3D Effects ⇨ The Boss, and use these settings: Width 12, Smoothness 87, Height 160, Brightness 87, Sharpness, Drop off: Gaussian, Direction 135, Angle 45.

Step 23. Select Mask ⇨ Remove.

Step 24. Making sure the lettering is still selected, apply a Perspective Shadow using the Drop Shadow command with the following settings: Click the Perspective Button, set the shadow Direction for 245 degrees, Light: 45 degrees, Fade 43, Opacity 81, Feather Width 9, Direction: Average.

Step 25. Group the letters and move them around to a location that looks good to you. This picture is included on the CD-ROM for you to experiment with and see how its done.

Combining Objects with Unique Filters

In this section are some special techniques for applying filters to select objects, before merging them with objects beneath them.

Using the Impressionist and the Puzzle Object Lens

Photo-Paint 8 comes with many new filters and special effects that can be applied to a single object on your canvas. Figure 12-29 shows the legs of a ballerina set in the foreground of an image. The legs were treated with a multicolor lighting effect (see the full-color image on the CD-ROM), and the Impressionist Object Lens was applied (Object ⇨ Create ⇨ New Lens ⇨ Impressionist). Behind it, the head was treated with the Puzzle effect (Effects ⇨ 2D Effects ⇨ Puzzle), using the Hard Light Merge mode. Merge modes can be selected from the Objects panel from the Docking window. The two objects were combined on the same canvas for a startling effect.

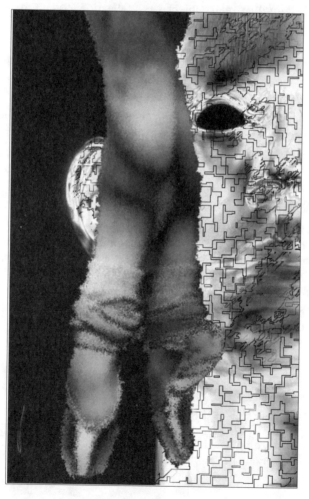

Figure 12-29: Combining two objects that have been treated with distinct filters.

Secrets of applying effects selectively

Figure 12-30 shows a photograph, and Figure 12-31 shows the same photo after some effects and cloning brush strokes are applied.

Figure 12-30: Jerry.

Figure 12-31: The same photo as a work of art.

This photograph was treated by the Whirlpool ⇨ Brush Stroke effect, and lenses were applied to the left while the central human figure in the photo emerges unscathed. In the image, interesting special effects and cloned brush strokes were applied at the sides, while the center retains the realism of a photograph. You can use objects and lenses to limit where special effects are applied on your canvas. You can also use them to restore original colors lost by special effects to selected portions of your image.

STEPS:

Adding Special Effects to a Photo

Step 1. To begin, select a photo you'd like to clone and add special effects to. Create a blank canvas the same size as your photo.

Step 2. Click on the Clone Brush tool and choose the Scalloped Dab brush. Click on the Brush Nib labeled 64, down near the bottom of the Brush Nib menu. (See the Property Bar after selecting the Clone Brush tool.)

Step 3. Right-click on the image you are cloning from, and then begin painting strokes on your new blank canvas. Start your strokes in the same area you right-clicked on the original image.

Step 4. Apply the Perspective effect (Effects ⇨ 3D Effects ⇨ Perspective), pulling the image up towards the center middle. In this image, we took the visual cue from the way the ladder in the back forms a natural angle and division between Jerry in the front and the receding street life. (See Figure 12-32.)

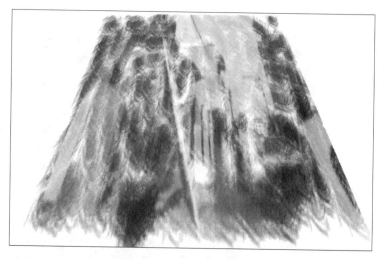

Figure 12-32: The Perspective Effect applied to the background brush strokes.

Step 5. Copy the main photograph to the Clipboard and paste it over the special effect background of the new image as an object, using the Invert Merge Mode.

Step 6. Apply the Whirlpool Effect (Effects ⇨ 2D Effects ⇨ Whirlpool) to this new, pasted object using the Brush Strokes setting (see Figure 12-33).

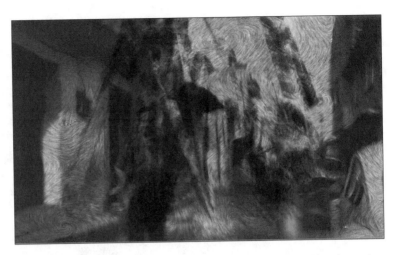

Figure 12-33: The Brush Stroke Whirlpool effect applied to an object layered over the background.

Step 7.   You need to restore some of the original Jerry image to give the picture a center. Again, past the image from the Clipboard onto the composite image you are creating.

Step 8.   Create a mask over the area that includes the main figure (in this case, Jerry), feather it for a smooth transition, and click on Object ⇨ Clip to Mask. This causes the newly pasted, normal Jerry to shrink down to the size of the mask, including the feathering effect.

Step 9.   Position this unaffected object so that the transition from surreal to real seems most natural.

Step 10. To the far right, we wanted to restore some of the colors of the background and not have the Inverted effect apply to the entire area. (The Inverted Merge mode is what causes the background to the right to appear blue, dark blue, and white, which is only evident in the color version of this image, included on the CD-ROM with this book.) To restore coloring to part of the background, we created a highly feathered mask at the far-right edge of the image, about two inches wide. We converted it to an object (click on the Create Object: Cut Selection icon on the Property Bar, or use the same command in the Object menu) and applied the If Darker Merge mode.

Step 11. To this same object, we increased the Saturation and Lightness (Image ⇨ Adjust ⇨ Hue/Saturation/Lightness) slightly, which made the far-right segment luminous and brightly colored. See Figure 12-34.

(continued)

STEPS *(continued)*

Adding Special Effects to a Photo

Figure 12-34: Objects are used to protect areas of the canvas from special effects applications.

Step 12. The hourglass filters on the far right are actually lenses. Again, we created a rectangular mask about half an inch wide (select View ⇨ Rulers to see exact measurements) and clicked on Object ⇨ Create ⇨ Lens From Mask. This brought up the Lens menu, with Psychedelic selected. You'll then see a slider allowing you to choose how much of this effect to apply. We chose 115 and closed the dialog box, which applied the lens.

Step 13. Still selecting the rectangle mask that was turned into a lens, the hourglass effect we created by clicking four times on the lens until the bounding boxes around the lens become small circles. You'll also see the phrase Perspective of the Object on the status bar, at the bottom of the screen. Manipulating the bounding boxes now changes the lens's Perspective. In this case, we dragged the upper-right bounding box all the way to the left, and the left bounding box to where the right used to be, which created an X or an hourglass effect.

Step 14. The Invert Merge mode was applied to this lens. It was then duplicated twice (Object ⇨ Duplicate), and the duplicates repositioned to create multiple layering of these hourglasses. The color version of this image with all the objects intact is included on the CD-ROM, so you can see how the objects were layered and applied.

Step 15. Because this image was composed partially of page-sized objects duplicated and moved around the canvas, the edges are not quite even at the upper right of the canvas, as shown in Figure 12-35. To fix this, a feathered rectangle was selected from right beneath the blank area. On the Property Bar, click on Object: Copy Selection. Then the new rectangle object can be moved upward to cover the blank area. To smooth the rough edges, we used the Smear Effect tool (click on the bottom tool on the toolbox; the Effect Tool will appear on the flyout), using the Big Soft Cover brush type (brush types appear on the left of the Property Bar, after the Effect tool is selected). Only a few strokes were necessary to blend and smear the colors a little bit.

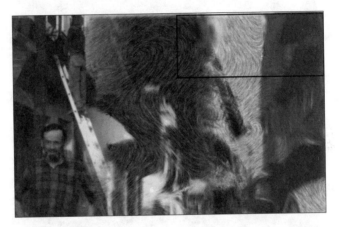

Figure 12-35: The ragged edges of this image are evened up by copying and moving similar pixels over the blank area and painting with the Smear Effects Brush.

Step 16. To frame the image, create a mask border near the edge, but leaving about 12 pixels free on all sides. Select Mask ⇨ Shape ⇨ Border and select 12. You'll see the "marching ants" border around your image. If it doesn't reach exactly to the edge of the canvas, you can resize it using the Mask Transform tool (same space on the toolbox as the Object Picker tool) and, on the Property Bar, select Size. Then just reposition the bounding boxes around the mask to the edges of the image.

Step 17. In the image shown here, we selected the Cubist Artistic brush. (Select the Brush tool, and on the drop-down menu on the Property bar farthest to the left, click on the last icon in the list. That's the Artistic Brush tool. Chose Cubist from the Brush Type drop-down menu, to the right on the Property Bar.) We brushed lightly with the rectangular-shaped strokes inside the mask, one pass with dark orange, and another pass with yellow. The Cubist brush effect applies multicolored strokes.

Step 18. To make the frame look "raised," apply the The Boss effect (Effects ⇨ 3D Effects ⇨ The Boss) two or three times.

Using Masks to apply effects to select image portions

The image in Figure 12-36 shows how to treat only select portions of a picture with a filter or effect.

Figure 12-36: Masking and feathering portions of an image to create effects to each segment.

STEPS

Using Masks to Selectively Apply Effects

Step 1. The sky was separated from the rest of the background, feathered, and copied to the Clipboard.

Step 2. That same segment of sky was then treated with Image Alchemy's Tree effect (Effects ⇨ Fancy ⇨ Alchemy ⇨ Style ⇨ Trees). The brush color and background were changed from Solid Color to From Image.

Step 3. The original sky was then pasted back into the treated image, reducing the Opacity (Docking Window ⇨ Objects Panel ⇨ Opacity slider) so that some of the special effect shows through, while retaining a good deal of the original sky. This procedure creates a slightly different effect than using Edit ⇨ Fade Last Command.

Step 4. The grass hill was selected with a mask tool, and feathered and separated from the canvas. Again, an Image Alchemy effect was applied; this time, the Autumn effect. As before, in the Paint Alchemy dialog box, the Brush Color and Background Color were changed from Solid Color to From Image.

Step 5. The original grass hill was pasted back over the treated area, using the Soft Light merge method.

Step 6. Finally, the tree and bird itself were lifted from the image and pasted back in with a slight Drop Shadow, and embossing was applied (Objects ⇨ Drop Shadow, and then Image ⇨ 3D Effects ⇨ Emboss). Embossing and shadowing enables the tree and bird, which are the main focal points of the picture, to appear more distinct from the rest of the image.

Step 7. A Red-Green-Blue lighting effect was applied to the entire image, which is not evident in the figure above but can be seen in the full color version on the CD-ROM of this book.

Secret

When selecting different portions of an image for editing as described previously, feather the selections generously (Mask ⇨ Shape ⇨ Feather) so that the various techniques used will blend into each other nicely, without abrupt transitions.

Summary

▶ Clipping an object down to the parameters of a mask is a powerful, flexible, and creative tool. With it, you can transform objects without permanently losing their shape and qualities.

▶ Working with parent and child objects lets you combine the shape and texture characteristics of two overlapping objects.

▶ Photo-Paint's Brushwork power is greatly extended by using a stylus. It's possible to achieve a personal, unique painting style that goes beyond what most often passes for "digital art."

▶ You can set up a tracing canvas, creating a guide layer that is later removed from the document.

▶ Exploring Photo-Paint 8's new features leads to some nice creative surprises.

Chapter 13

Dream 3D

In This Chapter

You learn how to use the following CorelDraw 8 features:

▶ Scene Wizard templates

▶ Perspective windows

▶ Low, medium, and high res rendering

▶ Virtual Trackball

For CorelDraw users, CorelDream 3D holds the least rewarding "out of box experience." Many factors — such as the little castles you have to line up perfectly, the paths you have to build along splines, and the difficulty of knowing what you're looking at — have kept many users from exploring Dream 3D. However, CorelDraw 8's version of Dream 3D includes a Scene Wizard that gives you more than just while-you-wait instant 3D pictures. The Scene Wizard provides starting points for you to include models that you choose, position objects the way you like, and even import graphics from CorelDraw and Photo-Paint. In fact, you can create some unique works of art with Dream 3D just by knowing how to manipulate and edit existing objects, without having to learn practical 3D modeling (the subject of the next chapter). So don't just skip over this somewhat intimidating program. Stop in and have a little fun.

Note

You should be aware, though, that of all Corel applications, Dream 3D requires the most horsepower. Even with 16MB of RAM, with this program we tend to make a lot of trips to the coffee maker in between steps. If you're patient, however, the results are rewarding. Three-dimensional modeling is the wave of the future, and nothing else looks quite like it.

Before You Get Started

Several of the projects we've created with Dream 3D can be found on the CD-ROM that accompanies this book. The projects are saved on the CD-ROM as complete Dream 3D projects, so you may load them, deconstruct each piece, and work along with the project if you wish. If you lose your place, you can always reload the finished work again from the CD-ROM.

However, to make Dream 3D projects on your computer look like the projects shown in this book, please read the following:

The way we've used Dream 3D in this book is by showing four perspectives on the screen simultaneously. That way, when you move an object up, for example, you can see the results of your movement from various angles. When working with 3D, this instantaneous feedback is all-important. Many times, you'll think you are moving an object up toward the top of your screen, and later, when you look at the scene from another angle, it turns out you were moving it forward, not up.

However, when you open CorelDream 3D, you'll only see one perspective window, not four. The problem with working with only one perspective window is that, in order to switch to different viewing angles, you have to right-click any white, blank area in the window, select View, and then choose a view type. Each time you change views, you'll have to do this.

On the CD-ROM that accompanies this book, we've included templates that will enable all of your 3D projects to open with four perspective windows up and running. To work alongside the lessons in the book, you pretty much need to load and work with these templates. This makes what you see on your screen match the screen layout shown in the book. You may load the *CorelDRAW 8 Secrets Dream 3D* template or load the project itself from the accompanying CD-ROM.

Loading the recommended templates

Note

The following directions require that you insert the *CorelDRAW 8 Secrets* CD-ROM in your CD-ROM drive. If you've installed CorelDraw 8 to run from your CD-ROM, then these instructions will not work for you. You must first exit from all CorelDraw programs, insert the *CorelDRAW 8 Secrets* CD-ROM, open the folder titled "Chapter 13," and copy the file called "Corel Secrets Workspace Template.d3d" to your hard drive. You may then remove the *CorelDRAW 8 Secrets* CD-ROM and replace the CorelDraw program CD-ROM as you would normally. Finally, to load the required Corel Secrets templates and follow along with this book, start with the third step that follows.

STEPS:

Loading Templates

Step 1. Put the *CorelDRAW 8 Secrets* CD-ROM in your CD-ROM drive.

Step 2. Open the folder titled "Chapter 13."

Step 3. Double-click on the icon titled "Corel Secrets Workspace Template." If Dream 3D is installed on your computer, that file opens automatically in Dream 3D. Take a minute to look at all four windows.

The larger window to the left that fills most of the screen is the Reference window, also known as Perspective Window of Doc1:1. This window displays the projections of your 3D objects on three different walls. Looking at this window gives you an idea of how your objects are positioned in three dimensions.

The window to the upper-right shows the view of your objects from above. This window, called Top View, or Perspective of Doc1:2, is good for checking objects that have been moved forward or backward.

The window below shows the view from the right. Look at this window to see if objects moved from top to bottom are really where you want them. This window is called Right View, or Perspective of Doc1:3.

The fourth view, or window, shows the view from the front. Doesn't it look just like the first view? Not really. Moving objects in the fourth window will only move them up or down. This limitation is desirable, because objects moved in the first view can be moved along all three axes, which can get confusing. This fourth window is called Front View, or Perspective of Doc1:4.

If objects appear too close or too far away in any of these views, use the Zoom tool to move closer or farther away from the objects. The Zoom tools work similarly as in other CorelDraw programs.

Now that you are a little acquainted with the four perspective windows, select Window ⇨ Workspace ⇨ Save. You'll be asked to name your workspace. Do so.

From now on, any project you begin or file you open in Dream 3D will open with these four windows showing. You'll also notice that the title of the workspace you saved appears as one of the choices under the Workspace menu. (Select Window ⇨ Workspace to see these choices.)

As mentioned previously, make your screen open with CorelDraw 8's default workspace by selecting one of the default settings from the same Workspace menu.

To restore the default screen, simply select Window ⇨ Workspace, and then choose the default setting for whichever screen resolution you work at. After choosing the default screen, your workspace will again consist of one perspective window and the hierarchy window (which we explain in the next chapter).

If you have trouble working with the template, check out the sidebar titled "What If the Template Doesn't Look Right to Me?"

Working without the template

Without the template, you can still follow along with the tutorials from the conventional CorelDream 3D view by changing views every time you move an object. In the following projects, the accompanying pictures show three, or sometimes even four, views at a time. To follow along without multiple views, right-click on any blank, white space inside the image window and select View ⇨ Type (see Figure 13-1). Choose one direction from the menu. The change on your screen is instantaneous. You'll see all of the screen objects from whichever view you select. The main view, the view that shows all of the 3D projections, is called the Reference view. Right-click on any blank area again to switch to a different view. You may do this as often as you wish, switching views back and forth to move an object into just the right position.

Figure 13-1: Right-clicking on any blank, white space in a window brings up a shortcut to change views on the fly.

Scene Wizard Templates

The Scene Wizard is more than just a collection of ready-made templates. Although you can use a Scene Wizard as a complete template, adding, perhaps, a company logo or personal art object, Scene Wizard also functions as a starting point to create more individualized scenes and projects. See Figure 13-2.

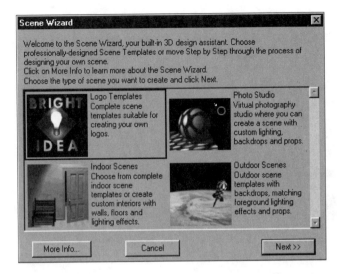

Figure 13-2: The Scene Wizard screen asks you to select from four different scene templates.

Each of the four main Scene Wizard categories (Logo Template, Photo Studio, Indoor Scenes, and Outdoor Scenes) moves through several phases of creation, asking you for input as your scene is built. For example, the Photo Studio template might look rather unremarkable at first glance, but click on Next, and you'll see that you can choose from 24 lighting effects and angles for your project. So actually, the Photo Studio template is your key to beginning a project with excellent lighting effects already in place. This gives you more time to be creative, rather than having to fuss with light faders.

Additionally, when using the Outdoor Scenes template, you'll notice that twelve scenes have been created for you, but you need not stick with their chosen backdrops. The real work in creating those templates went into getting effective lighting, fog, and camera angles. You could change the background of one of those scenes and be well on your way to creating an outdoor scene all your own.

Experimenting with the Indoor Scenes template is informative because you can have some say in how the room structure is built. If you choose Step by Step after clicking on Next, you'll see the Configure Your Room screen, as shown in Figure 13-3. You are given eight Room styles from which to choose, including various wall-and-floor combinations, and subsequently, eight Indoor Mood Lighting choices, including TV studio, Shadow effects, and multiple spotlights.

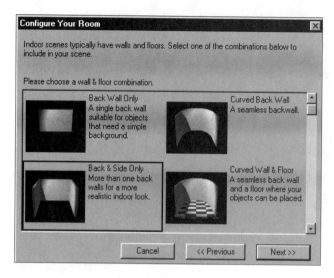

Figure 13-3: The Configure Your Room screen is available from the Indoor Scenes template.

For company logos, don't be deceived by the simple bulb image on the opening screen of the Scene Wizard. Inside are ten customizable company logo templates, each producing an unusual effect. So, the Scene Wizard is a collection of templates that give you room to bring a personal touch to even a simple project, without your having yet learned a stitch about 3D modeling.

Secret

Scene Wizard employs only basic serif and sans-serif fonts in its scenes. That's because each user has different fonts on his or her system. But you can easily replace the default Scene Wizard fonts with another font.

One important note: You can apply these Scene Wizard templates to already existing scenes. If you've created a 3D environment with some objects, but have not yet found the right lighting, try applying one of these templates to your project. If you decided that a cloudy sky would be the perfect backdrop for some 3D objects you've created, you need not make one from scratch. Just apply the one included in Outdoor Scenes.

After you've selected a scene and have finished choosing options for it, click on Finish, and your computer screen will fill with four perspectives of your scene, as shown in Figure 13-4. Perspective One is front and center. The other three perspectives fill the right side of your screen. (This will be the case if you've loaded the template as outlined at the beginning of this chapter, keeping in mind that you'll have to save the template and load it as a workspace. If you chose not to do this, you'll only see the single Perspective view.)

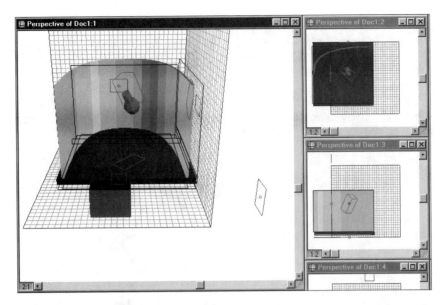

Figure 13-4: The four perspective windows appear after Scene Wizard creates an indoor scene.

Everybody who uses a 3D program like Dream 3D for the first time always has the same response after clicking on the Finish button at the end of the Scene Wizard process. Namely, "Where is it? Where is my work of art?"

What you see are simple models of the objects that are involved in creating your scene. These objects can be moved around, built upon, cast with different lights, shaded with different textures, and rendered against different backgrounds. After you have finished manipulating the objects in this wire-mesh mode, you can chose to render, or ray-trace, your scene into a real picture, something you can actually send to your publisher or to Mom.

Ray-tracing refers to the amazing mathematical process that brought us this new world of 3D modeling. Ray-tracing, miraculous as it is, also takes a really long time on most computers. That's why you are encouraged to spend a lot of time working in the wire-mesh mode building your scene and making sure the cameras are really pointing to the objects you think they are pointing to. Then, when you render your object (select Scene ⇨ Render, and chose from various quality settings—we'll get into that later), you'll have a better chance of seeing what you hoped to see.

What If the Template Doesn't Look Right to Me?

If the views shown in the four windows do not look similar to the four-at-a-time views shown in this book, you may need to adjust each screen one by one until the objects are centered. Click inside one window, and do the following:

Use the Zoom tool to zoom in or out until you've located the objects inside the wire-mesh screen. You should see some gears and the word "Industrial."

Use the scroll buttons on the bottom and right side of the window to reposition the objects so that they are in the center of the screen. The numbers at the bottom left of the window (1:2, 1:8, and so on) represent the zoom values. If the template originally places the objects so that they are too close for viewing, the zoom value will read something like "2:1" or "8:1." If the template placed the objects too far away for accurate viewing, the zoom value will perhaps read "1:4" or "1:8."

To view the three smaller windows to the right, use zoom values of 1:2. To view the main, larger window on the left, use a 1:1 zoom. But first, the objects must be located and centered. If the objects and the wire-mesh screen are quite far away, you might initially only see a small, blue screen in your window. Once it's centered, use the Zoom tool to bring the object closer so that it fills most of the screen. If the objects in the window are too close, you might only see a huge section of the wire-mesh screen filling the entire window. Zoom out to 1:2, and reposition and center the objects.

After centering and resizing your view of the objects, you can change the viewing angle of each window by right-clicking in any white, blank space in the window. Or choose View ⇨ Type, and then click on the type of view you want for that particular window.

The Dream 3D projects in this book are arranged as follows:

- The largest view (the view on the left side of your screen) uses the Reference view, meaning it shows projections of its objects on several walls to simulate 3D space.

- The second view (the view at the top-right) uses the Top view. This view is good for moving objects from forward to backward, because you can view everything from the top.

- The third view (the screen in the middle-right) provides a view from the right. This view is useful for moving objects up or down, meaning higher or lower.

- The fourth view (the view from the front) is good for moving objects from right to left or from left to right.

Choose Window ⇨ Save Workspace, and name your workspace anything you wish. After naming it, the workspace will be included in the list of available workspaces shown on that same menu. Now, anytime you open a new project, you can load this workspace, and your new project will offer the same four views of your saved workspace.

Secret

If you are using a smaller monitor, you may not see all of the windows that Dream 3D opens by default. The Objects Browser and Hierarchy of Doc.1 (or current document) are actually open and available, but you may only see the blue bounding window at the bottom of your screen. To view the Objects Browser, if it's not already visible, select Window on the Dream 3D menu, scroll down, and click. Then, locate the corner of the window and drag it into view.

Dream 3D scenes include a background — a bitmap, a color, or color gradient. However, you will not see your background until you render the scene, as it is not visible in the Perspective or Modeling mode.

Perspective Windows

Each perspective window represents the point of view of an existing camera. You know you are viewing Perspective One, because the window is labeled, Perspective of Doc1:1. The other perspective windows are labeled Perspective of Doc1:2, Perspective of Doc1:3, and so on. Looking at Figure 13-4, the blue box-like object near the front of the screen is really a camera facing away from you, toward the objects visible in that perspective window. You also notice a rectangle with a small circle in it projected onto the opposite surface from you. That rectangle represents what a camera is pointed at, in this case, Camera One, Perspective One. If you double-click on the camera, you'll see the Object Properties dialog box. (In Dream 3D, cameras and lights are thought of as objects.) The current tab says Camera, confirming the type of object with which you are working.

To see that you can switch to more than one camera even now, move to the Window menu and remove the checks by all of the Perspective options except Perspective of Doc1:1. Now, maximize Perspective of Doc1:1. Drag the scroll bars up, and you'll see a camera facing down on the objects. Drag the scroll bars to the left, and you'll see another camera. You can now return the other perspective views to their former positions on your screen by selecting them from the Window menu. Click the Windowed or Restore button to make Perspective of Doc1.1 return to its former size.

The red object that appears to be floating in air is a light. Double-click on it, and you'll see more information about the type of light it is, its positioning, and its brightness features. You'll see that the Object Properties dialog box for this light offers more tabs than a camera. These special lighting features, such as linking lights to geographical planes and viewing lights through gels, will be covered later in this book. You'll also notice a red-orange rectangle projected on the floor and opposite walls of the light. The projection onto the floor represents where the light is facing. The projection on the opposite wall represents where the light fixture exists on that particular 3D plane.

Using the other perspective windows

The other perspective windows off to the side of the screen represent the views of other cameras. For example, if you maximize the window called Perspective on Doc1:2, you'll see the objects created by Scene Wizard from the top down. You will not be able to see a camera or light present in all views.

Why is the "top-to-bottom" camera helpful? After all, you're probably not going to render scenes from this unflattering perspective. But once you get to know Dream 3D, you'll be joining objects together. In order to do this well, you'll need to see objects as they join in *all three* dimensions.

Finding the floor

Doesn't sound too hard, does it? (Depends what you did last night.) Guess again. The picture in Figure 13-5 shows a bicycle that appears to be seated directly on a surface. But the way 3D space works, we're not sure yet if it is or not. Figure 13-6 shows the same object viewed from another perspective window. But to be 100 percent sure, you'd have to see it from all three angles.

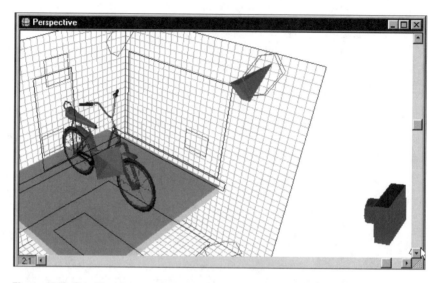

Figure 13-5: This bicycle may or may not be sitting directly on the surface.

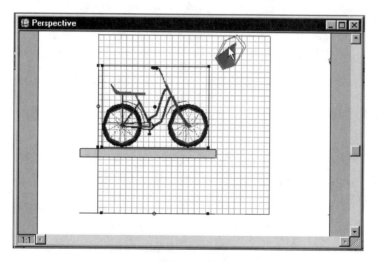

Figure 13-6: We can see the same object from an additional plane to help us position the bike.

Figure 13-7 shows the bicycle as we first dropped it down onto the surface. There's the bicycle, embedded inside the floor. 3D programs are like that. They'll let you cross and mesh objects as you wish. The trick is to get them to mesh together in a way that makes geometric sense. Looking again at the main perspective window (the largest) in Figure 13-7, you'll notice that it provides projections on three sides so that you can tell where exactly the camera is hitting the opposite wall and where the light beam is falling. Notice that the other two perspective windows, Perspective of Doc2:3 and Perspective of Doc2:2, only provide a view of one axis. But that help is enough.

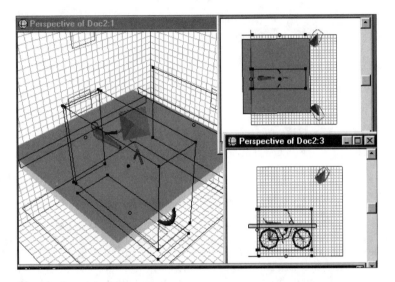

Figure 13-7: These three views of a bicycle show that it is positioned incorrectly on a platform.

If we were to use the Selection Arrow (the pointer in the upper left-hand corner) to click the bike in Perspective One and attempt to pull the bicycle up on top of the platform, we would really be pulling it towards us, along its x axis. From Perspective One, known as Perspective of Doc2:1, we cannot pull an object up, along its y axis. But look at Perspective of Doc2:3. You are given a direct cross-table view. Consequently, your pointer can reposition the bicycle up and down by dragging the bicycle in that window only. Notice that the smaller view is from a camera positioned to aid you in moving the bicycle towards the middle of the platform. If you tried to reposition the bicycle in and out by dragging in Perspective Three, you couldn't do it. It is by using the Selection Arrow tool in each of these three views that we were able to position the bicycle truly on top and in the center of the platform. Figure 13-8 shows the properly positioned bicycle.

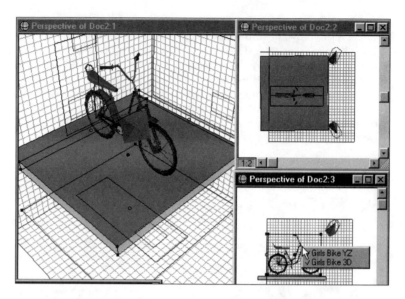

Figure 13-8: The properly positioned bicycle is shown in all three perspective windows.

Understanding the window names

While you may have many scenes open in Dream 3D at once, take note that the "Doc" referred to in Perspective of Doc2:3 means that there was another scene opened before this one was. (Hence, the title "Doc2:X.") The "3" in Perspective of Doc2:3 means that this window represents the third camera created to view this scene. It is possible to have many camera views (perspectives) associated with a scene. Therefore, you could potentially have a window titled Perspective of Doc4:5. A perspective window titled as such would represent the fifth camera view created for the forth document, or scene, that was open at this time.

Secret

When you position an object in one perspective window, be sure to keep an eye on how it moves in the other windows. Check the object's position in each window before moving your object too far along one plane. You might end up with only a piece of your object in the actual rendered viewing area.

Photo Studio Scene Wizard

The bicycle pictured in Figure 13-9 is the rendered (ray-traced) version of the scene modeled previously. Each model is a combination of groups of objects connected together at specific joints. These objects are treated with colors, and shaders and textures are available that can modify those colors. Lights are objects also, shined onto surfaces that cause shadows to be cast onto backgrounds. And the cameras that show the view from a specific angle are also objects, in that they can be made to possess various lens qualities and moved around the scene at will.

Figure 13-9: The rendered bicycle picture.

Figure 13-10 shows you how it all began, with one of the Scene Wizard templates, specifically, the Photo Studio template. The light setting "Left 30%/Right 100%" was chosen, as you can see from the figure. Each light combination brings out different surface qualities of the object(s) in the scene and casts unique types of shadows. After selecting a type of lighting, the Scene Wizard prompts you to select from one of six backgrounds, ranging from sky to wallpaper to no background at all. Following this choice you can select a prop for your scene, perhaps a stool on which to place an object, or, as in the case of the bicycle, a marble checkerboard floor on which to set the object. These choices are built into your scene. Of course, when you select Finish, all you immediately see is the wire-mesh "cut-out" box that represents the 3D universe used in building your scene. This three-sided projection area is the perspective window of Doc1:1.

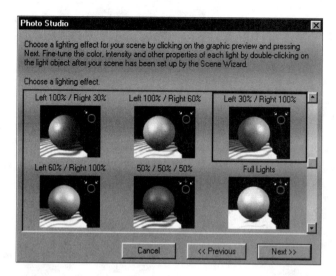

Figure 13-10: The Photo Studio Scene Wizard prompts you to choose from a variety of lighting effects.

Rendering

If you've jumped ahead a bit and placed an object of your choice on one of the props provided by Scene Wizard, you might want to go ahead and render this object to some format or picture file, and see what it *really* looks like.

When you choose Scene ⇨ Render, you'll see a drop-down menu of rendering choices. (See Figure 13-11.) Some specialized rendering choices are available in this menu, but what concerns you now is knowing the following:

■ How to render a picture quickly, just to make sure all the objects that concern you are really in your view (see "The Production frame," which follows).

■ How to render at a higher quality a picture of a scene you really like

We explain rendering choices thoroughly later in this chapter, but for now, know that the Render Settings menu item contains choices regarding type of file output, size and resolution, as well as which camera should be used for the rendering. Below that is the Render menu. At first, render with Low Res Review to check your scene. This is similar to a photographer taking a picture with a Polaroid camera first, just to be sure that the lens sees what he or she does. Use Medium Resolution when you are fairly happy with the results and want to preview the subtle blends and textures that Low Res

Review is not going to pick up. Finally, render with High Resolution when you're entirely happy with your work. Rendering at High Resolution can take several hours and appears to require more than 100MB of contiguous hard drive space on your computer to use as swap space. The rendering choice labeled "CPT Pre-Production Medium" creates a file 800 × 600 pixels at 150 dpi. The choice labeled "CPT Pre-Production High" creates a 1024 × 768 pixel file at 300 dpi. The trouble with using the last two modes for rendering is that, once you feel comfortable adjusting the Production frame (we'll discuss that next), those settings might not match your picture's proportion.

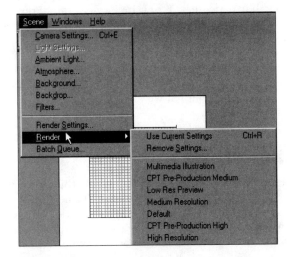

Figure 13-11: The Scene menu with the Render drop-down menu exposed.

At the end of the rendering process, you'll be given the choice to save your picture in one of several file formats.

After ray-tracing a scene, Dream 3D returns you to a maximized version of Perspectives Two or Three. This can be disconcerting to a new user. To return to the default perspective window setting, first click the Restore (windowed) button of the maximized window's control menu. Now select Window from the menu and click Perspective of Doc1:1. It will appear maximized as well. Again, click the Restore button from that document's control menu. You'll now have all four perspective views available as they were before.

Rendering and your camera

When you finally render a picture, you're going to have to choose one view to render to. It will be a view seen by one of the three or four perspective windows with which you've been working while developing your scene. So as you're working along, moving and editing objects, start thinking about which one of those views really looks like a picture. When you are happy with how things look, select Scene ⇨ Render Settings and click the Camera tab. Generally speaking, the title of each perspective window relates to the camera number. For example, the view Perspective of Doc3:4 would be a view of what the fourth camera sees. From the Camera tab of the Render Settings dialog box, open the drop-down menu and select the camera that corresponds to the view you'd like to render. After you select a camera, do a Low-Res Review render to be sure you've picked the right one. If you haven't, simply select a different camera. If you don't like any of the views, readjust the Production frame, and rotate objects and lights until one of the cameras suits you. In the next chapter, we talk about manipulating camera angles, lens qualities, and views.

The Production frame

Select View ⇨ Production Frame, and you'll see a black, thin box frame squared around your objects. This is the Production frame. It represents what you will actually see when you render a scene. It's important to keep this frame in view because none of your editing outside the production frame (except for adjusting lights, of course) will show up in your rendered output.

You can resize and move the Production frame by selecting it and using the bounding boxes to resize and drag it from inside the boundary. Figure 13-12 shows the results of the Production frame being sized around a large area. Figure 13-13 shows the results of the Production frame "shrunk in" closer around the rendered objects.

Object placement

Let's review the concept of looking at several perspective windows one more time. Figure 13-14 shows the Objects Browser and three perspective windows, one large and two small windows. The kayak clip art object was dragged to the main Perspective window; however, look closely, and you can see it from two other camera views in the two other perspective windows. Perspective of Doc1:2 presents an overhead view, and Perspective of Doc1:3 presents a view from the left. To be sure that your object is positioned correctly, you must check each perspective to see if the object is truly lined up in the way it appears from Perspective One. Sometimes, for example, a boat can appear to be in the water in Perspective of Doc1.1, but when viewed in another perspective window, it's clear that the boat is slightly above the waves. Check your object's location in several perspective windows before ray-tracing your picture.

Figure 13-12: Because the Production frame is sized around a large area, the rendered picture shows the wider area.

Figure 13-13: The Production frame has been resized to closely surround the main objects, and the rendered picture reflects this.

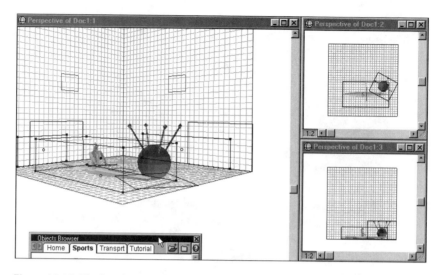

Figure 13-14: The kayak was dragged and dropped onto the scene. The three views help determine where the object is really located.

Logo Templates

It would be a shame to think that the only thing the Scene Wizard "Arabica Coffee" is good for is making a coffee commercial. (See Figure 13-15.) We're going to take advantage of the dramatic lighting and background scheme provided by this Scene Wizard and add new text, get rid of the cup of joe, and learn about three important Dream 3D features while we're at it. When we're finished with this, you'll understand a bit about grouping and ungrouping objects to recolor them, using and editing shaders that affect the texture of your object, and using the Virtual Trackball to rotate objects in any direction.

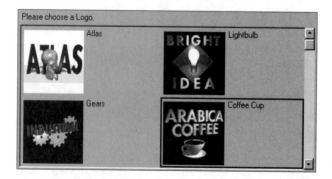

Figure 13-15: The Logo Templates Scene Wizard offers several selections from which to choose. Here the "Arabica Coffee" logo is selected.

If you'd like to follow along, click the Logo Templates Scene Wizard, click Next, select the cup of coffee logo, and again click Next. You'll be prompted to write in some text. Type **Caldwell Bowling**, one word for each space.

Next, we'll deconstruct and remove the cup of coffee from the scene, as shown in Figure 13-16 . You'll see that the cup of coffee is made up of groups of objects. The coffee steam plumes are three individual objects that remain ungrouped. The saucer is a single object as well. The cup of coffee, however, is a construction of several objects. Using the Selection Arrow, click a steam plume. A bounding box appears around one. While one steam plume is selected, click the Arrange menu. You'll see that Ungroup is not an option because each steam plume is a single object. Press the Delete key, and that plume of steam is gone. Do so with the other two plumes. Now select the saucer. Clicking delete rids us of that in one easy operation. But click the coffee cup and look inside the Arrange menu. You'll see that Ungroup is an available option. The coffee cup is really two joined objects. Still, pressing Delete once removes the entire cup from the screen. That's because the objects are grouped and will respond together to such commands. We now have the words "Caldwell Bowling" alone on the screen. Actually, lights, cameras, and backdrop are still alive and well, so "Caldwell Bowling" is not really alone at all. The lighting and backdrop manipulation that was created with this Scene Wizard template will still apply to whatever we create next, as long as we don't change those entities ourselves.

Figure 13-16: Removing the cup of coffee and its related objects.

Open Object Browser and click the Sports tab. Drag the bowling ball and pins icon, and drop it in the picture. Figure 13-17 shows our first attempt. Notice the bowling pins are placed clumsily in front of the letters. And yes, once again, no amount of repositioning the bowling pin in Perspective One is going to move the pin *behind* the letters. As you can see in Figure 13-17, the window labeled Perspective of Doc5:2 shows a camera angle best suited for dragging the bowling pin in and out. So drag the bowling pin backward, behind the letters with the Selection Arrow. Your view should be a view from above, as shown in that same figure, in order to move the pin correctly. Finally, the correct placement is shown in Figure 13-18.

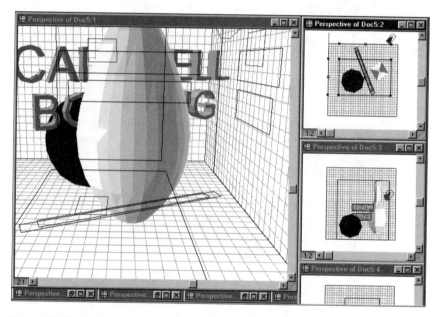

Figure 13-17: The first placement of the bowling ball and pins.

After moving the pin in front of the letters, get ready to color the bowling ball. Because the scene's background is black, it won't do to have the bowling ball be the same color. However, most objects need to be ungrouped to be recolored. Select Arrange ⇨ Ungroup, as shown in Figure 13-19, to ungroup the bowling pin and ball. It will then be possible to select the bowling ball individually.

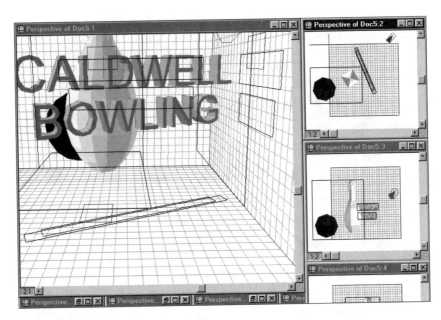

Figure 13-18: The bowling ball and pins are correctly placed.

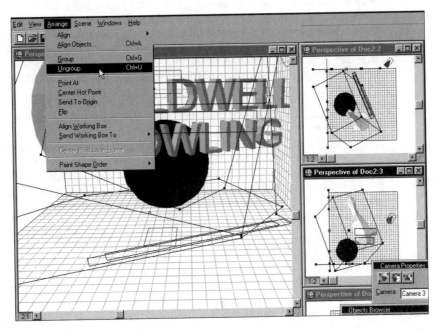

Figure 13-19: After selecting Arrange ➪ Ungroup, you can select the bowling ball and the pin individually.

When recoloring objects in Dream 3D, you can either drag a color Shader to the object you want to recolor, or click the color Shader while the object is selected, and click the Apply button. Figure 13-20 shows the Shaders Browser.

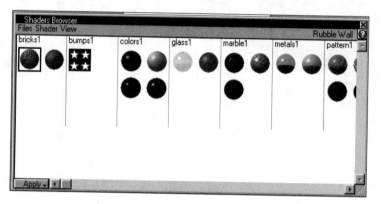

Figure 13-20: The Shaders Browser.

The reason it's called Shaders Browser and not Color Changer or something else is that many components are involved in creating a modified surface for your objects, and color is just one of them. Because 3D rendering is so accurate and can create such finely detailed appearances on surfaces, you can make precise changes in an object's reflective qualities, such as how metallic it looks, the degree of wood grain that should show through the color, and so on. When you double-click on any Shader ball in the Browser menu, you'll see the dialog box shown in Figure 13-21.

We cover the Shader Editor dialog box in detail later in this chapter, but you should know that inside it are sliding faders to modify how shiny or bumpy your object's surface is. For example, if your surface has a plaster-like texture, how deep should the pits and bumps be? If your scene includes a light shining on your surface, should the surface reflect mostly the light's color, or should it maintain a deep color quality of its own? All of these surface qualities and more—many more—are editable in the Shader Editor dialog box.

Getting back to modifying your bowling ball, select Marble from the Shader Browser, and double-click on it. This brings up the Shader Editor dialog box. You'll find that the dialog box opens to the Color tab. Double-click the color square itself and a three-fader Color dialog box opens in the upper-right corner of the screen. The three faders are RGB controls. To make your bowling ball blue like mine, drag the R fader to the left and the B fader to the right. The color rectangle on the Shader Editor itself will reflect the color change. As shown in Figure 13-22, the Color dialog box doesn't limit you to RGB color editing. Other modes are available from the drop-down menu.

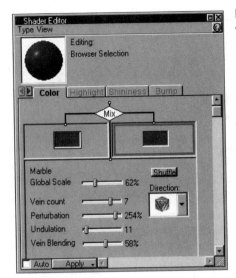

Figure 13-21: The Shader Editor dialog box lets you modify the surface of the bowling ball.

Figure 13-22: The Color dialog box enables you to edit your object in RGB color mode, among others.

Figure 13-21, the Shader Editor dialog box, shows the edited marble settings we used to make the marble surface more apparent in the scene itself. The changes will be reflected in the small square (with the sphere inside). Click the Apply button to change the bowling ball surface to match what you've created in the Shader Editor.

Figure 13-23 shows the ball and pin while still ungrouped, with the Shader Browser open. The bowling ball has a new color and texture.

With your Selection Arrow (the arrow on the upper-right of the Dream 3D toolbar), move into any perspective window in which it's easy to make a clear selection of both the ball and the bowling pin. While pressing Shift, select both objects and choose Arrange ⇨ Group from the menu. You'll notice the second object you select is surrounded with red bounding boxes, rather than black. That's because you can make the second object respond in certain ways to any editing you perform on the first object. This is called *linking*, and we deal with this form of editing later in this book. For now, you need both objects selected because you're going to tilt the bowling pin and ball to simulate a collision between the two.

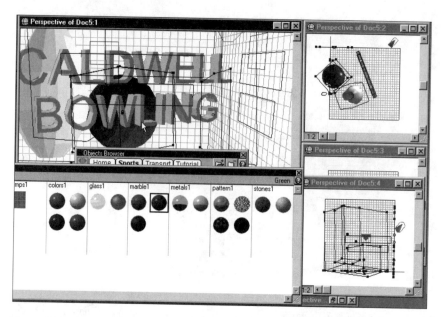

Figure 13-23: The ball and pin are still ungrouped, and the Shader Browser is still open.

Secret

With Dream 3D, you cannot use the Selection Arrow tool to drag a square around multiple objects you'd like to select. You'll have to select one, and then the other. That's because as you learn more about Dream 3D, you'll see that the *order* in which you select objects affects how they relate to each other.

The Virtual Trackball

The Virtual Trackball, shown in Figure 13-24, rotates the angle of objects in three-dimensional space. It is the second tool from the top of the Dream 3D toolbar. Usable in any view, you can rotate objects a little bit to the right, and then up, for example. (It combines X-Y-Z rotation with Pitch, Roll, and Yaw. More on that later in this book.) It is perfect for creating the random kinetic appearance of a bowling ball hitting the pins.

Secret

If you don't see the Virtual Trackball, but instead see a single curved arrow at that toolspace, press and hold your mouse button down a little longer over the toolspace. The Virtual Trackball will appear. The single curved arrow is the One Axis Rotation tool.

Figure 13-25 shows what happens when you move the Virtual Trackball tool into one of the perspective windows, click on an object, and begin dragging in a certain direction. Along with the usual bounding boxes, you'll see a circle around the entire perimeter of the object(s) you are manipulating. Look closely at that figure and you'll see a little arrow in the perspective window, Doc2:2. That arrow means you've placed the Virtual Trackball over an area that can be rotated or twisted in some way. Notice that the same circle is present in the other perspective windows as well. In this example, we've used the Virtual Trackball to raise the pin farther up off the ground, while the ball is tilted downward, simulating impact.

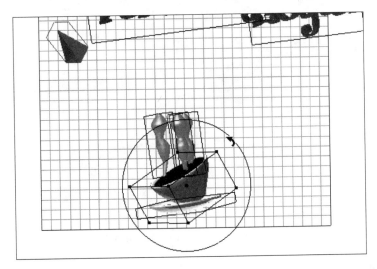

Figure 13-24: The Virtual Trackball rotates the angle of objects in three dimensions.

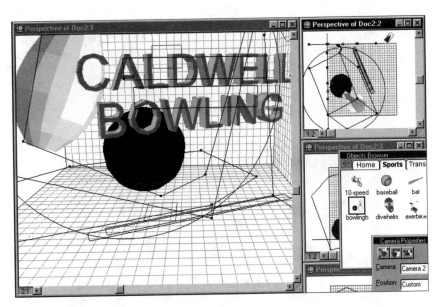

Figure 13-25: The Virtual Trackball moves both the ball and pin together.

Figure 13-26 shows the bowling pin and ball now tilted. I also moved the pin closer toward the letters. That's because the white coloring of the pins will produce an excellent shadow surface for the letters. Besides, ray-traced objects look so good close up that you don't have to worry about hiding imperfections, as with bitmaps.

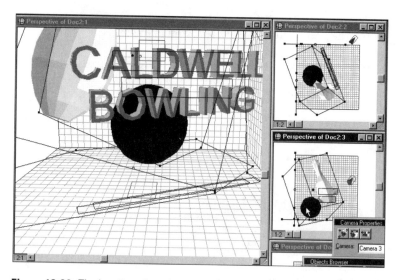

Figure 13-26: The bowling pin and ball, now repositioned, are ready for rendering.

While working on a project such as this, you should be doing Low-Res Review renderings every time you make a change. By doing these frequently (Choose Scene ➪ Rendering ➪ Low Res Review), you'll see what changes to make to your Production frame, when objects have moved out of camera view, and so on. After you've checked everything, try a Medium Resolution rendering to be sure you've placed the objects in the most flattering light, showing off their textures and shadows. Then, it's time for the High Resolution render. Figure 13-27 shows the bowling ball scene rendered in High Resolution mode and saved as a TIFF file. (We talk more about saving to different file types later in this chapter.)

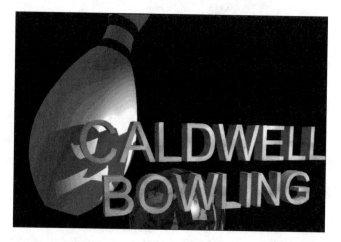

Figure 13-27: The bowling scene is shown here rendered in High Resolution mode. And to think this all started with a cup of coffee!

Creating a Unique Scene

Now, create an entirely unique scene. Start with a Scene Wizard called Foggy Morning.

STEPS:

Making a Scene

Step 1. First save and delete anything that's already open on your Dream 3D screen. When you save a project as the default file type (.D3D), you are not erasing or replacing any Scene Wizard files, even if you started your project with a Scene Wizard.

Step 2. You do not have to delete every single perspective window to get rid of the current project. Just select "Perspective of DocX:1," where X is the number of the document you are working on, and delete it by clicking the "X" in the perspective window's Control menu. The other perspective window associated with that project will close, also.

Step 3. Now you are free to begin a new project without having eight perspective windows to wade through. Select File ⇨ New ⇨ Scene Wizard ⇨ Next ⇨ Outdoor Scene ⇨ Foggy Morning.

Your scene will open to be modeled, and what you'll see is a whole lot of nothing. That's because the Foggy Morning scene includes only cameras, lights, and a background. You will not see your background until you render it.

Step 4. Drag the Object Browser out to where you can see it. Open the Transportation tab, and place the airplane called *wrigfly2* onto Perspective One. (See Figure 13-28.)

Note that the plane is too close to the ground to stir much interest. Look closely at the perspective window labeled Perspective of Doc7:3. It is this window that enables you to move an object up and down, for example, closer or farther from the ground. Once again, trying to adjust an object along this geometric plane in Perspective One will do no good. Use Perspective Three, which is a view from the left. Place the Selection Arrow tool inside that window and drag the airplane up. Use Perspective of Doc7:2 (the view from the top) to drag the airplane closer toward the front of the viewing area. Figure 13-29 shows the plane in the air. Please remember that, to attain these four views, you can either load this project in its entirety, which is found on the CD-ROM that comes with this book, or load the template, also provided, as outlined at the beginning of this chapter.

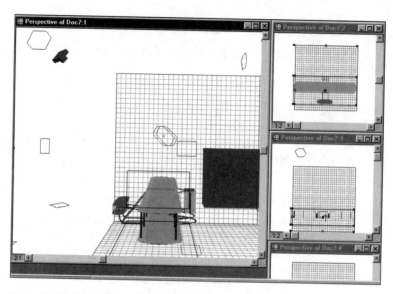

Figure 13-28: The wrigfly2 airplane object is placed into the Scene Wizard, Foggy Morning.

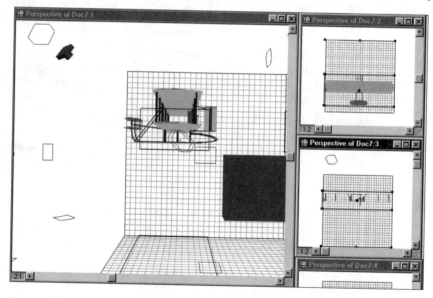

Figure 13-29: The plane is now airborne.

After checking and repositioning the Production frame, render the plane now. But before doing so, tilt the right wing toward you so you can see some of that nice wood grain in the rendering. Figure 13-30 shows the airplane in Perspective Three, which shows the best angle for tilting. Right next to it is the Low-Res Review rendering we did immediately after, just to check our work. Figure 13-31 shows the fully rendered plane against the preset Foggy Morning backdrop.

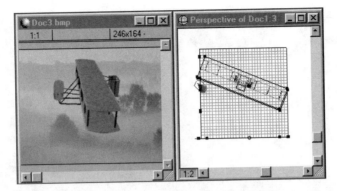

Figure 13-30: It's easy to tilt the airplane the way we want by using Perspective Three. Next to it is the Low-Res Review to check our work.

Figure 13-31: The fully rendered "Foggy Morning with Airplane" picture.

While the bitmap of the foggy morning is attractive, the concept of fog in 3D programs means creating a simulated fog with lighting and special camera effects so that the other objects in your scene seem to be moving in and out of the fog, rather than the object being plastered onto a picture with fog in it. Figure 13-32 shows another scene rendered with the same airplane, but with the fog features calculated from the Scene ⇨ Atmospheres dialog box (more on this topic later in this book).

Figure 13-32: The same airplane is rendered in a scene that includes fog provided by the Dream 3D fog algorithm.

Figure 13-33 shows the Render Effects dialog box with the Backdrop tab showing. This is accessed by selecting Scene ⇨ Backdrop. A drop-down menu is available. Scroll through the options and select Map. The dialog box will now include a floppy disk icon. Clicking on it enables you to search your hard drive for a bitmap to use as the backdrop for your objects. Many file types are allowable, including CPT, TIFF, and BMP. You'll see a tiny picture of the bitmap you've selected. Looking closely at the figure, you'll see that you are given options for how the bitmap may be placed, tiled, or rotated. You can make a "quality versus speed" choice regarding the rendering of your bitmap. For this project, we did not change any of the default settings.

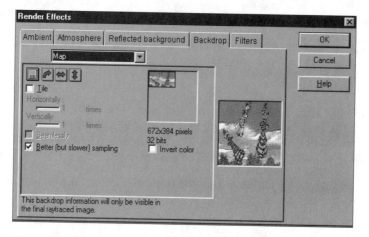

Figure 13-33: The Render Effects dialog box is opened to change the backdrop bitmap for the airplane scene.

Figure 13-34 shows the airplane rendered with the new bitmap. We called it "Chess Wars." Still, it needs embellishment. The plane is positioned at a boring angle, and besides, we want to tell you about how to position two objects so that it looks like they are touching one another.

Figure 13-34: The airplane is rendered with a new backdrop called "Chess Wars."

We decided that in order to negotiate a path through all of these attacking chess pieces, the airplane needed some glasses. Figure 13-35 shows our first humble attempt at positioning sunglasses from the Objects Browser onto the nose of the airplane. First, you must shrink the glasses somewhat. To do this, position your Selection Arrow over squares at the corners of the bounding box and drag inwards. You can do this in a precise, numeric way also, and we deal with that method in the next chapter. Figures 13-36 and 13-37 show two angles necessary to work with in order to really get the glasses up against the airplane's nose. Both of these perspective windows are provided by default by Dream 3D, so you don't have to create your own camera angles — yet, anyway. Please note that the bounding box containing the glasses is *tilted*, meaning that it will be necessary to do some positioning with the Virtual Trackball.

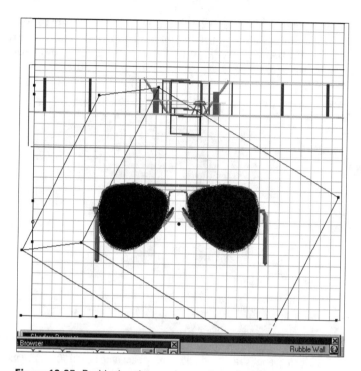

Figure 13-35: Positioning the sunglasses from the Object Browser.

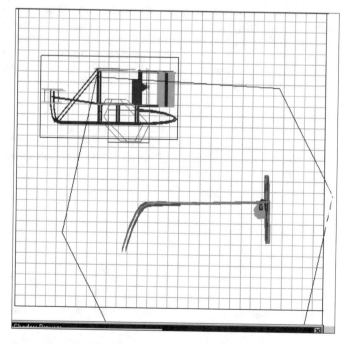

Figure 13-36: A sideways view of getting the sunglasses on the airplane's nose.

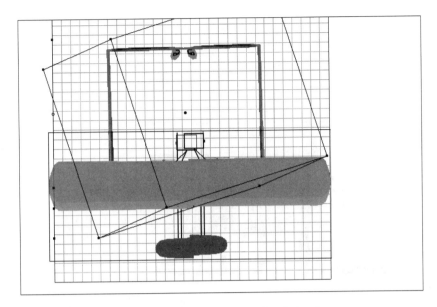

Figure 13-37: A top view of getting the glasses on the airplane's nose.

Figure 13-38 shows the glasses positioned correctly on the nose of the
airplane. Once the airplane and glasses are grouped together, the airplane
can easily be positioned at a much more interesting angle. The glasses add a
comic "face" focus. Now, move to the Edit menu and select Numerical
Properties. (Make sure you don't accidentally select Properties.) As shown
in Figure 13-38, the Numerical Properties dialog box displays data boxes for
the size and positions of both the glasses and the airplane. Dream 3D
provides highly precise control over the exact positioning and sizing of
objects that are joined. The method we're showing you here in this chapter,
positioning by hand through various perspective windows, is not
appropriate for creating the complex objects of which Dream 3D is capable.
But such a method serves well for now.

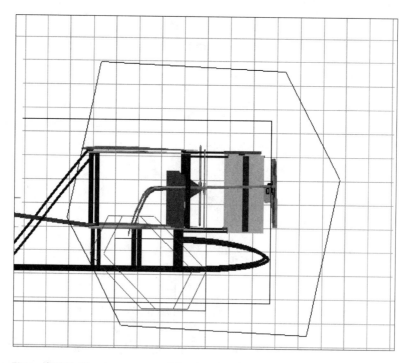

Figure 13-38: The glasses are positioned correctly and the airplane is reoriented in space.

Now that the plane looks good, let's move a camera around to the front and slightly below eye level to take advantage of the comical, off-angle appearance. The steps to do this are as follows:

STEPS:
Positioning the Camera to the Front

Step 1. In the Reference window (Perspective One, the largest window), zoom out so that you can see several cameras.

Step 2. With the Selection tool, choose one of the cameras, and move it toward the front of the airplane, facing it.

Step 3. Select both the Camera and the Airplane/Glasses group. Then choose Arrange ⇨ Point At (or press Ctrl+M). The camera will now face the center of the object or group.

Step 4. Using various views to check your positioning, move the camera slightly below eye level and to the front. Choose Scene ⇨ Render ⇨ Low Resolution Preview to make sure the camera is positioned where you want it.

Step 5. Don't forget that you can load the Chess Wars file from the accompanying CD-ROM (found in the Chapter 13 folder). Use that file to experiment with various camera angles, moving them around and rendering at low resolution until you come up with something you like.

Figure 13-39 shows the newly created camera pointing at the airplane's bespectacled face.

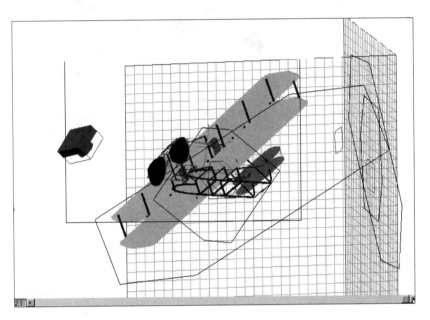

Figure 13-39: The new camera is pointing directly at the airplane's front.

Advanced users of 3D programs will howl that we have not discussed the Hot Point, which is the adjustable focus point on which any camera or light will focus. Yes, it can be moved and edited. This topic is covered in the next chapter.

Figure 13-40 shows the rendered version of the airplane in Chess Wars. A light was added, directed primarily at the glasses. This was done by selecting the Create Light tool from the toolbar and placing it in Perspective One. In the next chapter, you'll explore light positioning. You'll also learn about hierarchy, how to create objects from the tools in the toolbar, and how to join objects with the Numerical Properties dialog box. You'll also work further with this picture, adding text and changing the backdrop.

Figure 13-40: The rendered version of the airplane.

Summary

▶ Scene Wizard templates give you more than just while-you-wait instant 3D pictures. You can work on them to come up with exciting, original scenes.

▶ Perspective windows show different points of view of existing cameras.

▶ When you position an object in one perspective window, be sure to keep an eye on how it moves in the other windows.

▶ The Virtual Trackball rotates the angle of objects in three-dimensional space.

▶ By following the steps explained in this chapter, you can create an interesting and unique scene using Dream 3D.

Chapter 14

Advanced Dream 3D Techniques

In This Chapter

In this chapter you learn about:

- ▶ Using the Hierarchy window
- ▶ Adding text to scenes
- ▶ Editing shaders and shader channels
- ▶ Using the Alignment and Numerical properties dialog boxes
- ▶ Adding backdrops
- ▶ Using the Render Area, hot points, and the 3D Paint tool
- ▶ Creating objects from scratch in the Modeling window
- ▶ Duplicating with Symmetry
- ▶ Importing 3D objects into CorelDraw and Photo-Paint
- ▶ Rendering Dream 3D projects with Geometrical Channel information

The Hierarchy Window

First, we'll look at an important window that is created along with the Reference window every time you begin a Dream 3D project. This is the Hierarchy window. The hierarchy is a diagrammatic arrangement of all the objects in your scene. You can view it as one of your windows, from the same menu you'd use to view a perspective window. (After opening a file, choose Window ⇨ Hierarchy of Doc X:X.) A file must be open before the Hierarchy windows appears. Now we'll complete the "Chess Wars" picture begun in the preceding chapter by adding text, and we'll bring text into the picture by using the hierarchy. By dropping the Text icon onto the hierarchy list, you can easily control where your new text object should go in relation to other objects. Remember that in Dream 3D, objects include lights, cameras, and models. Figure 14-1 shows the Text tool being dragged below Camera 4.

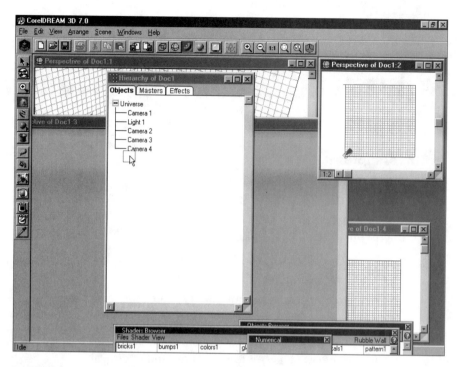

Figure 14-1: First drag the Text tool to the Hierarchy window.

After dragging the Text tool onto the main perspective window or the hierarchy, you'll see the Text dialog box. (See Figure 14-2.) It gives you control over letter bevel size, the depth of your text object, and the usual font control tools such as letter and word spacing. Remember, though, that your text object's depth can be controlled in the Perspective windows with the same tools you use to resize all objects.

Secret

When you are choosing a font size, here's a quick rule of thumb: Cut the font size in half, and you'll know your text object's approximate height in inches. The default text font size when you open the Text dialog box is 72. This setting creates a text object approximately 36 inches high.

After you've chosen your text and closed the dialog box (by clicking on the Done button), the hierarchy names your text object appropriately. (See Figure 14-3.)

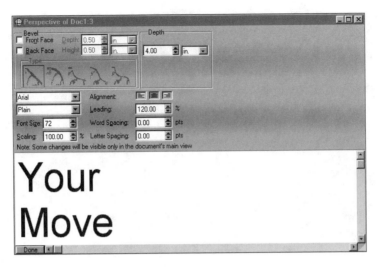

Figure 14-2: Use the Text dialog box to set various text attributes.

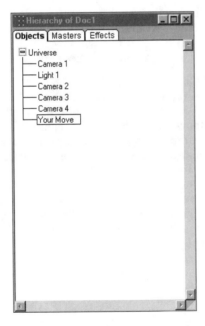

Figure 14-3: The hierarchy list now shows
the text you've added.

As you can see from Figure 14-4, objects you've just created initially appear
partially out of sight, or sometimes completely out of site from the main
Perspective window (Perspective of Doc1:1). We had to hunt through two
additional views to see where the text we created would be initially visible.

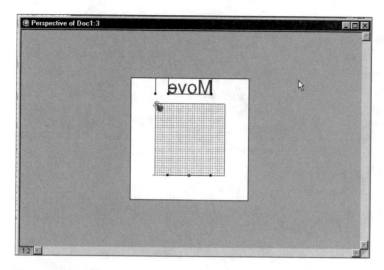

Figure 14-4: The text object just created initially appeared here on our screen.

Look at the window label in Figure 14-4. It says Perspective of Doc1:3. Now look back at the window label of the Text dialog box. It also says Perspective of Doc1:3. It should come as no surprise that this window is the only place you can initially locate the text object you have just created.

This text was actually created in its own scene, as we are creating it here, and then it was cut and pasted into the "Chess Wars" picture. We then decided to separate the words "Your Move" into two groups of letters and place the words at different distances from the camera. Figure 14-5 shows how initially the two words appeared one behind the other, unreadable when viewed from above. We had to change to another perspective window to select each group of letters and move them to a new position. (See Figure 14-6.) Note that Figure 14-6 also shows a camera added "front and center" to make it easier to know what you're viewing. One way to add a new camera is to choose the Camera tool from the toolbox and click and drag briefly in the Perspective window that most closely represents the angle you will be viewing from. Adding a new camera is a good way to experiment with different views. After you've repositioned the camera, select both it and the object at which you'll be pointing it. Choose Arrange ⇨ Point At, and your camera will face the object. See Figure 14-6.

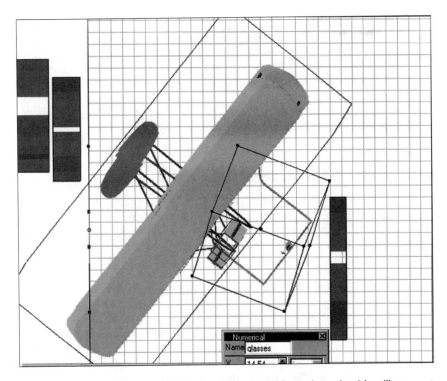

Figure 14-5: The letters appear as blocks when viewed from above, but it's still apparent that they need to be moved.

Figure 14-6: The "Chess Wars" letters have been added correctly. Note the camera front and center.

Tip

If the objects on your screen appear only as boxes or outlines of shapes, make sure View ⇨ Default Quality ⇨ Bounding Box is not selected. It's best to work with Preview or Better Preview quality. (Unless you have a very fast computer, Better Preview is too time-consuming for rendering in between quick edits.) Also, if you load the file "Your Move" in order to work alongside this project, you may not have the required font on your computer. If the letters appear blank, double-click on the outline of the letters and select a new font. You'll now be able to see the letters.

Coloring and Shading Text

Figure 14-7 shows the Shader Editor dialog box opened and one of the Glass shaders being selected. We could have instantly applied the preset color and texture to the text, but instead, we double-clicked on one of the Glass shaders, and the Shader Editor dialog box opened. Dream 3D gives you control over many aspects of the surfaces you create for your objects. That's because surfaces have more than just color qualities. Glass has varying degrees of reflectivity, light absorption, and texture, depending on the type of glass shading you wish to simulate. For this texture, we chose to merely adjust the quality of shininess when we applied the texture to the text. (See Figure 14-8.) To do so, simply click on the tab that represents the name of the texture feature you want to adjust. Turning up the Shininess slider causes a surface to reflect more of the light's color and brightness. Less of the object's innate color shows through.

Figure 14-7: The Shader Editor dialog box gives you control of surface qualities.

Figure 14-8: Adjust the shininess with the Shader Editor.

Figure 14-9 shows the process for applying a bitmap as your shader color. Once inside the Shader Editor, select Type ⇨ Texture Map, and click on the floppy disk icon. The Browse menu opens, enabling you to search your hard drive for a file to use as a bitmap. Dream 3D is capable of painlessly converting files of many types into color bitmaps for text objects.

You can make many more adjustments to shaders, such as controlling the surface texture or reflectivity of a surface with a bitmap image. (We explain some of these adjustments later in this chapter.) As you close the program, you're prompted to save the shader with its new adjustments as a separate file. You will then see the new shader in the dialog box with the preset sliders. Figure 14-10 shows the bespectacled airplane careening between the words Your Move, which have now been changed to a Calligraphy font and shaded with customized Glass and Wood textures. As you may recall from the preceding chapter, the bitmap background that has been applied to this scene will not be visible until you render the scene.

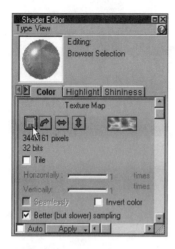

Figure 14-9: Choose a bitmap to color a text object.

Figure 14-10: The Chess Wars image has text modified, ready to be rendered.

Backdrops

Your backdrop or background image is not just wallpaper; it's an integral part of the scene. When you add a bitmap to a shader, you select Type ➪ Texture Map from the Shader Editor dialog box. Also, to create a backdrop for your scene from a picture in a different file format, you must select

Scene ➪ Backdrop and scroll down to the word *Map*. When rendering, Dream 3D precisely calculates how the chosen lighting setup will reflect on your backdrop or background. Light intensity, color, spread, elevation, and angle all interact with the objects to produce detailed lighting effects against your bitmap. Figure 14-11 shows the final Chess Wars rendered scene. The upper portion of the Chess Wars bitmap was removed in Photo-Paint and replaced with one of the Waterdrop Texture fills from Photo-Paint's presets. This edited backdrop creates a much more attractive image than the jaggy bitmap you get with a photograph.

Figure 14-11: The Final Chess Wars picture appears with text and chess pieces.

More Dream 3D Tools

Some helpful tools exist that you should know how to use to get the best results in Dream 3D. These tools include the Render Area tool and hot points. You'll also learn about the projections, which are the small rectangles you can see in the Reference window. Then there's the 3D Paint tool, which enables you to paint colors on an object while maintaining the object's lighting, curve, shadow, and reflective qualities.

The Render Area tool

Whenever you make a change to an object in your scene — whether it's adding a new shader or changing the distance between objects — it's useful to render just the area you have changed. To do so, click on the Render Area tool, found near the bottom of the toolbar, and drag a rectangle around the area you want to render. See Figure 14-12. Please note that, when you render the area, you won't see a new Window open up showing the preview, as when you click on Scene ⇨ Render and choose a setting. Rather, when you use Render Area, the new detailed view will appear in whatever Perspective you are working with at the moment.

Figure 14-12: The Render Area tool appears near the bottom of the toolbar.

Hot points

Every object in Dream 3D has a hot point. This is the small circle, usually in the middle of the object itself. The hot point is the point at which a light or a camera will face an object. It is also the reference point that the Numerical properties dialog box and the Alignment dialog box use to calculate distance measurements. The hot point is also the rotation axis. If you rotate an object 45 degrees, it will rotate around that point. If two objects are grouped, the hot point becomes the center of those two objects. You will always see the hot point as a small circle inside any object, as projected in your Perspective window.

You can move an object's hot point. For example, to simulate a batter swinging a baseball bat, the bat should appear to rotate at the point the batter's hands hold the bat, not at the exact center of the bat. You can drag an object's hot point anywhere you want. If you want a light or a camera to shine somewhere other than the direct center of that object, simply drag the hot point to the desired location.

Secret

An object's hot point can even be located outside the object itself.

Projections

While looking at the main perspective window, you've seen how each object in your window has a projection on both walls, and on the floor, if available. These projections serve to locate your object in 3D space. You can move each projection of the object as if it was the object itself. For example, if you need to move an object along its Y axis only, this is hard to perform on the object itself in the main perspective window. But dragging the projection of that object along the appropriate wall moves the object itself along the corresponding axis. The object's projection includes its hot point. If you need to move an object's hot point, sometimes it's easier to move its projection instead.

The 3D Paint tools

The 3D Paint tools enable you to paint directly on 3D objects. Applying a 3D Paint tool does not alter the lighting effects (such as shininess or glow qualities) that have been created around your object. When you paint with 3D Paint, you select a shader and a brush size (the Brush dialog box opens when you select the 3D Paint Brush tool) and begin applying paint to the chosen object. Dream 3D comes with Shape tools also, for applying paint in exact shapes. Because you are using shaders from the Shaders browser to select paint, you are not merely applying color; all the qualities of the chosen shader become part of the brush, such as bump, reflection, and shininess. (You may also use the Eyedropper tool to pick up a shader from an object already in your scene.)

Tutorial #1: Alien Visitors

For this project, you'll build 3D objects from scratch, place them in 3D space (as well as outer space), and render them against a background bitmap, adding some lighting to show off a 3D object's reflective surfaces.

Creating objects

Start with a new Dream 3D Empty Scene, and drag the Free Form tool (on the toolbar) into the Hierarchy window. Be sure you drag it into the Hierarchy window and not the main Perspective window.

You'll be taken to the Modeling window, shown in Figure 14-13, and prompted to name the object you are about to create. Name it "Alien." After doing so, you'll see the empty Cross Section plane (the darker blue mesh near the front of the box) and the Sweep plane (the lighter blue mesh that makes up the remainder of the box). You will draw on the Cross Section plane. However, to adjust how deep your object is (how long its Extrude path is), you'll adjust the pink line you see stretching halfway across the Sweep path. Notice that that pink line is actually visible on two sides of the model. That's because you can add different Extrusion paths for the different dimensions of your object. You can bend, curve, lengthen, or shorten those Sweep path description lines to make your object protrude or contort in various directions along its X and Y axes. The "Front" of your object, what you actually draw, is designed on the Cross Section plane, which is the front part of the Modeling window.

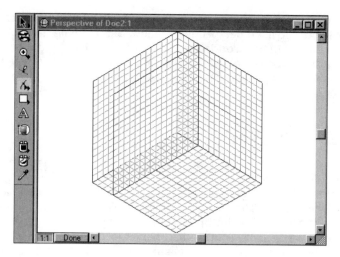

Figure 14-13: The Modeling window looks like this before anything is drawn on it.

Notice that the toolbar and the menu are different. The choices will revert to their original values when you leave the Modeling window (click on Done at the lower-left of the window).

Press and hold your mouse over the Rectangle tool (also on the toolbar), and select the Draw Rounded Corners Rectangle tool when it appears. Draw something similar to the shape that appears in Figure 14-14.

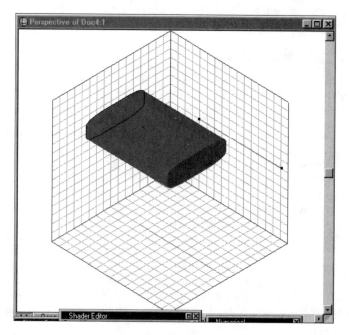

Figure 14-14: A shape is created with the Rounded Corners Rectangle tool.

Click on and hold the Convert Point tool until other icons appear. Select the plus sign, which is the Add Node tool. What you are doing is creating points at which your new object can bend and be curved. Otherwise, your options are limited to simply making the pink Extrusion path lines shorter or longer. Using the Add Node tool, click on the upper Extrusion path line to create new nodes, as shown in Figure 14-15.

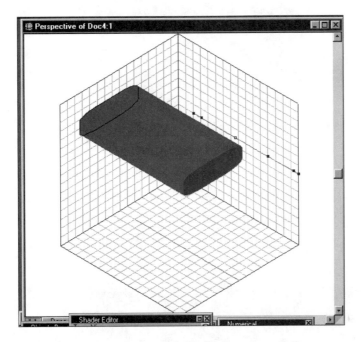

Figure 14-15: New nodes are added to the Extrusion path line.

Select Geometry ⇨ Extrusion Envelope ⇨ Symmetrical, and shape the lines as shown in Figure 14-16. This option enables you to create an object with two parallel paths while drawing only one, much as drawing half of a wine glass and holding it up to a mirror reproduces the other half of the glass. You'll need to select the Bézier tool, using it just as you would in CorelDraw, to bring curvature qualities to the lines. This gives the object a more rounded, less boxy quality. Use the Selection tool, still found at the top of the toolbar, to move the nodes, and hence, to move the lines. Notice that the object reflects every change you make to the lines. Don't worry if the lines you move appear to overlap with the object. They exist on two different planes, just like in science fiction stories.

What about the other pink line at the lower part of the mesh box? This is the other Sweep Path Description line; it can be used to create protrusions and shape changes along the X coordinates, "moving away from or closer to" the front of the screen. Figure 14-17 shows how to adjust these lines to add a more snazzy, sports car appeal to our alien vehicle.

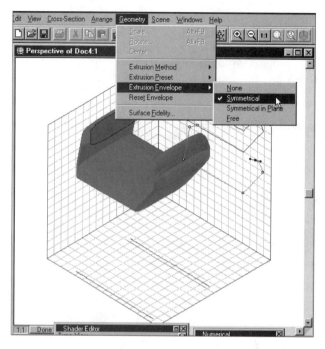

Figure 14-16: Adjust the extrusion lines with the symmetrical extrusion.

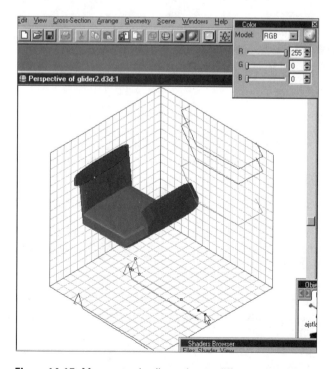

Figure 14-17: Move extrusion lines along a different plane.

Click on Done to return to the Perspective windows.

Using the Numerical properties dialog box

Our alien ship looks a bit thick, so we'll make it shorter — decrease its Z axis size by using the Numerical properties dialog box. To open the Numerical properties dialog box, right-click on an object while it's selected, and select Numerical Properties. Figure 14-18 shows the Numerical properties dialog box next to the alien ship. When one object is selected, the Numerical properties dialog box displays the XYZ coordinates of the object — where it is located in your scene. You'll also see the Yaw, Pitch, and Roll coordinates, which indicate the degree of rotation in any direction. At the bottom of the Numerical properties dialog box is the size of the object, again expressed in XYZ coordinates. Your job here is to decrease the Z parameter of the ship — make it shorter from top to bottom. To do this, you must uncheck the Keep Proportion check box, which is checked by default. (Look again at Figure 14-18, where the mouse pointer is.) Doing this makes the ship sleeker but keeps the width and depth the same.

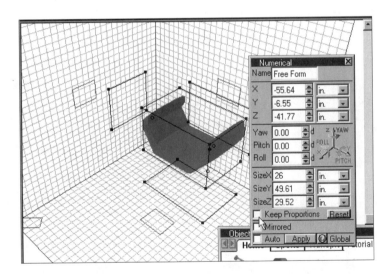

Figure 14-18: Use the Numerical properties dialog box to change only the height of an object.

Creating shaders from scratch

We want to color our alien ship with something totally different. To do this, let's create our own shader. Select Shader Browser ⇨ File ⇨ New, and the dialog box shown in Figure 14-19 appears. You must name your shader before doing anything else. To make it easier to keep all the materials used for this project together, name the shader "Alien."

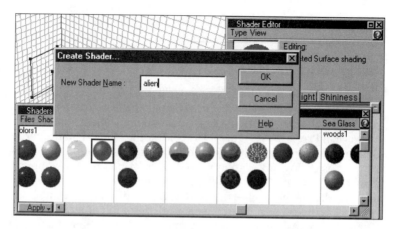

Figure 14-19: Give the shader a new name in the New Shader Name field of the Create Shader dialog box.

Select Shader Editor ⇨ Type ⇨ Texture Map, as shown in Figure 14-20, and open a picture file you'd like to use.

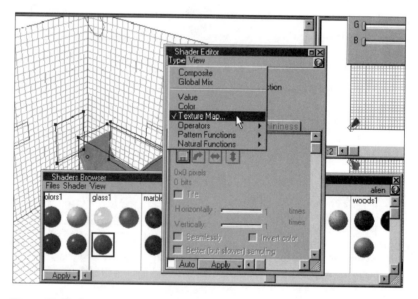

Figure 14-20: Create a new shader by using a bitmap.

Shader Editor channels

Having selected a bitmap for the shader color, we've only just begun. The Shader Editor contains many channels. If you are familiar with Pixar Typestry or RenderMan technology, then you'll know what we mean here. You can use colors or pictures to adjust many qualities of the shader. For example, if you drag any compatible bitmap (.BMP, .CPT, .TIFF, and so forth) onto the Shader Editor's Bump channel (see Figure 14-21), that picture will be broken down into its shades of gray, and the information will only be used to create higher or lower bumps (raised or embossed areas) in your picture. Think of the process as resembling a Photo-Paint mask using a picture to create different levels of masking protection. Similarly, if you drag a picture and drop it onto the Shader Editor's Shininess channel, that picture will be used to determine how shiny certain areas of your surface will be. If you select a color, or a gradient, the color pixels involved will be converted to gray scale and applied accordingly. The tabs on the Shader Editor access channels for Color, Highlight, Shininess, Bump, Reflection, Transparency, Refraction, and Glow.

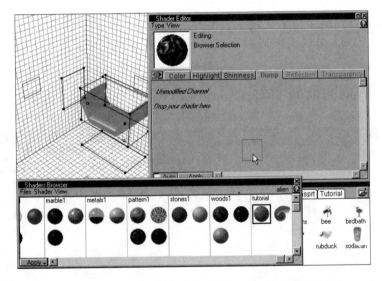

Figure 14-21: A bitmapped being is dragged into the Shade Editor's Bump channel.

Figure 14-22 shows the alien ship after applying a newly created shader. After you've created a shader, it is applied just as easily as the presets.

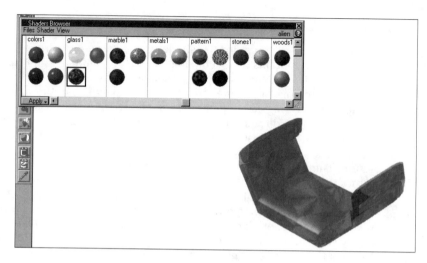

Figure 14-22: The new shader is applied to the alien ship.

Duplicating objects

No alien ship would go on a dangerous journey alone, so let's create some friendly company. While a ship is selected, click on Edit ➪ Duplicate, and use the Virtual Trackball in various Perspective windows to reposition the newly created ships in a pleasantly random pattern. (See Figure 14-23.)

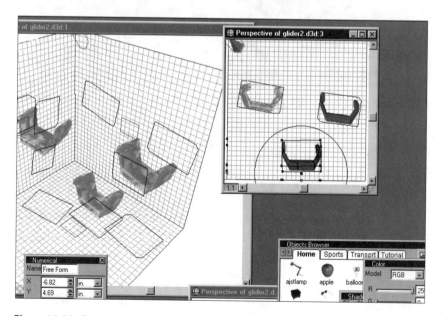

Figure 14-23: Duplicate and rotate the alien ship.

Adding a new light

Let's add a new light near Camera 4. This is easiest to do by dragging the New Light tool onto the Hierarchy window and dropping it near your preferred position. (See Figure 14-24.) Because you are adding the light near a known camera, you should have less trouble finding where the light shines its beam. Look for the outline of a red rectangle on the wall opposite where the light is positioned. If the beam is directly hitting an object, you'll see the outline of a red rectangle on the object itself. Double-click on the light to open the dialog box for changing the light's qualities, such as color, drop-off rate, and brightness.

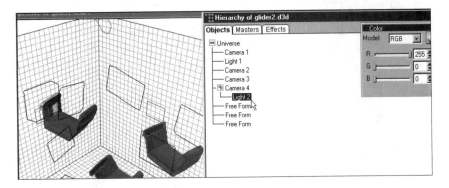

Figure 14-24: Add a new light to enliven the alien ships.

Preparing to render the picture

Don't forget to set up your Production Frame to limit the scope of the rendered image to things you really want to see. Figure 14-25 shows the Production Frame centered snugly around the three ships. Tightening up the field of vision will create an illusion of depth. We chose an "into the cave" backdrop bitmap to accent that effect further. Figure 14-26 shows the final rendered "Alien Visitors" image.

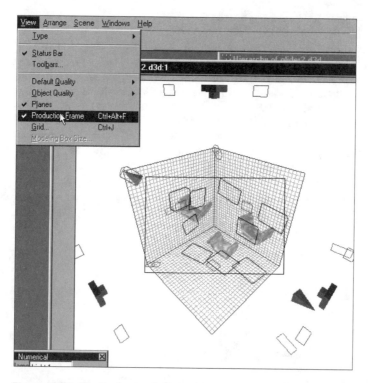

Figure 14-25: The Production Frame tightens its noose around the alien visitors.

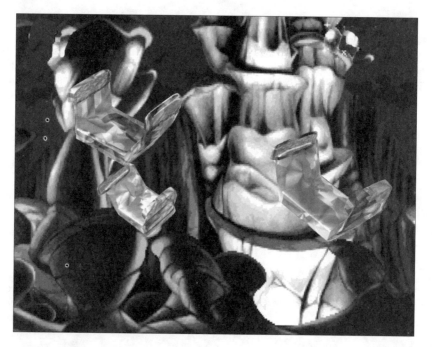

Figure 14-26: Alien Visitors is complete.

Tutorial #2: "Beer and TV"

In this project, you'll use the Alignment dialog box to reposition objects and cameras to obtain the best viewing distance and angle for a scene.

The Alignment dialog box

The objects shown in the following figures are from the Objects browser. They are all found under the Home tab of the Objects browser. (If the Objects browser is not visible, select Windows ⇨ Objects Browser.) Included in this project are TV, sodacan, and ajstlamp.

Figure 14-27 shows the unfortunate results of placing a camera too close to some objects to be rendered. The large rectangle to the right of Beer and TV is the camera. It's not supposed to be nearly that close. The upper screen shows a quick rendering of what that camera sees: just the TV screen. How can we mathematically move the camera farther to the right (the Y axis) without changing the up and down (Z axis) angle?

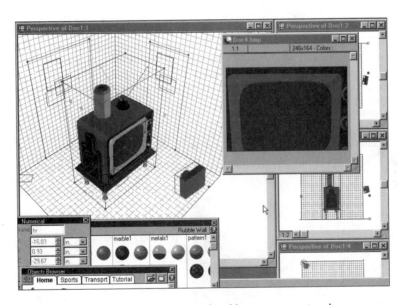

Figure 14-27: Beer and TV has been rendered by a camera set up by someone who's probably had too much of both.

Select Arrange ⇨ Align Objects, and the dialog box shown in Figure 14-28 appears. With both the camera and the TV selected, choose the Y Axis using the downward arrow to select which plane to adjust. You'll see a check box in which to select the type of alignment to use, as well as a data box to input the distance involved. In Figure 14-28, *Space* was selected as the type of alignment, and *170 inches* was selected for the distance. This method confines our movement to only the chosen axis, which is important when adjusting camera positions.

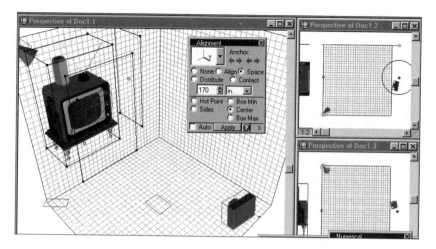

Figure 14-28: Adjust the camera distance via the Alignment dialog box.

Figure 14-29 shows the use of the Alignment dialog box to place the can precisely on the television. Clicking on the right-facing arrow expands the Alignment dialog box to show X, Y, and Z coordinates as completely adjustable, as they are shown here. By inputting distances in the data boxes for each coordinate, and putting a check in the check box indicating which type of alignment is required, you can place the can exactly where it should be on the television.

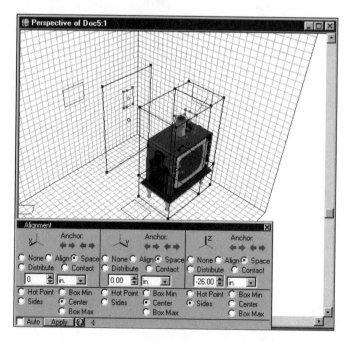

Figure 14-29: Use the expanded Alignment dialog box to position the can.

Figure 14-30 shows a lamp that will be positioned on the television also. But the way the lamp is angled now, it will face backward. We need to rotate it so that it faces at a nice, forward, casual angle. We will input a value in the Alignment dialog box to rotate the lamp on its Y axis, or Yaw.

Figure 14-31 shows the lamp rotated, and a new Yaw value of 120 degrees is shown in the data box. Although the results might not appear earth-shattering at the moment, we are trying to predict what the objects will look like when positioned on the TV.

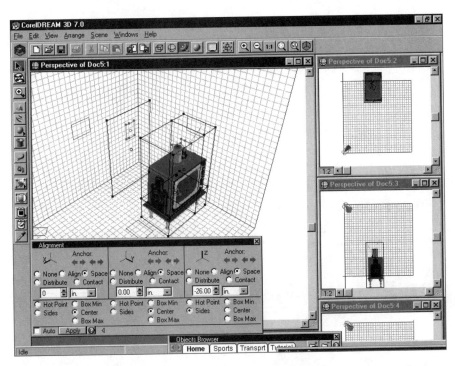

Figure 14-30: The lamp is ready to rotate on its Y axis (Yaw) so that it faces appropriately.

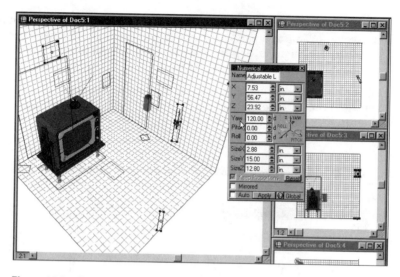

Figure 14-31: The lamp has been rotated with a new Yaw value.

Locating objects with the Numerical properties dialog box

Figure 14-32 shows the TV being rendered at a very unflattering angle. What we know is that the camera is quite far below the TV level, so this Camera 4 has a Z coordinate below zero, very far below zero.

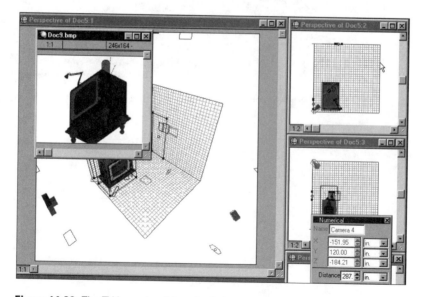

Figure 14-32: The TV is rendered from far below ground level.

Figure 14-33 shows that the camera, once located, has a Z value of –184.21 inches. Note the Perspective window on the bottom right, labeled Perspective of Doc5:3. This is the window that would most naturally provide a view of the missing camera. But as you can see, no camera icon appears in that Perspective window. The camera must indeed be quite far below the TV level. (To access the Numerical properties dialog box of any object, right-click on it and select Numerical properties.)

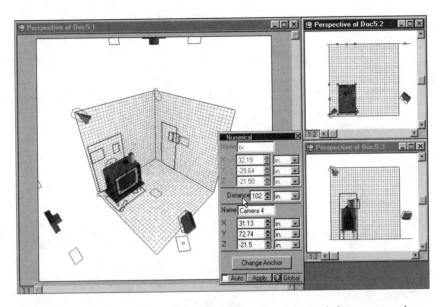

Figure 14-33: The Numerical properties dialog box shows the rendering camera to have coordinates well below eye level.

Let's fix this problem. In this instance, we've grouped two objects and then selected Arrange ⇨ Align Objects. (Remember, all the objects' options will be unavailable unless two or more objects are selected and unless you've made some numerical change or checked one of the data boxes in the Alignment dialog box.)

Note that in Figure 14-34, the dialog box shows location coordinates for the TV, below which appear location coordinates for Camera 4. In between is the distance separating the two objects, measured from their hot points. Figure 14-34 shows Camera 4's new Z coordinate of –22 inches to be adequate, for the camera has come into view in Perspective window 3. In fact, now the camera's Z coordinate is the same as the TV's. Also, by looking at the distance measurement, we can see that almost all of the distance between the camera and the TV lies along the Y plane, meaning that the camera is directly across from the face of the TV.

Look again at the numbers in both data box groups: the numbers for the TV and the numbers for Camera 4. You can see that, adding the TV's –29.64 inches along the Y coordinate to the Camera's 72.64, you'll come up with a distance value that matches the one in the Alignment dialog box. That means that the camera and the TV are in the same place, except for their position along the Y axis; they are "right across from each other," at a distance of 102 inches. This is a nice camera position, and it rendered the picture shown in Figure 14-35.

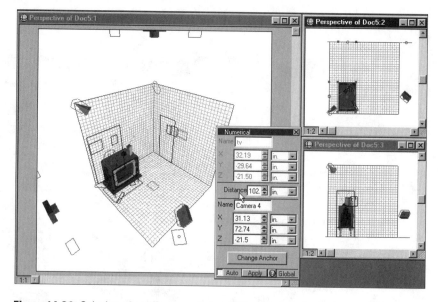

Figure 14-34: Calculate the differences between the numbers in the Numerical properties dialog box to properly position the camera in relation to the TV.

Figure 14-35: The rendered TV appears with ornaments.

Duplicating with Symmetry

Now you're going to create text, and you'll use the Duplicate with Symmetry command to create a mirror effect in the bitmap surface beneath the text.

Select the Text tool from the toolbar and drag it onto the main Perspective window. The Text dialog box appears. Type a short text entry in all capitals, and give the text the default Bevel amount by putting a check in the appropriate check box.

Close the Text dialog box, and the text will appear in the main Perspective window. We need to push the text high on the Z Axis. To do this easily, create a new view. While the text is selected, click on View ⇨ Type ⇨ Front, and position the text high on the wire mesh window. (See Figure 14-36.)

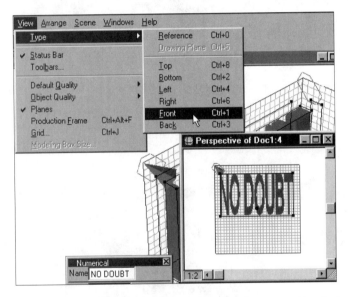

Figure 14-36: Use the Front submenu item to create a new, front-facing view to reposition text.

Stretch the text so that it reaches the entire length of the front-facing Perspective window you are using, and select Edit ⇨ Duplicate with Symmetry. Your text will be mirrored a few inches beneath it. (See Figure 14-37.)

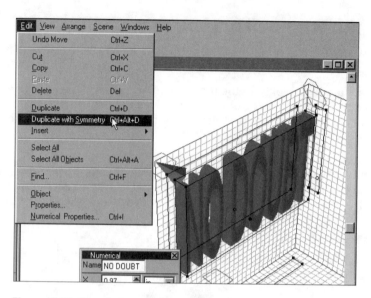

Figure 14-37: Stretch the text and select Duplicate with Symmetry.

Recolor the text using the Shaders browser. We used Stone from the Tutorial folder for the top text and Dark Wood from the Wood folder for the bottom. (See Figure 14-38.)

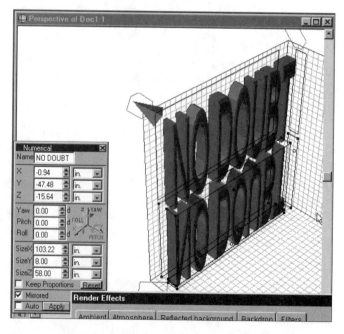

Figure 14-38: Each text instance has been enriched with selections from the Shaders browser.

Doing a fast render with the bitmap background, we found that the text tilted slightly to the left and did not create a believable "horizon" effect when rendered. In this case, you should group both text instances together and select the Numerical properties dialog box. This enables you to rotate them together on their Y axis until it matches the horizon. (See Figure 14-39.)

Figure 14-39: Rotate the grouped text instances so that they sit on the bitmap's horizon.

Now begins the arduous task of placing the text group exactly on the horizon. Figure 14-40 shows a quick rendering of the text against the bitmap. We're obviously way off here. Luckily, the Numerical properties dialog box is on hand to input changes in the Z coordinates, so we can get a direct hit . . . after a few misses, of course.

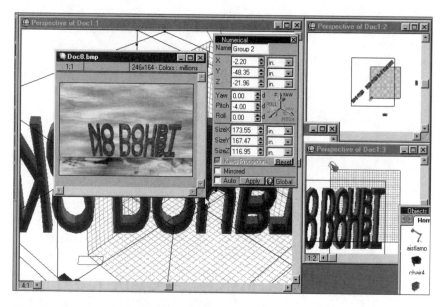

Figure 14-40: The Numerical properties dialog box helps position the text group exactly on the horizon, but it takes trial and error.

It's time to angle the bottom text portion a bit forward so that it appears to sit on the ground below the horizon, closer to the screen. To do this, you must ungroup the two text instances, and thus the rotating operation can be performed on the bottom text object only. (See Figure 14-41.) A negative value must be entered into the Roll data box to project text forward on its X axis. You may have to move the text object's hot point in order to rotate the text object on a new rotation point. That's because, depending on how your text objects are positioned, rotating them on the default "center" rotation point may not properly adjust the letters.

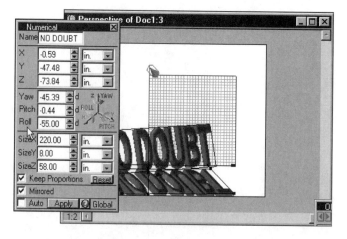

Figure 14-41: Rotate the bottom text on its X axis after ungrouping.

Figure 14-42 shows the final image to demonstrate Duplicate with Symmetry. We've succeeded, no doubt?

Figure 14-42: No Doubt.

Expert Advice

Here are some general tips to keep in mind as you're learning to use Dream 3D:

- **Using alpha channels.** When you save your rendered scene as a .CPT or .TIFF file, the objects in your scene are saved as Alpha channels and will open in all "alpha-aware" programs as selected masks. That means you can apply layering, photoediting, and painting techniques to the objects alone, even after they are saved in non-3D formats. However, if you save your rendered 3D artwork as a .TIFF file and then try to open that .TIFF file in a program that doesn't support Alpha channels, such as Paint Shop Pro 3, the file will not open.

- **Check your scratch disk.** If you have more than one hard drive, and if one of your drives is either much faster or less cluttered than the others, choose the fastest and emptiest hard drive for your scratch disk. The temp files Dream 3D creates are enormous. Give the program lots of room. We have found Dream 3D to behave well even using compressed drives created with Microsoft Drive Space 3, a benefit that we were not expecting. So Dream 3D seems to just appreciate the room to stretch, any way it can get it.

- **Use the Save Workspace feature.** We've spoken about the confusion that can occur while you are trying to organize your Perspective windows. Also, at times, the Hierarchy window, shader, and Objects browsers can get themselves stuck in a corner that's nearly impossible to reach. After you've arranged your windows in a way that seems productive to you, click on File ⇨ Save Workspace. From now on, any time you begin a new project or open an older one, the windows will open in the pattern you saved as a workspace.

- **Use Show Axis Information.** If it's hard for you to remember the directions or dimensions represented by the XYZ coordinates, select File ⇨ Preferences ⇨ Show Axis Information. This causes a small XYZ diagram to be placed at the foot of the selected object. This diagram helps orient you as to which way is which.

- **Work with deformers.** Dream 3D includes tools that can twist, bend, and stretch 3D objects for some very interesting effects. Figure 14-43, Earthquake Art, shows one of the basic Scene Wizards (Indoor Scene ⇨ Indoor Templates ⇨ Open Door) with a Bend and Twist deformer applied. To accomplish this, group all the objects you want to deform. Right-click on the group and select Properties. Choose the Deformer tab, and change the drop-down menu that initially reads "none." Select Bend and Twist from the Deformer list. Choose which axis to deform, and adjust the sliders until you are happy with the results as shown in the preview panel. The Shatter option also brings interesting results when applied in small percentages with the slider.

Figure 14-43: Earthquake Art illustrates the effects of the Bend and Twist deformer on one of the basic Scene Wizards.

■ **Drag and drop vector-type files directly into Dream 3D.** Drag the Free Form tool from the toolbar into the Reference window and drag to create a small box. The window automatically changes to the Modeling window. You can then drag any vector file (.CDR, .WMF, and so forth) onto the Modeling Box, to extrude and edit as you would any other Dream 3D file. Figure 14-44 shows a company logo created in CorelDraw. Figure 14-45 shows the same logo rendered as a 3D object and included in a Dream 3D scene.

Figure 14-44: A logo created in CorelDraw.

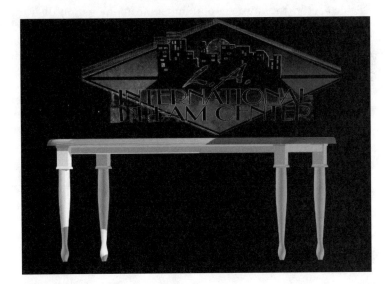

Figure 14-45: The same logo has been rendered as a 3D object and included in a Dream 3D scene.

Importing 3D Models into CorelDraw

CorelDraw can import 3D Model (.3DMF) files. Once opened in Draw, they can be rotated or viewed from different angles, and lights can be added, just as if you were still working in a 3D program. CorelDream 3D's native file format (.d3d) cannot be opened or imported directly into Draw. But any project you are working on in CorelDream can be saved as a .3DMF file and further manipulated and adjusted in Draw. CD #3 of your CorelDraw set comes with many .3DMF objects that can be opened and worked with in Draw. (In CorelDraw, select File ⇨ Import, and locate the 3DMF file you want to work with. After importing, you'll see a special set of tools for working with imported 3D objects.) However, you are not limited to importing single models. Entire scenes that include several objects, with lights and cameras, can be imported into Draw, without losing their 3D qualities. Objects will still respond accurately to camera position change, and surfaces will respond to lighting adjustments true to their texture and shape. While Draw's 3D toolbox and Property Bar choices are not full-featured, it's nice to have a few options at your disposal. This is quite an improvement over importing your 3D work into Draw as a 2D bitmap, and then finding out that the results are too dark and that there's nothing you can do about it. It's still best, however, to design and arrange as much as possible in Dream 3D, and then save your image as a .3DMF file and open it in Draw.

Some scenes, such as the City Block 3D Model, require more room than the default two-inch square workspace that 3D scenes are imported into. To change the size of both the workspace and the 3D model itself, increase the Scale Factor (the third set of numbers from the left on the Property Bar, set by default at 100 percent; see Figure 14-46). These numbers will be available as long as you see the thick, "shaded" bounding box around your 3D model (this shaded bounding box indicates that you are currently editing an object native to another program, such as a bitmap, a spreadsheet, or in this case, a 3D model). Adjusting the Scale Factor, as explained previously, increases the size of the object itself, but not your *relative distance* to it. To make the object appear closer, use the Camera Walk camera to move the viewing camera closer to the 3D model. (See Figure 14-47, which shows the 3D Toolbox in Draw.)

Figure 14-46: The 3D Property Bar allows you to change the scale of your image.

Figure 14-47: The CorelDraw 3D Toolbox.

Cameras and lights

Please note that when using Draw's 3D Model tools, you can have only one camera, but you can add as many lights as you like. Figure 14-48 shows a 3D model city block with two lights added for interesting shading. You can make the light icons invisible by clicking on the Display Light icons button on the Property Bar. When the city block is rendered and becomes part of your standard Draw workspace, the large light icons you see here (the bowl-shaped objects at either end of the city block) will not appear. Many unique views can be explored by zooming and panning camera angles, adding lights, and changing their colors and positions. These are true 3D objects, so the surfaces will respond accurately when you change such features in your scene. Figure 14-49 shows the same city block at a closer camera angle with more dramatic lighting, all of which have been added in CorelDraw itself, not Dream 3D.

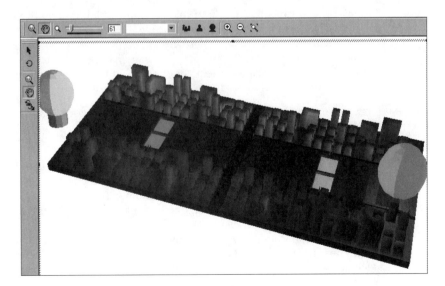

Figure 14-48: The city block 3D model, with two colored lights added.

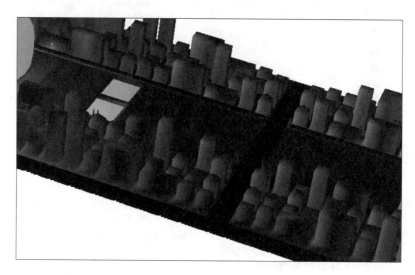

Figure 14-49: City Block with a closer camera setting.

Double-clicking on a light icon that appears in your scene changes the Property Bar to reveal setting options specifically for the light you clicked on. Click on Distant/Ambient to open the Illumination dialog box (see Figure 14-50), which allows you to change the type of light you are using (Distant, Point, Spot). Other features, such as light color, fall-off amount, and brightness, can be edited here. The Send to Back button allows you to illuminate your object with a light from behind, which creates a glow around it. On the Property Bar, click on the Add Light icon to add a light to your scene. It will immediately be added and appear selected, so you can move it around as you see fit. With any light, you can change its type (the light icon in the scene will change to reflect the type of light you've created), fall-off amount, brightness, and position.

Secret

For an interesting effect, try changing the light color, adding a new light with a different color, positioning it opposite the first light, and rotating the 3D object to expose more reflective surfaces.

Regarding cameras, there is no onscreen camera icon. Any changes you make to the camera settings will affect the single camera. To change camera position, click on the Camera Flyout tool on the 3D Toolbox (only available when a 3D object is being edited in Draw), and choose a camera type. Your mouse will then represent that camera's position. Click and drag in the 3D scene itself to see the 3D scene from a new perspective. Click on the Display Home Grid icon (found near the middle of the Property Bar when the 3D Object Selector tool is selected) to show a 3D "floor" for your scene. Use this floor to predict how objects will recede into 3D space, as shown in Figure 14-51.

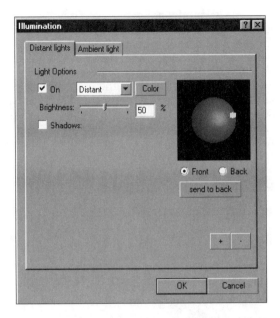

Figure 14-50: The lighting (Illumination) dialog box. Here you can change lighting features such as color and brightness.

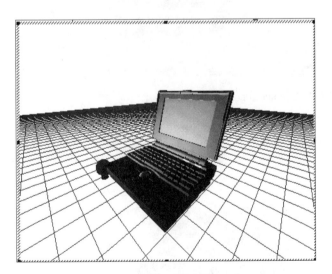

Figure 14-51: This 3D "floor," not visible in your final rendering, will be displayed when you click on the Display Home Grid icon.

Figure 14-52 shows a simple 3D model imported into Draw. Several tools appear on the toolbox on the left, and the Property Bar offers a set of options for each. As mentioned earlier, you may add a light to the scene, choosing from three different types. You can reposition the object within the scene boundaries using the Hand tool. Chose a camera to change the viewing angle, zoom factor. Figure 14-53 shows the use of the Object Rotate tool to rotate a camera, much as you'd use the Virtual Trackball in Dream 3D. Camera options on the Property Bar include the ability to change the camera's top, bottom, front, back, right or left view. Use the hand icon on the toolbox to reposition the object in the scene, and use one of the cameras to change your view of it.

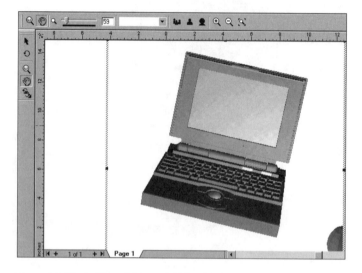

Figure 14-52: A 3D model imported into Draw.

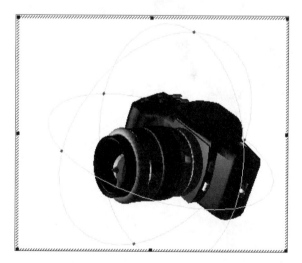

Figure 14-53: Use the Object Rotate tool to quickly change your view of an object.

Increasing workspace size

If you are using any of the Camera tools (Camera Pan, Camera Walk, Camera Rotate) to adjust your view of a 3D scene, you may notice that your objects quickly become larger than your scene workspace allows. To manually increase the size of the workspace, drag the bounding box corners. You'll now have more room to rotate and position your objects.

Tip

You can use the numeric X and Y coordinates displayed on the Property Bar to reposition objects with more accuracy, rather than drag them around your scene.

Rendering the 3D model in CorelDraw

While editing your 3D model in CorelDraw, you'll notice a thickened box outlining the 3D scene. 3D Objects can be moved around inside this scene, and, as mentioned previously, you can use the bounding boxes surrounding the scene to make it larger or smaller.

When you click outside the scene, the object will be rendered. CorelDraw will begin to shade in the objects, the light icon will disappear, and you'll get a good idea what your 3D model will look like as part of your entire Draw project. After the 3D model is rendered, you can move it around the page, resize it, skew it, and rotate it, just as with any other Draw object. You cannot change its shape with the Node tools, nor can you select part of it and fill it with a new color, as you would be able to do with a true Draw object. You can convert the 3D model to a bitmap (Bitmaps ⇨ Convert to Bitmap) and use Draw's bitmap filters, as found under the Bitmap menu. After an object is converted to a Bitmap, you cannot edit it as a 3D model again.

If you again would like to edit your 3D model in 3D, right-click on it and choose Edit in 3D. You'll again see the 3D tools to your left, and the Property Bar will change accordingly.

Secret

Moving back and forth between 3D editing and rendering is very memory-intensive. The wait time required for Draw to render the 3D model could be considerable. Also, when you minimize CorelDraw and work momentarily with another program, Draw will render the 3D model, whether you clicked outside the scene space or not.

When you incorporate a 3D model as part of your Draw project, you'll find that text will wrap around the rectangular bounding box surrounding the object, but text cannot be made to wrap closely around the shape itself, as you could do with an object created in Draw. However, you can place text on top of the object, as shown in Figure 14-54. The phrase "Such a Deal" was created as artistic text in Draw, rotated in a frame, and positioned as part of the computer screen. To rotate the artistic text frame, simply click twice on the frame, and then rotate by dragging on any corner. The cursor becomes the double-arrowed rotation symbol. You can also input numbers in the Angle of Rotation data box on the Property Bar. Figure 14-55 shows an exploded version of the text frames and laptop, revealing how they were combined to create the "text-on-the-laptop-screen" illusion.

Figure 14-54: A Draw project incorporating a 3D model.

Figure 14-55: The rotated text, and text shadow, were placed on the laptop screen.

As long as the laptop image shown in the above figure has not been turned into a bitmap, you can always return to 3D editing and change the rotation in 3D space, add lights, or change its size. You'll notice that rotating an object in 3D space creates a more realistic effect than converting a 3D object to a bitmap and changing its shape or position that way.

Importing 3D Objects into Photo-Paint

You don't really import 3D models into Photo-Paint. You simply open them (File ➪ Open) as you would any other picture type. Like CorelDraw, only 3D Model files (.3DMF) can be opened. Photo-Paint offers a similar 3D scene workspace for manipulating 3D objects, lights, and cameras. In Photo-Paint, however, you must work with a small preview screen (see Figure 14-56), using the camera and positioning tools in a much smaller space. Once rendered, the effects are the same as when working with 3D models in Draw, the surfaces responding with clarity to camera angle, lighting, and texture. Unlike CorelDraw, however, after a 3D model is rendered in Photo-Paint, you cannot again return to a 3D mode for further editing. After closing the 3D Import dialog box with its tabs for adjusting the lighting and size of your 3D models, your model will appear as a new image in Photo-Paint. It will appear as an object, with its background entirely transparent. You can then drag the new object onto an existing Photo-Paint project or use this current Photo-Paint image to begin a new one.

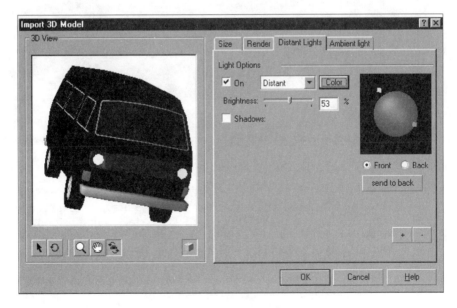

Figure 14-56: The Photo-Paint Import 3D preview screen.

Figure 14-57 shows a 3D model, Wine.3DMF opened in Photo-Paint. This model is found in your Dream3D folder (Corel\Graphics8\Dream3D\Samples) and is a .D3D file, which is Dream's native file type. But before being opened in Photo-Paint, it must be exported from Dream 3D as a .3DMF file. To facilitate this, open Wine.d3d in Dream and click on File ➪ Export, choosing .3DMF as the file type. You can then open this image in Photo-Paint. In this example, an additional light was added to the scene in Photo-Paint's Import 3D Model dialog box. This is done by clicking on the plus sign and moving the new light icon to a new location around the sphere. You can change the light's color and brightness, as well.

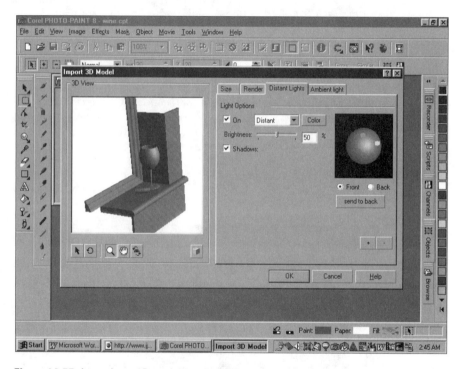

Figure 14-57: Importing a 3D model into Photo-Paint.

Figure 14-58 shows an image created in Photo-Paint by duplicating and applying filters to this 3D Wine model. To "stack" and position them as shown, the Order command was used often, so that none of the Wine copies would appear to be in front of the others. To quickly change the order of objects in Photo-Paint, select the object you want to reposition, and press Ctrl+Page Up to move the object forward in the sequence, and press Ctrl+Page Down to demote the object. Several of these Wine 3D models look a bit like line drawings. These were treated with the Find Edges filter (Effects ➪ 2D Effects ➪ Find Edges).

Figure 14-58: An image created by duplicating and arranging 3D models in Photo-Paint.

Figure 14-59 shows a Jet 3D model opened in Photo-Paint. The original model appears black when opened. By adding and repositioning new lights to the scene, you can reveal more texture and shape inherent in the 3D models. To add new lights to a 3D scene in Photo-Paint, open a 3D model to bring up the Import 3D Model dialog box, and click on the Distant Lights tab. Click on the plus sign, and a new light will be added to the scene, as evidenced by a yellow icon shown on a sphere, also found on the Distant Lights tab. Reposition the yellow icon around the sphere, and you'll see lighting qualities change on the object itself in the preview area. You can also use this dialog box to change the color and brightness of the light you've just created. To change the features of any other light, click on its yellow icon around the sphere and alter any lighting features you want.

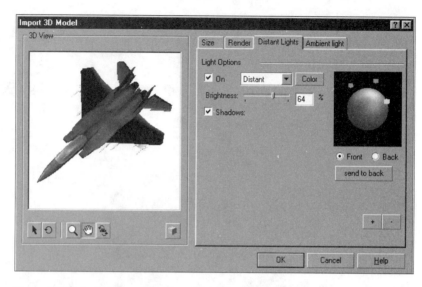

Figure 14-59: A Jet 3D model imported into Photo-Paint. Although the model appears poorly lit when imported, you can easily add and position new lights.

How 3D objects behave in Photo-Paint

3D models rendered in Photo-Paint become standard Photo-Paint objects. Unlike CorelDraw, the new object's boundaries will conform to the object itself, not to a rectangular bounding box that surrounds it. Please note that, in the completed jet portrait shown in Figure 14-60, the drop shadows accurately form around the edges of the jet planes themselves.

Figure 14-60: A portrait with 3D jet models. Note that the drop shadow follows the outline of the objects, not a rectangular boundary.

Photo-Paint backdrops for Dream 3D scenes

To import a complete Dream 3D scene into Photo-Paint, you must export your scene in Dream as a .3DMF file (File ⇨ Export) and then open it in Photo-Paint as described previously. Sometimes it's best, however, to simply use your Photo-Paint work as a background in Dream 3D (rather than import the Dream 3D scene). Environments rendered in Dream 3D are very realistic (such as fog and distance effects), and the shadow and texture effects generated in Dream 3D are more realistic than those in Photo-Paint. The image shown in Figure 14-61 was created using a Photo-Paint project as a background for 3D lettering and objects manipulated in CorelDream. The image was finished in Dream and exported as a .TIFF file. This image, however, was created with a flat Photo-Paint backdrop. In the following sections, we'll discuss the advantages of rendering in Dream 3D with reflected backgrounds.

Figure 14-61: An image created using a Photo-Paint background with Dream 3D objects.

Using Reflected Backgrounds

If you choose a reflected background (Scene ⇨ Background ⇨ Reflected Background tab) for rendering, then objects in your scene that have reflective values (marble, shiny wood surfaces) will reflect the background on their surfaces. Reflective backgrounds appear more like spheres than flat surfaces. Also, lights have a much more vibrant effect on a reflective background, and the reflective background will be visible beneath any transparent segments of your 3D objects. Your resulting image appears less flat.

Secret

For a reflective background to work, you must disable any normal backdrop you are using by selecting Use Background in the Background or Backdrop dialog box (Scene ⇨ Background or Scene ⇨ Backdrop).

To use a bitmap file as a reflected background, click on Scene ⇨ Background and choose the Reflected Background tab, and then choose Map from the drop-down menu. The bottom option is Map. Click on it to reveal a dialog box for opening a picture file on your computer to use as a reflected background. Reflected backgrounds are sometimes called Environmental Maps because not only is the color information used in the background, but the intensity of each color is used to determine the reflectivity of the surface.

Please remember that using a reflective background for rendering your scene is not the same as creating a reflective channel for a shader. (Double-clicking on any shader in the Shader Browser reveals a dialog box with tabs for adjusting features such as bumpiness and reflectivity. Adding reflective surfaces to shaders would not be applied to a background, but rather to any surface to which you apply the shader.)

Rendering with Geometry Channel Information

In Dream 3D you can render your picture with extra channels attached. These channels can be opened in Photo-Paint later, converted to masks, and used as a template for additional editing, such as adding fog, new lighting effects to the brightest or darkest points in your picture, or effects that will accent the distance between foreground and background in your picture. Some of these masks (called G-buffer channels because they contain exact geometrical information) are simple "cut-outs" that separate background material from 3D objects, allowing you to edit only one or the other. Other channel information is much more complex, such as the Surface Coordinate channel, which enables you to specifically create new texture effects for your 3D objects. (Remember that you must convert a channel to a mask before applying its affects.)

These channels have no effect on your project while working in Dream 3D. They are created when you render your picture as a bitmap or .CPT file (Scene ⇨ Render ⇨ Use Current Settings). There are six types of optional G-buffer channels (Scene ⇨ Render Settings ⇨ File Format ⇨ G Buffer; see

Figure 14-62), and you may select those which may be of use to you later. Simply place a check mark by the type of channel you want saved with your image. For example, if you want to create clouds that appear to hang in between your objects, then click on the 3D Position channel. Then load this channel in Photo-Paint and create clouds in this channel. When applied, the clouds you create will appear to be suspended between the objects rather than plastered on top of everything else. (Figure 14-63 shows the various channels available when you save an image as such. The mouse cursor is shown transforming the channel into a mask, which is necessary to see the effects.)

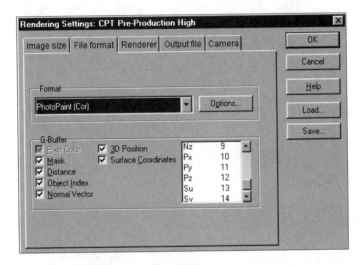

Figure 14-62: You can select G-buffers from the File format tab of the Render Settings dialog box.

Likewise, load the Distance channel in Photo-Paint to create a blurring effect, which makes your vanishing point more realistic in your final picture. The Normal Vector channel stores information about which direction the objects in your picture are facing. So, if you were to add new lighting effects, load this channel, and apply them there. This technique is far superior than simply turning up the brightness in certain segments of your picture. That's because these G-buffer channels contain graduated information, creating masks that vary in degrees of protection. Except for the Mask channel, they are not simple cutouts.

Figure 14-63: When you open an image with G-buffers in Photo-Paint, several new channels will appear in the Channels docker.

Keeping track of G-buffer channels

When you open your image in Photo-Paint or some other editing program, the channels will be labeled by number, not by type. To keep track of which channel is which, the File format tab of the Render Settings dialog box (in Dream 3D) lists each channel according to its number and type. Just match the channel number in Photo-Paint with the channel type as it appears here in this list. For example, when you save an image as CPT Pre-Production, as shown in the Render Settings dialog box, the Distance Channel is Channel #5. When you open Photo-Paint, clicking on the Channel Manager docker reveals all the saved channels. You'll see a reminder that pressing Alt+8 will select this particular channel.

Remember, to make a channel operative, you must change it into a mask (click on the Channel to Mask icon at the bottom of the Channel docker) before applying it. Depending on the type of channel information you are working with at the moment, you can either change the mask first and then alter and edit the channel using a special effect or a brush, or change the channel to a mask right before applying the mask to your image. In the following examples, we applied the mask information by copying the mask to the Clipboard and pasting it back onto the image, making sure we had the RGB Channel icon selected when we pasted it.

Figure 14-64 shows the effects of painting Photo-Paint's Cubist brush onto Channel 6 (Press Alt+9), which is the Object Index channel. This channel keeps track of the distance between your 3D objects. Notice that when you apply the channel, the brush strokes appear to occupy the same space as the objects on which they were applied. If you had not used channel information, you would merely have been painting on top of the entire image, with no 3D value.

Figure 14-64: Applying brush strokes painted onto a mask generated from Channel 6 spreads the strokes across the objects as they exist in your 3D environment.

Figure 14-65 shows the effects of applying Swirl brush strokes to the Distance channel (Channel 5; press Alt+8) and filling a Surface Coordinate channel with a bitmap fill. Remember that when you apply fills and brush strokes to channels, color information simply creates higher and lower areas of luminance, texture value, or whatever value that particular channel is controlling. In RBG images, color information is stored in the first three channels and has little to do with Dream 3D's special effects channels that we are discussing here.

Figure 14-65: Applying Swirl brush strokes to Channel 5, which is the Distance channel, makes the strokes recede appropriately into the background.

Secret

When choosing a file type for rendering, keep in mind that .PCX and .BMP files will not store channel information. Saving a file with Channel information as a .TIFF makes channel information available in a wide variety of photo-editing programs. If you know you are going to be doing more editing in Photo-Paint, save your work as a .CPT file, and your channels will follow the exact numbering sequence as shown in the Dream 3D Render Settings dialog box. Avoid saving more channels than you'll really use, because each channel increases file size and rendering time significantly.

More Fun with Dream 3D

If you've enjoyed dabbling in this basic introduction to Dream 3D, here's what we recommend you do next:

- Access the huge 3D clip art selection that comes with the CorelDraw CD-ROM. Import your own bitmaps as backgrounds, and experiment with building scenes.

- Experiment with creating objects with various extrusion methods. This chapter and the previous one have only touched on one such method, the Symmetrical Extrusion. There's much more to learn and apply.

- Learn to apply lights and cameras at interesting angles and with attractive color combinations.

- Import 3D modeling objects from other programs such as Ray Dream's Designer 4.2. Dream 3D allows importing standard .DXF modeled objects.

- Try the opening tutorial that comes with the CorelDraw 8 manual. It introduces many Dream 3D features in a short time.

Summary

In this chapter you learned how to:

▶ Create text and add it to an existing scene

▶ Use hot points and object projections

▶ Use the Hierarchy window

▶ Model 3D objects from scratch

▶ Use the Numerical properties dialog box

▶ Edit shaders and create them from scratch

▶ Use the Alignment dialog box

▶ Duplicate objects with symmetry

▶ Import 3D objects into CorelDraw

▶ Import 3D objects into Photo-Paint

▶ Render your Dream 3D projects with G-buffer channels

Part III

Utilities, Clip Art, and Templates

Chapter 15

Corel OCR-Trace

In This Chapter

You learn about:

▶ The OCR-Trace interface

▶ Tracing black-and-white bitmaps

▶ Tracing colored bitmaps

▶ Optical character recognition

The CorelDraw 8 package contains virtually everything you need to work with all types of graphics, including the two major graphics formats — vector and bitmap. As you've seen in earlier chapters, the primary application in the package, CorelDraw, provides everything you need to create and edit vector images. And Photo-Paint lets you perform all kinds of magic on paint-program bitmap images.

As Chapter 8 mentioned, vector and bitmapped graphics each have both benefits and limitations. For this reason, sometimes it's useful to convert bitmapped images to a vector graphics format. Bitmapped images, for example, are not easily resized without degrading image quality, and you can't always reshape and resize portions of bitmaps successfully. In addition, the lack of editable paths in paint-program images sometimes makes recoloring objects difficult.

Here's where the nifty utility OCR-Trace comes in handy. Basically, what OCR-Trace does is to trace — create outlines or paths — around objects in a bitmapped image. You can then make simple alterations to the paths (and their fills) in OCR-Trace, or you can import them into CorelDraw for a full range of vector image editing.

Sound too good to be true? Well, it's not. And this chapter shows you how to turn paint-program bitmap images into vector paths you can edit in CorelDraw. In addition to tracing bitmaps, OCR-Trace performs basic optical character recognition (OCR) functions. As you probably know, OCR is the process of turning scanned text pages into text that is editable by a word processor.

In this chapter we look at both tracing bitmaps and converting scanned text into editable text. Once you learn the secrets of this utility, OCR-Trace proves itself an extremely powerful tool to use along with your other business and graphic design applications.

The OCR-Trace Interface

In many respects, the OCR-Trace interface (shown in Figure 15-1) is virtually identical to that of CorelDraw and the other applications in the package. You can configure options and customize menus and toolbars the same way you do in CorelDraw. Many of the tools, including Zoom, Pan, and the Pick tool, work according to the same principles. Rather than rehashing material discussed elsewhere in this book, this chapter focuses on parts of the OCR-Trace interface that are different from the other CorelDraw 8 applications. Those are the tools used specifically for bitmap-tracing and OCR.

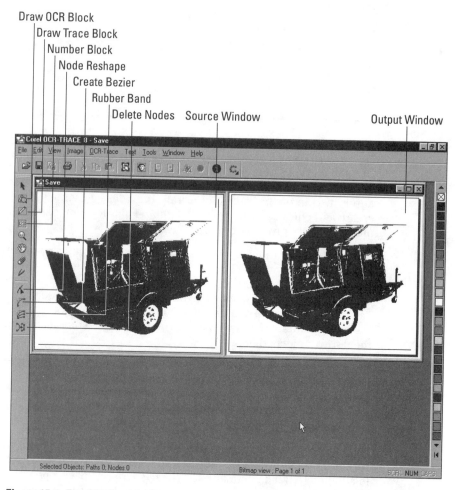

Figure 15-1: The OCR-Trace interface has many features in common with other CorelDraw 8 applications.

Here's an overview of the main features of the interface:

■ **The Source window** displays the image (or text, when performing OCR) to be traced.

■ **The Output window** displays the results of the trace or OCR procedure. You can also use this window to perform OCR-Trace's image editing functions, such as deleting paths, deleting notes, creating Béziers, erasing objects, and so on.

■ **The Draw Trace Block tool** enables you to define an area of a bitmap you want traced. This tool lets you pick and choose objects to be traced, eliminating the need to wait for the program to trace the entire image. This can be a big time saver, because large images can take quite some time to process. By selecting specific blocks to recognize, you don't have to edit portions of the scanned image you don't need. Figure 15-2 shows this tool in action.

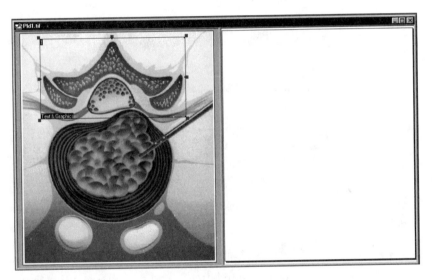

Figure 15-2: Use the Draw Trace Block tool to define areas in a bitmap image to trace.

■ **The Node Reshape tool** lets you edit nodes and Béziers in the Output Window. It works similarly to CorelDraw's Shape tool, discussed in Chapter 2.

■ **The Create Bézier tool** lets you add Bézier curves to the image in the Output window. It works similarly to the Bézier tool in CorelDraw, discussed in Chapter 2.

■ **The Rubber Band tool** lets you manipulate nodes and paths in an elastic fashion.

■ **The Delete Nodes tool** lets you delete nodes on paths. For information on the benefits and uses of deleting nodes, refer to the discussion of the Shape tool in Chapter 2.

- **The Draw OCR Block tool** enables you to define the area of text on a scanned page that you want recognized and converted to editable text. You can also use this option on a page where you want to perform OCR and trace bitmaps at the same time. By default, Draw OCR Block blocks are "Text & Graphic" mode. You can change them to recognize just text, ignoring graphics, by clicking the right mouse button in the block and then selecting Text Only. To define an area, simply draw a box around the text, as shown in Figure 15-3.

- **The Number Block tool** enables you to number multiple blocks in the Source Window. This tool becomes available when you use Draw OCR Block and Draw Trace Block to define areas for processing. It lets you choose the order in which areas are processed. The procedure for using this tool is as follows: Draw multiple blocks in the Source Window. Select the Number Block tool. Click in the blocks in the order you want them numbered. If you don't number blocks, they are processed in the order in which you draw them.

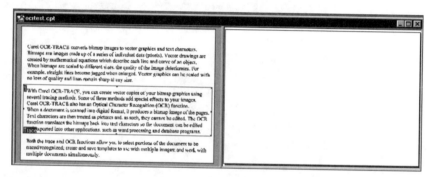

Figure 15-3: You can use Draw OCR-Trace to define areas in scanned text to recognize.

Tracing Black-and-White Images

Tracing black-and-white bitmaps and editing the output is much easier by far than working with color and grayscale images. In most instances, OCR-Trace creates a vector image that requires little touch-up.

To trace a black-and-white bitmap, you must first, of course, bring a source image into the program. You can do this in a number of ways:

- You can scan the image directly into OCR-Trace, which works the same as scanning into Photo-Paint, discussed in Chapter 8.

- You can use the Open command on the File menu.

- You can drag and drop the image from another OLE-aware program, such as Photo-Paint. You can also drag and drop from Corel Multimedia Manager, Windows Explorer, or any of several other clip catalogs or file management programs.

■ You can cut or copy (Edit ⇨ Cut) from another Windows application and paste (Edit ⇨ Paste) into OCR-Trace.

No matter how you bring the source image into OCR-Trace, it is displayed in the Source Window. You can now choose to trace all or a portion of the image. To trace all of the image, choose OCR-Trace ⇨ Perform Trace ⇨ By Outline. (You can also click on the Outline Trace button on the toolbar.) To trace a portion of the image, use the Draw Trace Block to define the area, and then choose Perform Trace.

You really have several options for tracing, including Outline and Center Line. The other options on the Perform Trace flyout on the OCR-Trace menu — Sketch, Woodcut, Mosaic, and 3D Mosaic — are special effects, which are discussed later in this chapter in the section "Using special effects in OCR-Trace." For creating vector paths, you'll work primarily with two options, Outline trace and Center Line trace. Outline trace creates filled paths by tracing the black areas of the image and then filling them with a black solid fill, as shown in Figure 15-4. The Center Line trace option creates paths by tracing the outlines and filled areas without filling the closed paths, as shown in Figure 15-5.

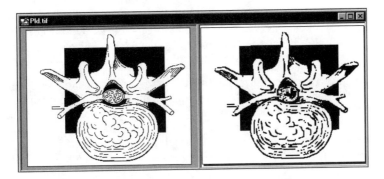

Figure 15-4: An image has been traced with the Outline trace option. Use this method to re-create the image, complete with fills.

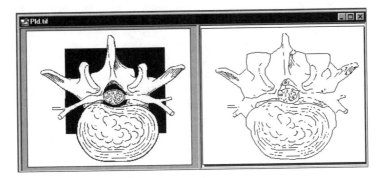

Figure 15-5: An image has been traced with the Center Line option. This method draws outlines around filled areas and traces lines.

As you can see from Figures 15-4 and 15-5, Outline trace re-creates the image in vector format. Center Line, on the other hand, re-creates only the outlines of the image. In either case, once the image is traced, you can use OCR-Trace's tools to edit the image, or you can import the image into CorelDraw and edit it there. Typical editing in OCR-Trace would include using the color palette in conjunction with the Pick tool to recolor closed paths, or to use the Bézier and other node editing to manipulate and close paths.

Note

You can adjust several factors of how OCR-Trace performs a trace by adjusting the options in the Trace Settings dialog box. Mostly, these options are the same whether you trace a black-and-white image or a color one. Rather than going over them twice, I discuss the options in Trace Settings in the next section.

Tracing Color Images

The procedure for tracing a color bitmap in OCR-Trace is primarily the same as for black-and-white images as just described, but the results can be quite different. First, not all color images can be successfully traced in OCR-Trace. Many photographs, for example, contain far too many colors and patterns for OCR-Trace to figure out how to create paths for all of them. When that's the case, you can increase your chances of success by first editing the image in Photo-Paint. Refer to Chapter 9 for a discussion of how to remove objects from images by turning paths into selections.

When you trace a color image in OCR-Trace, the program is capable of separating it into only 257 colors, for which it creates separate paths for each occurrence of a color and separate layers for each color. Actually, the program supports 256 colors and creates a separate layer for plugging holes, or areas for containing colors for which it was unable to create a layer. To view the layers, choose View ⇨ Dockers ⇨ Layer Manager after tracing a full-color image.

As you can imagine, you'll have a rough time getting successful traces of images containing thousands or millions of colors. OCR-Trace works best on scanned drawings or artwork with white or solid backgrounds and less than 256 colors. Other types of images can cause you to perform far too much touch-up to make it worth your while.

Secret

After the image is traced, you can edit each path by using the Layer Manager in Document Information to go to the layer containing the desired path. The Layers portion of the Document Information dialog box functions like the CorelDraw Layers roll-up, which is discussed in Chapter 3. You can turn off the display of individual layers, delete layers, and so on. Or you can bring the image into CorelDraw and edit layers with the Layers roll-up.

Improving your trace results

You can adjust several factors involved in the decisions OCR-Trace makes when it processes a trace from the Property Bar dialog box (View ⇨ Property Bar), shown in Figures 15-6 and 15-7. Each type of trace—Outline, Center Line, and the special effects—has its own sets of controls. And, as with the Property Bar in other CorelDraw applications, the Property Bar itself is context-sensitive. You can change Property Bar contexts with the first button on the Property Bar. This section discusses Outline and Centerline options. The others, which are special effects, are discussed in the next section.

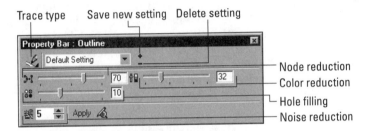

Figure 15-6: Use the Property Bar to modify the way OCR-Trace traces bitmaps. These options enable you to adjust settings for Outline trace.

Figure 15-7: Use these options to adjust Center Line traces.

Following are the settings for Outline trace and Center Line trace and how they affect the way the program performs:

- **Node Reduction.** If you've read much of this book, you already know what nodes are and the benefits of reducing the number of them on a path. Nodes, of course, mark a place in a path where it changes directions or joins. Using this method smoothes lines, taking many of the kinks out and eliminating small line segments. This option works the same whether you are using Outline or Center Line trace.

- **Color Tolerance.** Available only when performing an Outline trace, this option determines the accuracy for the color representation of the vector graphic. Color tolerance refers to how different (in hue) the source colors can be before the program can convert them to the same color in the vector graphic. The lower the color tolerance, the more unique colors will appear in the resulting graphic, and the more closely it will resemble the original image. Keep in mind that the more colors you allow, the more layers you will get in the resulting graphic. Editing an image with a couple of hundred layers is no picnic.

- **Hole Filling.** When you are working with color bitmaps, after an image has been traced, small holes are often left in the resulting vector graphic. Hole Filling creates a background layer of small rectangles of each area's average color. These rectangles fill the holes. By increasing the number in Hole Filling, you increase the number of rectangles, increasing the accuracy of the colors in the resulting traced image.

- **Noise Reduction.** When you are working with either Outline or Center Line trace, this option enables you to screen out small, unwanted, or not easily edited objects. Noise Reduction works by eliminating areas of color smaller in pixels than the value set in this field. Using this option can require some tradeoffs. If, for example, your bitmap contains fine details, they could be lost if Noise Reduction is set too high. If it is set too low, you could wind up with a lot of tiny paths that are difficult to fill and delete.

- **Iteration.** When processing a trace in Center Line mode, OCR-Trace eliminates the outline from the outside in, searching for the center of the line. Adjusting this value affects how quickly the trace processes and the thinness of the ensuing lines. The higher the setting, the thinner the resulting outlines.

Secret

While the settings in Trace Settings can greatly improve the quality of output from OCR-Trace, it's often difficult to predict how the program will analyze and trace your images. All images are different and have their own properties. It's often difficult to avoid a few trial-and-error traces before getting the best results. In these cases, the speed with which OCR-Trace traces can greatly affect how long you will have to work with an image to get it just right.

The physical size — in inches or pixels — plays less of a role in determining how long a trace takes than do image resolution and file size (remember that dpi and file size are closely related). You can reduce an image's file size in Photo-Paint with that program's Resample function (discussed in Chapter 8). There's really no reason to use images higher than about 200 dpi in OCR-Trace. And keep in mind, too, that once you make the conversion from bitmap to vector, the traced image is easily resized in CorelDraw — so the size of the source image is not all that critical during a trace.

Using special effects in OCR-Trace

OCR-Trace ships with four special-effects trace options. They are Woodcut, Sketch, Mosaic, and 3D Mosaic. Unlike Outline and Center Line trace, these options are for creating specialized artwork rather than tracing bitmaps in order to edit them as vector graphics. Figures 15-8 through 15-11 show the four effects available in OCR-Trace.

Figure 15-8: An example of OCR-Trace's Woodcut tracing option.

Figure 15-9: An example of OCR-Trace's Sketch tracing option.

Figure 15-10: An example of OCR-Trace's Mosaic tracing option.

Figure 15-11: An example of OCR-Trace's 3D Mosaic tracing option.

You can control several aspects of each effect from the Property Bar (when you select the proper context, or course), such as the angles of the lines in a Woodcut, or the number and size of the pyramids, fans, or bricks in a 3D Mosaic pattern. Depending on the effect you choose, the options can be pretty extensive. To find out what each option does and how it affects the resulting output, you should experiment with different settings. To get a description of what each option does, hover your mouse pointer over the option in the Property Bar. This gives you a context-sensitive pop-up help caption explaining the option.

Optical Character Recognition

If you've ever used optical character recognition for bringing hard copy text into your word processor, then you know how much time it can save. It's must faster and often more accurate than retyping. Although OCR-Trace is not as powerful and feature-rich as most dedicated OCR programs, such as Caere's OmniPage, it works well enough for occasional text recognition tasks.

The most common way to get a text source page into OCR-Trace is to scan it. However, you can also import images from fax software, such as Delrina's WinFax — as long as the fax program has the capability of exporting to a format supported by OCR-Trace, such as TIFF.

As with Photo-Paint (discussed in Chapter 8), you can use the TWAIN-compliant software that came with your scanner to scan a text page, or you can use CorelScan, the scanning utility bundled in the CorelDraw 8 package (discussed in Chapter 19). After you scan a page, it shows up in the Source Window. From here you can elect either to recognize the entire page or use Draw OCR Block in the toolbox to select specific portions of the page to recognize. Figures 15-12 and 15-13 show the two methods.

To recognize the text, simply choose Perform OCR from the OCR-Trace menu, or click on the Recognize Text button on the toolbar. If the scan is clean — 200 dpi or higher, straight, and free of noise (including dirt and interference from colored paper or backgrounds) — the recognition should perform without a hitch. The recognized text displays in the Output Window. You can now export the text (File ⇨ Export Text) to an ASCII text file or to one of many supported word processor files. Or you can cut or copy (File ⇨ Copy) the text and paste (File ⇨ Paste) it into CorelDraw and edit it as Paragraph Text (discussed in Chapter 4).

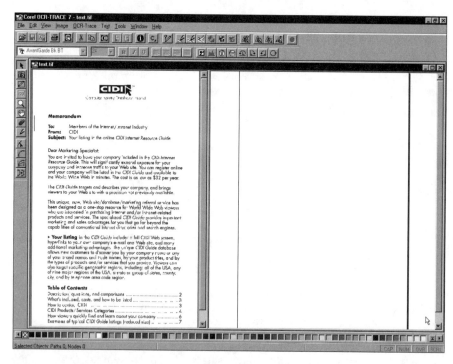

Figure 15-12: A full page of text is ready to recognize in OCR-Trace.

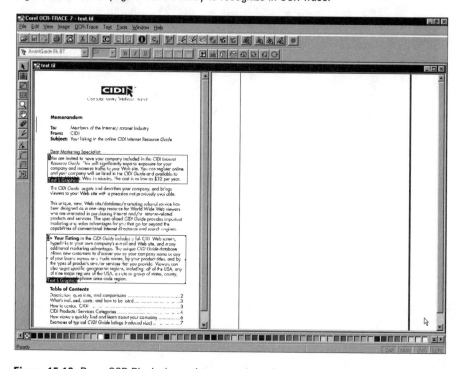

Figure 15-13: Draw OCR Blocks is used to recognize selected portions of a page.

When working in either the Source or Output windows, you can use the Zoom tool to magnify portions of the source or output, just as you would in any other CorelDraw application. This can make it easier to see which portions of the Source document you want to block for recognition. In the Output Window, zooming in enables you to better judge the results of a recognition session or edit portions of the output.

Secret

Don't forget that you can use the right mouse button. In the Source Window it provides options for changing views, adding pages, and several other useful functions. In the Output Window, the right-mouse pop-up provides quick access to several editing tools.

Changing OCR settings

OCR-Trace provides extensive options for modifying the settings the program uses while performing text recognition, including spell checking during recognition, special settings for pages that contain multiple columns or tables, and many, many other options. You control how OCR-Trace recognizes text from the OCR Settings context sheet on the Property Bar, shown in Figure 15-14. (In previous versions you used the OCR Settings dialog box.)

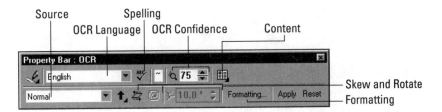

Figure 15-14: Use the OCR sheet on the Property Bar to control how OCR-Trace recognizes text.

As you can see, OCR Property Bar contains several options for controlling how OCR-Trace recognizes text. You can also click the Formatting button to change the OCR output options, such as fonts and page formatting. To see what the various options are on the Property Bar, hover your mouse over the option in question. The following list provides an overview of the various options available on the Property Bar and what you can do with them:

- The **OCR Language** drop-down of the Property Bar enables you to select a language with which to perform your recognition.

- The **Spelling** button determines whether the program should check spelling as it recognizes text.

- **Replacement Character** tells OCR-Trace which character to substitute for characters it doesn't recognize. The default is a tilde (~).

- **OCR Confidence** controls how thoroughly OCR-Trace trusts its own judgment. Each time OCR-Trace has trouble discerning a character, it inserts a reject character (a tilde ~ by default). A low confidence level decreases the number of rejects; a high confidence level increases the number of rejects. In other words, OCR-Trace guesses less often when you set a high confidence level.

- The **Content** option on the Property Bar enables you to tell OCR-Trace whether it is scanning a page of single-column text, a page containing multiple columns, or a table. The program then tries to reformat the output accordingly.

- The **Source** option on the Property Bar lets you provide information about the source page prior to recognition. This not only can speed up recognition but also improve the accuracy. From here you can tell the program whether the source is a normal scanned page, a dot-matrix page, or a fax. You can also set the page orientation at which you scanned the page, and you can adjust the skew level of the source page. Skew, in this case, refers to pages that are not set straight in the scanner or photocopies that did not print straight.

- The **Skew** and **Rotate** buttons enable you to straighten and change the page orientation, respectively.

- The **Formatting** button opens a dialog box that controls the output from the recognition process, shown in Figure 15-15. You can, for example, elect to keep all the page formatting or just the text formatting, such as bolds, indents, and so on. You can also choose the output font.

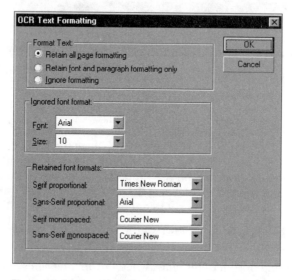

Figure 15-15: Use this dialog box to control the output from an OCR session.

As we mentioned earlier, in most cases OCR-Trace does a fair job of recognizing text. However, if the results are not to your liking, you can use these options to tweak the final output. OCR does you little good if you have to spend much time editing the results.

Working with multiple-page documents

Many text-recognition jobs entail processing several pages. The way traditional OCR programs handle this is to have you scan several pages before executing the recognition. You can do this manually or via a scanner sheet feeder, which scans 20 or more pages in succession automatically.

Unfortunately, you can't scan multiple pages into OCR-Trace. But you can open several scanned pages in the same OCR-Trace document and then process them all. You have several ways to do this. You can open them all at once with the Open command on the File menu; you can add them to an existing document with Add Page (File ⇨ Add Page); or you can drag and drop them into Page Manager from Windows Explorer or another OLE-aware application, such as Corel Multimedia Manager. Figure 15-16 shows the Source window containing several pages ready for recognition.

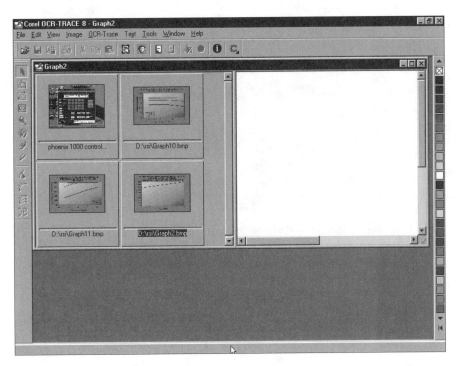

Figure 15-16: Use Page Manager to add and delete pages from the current document.

The most efficient way to get several scanned pages into OCR-Trace is through Open or Add Pages (also on the File menu). When you use the Open command, you can select all or some of the files in a directory by either Ctrl-clicking on each file or Shift-clicking on the first file and then Shift-clicking again on the last file you want to import. When you click OK, OCR-Trace opens all the files and places them in the same document or session.

You can now recognize all the pages at once by choosing OCR-Trace ⇨ Perform OCR, which opens OCR Multiple Pages, shown in Figure 15-17. From here you can select pages to recognize, or you can choose All Pages to recognize the text on them all. Red check marks inside the page icons in OCR Multiple Pages means that the page is selected to be recognized.

Secret

A further note on multiple-page documents. We should point out that you can go through and define blocks on each page for recognition with Draw OCR Block, as explained earlier in this chapter. OCR-Trace then ignores the other text on those pages. You should know, too, that you can also trace multiple pages of bitmapped images with the method we just described. You'll find that handy when you need to trace several images. You can just leave the computer working on it while you have lunch or work on something else.

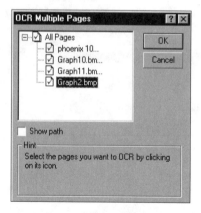

Figure 15-17: Page Manager lets you choose specific pages for recognition or recognize them all.

Summary

▶ You can create vector images from bitmaps that can be edited in CorelDraw with OCR-Trace.

▶ When you trace black-and-white images in OCR-Trace, they are placed on one layer, on which you can then edit and fill paths either in OCR-Trace or in CorelDraw.

▶ When you trace colored bitmaps in OCR-Trace, each color is placed on a separate layer, on which you can edit paths or which import into CorelDraw.

▶ You can turn scanned text into text editable in a word processor (or CorelDraw) with OCR-Trace OCR capabilities.

Chapter 16

Customizing Clip Art, Textures, and Templates

In This Chapter

You learn lots of tips on working with:

▶ Clip art

▶ CorelTexture

▶ Templates

The CorelDraw 8 package comes with many extras besides the applications: thousands of pieces of clip art, numerous templates, and a wonderful little program for creating your own textures that can be applied to CorelDraw, Photo-Paint, and Dream 3D. In this chapter, you learn to customize clip art, changing it significantly and giving it a far broader application than the usual window-dressing clip art gets relegated to. You also learn about CorelTexture, a program that allows you to create textures with so many variations that it's nearly impossible to make the same texture twice. Last, you learn how to customize Draw's templates so that, if you work with the same template often but find that you keep making the same changes each time, you can save those changes as part of the template — and even give it a new name. This chapter shows you how to maximize many of the extras that came on your CorelDraw 8 CD-ROMs.

Customizing Clip Art

Most clip art objects are groups of smaller art objects. A typical piece of clip art, for example, often consists of a solid black background that frames the shape of the entire picture. First, though, let's look at what you can do with clip art without ungrouping it. Figure 16-1 shows a rocket, a piece of clip art included with CorelDraw 8. Figure 16-2 shows an envelope applied to the rocket.

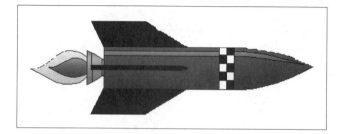

Figure 16-1: This rocket clip art object comes with CorelDraw.

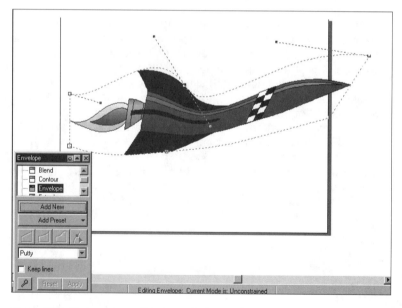

Figure 16-2: The envelope effect is applied to the rocket.

As you can see from the envelope bounding box around the rocket, the envelope can be modified by manipulating the curve handles, giving the rocket a unique twist. You can do this without having to ungroup the rocket and deal with its individual components.

Figure 16-3 shows the rocket after the Contour effect was applied to the wings on both sides. The Contour effect has stretched and curved the wings according to the envelope that was applied. For this to be done, the wings must first be ungrouped but not moved away from the rocket itself. Before applying the Contour effect, be sure to select only the wing and not the rest of the rocket.

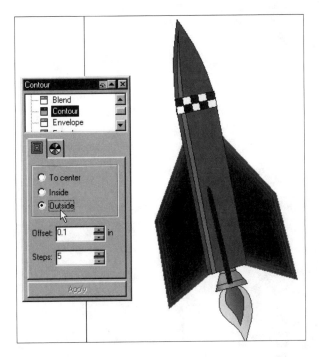

Figure 16-3: The rocket looks like this after a Contour effect was applied to the wings.

Figure 16-4 shows an unmodified clip art object, Little Red Riding Hood, available from the Fantasy folder of your clip art CD-ROM.

You can ungroup Little Red and then reposition the curves and lines on the hood. Figure 16-5 shows the beginnings of Little Red leaving her riding hood behind.

Figure 16-4: Little Red Riding Hood appears as clip art.

Figure 16-5: Little Red begins to lose her hood.

When you first ungroup this piece of clip art, select one of the objects and switch to the Shape Tool. You'll notice dozens and dozens of nodes outlining Little Red's red hood. In order to manipulate the hood, the first thing you must do is delete about 95 percent of those nodes. One of the main rules in altering the shape of clip art is simplifying the curves. If you don't, you may end up with untraceable twists and turns, not knowing which node is affecting which line. To delete a node, right-click on it and press the D key, or scroll down the shortcut menu to the Delete command. To delete many nodes at once, particularly nodes that are redundant and not needed for the shape's integrity, use the Node Auto-Reduce option to simplify the shape and reduce the sheer number of nodes.

You can do a lot with Ms. Red — perhaps you'd like to give her a more modern hair style? Or something more drastic? Look at Figure 16-6. By rearrangement of the lines and nodes, a shadowy cave was created. Another piece of clip art was inserted and treated with the Interactive Transparency tool. This was to create the impression of Red emerging from a cave after passing by a mysterious lake.

Figure 16-6: Little Red emerges from a dark Scottish loch . . . many miles away!

The next piece began as a simple circular clip art sun (see Figure 16-7). The sun was treated with CorelDraw 8's new Interactive Distortion tool (Zipper effect). This Zipper effect allows you to alter the jaggedness and frequency of each duplicate sun. The sun was duplicated, resized, and the copies were treated with various blends using the Interactive Blend tool. Also, using Interactive Transparency allows you to show off the various blends and shapes of the layers underneath.

Figure 16-7: What started as a simple circle with a face was transformed into this multilayer piece with many complex blends and distortion qualities.

Recoloring clip art

Figure 16-8 shows a gazelle from the Animals folder of the clip art CD-ROM. One nice feature of Draw's clip art is that even the smallest shapes that make up the whole clip art object can be colored individually. The boundaries are firm. This quality is helpful when you are using fills to recolor clip art. If the boundaries between the clip art individual pieces are solid, you don't need to spend lots of time closing gaps in order to keep the fill in the area you want.

Figure 16-9 shows that same gazelle treated with many blends of fountain fills and texture fills. The legs and flank were repositioned slightly to give the gazelle more "spring."

Figure 16-8: A clip art gazelle includes shapes that can be manipulated individually.

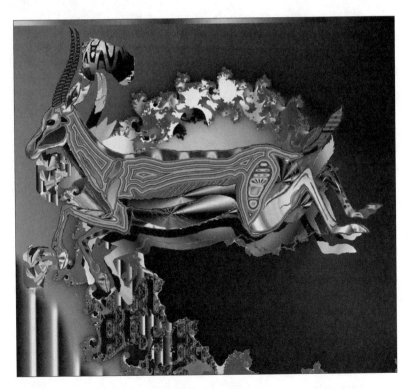

Figure 16-9: This clip art gazelle has been treated with every type of fountain fill known to humankind.

Figure 16-10 shows a clip art bird that was ungrouped; each piece has been treated with a unique fountain or texture fill. The background behind the bird was filled with a spiral pattern that draws your eyes to the bird.

Figure 16-10: This clip art bird has been filled with texture fills.

And finally, Figure 16-11, Wings of Desire, is a study in contrasts using clip art. (This piece was developed in CorelDraw, exported to Photo-Paint, and then finalized in CorelDraw.) The girls walking at the lower-right of the picture are clip art images converted to black and white only. The two women sitting in the middle are grayscale clip art pieces. The images behind and above them are clip art figures converted to masks and filled with sky and other textures. The woman in the back talking with one of the "angels" is a clip art image converted to black only.

Figure 16-11: A study in contrasts has been created with clip art.

Clip art and composition

Sometimes placement makes all the difference. How you position simple clip art objects, perhaps lightening the color value to draw attention to text nearby, can breathe new life into a tired medium.

In Figure 16-12, you see one piece of artistic text and a man with a worried look on his face.

Figure 16-12: A clip art businessman is alone with his troubles.

Let's try to do some interesting repeating and arranging. Figure 16-13 shows the artistic text with a shadow added, duplicated four times, each time reduced in size.

Figure 16-13: Duplicates of the text are gradually reduced in size and a shadow is added. More troubleshooting lies ahead.

But how to arrange it? In Figure 16-14, the text and clip art are arranged to create a sense of "trouble spiraling into a crisis."

Figure 16-14: The clip art and artistic text are rearranged for a pleasing effect.

In Figure 16-15, you see some fairly blah clip art selections.

Figure 16-15: These three clip art objects don't inspire much.

But once we've rearranged, lightened the color, rotated, and added a frame, the clip art actually complements the text rather nicely. The results are shown in Figure 16-16.

Figure 16-16: Reducing the color value and moving the clip art increases its artistic effect.

CorelTexture

CorelTexture is accessed by choosing Graphic Utilities from the CorelDraw 8 menu (Start ⇨ Programs ⇨ CorelDRAW 8) and selecting CorelTexture. It can also be launched from within CorelDraw, using the Application Launcher. If you will be creating only small texture bitmaps or rendering to the application window, the program is not a memory hog and can render nicely in the background while you work in another CorelDraw application.

The opening screen of CorelTexture allows you to begin work entirely on your own, receiving guidance from a wizard (for example, "Do you want your texture to look like wood or stone?" "Do you want grainy wood or smooth wood?"). Or you can start with one of CorelTexture's presets and build from there. For now, let's choose the latter course.

Using layers in CorelTexture

CorelTexture builds textures based on layering elements of an object's surface. Think of building a texture as resembling making a sandwich. Each layer of a texture brings a different element to the whole. One layer determines the texture's simple physical properties: wood, stone, water, clouds. Another layer contributes lighting effects to the texture. A further layer influences how "bumpy" the overall texture effect is. Building a texture is simply a matter of manipulating these layers to your own satisfaction. Each of the layers is described next.

The Form & Geometry layer

When you begin layer editing, you'll see a preview screen with the layers one upon another, each contributing some feature to the whole, which changes as you manipulate the individual layers. At the bottom is the Form & Geometry layer, which is used to establish the texture's basic appearance and edge qualities, such as bevel and extrude amount. Think of this as the bottom slice of bread in the texture sandwich.

The Lighting layer

The top layer is the Lighting layer, where you add lights and move them, controlling their intensity and color. This is the top slice of bread.

The Surface Properties layer

Right under the Lighting layer is the Surface Properties layer. This layer dictates how dramatically the lighting effects influence the texture. Four powerful slider controls are found here to change how the light plays on your texture's surface.

The Shader layers

"Sandwiched" in between these layers are various shaders. These shaders provide algorithms that further alter the texture's appearance. For example, you can mix a Marble appearance with an Aluminum Foil layer right underneath it. Each type of algorithm comes with its own shader controls. These controls affect characteristics such as the size of clouds, the depth of the marble's veins, how "crinkly" the aluminum foil looks, and so forth.

The final texture, then, is one big sandwich. With adroit and creative manipulation of the layers, you can create one-of-a-kind textures every time you use this application.

Saving layers

You can save any of the individual layers you've edited, as well as entire textures. You can then use saved layers later to make other textures. Figure 16-17 shows the mouse pointer accessing the Save Layer menu. Here, a new Form & Geometry layer is being saved. Looking at Figure 16-17, you can tell that the Form & Geometry layer is being saved because the white "broken-line box" appears on the bottom layer, which is always the Form & Geometry layer. The layer has been named "Bevel Frame" because beveling has been added and because the form has been changed to resemble a picture frame.

This layer is being saved

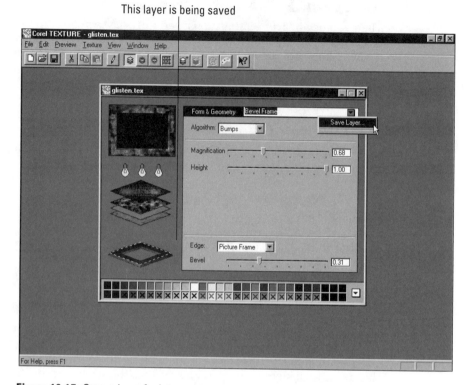

Figure 16-17: Save a layer for later use.

Why not call the layer in Figure 16-17 "Cloud Frame"? After all, the preview box clearly shows a cloudy texture on the frame. But remember, just the layer is being saved, not an entire texture. This particular layer has nothing to do with the "cloudy" effect seen in the texture. The cloudy effect is a function of one of the Shader layers (one of the slices of meat in the sandwich). If I were particularly happy with the cloud effect and wished to save it, I would click whichever Shader layer has a Cloud algorithm and then save that layer.

Before saving to a file, you'll need to determine the image's size and resolution. First select File ⇨ Image Setup and input your parameters. Next select Texture ⇨ Render to File and choose your file type. When you select Save, you'll be prompted to name the bitmap, and after clicking OK you'll see a blue progress bar that fills up as the bitmap is saved to file. When you are saving a large texture, this progress bar is sometimes your only indication that your computer hasn't frozen up. Saving textures at resolutions higher than 150 dpi will not particularly improve the texture's appearance, but it will greatly increase file size.

After saving a layer, you can select it from one of the preset layers that you use in your textures.

Saving textures as bitmaps

Individual layers are saved in a particular resolution and size that you specify. They are saved as .TEX files, and as such, they cannot be imported into any other application. Before you can apply a texture elsewhere, you must convert the texture into a bitmap. You can save a texture to the application window or to a file. When you're ready to save a texture as a file, you'll find that most graphic file types are supported. To save one as a bitmap, make sure you're happy with the texture, and then select Texture ⇨ Render to Window or Texture ⇨ Render to File.

Figure 16-18 shows CorelTexture's Texture Editing screen.

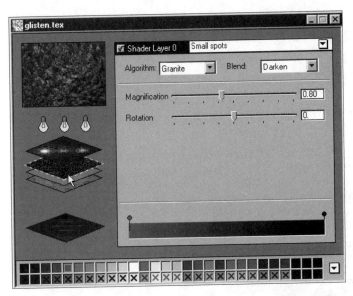

Figure 16-18: The Texture Editing screen gives you a number of useful options.

The Texture Editing screen sits inside the main screen, which contains all of the standard menu commands, such as File, Open, View, and Help. The Texture Editing screen is where the action is. The mouse pointer is seen selecting one of the Shader layers, one of the pieces of meat in this great sandwich of a texture. The layer's algorithm is Granite, and sliders can be used to adjust the amounts of magnification and rotation.

At the bottom of the main screen are color controls for each layer. They are set up as a gradient, measured between two color pins at either side of the spectrum. In this case, the darker gradient of the granite is not allowing much granite effect to show through, as you can tell from the Preview box, which seems to look much more like bumpy aluminum foil. To make the granite show through more, you must drag a color box of a lighter shade of gray to replace the darker-gray color pin. Figure 16-19 shows the mouse pointer dragging a color box that is almost pure white (to replace the original gray color pin at the left).

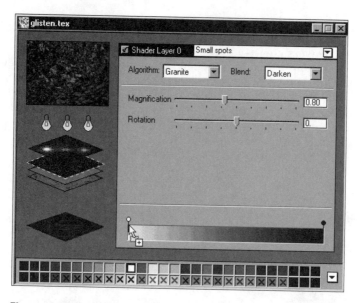

Figure 16-19: Dragging a color box changes a layer's color value.

Figure 16-20 shows the new texture rendered to a window. Rendering to a window is the best way to check a texture's true characteristics before rendering it to a file. As you can see, some granite effect is mixed in with the "wrinkle" coming through from an underlying shader. To render to a window, select Texture ⇨ Render to Window from the main screen.

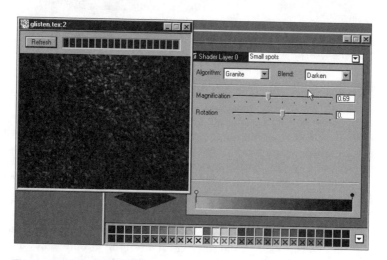

Figure 16-20: An edited texture is rendered to the window.

The Lighting layer can be edited extensively. Figure 16-21 shows a color box being dropped onto one of the three lights. Notice the label Light #2 is now shown as a colored light, whereas the other two lights are still white. You can use the mouse pointer to move lights around the surface. Just click and drag the light you want to move.

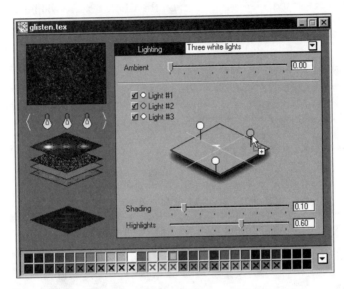

Figure 16-21: A color box is added to Light #2.

Any changes you make cause the Preview box to immediately refresh itself, showing the new texture.

CorelTexture's main menu

You could use CorelTexture's main menu only for rendering textures and setting file type, size, and resolution. However, some additional controls on the main menu make texture editing even easier.

Preview Selected Layer Only

Sometimes it's important to see the effect that one single layer is having on the texture. To see only one layer at a time, select a layer and choose Preview ⇨ Preview Selected Layer Only.

Add Layer

You may add an additional layer to the sandwich. By default this is a Shader layer, and you may choose which type of algorithm you want to apply to the layer. The nine algorithm types include adding a bitmap as a layer, a simple color gradient layer, and various natural textures. To add a layer, select Texture ⇨ Add Layer.

Change Layer Orientation

You can alter your layer's positioning in the sandwich. It need not be straight and flat. You can rotate your layer and change its distance from the other layers along any axis. The closer layers are to each other, the more pronounced the effects are. The farther apart they are, the more subtle their interaction. If one layer is rotated, its overall effect on the whole texture will be "skewed" along the axis of the rotation. To change your layer's orientation, select Texture ⇨ Layer Orientation.

Generate Tiling Image

Secret

You can use CorelTexture to render any image as a set of tiles. To create a tiling image, select Texture ⇨ Generate Tiling Image. To test the appearance of your tiling effect, select Preview ⇨ Test Tiling.

A complete texture

Figure 16-22 shows a wood texture rendered at 150 dpi, image size 320 × 240 dpi. A small area light was added to the upper right to provide more of a "smoky" appearance. Total time in creation and rendering, approximately six minutes. After you've finished a texture, you may save it in any file format you wish and import into your CorelDraw or Photo-Paint projects.

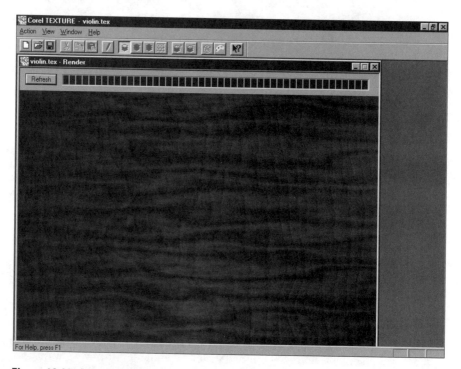

Figure 16-22: An edited "wood" texture has been treated with a light in the upper-right corner.

Templates

Another great feature of CorelDraw is *templates*. Templates give you quick control over the look of text, lines, and other objects. Using a template, you begin typing on your page, and the text is automatically rendered in the Harrington font, 72p, for example. A template enables you to begin creating a line that will automatically be blue, with a width of $1/8$ inch, for another example. Templates, therefore, store stylistic information about what goes on a page, so that you can simply start creating, without having to make formatting choices. Templates store information about text and paragraph alignment, number of columns, positioning of graphics on a page, headline and date placement. They are marked out with "placeholder" text and pictures. Typing over (or inserting a graphic in place of) one of these placeholders erases the placeholder, but your new object will retain the stylistic information of the placeholder.

The following templates are included with CorelDraw and are accessible by selecting File ⇨ New from Template, rather than File ⇨ New:

- Advertisement
- Business Card
- Brochure
- Calendar
- Card
- Certificate
- Envelope
- Fax Cover
- Invitation
- Invoice
- Label
- Memo
- Menu
- Misc
- Newsletter
- Purchase Order
- Product Marketing

CorelDraw includes templates from a company called Paper Direct, which sells predesigned paper. You can use the Paper Direct templates included with CorelDraw to see how your work will appear when printed onto this special paper.

To understand how templates work, you first need to understand Draw's Style feature. When you enter text to your documents, CorelDraw keeps track of all the style elements involved in your creation. Style elements may include any outlines around the text, margin settings, the kinds of bullets you use, headings, and so on.

You can the view the style of your document by selecting Layout ⇨ Graphics and Text Styles. This brings up the Graphic and Text Styles docker. Right-click on any style in the docker, and select Properties. You'll see the Style Options dialog box. You'll see panels for changing the Style Font, Fill, and Outline (see Figure 16-23). However, the best way to create or edit a style is to create a text and fill example you want to save and instantly apply later, then right-click click on it and choose Styles ⇨ Save Style Properties. This brings up the Save Style As dialog box, allowing you to name your style and choose which components of your text example to save (see Figure 16-24). For example, if your style example employs a fill that you don't want to save as part of your style, simply leave Fill unchecked.

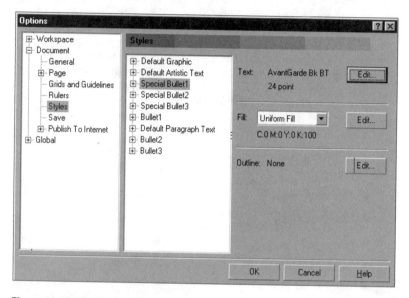

Figure 16-23: The Style Options dialog box reveals information about the selected style.

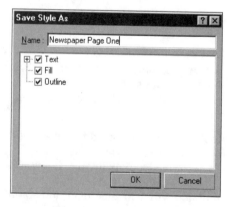

Figure 16-24: Save your style in the Save Style As dialog box.

Styles are covered elsewhere in this book. But please note that you can create an object of any shape, fill it, and save its outline and fill qualities as a style. This can be done in two steps. Later, the style you saved can be just as easily applied to another object.

First, after creating the object with your chosen Outline and Fill features, right-click on it, and select Styles ⇨ Save Style Properties. You'll see the Save Style As dialog box. Both Outline and Fill will be checked. If you want your style to ignore one or the other, uncheck the parameter you do not want included. After your style is named, it will be available any time by right-clicking on any object and selecting Style ⇨ Apply. You'll see your new style listed with the others.

Saving templates

By saving your document as a template, you are creating a convenient way to reproduce your work faster the next time — by automatically adding text or a particular graphic, without your having to worry about font selection, size, outline width, and so on. When you save a document as a template, you are saving a collection of styles that can all be instantly applied. A document saved as a template enables you to open the template later, replace the "marker text" with new text, and just get to work. In the case of a newsletter, for example, you would need merely to replace the volume number and date, without having to format the text appropriately for volume number and date styles.

When you save a style as part of a template, CorelDraw remembers the placement of graphics on the page, as well as any other features on your page that exist in the current document. If you decide to save the current document as a template, select File ⇨ Save As, and instead of saving your file as a .CDR document, choose .CDT, which is the template file type.

Adding a template to the Template Wizard

One quick way to create a template is to open the Template Wizard (Select File ⇨ New from Template) and select a template that approximates something you'd like to create. Reposition text and graphic objects on the page to your liking, and type in new text with any formatting changes you want. Choose Tools ⇨ Scripts ⇨ Script and Preset Manager. Scroll down to the script called Temp Wiz. Click Temp Wiz, and follow the onscreen prompts for saving your document as a template.

After creating your template, you may load it by selecting File ⇨ Open and choosing the .CDT file you created, or by choosing File ⇨ Open from Template. Once your template is part of the Template Wizard menu, you'll get these results:

- You get a graphical preview of your template.

- You will see it in a list with all the other Wizards for easier selection.

- An option is provided to load the template without the contents. This option loads only the blank text and graphic boxes with styles attached.

To add a template you've created from scratch to the Template Wizard list, first make sure your current document is exactly the way you like it. Remove any features of the document that you do not want to be part of the template's formatting. Next, open Tools ⇨ Scripts ⇨ Script and Preset Manager and scroll down to the document called Temp Wiz. You'll be prompted to provide information about the template you are saving that will be used in the Template Wizard preview, the next time you use it.

Later, you can load this template just as you would any other template by selecting File ⇨ Load from Template.

Summary

In this chapter, you learned:

▶ How to modify clip art to increase its artistic value and make it applicable to a wider variety of projects

▶ How to use clip art compositionally to your advantage

▶ How to use CorelTexture to create some new and unique texture effects that you can apply to your CorelDraw projects

▶ How to work with the templates included with CorelDraw

▶ How to create, work with, modify, and save custom templates

Chapter 17

Using Bitstream Font Navigator

In This Chapter

▶ You look at various aspects of font management, and see how Font Navigator is a great tool for this job.

▶ You discover how Font Navigator allows you to see which fonts are available from the CorelDraw 8 CD-ROM, and which fonts are already installed.

▶ You learn how to use Font Navigator to store fonts as groups, and how to load a font group for a particular project or application and then uninstall fonts when you are done.

▶ You see how to remove redundant and identical fonts from your computer, and how to uninstall fonts yet keep them available for reinstallation later.

Secrets of Font Management

Perhaps you've noticed that CorelDraw 8 comes with thousands of fonts. Loading all of these on your computer can slow your system down considerably. When you load more than two or three hundred fonts on a computer, performance detriment will surely follow because Windows must initialize each of those fonts every time you boot up your computer, in order to make them ready for you to use in a document. Still, lots of the fonts that come with CorelDraw 8 are quite nice, and who's to say which ones you'll *never* ever use? It would be nice to keep all the good fonts available, but not necessarily loaded on, taking up memory and system resources. That's where *font management* comes in.

Locating Bitstream Font Navigator

CorelDraw 8 includes Bitstream Font Navigator, which is a separate, bonus application that appears with other CorelDraw Productivity tools (Start ⇨ Programs ⇨ CorelDRAW 8 ⇨ Productivity Tools). It allows you to see examples of each font found on the CorelDraw CD-ROM and load the few that you want to use for your current projects. The fonts that are not loaded are still available through Font Navigator at a moment's notice.

Secrets of grouping fonts

Font Navigator also allows you to *group* fonts. Even fonts that are not loaded onto your computer can be categorized and placed in a special viewing folder according to any criteria you want. You may want to make groups of your favorite decorative fonts — professional "boardroom" fonts, or fonts for brochures and newsletters, for example — loading these specialized groups onto your computer *only* when you are working on a project that calls for them. Font Navigator makes it easy to load and unload these groups, helping to keep your computer running clean.

Preparing Font Navigator for use

When you start Font Navigator, you'll notice the panel on the left is filled with fonts. (See Figure 17-1.) This left panel is labeled Contents of Font Catalog. The best thing to do is create a font catalog with all the fonts on the CorelDraw 8 CD-ROM. That way you can instantly install them by dragging them and adding them to your installed list of fonts, which is the panel on the right side of the screen. Notice at the lower-right of the screen is a font viewing area that shows you a sample of what the font looks like. After allowing Font Navigator to catalog all the fonts on the CD-ROM, you can drag any font you like to the panel on the right, which loads the font permanently, even after the CD-ROM is removed.

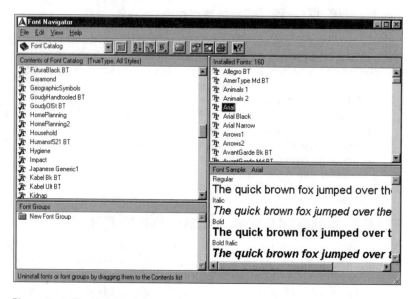

Figure 17-1: The Font Navigator main screen.

Creating a Font Catalog

To make a font catalog of all the fonts on the CorelDraw 8 CD-ROM, click on Find Fonts, and click on the plus sign next to the CD-ROM symbol in the Find Fonts dialog box. Now click on the plus sign next to the Fonts folder. Click on OK, and Font Navigator will begin cataloging the fonts so that you can later see some examples and drag fonts to the Install panel, if you choose.

To make a font catalog from some other group of fonts, simply use the same Find Fonts menu to locate that collection. Then you can use the same process described above, moving selected fonts from left to right, installing them for use on your computer.

Installing fonts

You now have over 1,000 fonts to choose from, which you can either group or simply drag to install. (See Figure 17-2.) As you install fonts one by one, notice that the number on the title bar of the Install Fonts panel increases by one each time you drag a font from left to right; conversely, you can uninstall a font by dragging it from right to left. Rather than drag fonts one by one, you can press Ctrl and click on each font that appeals to you, and then drag all of those selected fonts over at once. If you don't want to drag at all, you can right-click on any font and choose Install Fonts. Every font you've selected will then be installed.

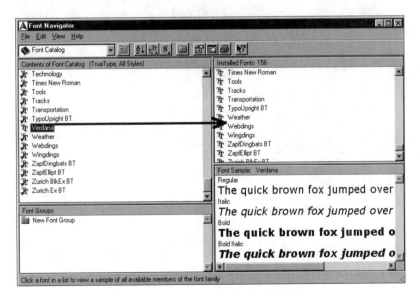

Figure 17-2: Dragging a font from left to right installs it on your computer.

If you know the name of a font you're looking for, scroll down to it quickly by typing the first letter of its name. You'll see a tiny window appear, prompting you to spell out the entire name or simply scroll and click.

Exploring font details

You can learn more about a font before installing it. Right-click on any font, and you'll see the Explore Font option (see Figure 17-3). Select that, and you'll see a panel showing the font in a sentence. However, click on Options at the upper left of the panel (see Figure 17-4), and you'll be able to view the font as it appears in a paragraph (Block Text Sample); see how it looks underlined, reversed, and rotated (Capabilities Sample); and see how the font appears in eight different sizes (Waterfall Sample). You can also type in your own Block Text Sample or Single Line Sample, if you want to replace the ones provided (Change Text).

To view a font's character chart, right-click on the font, then choose Properties. Click on the Character Chart tab. To view a larger version of the character, change its size with the Size drop-down menu at the right. A character chart is not much help unless you are told which keystroke combination activates it. Click on any character, and you'll see its keystroke at the bottom of the viewing panel.

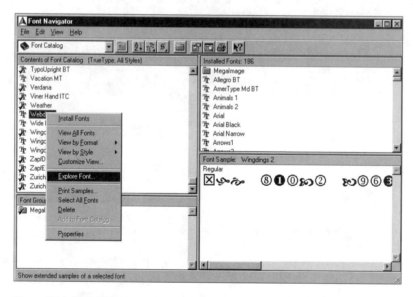

Figure 17-3: To find out more about a font, right-click on it and select Explore Font.

Perhaps, while choosing which fonts to install, you won't want to view them all at once in one huge, unwieldy list. Right-click on any font in the Font Catalog panel, and you'll see options for viewing groups of fonts according to font format (True Type, PostScript Type 1), and font style (Sans Serif, Decorative, Script, and so on). To restore the panel to include all fonts, right-click on it and select View All Fonts.

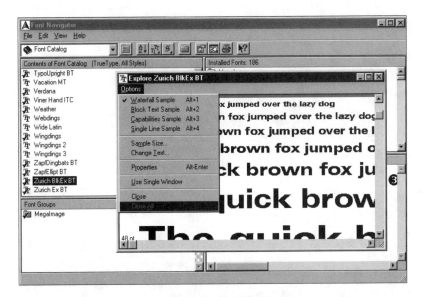

Figure 17-4: Click on Options to see the chosen font at work.

How to create font groups

The area to the lower-left of the screen is for creating font groups. These font groups are font collections *you* combine yourself within their own folders and then move at will from the Uninstalled panel (the left side) to the Installed panel (the right side) and back again. Font groups function the same on your computer as individual fonts. They are not limited just because they are part of a group.

When dragging to uninstall fonts (or font groups) from the right to the left, don't drag them back down into the Font Groups section. Just drag them straight across to the Catalog panel.

STEPS:

Creating a Font Group

Step 1.   Click on File ⇨ New Font Group. A folder will appear in the Font Groups panel, on the lower left of the screen.

Step 2.   Name your group.

Step 3.   Now simply drag fonts from either the right or left panel into the Font Groups folder (see Figure 17-5).

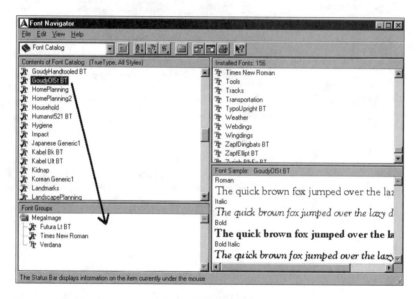

Figure 17-5: To add fonts to the group folder, simply drag them there.

Frequently installing or uninstalling fonts does no harm. Here's one warning: If you load a document that requires certain fonts, make sure they are installed at that time.

Automatically loading font groups

Font groups can be automatically loaded every time a certain program loads. Say you have one set of fonts you use every time you run CorelDraw, and a more decorative set that you employ for a Photo-Paint session. You can specify one group of fonts load automatically whenever CorelDraw starts. Then another set can load when your desktop publishing program starts.

STEPS:

Creating a font group

Step 1. Create a font group by selecting File Í New Font Group. Name your group.

Step 2. Drag fonts into the group folder, keeping in mind the project or program with which you'd like to associate this font group.

Notice that you can right-click on the font group and select Install. This will install all the fonts in the group onto your computer. But you learn how to associate an automatic installation with one particular document or program in the next section.

Associating fonts with a program or document

The following procedure shows you how to associate fonts.

STEPS:

Associating fonts

Step 1. Right-click on the font group folder and select Properties (see Figure 17-6). Make sure the General tab is on top.

Step 2. Notice the Association text box, and the Browse button right next to it. You can associate this font group with any executable file on your computer, for example. Also, you can type in the path and name of an actual document (for example, **C:\MyFiles\Homework.doc**), and the fonts will load whenever that application starts or the word-processing file loads.

Step 3. Use the Browse button to search for a file, or type it in if you know the entire path and filename.

Step 4. Click on OK. The next time the above conditions are met, the fonts in this group will automatically load.

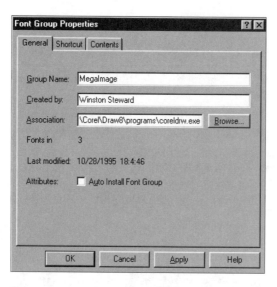

Figure 17-6: The Font Group Properties dialog box allows you to associate a font group with a particular program or project.

Creating a shortcut to a font group

You can create a shortcut to a particular font group, place that shortcut on your Windows Desktop, then right-click on the font group after activating the shortcut, and select Install from the menu choices. This way you have quick access to, as well as control over, how many fonts are on your computer at once. To do so, right-click on the font group in Font Navigator and choose Properties. Now click on the Shortcut tab and place a check next to the Create a shortcut for this group option.

You can choose to put the shortcut in a Program group (such as CorelDraw) or create a shortcut right on your desktop. You can also chose to put a shortcut in both places. Simply mark the appropriate check box, using the Browse menu provided to search for the program group in which you want to store your shortcut. Click on Apply or OK, and the shortcut will appear where it should.

Once you have a shortcut, right-click on it and select Install (see Figure 17-7). In the example shown, these fonts will also start up when CorelDraw is opened, as well as by the action represented here.

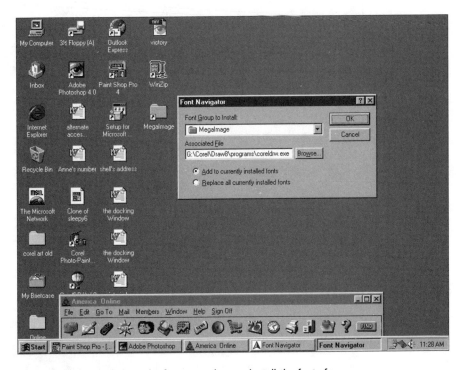

Figure 17-7: Right-click on the font group icon to install the fonts for use.

Uninstalling Fonts and Font Groups

To uninstall any individual font, right-click on any font that appears in the Installed Fonts panel (right side of the screen) and select Uninstall Fonts (see Figure 17-8).

Regarding groups, note that after fonts are installed *as a group* on your computer, they remain in a folder as shown in the Installed Fonts panel of Font Navigator. This organizational feat is quite helpful, because you can simply uninstall all the fonts in that group by right-clicking on the font group icon in the Installed Fonts panel, then clicking on Uninstall Fonts. After all, what's the point of being able to choose exactly which fonts to install if you can't uninstall them just as easily? Otherwise, you'd still end up with the same amount of clutter eventually.

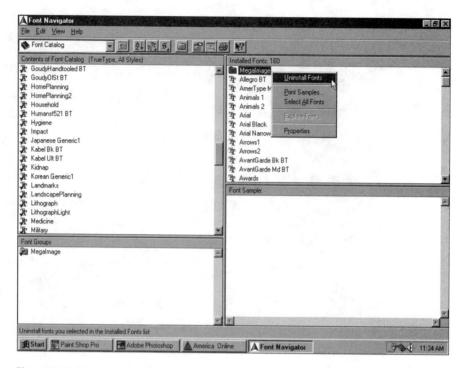

Figure 17-8: You can uninstall entire groups of fonts using the right-click pop-up menu.

Deleting Duplicate Fonts

If you've loaded many fonts on your computer, you may have noticed how fonts with entirely different names can actually look suspiciously the same. The phenomenon is not in your imagination. Some font vendors will change the name of a common font slightly and release it themselves under a different name.

You can quickly delete all duplicate fonts on your computer by selecting File ➪ Settings ➪ Duplicate Fonts. This opens the Duplicate Font Members dialog box. You'll see a list of fonts that are truly duplicated on your computer. A check will appear next to the font that is loaded and thus ought *not* to be erased. Move through the preview panel and select any fonts you want to delete. Press the Ctrl key to select multiple, noncontiguous fonts. Click on Delete to remove selected fonts from your hard drive. Remember, this action is more drastic than simply uninstalling them.

To learn more about a font before deleting it, click on the Properties button and the Sample Text tab. You'll see sample text. Note that you can type in your own text, as well.

Note

The previous procedure only works for fonts that are truly identical in name and character, and not for locating and removing redundant fonts that are named differently. However, Bitstream Font Navigator has a way for you to identify redundant fonts on your computer.

STEPS:

Identifying redundant fonts

Step 1.   Right-click on any font and select Properties from the pop-up menu.

Step 2.   Choose the Analog Name tab to see the window shown in Figure 17-9. (Not every font will have an Analog Name tab — only those in which a known duplicate font exists.)

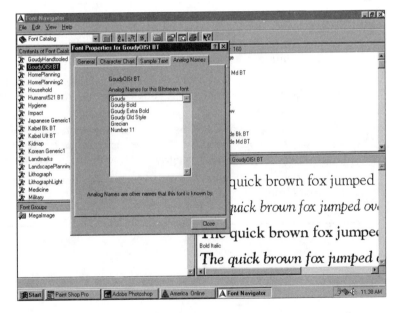

Figure 17-9: Use the Analog Name tab to examine possibly redundant fonts.

Step 3.   In the Analog Name tab, view the names shown. Some fonts have as many as five identical or nearly identical font types circulating about. Some may be on your computer, simply taking up space.

Step 4.   After viewing the redundant font name, search your own installed fonts to see if one of them exists on your computer.

(continued)

STEPS *(continued)*

Identifying redundant fonts

Step 5. To make searching a bit easier, remember the first letter of the font you are looking for. Click on Font Navigator's right panel, then type the first letter of the font. The Installed Font list will move forward to show the fonts beginning with the letter you typed.

Step 6. After locating the redundant font, right-click on it and select Delete.

Summary

▶ CorelDraw 8 comes with thousands of fonts. There is a great need for a tool to facilitate working with these fonts efficiently.

▶ Bitstream Font Navigator creates font catalogs to make it easy to see which fonts are already loaded on your computer, and which are available for loading.

▶ Font Navigator also allows you to store selected fonts as groups. These groups can be loaded by a mouse click, or can be loaded automatically whenever a particular program or document is accessed.

▶ Font Navigator makes it easy to locate and remove duplicate or redundant fonts from your computer.

Chapter 18

Corel Scripts

CorelDraw comes with a fully integrated scripting program, an application you use to create *scripts*, which are a lot like the macros you may have used in word processing programs. Scripts contain a set of instructions for carrying out tasks, such as opening files, filling polygons, extruding blends, or even creating multistep operations that require dialog boxes. Corel Script Editor also contains tools for creating dialog boxes. The basic scripting program, called Corel Script, loads right into CorelDraw (and Photo-Paint).

The easiest way to use the scripting program is to use the preset scripts that come with CorelDraw and Photo-Paint. To do this, you need not enter any code yourself. Recording scripts is simply a matter of performing a CorelDraw task while Script Recorder is recording. However, if you know a little Visual Basic, you can develop complex scripts yourself with Corel Script Editor. Scripts you create in Script Editor can be used in other applications, such as Corel Ventura and CorelDraw 8.

Opening Scripts in CorelDraw

To work with existing scripts, just select View ⇨ Dockers ⇨ Script and Preset Manager. You'll see the Script and Preset docker. Two folders are displayed, and clicking on either opens a variety of pictorial script icons for your viewing.

For more options, select Tools ⇨ Scripts. You're then presented with three options: Script and Preset Manager, Run Script, and Corel SCRIPT Editor. See Figure 18-1.

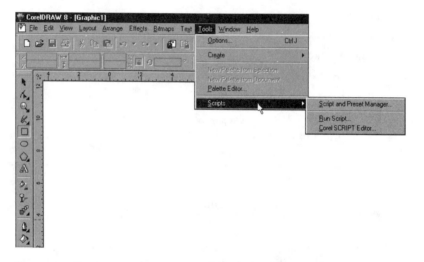

Figure 18-1: These script options appear in CorelDraw.

Run Script opens a Browse menu that enables you to select a script from any directory and run it as a program, right within CorelDraw.

The first option on the flyout, Script and Preset Manager, is a docker of icons representing two groups of scripts: those that come with CorelDraw as presets, and those that you create by yourself or by editing the presets. In this chapter, most of the discussion focuses on the Script and Preset Manager.

Click Tools ⇨ Scripts ⇨ Corel SCRIPT Editor to open a standalone application that enables you to create your own scripts and edit existing ones more to your liking. You may access it here in CorelDraw, in Photo-Paint, or from the Windows Program menu, by choosing Programs ⇨ CorelDRAW 8 ⇨ Productivity Utilities ⇨ Corel SCRIPT Editor. To learn more about this feature, see "Learning How to Compose Scripts," later in this chapter.

Saving Scripts

For all their power, CorelDraw scripts exist as simple-text files until they are compiled into a language similar to Basic right before you run them. Therefore, when you compose a script with Script Editor, you are actually working with a simple-text editor.

CorelDraw installs some scripts in three locations on your computer:

- C:\Corel\Scripts
- C:\Corel\Draw80\Draw\Scripts\Presets
- C:\Corel\Draw80\Draw\Scripts\Scripts

In working with Script Editor, the locations of scripts as they are saved are particularly important, because you may be spending time recording scripts within CorelDraw and then editing them via the Script Editor as text files. The preceding directory references will help you know where to find them. The first directory referenced is for scripts you compose using Corel Script Editor. The other directories are the default directories containing presets and scripts you record by simply performing tasks in CorelDraw. Once you open Script Manager in CorelDraw, you'll see them. Clicking on these directories provides access to scripts that you can immediately run in CorelDraw.

Working with Scripts

It's possible to work with scripts and never compose one yourself. You'll still find them marvelously convenient. Once you get the hang of working with scripts, you're likely to spend untold hours recording many of them. Here are four approaches to working with scripts:

- Using only preset scripts
- Recording your own scripts
- Editing existing scripts
- Composing scripts from scratch

Using only preset scripts

You can accomplish a lot using only the preset scripts that come with CorelDraw. To use these, select Tools ⇨ Scripts ⇨ Script and Preset Manager (or View ⇨ Dockers ⇨ Script and Preset Manager) and open one of the two folders (see Figure 18-2), each containing various preset scripts that you can instantly apply. These are explained in detail a little later in the chapter.

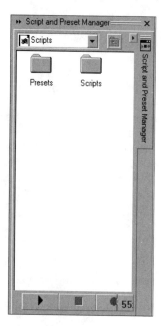

Figure 18-2: These two folders contain preset scripts for immediate application to your artwork.

Recording your own scripts

You can also record your own scripts and save them for later use. That way, you can have scripts at your disposal that are specifically suited to your own needs. After recording a script, you can apply it instantly to any appropriate situation.

Figure 18-3 shows the row of buttons found at the bottom of the Script and Preset Manager. Farthest to the left is the Playback button, for playing scripts. Press this button to play any script, one of your own or a preset. The middle button is the Stop button, highlighted while a script is recording or while a script is playing. Pressing it while recording ends the recording of your script and prompts the Save Script screen (see Figure 18-4). Pressing Stop while a script is playing abandons playback. Stopping playback does not reverse any operations performed before Stop was pressed.

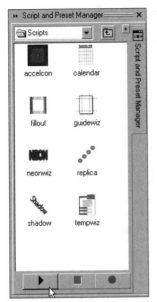

Figure 18-3: The Playback, Stop, and Record buttons appear at the bottom of the Script and Preset Manager.

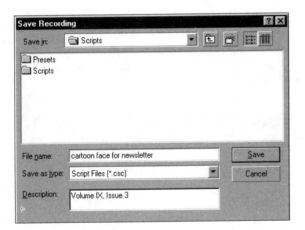

Figure 18-4: The Save Recording dialog box is prompted by pressing the Stop button.

Editing scripts

After learning a bit about composing scripts by exploring Script Editor's thorough Help files, you can open existing scripts and edit them. You can perhaps alter a script that turns an object red so it turns the object blue instead; or you can change the direction of an extrusion path. Learning to edit existing scripts is a marvelous introduction to learning to compose your own scripts from scratch.

Composing scripts from scratch

If you know even a small amount of Visual Basic, you can use Script Editor to compose scripts entirely by yourself.

Working with Preset Scripts

Open the Script and Preset Manager, and open the *Presets* folder. This folder holds more than 70 predefined scripts. Create a rectangle using the Rectangle tool in CorelDraw, with the default line width and no fill, as shown in Figure 18-5. Now select the preset *3dplaque*. While the empty rectangle is selected, press the Play button on the Script and Preset Manager. After a minute or two, the empty rectangle looks like a filled and bordered rectangle, also shown in Figure 18-5 (but in color, of course). By the way, playing back scripts takes time. Sometimes it appears as if no disk activity is taking place. Your computer may appear to have "frozen up," but be patient. We've had scripts take as long as three minutes to complete.

Abandon the preceding rectangle. On a new page, now enter a string of artistic text, preferably with a 72-point font. Select the preset below *3dplaque*. It's called *arches*. While the text and the *arches* preset are selected, click the Playback button on the Script and Preset Manager. The results should resemble Figure 18-6. In this example, upon playing back the script, we found the Perspective Effect to be a bit imposing, so we right-clicked on the text and selected Current Effect Roll-up, which was Extrude, and chose the Perspective Tab. From here we could adjust the perspective depth to make the text something more readable.

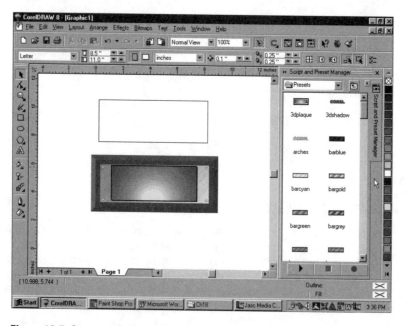

Figure 18-5: Create a 3D plaque like this one with a preset.

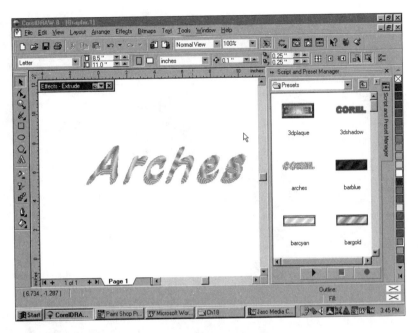

Figure 18-6: Text has been treated with the *arches* preset.

Figure 18-7 shows the *button* and *design01* presets applied. In this example, you can see that the small representative picture shown in the Script and Preset Manager gives you a pretty good idea of what the results will look like when applied to an onscreen object. The large button was created as a simple circle with no fill. When we selected the circle, clicked on the *button* icon in the Script and Preset Manager, and pressed Play, it transformed the large circle into an object that looked just like the icon.

Similarly, as shown in this same figure, after we clicked *design01* in the Script and Preset Manager, the polygon below the button took on the same Fill and Extrude qualities as represented by the *design01* icon. To make it easier to see which script icon edited which object in this figure, We've positioned the button and polygon object in the same relative positions they occupy in the Script and Preset Manager menu.

Remember

Figure 18-8 demonstrates *design19* and *earthgld*. Remember, the effects shown here are applied to simple text with no editing whatsoever. Only the effect was applied.

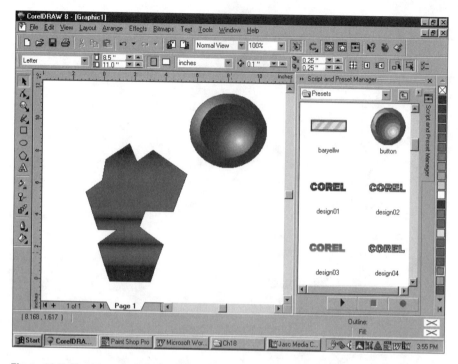

Figure 18-7: The *button* and *design01* presets have been applied.

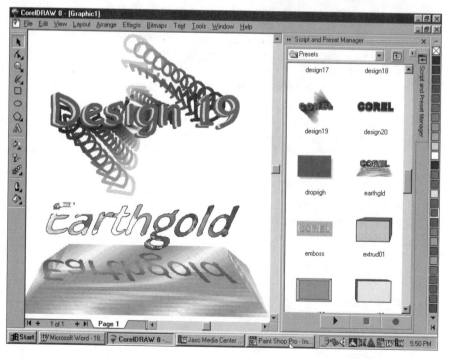

Figure 18-8: The *design19* and *earthgld* effects have been applied to simple artistic text.

Figure 18-9 shows four worthwhile text effects; the words that have been used to demonstrate the effects are the same as the effects' names. In color, they are each eye-catching and unique.

Figure 18-9: Four excellent preset text effects are demonstrated.

Secret

Spectrl1 and *Spectrl2* should only be rendered on simple fonts with very few serifs. Otherwise, portions of your text will disappear when the effect is finished rendering.

One way to look at these presets is as jumping-off points for further creativity. You might try changing the perspective to Small Back, or changing the colors of the extruded portion of the text to contrast more with the text face. Some are perfect right out of the box.

Click on the Up One Folder icon in the Script and Preset Manager, and select the Scripts folder. This menu has a handful of quick special effects. One is called *accelcon* (for accelerated contour) because it creates a deeply contoured version of any object you select. Figure 18-10 shows two preset effects applied consecutively. These objects started as simple Bézier curves. The preset called *fillout* was applied first. This preset thickens the outline of the selected object and fills the outline with a color gradient of your choice. Next *replica* was applied, which duplicates or clones (your choice) the selected object as many times as you specify.

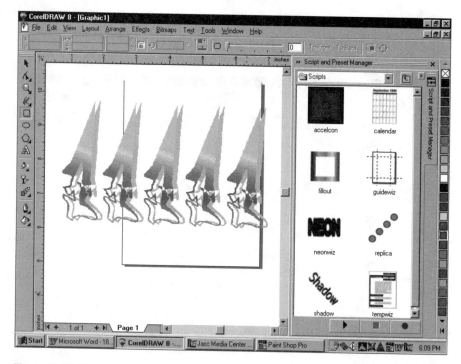

Figure 18-10: Two preset scripts were applied to a simple Bézier curve to create this effect.

Remember

Remember, *cloned* objects retain their links to the master object, so most effects or editing applied to the master object will change the cloned objects as well. A *duplicated* object is not linked to the master object.

The template scripts

Inside the Scripts folder (one of the folders you see in the Script and Preset Manager) are three hidden templates: one to create an instant calendar, one to set up grids on your page, and one to alter the templates included with CorelDraw. Pictured in Figure 18-11 is the Template Customization Wizard. You'll see this opening screen when you click on the Template icon in the Presets folder of the Script and Preset Manager. Template customization is explained in more detail in Chapter 16.

Figure 18-11: The Template Customization Wizard opening screen welcomes you.

It took about five minutes for the *calendar* script to create the calendar shown in Figure 18-12. After clicking on the icon, you're prompted to provide year and month, page orientation, font selection, and an optional link to a picture. After a brief interval, the calendar will be finished.

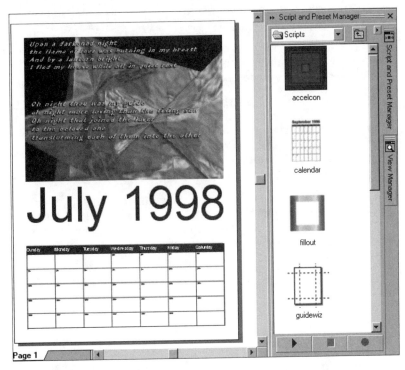

Figure 18-12: This calendar was created by selecting the script labeled *calendar*.

Other presets

Other presets are available on the bonus CD-ROMs that come with CorelDraw 8. Without a doubt, CorelDraw users will be posting helpful scripts on Web sites for the public to download, providing features such as the ability to open one of the last four pictures you were working on with a single mouse click or to change text to a particular font with one motion. Just by understanding how to use ready-made scripts, you can see that the Corel Script tool is quite helpful. Scripts need not be relegated to the cumbersome menu of folders in the Script and Preset Manager (and it will become cumbersome after you have more than a handful of scripts in one folder). Scripts can become icons on a toolbar, appear as items on a menu, or be launched with a hot-key combination. You'll learn to set these options later in the chapter.

Recording Your Own Scripts

Recording your own scripts is an intermediate step for somebody new to Corel scripts. By recording your own scripts, you need not learn any scripting language; you'll learn a lot more about the possibilities (and limitations) of scripts. When recording your own scripts, you work right inside CorelDraw. You need not have Script Editor open. Your only interface with the script program is the Script and Preset Manager. Using the Manager, you can record, stop recording, and save your scripts to hard disk, and you can play back your scripts.

To prepare to record your own scripts, have the Script and Preset Manager open and moved to the upper-right of your screen. Open and position conveniently any roll-ups and toolbars that you'll be using for your scripts.

After your screen is organized, press the red Record button and begin your procedure. You can tell you are recording because the red button will be grayed out. When you finish, press Stop. You'll be prompted to save your script. (Scripts are saved as .CSC files.) At the bottom of the save screen is an area to write a description of your script. As your scripts become more complicated and grow in number, you'll be thankful for this option.

Corel Script remembers any roll-up parameters you adjust and execute during your script recording. However, it helps to have all the roll-ups in place that you intend to use during the script. It's time to note one remarkable fact: To play back the script, you need not have any roll-ups that were required for the recording present on the screen. Your script will be carried out with a "clean screen."

Advice on scripting

Tip

Here are some scripting pointers to remember:

- Contrary to what you may have learned using macros, Corel Script remembers only mouse clicks. You cannot create a macro from your favorite hot-key combinations. For example, you can't create a script to open the most recently used file by pressing Ctrl+O. Even though that is a valid hot-key combination, Corel Script will not record it as part of a macro. With the exception of remembering text you enter while a text tool is being used, Corel Script does not record keyboard commands. You cannot incorporate existing hot-key combinations into your recorded macro. However, after you've created a macro with mouse clicks and/or text, it can be saved as a hot-key combination, which we explain later.

- When you record a script to perform a task on a selected object — for example, to execute a complex fountain fill on a rectangle or an ellipse you have selected — Corel Script performs the task on the selected object no matter where it is on the page. You need not position the object in the exact same portion of the page as you did when you recorded the script. Additionally, you don't need to reproduce the exact screen position of any roll-ups you used during recording in order to play back the script later. Corel Script is capable of locating the roll-up on the screen, even if it moved from a prior position.

- Corel Script remembers where on the screen you created objects while recording your script. Upon playback, it re-creates those objects in the exact same position where they were created during recording. This means that if you moved far off the page to record a script, perhaps because your page was getting crowded, Corel Script creates that object far off the page during playback. While you play back a script, if nothing seems to be happening, wait a second or two, change your Zoom setting to 25 percent, and see if your script was carried out somewhere in the far reaches of the workspace.

- If you create scripts to perform tasks that involve selected objects, such as blends between two objects or Text to Path routines, make sure you have those two objects selected before you record your script. If you create a script that includes the need for Corel Script to select the objects first, two things might happen. First, it may select the two objects in the wrong order to perform your operation. Second, it may not select the two objects you have in mind, if more than two objects exist on the screen. So it's best to have the objects selected before you record your script.

- Before you play back your script, make sure you've selected any objects involved. If you forget, you may sometimes get an error message. But at other times, you'll get no response at all after pressing the Playback button.

So far, you've seen how to record scripts to perform simple tasks that involve two or three steps. However, Corel Script is very competent at recording complex, lengthy procedures. The program does not appear to be a memory hog, which has tremendous implications.

For example, how many times have you developed a piece of work, looked back at it later, and wondered how you accomplished it? Trying to reproduce the same winning technique exactly can sometimes be frustrating. But with Corel Script, you can record the process. If, at a particular moment, you are feeling especially creative, just turn on Corel Script, start creating, and see what happens. No longer are your "magic moments" relegated only to the moment. Once you've recorded the script, you can play it back, watch what you did, and even stop the playback in the middle to examine the procedure a bit closer. With even a small amount of Script editing knowledge, you can alter a script you've created to use different colors or tool settings.

Examples of recorded scripts

Figure 18-13 shows the Script and Preset Manager with some personally created scripts in the viewing window. By default, any scripts you record will be stored in this folder for immediate viewing. If, for example, you use this window to explore scripts included on one of the extra CD-ROMs included with CorelDraw, this window will be filled with the contents of a specific folder. To find your way back here, note that the default folder for scripts you create is C:\Corel\Draw80\Draw\Scripts. Use the Up One Folder browse tool to find your way back to this folder, and all the scripts you create should be here. If you edit scripts later using the Script Editor, take care to save them in this default location, or you'll have to go searching for your edited script.

Figure 18-13: The Script and Preset Manager viewing window shows scripts you have recorded.

Figure 18-14 illustrates several principles. Notice the mouse pointer pointing to a recorded script called *Yellow to Blue fill.* We recorded that script by creating a simple rectangle, pressing Record, opening the Fill dialog box, choosing those two colors, and then filling the object. Corel Script recorded our filling operations. Notice that, as part of saving the script, an icon is created showing the final product of the script. In the example shown in Figure 18-14, we selected text rather than a shape before playing back the command. As you can see, the playback script worked just as well on the text as on a shape object.

Figure 18-15 shows the mouse pointer near the script labeled *Scale 150 percent.* We recording this script by selecting an object and adjusting the Scale Factor on the Property Bar. You can record and save as many scale-adjusting scripts as you like. These can be applied to any object.

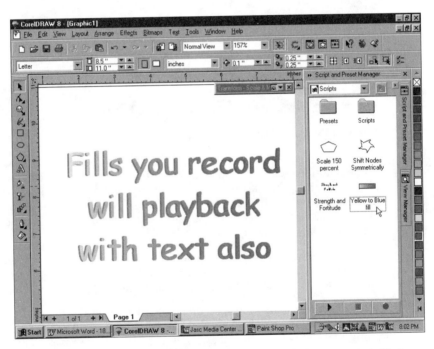

Figure 18-14: The Script and Preset Manager main screen displays some text effects.

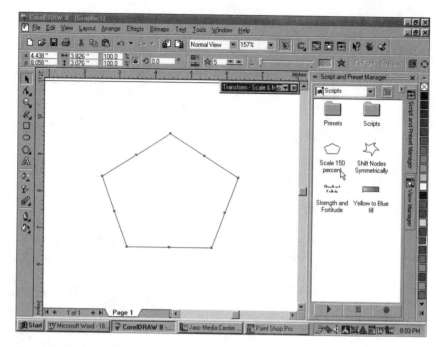

Figure 18-15: A user-made Scale Adjusting script is ready to run.

Secret

While recording a script, take your time. The script process will not remember time intervals between commands implemented. It is fine to pause and check a note you've written to yourself, or take a second to think carefully about the command you are about to execute. Your script will still commence at lightning speed.

Figure 18-16 shows the pointer near a script entitled *Rotate 45 Degrees*. Not surprisingly, this script rotates any object 45 degrees. Note that the icon saved with a script does not always reflect the script's purpose very well.

What Corel Script saves as an icon is the object that the command was performed on while recording. You can replace the icon with another chosen picture by right-clicking on the icon in the Script and Preset Manager, which brings up a pop-up menu with the Create Thumbnail command. This command replaces the existing thumbnail image with any image you have selected at the moment (see Figure 18-17). In this case, the image will be replaced with a picture that has more to do with rotating. Figure 18-18 shows the new image reproduced as the icon for the command.

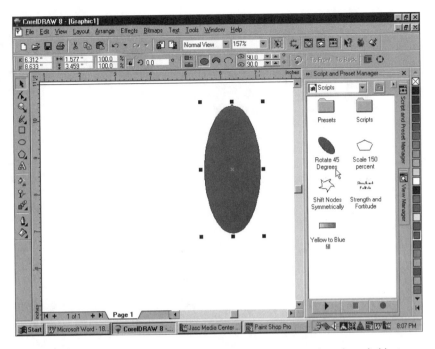

Figure 18-16: This user-created *Rotate 45 Degrees* script rotates the selected object 45 degrees.

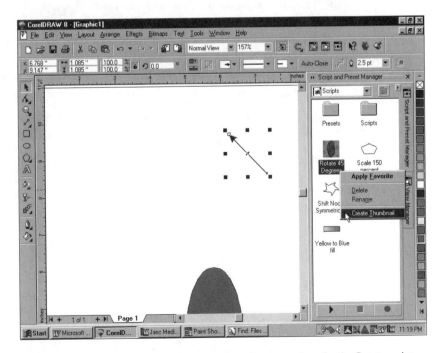

Figure 18-17: Select Create Thumbnail to replace the current icon for the *Rotate* script.

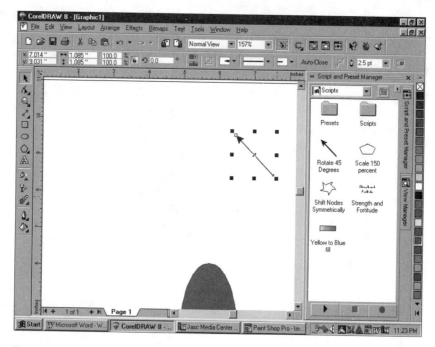

Figure 18-18: The new Thumbnail icon appears for the Rotate script.

Figure 18-19 shows the mouse pointer about to execute a script to create a complex line object with many curves. Corel Script recorded the entire procedure of creating and adjusting the line until we were happy with it. The script was saved and can be played back to create the same image at any time. Why is this better than cutting and pasting? Because you can use the script in later sessions. This routine rather resembles Draw's capability of creating and saving Power Lines.

Figure 18-20 shows a remarkable script action. By pressing Play, we can have these two objects blended in 60 steps. When we created this script, the Blend roll-up was on the screen. But we can play it back with the Blend roll-up off screen, and yet the procedure is carried out flawlessly. This example shows a major benefit to using scripts: You can carry out tasks that require roll-ups without their having to be present, cluttering up your screen!

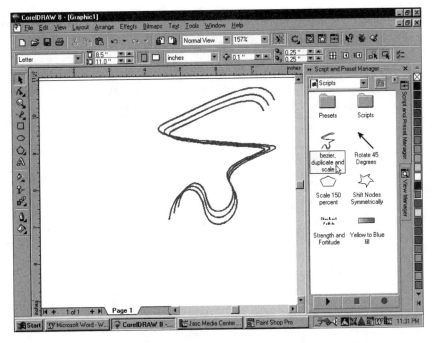

Figure 18-19: A user-created script helps create a complex, curved line object.

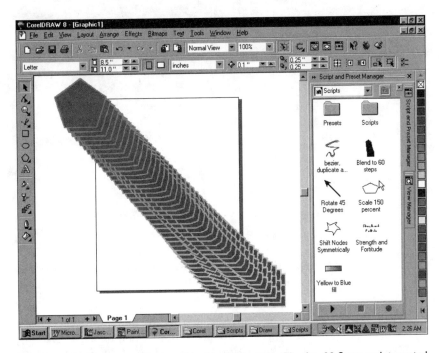

Figure 18-20: These two objects will be blended using a *Blend to 60 Steps* script created by the user. Notice that the Blend roll-up is nowhere in sight.

Running Scripts with Buttons and Hot-keys

Here's how to create a button on a toolbar from one of your Corel scripts.

STEPS:

Creating a Toolbar Button for a Script

Step 1.   You must first relocate your script to the directory where CorelDraw's Customize Tools menu will be capable of seeing and working with them. To do this, use Windows Explorer to open the folder containing the script you made, and copy it to the Corel\Scripts folder. The script you made will most likely be found in Corel\Draw\Scripts.

Step 2.   Now Select Tools ➪ Options ➪ Customize ➪ Toolbars from the CorelDraw menu. Customize and Toolbars appear as expandable folders in the command tree shown.

Step 3.   In the Commands area, open the folder that says *General Scripts*.

Step 4.   Click on the icon for the script from which you want to create a button. See Figure 18-21.

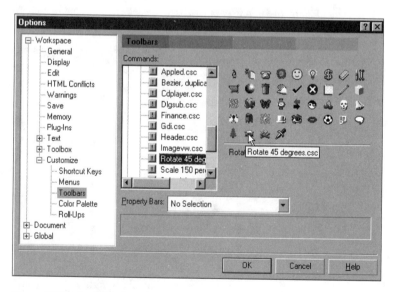

Figure 18-21: From the Customize Toolbars dialog box, select a script from which to create a button.

Step 5.   Move your mouse pointer to any of the buttons in the rows set aside for you to choose from. (Again, see Figure 18-21.) Get ready to drag that button to any toolbar on the CorelDraw main screen.

Step 6. Drag the button of your choice up to a toolbar, as shown in Figure 18-22. This button is "loaded" with your script command and is now ready for service.

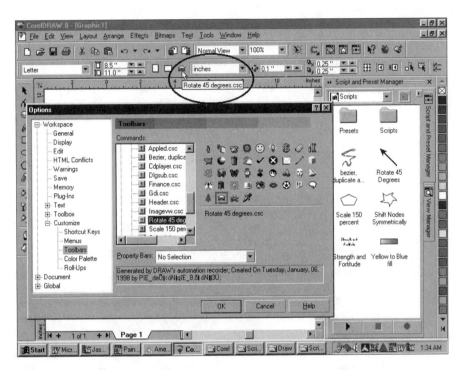

Figure 18-22: Drag a button loaded with your script up to an existing toolbar.

If you drag the button "out into the open" on the main CorelDraw screen, it opens as a free-floating toolbar and adheres to the same rules that all CorelDraw toolbars operate under. If you intend to create buttons for many of your scripts, this step we just described — creating a free-floating button — is really the first step in creating an entire toolbar of your scripts. Having created a free-floating button, make this into a full-fledged toolbar by opening other scripts you want to move and attaching them to this free-floating button. This new toolbar can be as large as you want. When you're finished, close the Options dialog box. No further "saving" is necessary.

To create a hot-key combination to activate your script, look again at Figure 18-21, the Toolbars area of the Customize dialog box. Instead of operating with the Toolbars tab, open the Keyboard tab. The same procedure applies as previously outlined, except instead of dragging a button to a toolbar, type in a hot-key combination that will execute your command.

You can also use this same dialog box to attach scripts to an existing roll-up.

Learning How to Compose Scripts

Even a light background in the Visual Basic language is enough to get started using Corel Script. If you don't know it, many excellent, user-friendly books are available on the subject. It is one of the easiest computer languages to learn. Corel Script is a cross between Visual Basic and simplified CorelDraw-specific command code.

The rest of this chapter provides hints on how to use the Corel Script online manual. After working with the online manual and learning a bit of Visual Basic, you'll be writing and editing scripts in no time.

Corel Script's online manual comes complete with example scripts. Every command is explained in detail with examples given, and ready-made scripts are offered to create custom dialog boxes that you can apply in any situation. The online manual also includes an organized compendium of commands used for CorelDraw and Corel Photo-Paint. It further includes instructions on how to use Corel Script to create scripts for other Corel applications such as Ventura 7.

Secret

Here are three quick tips to remember:

- Because Corel Script is just text, you can literally copy an example script right out of a Help file and paste it into Corel Script Editor. (You must place the proper application-specific headings, of course.)

- Please note that many scripts in the online manual are application-specific. If it says the script works only with CorelDraw 7, you can try adding the `.WITHOBJECT CorelDraw.Automation.8` command line and removing the one referring to CorelDraw 7, but the results are not predictable.

- Corel Script supports drag-and-drop. Open CorelDraw with the Script and Preset Manager viewing window available. Now open Script Editor. Drag any script icon from the Script and Preset Manager, drop it onto Script Editor, and the script will open, ready for editing.

Using the Corel Script online manual

The only way to access the Corel Script online manual is from outside CorelDraw. Select Program from the Windows Start menu, choose CorelDraw ⇨ Productivity Tools ⇨ Corel SCRIPT Editor, and select Help on the menu. Click the Contents tab and open the Corel Script "book," which is shown in Figure 18-23. You may wish to browse the "Using this online reference" article, which is two items above the Corel Script online manual itself. This article contains a book-by-book breakdown of what is available in the manual. (See Figure 18-24.)

Figure 18-23: Open the Corel Script online help manual.

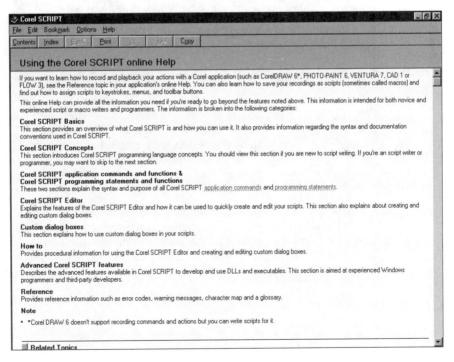

Figure 18-24: Here, we have accessed the "Using the Corel SCRIPT online Help" article.

Figure 18-25 shows the articles included in the Corel Script Basics book. Of particular interest to beginners are the "Sample script," the "Corel SCRIPT programming language," and the "Sample scripts" articles.

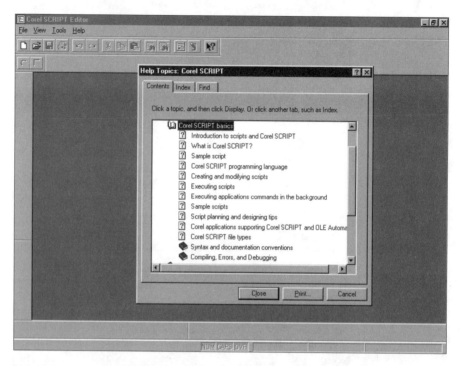

Figure 18-25: These articles are included in the Corel Script Basics book.

Figure 18-26 shows a sample script, available by clicking on the Sample Scripts article in the Corel Script Basics book. (You cannot see the entire script description in this picture.) Every parameter and command are explained. Remember that this script can be copied and pasted right into Script Editor itself. You may then use CorelDraw's Tools ⇨ Scripts ⇨ Run command to run the script.

It's very easy to lose your place while using these Help files. Don't forget to create bookmarks as you go. As soon as you create a bookmark, you'll be able to open Help to that exact location the next time you click on the bookmark tab and scroll down. Help can store an unlimited number of bookmarks.

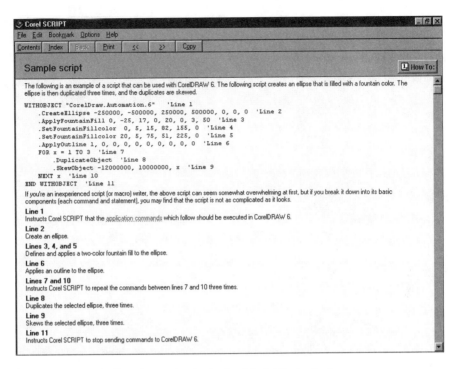

Figure 18-26: A sample script appears in the Corel Script Basics book.

Understanding Corel Script Programming Statements

From within the Corel Script Basics book, click on the "Corel Script Programming Language" article. Scroll down to a right-facing arrow that reads "Click here for a listing of all programming statements and functions." They mean it. Click on the right-facing arrow. Figure 18-27 shows what you'll see.

In Figure 18-27, the mouse pointer is shown hovering over one of the programming statement examples. Clicking on it takes you to an example of the use of that programming statement, with descriptions of the syntax used.

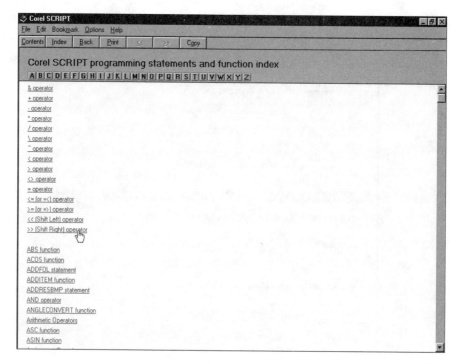

Figure 18-27: All of Corel Script's programming statements and functions are listed.

Creating custom dialog boxes

This online manual also includes instructions for creating custom dialog boxes. With Corel Script, making dialog boxes is just about as easy as dragging and drawing the features you want to include right onto the box. The Corel Script online manual contains many interactive dialog boxes that you can edit to suit your needs. The programming component (such as causing one box to close while another opens when the user clicks) has been taken care of. All you need to do is change the labels and link the dialog boxes to a script of commands for the boxes to control.

Photo-Paint and Scripts

In some ways, Photo-Paint's scripts are more flexible than CorelDraw's. In Photo-Paint you can use a script to open files, print, arrange toolbars and dockers just the way you like them, and other "extra-document" chores (tasks that involve more than manipulating objects in the current document, which is what scripts are pretty much limited to in Draw). These tasks also include faxing your Photo-Paint project and importing a file from a particular folder. Scripts can be recorded to perform these tasks all with a single mouseclick.

Photo-Paint comes with two folders of scripts, which are accessed by clicking View ➪ Dockers ➪ Scripts. You'll see the Scripts docker to the right of the workspace. Click the Effects folder to see 59 different effects you can apply to your canvas (see Figure 18-28). To apply an effect to the background (for example, *diffuse blur* or *shear*), simply make sure no object on your canvas is currently selected, and double-click on the effect. To apply an effect to an object (for example, *lens flare* or *3D rotate*), select the desired object and double-click on the effect.

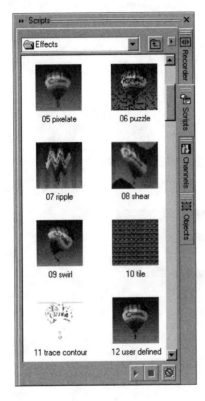

Figure 18-28: The Scripts\Effects folder shows 59 preset effects applied by a single mouseclick.

Most of Photo-Paint's scripts are not interactive, meaning you won't see a dialog box while the script is running, asking you to make choices. This can be an issue. For example, when you apply the *ripple* script, you have no say regarding how much ripple is applied. Also, changing the amount of ripple in the Ripple dialog box and then running the script has no effect on how the script is applied. Each script comes with its own settings.

To alter the amount of an effect, you can use Edit ➪ Fade Last Command, but with certain effects like *shear* and *perspective*, Fade Last Command doesn't reduce the effect amount. Rather, you'll see the object as it was, with a "ghost" of the effect superimposed over it.

The Photo-Paint Scripts folder

Also found in the Scripts docker is the Scripts folder. It contains scripts for creating text, masking, and movie building, as well as object cropping effects. Activate these scripts simply by double-clicking on them.

To create text effects, you need not create an image first. Just double-click the script, and a dialog box prompts to you enter a line of text. (See Figure 18-29.) Movie scripts require you either to load a movie or set aside a series of files from which you want to create a movie. (The *MovieBuilder* script prompts you to browse your hard drive for files to be sequentially converted into movie frames.) The various *Object* scripts require that objects on your canvas be selected. The *FlamingText* script actually creates a ten-frame "flaming" movie (an .AVI file). You'll be prompted to type in the text that will appear to be on fire.

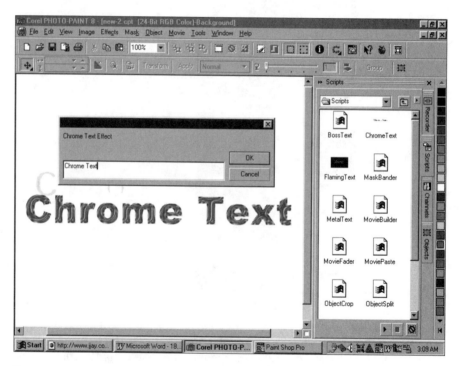

Figure 18-29: To create text effects, double-click a script and enter text in the dialog box.

After creating an object with a script, you can edit it further. Figure 18-30 shows text created with the *MetalText* script. Figure 18-31 shows the same text after applying the Whirlpool, Wiremesh effect, and a Drop Shadow, positioned more like a background glow (turquoise) than a shadow. A Custom Pastel brush was used along the edges of the letters, with bright colors, and a transparency setting of 55. Before you can edit this *MetalText* object, you must select the Object picker from the toolbox and click on the text.

Figure 18-30: Text created with the *MetalText* script.

Figure 18-31: The same text after editing with paint brushes, effects, and fills.

Recording scripts

Note

Recording scripts is covered somewhat in Chapter 9 of this book, but we'll go into more detail here. In Photo-Paint, most tasks can be recorded. Paintbrush strokes, adding fills, creating objects, browsing your hard drive, and importing objects or other documents — all these and other tasks are fair game for your recorded script. Proceed with caution when making a script that involves including a file from outside your Corel folder on your computer. If you move a file, forgetting that that file is essential for your Photo-Paint script, then the script will fail. Nonetheless, Photo-Paint scripts will remember fill and color settings, brush nib sizes, transparency and soft edge amounts, and all the other experimental and serendipitous settings you might build into your tools when creating a painting. For this reason, recording a script in Photo-Paint can really be a bit like a piano player leaving the tape recorder on when feeling especially inspired. But in a sense, Photo-Paint's tools are one better, because you can later re-create that same script on a different canvas, add to it or remove portions of the script, and even play it back on a canvas at a higher resolution.

As you record a script, each action appears as a line of text in the Recorder docker. (See Figure 18-32, shown with an image — a series of overlapping objects created from converted brush strokes, which are saved as a script.) Notice the small arrow pointing at the line of the script currently active; in this case, the top line. You begin recording a script by clicking the red Record button at the bottom, and, when you are done, click the Stop button. Pauses in between commands are not remembered, so you may take your time looking up the next step or clearing your head to be certain of what you are doing next. Make a mental note of when you began your script: Did you create a blank document and then press the Record button? Did you type some text and then press the Record button? Or did you press Record before doing anything at all? Happily, when you save your script (click the floppy disk icon at the top of the Recorder docker), you'll be provided room for two quick lines of notes to yourself. Unless you type text into this Description area, your name and the date will appear there. After recording a script, a pictorial icon of it appears in the Scripts docker, in the subfolder called Scripts.

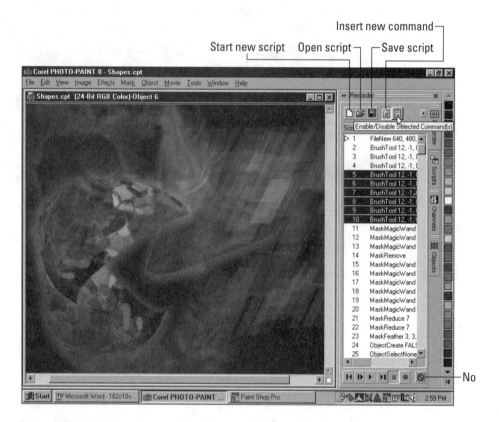

Figure 18-32: An image created with a script; each command is numbered. The current command is highlighted, with an arrow pointing at it.

To save scripts you've recorded, click on the floppy disk icon at the top of the Recorder docker. The folder icon to its left is for opening a script, although any scripts you create will automatically appear in the Scripts folder, available when you click on the Scripts docker. Click on the folder icon to browse your hard drive. Click on the icon farthest to the left to clear the script area and start again on a new script.

Secret

Did you create something that you are happy with but forgot to record it as a script? Open your Undo list (Edit ⇨ Undo Special ⇨ Undo List), and view all the commands noted there. Click on the Save button. You can now save your Undo list as a script. This Undo list contains the same type of information that a script does.

You can select any line or group of lines within a script and disable, delete, or make them active. Scripts can have errors, and at times you may want to disable a particular line in a script to determine if that is the line or group of lines giving you trouble. Click the Enable/Disable Selected Commands icon, second from the right at the top of the Recorder docker. It functions as a toggle. (See Figure 18-32.) To select more than one line at a time, simply click and drag through the list with your mouse, highlighting the chosen lines. To delete a line or group of lines, select the commands you want eliminated, and click the No icon at the bottom-right of the Recorder docker.

Inserting commands

In Photo-Paint, you can jump into the middle of a script and add new commands. Simply double-click on a command and click on the Insert New Commands icon, at the middle-right of the Recorder docker. Then click on the red Record button at the bottom right of the docker. The command "Set Document Info" is inserted immediately. This is how Photo-Paint keeps track of your work up to that point, recording everything you are about to do as new commands to be inserted after the command you double-clicked. The commands below your new recording are unaffected—if your script had 50 commands and you added 15 new commands after command 25, then commands 26 through 50 would appear after the new 15 you just inserted. The old command 26 would be the new command 41.

Correcting errors in scripts

At times, after recording an especially lengthy script and attempting to play it back, you may be told that an error exists. Photo-Paint will not even allow you to load such a script. To fix it, open the script in Script Editor (right-click on the script in question and click on Edit Script). When it's loaded, click on

Debug ⇨ Run (see Figure 18-33). The Debug program will run, and you'll see a window reporting your error. The first number appearing in parenthesis (in this case, 221) is the number of the offending command line (see Figure 18-34). Click on Search ⇨ Go to Line, as shown in the figure, and enter the offending line. You'll find your mouse cursor moved there.

As shown in Figure 18-35, the offending command in this case involved an erroneous command involving the Fancy ⇨ Alchemy command. In this case, it was easy to select and delete the offending "runaway digits." After erasing all those digits and saving the command, the script worked fine in Photo-Paint.

At times, however, after locating an offending line, it might be best just to erase the entire command. Remember the line number, though. When you open the script again in Photo-Paint, you can move the mouse to the line preceding your bad command, and then double-click to highlight the location. Then click on the Insert New Command icon and click on the red Record button. Repeat the command as you originally wanted it, click on the Stop button, and save your script. The script will now contain the new command.

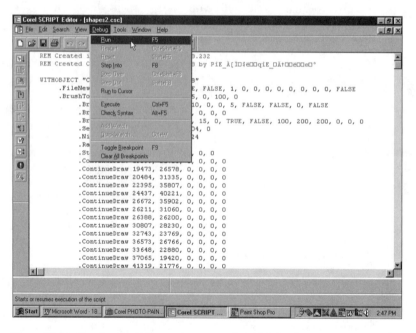

Figure 18-33: Running the Debug program reveals which line has an error preventing you from running your script.

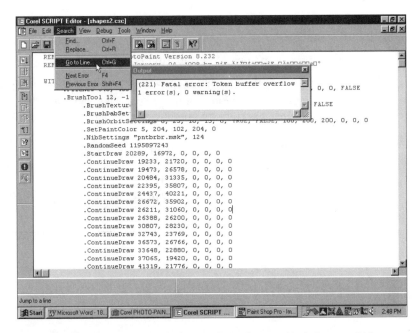

Figure 18-34: When the results are reported, the first number indicates which command is causing the problem.

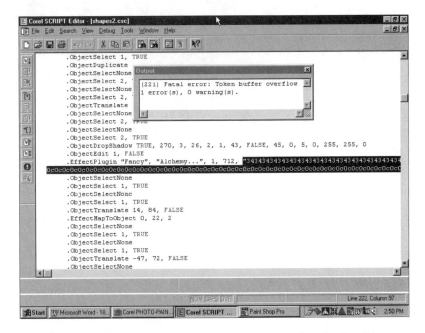

Figure 18-35: When the line is highlighted, you can remove the offending digits.

Summary

▶ You can simply use the preset scripts that come with CorelDraw.

▶ You can learn to record your own scripts from within the CorelDraw program.

▶ If you know even a small amount of the Visual Basic language, you can easily learn to edit recorded scripts by opening a recorded script in CorelDraw's Script Editor.

▶ By exploring the Corel Script online manual, you can combine your knowledge of Visual Basic with the information in the manual to create your own fully functional scripts from scratch.

▶ You can create and work with scripts in Photo-Paint as well as CorelDraw.

Chapter 19

Other Utilities

It may be hard to believe that after all of the preceding chapters about CorelDraw's supporting applications, there's still more to talk about. But there is. Your understanding of the CorelDraw 8 graphics suite isn't complete until you know at least the basics of two highly useful utilities — CorelCapture and CorelScan.

The first utility, CorelCapture, enables you to easily capture and save what people in the computer journalism business call *screen shots*. Screen shots (also called screen captures) are pictures of computer monitor screens. After you capture a screen, you can use it in a manual, on the Internet, or just about anywhere you want. As we move through the discussion on how to use this nifty little utility, I'm sure you'll think of lots of ways to use screen shots.

CorelScan simply makes scanning easier — whether into a CorelDraw application or another TWAIN-compliant program (TWAIN stands for Technology Without An Interesting Name). It is a set of wizards designed to help you set up your scanner and then make the proper settings for the source image and the intended use, or application, for the final scanned artwork. CorelScan is designed to help novices scan more effectively, but if you've been using your scanner for a while, you too may find that it makes scanning easier.

CorelCapture

When friends and acquaintances look over our books, they usually ask, "How did you do all of these graphics?" Many of them we create in CorelDraw or Photo-Paint. But all of the screen captures (and partial screen captures) are done with CorelCapture. CorelCapture takes much of the work out of the capturing, saving, and organizing process. All we do is press a key. CorelCapture captures the screen we designate, converts it to grayscale, prints it, and then saves it with a filename in a predesignated sequence—all while we keep working.

Today, people have many uses for screen captures—as instruction sheets for employees, in software and hardware documentation, for Internet presentations, and in application Help files, to name a few. CorelCapture can provide screen captures suited to just about any use you can think of, even multimedia presentations.

Creating a screen capture

One of the joys of CorelCapture is that it's so remarkably easy to use. It requires little (and sometimes no) setup, and then it just sits there, waiting in the wings to activate each time you need a screen shot. In previous versions of CorelCapture, you worked from a dialog box. In keeping with Corel's move toward uniformity, version 8 uses a Property Bar-like interface , shown in Figure 19-1. The Property Bar works identically to the Property Bars inside the other CorelDraw suite applications, except that in this case it works with all applications. Like previous versions, the interface is straightforward—no hidden menus or dialog boxes, and it's logically arranged. Setting up usually entails a quick and simple progression through the six sections of the CorelCapture dialog box, often in the order they appear.

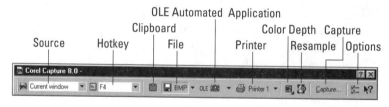

Figure 19-1: Use the CorelCapture Property Bar for setting up screen captures.

Setting activation options

Activation means "When do I take the screen shot?" In other words, here's where you tell CorelCapture when you press a key, or a combination of keys, to capture the screen. By default, CorelCapture executes a capture when you press F7. You can change that to any function key from the Hot Key drop-down list, or you can choose User Defined from the list and set just about any Ctrl, Alt, or Shift+keystroke combination.

You may be asking yourself, why not just leave it at F7? Here's why: when CorelCapture is active — in capture mode — even though it waits in the background, it overrides hot keys in the active application. Say you're working in an application, Microsoft Word, for instance, and you normally use F7 to activate the spell checker. If CorelCapture is open and active, pressing F7 will instead take a screen shot. So changing the hot key simply enables you to set a keystroke combination that won't interfere with the way you work.

Secret

When setting CorelCapture activation, consider how long you want the program to wait once you press the hot key before it actually captures the contents of the screen. Does this seem like a no-brainer? Right away, right? I mean, why wait longer than you have to?

Here's why: Often, you'll want the screen shot to include an open menu or flyout, or you may want the mouse to display doing something or other. Giving yourself a little time to set up the screen before CorelCapture goes to work enables you to prepare for the screen shot. You can set a delay from 1 to 60 seconds with the Initial Delay Before First Capture option in the Options dialog box, which appears when you click on the Options button (second from the right) of the CorelCapture Property Bar. The default is five seconds, which we find is usually long enough. (The Options dialog box is shown in Figure 19-2.)

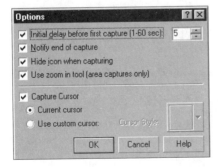

Figure 19-2: Use the Options dialog box to tell CorelCapture how long to wait before performing a capture, among other settings.

Telling CorelCapture what to capture

Sometimes you don't want to capture the contents of the entire screen. Occasionally, the active window or dialog box will do. You control which portion of the screen CorelCapture grabs with the Source drop-down (first option) of the CorelCapture Property Bar.

Most of the options in the Source drop-down are self-explanatory. You may, however, wonder about the third option, Animation Window. As you'll see in a moment, CorelCapture lets you create animated movies from your screen shots. This option enables you to capture roll-ups and toolbars as active windows, which can be helpful when creating animation sequences.

The last three options — Rectangle Area, Elliptical Area, and Free-hand Area — let you select portions of the screen with your mouse. To use one of them, you select the desired shape option (Free-hand lets you capture oddly shaped objects), click on Capture, and return to the application from which you want to capture a portion of the screen. Now press the hot key to initiate the capture. While CorelCapture cycles through the duration pause you set in Activation, set up the screen objects as you want to capture them — open a menu, a flyout, or whatever. When working in Rectangle or Elliptical mode the mouse cursor turns into a butterfly net, drag a marquee around the portion of the screen you want to capture. When you release the mouse, CorelCapture will capture the area you selected.

In Free-hand mode you use a different method. Press the hot key to initiate the capture. The mouse cursor displays as a registration mark. Click once to start the capture and then move the mouse cursor diagonally to the other end of the area you want to capture. Now click on again to capture the area between the two places you clicked on.

During a Free-hand capture, a magnified version of the area where the mouse cursor is hovering is displayed in the upper-left portion of the screen, allowing you to choose a place to click on more precisely. In addition, Capture displays a diagonal line across the area that will be captured as you position the cursor for the second click, showing you the area that will be captured.

Telling CorelCapture where to send the captured image

One of the really slick features of CorelCapture is that you can send the captured screen shot wherever you need it — a file, your printer, the Clipboard, or an OLE-aware client. You can even send it to two destinations at once. While capturing screens for this book, for example, we sent each capture to a file and my desktop printer. This saves me the extra time of having to open them in another application to print them later.

Where CorelCapture puts the image is controlled from the Destination buttons on the Property Bar. To save to a file, for example, choose a file format, as shown in Figure 19-3. To save to an OLE application, choose the application; to print to a specific printer, network or otherwise, choose the printer. Again, these options are for the most part self-explanatory. The File option saves the image to a filename you designate by choosing Options from the File drop-down list. This brings up the Capture As dialog box. You can name files individually or tell CorelCapture to name them sequentially, as you'll see in the later section, "Setting up automatic naming."

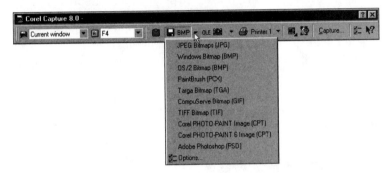

Figure 19-3: Use the Destination section of CorelCapture to designate where to send the screen capture.

The one option that probably needs explaining is Animation File. This, of course, designates an .AVI movie file in which to save consecutive captures. We explain creating movies with CorelCapture in the sidebar "Lights, Camera, Action!"

Next to the Source drop-down list is OLE Automated Application. This sends the capture to an OLE-aware Corel application of your choice—either CorelDraw or Photo-Paint. When you select this option, after CorelCapture captures the screen, it launches the application you designate in the drop-down list and pastes the capture into a new document.

When you select the Printer option on the Property Bar (next to OLE Automated Application), a list of available printers is displayed, enabling you to choose and set up a printer as you normally would from that printer's Print Setup dialog box. To configure the printer, choose the Options command from the Printer drop-down list.

Telling CorelCapture how to process the screen shot

Secret

We told you CorelCapture was full-featured and handy. In many screen capture utilities, you must open the captured image in a bitmap editor, such as Photo-Paint, to tailor it to your needs. But not in CorelCapture. Using the Color Depth and Resample options of CorelCapture allows you to change color depth and resize the image. The options on the Color Depth drop-down are self-explanatory. (If you don't understand color depth, see Chapter 5.) Clicking the Resample button displays the Resample dialog box shown in Figure 19-4. If you are unfamiliar with resampling, it is discussed in Chapter 8. With these options you can set the color depth, resolution, and physical size of the image on the fly—often eliminating the need to resample the image later.

When setting these options, you tell CorelCapture what kind of output you need—Screen, Printer, Clipboard, or a combination. For this book, for example, we set the Color Depth to Grayscale, set the File option to TIFF, and also told CorelCapture to send the image to the printer.

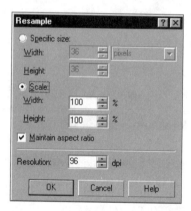

Figure 19-4: Use this dialog box to set resolution and image size on the fly.

Note

Again, if you aren't familiar with color depth, you can learn more about it in Chapter 5. The importance of dots-per-inch resolution is covered in Chapter 7.

Secret

Here's a way to adjust screen shots on the fly. Resample can be used to resize. Set the width to a different size than the capture and check Maintain aspect ratio. It will be captured at the new size and resolution. This feature is great for enlarging screen grabs for editing, or for capturing images at exactly the right size for a layout, such as a Web pages.

Naming and saving files

At the risk of seeming too enthusiastic, let us rave again about the thoroughness of the CorelCapture application, as this next discussion demonstrates. Not only does this utility let you control color depth and resolution, but you can also designate file format and filename from the File option of the CorelCapture Property Bar. We showed you how to choose which file format to save to earlier in this chapter. However, you can also choose one when setting up naming conventions for the captured file. Now, let's look at how to setup naming conventions. To do so, you choose the Options command on the File drop-down, which displays the Capture as dialog box shown in Figure 19-5. The options here are extensive and not necessarily obvious. Let's look at them one at a time.

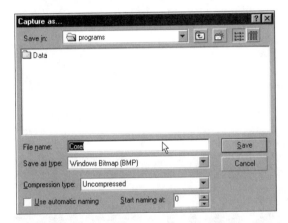

Figure 19-5: Use the File section of CorelCapture to designate filenames for your captures or to choose automatic file naming.

Designating a filename and format

In previous versions of CorelCapture you used the File sheet in the CorelCapture dialog box to set up file naming conventions. In version 8 you use the Save As-like dialog box interface in Capture as. This works quite similarly to any Windows Save As dialog box. You simply go to the folder where you want to save the file and use File name to name the file.

To designate the type of file (.TIFF, .JPEG, Adobe Photoshop, and so on), choose the desired format from the Save as type drop-down list. Many formats also support compression schemes, such as LZW compression for TIFF images and RLE compression for JPEG and Photoshop formats, that you can control from the Compression type drop-down list. When you choose a file format, CorelCapture automatically tacks the format extension (.TIFF, .JPG, .PSD, and so on) onto the end of the file. So do not include the extension in File name, or you get the extension twice (IMAGE.TIFF.TIFF), which is annoying and nonsensical.

Setting up automatic naming

We keep referring to how we used CorelCapture for this book. But it's a perfect example of a typical application for this utility. When you need multiple sequential captures, automatic naming is a lifesaver. Here's the procedure for setting up automatic naming:

STEPS:

Setting Up Automatic Naming for Screen Captures

Step 1. Type the first few characters for the naming scheme in File name. Keep in mind here that CorelCapture adds zeros to the automatic name, depending on the number you start with. For example, if you start with 1, the program tacks on two zeros, like this: *001*. The next will be *002*, and so on. So unless you plan to use the files only in a Windows 95 environment, where long filename conventions are observed, you should type no more than five characters in File name. For this book, for instance, we typed **cds** to identify the book (*CorelDraw Secrets*) and then a number designating the chapter number (01, 02, 18, 19, and so on). When CorelCapture tacked on the automatic name, it added three characters (001, 002, 018, 019, and so on) and the extension. Figure 19-6 shows a list of files created with CorelCapture for Chapter 2 of this book.

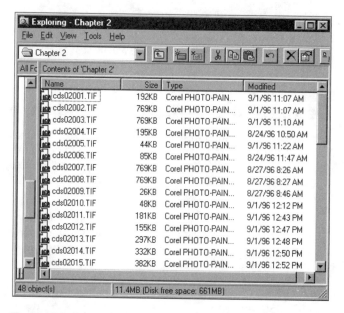

Figure 19-6: Several files have been created with CorelCapture's automatic naming function.

Step 2. Select automatic naming, and then set the number with which you want the naming to begin in Start naming at. Don't add zeros before the number, as CorelCapture adds them automatically.

Step 3. Use the Save in drop-down list and window to designate the desired drive and directory. If you want to save the files to a network drive, choose Network Neighborhood from the Save in drop-down list and then use the window to go to the desired computer, drive, and folder.

That's it! Now, each time you press the hot key, CorelCapture captures the screen, gives it the next name in the sequence, and saves it in the folder you designated. Voilà!

Capturing the cursor and creating borders

Often when capturing a screen, you'll also want to capture the cursor to help demonstrate your point (as we've done several places throughout this book). You may occasionally want to place a colored border around your screen shots, sprucing them up a bit. You can control whether the cursor is captured in the Property Bar Options dialog box (see Figure 19-7). And you designate whether CorelCapture should add a border to the captured image by choosing the Object with Border option in the Source drop-down list.

When capturing the cursor, you can capture the current cursor or tell CorelCapture to substitute a custom cursor by selecting Use custom cursor and then choosing a cursor from the Cursor Style drop-down list. You might find this handy for using the cursor to highlight areas.

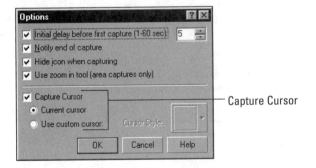

Figure 19-7: Use this dialog box to tell the program to capture the mouse cursor.

To capture the cursor, simply check Capture Cursor. The next time you press a hot key, the cursor will be included in the screen shot. This option works great for Current Window, Client/Animation Window, and Full Screen settings. However, because you use the mouse to capture partial screens with Rectangular Area, Elliptical Area, and Free-hand Area, you cannot capture the cursor when using these settings. Now get out there and capture some screen shots!

Lights, Camera, Action!

Secret

Talk about *Star Wars*! Did you know that you can create movies consisting of your mouse movements and other actions in Windows applications? What a great way to create training tools. Say, for example, that you are a systems administrator, and that you want to place files on the network (even the Internet) showing workers how to perform specific tasks on their computers. Can you think of a better way to show them than having them launch a movie containing animated screen shots demonstrating the task in action? (And, if you're really energetic, you can even open the movies in a digital film-editing application, such as Adobe Premiere, and record narration to accompany the clips.)

Recording animated sequences in CorelCapture is relatively easy but slightly involved. The following steps show how:

STEPS:

Recording Animated Sequences in CorelCapture

Step 1. Choose Animation Window from the Source drop-down list. Notice that the File option changes to .AVI.

Step 2. On the File drop-down list, choose Options. This option tells CorelCapture to perform several captures, one after the other, the number of times you designate in the field to the right. Each time you press the hot key, CorelCapture captures the number of screens you set. To capture another set of screens, simply press the hot key again, and again, until you've finished recording the procedure. Keep in mind though, that if you're working at high resolution (1024×768 is the standard or higher) and color depth (24-bit color), each capture may require close to half a megabyte or more of disk space. You'll have better luck setting your screen size to 640×480 and your color depth to 256 colors. Your movies won't take up nearly as much space, and they'll capture and run faster.

Step 3. In the File section of CorelCapture, set the interval between captures. This option tells CorelCapture how many seconds to wait before performing the next capture, up to the number you designate in Repeat Captures. The lower you set this option, the smoother your movie will run, but the larger your movie file will be. Higher settings will cause jerky movies, but file sizes are smaller and more easily managed.

Step 4. In the File section of CorelCapture, set the Animation Duration (sec).

Step 5. In the Destination section of CorelCapture, select Animation File, and then choose the movie file format: Microsoft Video, QuickTime for Windows, or MPEG. Keep in mind that to run a movie format on a computer, the drivers for that format must be installed on that computer. To ensure that the movie will run on any Windows 95 or Windows 3.*x* machine, Microsoft Video (.AVI) is a safe choice.

Step 6. In the Image section of CorelCapture, set the image size in pixels and the color depth. To do so, you must use the Custom setting in the Settings drop-down list in the Image section of CorelCapture. The best method to use for movies is to set your screen resolution and color depth in the Windows Display control panel and then choose Screen from the Settings drop-down list in CorelCapture.

Step 7. In the File section of CorelCapture under Animation Settings, name the movie file in the Movie File Name field. Then set the Frame Rate (msec). This option determines how long each captured screen is displayed when you play the movie in a media viewer, such as Windows' Media Player. The rate is set in milliseconds. Each screen captured is treated as a movie frame. What you actually set with this option is *Frames Per Second* (FPS). The faster the frame rate, the smoother the movie and the larger the file. Be sure, too, to set the directory where you want the movie to be saved.

That's it. You are now ready to capture a movie of the actions you perform in an application (or in Windows in general). To capture the movie, return to the desired application, set up the screen as you want the movie to start, and press the hot key. CorelCapture starts capturing screens based on the settings you made. For the best results, move the mouse slowly and deliberately and pause at points, such as when selecting menu commands or when setting options in dialog boxes, that you want to be sure to capture. When you finish, press the hot key again. CorelCapture will build and save the movie. (If you don't designate a directory for saving the file with Options, as described above, it will be saved in the same directory as CorelCapture. If you want to make sure your movie is well designed and well organized, write a script and practice it a few times before actually recording the captures.)

One other thing before leaving this discussion of capturing movies: The procedure we just described is straightforward, but a number of variables, such as screen resolution, color depth, and even the rate at which you move the mouse and perform other functions on screen, can affect the final movie. We wish we could assure you that you won't have to perform some trial runs to perfect your technique and tweak CorelCapture settings. But that would be like trying to tell you that you don't have to practice to learn to play piano.

CorelScan

If you own a scanner, you probably already know how to use it. And, if you're like us, you probably like to use the interface software that came with your scanner, and you're probably thinking about skipping this section. Before you go on, let us assure you that electing to use CorelScan does not preclude you from also using the scanner software you already use.

If you are not wedded to your scanner software, be sure to check out CorelScan. It enables you to perform a wide range of procedures, such as color correction and setting up and saving scanner presets, that most built-in scanner front ends don't provide.

The first time you launch CorelScan, before using it, you'll need to set up the software to use your scanner. CorelScan consists of a series of dialog boxes, rather than a full-blown application window. CorelScan works more like a conventional Windows application wizard, providing a step-by-step approach to scanning and processing images. Let's take a look at the dialog box CorelScan greets you with when you first launch the utility. (See Figure 19-8.)

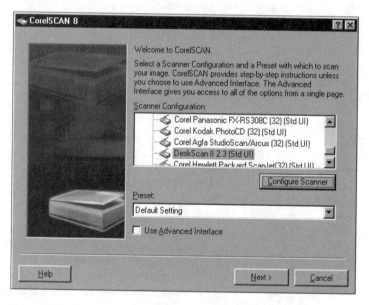

Figure 19-8: From this initial CorelScan screen, you set up CorelScan to work with your scanner.

The first time you use CorelScan, you must set it up to work with your scanner, which is why so few options are available. So if this is the first time you've fired up CorelScan, make sure that you select the proper scanner in the Scanner Configuration list. You should also click on the Configure Scanner button and make sure that the settings are correct for your scanner. Figure 19-9 shows the configuration one scanner; yours may be different.

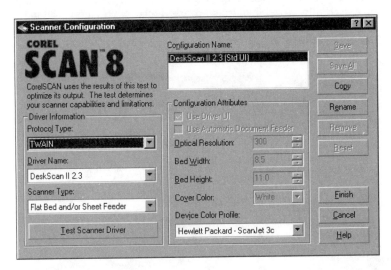

Figure 19-9: Use this dialog box to configure your scanner to work with CorelScan.

Next, make sure that you select the type of document you want to scan in the Preset drop-down list. Also, you should note that you can create and save your own presets.

Then click on the Next button. Depending on the Scanner Configuration option you chose, you'll get a dialog box designed to scan a document. Or, with some options, the document will be scanned automatically. In our case, we let CorelScan launch the ScanJet software, DeskScan, which we happen to like very much. You can do this also, or choose one of Corel's bundled drivers and interfaces. Either method you choose will work fine with CorelScan. If you choose to use your manufacturer's interface, at the end of the scanning process, the scan is dumped into CorelScan for further processing.

Choose OK, and then click on Next again. CorelScan runs your scanner interface and lets you make adjustments to the scan. After you've made these adjustments and made your final pass, the screen shown in Figure 19-10 is displayed, letting you choose the type of image or format you want CorelScan to process the image as. The program makes its best guess based on the information it receives from the scanner interface, but you can change it to whatever you like.

Depending on the type of image you choose, after you click on Next, CorelScan provides you with several processing options. For example, you might choose Color Photograph, which would open a particular dialog box for that option. From that point on, CorelScan is pretty straightforward, providing you with explanations for the processes the program suggests applying. For example, the next screen you would see in this process would offer to apply moiré removal, which our scan really needed. Take our word for it: If you let CorelScan make these decisions for you, you get better scans. At the end of the process, CorelScan provides a screen with options for saving your scan.

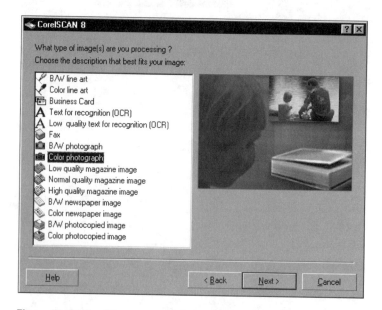

Figure 19-10: Use this screen to select the type of image you scanned. The type of image you select determines the next phases of using CorelScan.

Summary

▶ CorelCapture enables you to capture screen shots, save, resample, and automatically rename them on the fly. And you can even capture a series of screens in an animation sequence (or movie).

▶ CorelScan is a wizard-like utility that enables you to use preset scanning configurations, apply color correction, and make numerous other adjustments to images as you scan them.

Part IV

Electronic Media

Chapter 20

CorelDraw and the Web

In This Chapter

You learn tips for:

▶ Preparing images for the Web

▶ Designing attractive Web pages

▶ Choosing software to help you with Web page design

▶ Using CorelDraw to create Web pages

▶ Testing a Web page

▶ Using CorelDraw and Java

Preparing Images for the Web

In this era of behemoth images weighing in at 60MB and more, it's quite a pleasure to be able to transport an entire day's worth of Web page design work on one floppy disk. In fact, such portability is an indication that you are doing the right thing.

What should be in the back of your mind when designing a graphic for your Web page is an image of somebody surfing the Net, casually searching for a certain topic. He or she stumbles upon your Web page. This is your moment to shine. The viewer clicks and waits . . . 20 seconds . . . 30 seconds . . . still loading. Boredom hits. Your chance is gone. Your potential new viewer is now following a link to somewhere else. If a Web page is composed of smaller images, this scenario is less likely to happen. This is why Web site designers are always looking for creative ways to produce good work, while keeping the size of their images small.

CorelDraw creates beautiful images, with detailed fountain fills and sharp lines. Web graphics designed in CorelDraw won't have that fuzzy, "overcompressed" look that you see so often while browsing pages. You can create images in CorelDraw that are specifically designed for the limitations of a Web browser's color range, and for the patience of the average Web surfer. Still, images created in CorelDraw's native file format may be too big for the Web. But you do have tools at your disposal to make sure your images maintain their sharp, crisp "Corel look" while conforming to the norms of Web viewing.

To use CorelDraw or Photo-Paint images on the Web, you need to become proficient at shrinking the size, changing the resolution, and optimizing the color palette of images you create. Before we explain how to export entire CorelDraw documents as Web pages, we want to show you how to prepare individual images for Internet use. Later, we discuss how to create fully functioning Web pages right in CorelDraw.

Converting images to 256 colors

High-color images you create that are saved as JPG files can be viewed on the Web with minimal color loss. However, when possible, it's good to reduce the color content of your images, which decreases the amount of time a visitor to your site has to wait for the image to load. When reducing a high-color image to 256 colors, you can choose, to a degree, which colors are used. The conversion process involves blending combinations of the new 256-color palette to simulate what the image looked like before.

Corel applications enable you to choose from many 256-color palettes, and some palettes are better than others at preserving flesh tones and fountain fills, for example. This selection can minimize the distortion that naturally occurs when you reduce the colors an image contains. Most often, you'll be using palettes specifically designed for the two most popular Web browsers, Netscape and Microsoft Internet Explorer.

CorelDraw's Internet-optimized palettes

Figure 20-1 shows the Photo-Paint Color Table menu with the Netscape Navigator palette chosen. To reach this menu, select Image ➪ Convert To ➪ 8 bit ➪ Custom. Scroll through the drop-down palette menu to select a palette. Photo-Paint then converts your image to 256 colors. Then select Image/Color Table to view the palette. Remember to save your image as a .GIF or a .JPG for viewing on the Web. When converting a CorelDraw image to .GIF (the preferred format for Web page viewing), choose File ➪ Export and select .GIF.

If you want to use an image with more than 256 colors, choose the JPEG file format rather than .GIF. As a basic rule, small images such as buttons, thumbnails, and simple drawings are saved as .GIFs, while more elaborate, eye-catching main graphics can be saved as .JPG files.

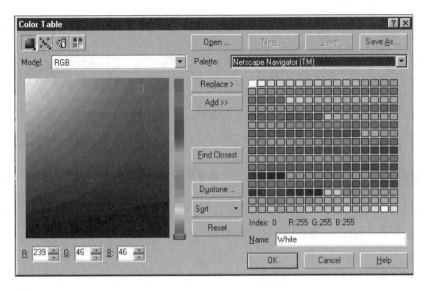

Figure 20-1: Use the Photo-Paint Color Table dialog box to choose a color palette for your Web page.

Secret

When you are converting a CorelDraw image to a bitmap, the default size will be much too large for the Web. An individual image on the Web should have a compressed size of no more than 100K. You may save your image in .JPG format to escape this limitation. If your viewers don't mind the wait, a .JPG image compressed to 100K can have an uncompressed size of more than one megabyte. The image quality will be higher.

Dithering

When converting an image to 256 colors, you should choose a type of dithering. Selecting dithering instructs Photo-Paint or CorelDraw to carefully blend colors to simulate the complicated color patterns found in your original image. If dithering is not selected, each spread of color in your image is quickly averaged and assigned a new value from one of the 256 choices. Of the two types of available dithering, Error Diffusion is the most accurate, but it takes longer to complete.

Image-format conversion

When converting an image for use on the Web, you have several choices to make:

- Image resolution for a Web graphic should be set to 96 dpi.
- Saving as a .GIF allows for setting a transparency color and 89A interlacing.

- Saving as a .JPG allows a larger file size to be used, and the file will not need to be reduced to 256 colors. Complex images look better at the larger file size.

- Selecting a transparency color enables you to save loading time by making the background color transparent. This is available as one of the .GIF options.

- Choosing 89A interlacing for your .GIF image allows Web viewers to see small portions of your image as it is loading.

Secret

When exporting a CorelDraw or Photo-Paint image for use on the Web, don't forget to crop as much background area as possible from around your image. However, you don't have to go to the trouble of building a mask to remove the background entirely. Later, you can select a .GIF transparency option to eliminate the background color from your image. But trimming most of the background makes the file size smaller.

Web Page Design

Even if you've never tried to create a Web page, you may have heard how notoriously easy it is to design one. Using HTML (HyperText Markup Language), you can quickly create all the essentials of a good Web page: some text, complemented by pictures to accent what the text is saying, and links to lead the viewer to other locations. HTML is called a *language*, and that description may scare some people away from it. But HTML is really just a collection of short phrases (called *tags*) that you place before and after items you want to place on your Web page. For example, to instantly design a Web page that says "Hello World," you would type

```
<HTML>
<HEAD>
<TITLE>My Web Page
</TITLE>
</HEAD>
<BODY>
<Hello, World.
</BODY>
</HTML>
```

If you were to type the preceding text into Windows Notepad and, instead of saving it as a .TXT file, save it with the extension .HTM or .HTML, you would have composed a genuine Web document. Without going into more detail about HTML, let's just say that it works by enclosing each part of a document — for example, the body of the document — between two tags.

If you were to type the tag <BODY>, type your text, and then finish with the tag </BODY>, every Web browser in the world would understand that the text you typed between <BODY> and </BODY> is the main text of your Web document. Those beginning and ending tags tell browsers how the text should be formatted (for example, that it should be formatted as the body of a paragraph, not as the heading of a paragraph). Many Web browsers have their own ways of formatting text and graphics for viewing, but HTML enables you to give a Web browser enough information about your text to make sure it appears the way you want it to; for example, as the main body of paragraph text. Many tags exist. For example, <HEAD> and </HEAD> are the beginning and ending tags for the heading in your document.

Learning HTML

Dozens of excellent books are available for teaching yourself HTML and getting started creating Web pages. However, many software products have been marketed, and each of these, in their own way, automate just about everything in the Web site design process. Office 97, Microsoft Publisher, HoTMetaL, and Corel WordPerfect 8 are examples of the new wave of publishing and word-processing products that let you design Web pages by typing text and inserting pictures anywhere you want. The program then converts your document to HTML. You can check your links, upload your documents to your server, and be done with it.

Some problems exist with this system of letting a software package do your HTML work for you. When your Web documents don't look like what you thought they would, you won't know why. Although the packages we mentioned previously, and others, enable you to create a Web document without knowing HTML, sometimes it's nice to be able to view your document as HTML and do a little "direct troubleshooting" on your own. Part of designing an HTML document is testing it and revising it to work in different circumstances. If you've designed your own HTML document, and you find that under Netscape 3.0 you get an error but under Netscape 4.0 you don't, you may be able to insert a couple of tags in the right places to suit the older version of Netscape. But if you don't know HTML, you are dependent on the savvy of the HTML-conversion software that your program uses. And no matter how sophisticated such conversion programs are, if they are more than one month old, they are already out-of-date. If you are remotely interested in creating Web pages, we heartily recommend setting aside the two or three weeks it may take to learn HTML for yourself. Then you should be sure to keep up with the newest versions of HTML, learning new tags as they come into widespread use. That way, your knowledge of HTML will grow along with the Web itself. The following Web sites can assist you in learning and staying on top of the latest developments in HTML:

- http://www.ncsa.uiuc.edu/demoweb/thml-primer.html

- http://www.access.digex.net/~tilt/cgh/

- http://kuhttp.cc.ukans.edu/lynx_help/HTML_quick.html

- http://developer.netscape.com/platform/html_compilation/index.html

Secret

When you learn a little HTML, you can improve your skills by doing a little detective work. For example, if you see a Web page that has made good use of structure (how the graphics are placed on the page, how the hyperlinks are arranged, where the tables are located, and so forth), you can download that page and view its HTML. (Simply download the Web page, and then open it in Windows Notepad.) The purpose is not to plagiarize the contents, but to see how the creator used the HTML tags and commands to create a good-looking document. If you know a little HTML, you'll be able to understand how the results were achieved.

For the Experts

For those of you more experienced in creating Web pages, we're going to cut to the chase and tell you what you want to know: how CorelDraw (and Photo-Paint) can facilitate creating Web sites and pages. Here it is in a nutshell:

■ You can save a CorelDraw or Photo-Paint document as an .HTM file. What the program really creates is a large group of images that takes up the entire size of the page, with Head, Body, Image SRC, and Title HTML tags attached. Your entire CorelDraw document — text, various images and all — is saved as .GIF or .JPG files. You can specify that each letter of text in your image is saved as an individual picture, which enables you to preserve clarity. The resulting .GIF or .JPG files will be saved in the same directory as the .HTM file that CorelDraw creates. The picture file will have the same title as your .HTM file's name, and the .HTM document links itself with this .GIF or .JPG file through Image SRC tags.

■ You can attach URLs to any CorelDraw or Photo-Paint object. The entire object will be clickable and will activate the URL. After you've

saved a CorelDraw or Photo-Paint document with hypertext links as an .HTM file, all text and objects that are not links will more or less be part of the background, although no <BACKGROUND> tags are used, in the HTML sense. The objects that had URLs attached to them will be recognized as separate image maps by the HTML document.

■ You can add forms to your Corel Web page, which include Submit buttons, check boxes, and text fields, just by pointing and clicking (Edit ⇨ Internet Object). For these forms to be functional, they must be saved as Corel Barista documents, or as HTML documents with CGI scripting. This same menu enables you to create Java applets. In the menu provided, you must specify the type of Java class applet you are creating as well as its parameters and variables.

■ For more complex Web pages, you can use CorelDraw to create Barista.class Web pages, which allow you to easily save frames and forms and multimedia files with your page. CorelDraw comes with several Barista Java applets, including ones that create scroll bars, pop-up menus, and toolbars.

Designing attractive Web pages

In this section are some tips to help novice Web page designers get started.

Change your units of measurement to pixels

It's tempting for a novice to create a Web page with a piece of notebook paper in mind. A single Web page can extend far below the bottom of the screen. Visitors may simply scroll down to see more of the page, or you can create links to lower portions of the page to spare people from scrolling. However, your page width is quite important. You do not want to make people scroll from right to left to see the whole thing. First, change the measurement of your workspace to pixels. (Select View ⇨ Rulers, right-click on the Ruler, and then choose Pixels from the drop-down panel. Click on the Resolution button, and set the resolution to 72. Close the dialog boxes.) After making that change, keep in mind that your pages should be no more than 550 pixels in width. That's because you need to leave some horizontal margin for the visitor's browser menu.

Secret

If you work in a 800 × 600 or 1024 × 1248 pixel environment, you don't need to reduce your screen resolution. However, you'll notice that 550 pixels look pretty small on your screen. You may want to reduce to 640 × 480 to see more detail.

Don't crowd your home page

The most common error of novice Web page designers is putting too much information on home pages. Here are some tips for designing a successful home page:

- Include an attractive logo. Put all your skills to work toward making this logo eye-catching and unique.

- Include a brief introduction to yourself, your company, and your services.

- Farm out everything else you want to say to a different page. On the home page, you should provide one link allowing the viewer to read about your past happy customers, another link to get details about your services, and another link to where people can find out more about you, something like a biography. Your front page, the home page, has to load fast. Think of your front page as an annotated business card.

- Provide labels on the links to those other pages in your site. Checking out your links takes valuable time on the part of the viewer. The average Web surfer's attention span approaches that of a hyperactive third-grade boy. Make sure your link labels are legible and clearly indicate what people will find when they log on to that page.

■ Provide helpful links to other sites offering relevant information, freebies, or services. Make sure you maintain the links regularly. (Are they still valid this month?) If you go to this trouble, people will come back to see what else you have to offer. Information abounds on the Web, but useful information is in short supply. Providing links where people can download drivers, e-mail addresses of various governmental agencies, and particularly generous vendors of products related to your site will make you quite popular over time.

■ Neatly arrange your hyperlinks along the bottom or at the upper left of your page. Keeping your links together on your page makes it easy for people to find them.

Keep your Web pages simple

Although more and more Web sites are incorporating animation, sound effects, and complicated scripting, some of the most popular sites employ none of these. Simple, informative, and well-organized Web pages are highly appreciated. The average Web visitor still prefers content over style. Sometimes a "beginner's page" will offer a service or viewpoint that hits a responsive nerve with the public, and it can become quite successful. If you create a Web page with the following five components, you can be rather happy with yourself:

■ Include a simple background graphic, composed of colors that don't interfere with the foreground text and graphics

■ Deliver interesting, to-the-point text. If you have something unique to say or sell, people will respond.

■ Feature a couple of tasteful .GIF or .JPG images. Lots of pictures are distracting and take too long to load.

■ Provide a way for people to contact you, interact, and do business.

■ Supply links to other informative sites. Creating a link in HTML takes about 30 seconds. Make sure your links are current, and always be on the lookout for new ones.

Provide thumbnails first, and then entire pictures on separate pages

When people log on to a page deeper in the site, they are ready to find out a bit more about you or your services. Provide a clickable thumbnail picture showing what lies beneath: artwork you are selling, car parts, or samples of music, for example. By providing a thumbnail for visitors to click, you allow them to determine whether opening the larger picture underneath is worth the time. Second, you can fit many thumbnails on a page. This enables you to build in a *catalog* or index of your work.

Include helpful Java applets

Java applets transform your Web page from a passive to an interactive document. Java applets put actual programs on your page that visitors can use. These programs include spreadsheets, small games, and a way to play musical and video selections that you provide, as well as the more typical information forms, hit counters, and scrolling marquees. With CorelDraw, you can quickly insert a Java applet in your Web page. This is done by selecting Edit ⇨ Internet Object ⇨ Java Applet. Click your left mouse button and drag to create the size applet you want to insert. For your Java applet to function, after you've created it, right-click on it and select Properties. Click on the Java Applet tab. In the Java Class text box, specify what class Java applet you are creating. If the code for your applet is going to be stored anyplace other than the main folder that contains all your files associated with this project, identify the folder path in the Code Base text box.

For visitors who can't work with Java applets, include alternate text for them to read, in the Alternate text box. For your Java applet to work, you have to identify the parameters associated with that applet (such as scrolling speed, user input type, and colors used for a flashing button), as well as variables for that parameter. The Java applet tab of the Java Properties panel provides spaces for you to type in each parameter and value.

Unlike forms created by using Corel's other Internet Object features, Java applets do not require you to provide scripting language and set up special folders according to your ISP's specifications. Java Applets can be created and deployed even by novice Web page designers.

Just like all objects created with CorelDraw's Internet Object feature, you can create an outline and a fill for your Java applet, as well as set its Text Wrap attributes. That is the purpose of the other tabs found on the Properties dialog box.

Choosing software for your Web-page design

If you find that you are spending far too much time fiddling with HTML books and trying to fathom how to create a page from scratch, follow along and take a look at tools that get you creating pages in less than an afternoon. In the following sections, you'll see a description of some of the best Web design software appropriate for new users. This list is far from complete, but it gives you an indication of what's available.

All the following products provide what-you-see-is-what-you-get Web page creation tools. You type text on the screen where you want it to appear, and drop pictures anyplace you think they should go. If your text has italics, various colors, and bolding, it will appear as such on the Web. All of the HTML tagging is done for you. You can just click and create tables, and instantly apply frames to portions of your page. These programs all automate HTML heading and body text formatting. Background .GIFs (watermark pictures behind your text) and transparency issues are taken care of. All of these mentioned here will allow you to embed sound, animation, and videos instantly. Of course, adding hyperlinks is as easy as clicking and typing the URL. The programs also provide some form of page-testing mechanism, so you can see how your page will really look and run.

Corel WordPerfect Suite 8

Corel WordPerfect Suite 8 converts full-featured word processing documents into Web pages with ease. Tables in your WordPerfect document are converted into HTML tables, and headings and body text are converted to their appropriate HTML counterparts. Images appear on your Web page pretty much where they do in your WordPerfect document. Images are saved as separate .GIF or .JPG files in the same directory as the HTML document itself and referenced accordingly. If your document has more than one page, other pages are saved together with the first page, all in one directory. This makes it easy to upload all your work at once to a server while keeping the relative directories intact.

Claris Home Page

Claris Home Page excels at allowing you to include as many frames as you wish in your document. There's a generous clip art library to begin with, and you may import any graphic and quickly convert it for Web use. Claris Home Page includes a nifty feature that estimates your page's download time for 28.8K or 14.4K modems.

HoTMetaL Pro 3.0

HoTMetaL Pro includes an extensive collection of ready-made Web page templates and over 400 multimedia files, including Java and Shockwave files. With HoTMetaL Pro 3.0, you can convert just about any word-processing document into a Web page. The program includes an extensive spell-checker, a thesaurus, and a search-and-replace utility.

Macromedia's Backstage Designer

Macromedia, creator of Director and Shockwave, has designed a Web page creation kit that specializes in allowing you to create return forms, password authentication and logon setups, complex database searching capabilities, and other high-end content features that used to be the domain of "experts" only. Through the use of *Backstage objects* rather than simple HTML objects, procedures such as searching through records online according to specialized criteria can now be built into your Web page as easily as inserting a graphic. Backstage Designer also comes with a healthy assortment of Java applets, and, of course, using Shockwave is your key to making animation, video, and sound available on your Web site without making visitors wait forever for the files to download.

InContext Spider 1.2

This program has the best template layouts we've seen. These templates are full of attractive designs, multimedia content, and even Java and Shockwave samples. Starting InContext Spider 1.2 with the Template dialog box begins an elaborate process for helping you choose the type of page you'd like to create. You can get results fast.

Microsoft FrontPage

Microsoft FrontPage provides the best word-processing tools of any HTML authoring tool. There's even a drag-and-drop thesaurus. Many templates are also available, along with a multiple undo feature and a feature that automatically fixes incorrect hyperlinks.

Netscape Navigator Gold

Not surprisingly, Netscape Navigator Gold's top feature is your ability to tool around in the familiar Netscape environment while creating your page. Navigator Gold does not, however, include clip art libraries, support for instant frame creation, or word processing extras such as spell checking and thesaurus assistance. Those familiar with the Netscape interface will nonetheless have an easy time creating Web pages with this program.

Creating a Web Page with CorelDraw

When you Export your CorelDraw or Photo-Paint project as a Barista or HTML document, the location of each graphic is noted and translated into HTML code so that your Web page will look the same as your original work. Objects that you have formatted as hyperlinks will be clickable and, when online, will link you to the appropriate location. If you've used Corel's Internet Objects menu to create a form (Edit ➪ Insert Internet Object), the form functions only if you've set up the appropriate CGI script. Discuss the inclusion of a CGI script form with your ISP's technical support personnel. They'll provide the necessary files and file-uploading instructions.

Artistic text created in CorelDraw is converted to a graphic. This can cause a loss in crispness. When converting your Web document, you have the option to convert each letter to an individual graphic. You're shown a preview panel of each letter. You can determine each letter's viewing quality and disk space usage. Higher-quality lettering results in larger file sizes, which increases loading time. Having a preview panel for each letter helps you make a more informed choice.

Because features of your Corel document are saved as graphics, there are limitations. For example, when you export a document as an HTML file, bulleted lists and headings placed in your CorelDraw documents are not converted to bullets and headings in HTML. They appear as they did in your CorelDraw document, but not with the flexibility of HTML objects. As mentioned earlier, HTML coding allows the Web browser to determine how to display formatting such as bullets, body text, headings, and quotes. This facilitates speedy loading of the page. Such is not the case for a page full of graphics. Therefore, creating an economically sized page in CorelDraw can be quite a challenge.

Remember that a CorelDraw object can be turned into an image map, a clickable image that visitors to your site can click on and be moved to a new location.

Figures 20-2 and 20-3 show two Web pages that were created using images from CorelDraw and Photo-Paint. The HTML was done in Windows Notepad.

Figure 20-2: The banner graphic "The Inside Track" was created in CorelDraw.

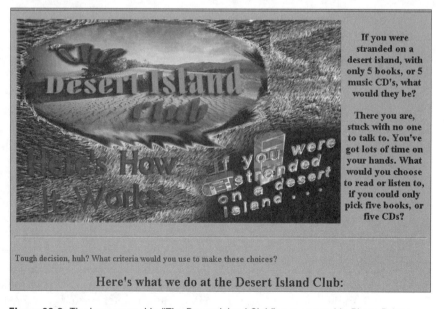

Figure 20-3: The banner graphic "The Desert Island Club" was created in Photo-Paint.

CorelDraw's Web-aware color palette options

When planning to create a Web document with CorelDraw, choose View ⇨ Color Palette. You'll notice color palette choices that bear significance, including one color palette optimized for viewing with Netscape Navigator and one optimized for Microsoft Internet Explorer. Choose one of these palettes before beginning your project, according to what you imagine your visitors' preferred browser will be.

Creating URLs in your CorelDraw document

A URL (Universal Resource Locator), is an address that you type into a clickable area of your document. When the user clicks on the URL, he or she is logged on to that address. URLs are typically used to link viewers of your Web site to other Web or FTP sites.

In any document, you have two steps for creating a clickable link that transports the viewer of your document to another location on the Web:

- **Creating a clickable object, marking out its boundaries, and indicating its location on the page itself.** This process is very important because the clickable object must have specific boundaries indicating where the clicking action will be effective. With its Internet Objects toolbox, CorelDraw takes care of this process for you. Any object you assign a URL will automatically be a clickable object. As you'll see briefly, you have the choice to designate that the clickable area will extend either as far as the object's bounding boxes or only to the object itself.

- **Indicating an address to which clicking on the object will log the user.** In HTML, this must be done exactly as specified in relation to the clickable object itself. Again, CorelDraw has included tools to take care of this coding process. Of course, you need to make sure the URL you are typing is correct.

Creating clickable objects in CorelDraw

Figure 20-4 shows a Web page in the making. A CorelDraw object with text has been designated for the viewer to click on. Then the viewer is transported to a page and instructed to fill out a form, give credit card information, or initiate some other form of payment. The figure shows a drop-down menu that includes the Internet Objects toolbox. This menu was revealed by right-clicking any blank toolbar space. As already noted, this Internet Objects toolbox will not create a script for allowing people to order an item from you, but it will make this object clickable and cause the viewer to log on to the URL you supply, if it truly does exist.

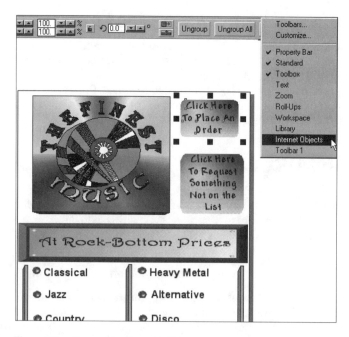

Figure 20-4: Reveal the Internet Objects menu.

Figure 20-5 shows the Internet Objects toolbar open with a URL supplied. Take a look at each component of the toolbar in the following list.

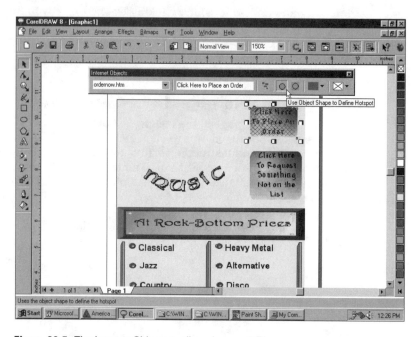

Figure 20-5: The Internet Objects toolbar shows a URL.

- Starting from the left, the first data box is for typing the Location URL. Often this will begin with `http://www`. In this case, the location URL sends the viewer to another HTML document on the same computer, specifically to an order form. Because it is a local address, only the filename itself is needed. In fact, it is advisable to keep all Web pages relating to a single Web site (the home page, the order form, the *What's New* page, and the *Send me e-mail page*) in the same directory. That's because you can easily upload all your Web site-related files to your server, and the file locations relative to each other will still be the same. That means your local URLs will still be accurate.

- Next is the Internet Bookmark, or Alternate Text data box. You should include text as an alternative to a graphic in case a particular viewer cannot view graphics or has set his or her browser preference not to view graphics. The text should reflect the same message as the missing graphic.

- The next button, with random small objects on it, is a toggle switch allowing you to highlight or not highlight the Internet objects on your page as Internet objects. Toggling this button to "off" does not hide the objects themselves; it hides only the colored "wiremesh" that CorelDraw provides to indicate Internet objects.

- The next button is titled *Use Object Shape to Define Hotspot*. Toggling this button to "on" sets the object's exact shape to be clickable. When the document is exported as HTML, it will include an image map of the object's exact boundaries to make it clickable. This feature works even with highly irregular objects.

- The following button, *Use Bounding Box to Define Hotspot*, means that the entire rectangular bounding area associated with the Internet object will be clickable. When the document is exported to HTML, the clickable image map created will extend to the full area of the object's bounding box. This option requires less accuracy on the part of the viewer. If the clickable area you have defined is a rather small button, it is advisable to use this bounding box option.

- The *Foreground Color of Hotspots* button enables you to choose what color you'd like the wiremesh Internet object marker to use.

- The *Background Color of Hotspots* button lets you fill an Internet object with a marker color rather than use a wiremesh covering. This option is helpful if the Internet object in question is rather small. To truly assess the clickable boundaries, you may need to fill the entire region with the marker color rather than just apply a wiremesh.

After assigning URL and *clickable region* options to an object, what happens? Nothing, until you save it as a CorelDraw .HTM file. This file will be in HTML and will contain an image map marking the exact location and boundaries of every Internet object you've defined in your document. The HTML document will also include the URLs you specified and the alternate text to be displayed by graphics-deficient browsers. You have the choice of saving this document as a Barista. class Java object. This topic will be discussed later in the chapter.

Indicating an address for a link

To indicate an address for a link, you have to know the exact location of the file you want to reference. If the URL is going to link visitors to another page of your own Web site, be sure that the page is saved in the same directory as the current page. Next, when you type in the link, include only the filename itself. Because you've saved the filename in the same directory as the first page, you have no need to type **C:\Webdocs\Page2.htm**, for example. You should type only **Page2.htm**. If you include the entire address, including the root directory, the Web page will work when you test it on your computer, but it will not work when you upload it to your server. Type only the relative address into the URL address data box of the Internet Objects menu (for example, **Signoff.htm**) and not the entire address.

You can also provide visitors with links to other Web sites of interest. In fact, most good Web pages include links to other sites. Make sure you enter the entire address, and check the reference yourself by logging on to the site once or twice to make sure it is still good. Nobody likes Web sites with links to other sites that are no longer valid. If you include a link to another site as one of your hyperlinks, include a couple sentences describing the new site referenced in your link. That way, your visitors will know better if the site to which you are sending them is one they're truly interested in.

Saving a document as a Web page

To save a document as an HTML file, select File ⇨ Publish To Internet. (See Figure 20-6, the HTML Export Wizard dialog box.) You're given a choice of file types among Corel Image Map HTML, Corel Barista, and Single Image. As mentioned earlier, saving pages in the Barista format is one way to deploy Java technology on your page. Barista-type Java applets provide features such as multiple columns, visitor-initiated sound and video playback, and simple data collection forms.

After specifying either the HTML or Barista file format for your page, click on OK. You then see a dialog box prompting you to choose a folder in which your Web images for this project should be stored. If you plan to store them in the same folder as the rest of your HTML files, you still need to type in the path. If you've chosen the Barista format, this option will not be available. You must also choose the type of HTML layout to employ. Choosing an option other than the most compatible (HTML tables) enables you to use some of the extra functionality of the newest browsers (Internet Explorer 4 and Netscape 4), but at the expense of compatibility with some lesser-known, older browsers.

Click on Next and choose a graphic file type. Remember that .GIFs provide transparent backgrounds and can emerge gradually on your screen (Interlacing), while .JPEG files can produce high-color images when needed.

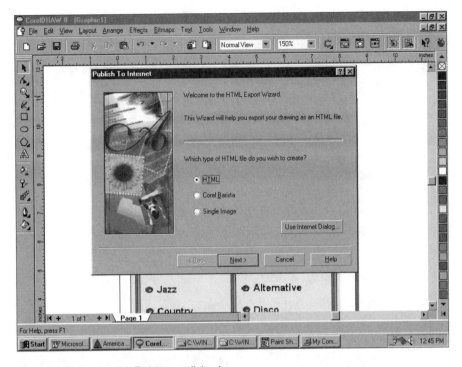

Figure 20-6: The Publish To Internet dialog box.

If you choose .GIF as your export file type and then click on Image Options, you'll see a screen that allows you to select which color should be transparent (see Figure 20-7). Use the slider to select a color numerically, or click on a color square. You can also use the provided eyedropper tool to choose which color should be transparent. Just locate your chosen transparency color in the image Preview Window, and click it with the eyedropper tool. If you want your image to gradually appear on the visitor's screen as it loads, click the Interlace check box.

Why assign a transparency color? Because transmitting any color data over the Web takes time, and if you can assign the background color as transparent, people visiting your site will be able to log on sooner because the Web browser's default background color will show through. Most often this background is gray, so avoid using much gray in your Web design if you are planning to use this option.

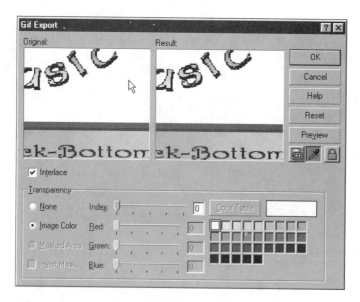

Figure 20-7: The Gif Export dialog box.

If you selected .JPEG as your export file type, click on Image Options from the main Publish To Internet dialog box, and you'll see a preview screen (see Figure 20-8) for determining the amount of compression to use on each image in your document. As you move the slider to increase or decrease the compression amount, the preview screen shows the amount of image degradation. This way, you can pick an adequate amount of compression without getting any ugly surprises later, when you see your whole page online.

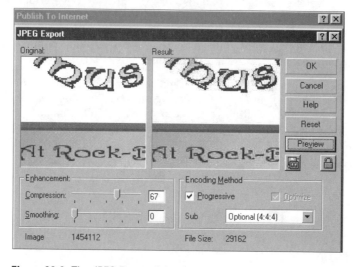

Figure 20-8: The JPEG Export dialog box.

Next you'll see a dialog box prompting you to name the pages themselves, the actual HTML filenames. You can also choose a title for each page. This title is important because it is the first information a Web browser reads to determine if your page should be returned as part of a search by a potential visitor to your site. Click on OK, and the appropriate files are placed in the folders you specified.

Secret

Although CorelDraw 8 lets you to save your Web document with a long filename, it's best to conform to the standard eight-dot-three character norm. Ultimately, you will upload these Web files to your server. The server software and certain Web browsers may not be able to work with Windows 95 long filenames.

Selecting Publish To Internet does not affect the current CorelDraw document. In fact, you may go online and view your new HTML file while the CorelDraw document is still open. When you select Publish To Internet, several files are created. One is the .HTM file, and the others are the .GIF or .JPG files, whichever format you selected during the saving process (unless you saved as a single image). These files should always be kept in the same directory. If you move them to a new directory, you have to move all of them. They are no longer dependent on the CorelDraw document, which can be moved or deleted.

Resizing images for your Web page

The following relates only to Draw images, not bitmaps. When a Draw image is converted to a bitmap, the resulting file size is much too large for the Web. Its best to manually convert those Draw images to smaller bitmaps before allowing Publish To Internet to take over converting the entire document to an actual Web page. To do this, you can export your CorelDraw image as a bitmap by first selecting a screen resolution of 72 rather your printer's default, which can be as high as 300. (By exporting a CorelDraw image beforehand, you have more control over the resulting file size rather than simply letting the Publish To Internet dialog boxes make all the decisions for you.) Then import that same image again as a bitmap into CorelDraw. The file size will be much more manageable for Web purposes.

Figure 20-9 shows the Bitmap Export dialog box.

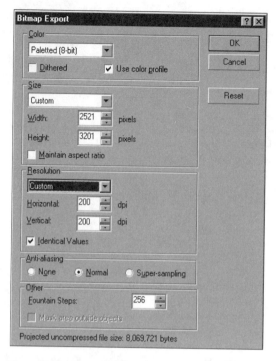

Figure 20-9: The Bitmap Export dialog box permits choices of number of colors, size, and resolution.

If you export a file as shown, with its default options, you're in big trouble. Take a look at the number at the bottom of the dialog box: *Projected uncompressed file size: 8,069,721 bytes.* As a creator of Web pages, you should hear an alarm ring in your head. Even with a fast modem, transmitting data takes a long time over the Web. If you export your Web page as it is with these default options, it would be almost impossible for anyone to view it. The following procedure outlines what you should do.

STEPS:

Adapting a Web Page for Export

Step 1.   First move down to the Resolution area of the dialog box and set the Resolution drop-down menu to Custom. Now place a check in the Identical Values box. Set both the Horizontal and Vertical data boxes to 72. This is the resolution for most computer monitors, and this is the medium you are dealing with now, not printed output. Anything higher than 72 dpi increases loading time without improving results for most viewers.

Step 2. Move up to the Size area of the dialog box, and set the Size drop-down menu to Custom. Sequence is important here, or you may end up with a Web page of uneven dimensions. This activates the Maintain aspect ratio check box, in which you should place a check.

Step 3. Keeping your eye on the number at the bottom of the dialog box, the Projected uncompressed size number, input a number in one of the Size data boxes that is about ⅓ the number there now. In this example, the current Width in pixels is 2521. To make your Web page small enough for timely viewing, you'll eventually need to dial that number down to 740 pixels. To change the Height in pixels dialog box to be in proportion with the Width, click once inside the Height numbers data box. The numbers instantly change to a height in proper proportion to your new Width setting. Conversely, if you set the Height in pixels first, clicking once in the Width numbers data box automatically changes those numbers appropriately. You may have to experiment with several numbers before finding the right size for the exported Web page. Keep in mind that your images should not be wider than 640 pixels or taller than 480 pixels. Otherwise, your Web page visitors will have to scroll to see the entire image. This 640 × 480 figure specifies the width and height of a typical screen, so your images should be even smaller than that, allowing for a browser's various menu bars and any text you have next to an image. Most Web images should not be larger than 550 pixels in width. The figures we're working with here relate to the most common screen resolution, which is 640 × 480. If your Web page visitors are working in 800 × 600 resolution mode, they can accommodate a wider image. However, it's a good idea to build your page for the lowest common denominator.

Step 4. When you are finished, click on OK.

Secret

Always create a Web page with the lowest common denominator in mind. Can a particular graphic do without so many colors? Also, keep in mind that your visitors will more than likely be using a 640 × 480 screen resolution. Can you shrink the file size a little more without too much degradation? Your visitors will be glad you did.

Testing your Web page

Contrary to the popular saying, you do want to try this at home! Two steps are necessary for testing your Web page. First, try it out on both Netscape and Internet Explorer without being online. Simply open the browser, and instead of logging on with your server, just open the local file, the HTML document you created with CorelDraw.

Figure 20-10 shows a Web home page designed exclusively in CorelDraw. The figure shows the page opened locally in Internet Explorer.

Figure 20-10: Test the operation of a home Web page designed with CorelDraw.

Check your page in two or three different browsers. You may find that objects and text line up slightly differently from browser to browser. You can make adjustments before going online. Also, it's important to make sure the transparency color selected affects only the background and doesn't degrade any of the images. As you can see, no background white color appears, and the images look fine. Finally, do the hyperlinks work? In this figure, the tester is shown placing his mouse over the word "Alternative." The mouse has turned into a pointing finger, so you can tell that a hyperlink was detected. If there were no hyperlink, the mouse pointer would not have become a pointing finger. At the lower left of the screen, notice that the link's address is displayed. Because the page is being tested on the creator's own computer, no http://www and so on appears. You simply see a link to another local .HTM file called Alterna.HTM. Clicking here, the visitor is logged on to a new Web page, presumably a list of records by alternative rock bands. Only by testing the link locally can the creator be sure it is really valid.

Some Web page features, such as Java applets, will not work on a local computer. If you've placed Java applets in your page (and this segues quite nicely into the final section of this chapter), you need to be online to test them. You can sometimes circumvent this limitation by logging on to your Internet service provider, opening a browser, and then checking out your own page locally, the page still on your own computer. You can see if the Java applets and other extra features work.

Similarly, you won't get a true sense of loading time by testing your page locally. You'll have to post your page on the Web and ask some long-suffering friends and family members to test your page for you. Then make them be brutally honest about how it really looks and how long it took to load.

CorelDraw and Java

Java is a computer language similar to C++ that was developed to create miniprograms that can be plugged into your Web page. These miniprograms, called *applets*, perform special functions such as creating an Audio CD Panel interface for visitors to select and listen to music you've made available. You can use Java applets to make interactive dialog boxes, marquee-style rolling text, information-gathering forms, and order forms. Following are some quick points about Java

Java is not like HTML. It is not as easy to learn. To create in Java, you need interpreters, code compilers, and a working knowledge of languages similar to C++.

You do not need to know Java to use Java applets, but you do need to know how to insert Java tags into your HTML document. These tags must include at least three applet attributes: the applet name; the applet's physical parameters, such as height, width, and alignment properties; and the alternative text to be displayed for non-Java-powered browsers. Some applets require more attributes to be specified with the applet tags in order to work correctly. In some cases, Java-specific language must be inserted at the beginning of the HTML document in order for the applet to work.

In many cases, Java applets cannot be tested locally with the methods we've just described. You need to obtain a Java applet viewer. These viewers are available online or come with various software packages such as Microsoft FrontPage and Macromedia's BackstageDesigner. In any event, the best site online to obtain Java help in time of need is still `http://www.Java.sun.com`.

CorelDraw can create Barista.class Java applets. This is done as easily as creating the Corel Image Map .HTM files that we discussed earlier in the chapter. However, what you are actually creating in CorelDraw is the Java applet's graphic component, together with its location on the page. It doesn't program the applet's actions. This is a bit like making the dialog box but deferring programming the script that makes the dialog box really do something.

CorelDraw does include Barista.class Java applets, but these are installed on your computer only if you select custom installation and then make sure that Internet filters are selected as part of your installation. If installed, these Java applets are stored in a folder called Barista under the CorelDraw folder.

Secret

To work with applets you create in CorelDraw and export to Barista, you must install your files in the Barista directory. The other .class files must be in the same directory as your created files. When you create a Barista.class document, a new directory of the same name is created under the Barista directory. It will contain HTML documents, one for every page you created in CorelDraw and then exported to Barista.HTM. If your document had three pages, you will find HTML documents p1.HTM, p2.HTM, and p3.HTM in that same directory.

Summary

▶ Preparing images for the World Wide Web includes converting images from their native CorelDraw or Photo-Paint format to formats and resolutions supported by the Web.

▶ Avoid crowding images and text on Web pages, and use thumbnails to guide people to pages below your home page.

▶ If you don't already know HTML, you should learn it. It's easy to use and universally accepted.

▶ With CorelDraw you can convert a document into a Web page.

▶ Some software programs complement CorelDraw by helping you create Web pages.

Chapter 21

Preparing Graphics for Multimedia

In This Chapter

▶ Working within the confines of 256-color mode

▶ Converting a 16.7 million-color image into 256-color mode

▶ Using interesting color schemes in your presentations

You've probably seen multimedia products in action, such as PowerPoint or Macromedia Director presentations that have been optimized for a top-flight computer. They probably looked great on the Pentium 200 on which they were created. The animation came in on cue, the sound effects were heard at the appropriate moments, and one slide segued neatly into the next. Meanwhile, back at the ranch, trying to get the same presentation to run well on an average machine can be a real chore. There's a good thirty seconds of hard drive chattering in between slides while the CPU tries to get all its ducks in a row. The animation that was supposed to hit the screen at a dramatic moment finally appears when the slide is about ready to close. So the creator who slaved all day trying to make a good presentation for the rest of the world to enjoy has to start almost from scratch.

These kinds of problems can be attributed to one cause: mistaken assumptions about computer speed, available RAM, color depth, and video card quality. Of course, graphics specialists tend to have the best computer equipment they can possibly afford, but if you send your PowerPoint or Astound presentation to a client on a floppy disk, you shouldn't assume that the client's equipment will be of the same caliber. You should follow certain basic rules when you're not sure on what equipment your presentations will be run. These rules generally apply to presentations created with Premiere, Director, PowerPoint, and Astound.

Gear your presentations to the lowest common denominator. Assume your standalone presentation will run on a 486-66 with 8MB of RAM and an old Trident 8900 video card with 1MB of RAM. Sadly, and most distressingly, you ought to assume the show will be viewed in 256 colors.

Working in 256 Colors

You have wonderful images you've developed for multimedia presentations. And unless you're developing some cinema noir Raymond Chandler project, these images are probably in 16.7 million colors. One way to work within the limitations of 256-color mode is to use few bitmaps in your presentation, and when creating fountain fills in CorelDraw, keep the number of steps around 20. CorelDraw's strength is its capability to create good-looking art without using bitmaps. And converting quality bitmaps to 256 colors always hurts.

Secret

If you know you are going to be spending the day creating a presentation in CorelDraw for a system that may be set to display only 256 colors, before you start the project, select View ⇨ Color Palette ⇨ Uniform. Similarly, to convert a bitmap to 256 colors, import it into CorelDraw, select Bitmap ⇨ Convert To ⇨ (Palleted) 8 Bit ⇨ Uniform.

Smooth blends, such as the ones displayed in Figure 21-1, should not be on your agenda for presentations that will be run on the typical computer. This image was created with Photo-Paint and Adobe Photoshop and rendered as a 300 dpi TIFF.

Figure 21-1: This image was created with Photo-Paint and Photoshop and rendered at 300 dpi.

Figure 21-2 is more like real life. This image was rendered to the screen (96 dpi), and it looks pretty good. As a 256-color image, the blends are not horrible. You can perform some tricks to make smaller, low-resolution images appear punchy and dramatic on the screen.

Figure 21-2: The same image was created again onscreen at 96 dpi.

Make sure you employ Dithering ⇨ Error Diffusion when converting your image to 256 colors.

You will have to sacrifice accurate color value in an effort to put some zip back into the picture itself. First, import the image into Photo-Paint and adjust the Level Equalization. Choosing AutoLevels probably won't make much difference, but if you take the time to set the highs and lows yourself, you can do some good.

Next, try altering the Highlights a little using Photo-Paint's Color Balance tool. There's really no rule here; just keep your eye on the image and adjust the sliders until you see an improvement in the definition that was lost when the image was reduced to 256 colors.

Finally, we hate to say it, but a little bit of old-fashioned Brightness-Contrast augmentation can also be helpful. These are tricks that don't increase an image's loading time or drag on your system resources during the presentation.

Secret

Many multimedia developers make the mistake of importing an oversized picture into the presentation and then using the presentation software's Resize tools to shrink the image to a size appropriate for the presentation. Even after resizing, you will end up using more CPU power to work with this imported picture than if you had reduced its size and resolution before importing it.

Working Around 256-Color Mode

If you want to see what a 16.7 million-color picture looks like when you open it in 256-color mode (which you shouldn't), take a look at Figure 21-3.

Figure 21-3: This is what a 16.7 million-color image looks like opened in 256-color mode.

If the presenter converted the picture to 256-color mode by choosing a palette and employing dithering, the results would not be so bad.

The picture in Figure 21-3 was treated with the Photo-Paint techniques explained earlier and also greatly profited from a trip to Photoshop's Despeckle filter. (In Photoshop, select Filter ⇨ Noise ⇨ Despeckle.) These extras help take the "dull layer" off the image that often results from the conversion process.

Secret

In the preceding example, we recommend using a Photoshop filter for treating an image. Because you've already converted your image to 256 colors, that filter will not initially be available. After opening your image in Photoshop, select Mode ⇨ RBG, and the filter should then be available. When you are finished, select Mode ⇨ Indexed Color. You can now save your image.

Opening a 16.7 million-color picture while working in 256-color mode will severely deplete system resources of the computer that is trying to run your presentation, making the computer sound like the train in that children's story ("I think I can, I think I can"). Actually, the computer can't open the image. We've had computers report General Protection Fault errors when opening 16.7 million-color images in 256-color mode.

Windows machines default to 256-color mode. Unless you're an artist or designer, there's no reason to learn about changing color modes. When you open a bitmap in 256-color mode, the Windows system palette does a fair job of rendering the bitmap. (It's only when you open a bitmap that was previously saved in 16.7 million colors that you run into problems.) Changing a computer's color mode involves loading new drivers, going back and searching for the floppy disks that came with the video card, restarting your computer, and performing other chores in which the average viewer of your presentation may not be interested. Additionally, standard consumer-grade computers that are more than two years old generally came equipped with video cards that could not comfortably handle high-color modes. As designers of multimedia titles, I'm afraid it's up to us to make sure our presentations run well under less-than-optimal conditions.

Using Interesting Colors

The need to convert images to 256 colors often arises out of a dependence on using bitmaps and complex images in projects. Graphic artists operate on the principle that these complex images are more impressive. Sometimes, however, the use of complementary and harmonious color arrangements can create a presentation that looks just as professional.

Here's a brief look at some principles for combining colors in multimedia presentations. As you know, the primary colors are red, blue, and yellow; and complimentary colors are their opposites on the color wheel. Red compliments green, blue compliments orange, and yellow compliments purple. Lots of Web pages out there have some form of lavender or purple backgrounds with yellow text. This combination is an example of complimentary color usage. Mixing a blue-green background with a light-orange text is another example of complimentary color usage.

Using Contrasts

In designing a presentation, the idea is to provide visually pleasing contrasts so the viewers understand what they are supposed to focus on and what is merely an aesthetic background. You have several ways to achieve good color contrast values in your work, and the examples mentioned previously are the most obvious.

You can compose a presentation that uses perhaps only two color hues, but with a large variation of the light and dark values of those hues. When objects are more lit up, your eye perceives them as being closer. Using this simple principle, you can create a multimedia presentation with fewer colors, tastefully varying the light and dark values of those colors, rather than switching to a new hue. When done correctly, these types of presentations can look quite professional and businesslike.

Similarly, you can build a presentation with warm and cool color contrasts. Using a landscape analogy, cool colors — green, blue, and purple, and, for multimedia use, brown — lend depth and visual weight to your project. Cool colors are generally used as background colors, just as in a landscape portrait. For example, a blue lake, green grass that goes on forever, and brown mountains provide depth and distance to a work of art. That's why blue, green, purple, and darker shades of brown are often called *receding colors*. Conversely, warm colors, such as yellow, orange, and red (and their common shades), provide excitement and appear closer to the eye than do the cooler colors. Red, yellow, and orange are often called *advancing colors*.

You can also build subtle contrast into your work by using a *split harmony* color scheme. Have your foreground (text or main image) favor yellow and orange, for example. Now select complimentary colors just to the right or left of your primary color (yellow) on the color wheel. In this case, these colors would be purple-blue and purple-red. The subtle alteration avoids the obvious yellow-purple combination but still provides a workable color scheme for your presentation.

To understand how these principles work, take some time examining the color wheel in CorelDraw, and get a feel for which colors and shades are across, or complimentary, from one another. Or, familiarize yourself with selecting color values for your work by viewing some of the templates that come with some of the big multimedia presentation packages, such as Macromedia Director, WordPerfect Suite 7 Presentations, and Office 97 PowerPoint.

Also keep in mind that adapting a color scheme does not mean you can never deviate from that scheme in the presentation. In fact, including a graphic that totally stands out from the color scheme is one way to make the scheme work for you. But color schemes are good for determining text color, background color, borders, line art, and any objects that your viewers are going to have to view over and over again on each slide. And luckily, adapting a good color scheme can save you from spending hours converting images that worked well in high-color modes to something that will work in 256-color mode.

Summary

In this chapter you learned:

▶ How to work around the 256-color limitation when working with high-quality bitmaps in your presentations

▶ How to use color schemes to diminish your reliance on photograph bitmaps when creating presentations

▶ How to use techniques that help make your presentations run smoothly and look good even on older computers or computers running under less-than-optimal conditions

Chapter 22

Distribution Options

Graphic designers spend a huge percentage of their time shuffling data around. Moving documents of Herculean file sizes to a service bureau can become a major task. Floppy disks, which have a small storage capacity, are often not a suitable medium for transporting your documents from place to place. As the size of your Draw files grows and grows, you might be wondering how in the world you are ever going to get them somewhere to print them out professionally.

Happily, you have several options. There are many media types that can hold the equivalent of hundreds of floppy disks, such as the following:

■ **Iomega Zip Drives**, which come in SCSI internal or parallel port external models

■ **SyQuest EZ Drives**, which come in SCSI internal or external models

■ **Iomega Bernoulli Drives**, which are cartridge drives available in internal or external models

■ **SyQuest Cartridge Drives**, another model of cartridge drive, available in internal and external models

■ **Iomega Jaz Drives**, which are SCSI drives and available as an internal or external drive

Recordable CD-ROM drives are discussed later in this chapter.

Portable Data Storage

All of the names and brands mentioned previously and the technology they represent put you in the business of transporting between 100MB and 1GB of data in your hip pocket. Such is the stuff of true freedom and power. After reading this chapter, you may never use floppies again.

The disks required for any of these media types described previously weigh less than a pound. The smallest is the Zip disk, which looks like an overgrown floppy disk; the largest is the cartridge for the Bernoulli drive, which is shaped like a CD caddy and is about as big as one of the pancakes they serve at Denny's restaurants. These devices vary greatly in storage capacity, reliability, and acceptance by service bureaus and print houses at large. The smallest storage device is the Zip drive, weighing in at a disk capacity of 100MB. The largest storage device is the Jaz drive, which can hold 1GB in a disk that is about as large as a beeper.

Now let's cut to the chase. As of this writing, your best buy per megabyte, dollar per dollar, is the Iomega Jaz drive. The cartridges cost between $89 and $100 and can hold 1GB of information.

When you're considering the various distribution options, however, it's important to understand the following terminology.

SCSI

SCSI (pronounced *scuzzy*) stands for Small Computer System Interface. SCSI devices on your computer employ a different technology than standard IDE or Enhanced IDE hard drives and CD-ROM drives. A bus card is placed in your computer, and information from the SCSI device is routed through this card, bypassing the normal channels. The SCSI technology "frees up" your CPU to do more computing chores, rather than managing peripheral devices like hard drives. SCSI adapters, which are a bit larger than sound cards, cost between $150 and $300 and are not hard to install. Adaptec is the most popular manufacture of SCSI cards for PCs. Following are the advantages of SCSI devices:

- They are extremely fast.
- You can quickly install up to seven devices, such as scanners, additional hard drives, and portable drives, without any denigration in performance.
- Because SCSI technology reduces utilization of the CPU for managing devices, you will notice an increase in overall computer performance.
- Because it is quite easy to link multiple SCSI devices, most of the movable media drives you'll see on the market are SCSI as well.

SCSI versus parallel port

One more bit of general information before we take a look at each device. A movable drive attached to your parallel port will inevitably be much slower than its SCSI counterpart. The parallel port is one of the oldest pieces of technology in your computer. It cannot transfer data nearly as fast as a standard hard drive, much less a SCSI hard drive. Newer computers have enhanced parallel port performance, which improves the situation somewhat, but by and large, data transfer to and from a parallel port removable drive feels like you are saving data to one giant floppy disk.

Universal Serial Bus connection

The *Universal Serial Bus* standard provides a way for newer computers to connect with devices such as mice, keyboards, monitors, and data storage devices — without having to install cards, adjust jumper switches, or set interrupts. USB is a standard of connectivity between PCs and devices that was developed by seven computer and telecommunication firms, with an eye towards increasing data flow via ISDN and other digital communication formats such as digital PBX. What USB provides for purchasers of large data storage devices is a way to escape the limitations we've been discussing with both parallel port and SCSI-based systems.

Devices connected through USB are truly "Plug-and-Play." Windows 95 recognizes them immediately, there is no limitation on the number of USB devices on your computer, and you need not worry about that familiar and maddening source of Windows General Protection Faults and freeze-ups: DMA and Interrupt conflict.

PCs built since 1997 are most likely to be USB compatible, and manufacturers of all types of peripheral devices are gradually developing more and more USB-based products. Check your Device Manager (Control Panel ⇨ System ⇨ Device Manager ⇨ Ports) to see if your computer is equipped with USB connnectivity.

Running programs

Today's portable drives and disks are faster than ever. Some are as fast as most hard drives. We were able to install Adobe Photoshop on a SCSI Zip disk and run it from there, noticing only a slight amount of speed loss. You can use some of the better movable drives to actually run applications. Zip disks, however, are not as durable as Jaz disks and can wear out just like their ancestor, the floppy disk.

Before you buy

If you've already picked out the service bureau or printing house you intend to work with, your choices in purchasing a portable drive will be limited by what that company uses. Call up and find out what sort of portable storage medium it supports. Most services can facilitate more than one type of device. For example, many have Zip drives and the older Bernoulli cartridge drives. If you haven't selected a service bureau yet, perhaps you ought to delay purchasing a portable hard drive until you do. One more general observation to make that is common between all the above devices: With the exception of the Zip drive, the internal model of each of these drives will cost about one hundred dollars less than the external version.

Your portable storage options

Figure 22-1 shows some of the best options available.

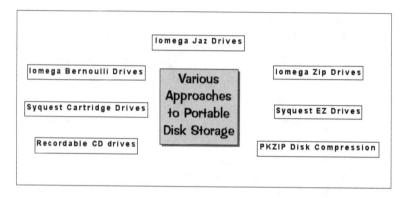

Figure 22-1: These are a few of the data storage options available.

Following are the specifics of each product.

The Iomega Zip drive

The Iomega Zip drive is the most popular portable drive with home computer users and is gaining popularity rapidly with service bureaus. The drives themselves cost between $120 and $200 and are very small. They are available in internal SCSI and external parallel port models. The Zip disks themselves cost between $10 and $18 each and can hold 100MB of information. Buying the Zip disks in bulk greatly reduces the cost. The external parallel port model, slow as it is, can be a lifesaver for laptop users who need to transport data from a laptop to a home or office desktop computer. Zip disks also have a low failure rate.

The SyQuest EZ Drive

SyQuest's EZ Drive is similar to the Iomega Zip drive; however, it holds 135MB of data rather than 100MB. The EZ Drive comes in external and internal SCSI models. The unit itself costs slightly more than the Zip drive. The disks are 15 to 25 percent more expensive than Iomega Zip disks, and it's hard to find a vendor that can keep them in stock. They are, however, faster than Zip drives, and many EZ Drive owners run applications from them interchangeably with their hard drive.

The external unit is not as thin and sleek as the Zip drive. While the Zip drives are becoming a fashion statement on Silicon Valley coffee tables, EZ Drives are tireless workhorses. Just like Apple computer owners vehemently insist that theirs is the better mousetrap, EZ Drive owners claim that this product performs head over heels above the Zip drive.

The Iomega Bernoulli cartridge drive

It would be hard to find a service bureau in the United States that doesn't have a Bernoulli cartridge drive. These drives represent the older "cartridge" technology that has enjoyed many years of popularity with graphic designers and others who must print their work. The standard Bernoulli drive available today works with a 230MB cartridge and is capable of running the older Bernoulli formats.

The SyQuest drive

As the phrase is used in service bureau lingo, "Yes, we have a SyQuest drive." The reference might not be to a literal driver produced by the SyQuest Corporation, but to the long-standing technology that SyQuest first developed. If there is a portable media "standard" recognized between graphic designers and service bureaus, it is the SyQuest drive. The drives support 44, 88, 200, and 270MB disks. There are both internal and external SyQuest drives. Surprisingly, given their acceptance in the field, disk failure rates can be high, especially when storing data for more than a year.

The Iomega Jaz drive

The Iomega Jaz drive is currently the fastest and highest capacity portable drive on the market. The drive itself sells for $400 for the internal model and $500 for the external model, both SCSI. Disks cost in the neighborhood of $100, making it by far the best "dollar per megabyte" deal. The Jaz drive is one of the newest on the market, certainly the newest of all the drives mentioned previously. Therefore, it is hard to say how the drive will rate as far as permanent storage capabilities. However, all signs indicate that Jaz drives function with all the speed and reliability of any 1MB hard drive that just happens to be portable. Because Jaz drives are new, you should not assume that your favorite service bureau supports them. However, they are quickly gaining in popularity.

When transferring large amounts of data within various directories from one drive to another, it's easy to forget what got transferred and what didn't. If you just did an archive two weeks ago and then went on to begin an important project, you might want to archive those new files as well. What do you do, transfer all the files again just because you can't remember where all the new ones are? Not necessarily. There are many new file-management programs that will synchronize files between two groups of directories, scanning both and updating the archived files with anything new. This process is much faster than copying all of the recently archived files over again. For example, on the Internet, search for a shareware program called Drag and File. This product synchronizes data transfers so that only new files are added.

Recordable CD-ROM technology

Recordable CD-ROM drives have now dropped to the price that standard CD-ROM drives were when they first entered the market six years ago. And if history is any indicator, today's luxury will become tomorrow's necessity. But CD-ROM recorders still have their drawbacks. For starters, the amount of free hard drive space on your computer must exceed the amount of data you want to archive on your CD-ROM recorder. You cannot use your computer while you are saving data to the CD-ROM. At this time, most CD-ROM recorders will save data at a rate equaling a double-speed CD-ROM drive. (Although many of the newer CD-ROM recorders will play CD-ROMs at the quad-speed rate.) Therefore, saving "an entire CD worth" of data will take about 45 minutes. And if there are problems, you'll have to throw the CD-ROM out and record again on a new one. Because the recording process actually "burns" the data into the CD-ROM via a laser, you cannot use the CD-ROM again once a session has gone awry. (At that point, it starts to matter that recordable CD-ROMs cost about $8 each.)

One more considerable limitation: When working with Jaz drives or other removable media, you can save some data today, leave the rest blank, and come back tomorrow and add some more. The way CD-ROM recorder technology works, one session becomes a hard drive. As far as Windows 95 is concerned, when you are finished recording CD-ROM data to disk, you have created a hard drive. Yes, you can come back later and record more data on your disk. But it will be archived and read later as yet another hard drive, moving one up the alphabet each time. You may have to alter settings inside Control Pane ⇨ System ⇨ Device Manager to accommodate this "run up" of hard drive labeling. Windows 95 is especially smart about adding additional devices automatically, but you can change this parameter in the Control Panel/System if you need to. And there is one potential situation that has led to more than one "oops" around our household: What happens when you are using data you cleverly archived on your recordable CD-ROM, but then want to use your CD-ROM for a CD-ROM-based program? If you take out the recorded CD-ROM while you are utilizing data from it, your computer will most likely crash.

In spite of all these complaints and caveats, nothing can beat the convenience of popping in a CD-ROM and retrieving last month's work you did for a client, or having all of your best artwork archived on one CD-ROM. The following are some of the advantages of CD-ROM recorders in graphic design work:

- CD-ROMs are 100 percent archival. Unless they are scratched, they won't fail a year from now just when you need them most.

- You can distribute your work to clients and potential customers on a CD-ROM, which is a medium anyone with a desktop computer is almost certain to have access to.

- The "dollar per megabyte" value exceeds even the Jaz drive. If all goes well with your session, you can save 640MB of data on a disk that costs $8, as opposed to a 1GB Jaz disk that costs $100.

There is a large variety of CD-ROM recorder software available to choose from. Not all packages are created equal. The most desirable feature in CD-ROM recording software is reliability of data transfer, followed closely by the product utilizing a simple interface that shows the directories and files on one side of the screen being neatly transferred over to synchronized directories on the other. The most usable and well-rounded CD-ROM recording software we have seen is Corel's CD Creator.

PKZIP

Sometimes a floppy disk isn't enough. What are you going to do if the file you need to send to somebody is 1.6MB? Send the information on a $20 Zip disk because the file exceeds a floppy disk's capacity by 200K? No! You use PKZIP.

PKZIP is a universally available program that compresses data to an infinitesimal portion of its previous size. It can shrink certain kinds of TIFF files down from 5MB to 112K. Using PKZIP, a 10MB Microsoft Publisher file will end up requiring only 590K of disk space. You "zip" your files using a simple command line in DOS or pointing and clicking your way in Windows. When you want to use the file, it is "unzipped" using a similar command line.

That being said, the actual executable files that comprise PKZIP are less than 100K total. If you place these two executable files in your DOS or Windows directory, you can run a PKZIP session from any directory or drive on your computer.

Although there are elaborate versions of PKZIP available for Windows and Windows 95, PKZIP itself works with a very simple command line. It works well through DOS or Windows, or in a DOS window. In five years of using PKZIP to shrink files and save them to floppy disks, we have never had PKZIP fail to recover a file due to an error in the program. You may locate a Windows version of PKZIP by logging on to your favorite Web search engine and typing **WinZip**. Retrieve the DOS version similarly by searching for a file called PKZIP.

One spin on the familiar PKZIP program that deserves special mention is Zip Folders, by Mijenix (download the 30-day, fully functional demo from `www.mijenix.com`). Although your files are zipped, you'd never know it. All your zipped files are fully functional in DOS or Windows. They appear in Windows Explorer in an unzipped state and can be opened, edited, and saved just as if they were not zipped. In reality, the files are fully zipped and thus use very little disk space. With Mijenix Zip Folders, you can enjoy the functionality of having all of your files handy, with the disk storage savings of zipped files.

You can use PKZIP to archive data across several floppy disks. When it comes time to unzip the data, the program prompts you to insert another floppy at the appropriate time. This is one of those simple programs that always works. What follows are two instances of using PKZIP command lines from DOS to zip a file:

- To zip a file called Myart.tif, log on to the directory where the file you want to zip is located, and type **pkzip myfile.zip myfile.tif** (watch the spaces!).

- To zip a large file across several floppy disks, type **pkzip -& a:\myfile.zip myfile.tif**.

- PKZIP works with any standard wildcard. For example, you can type **pkzip mytif.zip *.tif**. This would create one zipped file of every .TIFF file in the current directory.

- The nice thing is you need not remember any of this. If you have the pkzip executable file in your DOS or Windows directory, type **pkzip /h** and you'll receive a menu of switches that qualify the pkzip command and their explanations.

- For those DOS-deprived, the various Windows versions of PKZIP work just as well with the same results.

PKZIP is a proprietary product distributed on the World Wide Web and is included with various software packages. If you use PKZIP without registering it and sending the company a little bit of money, "nag lines" will appear on the screen every time you open or close the Windows-based version of the program.

Summary

▶ It is imperative for the graphic artist to be adept at managing large files. If managed poorly, the simple chore of moving large art files from place to place, as well as minimizing disk space loss, can take up more time than creating art.

▶ There are many movable storage options available, ranging from Zip disk drives that contain 100MB of data, to Jaz drives that can store 1GB of data, allowing you to access it as if it were a fully functional hard drive. Increasingly, recordable CD-ROM drives are becoming more popular and user-friendly.

▶ For smaller jobs, the PKZIP program, which compresses files down to their smallest possible storage space, provides a way to store and transport art files in convenient, small chunks. PKZIP is especially helpful when the need arises to move documents that are larger than a floppy disk's capacity, but not large enough to require a movable hard drive.

Appendix

What's on the CD-ROM?

It was difficult to decide what to put on the CD-ROM disc—CorelDRAW comes with so much stuff already. So, we looked around for some unique and useful utilities. We hope these goodies make your work with CorelDRAW more productive.

Each subdirectory on the CD has slightly different installation instructions and restrictions, so please check out the README.TXT file in the various subdirectories for instructions for using and installing these utilities.

Following is a description of the various subdirectories on the disc and what's in them:

/Artshow

This is a collection of the images on the second color insert by the artists who contributed. You can open these images in CorelDraw and check them out, but you can't reproduce them for any reason. The images belong to the artists.

/Bills_art

This is a collection of the artwork in the first color insert. All this art was created by one of the authors, Bill Harrel. You open this artwork in CorelDraw and Photo-Paint to see how it was created, but please don't use it in any of your layouts. Much of it belongs to Bill's clients and is used with their permission.

/CorelWeb

Corel WebMaster Suite is a collection of applications designed to help you create World Wide Web sites. The version included on the CD-ROM is a demo with certain feature and licensing limitations. See the accompanying README.TXT file for instructions on obtaining the full version.

/ImageClb

This is collection of sample images from Image Club. Feel free to use these images in your work. If you like them, check out the README.TXT file to find out how to get more.

/MetTools

This is collection of plug-in demos from MetaTools, including the popular Kai's Power Tools, a Photoshop plug-in that also works with Photo-Paint. You can find information for obtaining the full version of Kai's Power Tools and the other demos in the MetTools directory in the Acrobat files in the Acrobat subdirectory.

/Pegasus

This is a plug-in from Pegasus to help you work with .JPEG files. Because it is shareware, you should register it if you decide you can use it.

Enjoy!

Index

SYMBOLS & NUMBERS

* (asterisk), 168
⇨ (command arrow), 167
© (copyright character), 168
" (double quotes), 166
— (em dash), 166
- (hyphen), 166, 168
- (minus sign), 428
+ (plus sign), 7, 87, 345, 428
' (single quote), 166
~ (tilde character), 611
™ (trademark character), 168
256-color mode, 726–730
3D effects
   3D Mosaic effect, 603, 606, 608
   3D Rotate effect, 489–490
   adding, to photographs, 501–505
   Intersect tool and, 134–136
   masks and, 426
   for text, 134–136, 496–499
3D Model (.3DMF) files, 578–590
3D Paint Brush tool, 553, 555

A

ABK extension, 37
accelcon (accelerated contour) effect, 659
Accelerate Colors option, 252
Accelerate Shapes option, 252
Accelerate Sizing button, 35
Accurate option, 382
Actual Size tool, 346
Add A Printer icon, 300
Add button, 32
Add Layer command, 633
Add Menu button, 12
Add New button, 237, 238
Add Node button, 345

Add Node option, 239, 345, 557
Add Node tool, 557
Add paint mode, 397–398
Add Printer Wizard, 300, 301
Add tool, 345
Add/Remove Dropcap option, 20
Adjust option, 454
Adobe Systems
   Illustrator, 32, 309–310, 318
   PageMaker, 34, 65, 145, 158, 310, 321
   Photoshop, 256, 311, 424, 453, 465
   Premiere, 725
   Type I fonts, 145–146
Advanced sheet, 38
Advertisement template, 635
alchemy command, 485, 682
Alchemy dialog box, 435
Alien Skin, 317, 453, 465, 466–468
Align and Distribute dialog box, 105–112
Align Objects command, 565–569
Align sheet, 105–106
Align to Baseline command, 150
Alignment dialog box, 554, 565–568, 569
alpha channels (mask channels)
   basic description of, 424, 575
   importance of using, 575
   loading masks saved as, 426
Always Overprint Black option, 306–307, 308–309
Ambient slider, 487
Analog Name tab, 648–649
Angular button, 75
Angular Dimension option, 73–74
animation, 689, 694–695
Animation File option, 689
Anti-Alias button, 430
Anti-Alias option, 430
anti-aliasing, 343, 347, 349, 430
applets, 708–710, 715, 722–724

(continued)

(continued)

IDG BOOKS WORLDWIDE, INC.
END-USER LICENSE AGREEMENT

READ THIS. You should carefully read these terms and conditions before opening the software packet(s) included with this book ("Book"). This is a license agreement ("Agreement") between you and IDG Books Worldwide, Inc. ("IDGB"). By opening the accompanying software packet(s), you acknowledge that you have read and accept the following terms and conditions. If you do not agree and do not want to be bound by such terms and conditions, promptly return the Book and the unopened software packet(s) to the place you obtained them for a full refund.

1. **License Grant.** IDGB grants to you (either an individual or entity) a nonexclusive license to use one copy of the enclosed software program(s) (collectively, the "Software") solely for your own personal or business purposes on a single computer (whether a standard computer or a workstation component of a multi-user network). The Software is in use on a computer when it is loaded into temporary memory (i.e., RAM) or installed into permanent memory (e.g., hard disk, CD-ROM, or other storage device). IDGB reserves all rights not expressly granted herein.

2. **Ownership.** IDGB is the owner of all rights, titles, and interests, including copyright, in and to the compilation of the Software recorded on the CD-ROM. Copyright to the individual programs on the CD-ROM is owned by the author or other authorized copyright owner of each program. Ownership of the Software and all proprietary rights relating thereto remain with IDGB and its licensors.

3. **Restrictions on Use and Transfer.**

   (a) You may only (i) make one copy of the Software for backup or archival purposes, or (ii) transfer the Software to a single hard disk, provided that you keep the original for backup or archival purposes. You may not (i) rent or lease the Software, (ii) copy or reproduce the Software through a LAN or other network system or through any computer subscriber system or bulletin-board system, or (iii) modify, adapt, or create derivative works based on the Software.

   (b) You may not reverse engineer, decompile, or disassemble the Software. You may transfer the Software and user documentation on a permanent basis, provided that the transferee agrees to accept the terms and conditions of this Agreement and you retain no copies. If the Software is an update or has been updated, any transfer must include the most recent update and all prior versions.

4. **Restrictions on Use of Individual Programs.** You must follow the individual requirements and restrictions detailed for each individual program in the appendix of this Book. These limitations are contained in the individual license agreements recorded on the CD-ROM. These restrictions include a requirement that after using the program for the period of time specified in its text, the user must pay a registration fee or discontinue use. By opening the Software packet(s), you will be agreeing to abide by the licenses and restrictions for these individual programs. None of the material on this disc or listed in this Book may ever be distributed, in original or modified form, for commercial purposes.

5. **Limited Warranty.**

   (a) IDGB warrants that the Software and CD-ROM are free from defects in materials and workmanship under normal use for a period of sixty (60) days from the date of purchase of this Book. If IDGB receives notification within the warranty period of defects in materials or workmanship, IDGB will replace the defective CD-ROM.

(b) **IDGB AND THE AUTHORS OF THE BOOK DISCLAIM ALL OTHER WARRANTIES, EXPRESS OR IMPLIED, INCLUDING WITHOUT LIMITATION IMPLIED WARRANTIES OF MERCHANTABILITY AND FITNESS FOR A PARTICULAR PURPOSE, WITH RESPECT TO THE SOFTWARE, THE PROGRAMS, THE SOURCE CODE CONTAINED THEREIN, AND/OR THE TECHNIQUES DESCRIBED IN THIS BOOK. IDGB DOES NOT WARRANT THAT THE FUNCTIONS CONTAINED IN THE SOFTWARE WILL MEET YOUR REQUIREMENTS OR THAT THE OPERATION OF THE SOFTWARE WILL BE ERROR FREE.**

(c) This limited warranty gives you specific legal rights, and you may have other rights that vary from jurisdiction to jurisdiction.

6. **Remedies.**

(a) IDGB's entire liability and your exclusive remedy for defects in materials and workmanship shall be limited to replacement of the Software, which may be returned to IDGB with a copy of your receipt at the following address: Software Media Fulfillment Department, Attn.: *CorelDraw 8 Secrets*, IDG Book Worldwide, Inc., 7260 Shadeland Station, Ste. 100, Indianapolis, IN 46256, or call 1-800-762-2974. Please allow three to four weeks for delivery. This Limited Warranty is void if failure of the Software has resulted from accident, abuse, or misapplication. Any replacement Software will be warranted for the remainder of the original warranty period or thirty (30) days, whichever is longer.

(b) In no event shall IDGB or the authors be liable for any damages whatsoever (including without limitation damages for loss of business profits, business interruption, loss of business information, or any other pecuniary loss) arising out of the use of or inability to use the Book or the Software, even if IDGB has been advised of the possibility of such damages.

(c) Because some jurisdictions do not allow the exclusion or limitation of liability for consequential or incidental damages, the above limitation or exclusion may not apply to you.

7. **U.S. Government Restricted Rights.** Use, duplication, or disclosure of the Software by the U.S. Government is subject to restrictions stated in paragraph (c) (1) (ii) of the Rights in Technical Data and Computer Software clause of DFARS 252.227-7013, and in subparagraphs (a) through (d) of the Commercial Computer—Restricted Rights clause at FAR 52.227-19, and in similar clauses in the NASA FAR supplement, when applicable.

8. **General.** This Agreement constitutes the entire understanding of the parties, and revokes and supersedes all prior agreements, oral or written, between them and may not be modified or amended except in a writing signed by both parties hereto which specifically refers to this Agreement. This Agreement shall take precedence over any other documents that may be in conflict herewith. If any one or more provisions contained in this Agreement are held by any court or tribunal to be invalid, illegal or otherwise unenforceable, each and every other provision shall remain in full force and effect.

my2cents.idgbooks.com

CD-ROM Installation Instructions

Each of the programs and clip media included on the CD-ROM has slightly different setup and licensing instructions. For detailed information on using these programs and clip media, please see the README.TXT files in the subdirectories for the portions of the CD you want to use.

Changing Windows Read-Only Attribute

You may run into the problem of not being able to access files on the CD-ROM after you copy the files to your computer. After you copy or move the entire contents of the CD to your hard disk or another storage medium (such as a Zip disk), you may get the following error message when you attempt to open a file with its associated application:

```
[Application] is unable to open the [file].
Please make sure the drive and file are writable.
```

Windows sees all files on a CD-ROM drive as "read-only." This makes sense normally because a CD-ROM is a read-only medium—you can't write data back to the CD. However, when you copy a file from a CD to your hard disk or a Zip disk, Windows doesn't automatically change the file attribute from read-only to writable. Installation software normally takes care of this chore for you, but in this case, because the files are intended to be manually copied to your disk, you have to change the file attribute yourself. Luckily, it is easy. Follow these steps:

1. Click the Start menu button
2. Select Programs.
3. Choose Windows Explorer.
4. Highlight the filename(s) on the hard disk or Zip disk.
5. Right-click the highlighted filename(s) to display a pop-up menu.
6. Select Properties to display the Properties dialog.
7. Click the Read-only option so that it is no longer checked.
8. Click the OK button.

You should now be able to use the file(s) with the specific application without getting the annoying error message.